WATERBORNE PAGEANTS
IN THE RENAIS

European Festival Studies: 1450–1700

Series Editors:

J.R. Mulryne, University of Warwick, UK
Margaret Shewring, University of Warwick, UK
Margaret M. McGowan CBE, FBA, University of Sussex, UK

This series, in association with the Society for European Festivals Research, builds on the current surge in interest in the circumstances of European Festivals – their political, religious, social, economic and cultural implications as well as the detailed analysis of their performance (including ephemeral architecture, scenography, scripts, music and soundscape, dance, costumes, processions and fireworks) in both indoor and outdoor, urban and court, locations.

Festivals were interdisciplinary and, on occasion, international in scope. They drew on a rich classical heritage and developed a shared pan-European iconography as well as exploiting regional and site-specific features. They played an important part in local politics and the local economy, as well as international negotiations and the conscious presentation of power, sophistication and national identity.

The series, including both essay collections and monographs, seeks to analyse the characteristics of individual festivals as well as to explore generic themes. It draws on a wealth of archival documentary evidence, alongside the resources of galleries and museums, to study the historical, literary, performance and material culture of these extravagant occasions of state.

Waterborne Pageants and Festivities in the Renaissance

Essays in Honour of J.R. Mulryne

MARGARET SHEWRING
University of Warwick, UK

LINDA BRIGGS
Assistant Editor

Routledge
Taylor & Francis Group

LONDON AND NEW YORK

Frist published 2013 by Ashgate Publishing

Published 2016 by Routledge
2 Park Square, Milton Park, Abingdon, Oxfordshire OX14 4RN
711 Third Avenue, New York, NY10017, USA

First issued in paperback 2016

Routledge is an imprint of the Taylor & Francis Group, an informa business

British Library Cataloguing in Publication Data
A catalogue record for this book is available from the British Library

The Library of Congress has cataloged the printed edition as follows:

Waterborne Pageants and Festivities in the Renaissance: Essays in Honour of
    J.R. Mulryne / edited by Margaret Shewring, assisted by Linda Briggs.
        pages cm. – (European Festival Studies, 1450–1700.)
    Includes bibliographical references and index.
    1. Festivals – Europe – History. 2. Pageants – Europe – History. 3. Theater –
    Europe – History. 4. Renaissance. 5. Europe – Social life and customs.
    6. Mulryne, J. R. I. Shewring, Margaret.
    GT3530.W37 2013
    394.2694–dc23   2013013632

ISBN 13: 978-1-138-27701-4 (pbk)
ISBN 13: 978-1-4094-0023-3 (hbk)

Contents

J. R. (Ronnie) Mulryne

The inaugural conference of the Society for European Festivals Research, from which this volume derives, was held in March 2010 in honour of the Society's Co-Convenor, Professor Ronnie Mulryne, and in acknowledgement of his contribution to Festival Studies and to the study of Renaissance and later literature and theatre.

Ronnie's work has inspired generations of students and scholars, offering resources and a scholarly framework for the interdisciplinary study of European Renaissance culture, focusing most recently on Renaissance and Early Modern Festivals. He was Chairman of the Graduate School of Renaissance Studies at Warwick (later Centre for the Study of the Renaissance) from the 1980s until 2002, and Director of its research programme, 'Festivals of the European Renaissance'. He was the lead co-editor of the major collection *Europa Triumphans: Court and Civic Festivals in Early Modern Europe* (Ashgate, two volumes), as well as *Court Festivals of the European Renaissance* (Ashgate), and directed the extensive digitisation project published on-line with the British Library as 'Treasures in Full: Renaissance Festival Books'. He is currently editing one volume for the Society's European Festival Studies series, and serving as co-editor of a further two.

Ronnie's published work includes his founding editorship of *Shakespeare in Performance* (Manchester, 17 volumes), his many years as co-General Editor of *The Revels Plays* (Manchester), and his editing of plays of the Elizabethan and Jacobean periods such as Thomas Middleton's *Women Beware Women*, Thomas Kyd's *The Spanish Tragedy* and John Webster's *The White Devil*. His collections of essays, edited and co-edited, run to more than a dozen, spanning Renaissance topics such as *Theatre and Government under the Early Stuarts* (Cambridge), *Shakespeare and the Japanese Stage* (Cambridge) *Theatre of the English and Italian Renaissance* (Manchester) and *The Guild and Guild Buildings of Shakespeare's Stratford* (Ashgate). With Margaret Shewring he co-founded Mulryne and Shewring Ltd, publishing books on theatre in performance including *Making Space for Theatre* and volumes on the Royal Shakespeare Company's Swan Theatre, on the Cottesloe auditorium at the Royal National Theatre and on Shakespeare's Globe (with Cambridge University Press).

Ronnie has taught and researched, with generosity and distinction, at a number of UK and overseas universities including Birmingham (the Shakespeare Institute), Edinburgh and Warwick, and for shorter periods at California (UCSD) and Oxford (Jesus and Magdalen Colleges). His research association with the Société Internationale de Recherches Interdisciplinaires sur la Renaissance at the Sorbonne led to a series of published essays and to the award of the Ordre des Palmes Académiques (1992).

Ronnie has served as Chairman of national committees for the Council for National Academic Awards, the Arts Council of Great Britain, the British Council and the U.K.'s Arts and Humanities Research Board and has been a Trustee of the Shakespeare Birthplace Trust, a Governor of the Royal Shakespeare Company and Chairman of Governors of King Edward VI School, Stratford-upon-Avon (Shakespeare's School).

Many of the different strands in Ronnie's career were represented at a Dinner held in Venice during the Conference, when friends, family, conference members and colleagues gathered for a 'festival' reception, with music from Mascherata, and a celebratory banquet. Those present for the evening included: Iain Mackintosh, Ian and Nikki Brown, Simon and Juliet Erridge, Tony and Janet Bird, Alec and Anne Jolly, Michele Marrapodi and family, Eithne Mulryne, Grania Foster, James Morris, Richard Morris and Gavin and Kate Gemmell, with messages of apology and good wishes received from, among others, David Edgar, Seamus Heaney and Sir Ian McKellen.

We are glad to have this opportunity to recognise Ronnie's tireless and distinguished contribution to teaching, research and publication, and to honour his achievements with this collection of essays.

Acknowledgements

The acknowledgements for this volume fall into two categories and some people belong in both. The first group must include all those who did so much to make the conference in Venice in 2010 such a great pleasure to attend and to organise: not just the speakers and session chairs but colleagues and friends who helped to ensure the smooth-running of the occasion as well as those who travelled to Venice to be a part of it. There really are too many people to list here although special mention should be made of Sue Dibben, Kate Brennan, Claire Nicholls and Ros Lucas who helped to facilitate the organisation at Warwick as well as Chiara Croff, the University of Warwick's administrator in Venice, Roberta Warman and Cathy Charlton, who helped with the organisation from day to day in Venice, ably assisted by a small team of students also from Warwick: Alice Gahan (Theatre Studies), Rio West (English), Pesala Bandara (Renaissance Studies), and Linda Briggs (History) assistant editor of this volume.

Particular thanks are due to the University of Warwick's Institute for Advanced Study and Humanities Research Centre, both of which contributed to the funding of the occasion, and to the European Science Foundation which funded our Exploratory Workshop in the days immediately following the conference, also in Venice. This enabled relevant people to travel to both events and for the two occasions to inform each other. One major outcome of the conference and workshop was the establishment of the Society for European Festivals Research (SEFR). A second major outcome has been the establishment of research connections between SEFR and a European Science Foundation Research Network, PALATIUM, which concentrates its work on architecture in European palaces and great houses, 1400–1700.

Rachel Lynch, Managing Director of Ashgate Publishing Ltd has been generously supportive throughout and has encouraged us, with the Society for European Festivals Research, to embark on a series of publications on European Festivals in which this will be one of the first two books (co-general editors J.R. Mulryne, Margaret Shewring and Margaret M. McGowan).

A second group, to whom special thanks is due, is the contributors – some to both the conference and the volume, some just to the volume – who have responded promptly and with good humour to requests for further details, editorial information, illustrations and translations as the structure of the volume has taken shape. Together they have brought an international and inter-disciplinary range of scholarly expertise to bear on the study and analysis of Renaissance and Early Modern waterborne festivals. On their behalf as well as the editor's, thanks are due to numerous libraries, archives and image collections for permission to use images here. Each copyright holder is acknowledged at the appropriate point in the list of illustrations and/or captions. Three scholars who spoke at the conference and, both in their talks and in subsequent discussions, helped us to explore the topic of waterborne pageantry and festivities, are not represented in the essays collected here, since their work was already committed to other publications: Stephen Orgel, Julie Sanders and Nadine Pederson. Each made a distinctive contribution to the conference, for which I am very grateful.

Particular thanks are due to J.R. (Ronnie) Mulryne for his constant encouragement and generous help throughout the editing process as well as to Linda Briggs, assistant editor, who brought her particular expertise on the French Renaissance to bear and who, with Ronnie, worked on a number of the translations necessary to make such a collection into a coherent whole and to comply with our publishing guidelines, which require all contributions to appear in English. I am grateful to Richard Morris (postgraduate in Early Modern History, Trinity College, Cambridge) for his comments on, and proof reading of, a number of chapters. Finally my thanks go, too, to Rachel Lynch, Kirsten Weissenberg (Senior Editor) and their colleagues at Ashgate for their patience and meticulous attention to detail.

It has been a great pleasure to work with such an excellent team. I hope that they and our readers will pardon any errors which remain.

MS

List of Illustrations

Table

Colour Plates

The colour plates fall between pp. 198–199

Notes on Contributors

Maria Ines Aliverti is a Professor in the History of Art Department of the University of Pisa. She was a member of the steering committee of the European Science Foundation's Network on Theatre Iconography, 1987–2000. Her publications include: *Jacques Copeau* (Bari: Laterza, 1997), *Poesia fuggitiva sugli attori nell'età di Voltaire* (Roma: Bulzoni, 1993) and *La naissance de l'acteur moderne. L'acteur et son portrait au XVIIIe siècle* (Paris: Gallimard, 1998). She was both editor of, and contributor to, the Genoa cluster of Festival Books in J.R. Mulryne, Helen Watanabe-O'Kelly and Margaret Shewring (gen. eds), *Europa Triumphans: Court and Civic Festivals in Early Modern Europe* (Aldershot and Burlington VT: Ashgate, 2004); *Una scena di città attribuita a Sebastiano Serlio: Breve saggio di iconologia teatrale* (Pisa: ETS, 2008); she is currently editing *Il viaggio in Italia di Margherita d'Austria regina di Spagna (1598–1599). Ingressi, feste e cerimonie* (Pisa: Plus, forthcoming).

Sydney Anglo (FBA, FSA, FLSW) is Emeritus professor in the History of Ideas (University of Swansea). His principal interests are in the history of chivalry, tournaments, court festivals, the reception of Machiavelli, and the history of piano-playing. He has published many books including *Spectacle, Pageantry and Early Tudor Pageantry* (1969); *Images of Early Tudor Kingship* (1992); *The Martial Arts of Renaissance Europe* (2000); *Machiavelli – the First Century* (2005); *L'éscrime, la danse et l'art de la guerre* (2011). He was awarded the medal of the Arms and Armour Society in 2002.

Pesala Bandara recently completed her MA (with Distinction) in 'The Culture of the European Renaissance' at the University of Warwick. Her research interests include women's performance in early modern Scotland and the festival relationship between Italy and England in the sixteenth and early-seventeenth centuries. She is currently engaged in doctoral research in the Centre for the Study of the Renaissance, University of Warwick, on 'The Haringtons of Exton in their Cultural Context'.

Linda Briggs (Assistant Editor) is completing her PhD at the University of Warwick on 'Representations of the Monarchy and Peace-Making in the Royal Tour of France, 1564–1566'. Having received her MA in History and MLitt in Reformation Studies, both from the University of St Andrews, she now specializes in early modern ritual and visual culture and the French Wars of Religion. She has been an active member of the Society for European Festivals Research from its inception, and has recently co-organised the Society's conference in Bergamo,

Italy on 'The Iconography of Power: Ceremonial Entries in Renaissance and Early Modern Europe'. Her paper from the conference will appear in the forthcoming volume of the same name, also published by Ashgate.

Maria Grazia Cacciapaglia graduated *summa cum laude* in 2006 in History of Art at the University of Pisa with a degree thesis in 'Iconography and Iconology', entitled 'The Devil and the Hebrews: histories of anti-Semitism in Christian Art'. In 2009 she specialized *summa cum laude* in Medieval and Modern Art at the Scuola di Specializzazione in History of Art in Pisa. Part of her specialization thesis was published in 'Polittico' (Pisa University Press, 2012), with the headline 'The art of devotion. Santa Caterina da Siena's stigmata through her crosses'. Since 2009 she has collaborated with governmental offices which depend on the Ministry of Cultural Heritage, in Pisa and in Lucca. For three years she has studied the Cathedral of San Martino in Lucca, during its restoration, analyzing and cataloguing traces of frescoes, sculptures, capitals and all other material and artistic elements.

Marie-Claude Canova-Green is Reader in French and Comparative Literature at Goldsmiths, University of London. She has research interests in European court entertainments and has edited a four-volume collection of seventeenth-century ballet *libretti*. She has also published monographs on Molière and early modern French drama. Her most recent edited collection is *Writing Royal Entries in Early Modern Europe* (Turnhout: Brepols, 2013).

Monique Chatenet, *conservateur en chef du patrimoine*, undertakes research at the Centre Andre Chastel (CNRS, Paris) and teaches at the University of Paris, Sorbonne. She is the author of numerous books and articles on the topic of French architecture of the Renaissance and the life of the court in the sixteenth century. She has published two well-known monographs on the chateaux of Francis 1st, *Le Château de Madrid au bois de Boulogne* (Paris: Picard, 1987) and *Chambord* (Paris: Editions du Patrimoine, 2001), together with an edition of a study by several hands: *La cour de France au XVIe siècle. Vie sociale et architecture* (Paris: Picard, 2006). She has also directed numerous editions of collected studies, including most recently *Le Gothique de la Renaissance, actes des 4e rencontres de'architecture européenne* (Paris: Picard, 2011).

Richard Cooper is Professor of French and Vice-Principal of Brasenose College, University of Oxford. His publications include: *Marguerite de Navarre, Chrétiens et mondains, poèmes épars*, vol. 8 of *Œuvres completes de Marguerite de Navarre* (Paris: Librairie H. Champion, 2007), with G. Demerson, *Jean du Bellay, Peomata* (Paris: Société des Textes Français Modernes, 2007), *Litteræ in tempore belli: Etudes sur les relations littéraires italo-françaises pendant les guerres d'Italie* (Geneva: Libraire Droz, 1997) and *Maurice Scève, The Entry of Henri II into Lyon,*

September 1548, text with an introduction and notes (Tempe Arizona: Medieval and Renaissance Texts and Studies, 1997).

H. Neville Davies, formerly lecturer in English Literature at the University of Birmingham, has contributed 'The Queen's Entertainment at Elvetham' to a new edition of early modern sources for John Nichols's *The Progresses and Public Processions of Queen Elizabeth I*. His many other publications, predominantly on early modern English literature, include essays on royal entertainments and a critical edition of verse by Thomas St Nicholas, a hitherto unrecognised poet of the mid-seventeenth century.

Iain Fenlon is Professor of Historical Musicology at the University of Cambridge, and a Fellow of King's College. His principal area of research is music from 1450 to 1650, particularly in Italy. An early monograph on music of sixteenth-century Mantua explores how the Gonzaga family patronised the reform of liturgical music and the secular arts of spectacle. With James Haar he has written a study of the emergence of the Italian madrigal, and his 1994 Panizzi lectures on early Italian music print culture are published by The British Library. *Giaches de Wert: Letters and Documents* (Paris, 1999) provides editions with commentary on the composer's letters, including an important cache of autographs discovered in the late 1990s. Most of his writings, some of which are gathered together in *Music and Culture in Late Renaissance Italy* (Oxford, 2000), explore how the history of music is related to the history of society. His most recent book is *The Ceremonial City: History, Memory and Myth in Renaissance Venice* (Yale, 2007).

Michael Holden is a practising Theatre Consultant and graduated with an MA in Theatre Consultancy (with Distinction) from the University of Warwick in January 2013. As the founding chairman of the Lyric Theatre Hammersmith and CEO of the Shakespeare's Globe in Southwark during its building and opening seasons he has been central to the creation of two major London theatres. He has worked on more than 100 auditoria, including the Royal National Theatre, Barbican Arts Centre, Royal Scottish Academy of Music and Drama and Londonderry (Derry) Forum. The last project drew heavily on his experience as a Cultural Consultant for UNESCO. His current work is on the re-appraisal of the theatre buildings of the Elizabethan and Jacobean period in London from primary sources (forthcoming, 2014), and on the business of operating and managing these theatres, the subject of his doctoral research at the University of Warwick.

R.J. Knecht is Emeritus Professor of History at the University of Birmingham where he taught from 1956 until his retirement in 1994. His historical work has focused on the political and cultural history of sixteenth and seventeenth-century France. He has been chairman of the Society for Renaissance Studies and also of the Society for the Study of French History. His publications include *Renaissance Warrior and Patron: the reign of Francis I* (Cambridge: Cambridge University

Press, 1994); *The Rise and Fall of Renaissance France*, 2nd revised edn (Oxford: Blackwell, 2001), *Catherine de' Medici* (London: Longman, 1998), *The French Civil Wars, 1562–98* (Harlow: Pearson/Longman, 2000), *The Valois: Kings of France, 1328–1589* (Hambledon and London, 2004) and *The French Renaissance Court* (New Haven and London, Yale University Press, 2008). He is at present writing a biography of Henry III of France.

Evelyn Korsch is a researcher living in Venice. She studied History, Art History and Literature in Bonn and Zurich. Her PhD thesis (2009) deals with the triumphal entry of Henri III in Venice in 1574 as a non-verbal communication system. Korsch carried out several research projects regarding social, artistic and cultural aspects of Italian Renaissance history. Recently, she is working on social-economic themes including the luxury trade conducted by Armenian agents in Italy and their global networks in the seventeenth and eighteenth centuries. In 2012 Korsch, together with other researchers, founded an international working group funded by the German Research Foundation in order to study the material culture and consumption in Early Modern Europe. She has published articles regarding festival culture, the art market and princely collections, diplomatic gifts as well as the socio-cultural and economic aspects of luxury trade. Forthcoming publication: *Bilder der Macht. Venezianische Repräsentationsstrategien beim Staatsbesuch Heinrichs III* (1574) (Berlin: Akademie Verlag, 2013).

Iain McClure combines his research with teaching English at Epsom College in Surrey. His main research interests concern early modern English perceptions of 'the Orient' in general, and the Islamic world in particular. He has contributed an article on the crusading rhetoric of naval pageantry to *The Palatine Wedding of 1613: Context, Celebration and Consequence of an Anglo-German Alliance*, (Herzog August Bibliothek, Wolfenbüttel, 2013) edited by Sara Smart and Mara Wade. He is also working on a monograph based on his doctoral thesis on the 'Orientalism' of John Milton's writings, and has developing research interests in early Anglo-Russian relations and the discourses of monstrosity in early modern literature.

Margaret M. McGowan (Fellow of the British Academy) is Research Professor of The University of Sussex. Her research interests centre on the intellectual, cultural and artistic concerns of Early Modern Europe. Her publications include: *L'Art du ballet de cour en France, 1581–1643* (1963); *Montaigne's Deceits* (1974); *Ideal Forms in the Age of Ronsard* (1985); *The Vision of Rome in Late Renaissance France* (2000); and *Dance in the Renaissance: European Fashion, French Obsession* (2008). She gave the Leopold Delisle lectures in 2012, was awarded the Wolfson Prize in 2008 and the CBE for services to French Studies in 1998.

J.R. (Ronnie) Mulryne is Professor Emeritus of the University of Warwick, having previously been Director of the Centre for the Study of the Renaissance and Pro-Vice-Chancellor at the same University. He is author and editor of numerous publications, mainly in the areas of Shakespeare and Elizabethan/Jacobean theatre and contemporary theatre. Of particular relevance to the present volume is his General Editorship (with Helen Watanabe-O'Kelly and Margaret Shewring) of *Europa Triumphans*, a two volume collection of Court and Civic Festivals in Early Modern Europe (Ashgate, 2004; e-book, 2010), his edited collection, with Elizabeth Goldring, of *Court Festivals of the European Renaissance: Art, Politics and Performance* (Aldershot and Burlington VA: Ashgate, 2002), and his leadership of the digitisation project 'Renaissance Festival Texts' in the British Library's Treasures in Full series. He is currently co-Convenor of the Society for European Festivals Research.

Eric Nicholson has been a member of the Faculty of the Syracuse University in Florence since 1998. He holds a BA from the University of California, Berkeley, an MA from the Centre of the Study of the Renaissance, University of Warwick and a PhD from Yale University. His publications and translations include: *Sin and Fear: the emergence of a western guilt culture* (translator, St Martin's Press, 1990), articles in *A History of Women in the West* (Harvard University Press, 1993), *Place and Displacement in the Renaissance* (SUNY, 1995) and *Transnational Exchange in Early Modern Theater* (co-editor with Robert Henke, Ashgate, 2008).

David Sánchez Cano studied composition and guitar in Chicago (BM 1986, Roosevelt University) and musicology and art history in Berlin (MA 1997 and PhD 2006, Technische Universität Berlin), where he wrote his doctoral thesis on 'Royal Festivals in Madrid 1560–1690'. He has published various articles on festivals, dance, photography, and film in English, Spanish and German and is the co-author (with B. Borngässer and F. Scheffler) of *Madrid and the Prado* (Königstein, 2009). Currently he lives and works in Madrid as an independent scholar and translator.

Roger Savage taught for thirty-five years at the University of Edinburgh, where he staged productions of early opera and other forms of music theatre. He presented documentary programmes for BBC Radio 3 and is author of the entries on 'Incidental Music' and 'Opera production to 1860' for the second edition of the *New Grove Dictionary of Music and Musicians* (2000). His published essays include pieces on staging at court in the 1620s, Purcell's theatrical connections, Baroque stage presentations of the Native Americans and Metastasio's ideas on opera production. He contributed a chapter entitled 'Checklist for Philostrate' to J.R. Mulryne and Elizabeth Goldring (eds), *Court Festivals of the European Renaissance* (Basingstoke and Burlington, VT: Ashgate, 2002) and an introduction on the staging of European Festivals to J.R. Mulryne, Helen Watanabe-O'Kelly and Margaret Shewring (gen. eds), *Europa Triumphans: Court and Civic Festivals of the European Renaissance* (2 vols, Aldershot and Burlington VT: Ashgate, 2004).

Margaret Shewring (Editor) is Reader in Theatre and Performance Studies at the University of Warwick. Her teaching, research and recent publications concentrate on the performance context for Shakespeare and his contemporaries, Renaissance and Early Modern European Festivals and the design of space for performance on the contemporary stage. She was co-general editor of the two volume *Europa Triumphans: Court and Civic Festivals in Early Modern Europe* (Ashgate, 2004; e-book 2010) and a co-investigator for the digitised collection of Renaissance Festival Books on the website of the British Library. She is a co-founder of the Society for European Festivals Research and joint general editor, with J.R. Mulryne and Margaret M. McGowan of the new Ashgate Series of European Festival Studies.

Mara R. Wade is a Professor of Germanic Languages and Literatures at the University of Illinois at Urbana-Champaign. She has published over forty scholarly articles and is the principal investigator for the research group 'Digital Emblematica' at the University of Illinois. She edited and introduced the section on Scandinavian Festival Books in *Europa Triumphans: Court and Civic Festivals in Early Modern Europe*, 2 vols, J.R. Mulryne, Helen Watanabe-O'Kelly and Margaret Shewring, gen. eds (Aldershot and Burlington VT: Ashgate, 2004) and is currently writing a monograph entitled *Splendid Ceremonies: the Great Spectacles of the Early Modern Period in Electoral Saxony and Denmark, 1548–1709.*

Helen Watanabe-O'Kelly is Professor of German Literature at the University of Oxford and a Fellow of Exeter College, Oxford. She works on early modern court culture, German literature and gender questions. Among her books are *Melancholie und die melancholische Landschaft* (1978), *Triumphal Shews. Tournaments at German-Speaking Courts in their European Context 1560–1730* (1992) and *Court Culture in Dresden from Renaissance to Baroque* (2002). She has edited *The Cambridge History of German Literature* (1997), *Spectaculum Europaeum. Theatre and Spectacle in Europe, (1580–1750)* with Pierre Béhar (1999) and *Europa Triumphans: Court and Civic Festivals in Early Modern Europe* with J.R. Mulryne and Margaret Shewring (2004). Her most recent book is *Beauty or Beast? The Woman Warrior in the German Imagination from the Renaissance to the Present* (2010).

Mary M. Young graduated with distinction from Stanford University in 1980 with a BA in Art History. She joined the Masters' programme in Art History at Southern Methodist University where she was awarded scholarships for academic achievement and received her MA in 1992. Currently in the PhD programme in Humanities at the University of Texas at Dallas, she has completed her doctoral coursework and is preparing for her qualifying exams. Her principal field of academic interest is 'Ritual and festival culture of early modern Europe, especially grand-ducal Florence'.

Melanie Zefferino is a trained conservator, specialising in historic techniques, with an interdisciplinary background in the visual and performing arts. After graduating with honours in *Fine Arts and Conservation* at the Accademia Albertina she obtained a Master's degree in *Museum Studies* from the University of Leicester, and a postgraduate Diploma in *Archiving, Palaeography & Diplomacy* from the State Archives of Turin. She is now a final year PhD candidate at the University of Warwick, with joint supervision from the Theatre Studies and Art History Departments. Since 2009 she has been the keeper of the Ruffini Collection, formerly belonging to Prince Scipione Borghese. As a museum professional she has collaborated with the Victor Salvi Harp Museum, the Municipality of Villafranca Piemonte, Galleria Dieffe, the Tel Aviv Museum of Art with Associazione Italia–Israele in Florence and the Civic Museums of Castiglione Olona. She also worked for Bolaffi and the historic Lenci factory in Turin. From 2008 to 2010 she was board director of the Istituzione MusicaTeatro Moncalieri, managing the civic theatre and school of music there.

Introduction

Margaret Shewring

The rich diversity of chapters included in this collection is testament to the wealth of commentary invited by waterborne events throughout the Renaissance and Early Modern periods. Yet, surprisingly, no previous collection has attempted to address the extensive scope of waterborne festivals across Europe. This is all the more surprising given the hold on the poetic imagination of rivers,[1] fountains, lakes and seas as well as the essential role played by water – seas, rivers, lakes and canals – in the very survival of communities, cities and countries, providing routes for the transport of goods, services and individuals as well as employment and leisure activities.

The sea, occupying such a significant proportion of the maps devised by early cartographers, was depicted as at once enticing and dangerous – offering allurements to visit strange and distant new worlds but signalling, often through the depiction of rocks or sea monsters, that such adventures were not without their hazards. Seas provided borders for nations. They had to be traversed for the purposes of aggression or to confirm alliances.[2] They were treacherous in offering opportunity to pirates and hostile naval forces. As Roger Crowley writes of the Mediterranean:

> To those living on the shore, the million square miles of water, broken up into a dozen separate zones, each with its own particular winds and coastal irregularities and scattered islands, were intractable, vast and dangerous – so big that the two halves of the Mediterranean were different worlds.[3]

The seas pitted humanity against nature as sailors contemplated the winds and tides that could bring good speed or becalmed isolation. The hazards encountered

---

[1] The classic instance in English poetry of the period is Book 4, Canto 11, stanzas 8–53 of Edmund Spenser's *Faerie Queene*, which enumerates each of the principal rivers of England taking part in celebrations for the marriage of the Thames and the Medway. See also Samuel Daniel's court masque for 1610 in which Princess Elizabeth Stuart played the part of the Thames in *Tethys Festival* (Tethys being the wife of Neptune) at Whitehall Palace.

[2] See Peter Barber and Tom Harper, *Magnificent Maps: Power, Propaganda and Art* (London: The British Library, 2010).

[3] Roger Crowley, *Empires of the Sea, the Final Battle for the Mediterranean, 1521–1580* (London: Faber and Faber, 2008), p. 3.

by seafaring nations led them to invoke supernatural aid in their ventures, whether from the Gods of Christianity or Islam, or from Neptune, the Roman god who personified the power of the sea.

The conference at which a number of chapters for this book were first presented as papers took place in Venice, in Spring 2010, in honour of J.R. (Ronnie) Mulryne. Its intention was both to celebrate and draw on his scholarship, to acknowledge his achievements, in collaboration with academic colleagues, research fellows and postgraduate students, in making Renaissance and Early Modern festival books accessible in print and on-line and to focus on his keen interest in the imaginative as well as the practical life of spaces for performance.

Venice was the perfect location. The city in the lagoon still depends upon its canals and so presents a little-changed face to our contemporary world from its Renaissance and earlier past. It has been celebrated in paintings down the centuries as artists have been drawn to its distinctive qualities of light.[4] Venice lies at the intersection of the 'two halves of the Mediterranean', as is evident in its architecture, fine arts, ceremony and way of life.[5] For Shakespeare's merchant, Antonio, it is the fulcrum of the trade in luxury goods from the Byzantine world – a seriously risky venture in the sixteenth and early-seventeenth centuries as Salerio makes clear in envisioning the wreck of a proud argosy:

> Should I go to church
> And see the holy edifice of stone
> And not bethink me straight of dangerous rocks
> Which, touching but my gentle vessel's side,
> Would scatter all her spices on the stream,
> Enrobe the roaring waters with my silks,
> And, in a word, but even now worth this,
> And now worth nothing?
>   *The Merchant of Venice*, 1, i, 29–36.

The need to maintain a peaceful relationship with the Venetian lagoon is underlined by the annual celebration of the Sensa, an occasion pervaded with both Christian and traditional folk associations as the Doge, representing the city and sailing in the *Bucintoro* or state barge, plays his leading role in a ceremony of union with the sea.[6] Both Evelyn Korsch and Iain Fenlon concentrate on Venetian waterborne

---

[4]   See Paul Hills, *The Light of Early Italian Painting* (New Haven and London: Yale University Press, 1987) and Paul Hills, *Venetian Colour: Marble Mosaic, painting and Glass, 1250–1550* (New Haven and London: Yale University Press, c. 1999).

[5]   See Iain Fenlon, *The Ceremonial City: History, Memory and Myth in Renaissance Venice* (New Haven and London: Yale University Press, 2007) *passim*.

[6]   See Lina Urban Padoan, *Il Bucintoro* (Venice: Centro Internationale della Grafica, 1988) and Asa Boholm, *The Doge in Venice: the Symbolism of State Power in the Renaissance* (Gottenburg: IASSA, 1990).

festivals in this collection, while Helen Watanabe-O'Kelly discusses the festivities for Ernst August von Braunschweig-Lüneburg in Venice in 1685 and 1686.

To be, and to be seen as being, in control of the gift of water came to be regarded as a necessary requirement of a ruler concerned with the wellbeing of his people. This could be extended into the celebration of such powers as Maria Ines Aliverti outlines in her discussion of 'Water Policy and Water Festivals: the Case of Pisa under Ferdinando de' Medici (1588–1609)'. Irrigation and transport, but also gardens, fountains and grottos, man-made lakes and aqueducts could all be presented as features of the benevolent state, both in terms of the practical details of everyday life and in the cultural significance of this liquid environment for the pleasures of the mind and even the soul.

A long-standing bond with water is equally significant even in cities not bordering the sea. The rivers of France and Italy, for example, provided the arteries of their nation – sources of transport, trade and irrigation, and a location for festivals. In France numerous towns and cities, including Paris, Lyon, Rouen and Bayonne, staged elaborate water festivities during the early modern period including waterborne tournaments and firework displays, as Richard Cooper, Margaret M. McGowan, Monique Chatenet and R.J. Knecht detail in their chapters. Even a frozen river, as in Florence in 1604, as Mary M. Young shows, could offer opportunities for trade, sport and festivities. Spain, in its general lack of waterborne festivals, proved to be an exception to this widespread practice: as David Sánchez Cano demonstrates in his study of a small-scale water-pageant in the Buen Retiro in Madrid in June, 1657.

The chapters included here reflect the extraordinary range of waterborne pageants and festivities – from the celebrations associated with the election of civic officials (as in London at the annual Lord Mayor's show) to river processions that formed part of the welcome for a monarch or other noble ruler, or marked an investiture or coronation, the visit of an ambassador, the arrival of a foreign bride or bridegroom and the presentation of that person in a host city.[7] Sydney Anglo offers an authoritative overview in this volume of celebrations on the Thames and Michael Holden draws on the accounts held in the archives of the Watermen's Company in London while Iain McClure discusses an ambassadorial welcome and its place in the city's maritime politics. For Peter Ackroyd, writing his well-known London biography documenting the historical presence of the Thames and its memories, the great river 'brought in a thousand argosies. Venetian galleys and three-masted ships from the Low Countries vied for position by the riverside, while the water itself was crowded with wherries and ferries transporting the citizens from one shore to the other' on a daily basis. On special state and civic occasions

---

[7] In Naples (1506) and Genoa (1529) important guests arriving by sea were greeted using 'long piers' constructed out into the sea and bearing elaborate devices. See Bonner Mitchell, *Italian Civic Pageantry in the High Renaissance* (Florence: Leo S. Olschki Editore, 1979).

the Thames, he adds, became 'the river of magnificence, used as a golden highway by princes and diplomats'.[8]

Sometimes waterborne displays took the form of re-enactments of naval battles that were of particular significance to the identity of the host country. These *naumachiae* evoked moments of past glory as part of the state or national self-image and as projecting that image on the wider stage of international diplomacy.[9] A particular and repeated focus for such image-making was the Battle of Lepanto, as demonstrated here by Marie-Claude Canova-Green as she traces its representations from 1571 to 1656. Lepanto fired the imaginations of the Christian States and statelets as they vied amongst themselves to be seen as securing advantage over the Ottoman Empire, a powerful, exotic 'other' that was so feared by all of them. Examples of re-enactments of other naval battles in locations as distant from each other as Scotland and Savoy may also be found in this collection in Pesala Bandara's study of Mary, Queen of Scots' aquatic entertainments for the marriage of John Fleming to Elizabeth Ross, for which the Siege of Leith was reconstructed on a Scottish loch in May 1562, and Melanie Zefferino's engaging account of an unlikely naval reconstruction on Lake Cenis, high in the Alps. The latter, an occasion that took place during the journey from Chambery to Turin marking the engagement of Victor Amédée I of Savoy and the thirteen-year-old Marie Christine de Bourbon, recalled the historic achievements of Amédée V of Savoy's expedition to Rhodes in 1315 dedicated to aiding the Knights of St John defending Rhodes against the Turks.

Naumachiae were not restricted to the reconstruction of past naval battles. Waterborne celebrations could also utilise the vocabulary of story-telling and romance to pit the forces of the good, presented as brave, heroic and glamorous, very often using the iconography of classical gods and goddesses, against opponents of all kinds, both human and monstrous. Such heroic quests could be represented as being in the service of a community or of a lady, in the chivalric tradition underpinning such legends as that of St George slaying the dragon or of Jason and his quest for the Golden Fleece, feats commemorated in the British Order of the Garter and the Burgundian Order of the Golden Fleece. Seaborne quests might be presented by utilising personifications of the natural hazards faced in voyages of conquest or discovery. Such *naumachiae* drew on the martial skills of the participants as they sailed through difficult circumstances to assault island fortresses in order to rescue prisoners (usually a lady) held there as in 'the stories of old'.[10] They might even take the form of a fully staged *tournois à theme* as in

---

[8]   Peter Ackroyd, *London: the Biography* (London: Vintage, 2001), pp. 539–40.

[9]   The first *naumachia* on record represented the engagement between a Tyrian and an Egyptian fleet and was given by Julius Caesar in 46 BC on a lake which he had constructed in the Campus Martius.

[10]   'When a knight won his spurs, in the stories of old', Jan Struther (pen name of Joyce Anstruther, later Joyce Maxtone Graham and finally Joyce Placzek), *Songs of Praise*, enlarged edition (Oxford: Oxford University Press, 1931), Hymn 377.

the case of the 'L'Isola Beata' entertainments in the moat surrounding Ferrara's wall, on a theme taken from Ariosto. This was a festivity with which Duke Alfonso II d'Este marked the visit of Karl, Archduke of Austria in 1569 and, in so doing, sought to exceed the celebrated achievements of the Medici in staging waterborne occasions of all kinds.[11] That the dangers of participation in these *naumachiae* were real is attested by injuries and even fatalities. Equally, however, sea quests possessed the imagination of contemporaries in a pervasive way that had little to do with politics or action-packed re-enactments, as Eric Nicholson very skilfully shows in his discussion of the ambivalent, mutating figure of the mermaid, at once enticing and terrifying and omnipresent in literature and theatre.

Perhaps it is not surprising that such combats were often represented in the more controlled environment of court entertainments in halls of great houses and palaces using ingenious, innovative set designs that, as Roger Savage demonstrates, could evoke such 'sea spectacles on dry land'. Nor is it surprising that the desire of rulers to be at one with their land and people, shaping the natural environment in their people's interests, is reflected in the themes of many indoor court entertainments, notably the masques of the Stuart and Caroline courts in Britain, themselves much influenced by continental precedents.

Waterborne pageants and festivities temporarily transformed people's perception of the everyday into the extraordinary. They also displayed ingenious feats of engineering as artificial lakes were constructed on dry land in open landscapes or in the courtyards of palaces. Two chapters in this collection significantly advance our understanding of such scenic challenges entailed by in making space for the performance of water festivals in such localities together with the impact they exerted on spectators and the political implications they expressed. J.R. Mulryne unpacks the complexities entailed in the staging of a *naumachia* in the courtyard of the Pitti Palace in Florence to mark the wedding of Ferdinando de' Medici and Christine of Lorraine in 1589. H. Neville Davies brings new evidence to bear on the construction of the lake for a waterborne entertainment for Elizabeth I at Elvetham in 1591.

In a similar way to land-based royal and ducal progresses in the Renaissance and Early Modern period, waterborne spectacles may invoke legendary or folk-traditional stories, or make use of mythic figures to enhance the magnificence of the occasion. Such visual references often drew on the achievements of Ancient Rome.[12] They might refer, also, to national stories. For example, progresses for Elizabeth I drew on both pastoral imagery derived from classical sources and on

---

[11]   See Alessandro Marcigliano, *Chivalric Festivals at the Ferrarese Court of Alfonso II d'Este*, Stage and Screen Studies, 2 (Bern: Peter Lang, 2003), especially pp. 63–116. Marcigliano bases his discussion on the printed account of the occasion by Ercole Estense Tassoni which survives in 3 copies, two in the BCFe and one in the John Rylands Library in Manchester.

[12]   See Margaret M. McGowan, *The Vision of Rome in Late Renaissance France* (New Haven and London: Yale University Press, 2000).

the chivalric world of Arthurian legend. This was legendary material that was to feature again in the context of entertainments, masques and Barriers for the young Prince Henry Stuart in the early seventeenth-century, with the barely concealed intention of celebrating him as both a chivalric leader in the tradition of British rulers and as a potential defender of the Protestant cause in Europe.

The performance possibilities of water are also crucial to our understanding of waterborne festivals. Water provides a stage, natural or constructed. It separates the performers from spectators gathered to watch the occasion, whether from the bank, from bridges, from stands erected around a flooded courtyard or lake, or from a boat. If a river provides this natural *mise en scène*, it is unlikely that all of the spectators would have shared the same impression of pageant or performance. Sections of the festivity might float by, words drowned out by the sounds of the water as well as the general level of noise among the spectators. Indeed, if Peter Ackroyd is correct, then background noise was a constant presence in London in the sixteenth century, where

> the sound of water from fifteen conduits mingled with the noise of the Thames and its lapping tides, audible along all the lanes and thoroughfares which led to the river. Great wheels were used to pump water from the Thames into small wooden pipes, and their endless grinding and reverberation added materially to the overwhelming noise of the city.[13]

On festival occasions, music might carry rather better against such a soundscape, enhancing the pomp and ceremony of an event or making contact with the public by using popular songs or sea shanties. Volleys of gunfire might attract attention. Bells rung on the water might be answered by peals of bells from church towers and steeples along the way. And as for the sets built on barges – these could evoke the scale and magnificence of a procession, framing costumes and heraldic devices as well as displaying the banners of trades guilds or confraternities, and thus enhancing the spectacle. Such festivities require the skills of orators and singers, composers and musicians, writers and devisers of pageant-settings and costumes, campanologists and skilled sailors, shipwrights and stage managers. Waterborne festivities entailed huge challenges of organisation and 'stage' management.

Water may muffle or suppress sound, but it reflects light and provides a 'double image' in sunlight, so that the visual spectacle of the overall occasion may well be enhanced in daylight, adding to the enjoyment of spectators. By day, water provides the context for regattas and flotillas of all kinds as they become part of the spectacle. In the evening and at night-time, water serves as an enticing backdrop to firework displays – increasing their impact through the delights of reflected colour. The creative skills of pyrotechnicians were much in demand and the water could, of course, also provide an element of safety in quenching the spent fire and distancing spectators from exploding fireworks. These are phenomena

[13]   Ackroyd, *London: the Biography*, p. 74.

which Mara Wade discusses in a chapter that vividly evokes the widespread use of fireworks in festival celebrations in Saxony and Denmark in the sixteenth to the eighteenth century.

It is hardly surprising that waterborne festivities formed, and still form, a prime part of state and civic, public and private celebrations – as was evident in the recent festivities on the Thames for the diamond jubilee of Queen Elizabeth II.[14]

The roughly chronological structure of this book celebrates the diversity of spectacles and locations rather than grouping such activities together under the heading of one country or city, or according to one sub-genre or another of waterborne occasions. Each chapter makes a distinctive contribution to the description and contextualisation of the waterborne occasion or occasions on which it centres. Each, too, discusses or hints at the political, economic, social and cultural reverberations of such events in Renaissance and Early Modern Europe. Sometimes the analysis of these reverberations is the focal point of the chapter, sometimes it can be understood through the chapter's relation to other chapters in the collection.

The contributors to the book come from a wide variety of academic and curatorial disciplines and countries. The sources they draw on range from festival books, plays and poems to the material holdings of museums, the records of livery companies and written records held in civic archives as well as national library collections. These sources include evidence relating to scenography and choreography, music, fashion, painting, sculpture, architecture and urban planning. The manuscript, print and electronic sources drawn on by the writers of each chapter are included in the bibliographies of primary and secondary materials printed at the end of the relevant chapter, rather than gathered together at the end of the volume. Quotations are included in the body of the text, both the original language of the work being quoted and in an English translation. Variant spellings of proper names – Catherine de' Medici and Catherine de Médicis, or Henry III and Henri III – follow the usage of different countries and academic disciplines, and are consistent within chapters. Cross-referenced entries in the index offer any necessary clarification of the anomalies.

The book that follows this Introduction not only addresses a topic central to the cultural, political and economic life of the nation states of Early Modern Europe, but seeks in addition to bring to bear the disciplines of today's scholarship as practised by colleagues from many academic and curatorial backgrounds and national traditions. If we have succeeded in weaving a coherent overview from these multiple perspectives and if, in turn, we have succeeded in stimulating further study of this important topic, the collection will have fully served its purpose.

---

[14] See Susan Doran (ed.), *Royal River: Power, Pageantry and the Thames*, the catalogue for the exhibition of the same name at the National Maritime Museum, guest curator David Starkey (London: Royal Museums Greenwich, 2012).

Bibliography

Ackroyd, Peter, *London, the Biography* (London: Vintage, 2001).

Barber, Peter and Tom Harper, *Magnificent Maps: Power, Propaganda and Art* (London: The British Library, 2010).

Boholm, Asa, *The Doge in Venice: the Symbolism of State Power in the Renaissance* (Gottenburg: IASSA, 1990).

Crowley, Roger, *Empires of the Sea, the Final Battle for the Mediterranean, 1521–1580* (London: Faber and Faber, 2008).

Doran, Susan (ed.), *Royal River: Power, Pageantry and the Thames*, exhibition catalogue (London: Royal Museums Greenwich, 2012).

Fenlon, Iain, *The Ceremonial City: History, Memory and Myth in Renaissance Venice* (New Haven and London: Yale University Press, 2007).

Hills, Paul, *The Light of Early Italian Painting* (New Haven and London: Yale University Press, 1987).

Hills, Paul, *Venetian Colour: Marble Mosaic, painting and Glass, 1250–1550* (New Haven and London: Yale University Press, c. 1999).

Marcigliano, Alessandro, *Chivalric Festivals at the Ferrarese Court of Alfonso II d'Este*, Stage and Screen Studies, 2 (Bern: Peter Lang, 2003).

McGowan, Margaret M., *The Vision of Rome in Late Renaissance France* (New Haven and London: Yale University Press, 2000).

Mitchell, Bonner, *Italian Civic Pageantry in the High Renaissance* (Florence: Leo S. Olschki Editore, 1979).

Struther, Jan, *Songs of Praise* enlarged edition (Oxford: Oxford University Press, 1931), Hymn 377.

Urban, Lina Padoan, *Il Bucintoro* (Venice: Centro Internationale della Grafica, 1988).

Chapter 1
French Renaissance Waterborne Festivals in the Sixteenth Century

Richard Cooper

While Venice is famous for a profusion of waterborne festivals, not least those offered to an incoming Henri III, which are discussed in this volume of essays, and which were so elaborate that they were sent up in an amusing and fantastical pamphlet to which I will return at the end; while Portugal and even Spain has occasional waterborne festivals in Burgos,[1] Valencia[2] or Madrid,[3] Tudela or Tortosa;[4] France is less well known for its Renaissance aquatics. A number of chapters in this volume try to correct this, notably on Lyon, Paris, Fontainebleau and Bayonne, which allows me to focus on broader aspects of the subject.

Not that *aqua* is always essential for aquatics. Textbooks like that of Sabbatini,[5] explain how to create a realistic impression of movement of sea and waves on the stage, anticipated in the Sirens and Tritons leaping about in the *Balet comique de la royne*.[6] A good example is the performance in front of the château de Nantes in February 1596 of Nicolas de Montreux's *Arimène* for the duc de Mercœur. Among the five *intermèdes* was one of the rape of Helen (II), followed by a naval battle:

> *une mer coula artificieusement sur le theatre où flottaient les navires de Pâris,*
> *qui rencontrent en leur route des nefs ennemis*

---

[1]   S. Carrasco Urgoïti, 'Les Fêtes équestres dans les *Guerres civiles de Grenade*', in J. Jacquot (ed.), *Fêtes de la Renaissance* (3 vols, Paris: CNRS, 1956–75), vol. 3, p. 311; cf. N.D. Shergold, *History of the Spanish Stage* (Oxford: Oxford University Press, 1967), p. 242.

[2]   J.E. Varey, 'Les Spectacles pyrotechniques en Espagne (XVI–XVII siècles)', in Jacquot, *Fêtes*, vol. 3, p. 624.

[3]   See David Sánchez Cano's chapter in this volume, pp. 313–28.

[4]   C.A. Marsden, 'Entrées et fêtes espagnoles au XVIe siècle', in Jacquot, *Fêtes*, vol. 2, pp. 394–5.

[5]   N. Sabbatini, *Pratica di fabricar scene e machine ne' teatri* (Ravenna: P. de' Paoli and G.B. Giovannelli, 1638), in-fol.

[6]   J. Rousset, 'L'Eau et les tritons dans les fêtes et ballets de cour (1580–1640)', in Jacquot, *Fêtes*, vol. 1, pp. 235–45; see also the edition of the *Balet comique* by Margaret M. McGowan (Binghamton: Center for Medieval and Early Renaissance Studies, c. 1982).

[a sea flowed artfully across the theatre, bearing Paris's ships, which encounter enemy ships on their route]

and another (III) showing Andromeda chained to a rock, and how a sea monster that fires out water is defeated by Perseus:[7]

> *Sur le theatre parut une mer agitée, et les pentagones changeant de face parurent portant des grotesques et rochers [...]. A l'instant sortit le monstre de la mer, avec un haut bruit et jaillissement de flots.*

[On the theatre a stormy sea appeared, and five-sided revolving flats appeared, depicting rocks and grotesques [...]. Suddenly the monster rose from the sea, with loud noise and surging waves.]

The Antwerp Ommegangs, and François d'Anjou's 1582 entry,[8] made much of the ship on dry land, as did Brussels for the funeral of Charles V.[9] The marriage ceremonies in the Pitti Palace for Francesco de' Medici turn a courtyard into a lake, or have galleys or sea-creatures on wheels.[10] In Lyon in 1533,[11] the Arch at St Eloy sheltered a model ship in full sail, which lacked a helmsman, to the consternation of the sailors seeking guidance, until the arrival of the Virago Eleanor gave the answer to a sailor's prayer.

Gifts made to French monarchs by hopeful cities have a marine flavour, whether a representation of Perseus liberating Andromeda,[12] or the inevitable Neptune promising dominion of the seas, or a three-masted golden ship in full sail, filled with golden *écus*;[13] or again a golden statue of Charles offered in Montpellier,

---

[7] Rousset, 'L'Eau et les tritons', p. 238; R. Lebègue, 'Les Présentations dramatiques à la Cour des Valois', in Jacquot, *Fêtes*, vol. 1, p. 88.

[8] E. McGrath, 'Le Déclin d'Anvers et les decorations de Rubens pour l'entrée du Prince Ferdinand en 1635', in Jacquot, *Fêtes*, vol. 3, p. 181 and fig 9.

[9] S. Williams, 'L'Ommegangs d'Anvers et les cortèges du Lord-Maire de Londres', in Jacquot, *Fêtes*, vol. 2, pp. 353–4; J. Jacquot, 'Panorama des fêtes et cérémonies du règne', in ibid., vol. 2, pp. 469–71 and pl. XLVI.

[10] See the chapters by Maria Ines Aliverti and J.R. Mulryne in this volume, pp. 119–41 and 143–75; cf. C. Rinuccini, *Descrizione delle feste fatte nelle reali nozze de' serenissimi principe di Toscana* (Florence: I Giusti, 1608).

[11] D. Godefroy, *Le Cérémonial François* (2 vols, Paris: S. and G. Cramoisy, 1649), vol. 1, p. 808.

[12] A. de Ruffi, *Histoire de Marseille* (Marseille: C. Garcin, 1642), vol. 1, p. 230; Jean Boutier, Alain Dewerpe and Daniel Nordman, *Un Tour de France royal: le voyage de Charles IX (1564–1566)*, (Paris: Aubier, c. 1984), p. 400.

[13] Godefroy, *Cérémonial*, vol.1, p. 778: '*avec un don d'un navire d'or, avec trois hunes fort beau et grand, plein d'escus au Soleil, couvert et équipé comme s'il eust esté fait pour nager*' ('with a gift of a very fine and large golden three-masted ship, full of gold *écus*, rigged and fitted out as if built to sail').

standing on the shore of the Mediterranean, one foot on land, one on sea.[14] Nantes developed a speciality of offering gilded silver ships, taken from the city's coat of arms.[15] In Paris too, much is regularly made in the iconography of the ship on the city's shield,[16] and the same will apply in Caen, a maritime town, which makes no use of the sea in its entries, but has symbols including hands on tillers, anchors, lighthouses, storm-tossed ships,[17] or has seven virgins, representing the Virtues, pouring water into an '*estang*' ('pond').[18]

But France in fact has, throughout the sixteenth century, a good tradition of water festivals, of considerable variety, stimulated by an itinerant court covering hundreds of miles per year in the biggest country in Europe, and by the tradition of the *joyeuses entrées* at the beginning of each reign. I stress itinerant court, because of the convenience of river transport, which these festivals turn into something less mundane. To welcome Eleanor and the Royal Children to Bordeaux in 1530, a special boat was sent to Langon upstream on the Garonne, allowing the party to

> *vaguer sur la marine entre Langon et Bordeaux, en batteaux propres et experts, vitrez, peints, et dorez si magnifiquement, que la maison de verre du Roy d'Angleterre, tant estimé à la venue et entreveuë d'Ardres leur cedoit le lieu, quant à l'excellence des richesses et beautez.*[19]

[sail on the water between Langon and Bordeaux, in neat, manoeuvrable vessels, glazed, painted and gilded so magnificently that the King of England's glass palace at the Field of Cloth of Gold at Ardres was inferior to them in outstanding wealth and beauty.]

---

[14]   Boutier, *Un Tour*, p. 400.

[15]   For instance in May 1518, the city fathers commissioned a '*navire d'argent tout vermoille doré tant dehors que dedans*' ('a silver ship made inside and out of silver gilt'), see Nantes, Arch. Mun. AA 29, doc. 4 and 8.

[16]   Godefroy, *Cérémonial*, vol. 1, p. 733: '*grand navire d'argent voguant sur la mer*' ('a large silver ship sailing on the sea') with Roy Bacchus (King Bacchus) on board, surrounded by four '*monstres soufflans*' ('puffing monsters') for the winds, and many matelots, '*lesquels chantoient melodieusement*' ('singing tunefully').

[17]   See J. de Cahaignes, *Entrée du duc de Joyeuse à Caen le 5 avril 1583*, ed. T. Genty, Société des Bibliophiles Normands, 63 (Rouen: L. de Gy, 1900), pp. 3–6; J. de Cahaignes, *Discours de l'entrée du duc d'Epernon à Caen, le 14 mai 1588*, ed. R. de Formigny de la Londe, Société des Bibliophiles Normands, 66 (Rouen: L. de Gy, 1903), p. 12.

[18]   C. Bourgueville, *Les Recherches et antiquitez de la ville et Université de Caen* (Caen: J. Le Fevre, 1588), p. 106.

[19]   See the album 'Les Triomphes et nouvelles de la cour', in Godefroy, *Cérémonial*, vol. 1, p. 769; E. Fournier, *Variétés historiques et littéraires* (10 vols, Paris: P. Jannet, 1855–63), vol. 8, p. 252.

As part of the crossing of France by Charles V in 1539, the '*échevins*' (aldermen) of Orleans fitted out ten or twelve boats to meet François Ier at Gien on the Loire, and to fetch him to Orleans:

> *tous couverts de satin, où estoient galleries, cha[m]bres, cheminées, et cabarets en mode de navires; et y en avoit un special pour le Roy, où y avoit quatre chambres, galeries et jeux de paume.*[20]

> [all covered in satin, containing the kind of galleries, bedchambers, fireplaces and serveries found in ships; and there was a special one for the King, with four bedchambers, galleries and tennis courts.]

Nantes made a speciality of using expert local sailors to navigate the treacherous Loire to guide royal visitors safely.[21] In 1500 the town constructed two '*galliotes*' ('galiots') in which the '*seigneurs de la justice et aultres bourgeois furent au devant du Roy et de la Royne*' ('justices and other burghers went to meet the King and Queen'), Louis XII and Anne de Bretagne; one of the '*galliotes*', used for the king, was fitted with a cabin '*monté sur des arceaux*' ('mounted on arches'), rowed by 18 oarsmen, and strewn with straw.[22] The final part of the visit of François Ier and Claude on 8 August 1518 was made on the '*galions*' ('galleons') fitted out by Nantes and manned by crews recruited from Nantes and Le Croisic.[23] In 1532 Eleanor and the Dauphin were fetched from Ancenis in two '*galliotes*', each decorated with '*trente six grans pavoys armoyez et victrés*' ('thirty-six large shields, glazed and painted with arms') and topped with seven '*guyrouectes de fer blanc*' ('tin weather-vanes') and with '*ecussons*' ('coats of arms'); they had been converted from sailing barges, and fitted with a deck and glazed cabin, waterproofed with tarpaulin, and arrayed with rich internal hangings. It took a crew of 23 to sail the smaller '*galliote*' for the king and queen to Ancenis, and to navigate shallow waters in August, taking two days to cover the short distance and then, after the entry, needing a crew of 40 to take them back to Ancenis. The low water level, and the narrowness of the river in some places, meant that the craft had to be towed, and paddles provided to clear a path through the silt.[24] Once the

---

[20]   Godefroy, *Cérémonial*, vol. 2, p. 757.

[21]   P. Lelièvre, 'Entrées royales à Nantes à l'époque de la Renaissance, 1500–1551', in Jacquot, *Fêtes,* vol. 3, pp. 81–91; S. Garcia, 'L'Entrée de Henri IV à Nantes le 13 avril 1598: une manœuvre politique', in Anon., *Nantes et le pays nantais au moment de l'édit de Nantes* (Nantes: Société archéologique et historique de Nantes et de Loire-Atlantique, 1999), pp. 9–17.

[22]   Nantes, Arch. Mun., AA 27, doc. 1–2; Lelièvre, 'Entrées royales à Nantes', p. 81.

[23]   Nantes, Arch. Mun., AA 29, doc. 3 and 9; Lelièvre, 'Entrées royales à Nantes', p. 83.

[24]   Nantes, Arch. Mun., AA 30, doc. 10–11, 14, 19; Lelièvre, 'Entrées royales à Nantes', pp. 83–4.

guests were in Nantes, however, there is no evidence of the river being used as part of the ceremonial.

In the Royal tour of 1564–66, Charles IX and his mother, Catherine de' Medici, made use of ceremonial boats which had been fitted out for them by the municipalities,[25] travelling from Chalon-sur-Saône and Mâcon to Lyon in a '*basteau sumptueusement basty et maisonné*' ('sumptuously constructed and fitted vessel'), decorated by the Lyon municipality;[26] or up the Garonne to Agen[27] and then on to Bordeaux, on a craft rigged out by Toulouse,[28] before transferring to a boat provided by the Jurats of Bordeaux for the entry to that city,[29] before going off towards Bayonne, and being picked up by two craft sent by the elders of that town:[30]

> *deux Bapteaulx qui seront assès propres, selon la portée des rivieres de ce païs; oultre ce, qu'ilz seront accompagnez de douze gallions, lesquelz serviront de vous donner passe temps sur les rivieres.*[31]

> [two vessels, which will be very appropriate for the capacity of the rivers of this region; in addition, they will be escorted by twelve galleons, which will be able to provide you with entertainment on the rivers.]

So the river transport was part of the entertainment. Not that the boats were always grand: the royal party crossed the Etang de Berre from Martigues to St Chamant in some sort of skiff,[32] while Catherine borrowed some fishing boats to cross to the Etang de Leucate towards the Spanish border.[33]

As Margaret McGowan has written,[34] the lagoon in Venice makes it easy, whereas in France, they have to make use of navigable rivers, estuaries, river or seaports and, more rarely, the open sea. The estuaries at Nantes – the Venice of

---

[25]   Boutier, *Un Tour*, p. 122.

[26]   V.E. Graham and W. McAllister Johnson (eds), *The Royal Tour of France by Charles IX and Catherine de' Medici* (Toronto: University of Toronto Press, 1979), pp. 7, 188–9; Boutier, *Un Tour*, p. 371, n. 10.

[27]   Abbé Barrère, 'Entrée et séjour de Charles IX à Agen', in *Bulletin du Comité de Langue, de l'Histoire et des Arts de France*, vol. 1 (1852–53), pp. 472–6.

[28]   Graham and McAllister Johnson, *Royal Tour*, pp. 108–9.

[29]   Ibid., p. 108.

[30]   Ibid., pp. 30, 112.

[31]   Boutier, *Un Tour*, pp. 122, 372, citing E. Ducéré, *Charles IX à Bayonne* (Bayonne: A. Lamaignère, 1889).

[32]   Graham and McAllister Johnson, *Royal Tour*, pp. 95–6.

[33]   Ibid., Appendix IX, pp. 242–5.

[34]   Margaret M. McGowan, 'Festivals and the Arts in Henri III's journey from Poland to France (1574)', in J.R. Mulryne, Helen Watanabe-O'Kelly and Margaret Shewring (eds), *Europa Triumphans: Court and Civic Festivals in Early Modern Europe* (2 vols, Aldershot: Ashgate, 2004), vol 1, pp. 124–5.

the West – and at Bordeaux, were especially suitable, as reported by the Venetian ambassador to France in 1565, when describing the preparations for the *naumachia* on the Garonne, commenting that the river was

> *di tanta larghezza, che dà grandissima commodità a così fatti spettacoli, et potrà riuscir non ingrata vista se sarà dato il carico a persone che ne habbino qualche esperientia.*[35]

[so wide, that it lends itself very well to festivals of this sort, and it may offer a reasonable spectacle if entrusted to people of some experience.]

Perhaps the earliest French entries to make significant use of a seaport are those of Louis XII in 1502 and 1507 to Genoa, with its impressive long jetty.[36] In the earlier the king was shown '*plusieurs passe-temps nouveaux et esbastemens joyeux*' ('several new diversions and joyful entertainments') in the port, where the sailors did acrobatic tricks, climbing the rigging upside down, and diving off the tops into the sea below, swimming underwater, all to the accompaniment of music and cannonades.[37] The 1507 entry had the ships and the castle exchanging fire, plus a mention of the diverse origins of the ships, coming from France, Spain and all over the Mediterranean.[38] The artillery was

---

[35]   G. Suriano – Signoria, 6 April 1565, in BnF, *ms. ital.* 1724, f. 268.

[36]   Godefroy, *Cérémonial*, vol 1, p. 709.

[37]   Ibid., vol. 1, p. 709: '*Là vit les matelots monter les pieds à mont du bas des navires jusque dans les hunes, et descendre la teste contre bas jusques au fond des navires, et les uns se jetter d'amont les hunes jusques en mer, les autres nager sur l'eauë, et les autres dessous fort longuement, tirer l'artillerie, sonner instruments, courir esquifs, brigandins, et galiotes de navire à autre, et faire là mille autres algarades et jeux divers, en quoy prit grand plaisir*'. ('There he saw sailors climbing upside down from below in the ships right to the tops, then coming down again head-first into the ships, and some throwing themselves from the tops into the sea, others swimming in the water, and others swimming a long way underwater, cannon firing, instruments playing, skiffs, brigantines and galiots scurrying from ship to ship, and performing countless other assaults and various games, which greatly delighted the King.')

[38]   Ibid., vol. 1, p. 714: '*deux nefs et six galeres appartenans audit Seigneur, avec quatre autres galeres estans au Roy Catholique, toutes armées et equipées, qui l'espace d'une heure jetterent incessamment coups d'artillerie*' [...]. '*Et est à noter que audict port de Gennes y avoit autres galées, fustes, et nefs d'Alexandrie, Turquie, Barbarie, et autres lieux, où y avoit choses singulieres, qui pour la venue du Roy se resjouyssoient en joüans de plusieurs Instrumens, qu'il faisoit bon voir et ouyr*' ('two ships and six galleys belonging to the King of France, and four other galleys of the King of Spain, fully armed and equipped, which fired artillery salvos continuously for a whole hour [...]. Note that in the said port of Genoa there were other galleys, light galleys, and ships from Alexandria, Turkey, the Barbary Coast, and other places, on board which there were unusual things, and which rejoiced at the King's coming by playing various instruments, which were a pleasure to see and hear.')

so deafening '*qu'il sembloit que tout deust abismer*' ('that it seemed everything would be engulfed').[39]

These accounts appear to have directly influenced practice in France, as witness the 1508 entry to the river-port of Rouen.[40] In a manuscript account we learn that, when the king crossed the bridge, the ships in the port (50 or 60 of them) unfurled their flags and pennants, and played drum rolls, to the delight of the onlookers.[41] And just as in Genoa, the cabin boys swarmed acrobatically all over the rigging,[42] and the cannons roared so loudly, '*et estoit chose si impetueuse, qu'il sembloit que tout deust fondre*' ('and it was so violent, that it seemed everything would collapse').[43] This was copied again in Rouen in 1517, where the pennants flew, and the cabin boys frolicked, and the

---

[39] Ibid., vol. 1, p. 716: '*lesquelles galleres à la passée du Roy tirerent tres horriblement, qu'il sembloit que tout deust abismer*' ('and these galleys, as the King went by, fired their artillery so frighteningly, that it seemed everything would be engulfed').

[40] *L'Entrée du roi Louis XII et de la reine à Rouen 1508*, ed. P. Le Verdier, Société des Bibliophiles Normands, 60 (Rouen: L. de Gy, 1900), pp. xxxiii–iv.

[41] Ibid., pp. 14–15: '*et incontinent les bannyeres et estandarts du navire, qui pour lors estoit en la riviere de Seyne prez dudict port, furent desployez au vent. Et y avoit bien de cinquante à soixante grands navires tous à hune, et d'autres assez en plus grand nombre qui n'avoyent point de hune. En icelles hunes estoyent gros tambours qui sonnoyent* (p. 15) *si haultement qu'il n'y avoit cœur qui ne fust incité à joye, tant à raison de la grand multitude d'iceux tambours que de l'harmonie et resonance qui procedoit à cause du retentissement de l'eaue*' ('and immediately the banners and standards of the ship, which at that time was on the Seine near the said port, were unfurled in the wind. And there were some fifty or sixty large ships all with tops, and an even larger number without tops. From these tops large drums were beating so loudly, that there was no one whose heart was not moved to joy, both by the great number of drums and by the harmony and resonance as the sound echoed off the water').

[42] Ibid., p. 14: '*Semblablement en icelles hunes, appareils et cordaiges estoient petis pages de navires, qui faisoyent tant de menuz sauts, souplaisses de corps et petites autres joyeusetez, que c'estoit plaisant au Roy et aux seigneurs.*' ('Likewise, amidst the tops, ropes and rigging, there were cabin boys, who performed so many leaps, acrobatics, and other little sports, that the King and other lords were delighted.')

[43] Ibid., p. 14: '*Durant le temps que le Roy marchoit sur ycelluy pont, toute l'artillerye d'iceux navires grans et petis fut deschargée toute ensemble, qui estoit chose de grand bruit et admiration, et par plusieurs fois fut rechargée et deschargée; mesme grande partye de l'artillerye de ladicte ville avoit esté menée sur le tallut de ladicte riviere, qui par semblable fut tirée alors, et estoit chose si impetueuse, qu'il sembloit que tout deust fondre. Aultres plusieurs joyeusetez se firent en ladicte riviere, comme lances de feu, de fusées qui volloyent par l'air, et choses semblables qui longues seroyent à reciter.*' ('Whilst the King was walking across the bridge, all the guns of these ships, large and small, were discharged together, which was a noisy and impressive thing, and were then repeatedly reloaded and discharged: likewise much of the city's artillery had been stationed on the river embankment, and was then fired, with such fury that it seemed everything would collapse. Many other sports were performed on the river, such as flares and rockets flying through the air, and such things, which it would take time to recount.')

drums and artillery lifted the hearts of all;[44] and the same goes for 1532.[45] It was not until 1550, and then 1563, that Rouen was to recast these aquatic entertainments completely.

The arrival in Bordeaux in 1530 of Eleanor and the hostage children,[46] by river from Langon, was awaited by seven or eight score vessels in the port, both military and merchant, dressed overall,

> *chacune desdites navires portoit sur leurs hunes estendarts et enseignes de soye aux armes du Roy, avec autres fantaisies,*

[each of these ships carried on their tops silk standards and ensigns sporting the Royal arms and other devices,]

and was greeted by a massive fifteen-minute cannonade on the dockside,

> *et tant fut offusquée l'eauë et aussi le Ciel qu'on ne voyoit goute, et perdoit-on la cognoissance de l'eauë.*[47]

[and the water and sky were so darkened, that one could not see, nor make out where the water was.]

Madame de Nevers also arrived in a '*galion*' ('galleon'), '*tout prest tapissé et équipé de toutes choses necessaires; et y avoit instrumens fort melodieux*' ('decorated overall and fitted with everything necessary, and with most tuneful

---

[44]   *L'Entrée de François Premier, roi de France, dans la ville de Rouen, au mois d'août 1517*, ed. C. de Beaurepaire, Société des Bibliophiles Normands, 16 (Rouen: H. Boissel, 1867), f. b3vo: '*il voyoit en la riviere de Saine plusieurs gros navires à hune et aultres en grant nombre, les estandar[t]s desployés au vent. Aux quelz se faisoyent plusieurs joyeusetés tant par les pages d'iceulx navires estans aux dictes hunes et cordaux, que par gros tabours et artillerie desdictes navires qui deschargeoient plusieurs fois ...*' ('he could see on the Seine many large ships with tops, and many others, with their pennants fluttering. Various sports were performed on board, both by the cabin boys up in the tops and rigging, and by the big drums and artillery of the ships which fired several times').

[45]   *Les Entrées d'Eléonore d'Autriche, reine de France, et du Dauphin [...] dans la ville de Rouen, au mois de février 1532*, ed. A. Pottier, Société des Bibliophiles Normands, 9 (Rouen: H. Boissel, 1866), vol. 9, f. A3: '*Et pendant ce temps sonnerent grand nombre de grosses pieces d'artillerie de la part de ladicte ville. Avec l'appareil de tout le navire estant sur le port de ladicte ville: qui semblablement firent leur debvoir de tirer de leurs bordz grand nombre de ladicte artillerie.*' ('Meanwhile many pieces of heavy artillery fired from the town. With the ordinance of all the ship[s] in the city's port, which likewise did their bit in discharging from on board a large amount of artillery.')

[46]   See the accounts in Godefroy, *Cérémonial*, vol. 1, pp. 769–74 and E. Fournier, *Variétés historiques et littéraires* (10 vols., Paris: P. Jannet, 1855–63), vol. 8, p. 252.

[47]   Godefroy, *Cérémonial*, vol. 1, p. 770.

instruments on board')[48] and met up with that of the queen, each vessel '*jettant plus de mille coups d'artillerie par manière de salutation*' ('firing over a thousand salvos in greeting') and being joined by seven or eight other vessels,[49] including one for each corporation: '*chacun Mestier Juré de la ville avoit son batteau bien accoustré*' ('each city guild had its own well-decorated vessel'). Madame de Nevers was then manhandled by leading courtiers, '*mené par sous les esselles par Monsieur de Guyse, Monsieur de Saint Pol, et le Grand Maistre jusque vers la Reyne*' ('carried under her armpits by Monsieur de Guise, Monsieur de Saint Pol and the Grand Master to where the Queen was'), where she joined the queen and king, and all could disembark.

Under François Ier, Marseille was more imaginative in its use of the sea. Already in 1516 the King had been given a grand reception on his return from Italy.[50] Queen Claude and Louise de Savoie had already been welcomed there (3 January), saluted by the artillery of galleys and by a '*combat d'oranges*' ('fight with oranges').[51] They went to meet the king at Sisteron, and accompanied him to Marseille, where they were welcomed by a figure of Neptune on a ship, before visiting the galleys in the port, and witnessing another battle, for which the town had bought eleven thousand oranges. The king then went to visit the galleys, received with cannonades, and was taken on board a galley to visit a ship of the king of Portugal, which was transporting a rhinoceros as a gift to the Pope.[52]

This formula was amplified in 1533 by the Grand Maître, Montmorency, in his preparations for the arrival of Clement VII to celebrate the marriage of Henri d'Orléans and Catherine de' Medicis:[53] he sent to Livorno under the Duke of Albany a fleet of 18 (including four borrowed from Rhodes, nine Spanish galleys and his own *Capitainesse*, but missing one destroyed by lightning),[54] all fitted out in brocade, cloth of gold, damask of red, green and gold, with tapestries inside, and crewed by sailors in damask of the same colours.[55] While they brought the pope to

---

[48]   Ibid., vol. 1, p. 771.

[49]   Ibid., vol. 1, p. 774.

[50]   E. Baux, V.-L. Bourrilly and P. Mabilly, 'Les Voyages des reines et de François Ier en Provence et dans la vallée du Rhône (décembre 1515–février 1516)', in *Annales du Midi*, XVI (1904), pp. 31–64; R.J. Knecht, 'Court Festival as political spectacle', in *Europa Triumphans*, vol. 1, p. 21.

[51]   Baux, Bourrilly and Mabilly, 'Les Voyages', p. 40.

[52]   Ibid., p. 52.

[53]   Some sources were collected by A. Hamy, *Entrevue de François Ier avec Clément VII à Marseille, 1533* (Paris: H. Champion, 1900); see also J. Pelisson, *Panegyricus de Clementis VII* (Lyon: S. Gryphius, 1534); on the role of Montmorency see F. Decrue, *Anne de Montmorency* (Paris: E. Plon, 1885), pp. 211–12.

[54]   Hamy, *Entrevue ... Marseille*, p. 10.

[55]   Ibid., pp. 4–5, 11–12; Godefroy, *Cérémonial*, vol. 1, p. 817: '*sur le tilhac, qui est le bout de devant d'une galère, estoit la chambre dudit saint Pere, tendue par dehors, par dessus, et de tous costez de fin drap d'or, traisnant jusques à l'eau de la mer, et ayant en*

Marseille, Catherine was fetched from Nice and all made their entries by sea, with the fleet now numbering 70 (including a chartered merchant '*galion*')[56] and a crew of 1,500.[57] They were welcomed by salvos of artillery which shattered windows in the town,[58] but were described nonetheless as '*un paradis pour la vue et pour l'ouïe*' ('a paradise for eyes and ears').[59] The pope was transferred to smaller craft to disembark, escorted by the Royal children[60] and French cardinals,[61] then escorted across a boat bridge to the shore.[62]

During the month-long stay and long negotiations which followed, François took time off to launch new galleys,[63] and to have a trip round the bay, escorted by all the ships in the port, some twenty-eight of them, including galleys, brigantines and '*fustes*' ('light galleys'),[64] decorated in gold and rich tapestries, the flotilla venturing out a couple of leagues to sea, firing off the artillery, and stopping off at an island '*pour passer le temps et soy esbattre*' ('to pass the time and enjoy themselves').[65]

---

dedans plusieurs fleurs de lys d'or fort riches' ('on the upper deck, which is the front part of a galley, was the Holy Father's room, draped outside, above and all over, with fine cloth of gold, hanging down to water level, and decked inside with many rich fleurs de lys'); each chamber had '*huit grands estandarts et douze bannieres, toutes aux armes de France*' ('eight large standards and twelve pennants bearing the arms of France'), and the sailors were dressed in '*damas rouge et jaune, qui estoient gros frais et chose tres somptueuse à regarder*' ('red and yellow damask, which was a great expense and very sumptuous to behold'); vol. 1, p. 821: the pope's galley was '*dorée au bout de la poupe, et tapissée de drap d'or, et les forçaires qui menoient les galeres à l'arrivée estoient tous vestus de damas des couleurs du Roy*' ('gilded at the poop, and hung with cloth of gold, and the galley slaves who rowed the galleys to the point of arrival were all dressed in damask in the royal colours').

[56]   Hamy, *Entrevue ... Marseille*, p. 5, '*grand galleon de Servian*'.

[57]   Ibid., p. 16; Godefroy, *Cérémonial*, vol. 1, pp. 816–17.

[58]   Godefroy, *Cérémonial*, vol. 1, p. 820: '*tiré si grand nombre que toute la Ville en trembloit, et quantité de vitres en furent rompuës*' ('discharged so much artillery that the whole City shook, and many windows were broken').

[59]   Hamy, *Entrevue ... Marseille*, p. 11.

[60]   Godefroy, *Cérémonial*, vol. 1, p. 818.

[61]   Ibid., vol. 1, p. 820: '*environ une lieuë dedans la mer*' ('about a league out to sea').

[62]   Ibid, vol. 1, p. 820.

[63]   See Hamy, *Entrevue ... Marseille*, p. 21.

[64]   See the letter of Berthereau–Bailly de Troyes, Marseille, 15 Oct. 1533, BnF, *ms.* Dupuy 547, f. 273, cited in A. Hamy, *Entrevue de François Ier avec Henry VIII à Boulogne-sur-Mer, en 1532* (Paris: L. Gougy, 1898), p. ccclxxii: '*Demains se pourra commencer à negotier, après que le Roi qui veult aller sur mer entre cy [et] les isles avec toutes les gallaires qui sont en nombre xxviii de prestes et qui fait tres bon veoir.*' ('Tomorrow negotiations will begin, after the King, who wants to go to sea between here and the islands with all the galleys, of which 28 are ready and looking very good.') See also Hamy, *Entrevue ... Marseille*, pp. 20–21.

[65]   Godefroy, *Cérémonial*, vol. 1, p. 819: '*Le Roy prit apres disner toutes les Galeres qui estoient dedans le Port, et s'en alla en la haulte mer environ deux ou trois lieuës; et*

Various visits were made to the galleys, two new ones of which were launched. The same bill of fare was served to Charles IX in Marseille in November 1564, with another baptism of a newly-built galley.[66] Like his grandfather, Charles set off in a galley called *La Reale*, with 13 others in the flotilla, and headed for the Château d'If, where they met very rough seas, and had to seek sheltered anchorage for lunch, before watching the galleys form up into two squadrons, which engaged in battle.[67]

This formula served for other grand visitors to Marseille, notably Marie de Médicis on her arrival from Toulon (1600), in a galley belonging to the Grand Duke, *'aussi splendide et magnifique qu'il s'en est jamais veuë'* (as splendid and magnificent as was ever seen), all gold and silver right down to waterline, and accompanied by a flotilla of 17 ships. She was met at the Château d'If by courtiers and cardinals, and accompanied to a pontoon specially built for her disembarkation.[68]

The success of these trips round the bay was not lost on towns like Toulon, where Charles IX, a few days before Marseille (3 November 1564), had been taken out to sea for lunch by the Marquis d'Elbeuf with seven galleys.[69] Similarly, the idea of a naval exercise involving a mock battle, seen in Marseille, seems to

---

entra en une Isle pour passer le temps et soy esbatre.' ('After dinner the King took all the galleys which were in the port out on to the high seas two or three leagues away, and disembarked on an island to pass the time and enjoy himself') and ibid, vol. 1, p. 823: *'s'en est allé aux galeres qu'il a emmenées en esbat sur la mer, et ont tire fort artillerie, ce qu'il faisoit bon voir et ouyr'* ('he went to the galleys, which he has taken out to sea for a trip, where they fired a lot of artillery, which was good to see and hear').

[66] See the account by Abel Jouan in Graham and McAllister Johnson, *Royal Tour*, pp. 95–6: *'alla faire celebrer la Messe en une Galere neuve, qui n'avoit encores navigué, et fut baptisé, laquelle le Roy et la Reyne sa mere la nomerent Charlotte Catherine. Ladicte Galere appartenoit au Comte de Fisque'* ('he went to hear Mass in a brand new galley, which had not yet been to sea, and which was baptised and named by the King and Queen Charlotte Catherine. This galley belonged to the Comte de Fisque').

[67] Ibid., pp. 95–6: *'s'embarqua en une Gallere appelée la Reale, accompagnée de treize autres Galleres, pensant aller disner à la tour d'If, qui est une forte place, une lieue avant en pleine mer, sur un rocher'* ('he embarked in a galley called La Reale, escorted by thirteen other galleys, intending to lunch at the Tour d'If, which is a fortress on a rock, one league out to sea') (p. 96); *'Et en ce lieu, la tourmente se trouva si fascheuse, que lesdictes Galleres ne sceurent aborder et les falut mettre à l'ancre contre un autre rocher, qui estoit à un quart de lieue de là, et là le Roy disna. Puis s'en alla les mener en pleine mer, et fist faire deux Esquadrons qu'il fist combattre l'un contre l'autre.'* ('Here the storm was so violent, that the galleys couldn't land, and they had to be anchored by another rock, a quarter league away, and the King dined there. Then he took them out to sea, and drew them up in two squadrons, which he ordered to fight each other.'). See Boutier, *Un Tour*, p. 164.

[68] Godefroy, *Cérémonial*, vol.1, pp. 953–6.

[69] Report of Abel Jouan in Graham and McAllister Johnson, *Royal Tour*, pp. 94–5: *'avec sept galeres bien en poinct, dans lesquelles le Roy s'en alla pourmener après disner, où il prenoit grand plaisir'* ('with seven well-appointed galleys, in which the King went sailing after dinner, and much enjoyed it').

have inspired the sailors of Brouage, a key naval port, the following September, when Charles, after some overenthusiastic artillery which killed some onlookers,[70] saw a staged naval combat between a 35 or 40 ton merchant vessel and two pirate ships, which burned and sank it in the harbour, demonstrating to the king the dangers posed to shipping, especially by Spanish marauders.[71] This had been an accessory motivation for the Bayonne naval battle against a whale, wishing to show the king, conscious of the burning of the town by the Spaniards in 1557, '*la façon comme on pourroit deffandre la ville et assaillir les navires entrans en ceste riviere, s'ils vouloient rien entreprendre au desservice dudict Seigneur*' ('how one might defend the town and attack ships entering this river, should they attempt anything prejudicial to the King's interests').[72]

Once the visitors had arrived safely at the destination, a whole range of entertainments may have been prepared. One of the most common was the construction of a special ceremonial vessel, both for banquets and for viewing the entertainments. This was done in Lyon in 1548, in a joint effort by the city and Ippolito d'Este,[73] and became a feature in the Lyon entries of 1564[74], 1574 (with

---

[70]   Ibid., p. 124: '*qui en ne prenant pas garde à eux tuerent deux homes, et en blesserent quelques autres. Et puis apres disner les Mariniers donnerent plaisir au Roy d'un combat des vaisseaux contre vaisseaux sur la mer que en ce faisant brulerent une de leurs Navires*' ('who, not taking enough care, killed two men and wounded some others. Then after dinner the sailors treated the King to a sea-battle between the vessels, setting fire to one of their ships').

[71]   See G. de Tavannes, *Mémoires*, in J.-F. Michaud and J.-J.-F. Poujoulat, *Nouvelle Collection des Mémoires* (32 vols, Paris: Ed. du commentaire analytique du Code civil, 1836–39), vol. 8, p. 277: '*Ceux du pays des îles lui vouloient faire voir de quelle façon un navire marchand estant à la mer, par un navire de guerre ou pirate, est attaqué. Pour ceste cause, accomoderent un navire de 35 à 40 tonneaux et l'équiperent de voiles et y mirent un capitaine et huit ou dix marins, lequel entrant dans le havre dudit Brouage qui est très beau, fut ledit navire suivy de deux chaloupes equipées de guerre. Le navire marchand fut attaqué, pris et coulé.*' ('Those of the islands wanted to show him how a merchant ship at sea is attacked by a warship or a pirate. To this effect they fitted out a 35–40 ton ship, and rigged it with sails, and manned it with a captain and eight or ten sailors, which, on entering the fine harbour of Brouage, was pursued by two boats armed for war. The merchant ship was attacked, captured and sunk.'). See also L. Plédy, *Brouage* (La Rochelle: Pijollet, 1925), p. 17.

[72]   Graham and McAllister Johnson, *Royal Tour*, p. 43, note 68.

[73]   Maurice Scève, *Entry of Henri II to Lyon, September 1548*, ed. Richard Cooper (Tempe, Ariz: Medieval and Renaissance Texts and Studies, 1997); and the chapter in this volume by Margaret McGowan, pp. 37–49.

[74]   Graham and McAllister Johnson, *Royal Tour*, pp. 207–8.

a Venetian *Bucentaur*)[75] and 1595.[76] And it was done again in Rouen in August 1563, where

> *au dessus du Pont estoit un plat bateau, un dome d'arcades Ioniques, preparé pour le Roy, pour voir combattre un Fort au milieu de la riviere par quatre Gallions, et aultres combatz d'honneurs sur l'eau.*[77]

[above the bridge there was a flat vessel, with a dome supported by Ionic arches, fitted out for the King, from where to watch a Fort in the middle of the river being attacked by four Galleons, and other worthy battles on the water.]

On the royal tour of 1564–65, Charles IX was presented in Nantes with a galley specially fitted for his convenience.[78] In Bordeaux in 1565,[79] they built '*deux maisons sur l'eau*' ('two constructions on the water'), one on a 'barque' ('barque'), one on a 'courau' ('small boat'), which are elaborately described in the *livrets*.[80] From this vantage-point, the King could enjoy the salvos of artillery,[81] and could see '*voguer sept Gallions avecques autant d'Enseignes et divers Capitaines*' ('seven Galleons sailing with as many ensigns and various captains') and a small craft decked out as a sea shell, in which sat in splendour the '*Roy de la Bazoche dedans un esquif faict en manière de coquille de mer en bel equipage*' ('king of the Basoche guild in a skiff in the shape of a shell, in great state'). The question arises of how far the '*confréries*' ('fraternities') were involved in these water spectacles – such as the Basoche in Bordeaux,[82] the Connards in Rouen,[83] and the watermen's

---

[75]   Godefroy, *Cérémonial*, vol. 1, pp. 925–6: '*à l'endroit de l'Arcenal un bateau à la forme du Bucentaure de Venise, qui representoit un Chateau*' ('by the Arsenal, a boat in the form of a Venetian bucintoro representing a fortress').

[76]   Ibid., vol. 1, p. 933.

[77]   *Entrée de Charles IX à Rouen au mois d'août 1563*, ed. P. Le Cacheux, Société des Bibliophiles Normands, 88 (Rouen: A. Lainé, 1936), p. XXI.

[78]   Graham and McAllister Johnson, *Royal Tour*, p. 131; see Nantes, Arch. Mun., AA 33, doc. 16–17, where we learn that the King made a gift of it to M. de Cossé, and the city bought it back from him for future use.

[79]   Graham and McAllister Johnson, *Royal Tour*, Appendix XII, pp. 280–83.

[80]   Ibid., p. 281.

[81]   Ibid., p. 281: '*On eust pensé que Vulcain alors eust faict jouer toutes ses Flustes pour foudroyer la Ville*' ('You would have thought Vulcan had sounded all his instruments to bombard the city'); similar artillery to welcome him to Rouen in 1563: '*furent tirez des Galleres plusieurs volés de canons et d'autres endroitz*' ('various cannon salvos were fired from the galleys and other places'). See *Entrée de Charles IX à Rouen*, ed. Le Cacheux, p. XIa.

[82]   Godefroy, *Cérémonial*, vol.,1, p. 907; associated with the election of the Roy de la Bazoche, ibid., vol. 1, p. 915.

[83]   R. Herval, *Histoire de Rouen* (2 vols, Rouen: Maugard, 1947–49), vol. 2, p. 107.

'*confréries*' of St Vincent and St Georges in Lyon,[84] who had been involved in the Fête des Merveilles,[85] and were so again in the 1559 celebrations of peace.[86] A certain prominence was certainly given to the companies of sailors, recruited for the occasion, or working in the docks, who took part in the 1530 Bordeaux procession,[87] and again in that in Rouen in 1588.[88]

Under François Ier the detailed aquatic ceremonial was limited, as witness the 1515 entry to Lyon, where he was greeted by a ship towed across the river by a white stag, recalling the legend of Clovis in which such a stag pointed out a ford. At Bayonne in both 1526[89] and 1530, much use was made of boats on the Bidassoa, which formed a kind of pontoon for the exchange and return of hostages, constructed '*d'une si grande ingenieusité, que l'on ne pouvoit aucunement sçavoir si on estoit sur terre ou sur mer*' ('so ingeniously that one could not tell if one was on land or on water').[90] This was again to be a feature of the meeting in June 1565, so as to maintain the protocol between the two dynasties as to who was on whose territory.[91] By 1539 a more military flavour had crept in, as seen in Orleans when the Emperor arrived, crossing the very long bridge over the Loire, with an island in the middle, where they had placed artillery, which fired so loudly that it was

---

[84]   Cooper (ed.), *Entry of Henri II*, pp. 20–24; *Entrées royales et fêtes populaires à Lyon, du XVe au XVIIIe siècles* (Lyon: Bibliothèque municipale, 1970), pp. 19–21.

[85]   G. Paradin, *Memoires de l'histoire de Lyon* (Lyon: A. Gryphius, 1573), pp. 200–202: '*fort grand basteau, comme un Bucentaure, sur la riviere de Saone, auquel les plus apparens de la cité alloyent par esbatement jouër sus l'eau, avec infiniz passetemps. Ce grand basteau estoit conduit par dessoubs le dernier arc du pont, devers saint Nizier*' ('a very large vessel, like a bucentaur, on the Saône, on which the most prominent citizens would go to have fun on the water, with various diversions. This large vessel was taken under the last arch of the bridge towards St Nizier church').

[86]   B. Du Troncy, *Suytte de la description des grands triomphes faitz à Lyon après la publication de la paix* (Lyon: J. Saugrain, 1559), p. 5: '*en forme d'un chasteau quarré à quatre tournelles, et une grosse tour au milieu haut enlevée, au dessus de la quelle estoit representé le monstre occis par ledict chevalier sainct Georges. [...] Furent faictes quelques joustes sur l'eau par les susdicts de sainct George*' ('shaped like a square castle with four turrets, and a massive tower in the middle rising high, above which was an image of the monster killed by St George. There was some jousting on the water by the members of the St George's guild').

[87]   Godefroy, *Cérémonial*, vol. 1, p. 776: '*Pescheurs et Nautonniers à une banniere de jaune et incarnate*' ('fisherman and sailors with a yellow and red banner').

[88]   McGowan, 'Festivals and the Arts', in *Europa Triumphans*, vol. 1, pp. 202–9.

[89]   A. Champollion-Figeac, *Captivité du roi François Ier* (Paris: Imprimerie royale, 1847), pp. lxiii–lxiv, 510–12, 518–19.

[90]   L. Cimber et F. Danjou, *Archives curieuses de l'histoire de France,* 1ère série (15 vols, Paris: Beauvais, 1834–37), vol. 2, pp. 251–451; cf. Godefroy, *Cérémonial*, vol. 1, p. 766.

[91]   For sources see Boutier, *Un Tour*, p. 368, note 46.

heard seven leagues away.[92] The one piece of court ceremonial under François, which best shows this shift towards military aquatics, is the baptism of the future François II at Fontainebleau in 1543,[93] where on the '*estang*' (pond) of the newly completed château a bastion had been built, which was then assaulted by '*trois galeres qui batoient de ce costé ledit bastion*' ('three galleons, which bombarded the bastion from this side').

The accession of Henri II marked a change. The account of his coronation in Reims is quite different from all the others recorded by Godefroy for that century, by virtue of the sea-battle arranged on the Marne,[94] supposedly at the express wish of the king. This coronation set the style for the reign, including as it did two marine extravaganzas. By the second gate of the city, on the river bank, the king saw a

> *montagne faite en forme de rocher entr'ouvert, et dans le creux des Monstres marins, des Syrenes et des Satyrs, representez par des jeunes hommes environnez de lierre et de mousse.*[95]

[mountain built like a half-open rock, and in the crack sea monsters, sirens and satyrs played by young men swathed in ivy and moss.]

This mythological marine idyll, which would be copied elsewhere, was accompanied by an actual floating spectacle, of

> *un navire peint et azuré avec tous ses attirails, et conduit par des Sauvages, qui faisoient mille sauts et postures, comme voulans attaquer les monstres qui gardoient le rocher.*

[a ship painted pale blue with all its equipment, steered by Savages, who did countless leaps and poses, as if wanting to attack the monsters guarding the rock.]

This, to my knowledge, is the first use of savages, and was to be copied in Rouen in 1550,[96] and again in 1588 with a tribe of

> *Negres tous nuds qui avec leurs arcs et fleches bien empennées firent bien autant de mal que la miliace de canomnades qui fut alors tirée.*[97]

---

[92]   Godefroy, *Cérémonial*, vol. 2, p. 757.

[93]   Ibid., vol 2, pp. 143–6.

[94]   Ibid., vol. 1, p. 303.

[95]   Ibid., vol. 1, p. 305.

[96]   *L'Entrée de Henri II à Rouen 1550*, ed. Margaret M. McGowan (Amsterdam: Theatrum Orbis Terrarum; New York, Johnson Reprint Corp., 1974).

[97]   McGowan, 'Festivals and the Arts', p. 206.

[Stark naked Negros who, with their bows and well-fledged arrows, did as much damage as the mass of cannon-fire discharged.]

In Reims in 1547 the savages in their boat attacked the riverside mountain with grappling hooks, with abundant fireworks, and with both sides, sea monsters and savages alike, having to jump into the sea to avoid being burnt alive:

> *ils approcherent enfin de la veuë de sa Majesté, et se joignirent avec des crocs de fer pour venir aux mains, et combattre plus aisément; tous faisoient merveille à se defendre les uns et les autres jettans des flammes et des fuzées en forme de dards, et autres feux volans, en sorte que le mast du navire, la hune, et le pilot furent jettez en l'air par subtilité, pendant que les Monstres marins et les Sauvages se plongeoient à tout coup sous les eaux les uns sur les autres, pour n'estre incommodez des flammes.*[98]

[they finally came into his Majesty's view, and secured the ships to each other with grappling irons to allow hand to hand combat; they performed wonders defending themselves, each side firing flames and rockets like spears, and other fireworks, with the result that the ship's mast, its top and its pilot were all artfully shot into the air, whilst the Sea monsters and the Savages were suddenly diving underwater one after the other, so as not to be harmed by the flames.]

The king's delight in this entertainment inspired the Lyonnais to put on their own river battle, as it did Rabelais, in his account of the *Sciomachie*, to present the aborted river battle on the Tiber as an idea of Jean Du Bellay's to honour the birth of Louis d'Orleans, when it was actually planned as part of the Roman carnival, and abandoned because of the state of the river.[99] The organisers of the Paris 1549 entry had not scheduled a river battle, but included it at royal request, and to judge by the comments of some diplomats, not very successfully.[100]

Evidence of this change of style comes in Nantes[101] as early as 1548, for the entry of Mary, Queen of Scots.[102] In earlier entries, the river had only been used for ceremonial transport, but in September 1548, at the same time as the Lyon entry, the young queen was taken downstream from the town to La Fosse, on the bank of the Loire, and treated to a banquet at La Fosse[103] followed by a river battle, '*avecques chasteaulx portez en Loyr tyrant canons et triomphes et magnifficence*'

---

[98] Godefroy, *Cérémonial*, vol. 1, p. 305.

[99] R.A. Cooper, *Rabelais et l'Italie* (Geneva: Droz, 1991), pp. 68–9, 187–8.

[100] *The Entry of Henri II into Paris, 16 June 1549*, ed. I.D. McFarlane (Binghamton, Center for Medieval and Early Renaissance Studies, 1982), pp. 63–8.

[101] On the Nantes festivals see the archival records in Nantes, Arch. Mun., AA 27–AA 34; Lelièvre, 'Entrées royales à Nantes', pp. 81–91.

[102] Nantes, Arch. Mun., AA 31; Lelièvre, 'Entrées royales à Nantes', p. 87.

[103] Nantes, Arch. Mun., AA 31, doc. 1.

('with fortified ships brought to the Loire, firing cannon, and with triumphs and display').[104] Three years later, in 1551, another, highly ambitious, *naumachia* was put on for Henri II, as part of a grand entry involving no less than 12 triumphal arches.[105] As before, the naval part took place westwards at La Fosse, where a pavilion had been built for the king to watch the parade and combat, and where he was presented with a gilded ship, and with a silver stoat representing Brittany.[106] The city fathers had built a '*bastillon*' ('small fort') and had bought two '*challans*' ('barges') which, at the boatyards of Richebourg, they transformed over a month into '*galliotes*' ('galiots'), with cabins, oars, artillery and brightly painted decoration. At the same time they commissioned captains and sailors at Le Croisic to fit out for war three '*galions*' ('galleons') and one '*ramberge*' ('rowing barge'). All six vessels were decorated in taffeta of white, red, blue and yellow, sported flags, banners and standards, and were crammed with trumpeters and drummers.[107] The opponents in the *naumachia*, Bretons fighting against '*mores et autres gens d'estrange nation*' ('moors and other foreigners'),[108] launched assaults, attempted boardings, and fired artillery and especially Greek fire, which continued to burn in water:

> *Et lors commencerent les dits combattans au premier son des trompettes voltiger et courir les uns aux autres, decharger d'artillerie, et à la force de rames s'entreacoster, cramponner et donner assauts et alarmes, jetter dards, allumer lances à feu vif et gregeois, lequel ardoit et bruloit aussi bien en eau qu'il eut fait en paille seche, non sans danger et perils des dits combattans ... lesquelles choses faisoient fort bon à voir et à ouir.*[109]

[Then the trumpets sounded and those combatants began to dart about and rush at each other, firing artillery and, rowing hard, to engage, grapple, attack, sound the alarm, throw spears, light flares and Greek fire, which burned as well on the water as it would have done in dry straw, not without danger to these combatants ... all of which was very good to see and hear.]

In a later festival in Nantes in 1565, captains were again hired from Le Croisic, who constructed '*galions*' ('galleons'), '*chaloupes*' ('flat-bottomed boats') and a

---

[104] Nantes, Arch. Mun., AA 31, doc. 10; Lelièvre, 'Entrées royales à Nantes', p. 87.

[105] See the archive records in Nantes, Arch. Mun., AA 32; also the *livret* by the festival organiser, Bonaventure Coppegorge, *Joyeuse entrée du roy et de la royne*, August 1551, who was paid 27 *livres* for publishing the account; see also Lelièvre, 'Entrées royales à Nantes', p. 87 and S. Garcia, *Les Entrées de ville à Nantes, du milieu du XVIe à la première moitié du XVIIe siècle, mémoire de maîtrise* (Univ. de Nantes, UFR d'Histoire, 1996).

[106] Nantes, Arch. Mun., AA 32, doc. 2 and 9.

[107] Nantes, Arch. Mun., AA 32, doc. 2, 4, 9 and 40.

[108] See Coppegorge, *Joyeuse entrée*.

[109] Ibid.

'*galliasse*' ('galleass') for the battle, while, for the king's own use, they transformed a sailing barge in Nantes into a large galley, which they then presented as a gift to Charles IX.[110]

In Bayonne, as part of the royal tour, two *naumachiae* were put on, one involving two fleets, each of 12 galleys and one galleon, which joined battle with such force that the onlookers thought it was real war, and with such fierce cannon fire and thick smoke that the fleets could not be seen for half an hour, before the air cleared to reveal that one side was victorious.[111] The second sea-battle pitched the fleet against one large vessel,

> *basty en chasteau avec tourelles à l'antour. Et se defendoit à coups de*
> *fusils, d'artillerye et d'arquebuses, estant attacqué de mesme de façon que*
> *l'escarmouche dura bien deus heures; et enfin le chasteau ne fut prins.*[112]

> [constructed like a castle with turrets all around. It defended itself with fire from
> muskets, artillery and arquebuses, and was attacked by the same, and after two
> hours of skirmishing the castle was finally not taken.]

But otherwise on the royal tour of 1563–66, the ceremonies put on for Charles and his mother were less explicitly bellicose, no doubt in keeping with the propaganda message of pacification and reconciliation. In Rouen in 1563 (12–19 August),[113] the king was taken out on the galleys, where he saw a performance put on by an expert diver:

> *il alla dans les Galleres se promener sur l'eau, où estoit un homme qui par*
> *l'espace de demye quart d'heure demouroit au fons de l'eau, et en raportoit*
> *grande quantité de Poissons.*[114]

> [the king went for a trip in the galleys on the river, where there was a man who
> remained underwater for over seven minutes, bringing up lots of fish.]

There is a direct parallel in the king's stop on the river Touvre (Charente), where a '*feuillée*' ('arbour') was erected amidst the abundant streams and fountains of the river, '*laquelle est toute couverte de Cignes, bordée d'Escrevisses, et pavée de Truittes les meilleures qu'on sçaurait menger*' ('which is covered in swans, surrounded by crayfish and swarming with the finest trout you could eat'). The young king took great pleasure in watching local fisherman catching masses of

---

[110]   Nantes, Arch. Mun., AA 33, doc. 9–15.

[111]   Graham and McAllister Johnson, *Royal Tour*, p. 284, Appendix XIII: *L'entrée du Roy Charles neufiesme*, p. 289.

[112]   Ibid., p. 289.

[113]   *Entrée de Charles IX à Rouen*, ed. Le Cacheux, p. XXI.

[114]   Herval, *Histoire de Rouen*, vol.2, p. 86.

trout, and having over a hundred swans rounded up and brought to him.[115] This is much closer to the mythological marine églogue of Fontainebleau, put on specifically for carnival, 14 February 1564,[116] where the king sat between the two canals and saw the

> *trois Sereines qui estoient trois jeunes enfans ayant des voix excellentes, si bien tirées au Naturel qu'il sembloit qu'elles fussent nues et avoient du nombril au bas de grandes queues dorees, argentees et azurees, et retroussees comme celles des Daulphins, en la forme qu'on painct ordinairement les Sereines, et nageoient au milieu de l'eau.*

[three sirens, who were three young children with excellent voices, whose costumes were so life-like, that they seemed naked, and from the waist down they had tails in gold, silver and blue, curled like dolphins' tails, as one sees in pictures of sirens, and they swam in the water.]

They recited verses by Ronsard, whilst Neptune with trident, on a chariot drawn by four sea horses, offered his power and empire to Charles. The king came to the rock, which opened to reveal a fountain, and a (*castrato*) nymph sitting on a shell, who sang a sonnet to the king. The same mythological, almost balletic, character was seen in the nautical parade on the Seine arranged for the marriage of Joyeuse in 1581,[117] with the King in a floating chariot loaded with musicians, drawn by boats decked out as sea creatures, accompanied by tritons, turtles, dolphins, whales, etc.

The increasingly hybrid nature of the waterborne festival under Charles IX and Henri III is evident in 1565 in Chenonceau,[118] and especially in Bayonne,[119] about which Robert Knecht has written in this volume.[120] This hybrid nature of such river pageants is clearer still in the entry of Henri III to Rouen in 1588, with

---

[115] Graham and McAllister Johnson, *Royal Tour*, pp. 122–3: '*plaisir de veoir pescher des truittes à des hommes qui en prenoient grande abondance, et se feit amener devant luy bien huict ou neuf vingts Cignes tout en une troupe*' ('pleasure of seeing trout being fished by people who caught lots of them, and the king had brought before him a bevy of eight or nine swans').

[116] Ibid., p. 59 and Appendix I, *Le Recueil des Triumphes*, pp. 147ff..

[117] J. Rousset, 'L'Eau et les tritons', pp. 235–45.

[118] A. Boulay de la Meurthe, *Entrée de Charles IX à Chenonceau* (Tours: P. Bousrey, 1900; offprint from *Mémoires de la Société archéologique de Touraine*, 1900); N. Ivanoff, 'Les Fêtes à la cour des derniers Valois', in *Revue du Seizième Siècle*, 19 (1932–33), p. 119.

[119] For the programme see Graham and McAllister Johnson, *Royal Tour*, pp. 310–11; for iconographic sources see Boutier, *Un Tour*, pp. 396–7, note 62; on tapestries see Ivanoff, 'Les Fêtes', pp. 96–122 and F. Yates, *The Valois tapestries* ([London]: Routledge, 1975), pp. 55–60, plates I, III, VIII, IXa, Xa; J. Ehrmann, 'Les Tapisseries des Valois du Musée des Offices à Florence', in Jacquot, *Fêtes*, vol. 1, pp. 93–100.

[120] See pp. 67–77.

its interweaving of mythology and war. Over several days the king could follow a wide range of nautical entertainments from a pavilion built on the bridge,[121] savouring the

> *plaisir d'une guerre navalle, dressee avec neuf ou dix Galiaces, et autres vaisseaux de guerre tous magnificquement peincts, dressez et armez,*[122]

> [pleasure of a sea battle, mounted between nine or ten galleasses and other warships all magnificently painted, fitted out and armed,]

with salvos of artillery followed by hand to hand fighting, storming of castles and attacking of sea-monsters. According to the *livrets*, one company dressed as sailors, wearing identical sea-green taffeta suits with jackets and sea-breeches, while others were companies in silk and velvet of various colours, and yet others dressed as galley slaves, '*forsaires ou conducteurs desdites galeres et vaisseaux de guerre*' ('galley slaves, or captains of the galleys, or other warships'). A high point of the repertoire, of more acrobatic than bellicose flavour, was the '*plaisant jeu de l'anguille*' ('merry game of the eel'), the eel being suspended from cable stretched across the Seine, and grabbed for by sailors from the rigging of ships:

> *les tireurs de laquelle la prenant aux mains, leur vaisseau naval passant par dessoubs un cable haut eslevé leur falloit retomber de fort haut en l'eau, et là denoüer la corde avec les dents, de laquelle l'anguille estoit pendüe, et l'ayants faillie leur convenoit se sauver à nage. Et apres l'avoir plusieurs fois assaillie ... ils la denoüerent, et derechef renoüerent pour avoir plus de plaisir.*[123]

> [the people pulling at it, once they got their hands on it, as their vessel passed below a cable stretched out high up, had then to drop from a height into the water, untie with their teeth the cord attaching the eel, and if they failed, they had to swim for safety. After several attempts ... they undid it, then tied it on again for further entertainment].

The public seemed to enjoy the spectacle of high-diving, to the accompaniment of fifes, trumpets, tambours and arquebus volleys:

---

[121]   See Herval, *Histoire de Rouen*, vol. 2, p. 97, who cites the *Brief discours sur la bonne et joyeuse Reception*, Rouen, 1588 by Jean de Séville: '*furent données à sadite Majesté maintes recreations sur la Saine, sur le pont de laquelle luy fut dressée une magnifique lambrissée de beaux tapis*' ('His Majesty was shown various entertainments on the Seine, and on the bridge was hung a magnificent display of fine carpets').

[122]   From the account by Jean de Séville published in *Europa Triumphans*, vol. 1, pp. 204, 206.

[123]   Ibid., p. 206.

et ne voyoit on qu'hommes nager en l'eau et vaisseaux flotter, et entre autres y eut xv. ou xvi. braves nageurs qui se precipiterent par plusieursfois de dessus le pont d'aussi haut qu'une maison de trois ou quatre estages d'auprès sa Majesté, les uns tous vestus, autres n'ayans que leurs chemises et brayes, et ainsi merveilleusement precipitez nageoient avec une infinité d'autres qui faisoient à qui mieux mieux.[124]

[and all you could see was men swimming, and vessels afloat, among whom were 15 or 16 bold swimmers who jumped several times from the bridge, where His Majesty was, as high as a three- or four-storey house, some fully clothed, some just in shirt and breeches, and after these wonderful dives they swam about with countless others, vying with each other.]

A second *naumachia* involved artillery, hand to hand fighting, with, once again, plenty of men overboard,

autres encores jusques à grand nombre nageoient dedans la Seine après s'ettre precipitez d'enhaut du pont dedans icelle et autres de la proue des navires.[125]

[and others in large numbers swam in the Seine after diving from off the bridge into the river, and others from the prow of ships.]

Politics were not, however, forgotten and one spectacle involved the storming from the river of a castle built to resemble the Protestant stronghold of La Rochelle, which, however well fortified and defended, was finally taken with divine assistance, since '*Dieu des exercites donne la victoire à qui luy plaist*' ('the God of Hosts gives victory to whom he pleases'), the defenders once again '*se sauvant à nage*' ('swimming to safety'), and the fort of the miscreants '*du tout bruslée et rasée pour un perpetuel tesmoignage et rebellion*' ('burnt and razed to the ground as a perpetual witness of rebellion'). Since the public was '*assez cupide de voir quelque chose de beau et de nouveau*' ('very avid to see something fine and new'), the planners came up with a concluding novelty, reinterpreting the story of Jonah by staging the siege of a large, well-fortified city called Nineveh, built on the bank of the Seine, and fashioning a large floating whale. After the prophet Jonah had been thrown from one of the ships, he was

incontinent englouty par la balaine et quelque temps après revomy par icelle sur le pont de ceste ville de Ninive pour y prescher penitence.

[immediately swallowed up by the whale, and brought up again some time after on to the bridge of this city of Nineveh to preach repentance.]

---

[124] Ibid., p. 206.
[125] Ibid., p. 206.

Though the city was repeatedly attacked by a fleet of '*galliaces*' ('galleasses') in a frenzy of sound and smoke,

> *Cependant on ne voyoit que feu et fumée, on oyoit une milliasse de canonnades, on n'oyoit que piffres, tambours et fanfares de trompettes donnantes l'assaut*

> [all one could see was fire and smoke, all one could hear was massive gunfire, and the noise of fife, drum, and fanfares of trumpets sounding the attack]

with many jumping fully clothed from the bridge where the king was watching, and with a '*brave et asseuré Capitaine de marine*' ('bold and confident sea-captain'), and a few sailors balancing on floating planks to fire arquebuses at Nineveh, and despite the distracting intervention of a mermaid,

> *moytié homme et moytié poisson avec le miroir et le peigne tousjours miraculeusement à demy aparoissant sur l'eau chantant melodieusement,*

> [half-human and half-fish, holding mirror and comb, half-emerging from the water in a wonderful way, and singing tunefully,]

the city held out, even after its walls were breached, and the fleet had to withdraw.[126]

Such extravagance and fantastic invention were bound to attract criticism, as witness the spoof published in 1582 of Henri III's European tour on his way back from Poland to France to take the throne, *La Description de la superbe et imaginaire entrée faite par la reine Gijlette passant à Venise*.[127] We learn there that Venice was keenly awaiting the queen's arrival (that is the arrival of Henri III), and had, in anticipation, fattened up the *Bucentaurs* on aphrodisiac biscuits,

> *car les trois grans Bucentaures estoient gaillards pour avoir esté nourris six semaines durant de biscuit cantharide,*[128]

> [for the three great *Bucentaurs* were frisky after their six-week diet of cantharid biscuits,]

the *bucentaurs* imagined here not as boats but as huge monsters, on which the 50 '*magnifiques*' (grandees) of Venice could ride out to meet Royne Gijlette, '*montez sur le plusgrant des Buccentaures revestues à la Panthalonesque bien richement*'

---

[126]   For the final *naumachia* put on there in October 1596 for Henri IV, see Godefroy, *Cérémonial*, vol. 1, p. 945; Herval, *Histoire de Rouen*, vol. 2, p. 107.

[127]   (Paris: [A. L'Olivier], 1582); copies in the Bodleian, Douce G. 355 and the Bib. Mazarine, 56563.

[128]   *Description*, p. 11. Dried and powdered extract of cantharid beetle was believed to have aphrodisiac virtues, see *Trésor de la Langue Francaise*, s.v.

('astride the biggest of the *Bucentaurs* richly dressed like Pantaloon'),[129] akin to the ridiculous figure of Pantalone, *il Magnifico*, from the *commedia dell'arte*, a figure sometimes used for mockery of Venetians in general. They were accompanied by a Venetian lady, Signora Nespaula, who although '*vestue en façon de sereinne*' ('dressed as a mermaid'),[130] probably alluding both to Venetian courtesans and to the annual ritual of the marriage of Venice to the sea, also embodies a transsexual in-joke, since the Italian '*nespola*' ('medlar') was used, like its French equivalent, '*nèfle*' or '*mesle*', to represent testicles.[131] The theme of sexual ambiguity is not lost on the reader.

The banquet put on for the Queen/King was spread on a table laden with '*quantité de Monstres Marins ... faicts de sucre, et de paste*' ('lots of sea-monsters ... made of sugar and paste'),[132] and sugar was also the material used to construct a tall ceremonial tower, commanding a view of the whole lagoon (like San Marco), which collapsed after being nibbled away at its base, dumping all the performers into the sea.[133] Later stages involved a cannonade, as in other waterborne festivals:

> *A une heure apres midy, l'arsenac de la ville commença à faire jouer ses fleuttes, si furieusement que le Ciel estoit obscurcy de fumée.*[134]

> [At one in the afternoon the city's Arsenal began to sound its instruments so fiercely that the sky was darkened with smoke],

followed by a combat of rhinoceros and elephant. As in other waterborne festivals, a sumptuous vessel was provided for the illustrious visitor, who

> *entra en sa gondolette, qui avoit esté bastie fort superbement, par les Gentishommes à claires voyes residens à Maran, en façon d'un Palays à quatre tourelles,*[135]

---

[129]   *Description*, p. 16.

[130]   *Description*, p. 19.

[131]   *Pantagruel*, ch. 1, '*année des grosses Mesles*': see Rabelais, *Œuvres completes*, ed. M. Huchon (Paris: Gallimard, 1994), p. 218.

[132]   *Description*, p. 24.

[133]   *Description*, pp. 26–7: '*par la grace de Dieu tombe du costé de la mer ... Les joueurs et musiciens tomberent en pleine mer, on ne vist jamais musicque voguer à la Venitienne, ny Panthalon musicien nager en ephant si humide*' ('by the grace of God fall on the side towards the sea ... The players and musicians fall right into the sea, and no one had ever seen music floating in the Venetian manner, nor a Pantaloon musician swimming in such a wet garment').

[134]   Ibid., p. 35.

[135]   Ibid., p. 47. Marans (Charente-Maritime) is in the Marais Poitevin.

[boarded his small gondola, which had been magnificently fitted out in openwork
by the gentlemen living in Marans as a Palace with four turrets,]

and watched the aquatic battle royal between Venetians and, once again, Protestants
from La Rochelle, each represented as sea creatures, the Venetians as '*cancres*'
('crabs') and the Rochellois as '*casserons*' ('small cuttlefish', a local term). The
crossbowmen from the towers of the queen's/king's gondola fired into the canal

> *pour faire sortir les Casserons Rochelois en nage, et venir à la rencontre des
> Cancres Venitiens qui estoient aux aguets.*[136]

[to force the 'cuttlefish' of La Rochelle to swim out and encounter the Venetian
crabs who were on the look-out.]

Unable to remain afloat, the Huguenot cuttlefish sank to the bottom, where they
were devoured by the Catholic crabs. This is clearly an allusion to the lengthy
siege of La Rochelle by the future Henri III in the spring of 1573, but with a
very different outcome, since, despite the intervention of the French navy, the
Huguenots were able to withstand the assaults, and the Catholics withdrew.

Although not all French towns were equipped for waterborne festivals or
naumachiae, it is evident that they became very fashionable over the course of
the century, and that planners made use of whatever facilities they had to hand,
whether an artificial lake at Fontainebleau, or the inland river at Chenonceau, or the
estuaries at Rouen, Bordeaux, Nantes and Bayonne, or the open sea at Brouage or
Marseille, where they could call upon the embryonic French navy. The shipyards
of Marseille or Nantes provided carpenters capable of both building anew or
transforming existing craft into ceremonial vessels for transport or combat, while
sailors could be borrowed from places like Le Croisic, or from the companies of
boatmen on the Rhône. Local *confréries* like the Basoche or the Connards, or the
two Lyon guilds, could be given a floating role as lords of misrule, but the planners
could also draw on the expertise of people like Jehan Bouchet, experienced in
entries or mysteries. The craft built for the waterborne festivals could be very
grand, large enough, as in Lyon, to accommodate a hall for banqueting or dancing,
with movable floor.[137] Under Henri II the festivals took on a markedly military
flavour, with elaborate *naumachia*, involving participants representing not only
French sailors, but Moors, galley-slaves or savages. Under Charles IX and Henri
III the style swung more towards hybrid festivals combining war with mythology
and fantasy, as if the nation were tired of war. What remains constant is the
high, and increasing, cost of these extravaganzas, with the Venetian ambassador
estimating the expenditure on the 1565 Bayonne celebrations at a million francs,

---

[136] Ibid., p. 47.
[137] Cooper (ed.), *Entry of Henri II*, p. 23, f. K2v, L2v.

a figure '*difficile a credere*' ('hard to credit'),[138] while his masters in Venice were themselves to spend no less lavishly to welcome Henri III.

Bibliography

Manuscript Sources

Archives Municipales de Nantes
AM Nantes, Series AA 27, docs 1, 2.
AM Nantes, Series AA 29, docs 3, 4, 8, 9.
AM Nantes, Series AA 30, docs 10, 11, 14, 19.
AM Nantes, Series AA 33, docs 16, 17.
Bibliothèque nationale de France, MS. Ital. 1724, fol. 268.
BnF, MS. Dupuy 547, fol. 273.

Printed Primary Sources

Bourgueville, C., *Les Recherches et antiquitez de la ville et Université de Caen* (Caen: J. Le Fevre, 1588).
de Cahaignes, J., *Discours de l'entrée du duc d'Epernon à Caen, le 14 mai 1588*, ed. R. de Formigny de la Londe, Société des Bibliophiles Normands, 66 (Rouen: L. de Gy, 1903).
de Cahaignes, J., *Entrée du duc de Joyeuse à Caen le 5 avril 1583*, ed. T. Genty, Société des Bibliophiles Normands, 63 (Rouen: L. de Gy, 1900).
Du Troncy, B., *Suytte de la description des grands triomphes faitz à Lyon après la publication de la paix* (Lyon: J. Saugrain, 1559).
Entrée de Charles IX à Rouen au mois d'août 1563, ed. P. Le Cacheux Société des Bibliophiles Normands, 88 (Rouen: A. Lainé, 1936).
Entrées royales et fêtes populaires à Lyon, du XVe au XVIIIe siècles (Lyon: Bibliothèque municipale, 1970).
Godefroy, D., *Le Cérémonial François* (2 vols, Paris: S. and G. Cramoisy, 1649).
L'Entrée de François Premier, roi de France, dans la ville de Rouen, au mois d'août 1517, ed. C. de Beaurepaire, Société des Bibliophiles Normands, 16 (Rouen: H. Boissel, 1867).
L'Entrée de Henri II à Rouen 1550, ed. Margaret M. McGowan (Amsterdam: Theatrum Orbis Terrarum; New York, Johnson Reprint Corp., 1974).
L'Entrée du roi Louis XII et de la reine à Rouen 1508, ed. P. Le Verdier, Société des Bibliophiles Normands, 60 (Rouen: L. Gy, 1900).
Les Entrées d'Eléonore d'Autriche, reine de France, et du Dauphin [...] dans la ville de Rouen, au mois de février 1532, ed. A. Pottier, Société des Bibliophiles Normands, 9 (Rouen: H. Boissel, 1866).

[138] Suriano – Signoria, 8 July 1565, in BnF, *ms. ital.* 1724, f. 293v.

Paradin, G., *Memoires de l'histoire de Lyon* (Lyon: A. Gryphius, 1573).

Pelisson, J., *Panegyricus de Clementis VII* (Lyon: S. Gryphius, 1534).

Rinuccini, C., *Descrizione delle feste fatte nelle reali nozze de' serenissimi principe di Toscana* (Florence: I. Giusti, 1608).

Sabbatini, N., *Pratica di fabricar scene e machine ne' teatri* (Ravenna: P. de' Paoli and G.B. Giovannelli, 1638), in-fol.

Scève, Maurice, *Entry of Henri II to Lyon, September 1548*, ed. Richard Cooper (Tempe, Ariz: Medieval and Renaissance Texts and Studies, 1997).

Tavannes, G. de, *Mémoires*, in Michaud J.-F. and Poujoulat J.-J.-F., *Nouvelle Collection des Mémoires* (32 vols, Paris: Ed. du commentaire analytique du Code civil, 1836–39), vol. 8.

The Entry of Henri II into Paris, 16 June 1549, ed. I.D. McFarlane (Binghamton: Center for Medieval and Early Renaissance Studies, 1982).

Secondary Sources

Anon., *Nantes et le pays nantais au moment de l'édit de Nantes* (Nantes: Société archéologique et historique de Nantes et de Loire-Atlantique, 1999).

Barrère, Abbé, 'Entrée et séjour de Charles IX à Agen', in *Bulletin du Comité de Langue, de l'Histoire et des Arts de France*, vol. 1 (1852–53).

Baux, E., V.-L. Bourrilly and P. Mabilly, 'Les Voyages des reines et de François Ier en Provence et dans la vallée du Rhône (décembre 1515–février 1516)', in *Annales du Midi*, XVI (1904), pp. 31–64.

Boulay de la Meurthe, A., *Entrée de Charles IX à Chenonceau* (Tours: P. Bousrey, 1900; offprint from *Mémoires de la Société archéologique de Touraine*, 1900).

Boutier, Jean, Alain Dewerpe and Daniel Nordman, *Un Tour de France royal: le voyage de Charles IX (1564–1566)* (Paris: Aubier, c. 1984).

Champollion-Figeac, A., *Captivité du roi François Ier* (Paris: Imprimerie royale, 1847).

Cimber, L. and F. Danjou, *Archives curieuses de l'histoire de France, Ière série* (15 vols, Paris: Beauvais, 1834–37).

Decrue, F., *Anne de Montmorency* (Paris: E. Plon, 1885).

de Ruffi, A., *Histoire de Marseille* (Marseille: C. Garcin, 1642).

Ducéré, E., *Charles IX à Bayonne* (Bayonne: A. Lamaignère, 1889).

Ehrmann, J., 'Les Tapisseries des Valois du Musée des Offices à Florence', in J. Jacquot (ed.), *Fêtes de la Renaissance* (3 vols, Paris: CNRS, 1956–75), vol. 1.

Fournier, E., *Variétés historiques et littéraires* (10 vols, Paris: P. Jannet, 1855–63).

Garcia, S., 'L'Entrée de Henri IV à Nantes le 13 avril 1598: une manœuvre politique', in Anon., *Nantes et le pays nantais au moment de l'édit de Nantes* (Nantes: Société archéologique et historique de Nantes et de Loire-Atlantique, 1999), pp. 9–17.

Garcia, S., *Les Entrées de ville à Nantes, du milieu du XVIe à la première moitié du XVIIe siècle, mémoire de maîtrise* (Univ. de Nantes, UFR d'Histoire, 1996).

Graham, V.E. and W. McAllister Johnson (eds), *The Royal Tour of France by Charles IX and Catherine de' Medici: Festivals and Entries, 1564–66* (Toronto: University of Toronto Press, 1979).

Hamy, A., *Entrevue de François Ier avec Clément VII à Marseille, 1533* (Paris: H. Champion, 1900).

Hamy, A., *Entrevue de François Ier avec Henry VIII à Boulogne-sur-Mer, en 1532* (Paris: L. Gougy, 1898).

Herval, R., *Histoire de Rouen* (2 vols, Rouen: Maugard, 1947–49).

Ivanoff, N., 'Les Fêtes à la cour des derniers Valois', in *Revue du Seizième Siècle*, 19 (1932–33).

Jacquot, J. (ed.), *Fêtes de la Renaissance* (3 vols, Paris: CNRS, 1956–75).

Jacquot, J., 'Panorama des fêtes et cérémonies du règne', in J. Jacquot (ed.), *Fêtes de la Renaissance* (3 vols, Paris: CNRS, 1956–75), vol. 2.

Knecht, R.J., 'Court Festival as political spectacle', in J.R. Mulryne, Helen Watanabe-O'Kelly and Margaret Shewring (eds), *Europa Triumphans: Court and Civic Festivals in Early Modern Europe* (2 vols, Aldershot: Ashgate, 2004).

Lebègue, R., 'Les Présentations dramatiques à la Cour des Valois', in J. Jacquot (ed.), *Fêtes de la Renaissance* (3 vols, Paris: CNRS, 1956–75), vol. 1.

Lelièvre, P., 'Entrées royales à Nantes à l'époque de la Renaissance, 1500–1551', in J. Jacquot (ed.), *Fêtes de la Renaissance* (3 vols, Paris: CNRS, 1956–75), vol. 3.

Marsden, C.A., 'Entrées et fêtes espagnoles au XVIe siècle', in J. Jacquot (ed.), *Fêtes de la Renaissance* (3 vols, Paris: CNRS, 1956–75), vol. 2.

McGowan, Margaret M., *Balet comique de la royne* (Binghamton: Center for Medieval and Early Renaissance Studies, c. 1982).

McGowan, Margaret M., 'Festivals and the Arts in Henri III's journey from Poland to France (1574)', in J.R. Mulryne, Helen Watanabe-O'Kelly and Margaret Shewring (eds), *Europa Triumphans: Court and Civic Festivals in Early Modern Europe* (2 vols, Aldershot: Ashgate, 2004).

McGrath, E., 'Le Déclin d'Anvers et les decorations de Rubens pour l'entrée du Prince Ferdinand en 1635', in J. Jacquot (ed.), *Fêtes de la Renaissance* (3 vols, Paris: CNRS, 1956–75), vol. 3.

Mulryne, J.R., Helen Watanabe-O'Kelly and Margaret Shewring (eds), *Europa Triumphans: Court and Civic Festivals in Early Modern Europe* (2 vols, Aldershot: Ashgate, 2004).

Plédy, L., *Brouage* (La Rochelle: Pijollet, 1925).

Rabelais F., *Œuvres complètes*, ed. M. Huchon (Paris: Gallimard, 1994).

Rousset, J., 'L'Eau et les tritons dans les fêtes et ballets de cour (1580–1640)', in J. Jacquot (ed.), *Fêtes de la Renaissance* (3 vols, Paris: CNRS, 1956–75), vol. 1.

Shergold, N.D., *History of the Spanish Stage* (Oxford: Oxford University Press, 1967).

Urgoïti, S. Carrasco, 'Les Fêtes équestres dans les *Guerres civiles de Grenade*', in J. Jacquot (ed.), *Fêtes de la Renaissance* (3 vols, Paris: CNRS, 1956–75), vol. 3.

Varey, J.E., 'Les Spectacles pyrotechniques en Espagne (XVI–XVII siècles)', in J. Jacquot (ed.), *Fêtes de la Renaissance* (3 vols, Paris: CNRS, 1956–75), vol. 3.

Williams, S., 'L'Ommegangs d'Anvers et les cortèges du Lord-Maire de Londres', in J. Jacquot (ed.), *Fêtes de la Renaissance* (3 vols, Paris: CNRS, 1956–75), vol. 2.

Yates, F., *The Valois Tapestries* ([London]: Routledge, 1975).

Chapter 2

Lyon: a Centre for Water Celebrations

Margaret M. McGowan

Four years before he organized the memorable royal entry into Lyon (1548), Maurice Scève had published a collection of love poems which he called *Délie*.[1] Although they were informed by the work of earlier Italian poets,[2] they were also inspired by the topography of the city of Lyon and, in particular, by the two great rivers: the fiery Rhône and the calm and placid Saône, whose waters ran into each other at the heart of the city. Scève used their confluence to express the ineradicable nature of his feelings for his mistress:

> Plutost seront Rhosne, et Saone desjoinctz
> Plutost le Rhosne aller contremont lentement
> Saone monter tres violemment
> Que ce mien feu, tant soit peu diminuer … (XVII)

> [The Rhône would rather be separated from the Saone,
> The Rhône would rather flow slowly backwards
> And the Saone advance violently
> Than my fire would diminish in the slightest.][3]

Through lines such as these evoking accurately the presence and character of the two rivers, and deliberately distorting them, Scève showed how the landscape of the city had entered his imagination; and it was to remain part of his creative life. As he contemplated the design of the double arch of Saint Paul for the royal entry,[4]

---

[1]   Maurice Scève, *Délie: object de plus haulte vertu* (Lyon, 1544); Maurice Scève, *Délie: object de plus haulte vertu*, ed. Eugene Parturier (Paris: Librairie M. Didier, 1961).

[2]   The sources of Scève's poems were identified and explained by Dorothy Gabe Coleman, *Maurice Scève: Poet of Love: tradition and originality* (Cambridge: Cambridge University Press, 1975).

[3]   In addition to Dixain XVII quoted here, Scève developed the theme of the rivers in XXVI and CCVIII. It is interesting to note that Charles Fontaine, in his *Salutation à Charles IX*, at his entry into Lyon in 1564 (f. 132), uses the confluence of the two rivers as a symbol of political union.

[4]   Two sources have been invaluable for this study: Georges Guigue's facsimile edition of *Henri II's entry into Lyon 1548* (Paris: 1927), printed together with the complete record from the municipal archives of all the payments incurred; and Richard

the rivers returned again to his thoughts. There, Henri II could contemplate the two rivers turned into stone, yet retaining their natural attributes: the Saône on the right – a female figure languid among the reeds and marshes, apparently asleep; on the left, the fiery personage of the Rhône, alert and ready to welcome the ships that raced along its waters.

The prominence given to the rivers in the entry reflected their importance for the city whose international status derived partly from its early development by the Romans, but especially from its position on a navigable river (the Rhône) which linked Lyon to Mediterranean ports in the South and to German and Dutch commercial centres in the North.[5] From earliest times, the rivers had been the focus of civic celebrations; the annual veneration on 2 June of Saint Pothin (for instance) had been marked, since the fourteenth century, by processions along the river from the five main churches of the city whose representatives sang matins by candlelight on the outward journey to Saint Martin d'Ainay and evensong on their return.[6]

Given this kind of tradition, it was inevitable that the rivers regularly provided a magnet for spectacles arranged to greet visiting dignitaries. Thus, a white stag welcomed François Ier in 1515, drawing a massive boat (charged with symbolism) along the Saône;[7] and water festivals of marine deities paid homage to Queen Eleonore in 1533,[8] while François was entertained again by the Admiral of France '*sopra al suo gran naviglio*' ('on his own great ship') in July 1545.[9] Nothing, however, could match the explosion of aquatic activity which was prepared for the coming of Henri II and Catherine de Medici 15 years later.

Cooper's learned edition, *The Entry of Henri II into Lyon, September 1548* (Tempe, Ariz: Medieval and Renaissance Texts and Studies, 1997), in which are printed the reactions of visiting ambassadors and other contemporaries; most citations in this paper are taken from this edition. The arch at Saint Paul is described, sigs F3'–4, and is shown in a woodcut, sig. F4'.

 [5] For a comprehensive account of Lyon's significance within France, see Yann Lignereux, *Lyon et le roi: De la 'bonne ville' à l'absolutisme municipal (1594–1654)* (Seyssel: Champ Vallon, 2003).

 [6] See *Entrées royales et fêtes populaires à Lyon, XVe–XVIIIe siècles* (Lyon: 1970), p. 20, where it seems that bishop Saint Pothin had been commemorated at Lyon since 830. For the involvement of local corporations in civic celebrations, see Richard Cooper's chapter, 'French Renaissance Waterborne Festivals in the Sixteenth Century', pp. 9–36 in this volume.

 [7] The municipal archives record the costs of building the boat, for the work involved in its movement across the water. These are collected in Georges Guigue's edition, *L'Entrée de François Ier ... en la cité de Lyon, le 12 juillet 1515* (Lyon, 1899), where the symbolism attaching to the figures the boat carried are explained.

 [8] See *Entrées royales ... à Lyon*, p. 73.

 [9] Letter from Alessandro Zerbinati to the duke of Ferrara (Lyon, 1 August 1545), in Carmelo Occhipinti, *Carteggio d'arte degli ambasciatori estensi in Francia (1536–1553)* (Pisa: Scuola normale superiore, 2001), p. 113.

In September 1548, the rivers were naturally the principal focal point of spectacle, entertainments offering respite from the insistent political messages on the triumphal arches, and from the pleas for privileges from the citizens in all their speeches. Every day during their week-long stay, the king and his court went by boat from the Archevêché (where he lodged) to the scenes of celebration. His gondola,[10] in which he frequently travelled, was accompanied by a large flotilla of vessels which kept pace with the royal party, moving to the sound of music which played continuously, its harmonies oftentimes impossible to distinguish above the noise of cannon fire or from the blasts of trumpets, pipes, horns and drums. So impressive was the daily sight of these ships in strict formation that the Italian account of the entry likened it to that standard reference to heroic performance: the departure of Jason on his way to Colchos to triumph over the Golden Fleece.[11] Although such comparisons seem outlandish now, they fitted in with the views of Scève himself and of other witnesses to the water triumphs since they all lavished such care on their descriptions of the movement of ships, their fabrication and their magnificent rigging.

To accommodate all the vessels, '*lesquels estoient fabriqués à neuf*' ('which had been built afresh'), the port at L'Archevêché had been re-constructed, a second tower made to balance the existing one, 16 classical columns set between them with marine deities in their niches, and rounded steps down to the river. The whole ensemble, described '*à la Romaine*' ('in Roman fashion'), was made to resemble Sebastian Serlio's engraving of the Belvedere Court.[12] Apparently, vessels 'without number' came to settle in this harbour, although the exact figure is difficult to determine. Preparations for the construction of boats had been under way since mid June; by early July, however, it was obvious that the four galleys which had been commissioned would be quite insufficient. So the consuls had recourse to purchasing eight more vessels. In addition, there was the king's ceremonial boat, the *Bucentaure*, which was always accompanied by five or six other boats. Then there were two large *galliasses*, modelled on ancient examples,[13] and designed for the sea battle, to be filled with soldiers armed with every possible modern weapon. Finally, there were boats carrying municipal officials, city dignitaries, the Enfants de la Ville

---

[10]   The gondola is described in detail in the *Relation des entrées solennelles dans la ville de Lyon, de nos Rois, Reines, Princes, Princesses* (Lyon, 1752) [largely copied from Scève's text], p. 58: '*subtile et légère*' ('subtle and light'), having at its centre a square pavilion '*comme un lit*' ('like a bed'), with curtains in black velvet and Turkish carpets on the floor.

[11]   Cited in Cooper, *Henri II into Lyon*, p. 141.

[12]   For the effort to make this entry a veritable '*fête à l'antique*', see my discussion of French structures modelled on Roman examples in *The Vision of Rome in Late Renaissance France* (New Haven and London: Yale University Press, 2000), pp. 326–7.

[13]   Cooper, *Henri II into Lyon*, p. 122, has argued convincingly that Du Choul influenced the form of these ships and possibly the decoration of others. Du Choul's reconstructions in *De re nautica* are still in manuscript.

and those tradesmen anxious to get close to the action. So great was the volume of vessels on the river that observers could not distinguish land from water.[14]

It is noticeable that all attention is focused on military activity – a marked shift in taste from earlier entries to accommodate Henri II's preferences.[15] Imagine the size of the undertaking, if it was to be perfect! Three months hardly seemed adequate to assemble materials and workmen necessary to construct such a fleet. And observers, especially the chronicler Jean Guéraud and Italian reporters, emphasized the range and variety of vessels used, as the municipal records also demonstrate in detail.[16] While carpenters laboured six days a week to construct galleys and workmen knocked down buildings along the route to the river, clearing the way for the transport of ships from dry land to the water, chandlers worked on the mechanisms to fit fireworks into the galleys and to attach ropes that would pull vessels through the water.[17] Yet, the consuls realized that all that effort was not enough. Therefore, they accelerated the pace of the work, ordering carpenters to labour seven full days a week; and they authorized the purchase of ships from afar.[18] Manpower, too, had to be put in place: 70 sailors recruited to man the galleys and 14 skippers employed to guide them up and down the river.[19] The city fathers were anxious that there would be no slip-ups in the complex water performances they planned; so, three expert fencers were taken on to train 12 'gladiators' to perform a pyrrhic and to fight on the two *galliasses* during the sea battle. To ensure

---

[14]   For the detail and quantity of ships see *Relation*, pp. 67–71; for the specific observation, p. 69: '*la rivière tellement garnie de batteaux pleins de monde, que l'on ne pouvoit discerner l'eau de terre*' ('the river so decorated with boats full of people that one could not distinguish water from land'). The narrator at Rouen had a more startling expression: both land and sea '*sembloit être couvert d'un seul drap noir, marqueté de faces humaines*' ('seemed to be covered with a single black sheet, inlaid with human faces'), see *L'Entrée de Henri II à Rouen, 1550*, ed. Margaret M. McGowan (Amsterdam: Theatrum Orbis Terrarum; New York, Johnson Reprint Corp., 1974), sig. M3.

[15]   See Richard Cooper's discussion of this shift in his chapter in this volume, pp. 9–36.

[16]   For such detailed observations, see the dispatches of Giorgio Conegrani to the Duke of Mantua (Appendix A in Cooper, *Henri II into Lyon*, pp. 301–15); the letters of Ambassador Giulio Alvarotti to the Duke of Ferrara (Appendix B in ibid., pp. 315–16); and Jean Guéraud's diary (Appendix E in ibid., pp. 322–4).

[17]   See Guigue, *Henri II's entry*, in which he publishes the complete archives relating to the entry; for work on the galleys, pp. 182, 220, 237, 243–4, 249, 259, 264, 270, 276, 281, 299.

[18]   Guigue, ibid., pp. 239–40, 285. Conegrani, Alvarotti and Guéraud all mention the purchase of boats from Marseilles and from Venice; Alvarotti specifies the different types of foreign boats. Similarly, at Rouen in 1550, local expertise was deemed inadequate and the town councillors sought skills from a distance, '*avoient mandé & venir de loingtain pays*' ('had ordered (them) to come from distant lands'), Cooper, *Henry II into Lyon*, sig. Q1V.

[19]   For their cost, see Guigue, *Henri II's entry*, pp. 179–80, 356.

success, they were paid for rehearsals, as were sailors from Saint Vincent who tried out the galleys on the water for two days prior to the *naumachia*.[20]

Of all the craft constructed in 1548, the most magnificent was the *Bucentaure*, the king's boat. Its structure inspired from the Doge's ceremonial barge it was, in the words of ambassador Alvarotti, '*cosi bello et forse più de quello de Vinetia, ma non gia però cosi grande a un gran pezzo*' ('more beautiful and stronger than the Venetian original but not of such weight').[21] The *Bucentaure*, described by Guéraud as a floating palace, was built in what Scève claimed was classical style. On its solid base was constructed a large hall, 32.5 feet long, 15 feet wide and 30 feet high, its doors framed with cornice, pediments and fluted columns, its long windows similarly conceived *à l'antique*; everywhere decorated in the king's colours, black and white, and emblazoned with his device of the triple crescent moon. Above the hall was a balustraded viewing gallery around which guests could walk, while the king had a viewing platform of his own, situated on the prow of the boat from which he could enjoy the dancing which took place regularly in the body of the hall.[22] Since much time was spent by the king and his court, watching the water festivals from the *Bucentaure*, it was necessary to provide food and drink. This was achieved in the most ingenious way: when the king wanted to eat, a collation already prepared descended on a panel from the ceiling, at will and instantaneously, supported by four stout silk ropes controlling the apparently imperceptible movement. When the king wished to drink, part of the floor rose up before him, revealing a table laden with fine liqueurs and rare sweetmeats shaped into the devices of the royal party.[23] Denis Sauvage, in his *Histoire de Lyon*, was most impressed by the invisible workings of the mechanism: the gods (he thought) had to be responsible.[24] The ship itself called forth even greater enthusiasm: Cleopatra's golden prow (Sauvage declared) was nothing compared

---

[20]   Details in Guigue, ibid., pp. 177–8, 301, 357. The well-known organizer and writer on festivals, C.F. Ménestrier, recommended such rehearsals to ensure that complex and spectacular events succeeded. See Lucien Bely, 'Des entrées et receptions solennelles des princes et grands seigneurs', in Gérard Sabatier (ed.), *Claude François Menestrier, les Jésuites et le monde des images* (Grenoble: Presses universitaites de Grenoble, 2009), pp. 167–80.

[21]   Cited in Cooper, *Henri II into Lyon*, p. 21.

[22]   Details concerning the *Bucentaure* and the Hall are given in Cooper, *Henri II into Lyon*, sigs I 1"–2; Guéraud, pp. 322–4; and Sauvage, pp. 325–6.

[23]   Descriptions of the mechanism and admiration for its ingenuity can be found in *Relation*, pp. 56–7, 65–6; Cooper, *Henri II into Lyon*, sig. I 2; and Sauvage, p. 326.

[24]   '*Comme si les Dieux celestes et terrestres eussent miraculeusement envoyé de hault et de bas la collation aux assistans*' ('as if celestial and terrestrial deities had miraculously sent, from above and from below, the collations to the guests'), Sauvage in Cooper, *Henri II into Lyon*, p. 326. This judgement is a variation on the text in *Relation*, pp. 65–6: '*comme si les esprits celestes leur envoyassent d'en haut la collation, et ceulx des eaux les voulussent amener de leur maison acquatique*' ('as if celestial spirits had sent them the collation from above, and those of the sea wished to lead them into their aquatic domaine').

to the singularities of the king's boat.[25] The use of the *Bucentaure* proved so successful that the citizens of Lyon created similar structures, albeit less elaborate, when Charles IX came in 1564 and for Henri III on his return from Italy in 1574.[26]

What games were played on the water? These involved the traditional jousting and acrobatic antics of fishermen from the Saint Vincent and Saint George districts.[27] Then came the highlight, in terms of nautical skill and enterprise, and military tactics on the water, the *naumachia* (or sea battle). Scève, aided by Du Choul, thought they were re-enacting an ancient form of festival, but (they also avowed) that they had added ingenious, modern touches.[28] Although they did not attach cosmic meanings to their aquatic display as the organizers of the entry into Rouen were to do in 1550,[29] the importance which Scève and his colleagues attached to this event may be judged by the amount of detail provided: not only of the different ships, their movements in the contest, but also the swiftness of the oarsmen, the actions of the combatants, the length of the battle and the noise of clamour.[30] Finally, a most spectacular vision: a firework display engineered on two galleys moored on the Saône at mid-river; and, the following day, the storming of a mock castle, constructed on a galley which, after being attacked by a crowd of boats, blew up scattering a thousand shafts of fire into the sky.[31]

---

[25]   Sauvage: '*la pouppe d'or de Cleopatra ne leur eussent sceu faire honte, singulièrement accosté au Bucentaure*' ('the golden prow of Cleopatra would not have shamed it, singularly likened to the *Bucentaure*'), Cooper, *Henri II into Lyon*, p. 326.

[26]   For the two '*galeottes*' made for Charles IX and the Queen Mother in 1564, see Victor E. Graham and W. McAllister Johnson (eds), *The royal tour of France by Charles IX and Catherine de'Medici: festivals and entries, 1564–1566* (Toronto: University of Toronto Press, 1979), Appendix V, p. 207 and *Relation*, pp. 88–90; for Henri III's boat, ibid., p. 94.

[27]   *Relation*, p. 65. Georges Guigue's edition of *L'Entrée de Louis XII le 17 juillet 1507* (Lyon, 1885), pp. 3–4, shows how well-established this tradition of using local corporations was: '*les pescheurs de Sainct Vincent ... [were paid for having] jousterent sur Saone à Sainct Jehan*' ('the fishermen from Saint Vincent (were paid for having) jousted on the Saône at Saint Jean').

[28]   *Relation*, p. 67, '*une naumachie ou bataille navale de galeres suivant quant à la façon, elles [the two galleys] étoient d'enrichissement et de beauté, proues et pouppes de nouvelle et folâtre invention*' ('a *naumachia* or naval battle according to the manner, they (the two galleys) were richly decorated and beautiful, prows and stern of new and wild invention').

[29]   The demonstration of cosmic arithmetic at play in the aquatic scenes at Rouen has been well studied by Luisa Capodieci, 'Sic Itur ad Astra. Narration, Figures célestes et platonisme dans les entrées de Henri II (Reims 1547, Lyon 1548, Paris 1549, Rouen 1550)', in Nicolas Russell and Hélène Visentin (eds), *French Ceremonial Entries in the Sixteenth Century: Event, Image, Text* (Toronto: Centre for Reformation and Renaissance Studies, 2007), pp. 73–109.

[30]   Cooper, *Henri II into Lyon*, sigs K 3–L 1; Conegrani, p. 312; and Guéraud, p. 323.

[31]   *Relation*, p. 72 and Cooper, *Henri II into Lyon*, sigs L 3–4.

Such feats of vision are not easy to transcribe in words. In accounts of royal entertainments we have become accustomed to the use of what we would regard as hyperbole, the upgrading or overstatement of facts as writers sought a language adequate to convey their own colossal aims, the expectation of princes, and the marvels of their technical achievements.[32] Remember the king's boat more remarkable than the golden prow of Cleopatra's barge; remember the gods who seem to have provided food and drink.

Reporters managed to convey the visual excitement by choosing one particular element and concentrating attention upon it. For the fireworks (for instance), the focus was on the rotating wheel with its backwards and forwards thrust; the narrative then moved to the spectacular effects produced from this movement: the showers of sparks, spread in all directions against the night sky; and a final comparison: the illumination was so great that the world turned upside down as stars seemed to have been torn out of heaven.[33] The assault on the exploding castle posed more problems for the ardent reporter since the rains came and dampened the spectacle; yet Scève struggled to convey a sense of brilliance by likening the lights to stars.[34] To persuade the reader of the unusual nature of an event, writers frequently evoked the size, eagerness and enthusiasm of the crowd, most often depicted as a multitude of bodies scrabbling over rooftops, crushed into windows, or jostling for position along the royal route: the people 'thick as grains of sand', as one observer reported.[35] For water festivals, however, reporters offered something different. They searched for uncommon, arresting images. For example, *'lesquelz [bâteaux] estoient certes en si grande quantité, que les poissons se pouvoient dire couvertz, comme soubz l'umbrage d'une croûte de glace contenant uniment tout le dessus de la rivière'* ('the sheer quantity of boats crowded on the river on the

---

[32] For a discussion of the necessity of hyperbole in the description of such events, see my article, 'The French Royal Entry in the Renaissance: The Status of the Printed Text', in Russell and Visentin, *French Ceremonial*, pp. 29–54.

[33] *Relation*, p. 72, *'de mode qu'il sembloit que ce fussent étoiles qui se fussent arrachées du ciel'* ('in a fashion that it seemed as though it was the stars which had been snatched from heaven').

[34] Cooper, *Henri II into Lyon*, sig. L 4v: *'grand spectacle de torches, lanternes, et chandelles le long du bort de la rivière, voulants ce sembloit* [note Scève's caution] *contendu de nombre à la multitude des estoiles (s'il eust fait cler) et resister à la pluye qu'il faisoit'* ('a great spectacle of torches, lanterns and candles along the river's edge, seeking in number to rival the multitude of stars (if it had been fine) and resist the rain which was falling').

[35] Description of the crowd at the *naumachia* organized in Paris (3 July 1549): *'les rives couvertes de peuple dur comme sable'* ('the river banks were covered with people crowded together as if they were grains of sand'), *The Entry of Henri II into Paris, 16 June 1549*, ed. I.D. McFarlane (Binghamton: Center for Medieval and Early Renaissance Studies, 1982), p. 67, where he cites from François Belleforest, *Les Chroniques et Annales de France* (Paris, 1600), ff. 576 r–v.

night of the sea battle, was felt even by the fishes who might surmise that they lay in shade beneath a crust of ice spread over the entire waters').[36]

By far the most difficult event to re-enact on paper, and the most significant for the planners given the king's martial tastes, was the *naumachia*; and here, Scève displayed extraordinary vigour as he simulates in words the battle, its magnificence and its noise. The spectacular contest developed in three waves with the two galleys, appropriately decorated all around with the labours of Hercules, manoeuvring around each other at first, then engaging in conflict, soldiers using every one of their many weapons to vanquish their opponents; then middle-sized vessels got involved, prows locked together as they rammed home their advantage; and finally, it was the turn of the smallest craft. Scève succeeds in conveying the pandemonium, the excited emotions and the fears aroused by piling on the words, listing the '*chamaillis d'armes tranchantes*' ('clash of cutting blades'), the accompanying noise of trumpets and arquebuses, and by interrupting his text with images of the shafts of flame that skidded across the water. Spectators expected fatalities, their feelings vying between intense joy and overwhelming fright as one ship went down; the king's colours triumphed, and it seemed – truly – that the fight was to the death. Thus, Scève's heightened tones simulated real warfare; he paints the crowd reacting to the violence '*mortelle et à oultrance*' ('mortal and to the death').[37] Yet, as the *Relation* makes clear, no one was hurt: '*tel le fust l'issue de cette bataille navale, sans offense de quelque personne que ce fût*' ('thus ended the naval battle without hurt to any person whatsoever').[38]

Descriptive power, and reassurance that something magnificent had been attempted, were what the consuls of Lyon wanted when they ordered Scève's narrative to be printed, with pictures, at the city's expense.[39] The reverberations which came from this printing were considerable. When the king entered his capital in June 1549, on the arch facing Saint Jacques de l'Hospital, he saw river statues – the Seine and the Marne[40] replacing the Saône and the Rhône he had admired at Lyon. Water sports, however, were not formally part of the Paris entry but, at the express command of the king, '*expressément commandé et ordonné par le roy*',[41] on 3 July, there was a spectacular castle-storming when a fort built for the purpose on L'Isle Louviers was overpowered by cannon fire and by the artillery

36   Cooper, *Henri II into Lyon*, sig. L 3.

37   Ibid., sig. L lr: '*à cest assault fut faict un tel chamaillis d'armes tranchantes, que l'on eust juré asseurement combattoient mortellement et à oultrance, qui ne fust sans esbahissement et peur à plusieurs regardants*' ('during this assault such a clash of cutting blades occurred that one would have sworn truly that they fought to the death, and that several spectators suffered from wonder and fright').

38   *Relation*, p. 70. It is probable that dummies were used to impress the crowd.

39   See Guigue, *Pièces justificatives* [*Henry II's entry*], pp. 187–9; Cooper, *Henri II into Lyon*, discusses the dating of these instructions, pp. 130–31.

40   McFarlane, sigs B iiiv–ivr.

41   Ibid., p. 63, where he is citing from the municipal archives.

force from the seven *galliasses* which had detached themselves from the convoy of some 33 galleys which had sailed in formation down the Seine.[42]

At Rouen, the following year (October, 1550), water festivals were an integral part of the royal entry, and were very extensive. In fact, there was a triple triumph: a display of Neptune's power as his subjects performed feats of aquatic skills for the king.[43] Thetys, Amphitryon and their nymphs saluted the queen with diverse, intricate water sports; and a *naumachia*, done twice on successive days, to which the Rouennais added a political message as the Portuguese galley was each day overcome by the French.[44]

The author of the official account at Rouen, although providing ample testimony to the magnificence of all the shows and architectural delights, was at pains to stress the inadequacies of his pen.[45] He recalled the artist Timotheus who, in painting the sacrifice of Iphigenia, had covered Agamemnon's face as the father's distress was too awful to depict. Similarly, the recorder at Rouen feels constrained to draw a veil over the '*magnificence, pompe et excellence de ce Triumphe*', so overcome is he by their splendour that he fears to add anything of his own: all he can do is to provide the glimmer of a painting, '*sinon, vous presenter icy l'umbre de la peinture*' ('notwithstanding, to present you here with the mere shadow of the painting').[46] Mock modesty, perhaps, for he goes on to expatiate for many more pages on the remarkable event. Indeed, the passage is so striking for the insights it gives into the descriptive and artistic preoccupations of the recorders of royal entries that it is transcribed and translated in full in the Appendix to this chapter.[47]

In describing the occasion at such length, however, he reproduces literally passages from Scève's Lyon's text. Perhaps it was his sense of inadequacy that encouraged him to borrow the striking image of the fish feeling they were beneath a

---

[42]   The account of the *naumachia* can be found in Belleforest, ff. 576'; it is reproduced in full in McFarlane, p. 67. The archives make clear that the city found it extraordinarily difficult to recruit a sufficient number of skilled sailors for the task indicating, perhaps, that the sea battle had not been part of the original plans. Reference is also made to these water sports by the Ferrarese ambassador who wrote to his master on 5 July, see Occhipinti, p. 231. For a detailed analysis of these military antics on the water, see Monique Chatenet's chapter in this volume, pp. 51–66, where she discusses the military hopes underlying the 1549 spectacle. A further '*jeu naval*' was performed at Lyon on the Saône to entertain the future duc de Nevers in July 1549, see Leonardo Arrivabene to the duchess of Mantua (Mantova, Archivio di Stato, AG 642). I thank Monique Chatenet for drawing my attention to this letter.

[43]   McGowan, *Henri II à Rouen*, sig. L.

[44]   Ibid., sig. P 3'.

[45]   Ibid., sig. K 2.

[46]   Ibid.

[47]   See pages 46–7, below.

crust of ice,[48] or to describe in exactly the same terms the naval contest as '*mortelle et à oultrance*' while affirming the safety of all the combatants: '*nul des matelots en fût offence*' ('not one of the sailors was hurt').[49] Observers of the *naumachia* strained language to the uttermost in their attempt to capture the impact of it all.

  Thus the glory of Lyon was perpetuated;[50] but at what cost! The shows arranged for Henri II and his queen bankrupted the city and several consuls found themselves in prison.[51] That experience did not, however, prevent future generosity. Throughout the sixteenth and seventeenth centuries, Lyon delighted important visitors with extravagant displays, especially on the water.[52] Menestrier has left eloquent accounts of the *Réjouissances* which he masterminded for Louis XIV in 1658 and again in 1660, for instance.[53] Perhaps the ultimate in naval construction was reached in 1701 for the grandsons of the Sun King, the duc de Berry and the duc de Bourgogne. For their delectation, two boats were constructed, each 65 feet long, supreme in their art as to size, safety and good taste. From their vantage points on the river, the princes could enjoy all the spectacles prepared for them. It was as though Henri II's *Bucentaure* had come back to life – in double vision.[54]

Appendix

Extract from the official account of the water festivals at Rouen, October 1550.

> *Ains destitué de termes propres, pour dignement representer et mettre en lumiere, le discours d'icelluy triumphe: il me conviendra, en c'est endroict suyvre le conseil*

---

 [48] Ibid., sig. P 4: '*Lesquelz [bateaux] estoient en si grande quantité, que les Poissons se pouvoient bien dire couvertz, comme souz l'umbrage d'une crotte de glace*' ('which (boats) were in such large quantity that the fishes might surmise that they lay in shade beneath a crust of ice').

 [49] Ibid., sig. M 1".

 [50] It was to re-surface in Florence in 1565 when Vincenzo Borghini, prior of the hospital of the Innocenti, took notes from Scève's text to develop ideas for festivals celebrating the wedding of Francesco de' Medici with Joanna of Austria. I thank Iain Fenlon for drawing my attention to Borghini.

 [51] On the financial difficulties and bankruptcy, see the detailed discussion of Cooper, *Henri II into Lyon*, pp. 15, 27, 30 and 143; for the lavish expenditure of Ippolito d'Este who paid for many of the boats, see ibid., pp. 2–4, 28–30.

 [52] Restricting information to visiting monarchs: reference has already been made to Charles IX (1564) and Henri III (1574). Henri IV was extravagantly entertained twice, in 1595 and 1600; and Louis XIII was received three times (1622, 1630 and 1632).

 [53] C.F. Ménestrier, *L'Autel de Lyon consacré à Loys Auguste et placé dans le Temple de la Gloire* (Lyon, 1658); *Les Réjouissances de la Paix, faictes dans la ville de Lyon le 20 mars, 1660* (Lyon, 1660).

 [54] *Relation*, pp. 276–7 gives a detailed description of the two vessels, and of the size and purpose of several accompanying boats.

de Timothee peintre tresexcellent. Lequel au tableau, ou il effigioit l'inhumaine immolation d'Iphigenia, fille d'Agamenon apres avoir delivré les princes assistens, extresmement affligez, de veoir un si indigne & cruel spectacle: ne pouvant de son art exprimer au vif: l'excessive oppression du coeur paternel: Couvrit le visage d'Agamenon: laissant à penser aux spectateurs, l'extreme douleur: qui surmontoit lenergie de son sçavoir. A semblable raison: toutesfois à subiect dessemblable: ie suis forcé: mettre un voile de silence: sur la magnificence: pompe: & excellence de ce Triumphe: pourceque: l'admirable succez d'icelluy: m'a tellement estonée: que ie ne puis: & ne doy aussi autre chose promettre du mien: sinon: vous presenter icy seulement: l'umbre de la peinture: Car de m'ingerer vous en representer l'image, seroit à moy entreprise trop hardie, veu que l'eloquence mesme, au progrez de l'histoire, se pourroit trouver mute, ou privée de voix articulée.

[Thus, deprived of appropriate words to represent and bring into the light the description of this triumph, it is fitting in this place to follow the counsel of that excellent painter Timotheus who, in the painting where he depicted the sacrifice of Iphigenia, daughter of Agamemnon, after having freed the princely witnesses overcome with sorrow from seeing this unworthy and cruel spectacle, not being able through his art to depict the excessive sorrow of the father's heart, covered the face of Agamemnon, allowing the spectators to guess at the extreme distress which overcame the power of his (the painter's) knowledge … For a similar reason, although the subject is quite different, I am obliged to put a veil of silence over the magnificence, pomp and excellence of this triumph, because its wonderful outcome has so astonished me that I cannot, and should not, promise from myself anything other than, presenting you with a mere shadow of the painting. For to undertake to present you with the exact image would be, for me, too difficult an enterprise since even eloquence, through the progress of history, would find herself mute, deprived of a speaking voice.]

Bibliography

Primary Sources

Entrées royales et fêtes populaires à Lyon, XVe–XVIIIe siècles (Lyon, 1970).
Fontaine, Charles, *Salutation à Charles IX*, at his entry into Lyon in 1564.
Guéraud, Jean, *Chronique*, in *The Entry of Henri II into Lyon, September 1548*, ed. Richard Cooper (Tempe, Ariz: Medieval and Renaissance Texts and Studies, 1997).
Henri II's entry into Lyon 1548, facsimile edition, ed. Georges Guigue (Paris, 1927).

L'Entrée de François Ier ... en la cité de Lyon, le 12 juillet 1515, ed. Georges Guigue (Lyon, 1899).

L'Entrée de Henri II à Rouen, 1550, ed. Margaret M. McGowan (Amsterdam: Theatrum Orbis Terrarum; New York: Johnson Reprint Corp., 1974).

L'Entrée de Louis XII le 17 juillet 1507, ed. Georges Guigue (Lyon, 1885).

Ménestrier, Claude-François, *L'Autel de Lyon consacré à Loys Auguste et placé dans le Temple de la Gloire* (Lyon, 1658).

Ménestrier, Claude-François, *Les Réjouissances de la Paix, faictes dans la ville de Lyon le 20 mars, 1660* (Lyon, 1660).

Relation des entrées solennelles dans la ville de Lyon, de nos Rois, Reines, Princes, Princesses (Lyon, 1752).

Sauvage, Denis, 'Histoire de Lyon', in *The Entry of Henri II into Lyon, September 1548*, ed. Richard Cooper (Tempe, Ariz: Medieval and Renaissance Texts and Studies, 1997).

Scève, Maurice, *Délie: object de plus haulte vertu* (Lyon, 1544).

Scève, Maurice, *Délie: object de plus haulte vertu*, ed. Eugene Parturier (Paris: Librairie M. Didier, 1961 [c. 1939]).

The Entry of Henri II into Lyon, September 1548, ed. Richard Cooper (Tempe, Ariz: Medieval and Renaissance Texts and Studies, 1997).

The Entry of Henri II into Paris, 16 June 1549, ed. I.D. McFarlane (Binghamton: Center for Medieval and Early Renaissance Studies, 1982).

Secondary Sources

Bely, Lucien, 'Des entrées et receptions solennelles des princes et grands seigneurs', in Gérard Sabatier (ed.), *Claude François Menestrier, les Jésuites et le monde des images* (Grenoble: Presses universitaires de Grenoble, 2009).

Capodieci, Luisa, 'Sic Itur ad Astra. Narration, Figures célestes et platonisme dans les entrées de Henri II (Reims 1547, Lyon 1548, Paris 1549, Rouen 1550)', in Nicolas Russell and Hélène Visentin (eds), *French Ceremonial Entries in the Sixteenth Century: Event, Image, Text* (Toronto: Centre for Reformation and Renaissance Studies, 2007), pp. 73–109.

Coleman, Dorothy Gabe, *Maurice Scève: Poet of Love: tradition and originality* (Cambridge: Cambridge University Press, 1975).

Graham, Victor, E. and W. McAllister Johnson (eds), *The royal tour of France by Charles IX and Catherine de' Medici: festivals and entries, 1564–1566* (Toronto: University of Toronto Press, 1979).

Lignereux, Yann, *Lyon et le roi: de la 'bonne ville' à l'absolutisme municipal (1594–1654)* (Seyssel: Champ Vallon, 2003).

McGowan, Margaret M., 'The French Royal Entry in the Renaissance: The Status of the Printed Text', in Nicolas Russell and Hélène Visentin (eds), *French Ceremonial Entries in the Sixteenth Century: Event, Image, Text* (Toronto: Centre for Reformation and Renaissance Studies, 2007), pp. 29–54.

McGowan, Margaret M., *The Vision of Rome in Late Renaissance France* (New Haven and London: Yale University Press, 2000).

Occhipinti, Carmelo, *Carteggio d'arte degli ambasciatori estensi in Francia (1536–1553)* (Pisa: Scuola normale superiore, 2001).

Russell, Nicolas and Hélène Visentin (eds), *French Ceremonial Entries in the Sixteenth Century: Event, Image, Text* (Toronto: Centre for Reformation and Renaissance Studies, 2007).

Sabatier, Gérard (ed.), *Claude-François Ménestrier, les Jésuites et le monde des images* (Grenoble: Presses universitaires de Grenoble, 2009).

Chapter 3
Parisian Waterborne Festivals from Francis I to Henri III

Monique Chatenet

In the sixteenth century Paris had no tradition of waterborne festivals in the manner of Venice or Lyon. However, the topography easily leant itself to such occasions. The Seine is a peaceful river and, as there were not yet many bridges in the capital, it was often crossed by boat.

Thus in March 1546, after a turbulent game of soccer in Saint-Germain-des-Prés, Francis I and the duchess of Etampes embarked for the Louvre, followed by the entire court. This is recounted as follows by the ambassador of Ferrara, Giulio Alvarotti:

> *Era in quell'hora la riviera carica di barchete per passare quasi tutta questa corte. La banda di Monsr Delphino passò tirando per acqua molti razzi che spaventavano quelle damme.*[1]

---

[1]   Abréviations:

Comptes 1549 – A.N., KK 286A *Comptes de la ville de Paris 1549. Dépenses pour le combat naval du 3 juillet.*

BELLEFOREST 1617 – Nicole Gilles et François de Belleforest, *Les Chroniques et Annales de France dès l'origine des François et leur venüe ès Gaules, faictes jadis briefvement par Nicole Gilles, ... jusqu'au roy Charles VIII et depuis additionnées par Denis Sauvage jusqu'au roy François II du nom, reveues, corrigées et augmentées ... contenantes l'histoire universelle de France dès Pharamond jusqu'au roy Charles IX, par F. de Belleforests, Comingeois, avec la suite et continuation d'icelles, depuis le roy Charles IX, jusques au roy ... Louys XIII à présent régnant*, par G. Chappuys, ... et autres (Paris: M. Sonnius, 1617).

CHATENET ET CAPODIECI 2006 – Monique Chatenet et Luisa Capodieci, 'Les triomphes des noces de Joyeuse (17 septembre–19 octobre 1581) à travers la correspondance diplomatique italienne et l'Epithalame de Jean Dorat', *Bulletin de la Société d'Histoire de l'Art Français* (2006), pp. 9–54.

CORROZET 1581 – *Les Antiquitez, croniques et singularitez de Paris ... avec les fondations et bastimens des lieux, les sépulchres et épitaphes des princes, princesses et autres personnes illustres ...* (Paris: N. Bonfons, 1581).

OCCHIPINTI 2001 – Carmelo Occhipinti, *Carteggio d'arte degli ambasciatori estensi in Francia (1536–1553)* (Pisa: Scuola normale superiore, 2001), Strumenti e testi 8.

A.S. Modena, *Ambasciatori in Francia 22, 9 mars 1546 (Alvarotti au duc de Ferrare).*

[At that time the river was full of boats allowing almost the whole court to pass over. The company of the Dauphin crossed the water firing many rockets, which terrified those ladies.]

It was only an improvised entertainment. The Dauphin had to wait for his coronation, or rather for his and Catherine de Médicis's entry into the capital in June 1549, to allow the devisers time to frighten the ladies with a well-organised naval battle which was to constitute the high point of the celebrations.

This event launched a fashion of waterborne festivals on the Seine. There were four in the sixteenth century, all examined in chronological order in this chapter. The four occasions celebrated the entry of Henri II and Catherine de Médicis into Paris (3 July 1549), Charles IX's seventeenth birthday (26 June 1576), the Peace of Saint-Germain (August 1570) and the Duke of Joyeuse's wedding (10 October 1581).

The Naval and Land Battle on the île de Louviers (3 July 1549)

Henri II was the initiator of the naval battle designed for his Parisian entry. On 14 May, as the preparations for the entry were well underway, the king ordered the Paris aldermen to fortify, at their own expense, the island of Louviers '*vis à vis des murs de la ville devant le couvent des célestins*' ('opposite the city walls in front of the convent of the Celestins') and to build '*un port en forme de havre*' ('a port taking the form of a small harbour') and a '*fort et bastillon pour monter dedans des gens de guerre de défence*' ('a fort and small bastion to accommodate the defending soldiers inside'); to set up ship-made bridges to join the island to its neighbours for the '*gens de guerre à pied qui viendront assaillir ledit fort*' ('infantry soldiers who would advance to assault the said fort'), and lastly to equip the ships '*en manière de galères*' ('like galleys') in order to attack the fort from the river.[2]

The île de Louviers (Fig. 3.1), which no longer exists, was situated upstream from, and in the immediate vicinity of, the future île Saint-Louis which was then made up of two separate islets called the île aux Vaches and the île Notre Dame. This imposing event is known in detail through the numerous documents studied by Ian McFarlane and more recently by Richard Cooper.[3] The expenses, which

---

[2]   A.N., K 957, *pièce* 16a, 14 mai 1549. *Lettres patentes de Henri II au prévôt des marchands et aux échevins de Paris.*

[3]   Anon., *The Entry of Henri II into Paris, 16 June 1549*, ed. with introduction by I.D. McFarlane (Binghamton, NY: Medieval and Renaissance Studies, 1982), pp. 63–8; Richard Cooper, 'Jean Martin et l'entrée de Henri II à Paris', in *Jean Martin. Un traducteur au temps de François Ier et de Henri II,* Cahiers V. L. Saulnier, 16 (Paris: Presses de l'école normale supérieure, 1999), pp. 97–111; OCCHIPINTI 2001, p. 231 (5 juillet 1549); A.S. Mantova, AG 642, fol. 126 (*juillet 1549; classé par erreur à 16 juin* ('classed by mistake as 16 June')).

Figure 3.1   The Isle of Louviers in 1550 on the map known as 'Saint-Victor' (photo: Chatenet).

reached 15,000 *livres* for this one day,[4] allowed a series of outstanding artists, including the painters Luca Penni, Charles Dorigny and Jean Cousin, to take part in the project under the direction of the Italian engineer Francisco Malacorda.[5] It was the king's own cabinet-maker Francisque Scibec (Francesco Cibelli da Carpi) who turned the run-of-the-mill rowing boats into dashing galleys.[6]

On 3 July 1549, the king and queen went in a 'gondola'[7] to the vicinity of the island to take supper in a huge floating salon displaying the colours of the

---

[4]   *Comptes 1549*, Total de la dépense: 141, 71 livres (20 s. 11 d.).

[5]   *Comptes 1549*, fol. 168v: '*Malacorda, conducteur et entrepreneur de la conduicte des ouvrages d'icelluy fort*' ('Malacorda, overseer and developer of the work on this fort'); fol 174: '*au sieur Francisco Malacorda, ingenieur depputé par le Roy a dresser ledit fort*' ('to Francisco Malacorda, the engineer appointed by the king to design the said fort').

[6]   *Comptes 1549*, fol. 174v: '*A Francisque Scibec, menuysier du roy ... pour avoir ... accomodé en forme de galleres trente trois basteaulx de diverses longueurs*' ('to Francisque Scibec, the king's carpenter ... for having ... prepared 33 boats of differing lengths in the form of galleys').

[7]   BELLEFOREST 1617, fol. 576. However, the accounts never use the word gondola.

queen,[8] very reminiscent of the *Bucentaure* of the Lyon 1548 celebrations.[9] To make the most of the spectacle, Catherine de Médicis then had herself conveyed to a '*grand échaffaud ... faict en theatre*' ('a large scaffold ... taking the form of a theatre')[10] that was erected by the city wall, near the *couvent des Célestins* where there were already the '*juges du combat naval*' ('umpires of the naval battle')[11] in the company of the aldermen, ambassadors and other important people from the court and the city.

As the spectacle began, 30 galleys first appeared upstream led by three big '*capitaneresses*' ('large galleys'),[12] exhibiting green, white and '*incarnat*' ('blood red') flags marked with the devices and coats of arms of the assailants.[13] The ships entered the small branch of the river to attack the '*havre*' ('harbour') with the support of artillery. The shots from the seven *galéasses*,[14] which left the port to meet them, were designed to thwart the plans of the assailants. In the midst of the thunder of artillery and the clouds of smoke, the galleys got the upper hand, and the defendants had no alternative but to set fire to the tower that blocked the entrance to the port in order to avoid it being taken over.[15] The salvos of the artillery were

---

[8]   *Comptes 1549*, fol. 179: paiement de 20 '*casaques blanc et vert pour ceulx qui estoient à la garde du basteau ou souppa le roy et la royne*' (the payment of 20 'white and green coats for those who stood guard on the boat where the king and queen dined').

[9]   *Comptes 1549*, fol. 180v: '*Construction tant d'une salle faicte sur un grant basteau ou le roy et la royne soupperent le jour du combat naval que des eschaffaulx faictz le long des murs de la closture de lad. ville viz a viz de la riviere ou estoit madite dame pour icelluy combat veoir plus a son ayse*'('Construction of a hall erected on a large boat where the king and queen dined on the day of the naval battle, on scaffolds along[side] the boundary walls of the said town, opposite the river [bank] where the said madam could view this combat at her ease'). The arrangement of the room is set out at fol. 182v.

[10]   *Comptes 1549*, fol. 180v: '*Un grant esschaffault le long du mur de closture de la ville devant le port des celestins ou la royne se retira pour veoir ledict combat apres avoir souppé en son basteau, ledit eschaffault de douze thoises de lon et de neuf a dix pieds de large faict en theatre.*' ('A large scaffold alongside the boundary wall of the town in front of the gate of the Celestins where the queen retired to view the said combat after having dined on her boat, the said scaffold being constructed in the manner of a theatre, twelve *toises* in length and nine or ten feet broad.'). [1 *toise* = 6.5 feet.]

[11]   *Comptes 1549*, fol. 184.

[12]   *Comptes 1549*, fol. 174v.

[13]   *Comptes 1549*, fol. 174–7.

[14]   Belleforest 1617, fol. 576; Henri Sauval, *Histoire et recherches des antiquités de la ville de Paris* (2 vols, Paris: C. Moette 1724), vol. 1, p. 692; *barques au nombre de 12 pour l'ambassadeur de Mantoue* (A.S. Mantova, AG 642, fol. 126, 16 juin [sic, for 'juillet'] 1549).

[15]   Belleforest 1617, fol. 576; Corrozet 1581, fol. 261v–2: '*en cet assaut fut bruslée une tour au milieu de l'eau*' ('in this attack a tower by the waterside was burnt down'). The Parisian accounts for 1549 also mention 'a tower which was burnt down'.

so powerful that the stained-glass windows of the nearby Celestines' church fell down – if we are to believe Corrozet, who might be exaggerating a little.[16]

Then the artillery, massed on the *'rempart'*[17] ('battlements', also called 'boulevard')[18] of the île aux Vaches, performed an impressive cannonade, while the troops crossed the bridges made of ships or landed from their pageant ships in order to put ladders against the walls of the fort. The fierce fights between the defenders, directed by the Duke of Aumale,[19] and the assailants, among whom there were a number of the most illustrious lords of the court, lasted until nightfall, but eventually the fort had to surrender, to loud cheers from the crowd assembled on both riverbanks.

The swords were not sharpened, the cannons fired blanks,[20] the guards of the fort made use of water poured from buckets;[21] yet the death of a nobleman and several casualties among the soldiers appointed by the City occurred, as reported *en passant* by the ambassador of Ferrara.[22]

---

[16]   CORROZET 1581, fol. 261v–6. *'De l'estonnement les verrieres des celestins tomberent toutes par terre'*. ('From the noise of the canons the windows of the Celestines' convent all fell to the ground.').

[17]   *Comptes 1549*, fol. 157, *'fort, havre et rempart faict en l'isle aux Vaches pour asseoir l'artillerie'* ('the fort, small harbour and battlements constructed on the Isle aux Vaches to accommodate the artillery').

[18]   BELLEFOREST 1617, fol. 576, *'boulevert de l'isle aux Vaches couvert de soldats'* ('the boulevard on the Isle aux Vaches swarming with soldiers').

[19]   Aumale is named by Corrozet and by the Mantuan ambassador. Other participants mentioned by the ambassador from Modena included François d'Andelot, François de Vendôme, the vidame of Chartres, and Galeazzo and Nicolo Tassoni (OCCHIPINTI 2001, p. 231).

[20]   A.S. Mantova, AG 642, fol. 126: *'artiglieria carica nondimeno di polvere solo'* ('the artillery weapons were however charged with powder only').

[21]   *Comptes 1549*, fol. 169: *'A Pierre Morelet, pour avoir fourny et livré deux douzaines de seaulx qui ont sery a porter l'eaue dedans les cuvettes dudict fort pour en gecter aux assaillans le jour du combat'* ('to Pierre Morelet for having provided and delivered two dozen buckets which were used to carry the water from the basins of the said fort in order to deluge the attackers on the day of the contest').

[22]   OCCHIPINTI 2001, p 231 (5 juillet 1549): *'Avantieri [3 juillet] combatterono uno castello fatto qua in una isoletta della riviera de Scena a similitudine di Bologna di Picardia, cui anco avevano dati da quaranta in cinquanta batelli in foggia di Galee. Nel castello vi fù il vidamo di Chiartres e con esso lui et una compagnia il signor Guido, il conte Theofilo, li dui Tassoni. Nel combattere, se anegò un gentiluomo del Re chiamato La Boscia, e certi altri della villa, e fu anco per annegarse Andelot, ma fu aiutato e si salvò'* ('Before the third of July they attacked a castle constructed on a little island off the river bank of the Seine similar to 'Boulogne' in Picardy, with the addition of forty to fifty boats in the form of galleys. In the castle, was the Vicomte of Chartres and with him and his men Signor Guido, the Count Theofilo, [and] the two Tassoni. In the combat a gentleman of the king's called La Boscia was killed, and some others of the villa, and also a certain Andelot came near to drowning, but he was given assistance and was saved.')

McFarlane and Cooper detect the origin of the battle on the île de Louviers in the festivities that took place on the occasion of Henri II's entry to Lyon in September 1548 and the Roman *naumachia* commissioned in March 1549 by the cardinal du Bellay to celebrate the birth of the duke of Orléans. Though the second event took place only on paper – the *naumachia* was postponed because of the Tiber floods, so that we know it only from Rabelais's text – there is no doubt that these notable festivities, while launching the fashion for this kind of entertainment, greatly contributed to the quality of the Paris battle.

However, even if the Lyon event was, like that of Paris, linked to the *magnificences* of an entry, the type of battle was rather different. In Lyon, as in Rome, a naval battle was staged *stricto sensu* where each camp strove to board the enemies' ships. In Paris we come across both naval and land actions, uniting the '*naumachia à l'antique*' ('traditional naval battle') to the medieval '*escarmouche*' ('skirmish') directed at a wooden *chateau* which, ablaze and partly wrapped in smoke, ultimately vanishes.

In this respect the Parisian entertainment has a more direct precedent, the battle organised at Fontainebleau on the occasion of the future François II's baptism in February 1544, as described in the printed account of the event:

> *Le jeudy ensuivant, 13e jour dudit mois, fut fait un bastion auprès et joignant ledit chevet dudit Fontainebleau là où se dressèrent les plus belles et braves escarmouches que l'on saurait réciter tant par terre que par eau, parce que sur l'étang de Fontainebleau joignant ledit bastion y avait trois galères qui battaient de ce côté ledit bastion.*[23]

> [The following Thursday, the thirteenth day of the same month, a bastion was constructed next to and joined with the aforementioned east end of the church at Fontainebleau where the most remarkable and splendid skirmishes one could describe took place both by land and by water, since on the pond at Fontainebleau adjoining the aforementioned bastion were three galleys which joined battle alongside the bastion.]

The sheer scope of the Parisian entertainment, which was far more ambitious than that of the Fontainebleau baptism, considerably modified the very nature of the spectacle. In Fontainebleau there were three galleys; in Paris there were 33. In Fontainebleau, the *escarmouche* concerned only the courtiers. In Paris, they were joined by a veritable army of more than 500 soldiers paid by the City.[24] To manoeuvre the galleys, the aldermen also hired hundreds of '*mariniers*' in Melun,

---

[23]   *C'est la triumphant baptesme de monseigneur le duc, premier filz de monseigneur le daulphin*, Jacques Nyverd, 1543 [1544 n. st.] (BnF, 8o Lb30, 99). (For the famous carnival in 1564, a fort was constructed in the middle of the pond at Fontainebleau, but without galleys.)

[24]   *Comptes 1549*, fol. 199 ff.

Corbeil, Villeneuve-Saint-Georges, Neuilly-sur-Marne, Charenton, Saint-Maur, Noisy, Gournay and so on.[25] They even requisitioned ferry boats from the port of Neuilly[26] to convey the troops to the island. Consequently, what took place in Paris was a fictitious battle looking like a real one – unlike that of Fontainebleau, which was just a court entertainment. This is eloquently backed-up by the report given by Giulio Alvarotti:

> *Avantieri combatterono uno castello fatto qua in una isoletta della riviera de Scena a similitudine di Bologna di Picardia.*[27]

[The day before yesterday they attacked a castle constructed on a little island situated by the bank of the Seine, similar to *'Boulogne' in Picardy*.]

This interpretation of the spectacle's theme bears no obvious trace of officialdom. Henry II's *lettres patentes* which order the battle, as well as the city's accounts containing all the details, drop no hint about the city in Picardy. What is more, the description of the fort's painted scenery in the city's accounts, and in particular the allegorical subjects represented there, suggest a symbolic battle with moral overtones. Both doors of the fort were stamped with Henry II's coat of arms and devices. Above one of them there was an allegory of Nature generously handing-out the milk from her breasts to humans and animals, whereas on the other door, the royal coat of arms held up by Strength and Prudence was surmounted by a variation on the Fontainebleau theme of *'Ignorance chassée'* ('Ignorance driven out').[28] Some *'tables d'actente'* ('programme notes') clarified the significance of these 'stories': their contents, alas, did not reach us.

Be that as it may, neither the iconography nor the heraldry seems to allude to Picardy or England. The interpretation reported by Alvarotti appears first and foremost as an echo of a fanciful rumour due to the fact that the recapture of Boulogne was an *idée fixe* in those days. Yet a similar interpretation can be found in a document beyond suspicion: a payment dated to May 1550. It concerns the demolition of a *'fort qui avoit esté faict sur la rivière de Seine à l'instar du fort de Boullongne'* ('fort which had been constructed on the bank of the Seine in the manner of the fort at Boulogne').[29]

---

[25]   *Comptes 1549*, fol. 186 ff.

[26]   *Comptes 1549*, fol. 194.

[27]   See note 22, above.

[28]   See Anne-Marie Lecoq, 'La fondation du Collège royal et l'Ignorance chassée de Fontainebleau', in Marc Fumaroli (ed.), *Les origines du Collège de France (1500–1560)* (Collège de France: Klincksieck, 1998), pp. 185–206. See also Appendix to this chapter, pp. 63–4.

[29]   Ernest Coyecque, *Recueil d'actes notariés relatifs à l'histoire de Paris et de ses environs au XVIe siècle* (2 vols, Paris: Imprimerie nationale), vol. 2, 1924, p. 400 (12 May

The capture of the city by the English in 1544 was indeed felt as a tragedy by the future Henri II (whose wife was Countess of Boulogne) and by his mentor, Montmorency. On 1 July 1549, only two days before the naval battle, the 'traitor' Vervins had been publicly beheaded at Les Halles. Though war was not officially declared until 8 August, the preparations for the siege by land and sea had already begun. Setting off from Scotland, Leone Strozzi's squadron of galleys was heading towards the Channel Islands to take up their battle position.[30]

No wonder, under the circumstances, that everyone thought about the contemporary relevance of the festival. Not only did the spectators, or those who actually built the fort, indulge in such comparisons but also, *a fortiori*, the authors of the spectacle. They did so in spite of whatever meaning was to be ascribed *officially* to the naval battle.

So it is important to judge the ephemeral constructions of the *île de Louviers* in this light. What does one see? A tower protecting a *havre*, a fort with walls of false bricks propped up by (fake) stone towers and a '*boulevard en pointes de diamans de gris, blanc et noir escarlette en façon de pierre de taille*' ('battlement walls shaped like diamonds of grey, white and black, in the likeness of dressed stone').[31] Boulogne (Fig. 3. 2), in the mid-sixteenth century, was first and foremost a stone lighthouse towering over the landscape[32] and extolled by contemporary accounts; there were also two small rose-brick bastions hastily devised by the French in 1548.[33] Boulogne was, last but not least, a *havre* situated far from the upper city and badly-protected. Surely it is possible to regard the striking elements of the Picardy site adopted by the *île de Louviers* as an allusion to a forthcoming recapture of the city, or perhaps even as a military preparation and a mental conditioning for this recapture?

1550). I am indebted to Marie Noelle Baudouin Matuszek for drawing my attention to this article.

[30]   Ivan Cloulas, *Henri II* (Paris: Fayard, 1985), p. 262.

[31]   *Comptes 1549*, fol. 174, '*Item, painct tous les murs de rouge en façon de brique et les tours en façon de pierre de taille, les boullevars faictz en pointes de diamans de gris, blanc et noir escarlette en façon de pierre de taille.*' ('Item, all the walls were painted in red, in the likeness of bricks and the towers in the likeness of dressed stone, with the battlement walls shaped like diamonds of grey, white and black set out in imitation of dressed stone.').

[32]   La tour d'Odre.

[33]   The forts of Châtillon and Pont-de-Brique. I am most grateful to Nicolas Faucherre and Emmanuel de Crouy Chanel for this information. See also, Pierre Héliot 'Les fortifications de Boulogne sous l'occupation anglaise (1544–1550)', *Revue du Nord*, XL, 157 (1958), pp. 5–38.

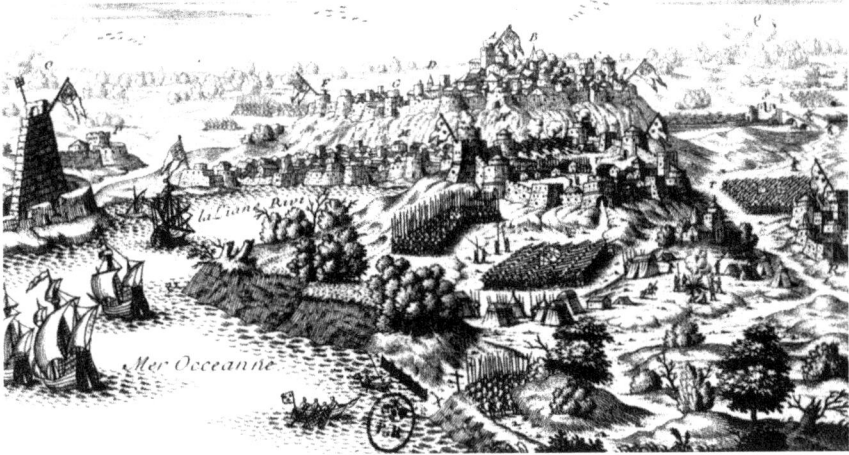

Figure 3.2   The siege of Boulogne (photo: Chatenet).

Charles IX's Birthday

One must wait for almost fifteen years for Paris to take advantage once again of a naval entertainment, recounted thus by Gilles Corrozet:

> *Le jeudy vingt septiesme jour [de juin 1566] le Roy vint aux Thuilleries et au Louvre pour après souper prendre plaisir à veoir quelques joustes qui furent faites sur la rivière de Seine entre la porte de Nesle et la porte neufve. Au milieu de l'eau estoit un fort fait en façon d'un monde qui estoit entouré de canon et fusées. Le feu y fut mis par des hommes habillez en diables tenans des flambeaux ardents de feux artificiels et ce fut fait pour remarquer le jour natal dudict seigneur Roy.[34]*

> [On Thursday the twenty-seventh [of June, 1566] the King came to the Tuileries gardens and the Louvre to take his pleasure after dining by way of seeing some jousts which took place on the bank of the Seine between the Porte de Nesle and the Porte Neufve. In the midst of the stream a fort had been constructed in the shape of a globe, surrounded by cannons and rockets. These were fired by men dressed as devils holding torches emitting fireworks created to celebrate the birthday of his said majesty.]

Corrozet's text must be related only to the finale of the spectacle, for Brantôme offers the description of a traditional naval battle, with the '*tenants*' ('defenders')

---

[34]   CORROZET, édition de 1586, fol. 186.

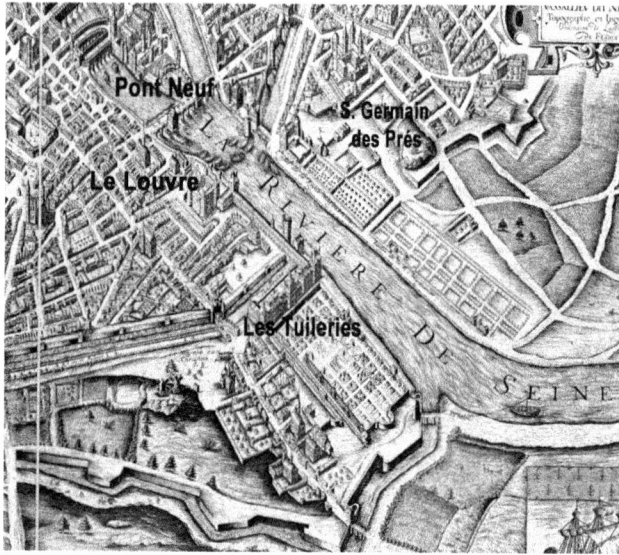

Figure 3.3   The Seine alongside the Louvre in the reign of Henri IV, on the map
               of Nicolay, 1609 (photo Chatenet).

on the big ship and '*assailants*' ('attackers') on small boats doing their best to
board the ship.[35]

What is far more interesting, however, is the spot chosen for the celebration
of the young king's birthday – the Seine just opposite the Louvre, which was the
favourite setting for the waterborne festivals to come in the *Grand siècle*. The
date of the event is significant, too. According to Jacques Androuet du Cerceau,
Catherine de Médicis, after making a start on the construction of the Tuileries in
1564, '*avait encommencé [1566] quelques accroissements de galleries et terraces
du costé du pavillon [du roi], pour aller au palais qu'elle a[vait] fait construire et
édifier au lieu appelé les Tuilleries*' ('had begun [1566] on extensions in the form
of galleries and terraces beside the [king's] pavilion, to allow access to the palace
she had set up and built in the place called the Tuileries').[36] It is clear therefore
that it was in those days that the idea of connecting the Louvre and the Tuileries
through the terrace covering the '*petite gallerie*' ('little gallery') which was then
under construction and the '*chemin de ronde*' ('circular route') at the top of the
city walls saw the light of day. So the Louvre, until then a self-sufficient isolated

---

[35]   See Brantôme (Pierre de Bourdeille, seigneur de), *Œuvres complètes*, ed. Ludovic
Lalanne (11 vols, Paris: Mme Vve J. Renouard, 1864–82), vol. 4, p. 347, in the Appendix
to this chapter, pp. 64–5.

[36]   Jacques Androuet du Cerceau, *Les plus excellents bastiments de France …*, ed.
David Thomson (Paris: L'Aventurine, 1988), p. 27.

fortress, turned definitively towards the river. This tendency was emphasised under Henry IV by means of the '*grande galerie*' and the Pont Neuf (Fig. 3. 3).

The Cardinal of Bourbon's Naval Discomfiture

I shall mention for the sake of completeness the '*combat dans l'île du palais*' ('contest on the palace island') which was organised on the occasion of the Paix de Saint-Germain in August 1570. Whatever its literary and iconographic appeal, thanks to Ronsard and the appearance of Charles IX as the Sun,[37] the *escarmouche* is hardly known and therefore one cannot really make out the detail of what occurred.[38]

So I shall pass directly on to the fourth and last event: the '*triomphe marin*' (waterborne triumph) organised by the Cardinal of Bourbon to celebrate Anne of Joyeuse's and Marguerite of Vaudémont's wedding on 24 September 1581 – an event which reverberated through a multitude of documents, notably including an abundant diplomatic correspondence.[39] Instead of a 'waterborne triumph', it was rather a 'waterborne discomfiture', for Cardinal de Bourbon was hardly more successful in his aquatic undertaking than his counterpart Du Bellay had been thirty years earlier in Rome.

To celebrate the wedding of the king's '*archimignon*' ('chief favourite') with the queen of France's sister, the Cardinal of Bourbon ordered the transformation of a big ship into a Chariot of Neptune. At the stern, the triumphal chariot was adorned with a huge statue of the god holding a golden crown above the throne where the king was to sit.[40] Supplied with wheels that seemed to float on water, it might remind one of the vision depicted in *Canto ventinovesimo* ('the twenty-ninth canto') of Dante's *Commedia*. Eight sea-horses were hitched to it. They were

---

[37]   See the fine article by John T.D. Hall, 'Ronsard et les fêtes de cour en 1570', *Bibliothèque d'humanisme et de Renaissance*, 35/1 (1973), pp. 73–7.

[38]   Despite a fragment of the accounts of the Court Entertainments ('*Menus plaisirs*') BnF, Ms. fr. 26150, fol. 1937–40, in which the following statement can be found: '*A Estienne Escuier, voicturier, 160 livres pour son paiement d'un batteau de roy de 7 toises de long et de 7 pieds de large qui a esté faict en forme de gallere pour le plaisir et recreation du Roy et qui a servy en ung combat que S. M. a faict en l'Isle du Pallais.*' ('To Estienne Esquier, victualer, 160 livres for his payment for a royal barge of 7 toises (approx. 45 feet) in length and 7 feet wide which was made in the form of a galley for the enjoyment and recreation of the King and those who took part in a combat which his Majesty commissioned on the *Isle du Palace*.')

[39]   See CHATENET et CAPODIECI (2006).

[40]   '*alla poppa (...) era una figura in forma di Nettuno, il qual tenea una gran corona dorata in mano sopra una sedia nella quale dovea essere ricevuto il Re*', ('at the stern stood a figure representing Neptune, which held a great golden crown in its hand, over the place where the king was to be received'), A.S. Mantova, AG 659, 20 October 1581, published in CHATENET ET CAPODIECI (2006), p. 40.

accompanied by eight sirens[41], four mermen, four whales, eight dolphins and a gigantic tortoise. The whole device, made of painted canvas '*a pochissima spesa*' ('at very small expense'), as reported by a spiteful witness,[42] was mounted on little boats. A sophisticated system of invisible ropes was devised in order to tow the chariot and its escort, allowing it to sail triumphantly up the river from an island located near the quay d'Orsay to the Louvre, in order to salute the king, the queen and the newly-weds, and to take them to the banquet organised in their honour at the abbey of Saint-Germain-des-Prés whose abbot was the cardinal of Bourbon. Was the current too strong that day? No one knows. The king, the queen, the entire court and the thousands of Parisians assembled on the riverbanks waited in vain for three hours, and when at last the ship made its appearance it was too dark to see anything! It is easy to imagine the boos and jeers from the audience … and also the hilarity of the members of the Roman Curia when a particularly ferocious letter, written by the Cardinal of Este's diplomatic correspondent, reached the Eternal City.[43] Henri III said a few unkind words,[44] but Queen Louise, whose benevolence was proverbial, suggested the cardinal should resume the performance on the next day – in her presence.[45] The cardinal complied with her wish. One wonders, though, how such a catastrophe could occur. The Cardinal de Bourbon, the current archbishop of Rouen, merely followed the well-known device put into practice 30 years before for the entry of Henry II into Rouen in 1550.[46] (Fig. 3.4). It is true that, on that occasion, the Chariot of Neptune simply crossed the Seine – it is undoubtedly much more difficult to sail up-river than just to cross it.

Such failures did not mar the history of Parisian festivals in the *Grand siècle*. But that is another story.

---

[41]   Eight for the ambassador of Mantua, as against six only for Ludovic de Parades. See CHATENET ET CAPODIECI (2006), pp. 40, 51.

[42]   Dated 17 October, 1581, Mons. De Parades to the Cardinal d'Este in Rome (A.S. Modena, *Ambasciatori in Francia 77*): '*La spesa era pochissima perché non erano quelli monstri fatti d'altra cossa che de tella depinta in su delle picole barche*'. ('The expense was very small because these monsters were made of painted canvas arranged on small boats.'). See CHATENET ET CAPODIECI (2006), p. 51.

[43]   Ibid.

[44]   Pierre de l'Estoile (*Registre journal du règne de Henri III*, (eds) Madeleine Lazard and Gilbert Schrenck (1579–81) (6 vols, Geneva: Droz, 1997), vol. 3, pp. 155–6) writes: '*Le roi … despité et marri, dit qu'il voioit bien que c'estoient des bestes qui commandoient à d'autres bestes*'. *Ludovic de Parades prête au roi des propos à peine moins désagréables: 'Mon cousin, voisi une belle despance, il est daumage qu'elle ne soit esté achevée a temps*'. ('The King, … jeered at and vexed, said that he could see that these were beasts leading other beasts. Ludovic de Parades gives the king a less aggressive tone: 'My cousin, this is a beautiful expense; it is a pity that it couldn't be managed in good time.').

[45]   CHATENET et CAPODIECI (2006), p. 51.

[46]   *L'entrée de Henri II à Rouen en 1550*, ed. Margaret M. McGowan (Amsterdam: Theatrum Orbis Terrarum; New York: Johnson Reprint Corp., 1970).

Figure 3.4   Entry of Henri II to Rouen, 1550, detail: the floating Pageant Car of Neptune (photo: Chatenet).

Appendix: Translations

See note 28

A Charles Dorigny, (pour avoir) painct deux portes d'icelluy fort en façon de pierre rusticque et au-dessus de la premiere porte painct deux figures tenans ung escu de France avec l'ordre et la couronne, et plus haut une Nature ayant les deux bras estenduz tenant en la main droicte une fleur de Liz et a l'autre un croissant; au costé droict de lad. Nature, painctz hommes, femmes et enffans de diverses sortes et au costé senestre de toutes sortes de bestes sur lesquelles tumboit du lait tant d'un costé que d'autre des mamelles de ladicte Nature. Item trois tables d'actente pour escripre la signification de lad. histoire; Item de l'autre costé painct deux autres figures, l'une Force et l'autre Prudence tenant un escu de France avec l'ordre et couronne et au-dessus une femme debout tenant en sa main droicte une couronne de laurier et en l'autre main une escorges (longe) et au dessoubz plusieurs gens venans et mangeans entre lesquelz y avoit ung ayant les yeux bendez en champ obscur et mellencollique. Item du costé droict painct grant compagnie de gens avec estralabes, spheres, regles, escaires compas, lymes, instrumens et plusieurs autres choses semblables en champ cler et joyeulx et au-dessus trois tables d'actente pour escrippre la significacion de ladicte histoire, le tout faict de toille de bonne paincture.

[To Charles Dorigny, (for having) painted two gates of this fort in the style of rustic stone. Above the first gate, two figures were painted holding a shield of France with the order [of Saint Michael] and the crown, and higher up a [figure representing] Nature, which had two arms outstretched holding in the right hand a lily and in the left hand a crescent. On the right of the said [figure of] Nature, men, women and children of diverse sorts were painted, and on the left were all sorts of beasts; milk from Nature's breasts fell on both the people and the animals. Item: three panels in which the meaning of the story was written. Item: on the other side [on the second gate?], two other figures were painted, one of Strength and the other of Prudence, holding a shield of France and the order and crown, and above this stood a woman holding in her right hand a crown of laurels and in the other hand a long rope. Below this, several people were coming and eating, between whom there was one who was blindfolded in a dark and melancholic field. Item: on the right side was painted a great company of people with astrolabes, spheres, rulers, set squares, compasses, files, instruments and several other similar things, in a bright and joyous field, and above this, three panels in which the meaning of the story was written, all made of canvas and of good paint.]

See note 35

Le roy Charles, doncques, ayant entrepris de faire un combat sur l'eau à Paris, devant le Louvre, il se mit dans son grand bateau couvert qu'on avait veu longtemps devant le logis du contrerolleur Dumas. Le roy tenoit et gardoit son bateau avecques les siens contre Monsieur et les siens, qui le vimmes assaillir. Ainsi que nous voulions monter et que le baron [de Montesquieu] estoit à demy monté, voycy Fervacques, qui a esté tousjours rude joueur, qui poussa de haut en bas ledict baron dans l'eau, qui s'alloit neyer sans moi qui courrus du bout du bateau et le pris par le collet, et le jette dans nostre batteau, lequel n'en pouvoit plus; mais il se remit tellement quellement, et aussytost se mist à genoulx et me remercia et qu'il me debvoit la vie; et despuis m'appella toujours son père, bien que je fusse plus jeune que lui. Il fut tué par amprès au siège de Saint-Jean-[d'Angély]'.

[King Charles, thus, having undertaken to hold a combat on the water in Paris, in front of the Louvre, took his place in his great covered boat that had, for a long time, been seen in front of the lodgings of the controller Dumas. The king held and guarded his boat, which we saw sail off, with his [company] against Monsieur and his [company]. Together we wanted to mount [the boat], and the baron of Montesquieu had half-mounted, when Fervacques, who had always been a rough player, pushed the baron into the water. The baron would have drowned without me, who ran to the tip of the boat and took him by the collar, and threw him into our boat, all that could be done; he recovered, and immediately fell to his knees and thanked me and [said] that he owed me his life; and from then he always called me his father, although I was much younger than him. He was subsequently killed at the siege of Saint-Jean[-d'Angély].]

Bibliography

Manuscript Sources

A.N., K 957, *pièce* 16a: *Lettres patentes de Henri II au prévôt des marchands et aux échevins de Paris, 14 mai 1549.*
A.N., KK 286A: *Comptes de la ville de Paris 1549, Dépenses pour le combat naval du 3 juillet.*
A.S. Mantova, AG 642, fol. 126 (*juillet 1549; classé par erreur à 16 juin*).
A.S. Modena, *Ambasciatori in Francia 22: 9 mars 1546 (Alvarotti au duc de Ferrare).*
A.S Modena, *Ambasciatori in Francia 77: 17 October 1581*, Mons. De Parades to the Cardinal d'Este in Rome.
BnF. Ms. fr. 26150, fol. 1937–40: Accounts of the Court Entertainments ('*Menus plaisirs*').

Printed Primary Sources

Androuet du Cerceau, Jacques, *Les plus excellents bastiments de France ...*, ed. David Thomson (Paris: L'Aventurine, 1988).
Anonymous, *C'est la triumphant baptesme de monseigneur le duc, premier filz de monseigneur le daulphin*, Jacques Nyverd, 1543 [1544 n. st.] (BnF, 8o Lb30, 99).
Anonymous, *L'entrée de Henri II à Rouen en 1550*, ed. Margaret M. McGowan (Amsterdam: Theatrum Orbis Terrarum; New York: Johnson Reprint Corp., 1974).
Anonymous, *The Entry of Henri II into Paris, 16 June 1549*, ed. with introduction by I.D. McFarlane, (Binghamton, NY: Medieval and Renaissance Studies, 1982).
Belleforest, François de and Nicole Gilles, *Les Chroniques et Annales de France dès l'origine des François et leur venuë ès Gaules, faictes jadis briefvement par Nicole Gilles, ... jusqu'au roy Charles VIII et depuis additionnées par Denis Sauvage jusqu'au roy François II du nom, reveues, corrigées et augmentées ... contenantes l'histoire universelle de France dès Pharamond jusqu'au roy Charles IX, par F. de Belleforests, Comingeois, avec la suite et continuation*

d'icelles, depuis le roy Charles IX, jusques au roy ... Louys XIII à présent régnant, by G. Chappuys, ... et al. (Paris: M. Sonnius, 1617).

Corrozet, *Les Antiquitez, croniques et singularitez de Paris ... avec les fondations et bastimens des lieux, les sépulchres et épitaphes des princes, princesses et autres personnes illustres ...* (Paris: N. Bonfons, 1581).

Coyecque, Ernest, *Recueil d'actes notariés relatifs à l'histoire de Paris et de ses environs au XVIe siècle* (2 vols, Paris: Imprimerie nationale: Edouard Champion, 1905–23).

de l'Estoile, Pierre, in *Registre journal du règne de Henri III*, (eds) Madeleine Lazard and Gilbert Schrenck (1579–81) (6 vols, Geneva: Droz, 1997), vol. 3, pp. 155–6.

Secondary Sources

Brantôme, Pierre de Bourdeille, seigneur de, *Œuvres complètes*, ed. Ludovic Lalanne (11 vols, Paris: Mme Vve J. Renouard, 1864–82).

Chatenet, Monique and Capodieci, Luisa, 'Les triomphes des noces de Joyeuse (17 septembre–19 octobre 1581) à travers la correspondance diplomatique italienne et l'Epithalame de Jean Dorat', *Bulletin de la Société d'Histoire de l'Art Français* (2006), pp. 9–54.

Cloulas, Ivan, *Henri II* (Paris: Fayard, 1985).

Cooper, Richard, 'Jean Martin et l'entrée de Henri II à Paris', in *Jean Martin. Un traducteur au temps de François Ier et de Henri II*, Cahiers V. L. Saulnier, 16 (Paris: Presses de l'école normale supérieure, 1999), pp. 97–111.

Fumaroli, Marc (ed.), *Les origines du Collège de France (1500–1560)* (Collège de France: Klincksieck, 1998).

Hall, John T.D., 'Ronsard et les fêtes de cour en 1570', *Bibliothèque d'humanisme et de Renaissance*, 35/1 (1973), pp. 73–7.

Héliot, Pierre, 'Les fortifications de Boulogne sous l'occupation anglaise (1544–1550)', *Revue du Nord*, XL, 157 (1958), pp. 5–38.

Lecoq, Anne-Marie, 'La fondation du Collège royal et l'Ignorance chassée de Fontainebleau', in Marc Fumaroli (ed.), *Les origines du Collège de France (1500–1560)* (Collège de France: Klincksieck, 1998), pp. 185–206.

Occhipinti, Carmelo, *Carteggio d'arte degli ambasciatori estensi in Francia (1536–1553)* (Pisa: Scuola normale superiore, 2001).

Sauval, Henri, *Histoire et recherches des antiquités de la ville de Paris* (2 vols, Paris: C. Moette, 1724).

Chapter 4

Water Festivals of the Reign of Charles IX of France

R.J. Knecht

Water festivals had become an established feature of French court entertainments by the time Charles IX ascended the throne in December 1560. They were of two kinds: civic festivals laid on by towns as part of the rejoicings associated with a royal entry and entertainments laid on at court exclusively for its members and guests. Charles IX was only a boy of ten at his accession – too young to be a fully-fledged king, so that his mother, Catherine de' Medici, had to govern in his name. She was given the title of 'governor of the kingdom', but was in effect regent. Her task was difficult, for two years after Charles's accession the first of a series of French religious wars broke out that tore the kingdom apart.[1] Not a propitious time, one might think, for water festivals; yet they did take place, if only because Catherine, who was no religious fanatic, believed that they might serve to bring Frenchmen, more especially the nobility, together in peace.

In 1563 the Crown issued the Edict of Amboise, the first of a long series of edicts of pacification which punctuated the Wars of Religion without much success.[2] Catherine's hopes, however, were high in 1563 and she set about asserting her son's authority by taking him and his court on an extensive progress across France which lasted roughly two years, from February 1564 to March 1566.[3] Another reason for the progress was Catherine's desire to meet her daughter, Elizabeth, and her husband, King Philip II of Spain. A meeting was arranged in Bayonne, near the Franco–Spanish border, but Philip II refused to attend. He sent his minister, the duke of Alba, in his place, but before the progress could take place, Charles IX had to be proclaimed of age to be king in his own right, a ceremony which took place, not in Paris as one might have expected, but in Rouen on 17 August 1563. Early in the following year, the court moved to the palace of Fontainebleau for a lavish sequence of entertainments in which Catholics and Huguenots were expected to sink their differences in a number of chivalrous exercises. These included a mock battle between twelve knights – six a side – dressed as Greeks

---

[1]   R.J. Knecht, *Catherine de' Medici* (London: Longman, 1998), pp. 96–100.

[2]   N.M. Sutherland, *The Huguenot Struggle for Recognition* (New Haven, Mass. and London: Yale University Press, 1980), pp. 142–57, 356–7.

[3]   P. Champion, *Catherine de Médicis présente à Charles IX son royaume, 1564–1566* (Paris: B. Grasset, 1937), pp. 31–4.

and Trojans. In another entertainment, the young king and his brothers, dressed as knights, rescued ladies trapped inside an enchanted tower on an island. Each entertainment was offered by a different courtier. Catherine's own contribution was a water festival in which sirens, swimming in a lake, sang verses composed by Ronsard greeting the king.[4] After the sirens, Neptune floated by in a chariot drawn by sea-horses. We have not only written accounts of this event, but also drawings attributed to Antoine Caron which were later used by the designer of the famous set of eight Valois tapestries.(Fig. 4.1)

Figure 4.1   Design for a Tapestry: a *naumachia* at Fontainebleau, 1564. Drawing by Antoine Caron. © National Galleries Scotland.

The 'Grand Tour of France' was a gigantic operation involving the displacement of some two thousand people and even more horses over a period of 829 days. The court moved on 201 days and stayed put on 628. In other words, it travelled on average one day in every four. Twenty-one stops lasted one week or more.[5] Such intensive mobility did not leave much scope for elaborate festivities save in some of the longer halts. Of course, wherever the king visited a town, he was offered an entry by the citizens. More than one hundred such entries took place during the progress, but few involved the use of water. Although severely

---

[4]   P. Laumonier, *Ronsard, poète lyrique* (Paris: Hachette, 1909), p. 219–22.

[5]   Jean Boutier, Alain Dewerpe and Daniel Nordman, *Un tour de France royal: Le voyage de Charles IX (1564–1566)* (Paris: Aubier, 1984), pp. 17–24.

hit by the recent civil war, Lyon put on an elaborate show minutely described in an account published in Paris by Mathurin Bréville in 1564.[6] This account states: 'As we have sufficiently described the earthly triumph honouring the coming of our Most Christian king, it seems only reasonable that we should speak of what took place on the lovely River Saône to exalt the excellence of His Majesty'.[7] This consisted, in the first place, of an enormous mock galley built for the occasion. The prow and poop were adorned with a painted frieze above which a balustraded gallery enclosed the seat of the pilot steering the vessel. Near the poop, covered with an awning of blue and white taffeta, a rich standard was raised. The entire vessel was covered with red and violet streamers. Inside were rows of benches and oars '*propices au navigage*' ('poised for navigation'). On the benches sat '*galiots fort adextres*' ('oarsmen') wearing outfits of red cloth. The magnificence of the occasion was further enhanced by another smaller galley – a real one this time. Dedicated to the Queen Mother, this too was beautifully decorated: the poop had a painted frieze, a balustrade and a blue and white awning that enclosed the pilot. On a raised platform in the middle of the galley was a room or *salle* flanked by five niches on each side serving as windows. Also within the ship were two portals bearing the inscription *R. Virtute Catharinae*. There were five benches in the *salle* and above them inscribed on a blue frieze verses praising Charles IX and his mother. The ceiling was coffered. In each coffer there was a golden or silver rose on a blue background. The roof made of, '*étain argenté*' ('silvered tin'), was painted to look like fish-scales. Clasping the prow with its claws was a carved lioness with a fish's tail.

We are not told whether Charles IX and his suite actually boarded a ship; only that they watched several '*passetemps*' on the ships '*sur l'eschine de la Saône someillante*' ('from the bank of the sleepy river'). At night, they were treated to a fireworks display in which an infinite number of rockets rose into the sky and fell to earth '*avec un bruit de tresbonne grace*' ('with a very gentle noise'). A large number of rowing-boats also gathered on the river whose owners – the *Gens de Rivière* – entertained the king by jousting with shields and fishing spears.[8] The court did not remain for long in Lyon. An epidemic of plague obliged it to beat a hasty retreat to the neighbouring town of Crémieu. On 3 November, however, at Toulon, Charles IX went out to sea on a galley and soon afterwards, in Marseille, he and his companions, disguised as Turks, took part in a mock naval battle.[9]

The climax of the 'Grand Tour' was the meeting that took place at Bayonne between the French court and a large Spanish delegation led by Elizabeth, Philip II's queen. A special effort was made by the French to impress their Spanish

---

6   Victor E. Graham and W. McAllister Johnson (eds), *The royal tour of France by Charles IX and Catherine de' Medici: festivals and entries, 1564–66* (Toronto: University of Toronto Press, 1979), pp. 187–209.

7   Ibid., p. 207.

8   Ibid., pp. 207–209.

9   Champion, *Catherine de Médicis*, pp. 165, 170.

guests by means of lavish entertainments. On 19 June 1564 was held the first 'Magnificence' – the 'Tournament of the Divers Nations'. The second, on 21 June, took the form of an elaborate indoor *mascarade*, centred around an assault on an enchanted castle. This was followed on 23 June by an outing to a small island in the River Adour. Several accounts exist of this festival. The most informative is the *Recueil des choses notables qui ont esté faites à Bayonne*, published in Paris in 1566.[10] It offers a wealth of detail about all the participants, the clothes they wore and quotes at length the verses sung during the entertainments.[11] Another account is a diary of the entire Grand Tour kept by Abel Jouan, who was a lowly member of the royal kitchen staff. He recorded all the places visited, the time spent in each and the distances covered. Jouan also pays some attention to the court's activities. Although a participant in the Grand Tour, he may not have been sufficiently important to witness all the festivities.[12] A third account of the meeting in Bayonne is a manuscript written by a certain Monsieur de Corbières about whom nothing is known.[13] Then there are the *Mémoires* of Charles IX's sister, Marguerite de Navarre. She was only twelve years old at the time and her *Mémoires* were not published until 1628, thirteen years after her death. Marguerite admits that she only remembers the meeting in Bayonne '*en gros*' ('in general'); '*les particularités s'estants evanouies de ma mémoire comme un songe*' ('the particulars have vanished from her mind as in a dream').[14] There are also two foreign descriptions of the Bayonne meeting: an anonymous manuscript letter in Spanish and an account in Italian published in Milan in 1565.[15] In addition there are drawings by Antoine Caron and the Valois Tapestries which appear to illustrate the festivities at Bayonne and Fontainebleau.[16] Judging from the costumes worn

---

[10]   *Recueil des choses notables qui ont esté faites à Bayonne, à l'entrevue du Roy Trèschrestien Charles neufieme de ce nom, et la Royne sa treshonorée mere, avec la Royne Catholique sa soeur* (Paris, 1566). Reprinted in Graham and McAllister Johnson, *The royal tour of France*, pp. 328–80.

[11]   For a discussion of the authorship of these verses see P. Laumonier, *Ronsard*, pp. 223–25, 743–54,who casts doubt on Ronsard's presence at Bayonne. He thinks Baïf is a more likely author of some of the verses.

[12]   Abel Jouan, *Recueil et discours du voyage du roy Charles IX de ce nom à present regnant accompagné des choses dignes de memoire faictes en chacun endroit faisant son dit voyage en ses païs et provinces de Champaigne, Bourgoigne, Daulphiné, Provence, Languedoc, Gascoigne, Baïonne, et plusieurs autres lieux, suyvant son retour audit lieu, és années Mil cinq cens soixante quatre et soixante cinq* (Paris, 1566). Reprinted in Graham and McAllister Johnson, pp. 71–143.

[13]   *Bibliothèque nationale de France*, MS. *Les Cinq cents de Colbert*, 140, ff. 495r–500v. Reprinted in Graham and McAllister Johnson, pp. 284–90.

[14]   *Mémoires de Marguerite de Valois*, ed. Y. Cazaux (Paris: Mercure de France, 1971), pp. 40–41.

[15]   Graham and Johnson, pp. 314–27.

[16]   Jean Ehrmann, *Antoine Caron* (2nd edn, Paris: Flammarion, 1986), pp. 189–200; Frances A. Yates, *The Valois Tapestries* (London: Routledge and Kegan Paul, 1975), pp. 3–5.

by the people represented in them, they both date from around 1575; in other words, ten years after the events they illustrate. Caron would have had access to the official *Recueil* published by Vascovan in Paris in 1566.[17]

Modern accounts of the Bayonne festivities are for the most part based on this one source, which tells us that the water festival was devised by Catherine de' Medici to entertain Charles IX and his sister Elizabeth. Assuming that they would have become weary of the 'magnificences' so far seen, the Queen Mother decided *'entremeler quelquechose de son invention pour leur donner plaisir'* ('to insert something of her own devising that would please them'). This was a rustic banquet on an island, called Aigueneau, in the river Adour. Situated close to the river bank, it was surrounded by canals. One of these was long, wide and straight. It was also flanked on both sides by meadows and copses. The *Recueil* informs us that Catherine built on the island *'une grande salle octogone'* ('a spacious octagonal hall') made of *'feuillée et charpenterie'* ('foliage and timber') which cost a great deal of money. It stood within a clearing measuring some 70 feet in diameter, surrounded by tall *'chesnes'* ('oak trees'), which Catherine used *'fit accommoder'* ('to provide shade'). In the middle of this space was an oak tree, at the foot of which was a fountain with a basin made of coloured seashells. In each angle of the octagon there was a table for eight people. The Queen Mother also provided an alley of turf, long and straight, leading from the landing stage on the island to the banqueting hall. It was bordered with artificial trees and shrubs.[18] Jouan describes the hall as *'une belle feuillée'*. The word *'feuillée'* implies foliage.[19] And Marguerite de Valois remembers the *salle,* or hall, very precisely. She writes that *'la sale qu'il sembloit que la nature eust appropriée à cet effet'* ('the hall seemed contrived by nature'). She explains that it consisted of a large meadow *'en ovale de bois de haute fustaye'* ('with an oval of tall trees') containing a number of niches, each of which contained a table for 12 people. Charles IX, Queen Elizabeth and Catherine de' Medici sat at a separate table raised on a dais made of *'quatre degrés de gazon'* ('four thicknesses of turf').[20] The Italian account states that she had built an edifice of foliage (*'un edificio di verdure fatto in ovale di si mirabile artificio'*).[21] The Spanish account describes it as an arbour (*'enramada'*) 100 paces long and equally wide, shaped like the capital of a pillar (*'redonda a mañera de chapitel'*) with circular openings all around (*'toda llena de ventanas redondas'*).[22] The evidence seems to rule out the idea of a building, octagonal or

---

[17]   Léon de Groër, 'Les tapisseries des Valois du Musée des Offices à Florence', in *Art, objets d'art, collections (Hommage à Hubert Landais)* (Paris: Blanchard, 1987), p. 132. [This work has no editor.]

[18]   Graham and Johnson, pp. 372–3.

[19]   Ibid., p. 117.

[20]   *Mémoires*, pp. 40–41.

[21]   Graham and Johnson, p. 323.

[22]   Ibid., p. 317.

otherwise and, for this reason, I suspect the reliability of Caron's drawing, which shows a building with a classical portico.

After dinner around 10 p.m. the royal party set off from Bayonne in a boat resembling a castle. The Spanish letter describes this boat as having standing room for 800 people![23] The royal party soon encountered a whale, described by one account as '*une petitte Baleyne finte soubs les ponts de Bayonne*' ('a small whale that had died under the bridges of Bayonne') and by another as '*une grande Baleine faite artificiellement*' ('a large artificial whale').[24] The beast was then attacked by men in boats. As they pierced the whale with long spears, red wine resembling blood gushed from its wounds. The fight lasted half an hour. A tocsin then sounded and the royal party was able to proceed closely followed by a flotilla of some 30 gaily decorated boats carrying the other guests. The Spanish account gives the number as 300 which, again, seems incredible. This same source also mentions a castle with four towers of fireworks on two boats, with one doing nothing as it was needed for the return journey.[25] Continuing on their way, the royal party ran into more surprises: first a huge turtle with six Tritons on its back playing cornets. The Spaniard did not think much of this artificial beast, describing it as clumsily made. It stuck its head out and paddled with its feet. Then Neptune appeared seated in a shell-shaped chariot pulled by three sea-horses. He recited a poem in three stanzas that were punctuated by the Tritons blowing their cornets. In the poem Neptune proclaimed his power over land and sea and his willingness to cede it to King Charles IX to whom he offered his golden trident. Arion then appeared riding two dolphins. Accompanying himself on a lyre, he sang a tribute to Elizabeth in five stanzas punctuated by a consort of six violins concealed in a wood on the river bank. Finally, three Sirens sang quatrains honouring Elizabeth, Charles, Philip and Catherine. As the royal party disembarked on the island, it was greeted by eight shepherds and 16 shepherdesses dressed in the Queen Mother's colours of green and white.[26] Abel Jouan says nothing about the royal party encountering sea-creatures on the way to the island or about dancing there. He merely states that they travelled by boat to the island where they were served by great lords and ladies disguised as shepherds and shepherdesses.[27] It could well be that he did not witness the event, for the Italian account states that '*andò la corte, solo li principali*' ('only leading members of the court went') to the island.[28]

After landing, the royal party saw in a large field two groups of dancers. One consisted of eight shepherds and 16 shepherdesses; the other of six shepherds and six shepherdesses. They were accompanied by six players of bagpipes. They wore clothes made of rich fabrics which the *Recueil* describes in minute detail. The

---

[23]   Ibid., p. 316.
[24]   Ibid., pp. 289, 373.
[25]   Ibid., p. 316.
[26]   Ibid., pp. 373–6.
[27]   Ibid., p. 117.
[28]   Ibid., p. 323.

shepherds carried crooks covered in white taffeta and the shepherdesses silver baskets containing silk flowers. The Spanish account states that the royal party was greeted 'in the prettiest grove' by 20 women ('*damas*') clothed in white satin with peasant hats ('*tocadas a la pastoral*') and ten young men dressed in tunics and tights with stoles of white taffeta. Holding *guadañas* ('crooks') tipped with silver and covered in white satin, they performed a pastoral dance to a musical accompaniment. Further on, in a meadow, were 12 women who wore clothes of gold and silver cloth and had bejewelled coiffures. With them were 12 beautifully attired young men, wearing different shoes, who, dancing and waving their hands, came forward and offered the queen and other ladies trinkets of gold and silver.[29]

After watching the dances, the royal party walked up the alley of grass leading to the banqueting area. On the way they encountered three nymphs, Orpheus and Linus, each of whom recited verses in praise of the Franco–Spanish *entente* to which all this merriment bore witness. Marguerite de Valois's description of this part of the festival differs radically from all the other accounts. She describes girls performing various provincial dances in the fields on either side of the alley. The Poitevines, she writes, were accompanied by bagpipes, the Provençales danced the *volte* with '*cimballes*', the Bourguignonnes and Champenoises with '*petit hautbois, le dessus de violon et tabourins de village*' ('small hautboys, violins and rustic tambourines'), the Bretonnes danced the *passe-pieds* and '*branlesgais*'.[30] One wonders how a child whose memory of the event, on her own admission, was so hazy could recall so precisely the various kinds of dance or the instruments that accompanied them.

The banquet itself is described briefly in the *Recueil*. The royal table was served by the shepherds and shepherdesses, who had danced for the king and his guests at the time of their landing on the island. Preceded by '*joueurs de musettes*' ('pipers'), five shepherds and ten shepherdesses marched in groups of three carrying the dishes in addition to the stewards who carried '*houlettes*' ('crooks') instead of their usual sticks. Once the royal table had been served eight shepherds and 16 shepherdesses served the eight tables, each shepherd being assisted by two valets. The Spanish account states that the Queen Mother and her four children sat at one table, while French and Spanish cardinals, noblemen and ladies sat at other tables It describes the banquet as '*muy soberbio y rico*' ('very superb and rich'). It consisted of all sorts of fish including huge salmon and sturgeon pies. The description of the service broadly tallies with that of the *Recueil*. Thirty of the queen's and king's pages wearing skirts and tights of yellow taffeta and little caps of crimson satin carried the dishes as far as the arbour where they handed them over to the shepherds and shepherdesses who had met the royal party at the landing stage. While the women served and removed the dishes, the men dispensed the drinks.

---

[29]   Ibid., p. 317.

[30]   *Mémoires*, pp. 40–41.

After the supper, according to the *Recueil*, six violinists entered wearing long red and yellow gowns as well as yellow and green turbans. They were followed by nine nymphs. The first of these came in alone, playing a lute. She was richly dressed in cloth of gold and adorned with jewels. The other nymphs followed and performed a ballet after which the royal party returned to their boat which was now brightly-lit by lamps. The Spanish account tells a different story. The banquet, it says, was followed by the entry of 12 bass-viol players dressed in yellow satin. Behind them came 12 women dressed in Turkish costumes made of gold and silver cloth. They had very pretty coiffures with pearls, precious stones from which sprang rich plumes. In their midst was a small child who played on a lute and sang a French song. All the women, whose dance lasted half an hour, wore black masks which they later removed showing them to be women specially picked by the Queen Mother on account of their beauty. As the royal party returned to the landing stage after the close of the entertainment at 1 a.m., many stumbled in the dark. Some were badly hurt. The *Recueil* says nothing about this. It merely states that on their return to Bayonne the royal party were escorted to their palace by numerous torch-bearers. Marguerite's account is again different. Following the banquet, she writes, a troop of musicians disguised as Satyrs entered a large luminous rock. This, she explains, was more brightly-lit by the beauty and precious stones of the nymphs, who appeared above the rock, than by the artificial lights. After descending from the rock, the nymphs performed a ballet so beautiful that the goddess Fortune was unable to contain her envy. She triggered a torrent of rain and a tempest which caused the royal party to take to the boats in total confusion. This was a source of much amusement the following day. As for Abel Jouan, he disagrees with the *Recueil* over the date of the banquet. According to the *Recueil* this took place on Saturday 24 June, the Feast of St John the Baptist. Jouan states that it was on the previous day and that the king and his guests, instead of returning to Bayonne directly after the banquet, preferred to watch the bonfire, called *La Jouannée* on an island in the River Gave, which was traditionally lit on the eve of the Feast of St John. On the way, they were able to admire along the whole length of the river fireworks shaped like whales, dolphins, tortoises and Sirens (*'toutes contrefaictes en artifice de feux'*). Such was their enjoyment that they did not return to their lodgings in Bayonne until after 2 a.m. Corbières, who dates the banquet to 22 June, states that the Spaniards admired the dancing after the banquet so much that they missed the boats that had waited to take them to the St John's Eve bonfire, so that some had to sleep on the island. Other accounts are in line with the *Recueil*. They state that six violins appeared after the banquet and that nine nymphs danced a ballet. They do not mention provincial dances before the banquet or the luminous rock or the St John's Eve bonfire.

Turning to the visual evidence, we have two drawings attributed to the contemporary artist, Antoine Caron, and two tapestries in the set of eight collectively known as the Valois tapestries. One of the drawings (at the National Gallery of Scotland, Edinburgh) is thought to show a water festival at Fontainebleau in 1564: the other (at the Pierpont Morgan Library, New York) is related to the festival in

Bayonne in 1565; the tapestries are at the Uffizi museum in Florence and their maker has freely adapted the drawings. Little is known about Caron. He was born at Beauvais in the early 1520s and eventually became attached to the French court. His name appears twice in Fontainebleau accounts for the years 1540–50 when he was paid the lowly wage of 14 *livres* a month, and in 1559–60 when he was paid for restoring decorations in the royal apartments. Among Caron's best known works are paintings of massacres and sketches depicting festivals at the Valois court. Whether or not he was actually present at these events is not known. As Yates pointed out in her book on the tapestries, the first drawing does not accord with any description of the festivities at Fontainebleau in 1564. The other drawing, sometimes called 'The Whale' can be related to the Bayonne festival. The foreground shows a row of courtiers standing beyond a balustrade – presumably on a boat-deck – flanked by trumpeters and drummers. They are watching a ferocious-looking sea monster (hardly a whale!) under attack from two sides by men armed with spears standing in rowing boats. These closely resemble the boats in the so-called Fontainebleau drawing. In the background one can see Neptune seated in his chariot, trident in hand, pulled by three sea-horses, the Tritons seated on a large turtle and, on the right, a classical building – presumably the banqueting house on the island – and, vaguely, two circles of dancers. The building is neither octagonal nor does it bear any relation to written accounts of the festival. It strongly suggests that Caron imagined his drawing, perhaps after reading the *Recueil.* The drawing, in which everything is happening at once, exemplifies the current fashion for 'compositions with numerous but minuscule actors being developed in a vast space'.[31]

The Valois tapestries remain controversial. Not everyone accepts the Yates thesis as to who commissioned them.[32] Fortunately that is not our concern. The tapestries were obviously intended to celebrate the court festivals organized by Catherine de' Medici, who figures is all of them save one, albeit rather discreetly. Only two are concerned with the water festivals at Fontainebleau and Bayonne. The first shows the combatants at Fontainebleau wearing costumes of many nations. There are American Indians on the island and Turks in one of the boats. No such fête is recorded as having taken place at Fontainebleau. Turning to the other tapestry we see a sea-monster similar to that drawn by Caron, also Neptune, the Tritons and sirens, but no classical building on the island, only trees. Ladies are walking up a tree-lined alley and some people are sitting at a circular table

---

[31]   Henri Zerner, *Renaissance Art in France: The Invention of Classicism* (Paris: Flammarion, 2003), p. 153.

[32]   Léon de Groër, 'Les tapisseries des Valois', pp. 125–34. Building on a theory first advanced by Jean Ehrmann, Yates identified the designer of the tapestries as Lucas de Heere and argued that they were commissioned by William the Silent for presentation to Catherine de' Medici. This hypothesis is demolished by de Groër who shows that they could only have been commissioned by Catherine herself. Much of Yates's argument, he suggests, rests on a mistaken identification of some portraits in the tapestries and a failure to appreciate changes in fashion between 1577 and 1581.

in an arbour. In the foreground are rustics, male and female, dancing to the accompaniment of bagpipe-players.

What are we to make of all this evidence? That water festivals took place at Fontainebleau and Bayonne is indisputable. What is less certain is that the written and visual evidence offer an accurate picture of what actually took place. One suspects that both have been enhanced with the passage of time.[33] The more credible are those nearest in time to the festivals. That would include the Spanish and Italian accounts but not that of Jouan who, I think, lacked the necessary kudos to attend the entertainments. His account has been described as: 'a kind of official account of the progress designed to immortalize it in print and every page of which surrenders itself to a propaganda of peace. The truth is often glossed over.'[34] This judgment seems to me more applicable to the *Recueil* of the Bayonne meeting – that published by Vascovan in 1566 – which is too rich in detail to be wholly credible. As for the *Mémoires* of Marguerite de Valois, they are, in my view, the least reliable of all in respect of the royal progress of 1564–65. Marguerite only began writing her memoirs in 1594. The original manuscript is lost; nor had she any archives at her disposal. Her memory was not infallible. She describes two and a half years she spent at Nérac as 'four or five years of felicity'. Why should we accept her account of the banquet at Bayonne in 1565 as anything more than a colourful flight of imagination designed to give life to an otherwise sparse account of her childhood?[35]

Bibliography

Manuscript Sources

Bibliothèque nationale de France, MS. Les Cinq cents de Colbert, 140, ff. 495r–500v.

---

[33]   For a valuable discussion of the authenticity of festival books see Margaret M. McGowan, 'The Status of the Printed Text', in Nicolas Russell and Hélène Visentin (eds), *French Ceremonial Entries in the Sixteenth Century: Event, Image, Text* (Toronto: Centre for Reformation and Renaissance Studies, 2007), pp. 29–53.

[34]   M. Simonin, *Pierre de Ronsard* (Paris: Fayard, 1990), p. 276: 'Le *Recueil et discours du voyage du Roy Charles IX,* sorte de journal officiel du voyage destiné à en perpétuer la mémoire par l'imprimé, s'abandonne à chaque page à un irénisme de propagande. La vérité est ici fort fardée ...'.

[35]   Eliane Viennot, *Marguerite de Valois* (Paris: Payot, 1995), pp. 186–92: 'Mais quelle mémoire lorsqu'il s'agit d'évoquer le festin de Bayonne en 1565!'

Printed Primary Sources

Jouan, Abel, *Recueil et discours du voyage du roy Charles IX de ce nom à present regnant accompagné des choses dignes de memoire faictes en chacun endroit faisant son dit voyage en ses païs et provinces de Champaigne, Bourgoigne, Daulphiné, Provence, Languedoc, Gascoigne, Baïonne, et plusieurs autres lieux, suyvant son retour audit lieu, és années Mil cinq cens soixante quatre et soixante cinq* (Paris, 1566).

Recueil des choses notables qui ont esté faites à Bayonne, à l'entrevue du Roy Trèschrestien Charles neufieme de ce nom, et la Royne sa treshonorée mere, avec la Royne Catholique sa soeur (Paris, 1566).

Secondary Sources

Boutier, Jean, Alain Dewerpe, and Daniel Nordman, *Un tour de France royal: Le voyage de Charles IX (1564–1566)* (Paris: Aubier, 1984).

Cazaux, Y. (ed.), *Mémoires de Marguerite de Valois* (Paris: Mercure de France, 1971).

Champion, P., *Catherine de Médicis présente à Charles IX son royaume, 1564–1566* (Paris: B. Grasset, 1937).

de Groër, Léon, 'Les tapisseries des Valois du Musée des Offices à Florence', in *Art, objets d'art, collections (Hommage à Hubert Landais)* (Paris: Blanchard, 1987).

Ehrmann, Jean, *Antoine Caron* (2nd edn, Paris: Flammarion, 1986).

Graham, Victor E. and McAllister Johnson, W. (eds), *The royal tour of France by Charles IX and Catherine de' Medici: festivals and entries, 1564–66* (Toronto: University of Toronto Press, 1979).

Knecht, R.J., *Catherine de' Medici* (London: Longman, 1998).

Laumonier, P., *Ronsard, poète lyrique* (Paris: Hachette, 1909).

McGowan, Margaret M., 'The Status of the Printed Text' in Nicolas Russell and Hélène Visentin (eds), *French Ceremonial Entries in the Sixteenth Century: Event, Image, Text* (Toronto: Centre for Reformation and Renaissance Studies, 2007).

Simonin, M., *Pierre de Ronsard* (Paris: Fayard, 1990).

Sutherland, N.M., *The Huguenot Struggle for Recognition* (New Haven, Mass. and London: Yale University Press, 1980).

Viennot, Eliane, *Marguerite de Valois* (Paris: Payot, 1995).

Yates, Frances A., *The Valois Tapestries* (London: Routledge and Kegan Paul, 1975).

Zerner, Henri, *Renaissance Art in France: The Invention of Classicism* (Paris: Flammarion, 2003).

Chapter 5

Renaissance Venice and the Sacred–Political Connotations of Waterborne Pageants[*]

Evelyn Korsch

Festivals in Venice

Festivals are synaesthetic artworks designed to appeal to all the senses. Baroque scholars of Ceremonial Science, such as Julius Bernhard von Rohr, have pointed out that on festive occasions public open spaces served not only as musical venues[1] but in addition could be illuminated and even perfumed. However, the principal focus of festivals remained visual performance, as the most effective medium for conveying meaning. Effectiveness in this sense takes in both a comprehension of what is seen by the onlookers – that is the decoding of images and gestures – and the sustainability of what is perceived, that is to say a continuing existence for the performed images in the public memory.

Renaissance authors were keenly aware of the prime significance of visualization: '*Lo Occhio si dice che e la prima porta/ Per la quale lo Intellecto intende e gusta*' ('They say that the eye is the first portal/ Through which the intellect comprehends and enjoys').[2] Dante used the phrase *visibile parlare* (to speak visibly) to refer to the means by which God in Creation made man conscious of his existence.[3] Similarly, one might say, a festival's aim is to render the abstract character of a message visible and comprehensible by material means. In the context of the state, an aim such as this forms the basis of political iconography. Festivals serve, that is to say, as specific *instrumenta regni* (instruments of rule). As multimedia productions of political, social and economic power, festivals

---

[*]   This article is based upon research undertaken in the context of my PhD thesis entitled 'The image of Venice after Lepanto – The triumphal entry of Henry III as a non-verbal communication system' (University of Zurich, 2009).

[1]   Cf. Julius Bernhard von Rohr, *Einleitung zur Ceremoniel-Wissenschaft der großen Herren* (Berlin, 1733; reprinted in Leipzig: Edition Leipzig, 1990), pp. 838–46.

[2]   This statement starts Feo Belcari's play *Abraham and Isaac* (1449); quoted by Michael Baxandall, *Die Wirklichkeit der Bilder. Malerei und Erfahrung im Italien der Renaissance* (Berlin: Wagenbach, 1999), p. 181.

[3]   Dante Alighieri, *La divina commedia*, vol. 2: *Purgatorio*, ed. Carlo Salinari, Sergio Romagnoli and Antonio Lanza (Rome: Editori Riuniti, 1980), Canto X, 95.

attempt by way of ostentatious pageantry to display and to justify a culture based on conspicuous consumption.[4]

As is well known, in their published work Renaissance writers stress the singular position and significance of Venice. This literary *topos* emphasizes in particular the unique position of Venice by reference to its watery location, its freedom and its prosperity. The latter two qualities are closely associated with the city's lagoon site.[5] Venice is, moreover, presented as the world's most beautiful city, an assertion justified by its perfect combination of three elements: architecture, water and the inherent quality of its natural light. Unsurprisingly, these features also emerge as basic aspects of the visual language of Venetian festival culture.[6] In particular, the synaesthetic power of Venetian spectacle results in considerable measure from the interaction between water and light. By day, reflections glint on the water. By night this effect is enhanced: moonlight creates an unreal impression, leading the spectator into an appreciation of ethereal beauty. Beauty, in turn, described by Renaissance authors as '*un altro cielo formato in terra ornato di stelle*' ('another heaven created on earth decorated with stars'),[7] evokes divinity and closeness to God.

Firework displays can have the effect of strengthening the divine character of festival by bringing together illumination and sound, ideally in an orderly environment. According to Neoplatonism, sound belonged to the cosmic sphere and so represented an appropriate medium of divine communication.[8] Thus, fireworks could be understood as expressing and complementing higher meanings. There were practical aspects to this too. The preferred means of launching fireworks in the Renaissance period entailed the construction of temporary and fancifully decorated 'swimming stages'.[9] Described as *macchine* these represented a special type of festival architecture – on land or water – offering a display of music, sound, light and movable elements. A festival type such as this not only imitated theatre scenography

---

[4]   For a definition of conspicuous consumption see Thorstein Veblen, *Theorie der feinen Leute. Eine ökonomische Untersuchung der Institutionen*, 6th edn (Frankfurt am Main: Fischer Taschenbuchverlag, 2000), pp. 79–107.

[5]   Cf. Francesco Sansovino, *Venetia città nobilissima et singolare, descritta in XIIII Libri, nella quale si contengono tutte le Guerre passate, con l'Attioni Illustri di molti Senatori, le Vite de i Principi, et gli Scrittori Veneti del tempo loro, le Chiese, Fabriche, Edifici, et Palazzi publichi, et privati, le Leggi, gli Ordini, et gli Usi antichi et moderni, con altre cose appresso Notabili, et degne di Memoria* (Venice: [Iacomo Sansovino], 1581; reprinted Bergamo, 2002), fol. 3r–4r.

[6]   For different types of waterborne pageants see Lina Urban, *Venezia e le feste sull'acqua* (Venice: Centro Internazionale della Grafica, 1992).

[7]   Cf. Marsilio Della Croce, *L'historia della publica et famosa entrata in Vinegia del Serenissimo Henrico III. Re di Francia, et Polonia, con la descrittione particolare della pompa, e del numero, et varietà delli Bregantini, Palaschermi, et altri vaselli armati, con la dechiaratione dell'edificio, et arco fatto al Lido* (Venice, 1574), p. 18.

[8]   Cf. Dean Arthur Miller, 'The Emperor and the Ritual. Magic and Harmony', in *Byzantine Studies/ Études Byzantines* 6 (1979), pp. 117–28.

[9]   Cf. von Rohr, *Einleitung*, pp. 846–53.

but also offered an actual stage for plays, concerts and simulated battles. Julius von Rohr emphasizes that all such events had to be arranged with the maximum of discipline and harmony, not only in order to reduce security risks but mainly to enable the onlooker to recognize the transmitted message.[10] Petrarch had pointed out that Venice was famous not only for its festival culture in general but also for maintaining public order during festival events. Pageantry and temperate behaviour were combined harmoniously it was said, whereby the continuance of the state was assured.[11] Petrarch furthermore associated harmony and order during Venetian festivities with the perfect order of the heavenly sphere.[12] By such an association of ideas Venice could be brought within an understanding of the legitimation of power such as commended itself in similar fashion to Byzantine emperors.[13]

This chapter will address the sacred connotations of Venetian political self-understanding during the sixteenth century and after, and the mythologically-based role of the city as Queen of the Sea. In this period waterborne pageantry contributed one of the basic elements of Venetian strategies of self-representation, including the appropriation of a quasi-divine image for the city. A brief analysis of some of the ideological and practical implications of this stance will, it may be hoped, make a contribution to the themes of this volume as a whole.

The Divine Foundation of the City

The Master of Ceremonies of San Marco, Giovanni Battista Pace, sets out in his ceremonial book of 1678 an account of the origins of the city, beginning with a quasi-mystical interpretation of its propitious foundation and setting:[14]

> *La sempre gloriosa veneta Republica trasse l'origine sua faustissima dal mare l'anno di nostra salute 421 il giorno dell'Annuntiatione di Maria Vergine destinato felice a tutta la Christianità. L'Eterno Padre considerando seco stesso perapunto nell'eternità di trovar sposa al di lui Unigenito Figliolo, rissolse, che si generassero nel ventre verginale in un istesso giorno Christo, e Venetia; ed ecco dello sposo, e della sposa li 25 marzo il pretiosissimo incalmo.*

---

[10] Cf. von Rohr, *Einleitung*, p. 849.
[11] Cf. 'Senilium rerum libri IV, 3', in Francesco Petrarca, *Epistole*, ed. Ugo Dotti (Turin: UTET, 1978), p. 686.
[12] Cf. 'Senilium rerum libri IV, 3', in Petrarca, *Epistole*, p. 688.
[13] Cf. Antonio Carile, *Immagine e realtà nel mondo bizantino* (Bologna: Lo Scarabeo, 2000), p. 57.
[14] Biblioteca Nazionale Marciana di Venezia (BNMV), It. VII 396 (7423): *Ceremoniale magnum sive raccolta universale di tutte le ceremonie spettanti alla Ducal Regia Capella di San Marco, alla persona del Serenissimo, de Ecc.mi Procuratori, et circa il suonar del campanile [...] dal Rev. do P. Giovanni Battista Pace* (1678).

Perché doveva esser asilio della cattolica fede, ecco che naque fra l'aque, e si rende immobile fra le turbolenze de flutti, e fra l'humane tempestose vicende.

Nata in grembo al mare, che salum latinamente si dice, dispone tutte l'operationi sue cum grano salis; è fortissima circondata da mobili mura diffesa dall'occhio, dall'unghie d'un leone di questa Ser.ma Dominante, rimarcabile impresa, com'anche dell'Evangelista San Marco glorioso, e faustissimo embloema; attufata nell'aque a guisa del sole più viva, più rinomata, e cospicua riluce, fatta spettacolo inimitabile, e da tutto il mondo ammirata. Apena nata qesta [sic] Regina dell'Adria, diede saggio della futura religiosa sua indole; perché visitata da sommi Pontefici fu da medesimi cresimata giusto il decreto di Iginio Atheniese anno 140, e come da compadri sorti così cospicui priviletti, che a niuna altra corona reale è seconda.

Fu anche illustrata di prerogative da varii Imperatori; ad ogni modo decretò vivere usque ad cineres *sotto la tutella pontificia, da cui conobbe ogni sua christiana grandezza.*

[The ever-glorious Republic of Venice took its most fortunate origins from the sea, in the year of our salvation 421, on the day of the Feast of the Annunciation to the Virgin Mary, [a day] destined to be a fortunate one for all of Christendom. The Eternal Father himself, considering rightly from eternity to find a bride for his only Son, decided that Christ and Venetia should be conceived in the virgin womb on the same day. This most precious conception of groom and bride [took place] on 25 March.[15]

Because she must be a secure refuge for the Catholic faith, Venice was born amongst the waters, made immovable among the turbulence of the waves and the tempestuous vicissitudes of human existence.

Born in the womb of the sea, which in Latin is called *salum*, Venice conducts all her affairs *cum grano salis* ('in awareness of the sea'). She is extremely strong, circled by movable walls and guarded by the eye and claws of a lion, the singular impresa (device) of the Most Serene Dominion [Venice], and the most propitious emblem of the glorious Saint Mark the Evangelist.

Plunged in water like the sun, she [Venice] shines gloriously bright, and has become a spectacle without compare, wondered at by all the world. At her birth this Queen of the Adriatic gave notice of her future religious nature; being recognised by the most eminent pontiffs, she was confirmed by a rite decreed by Hyginus of Athens

---

[15]   In Venetian dialect 'incalmo' means 'conception of a foetus' as well as 'pregnancy'; cf. Giuseppe Boerio, *Dizionario del dialetto veneziano*, 2nd edn (Venice: Tipografia di Giovanni, 1856), p. 333.

in the year 140, and in accordance with the accompanying privileges, [privileges] so outstanding that she is not second to any other royal crown.

She was distinguished also by the prerogatives granted by various emperors, and yet she resolved to live *usque ad cineres* (to the end) under papal rule, and so became acquainted with all its [the papacy's] Christian greatness.][16]

The strategy of presenting Venice as chosen by God as the bride of Christ, with both Venetia-Venice and Christ conceived on the same day, through the agency of the Virgin Mary, allowed the state, though officially a republic, not only to be seen as equivalent within the political hierarchy of Europe with states ruled over by kings (through God's grace), but even to surpass these states in rank because it took its origin directly from a divine source. Venetia appeared in this interpretation as the *alter ego* of Christ and thus became supreme as a defender of Christianity. She was furthermore guarded by the lion of St Mark as invincible protector. As a fortress of the Catholic faith, she was born in the water of the lagoon, not only impregnable against attack, but also transformed into an aesthetically incomparable spectacle admired by the whole world. The particular topography and beauty of Venetia-Venice led to its being mythologized as a virgin: '*il magnifico, et veramente maraviglioso theatro della città di Vinetia: la quale piantata in mezo all'acque ... cosi con debita ragione le doveva attribuire il meritato titolo di Vergine.*' ('The magnificent and truly marvellous scene of the city of Venice, planted in the midst of water ... had thus without dispute to be granted the merited title of Virgin.')[17] Venetia's birth in water brought her the title of Queen of the Adriatic and signified a rule based upon the will of God, a rule which therefore needed no further legitimation. Popes and emperors acknowledged her value to Christendom by granting her appropriate privileges.

The Legend of Pope Alexander III

According to legend, in 1177 Pope Alexander III, persecuted by Emperor Frederick I Barbarossa, fled to Venice, where he took refuge in the monastery

---

[16] BNMV, It. VII 396 (7423), fol. 5 (original emphasis). Translation: Melanie Zefferino/ Ronnie Mulryne/ Evelyn Korsch.

[17] Thomaso Porcacchi, *Le attioni d'Arrigo terzo Re di Francia, et quarto di Polonia, descritte in dialogo, nelquale si raccontano molte cose della sua fanciullezza, molte imprese di guerra, l'entrata sua al Regno di Polonia, la partita, et le pompe, con le quali è stato ricevuto in Vinetia, et altrove, con essempi d'Historie in paragone, et massimamente de' Principi di Corona, ch'altre volte sono stati ricevuti in Vinetia* (Venice: [Giorgio Angelieri], 1574), fol. 20v.

of Santa Maria della Carità.[18] The Doge Sebastiano Ziani immediately offered Alexander his help, equipping a fleet which overcame the Imperial armada and captured the Emperor's son Otto. Barbarossa in response came to Venice to kiss the Pope's feet. In gratitude for his help, Alexander presented the Doge with a golden ring, entrusting him with the lordship of the Adriatic. Henceforth, every year on Ascension Day Venetian doges celebrated the city's solemn marriage to the sea.[19] Moreover, the Pope issued a 'privilege' which granted absolution to every Christian who attended mass in San Marco on the feast day or during the following eight – later fifteen – days.[20]

Many differing versions of the origin of the so-called Peace of Venice came into existence. Francesco Sansovino, author of *Venetia citta nobilissima et singolare* (1581), accepted the diverse sources of the legend. However, he reported that '*quel Pontefice gratissimo al Senato, gli lasciò segni esterni dell'obligo suo, et dell'amorevolezza della Rep. verso di lui, col donar li gli stendardi, le trombe, l'ombrella, il seggio, la spada, et il dominio del mare con altre cose appresso.*' ('This pope, so grateful to the Senate, left it tangible signs of gratitude and love for the Republic by presenting it with the flags, the trumpets, the umbrella, the chair, the sword, the lordship over the sea, along with other similar things.')[21] In this way, the Serenissima received its insignia of sovereignty and the legitimation of its rule over the sea from papal – and thus from divine – hands.[22] To exclude any possibility of debate about Venice's divine appointment, the legend of Pope Alexander III was embellished with further details and given a place in the Venetian festival calendar. Numerous paintings and engravings illustrate the episode. To take a particular instance, the pope's donation to the doge became the central motif of a cycle of paintings in the Sala del Maggior Consiglio (Hall of the Great Council) in the Doge's Palace. Pictures with scenes representing the Peace of Venice were displayed in public spaces not only in Venice but in other cities also, without any significance being attached to whether the episode was based on legend or fact. The real value of the paintings lay in bringing to public attention a Venetian subject which visitors to these places could not easily avoid.

---

[18]   Cf. Biblioteca del Museo Correr Venezia (BMCV), Cod. Correr 383 which gives a detailed description of the legend. For the legend and history of the peace treaty see Corinna Fritsch, *Der Markuskult in Venedig. Symbolische Formen politischen Handelns in Mittelalter und früher Neuzeit* (Berlin: Dissertation, 2001), pp. 67–74.

[19]   For the connection between the Pope-Alexander-Legend and the Sensa see Lina Padoan Urban, 'La festa della Sensa nelle arti e nell'iconografia', in *Studi Veneziani*, 10 (1968), pp. 291–353.

[20]   Although this privilege was noted in the *Pacta* it is said to be a falsification of the fourteenth century. Cf. Padoan Urban, 'La festa della Sensa', p. 330.

[21]   Sansovino, *Venetia città nobilissima et singolare*, fol. 231r.

[22]   These insignia were accompanying the doge when he left the palace for *andate in trionfo*. Cf. Archivio di Stato Venezia (ASV), Collegio, Cerimoniali, reg. 1, fol. 7v.

Despite the overlay of legend, historical evidence does exist that Doge Ziani hosted both pope and emperor in 1177. Following the defeat of the emperor at the Battle of Legnano on 29 May 1176, and the consequent failure of Imperial policy in Italy, a meeting between the competing parties took place in Venice, during which the doge assumed the role of mediator. On 24 July 1177 a peace treaty was drawn up, and was ratified on 15 August. In accordance with this, the emperor recognized Alexander III as the legitimate pope and was forced to abandon his claim to authority over Rome. Barbarossa observed on this occasion the ritual of the *osculatio pedum* ('kissing of the feet'), a gesture of humility derived from Byzantine court ceremonial. Tradition has it that the pope then raised the emperor to his feet and gave him a kiss of peace.[23] By curtailing Barbarossa's ambitions, Venice was able to expand and consolidate her own position, including domination of the Adriatic Sea and the promotion of trade.

The diplomatic success of Venice as mediator became associated with a naval victory won by Doge Pietro Orseolo II on Ascension Day 998, in response to the threat posed by Slavic pirates to the population of Dalmatia. To commemorate this victory, the annual Feast of the Sensa was introduced, which initially consisted only in a simple rite of blessing the sea.[24] As a result of the papal privilege of the absolution of sins on Ascension Day a large flow of pilgrims came to Venice, which developed into a lucrative source of income for the city. Over the period of the Sensa celebrations a trade fair was set up in Piazza San Marco, becoming one of the largest such fairs in Europe.[25] This amalgam of diplomacy and trade represents a typical Venetian strategy, as a result of which political interests are connected with ritual actions and then placed in a profit-oriented context. In this way, state-organized festival culture served as a promotional measure for a trade in artworks and many other types of goods.[26]

On the occasion of their meeting in 1177 Alexander III and Frederick Barbarossa were rowed from San Nicolò on the Lido to the city's main island.[27] The pope had previously been brought from Chioggia on the Venetian lagoon to San Nicolò, in order to begin his triumphal entry from there. The symbolic importance of San Nicolò

[23]   The kiss of peace is an important ritual because as a symbol of reconciliation it establishes for this moment the same level of ranking for both protagonists.

[24]   Cf. Flaminio Corner, *Ecclesiæ Venetæ antiquis monumentis nunc etiam primum editis illustratæ ac in decades distributæ, Decas duodecima* (Venice: [Giambattista Pasquali], 1749), pp. 104–6. For the ceremonial in the sixteenth century cf. ASV, Collegio, Cerimoniali, reg. 1, fol. 8v.

[25]   Cf. Padoan Urban, 'La festa della Sensa', pp. 330–34.

[26]   From the sixteenth century this trade fair gained increased significance for the art market. The procurators of St Mark *de supra* were responsible for its organization.

[27]   Cf. Heinrich Kretschmayr, *Geschichte von Venedig* (3 vols, Gotha: F.A. Perthes, 1905 and 1920; Stuttgart, 1934; reprinted Aalen: Scientia Verlag, 1964), vol. 1, pp. 263 and 265.

is thus made clear. The itinerary adopted in this way corresponds to the ceremonial route taken by the Feast of the Sensa, and so takes on an added sacredness.

The Marriage of the Doge with the Sea: the Sensa

The rite of the Sensa, celebrated each year on Ascension Day, is described in detail in the *Ritum ecclesiasticorum* ('church ceremonial') of 1564.[28] A shortened version can be found in the ceremonial book compiled in 1593 by order of the Capi del Consiglio di Dieci ('Heads of the Council of Ten'):

> *Die Ascensionis Domini mane Dux conscendit Bucentaurum causa solemnitatis annuli, et veniunt sex Canonici Sancti Marci pluvialibus induti albis, incedentes inter Notarios Curiae maioris et secretarios Ducales. Solvens a ripa Sancti Marci Navis ipsa tendit portum versus Sancti Nicolai, et inter monasterium Sancti Antonii, et Sanctae Helenae occurrit Reverendissimus Patriarcha Venetiarum, pontificalibus ornatus cum canonicis suis, in quadam navicula, seu plato, proramque suam conscendit, acbenedicit appositam aquam in solio, et multis decantatis orationibus, movens se cum navicula sua, quae ad latus dextrum steterat Bucentauri, circuit navem ipsam Ducalem, spargendo in Dominum Ducem, et omnes aquam benedictam. Et ad latus dextrum revertitur Bucentauri, commitaturque exeuntem per duo castella portus Sancti Nicolai ad tertium pharum, ubi bucentaurus non ultra progrediens proram, vertit ad Castella ipsa et Dominus Dux surgens vertit se, et in mare aureum annulum iacit, Inqiens In signum veri perpetuique Dominii. Et Dominus Patriarcha dum vertere proram Bucentauri intuetur, Solium, seu situlam aquae Benedictae e prora sui plati spargit totam in mare. Et Gastaldiones D. Ducis suum quoque solium, seu situlam quam habent in Cimba sua plenam aqua benedicta spargunt similiter in mare. Quibus absolutis D. Dux ingressus cum Bucentauro per castella qua venerat, se confert ad templum Beati Nicolai in littore, ubi ad destensum e Bucentauro occurit Abbas, et Monachi Sancti Nicolai, sacris induti excipientes eius Ex.am cum ceremoniis etc. Ubi adest quoque D. Patriarcha praefatus, et missam in Ecclesia praedicta D. Dux audit solemnem: Et ad evangelium accensum tenet cereum, Cumque in Palatium est reversus epulum celebrat.*[29]

[Early on the morning of Ascension Day the Doge boarded the *Bucentoro* for the annual ceremony. Six Canons of Saint Mark's, dressed in white copes, accompanied him, processing between Notaries of the Greater Curia and the

---

[28]   Cf. ASV, Procuratori di San Marco *de supra*, Chiesa, reg. 98, fol. 25r–v, 77r–v, 151v–152r; and the supplemented version from 1752 in: Procuratori di San Marco *de supra*, Chiesa, reg. 99, fol. 273r–276r.

[29]   ASV, Collegio, Cerimoniali, reg. 1, fol. 8v (Original emphasis). Translation: J.R. Mulryne.

dogal Secretaries. Leaving the landing stage at Saint Mark's, the *Bucentoro* sailed towards the harbour at San Nicolò. Between the monastery of St Antony and Saint Helena they were met by the most reverend Patriarch of Venice, who went on board a small ship or barge dressed in his pontifical robes and accompanied by six of his Canons, and took his place at its prow. Here he blessed the surrounding water from his patriarchal seat and with many chanted prayers. Sailing in his barge, which had been positioned on the right-hand side of the *Bucentoro*, he circled the Doge's vessel, sprinkling the Doge and all his companions with holy water. Then he returned to the right-hand side of the *Bucentoro* and joined it in leaving by way of the two forts [guarding] the harbour of San Nicolò as far as the third island, where the *Bucentoro* was unable to proceed further but turned back towards the forts. Here the Doge stood up and turning cast a gold ring into the lagoon, saying 'In token of true and everlasting dominion'. The lord Patriarch, when he saw the bow of the *Bucentoro* turning, emptied a whole tub or container of holy water from the prow of his barge into the sea. The Doge's *gastalds* (high officials) likewise sprinkled their own boat, and emptied the full tub or container of holy water which they had in their boat similarly into the sea. When these matters were completed, the Doge proceeded in the *Bucentoro* towards the islands from which he had come, and betook himself to the church of San Nicolò on shore, where, leaving the *Bucentoro* he met the Abbot and Monks of San Nicolò as arranged, dressed in their sacred garments, welcoming him and his companions on both sides with certain sacred rites. There was also present the afore-mentioned lord Patriarch of Venice. The Doge heard solemn Mass in the aforesaid church and lit a candle to the apostle, and when he had returned to his palace he held a great banquet.]

Venice's legitimation as ruler of the Adriatic Sea stemmed from the gift of the golden ring by Pope Alexander in 1177. The originally simple rite of the Sensa, blessing the sea, was transformed into a public act of state involving foreign dignitaries. Particular importance was attached to the church of San Nicolò, dedicated to the patron saint of sailors, and to the *bucintoro*, the gilded state galley which, mentioned for the first time in 1253, was used only for ceremonial occasions.[30] According to the *Cerimoniale* the various protagonists in the rite were allocated different places at different dates. A gradual development of the occasion's pattern underlined the rite's importance, as did the continuity implied by the invitation announced each year referring to the following year's event, thus serving as a form of ritual self-affirmation.

For the Ascension Day festival the doge, the Senate and foreign ambassadors boarded the *bucintoro* and set out for the Lido. During the trip, the choir of San

---

[30] The *bucintoro* derives from the Byzantine Imperial ceremonial as documented by Constantine's VII *De cerimoniisaulae byzantinae*. See Lina Urban, *Processioni e feste dogali. 'Venetia est mundus'* (Vicenza: Neri Pozza Editore, 1998), p. 187. The construction of a *bucintoro* cost 70,000 ducats in 1606. See Padoan Urban, 'La festa della Sensa', p. 324.

Marco sang madrigals and motets.[31] As they came abreast of Sant' Elena they met the patriarch's *piatta*[32] and, with it, the clergy. Before the *bucintoro* reached the sea, the patriarch came on board. There he blessed first the doge and the Signoria and then he blessed the sea with holy water. The *bucintoro* next crossed the strait of San Nicolò, where the doge threw a golden ring into the water with the words: 'We marry you, O sea, as a sign of our true and eternal dominion'. Symbolically, the doge took dominion over the sea in the way that a husband assumes authority over his wife. Afterwards the *bucintoro* brought the group involved in the festival to the church of San Nicolò at the Lido, where the doge and patriarch were received by the abbot. A mass was said and finally the patriarch took leave of the doge, inviting him to the same ceremony for the following year. The doge returned across the lagoon on the *bucintoro* together with the Signoria and his guests, while the patriarch remained with the monks. The ceremony was completed by a banquet at the Doge's Palace, to which the doge invited all participants in the festival.

Symbolic Associations

Certain symbolic associations, confirmed by the newly created iconographic programme in the Doge's Palace, may be discerned as deriving from the foundation myth and the Sensa. These contribute in a notable way to Venetian conceptions of political self-understanding and image-building during the Renaissance and post-Renaissance periods.

Christ and Venetia

Venice is represented in Venetian iconography as a state created directly by God and thus a – perhaps the – paradise on earth.[33] She is also seen as infallible in her religious and public life, since the figure of Venetia is understood to be interchangeable with the Virgin Mary and with Iustitia. In this fusion of virginity and justice Venetia is conflated with Astraea, who leads the people into a new golden age – that is, into the Kingdom of God where peace and true Christian faith rule.[34] Venetia acts as a defender of Christianity and is further presented as the saviour of a pope. In this way she is seen as a coequal power with emperor and

[31] Cf. Ellen Rosand, 'La musica nel mito di Venezia', in Manfredo Tafuri (ed.), *'Renovatio urbis'. Venezia nell'età di Andrea Gritti (1523-1538)* (Rome: Officina edizioni, 1984), pp. 167–86, p. 173.

[32] Like a small *bucintoro*.

[33] See Staale Sinding-Larsen, *Christ in the Council Hall. Studies in the religious iconography of the Venetian Republic* (Rome: L'Erma di Bretschneider, 1974).

[34] For Astraea leading not only into a kingdom of faith but also to the rule of a global empire see Frances A. Yates, *Astraea. The Imperial Theme in the Sixteenth Century* (London and Boston: Routledge and Keegan Paul, 1975), pp. 1–28.

pope. As the virgin bride of Christ, Venetia is appropriately described on a secular level as a city never captured by enemies: '*è durato già tanti secoli ... inviolabile et immaculato*' (she 'has endured already for many centuries ... inviolable and immaculate').[35] Christ and Venetia are seen as associated.

The Doge and the Sea

In a similar fashion, the 'marriage' of the doge with the sea underwent a mythological transformation. The 'marriage' legitimizes the maritime supremacy of Venice and, since she was born as Queen of the Adriatic, she is seen as representing not only the bride of Christ, but also of the doge. Any conceptual conflict in this dual marriage is solved iconographically through identifying the doge with Christ. Thus not only is Venetia's virginity respected, but the sacredness of the doge's person and role is emphasized. This is crucial to understanding the doge's role as redeemer, a status newly assigned to him from the mid 1570s.

The Symbolism of Topography

Venice's position in the midst of water played a crucial part in the presentation of the city on festival occasions. In particular, during visits of foreign rulers a watery setting for festival events served to underline Venice's reputation for political and economic power as well as military strength. The most important festive event during the sixteenth century, the state visit of Henry of Valois, King of France and Poland, on his way from Cracow to Paris to take up the crown of France, exemplifies these aspects.[36] On 17 July 1574 Henry arrived at Marghera, where he was received by 60 senators sent by the Serenissima. The king boarded a golden gondola and was rowed to Murano. The itinerary proceeded by way of the islands of San Giuliano, San Secondo, Sant'Alvise and San Cristoforo. At Murano, the king spent the night at the Palazzo Cappello. On 18 July, the doge, the Signoria, senators and ambassadors of foreign powers collected Henry from his accommodation in a ceremonial galley. The ship headed for the Lido, where at San Nicolò the reception ceremony took place. The return journey featured the king's triumphal entry on the *bucintoro* accompanied by music, ringing of bells and gun salutes. Escorted by numerous galleys and boats the *bucintoro* passed the islands of Sant'Elena, San Servolo and San Giorgio Maggiore. The ship then turned into the Canal Grande, where every building was festively decorated and illuminated, and so brought

---

35   Sansovino, *Venetia* (1581), fol. 3v.

36   For details of the state visit cf. ASV, Collegio, Cerimoniali, reg. 1, fol. 43r–45r; Evelyn Korsch,   *Bilder der Macht. Venezianische Repräsentationsstrategien beim Staatsbesuch Heinrichs III. (1574)* (Berlin: Akademie Verlag, 2013), and see J.R. Mulryne, Helen Watanabe-O'Kelly and Margaret Shewring (eds), *Europa Triumphans: Court and Civic Festivals in Early Modern Europe* (2 vols, Aldershot: Ashgate, 2004), vol. 1 pp. 103–218 for a wide-ranging discussion of the visit and its significance.

the king to his accommodation at Ca' Foscari. On 27 July the king left Venice in a gondola accompanied by the doge, Signoria, senators and ambassadors. The gondola was rowed to Lizzafusina where Henry boarded a *piatta* for travelling to Padua on the Brenta river. The journey towards the Terraferma (mainland) entailed sailing by way of the islands of Santa Chiara and San Giorgio in Alga. Thus, during the state visit the entire city was circled on water.

In Venice's case the city limits are defined precisely by the city's position *in* water. The decision to accommodate the king at Murano for the visit's first night was based primarily on pragmatic considerations to get from there to San Nicolò, chosen as the starting point for the triumphal entry, without revealing the centre of Venice. The port of San Nicolò functioned as the main access route into Venice in the sixteenth century. (The port of Malamocco took over this role only in the eighteenth century.) The strait of San Nicolò was called 'due castelli' because it was guarded on one side by the Castel Vecchio, near San Nicolò at the tip of the Lido, and on the other by the Castel Nuovo Sant' Andrea, constructed on a sand bank.[37] Visitors arriving in the city were thus confronted with a demonstration of the military power of Venice. After the Victory of Lepanto on 7 October 1571 the Consiglio di Dieci decided to attach a large marble plaque on the side of the fort visible to travellers, commemorating this important event during the dogal rule of Alvise I Mocenigo. The victory at Lepanto over the Ottoman Empire was interpreted as a sign from God confirming the *magnificentia* of the Republic and its leading role as defender of Christianity.[38] In this way the victory became myth and as such served to enhance Venetian prestige.

On the day of his solemn entry Henry III was brought from San Nicolò to the centre of Venice, because, in this perspective, the city was able to present herself like a stage. At the rear of the *bucintoro*, a throne was erected from which the king could enjoy the spectacle. When the galley headed for the entrance to the Canal Grande, the Piazza San Marco with its significant buildings appeared before the eye of the Royal beholder: the Doge's Palace and the Procuratie as the seat of government, the Basilica San Marco as religious centre, the Zecca as the depository of treasure and the Libreria as the location of artistic and cultural collections. On the Piazza itself merchants had set up their stalls; part of the city's commercial activities took place there, in addition to the trade taking place at the Rialto.

---

[37]   It was a defensive fortification which combined various security systems because the Venetian fleet was stationed in the port of Corfu and could not assist immediately in case of need. For the two forts see Ennio Concina, 'Le fortificazioni lagunari fra il tardo Medioevo e il secolo XIX', in Giovanni Caniato, Eugenio Turri and Michele Zanetti (eds), *La laguna di Venezia* (Verona: Cierre, 1995), pp. 249–62.

[38]   After the separately concluded peace treaty between Venice and the Ottoman Empire in 1573 the image of the Republic as defender of Catholic faith suffered much criticism by the European rulers. Venice responded by intensifying mythological strategies of image building.

To sum up: the itineraries travelled by Henry III or other illustrious guests in the lagoon represented topographic quotations with multiple symbolic functions.[39] Festive ceremonial was performed in the same manner over centuries, with only a few variations.

Sacred–Political Connotations of the *via triumphalis*

When on 18 July 1574 the reception for Henry III came to its conclusion at San Nicolò, the doge, king, papal legate, senators and ambassadors boarded the *bucintoro* to travel towards San Marco. They did not stop there, however, but turned into the Canal Grande in order to bring Henry III to his accommodation at Ca' Foscari. The *bucintoro*'s route from San Nicolò to the centre corresponded exactly with that traditionally prescribed for the Sensa. This identical itinerary certified the Serenissima's claims to power, for the benefit of both the guest of honour and the invited foreign ambassadors. However, it was also a special mark of respect to the visitor for him to be collected by the *bucintoro* at San Nicolò. This great honour was accorded to both Pope Alexander III and the Emperor Frederick I Barbarossa in 1177 when negotiating the Peace of Venice. In contrast, in 1574 the papal legate, the Cardinal of San Sisto, who came to Venice to pay his respects to Henry III, was unable to take advantage of the *bucintoro* because it had to be prepared for the king. This refusal led to a ceremonial controversy, because it was laid down in the *Cerimoniali* that popes, cardinals, emperors, kings and princes were entitled to make their entry on board the *bucintoro*.[40] On the other hand, it could happen that the *bucintoro* was indeed made available, but entry into the city was not routed from San Nicolò. When in 1468 Emperor Frederick III visited Venice, the Signoria met him with the *bucintoro* at the island of San Clemente.[41] Even less spectacular was the arrival in 1556 of the Polish Queen Bona Sforza, who made her entry on the *bucintoro* starting from the Giudecca, and was then taken to her accommodation at residence of the Dukes of Ferrara.[42]

---

[39] For the context of sacred and secular significations of space see Edward Muir and Ronald F.E. Weissman, 'Social and symbolic places in Renaissance Venice and Florence', in John A. Agnew and James S. Duncan (eds), *The power of place. Bringing together geographical and sociological imaginations* (Cambridge: Cambridge University Press, 1986), pp. 81–103. For the function of the Piazza see Egle Renata Trincanato, 'Rappresentatività e funzionalità di Piazza San Marco', in Giuseppe Samonà, Umberto Franzoi and Egle Renata Trincanato (eds), *Piazza San Marco. L'architettura, la storia, le funzioni* (Padua: Marsilio, 1970), pp. 79–91.

[40] Cf. ASV, Collegio, Cerimoniali, reg. 1, fol. 13r–14r.

[41] Cf. ASV, Collegio, Cerimoniali, reg. 1. fol. 14r.

[42] Cf. Mario Savorgnano, *La venuta della serenissima Bona Sforza et d'Aragona reina di Polonia et duchessa di Bari nella magnifica città di Padova a ventisette di marzo.*

The city's position, in being surrounded by water, limited the opportunities for triumphal entries or processions on solid ground. During the procession for the founding of the Holy League in 1571 the Piazza San Marco resembled something akin to a maze, because the authorities tried to organize the crowds of onlookers in geometrical patterns following a regular scheme.[43] The actual processional route led from the Porta del Frumento of the Doge's Palace across the expanse of the Piazza San Marco to the main portal of San Marco, thus marking out a symbolic connection between the political and religious centres. On the occasion of a procession later in the same year celebrating the Victory of Lepanto, the itinerary was identical. Ephemeral constructions were usually omitted on festival occasions because of Venice's traditional self-perception as presenting an already perfect appearance, so making additional decorations unnecessary, and also in practical terms because of a lack of space in the Piazza San Marco.[44]

The city overcame these limitations by including the lagoon in the *via triumphalis*. The waterway, which initially might seem to offer a practical drawback, proved on the contrary to be an advantage because, for example, expensive and time-consuming building activities for straightening the route (as had to be done in Rome) were unnecessary. San Nicolò, with its port entrance between the 'due castelli', proved an excellent starting point because it offered both natural access and, protected by a military fortification, a safe area. Moreover the route to San Marco was long enough to stage a triumphal entry framed by the city as scenery. However, the crucial factor was the symbolic function of San Nicolò. Only a place with sacred–political connotations could initiate a *via triumphalis* ending in another place with sacred–political connotations such as the area surrounding the Basilica San Marco and the Doge's Palace. By making use of the Porta della Carta a *via triumphalis* could also be created between San Marco and the Doge's Palace, leading up the Scala dei Giganti to the chambers of government.

On the occasion of Henry III's entry a triumphal arch was erected at San Nicolò on the Lido in imitation of the arch of Septimius Severus in the Forum in Rome.

Con l'entrata nella inclita città di Vinegia, il dì 26 aprile 1556, et la sua partita per Bari (Venice, 1556), fol. 12r.

[43]   Cf. the etching *Processione generale per la lega contro i Turchi del 1571*, in Giacomo Franco, *Habiti d'huomeni et donne venetiane con la processione della ser.ma signoria et altri particolari cioe trionfi, feste et cerimonie publiche della nobilissima citta di Venetia* (Venice: [Frezzaria all'insegna del sole], 1610).

[44]   There were two exceptions: the guild of the butchers built a triumphal arch on the Piazzetta at San Marco on the occasion of the entry of the dogaressa Zilia Dandolo Priuli in 1557 and another one in 1597 for the dogaressa Morosina Morosini Grimani. Besides in 1571 two arches commissioned by the guild of the goldsmiths were erected at Rialto to celebrate the victory of Lepanto. See Lina Padoan Urban, 'Apparati scenografici nelle feste veneziane cinquecentesche', in *Arte Veneta* 23 (1969), pp. 145–55, here: p. 148; Lina Padoan Urban, 'Gli spettacoli urbani e l'utopia', in Lionello Puppi (ed.), *Architettura e utopia nella Venezia del Cinquecento (exhibition catalogue)* (Milan: Electa Editrice, 1980), pp. 144–66, here: p. 146.

This device associated Venice not only with the Roman Empire and its tradition of triumphal processions, but also brought to mind the *via sacra*, integrated into Rome's public performances as a route with the highest symbolic value. As the former processional route that crossed the ancient Roman Forum, the *via sacra* first became part of a modern *via triumphalis* in 1536 for the triumphal entry of Charles V – for which a new *axis urbis* was created.[45] The *via sacra* started at the arch of Titus, passed through the arch of Septimius Severus to the Temple of Saturn, and from there led up to the Capitol. The Capitol with the Temple of Jupiter Capitoline represented the religious centre of Rome, where all triumphal processions ended. Symbolic–topographic parallels between Rome and Venice are evident. The Roman Forum performed the same functions as the area around Piazza San Marco, since in both cases the political and religious centres of the cities were located there as well as trading activities. The portico of Rome's Curia Iulia – no longer extant – served as a meeting place of senators in the same way as the Loggetta at the base of the Campanile, while the Temple of Jupiter Capitoline paralleled the Basilica San Marco both as spiritual centre and the endpoint of processions.

The Roman parallel implicit in the *via triumphalis*, moreover, appealed not only to motifs embedded in Imperial iconography, but also could be seen as having a sacred aspect related to Christian practice, since the itinerary in part corresponded to that of the ceremony of *possesso* (claim to office) undertaken by a new pope.[46] In the case of the *possesso*, the route followed the *via papalis* from San Pietro to San Giovanni in Laterano, crossing the Roman Forum by way of the *via sacra*. The highlight and conclusion of the ceremony took place in the Lateran Basilica, where the mystic marriage of the pope, as bridegroom, to the Catholic Church, as bride, was celebrated. A special significance was acquired accordingly by the arches of Septimius Severus and Titus, which formed the endpoints of the original *via sacra*. The integration of the ancient monuments into the processional route served the popes as a strategy of legitimation. A symbolic continuity between the Roman Empire and the papacy would help to suggest the acquisition of political power to reinforce spiritual. Venice, in its turn, by drawing symbolically on the ceremonies of *ingresso* and *possesso*, could adopt both Imperial and the sacred implications for the purposes of its own political iconography. Allusion to the mystical marriage of the pope and the Catholic Church confirmed formally the city's divine mission as defender of Christianity and its role as *vicarius Dei*. The integration of a *via sacra* and the arch of Septimius Severus into the Venetian *via triumphalis* served furthermore not only as a means of referring to the Roman Empire, but also to the world empire of Charles V as a measure of political power.

---

[45]   Cf. Marialuisa Madonna, 'L'ingresso di Carlo V a Roma', in Marcello Fagiolo (ed.), *La festa a Roma dal Rinascimento al 1870 (exhibition catalogue)* (2 vols, Turin: U. Allemandi, 1997), vol. 1, pp. 50–65.

[46]   Cf. Marcello Fagiolo, 'L'Effimero di Stato. Dal Conclave al Possesso', in Marcello Fagiolo (ed.), *La festa a Roma dal Rinascimento al 1870 (exhibition catalogue)* (2 vols, Turin: U. Allemandi, 1997), vol. 2, pp. 8–25.

In this way Venice's rule over the land was legitimized, just as the Sensa already claimed such legitimacy in spiritual terms in reference to the sea. Venice could assert, in other words, that it would be too modest to define the city as *altera Roma* (another Rome), because it should rather be characterized as *Romam superans* (Rome surpassed).

In Conclusion

Waterborne pageants were of crucial importance for Venetian festival culture as media of political iconography based upon sacred connotations and mythology. The pageants transmitted the Republic's image as both Queen of the sea and defender of Catholic faith. Venice in fact created its own *via sacra* on water, ending in practice at San Marco, but in ideological terms continuing to the doge's seat on the Tribunale in the Sala del Maggior Consiglio. Festivals represented acts of state celebrated in the presence of foreign ambassadors in order to integrate the doge symbolically into the hierarchy of European monarchs. This developing system of visual, acoustic and topographical strategies provided a continuous process of self-affirmation for the city. From the mid-1570s on, these performances assigned a quasi-divine role to the doge as redeemer – a phenomenon technically known as Neobyzantinism.

Bibliography

Primary Sources: Manuscripts

Archivio di Stato Venezia (ASV):
Collegio, Cerimoniali, reg. 1
Procuratori di San Marco *de supra*, Chiesa, reg. 98
Procuratori di San Marco *de supra*, Chiesa, reg. 99
Biblioteca del Museo Correr Venezia (BMCV): Cod. Correr 383
Biblioteca Nazionale Marciana Venezia (BNMV): Cod. It. VII 396 (7423):
    Ceremoniale magnum sive raccolta universale di tutte le ceremonie spettanti alla Ducal Regia Capella di San Marco, alla persona del Serenissimo, de Ecc.mi Procuratori, et circa il suonar del campanile [...] dal Rev.do P. Giovanni Battista Pace (1678).

Primary Sources: Printed books

Alighieri, Dante *La divina commedia*, ed. Carlo Salinari, Sergio Romagnoli and Antonio Lanza (Rome: Editori Riuniti, 1980)

Benedetti, Rocco, *Le feste, et trionfi fatti dalla Sereniss. Signoria di Venetia nella felice venuta di Henrico III. Christianiss. Re di Francia, et di Polonia* (Venice: Libreria della Stella, 1574).

Boerio, Giuseppe, *Dizionario del dialetto veneziano*, 2nd edn (Venice: Tipografia di Giovanni Cecchini, 1856).

Corner, Flaminio, *Ecclesiæ Venetæ antiquis monumentis nunc etiam primum editis illustratæ ac in decades distributæ, Decas duodecima* (Venice: [Giambattista Pasquali], 1749).

Della Croce, Marsilio, *L'historia della publica et famosa entrata in Vinegia del Serenissimo Henrico III. Re di Francia, et Polonia, con la descrittione particolare della pompa, e del numero, et varietà delli Bregantini, Palaschermi, et altri vaselli armati, con la dechiaratione dell'edificio, et arco fatto al Lido* (Venice, 1574).

Franco Giacomo, *Habiti d'huomeni et donne venetiane con la processione della ser.ma signoria et altri particolari cioe trionfi, feste et cerimonie publiche della nobilissima citta di Venetia* (Venice: [Frezzaria all'insegna del sole], 1610).

Petrarca, Francesco, *Epistole*, ed. Ugo Dotti (Turin: UTET, 1978).

Porcacchi, Thomaso, *Le attioni d'Arrigo terzo Re di Francia, et quarto di Polonia, descritte in dialogo, nelquale si raccontano molte cose della sua fanciullezza, molte imprese di guerra, l'entrata sua al Regno di Polonia, la partita, et le pompe, con le quali è stato ricevuto in Vinetia, et altrove, con essempi d'Historie in paragone, et massimamente de' Principi di Corona, ch'altre volte sono stati ricevuti in Vinetia* (Venice: [Giorgio Angelieri], 1574).

Rohr, Julius Bernhard von, *Einleitung zur Ceremoniel-Wissenschaft der großen Herren* (Berlin, 1733; reprinted in Leipzig: Edition Leipzig, 1990).

Sansovino, Francesco, *Venetia città nobilissima et singolare, descritta in XIIII Libri, nella quale si contengono tutte le Guerre passate, con l'Attioni Illustri di molti Senatori, le Vite de i Principi, et gli Scrittori Veneti del tempo loro, le Chiese, Fabriche, Edifici, et Palazzi publichi, et privati, le Leggi, gli Ordini, et gli Usi antichi et moderni, con altre cose appresso Notabili, et degne di Memoria* (Venice: [Iacomo Sansovino], 1581; reprinted Bergamo, 2002).

Savorgnano, Mario, *La venuta della serenissima Bona Sforza et d'Aragona reina di Polonia et duchessa di Bari nella magnifica città di Padova a ventisette di marzo. Con l'entrata nella inclita città di Vinegia, il dì 26 aprile 1556, et la sua partita per Bari* (Venice, 1556).

Secondary Sources

Agnew, John A. and James S. Duncan (eds), *The power of place. Bringing together geographical and sociological imaginations* (Cambridge: Cambridge University Press, 1986).

Baxandall, Michael, *Die Wirklichkeit der Bilder. Malerei und Erfahrung im Italien der Renaissance* (Berlin: Wagenbach, 1999).

Caniato, Giovanni, Eugenio Turri and Michele Zanetti (eds), *La laguna di Venezia* (Verona: Cierre, 1995).

Carile, Antonio, *Immagine e realtà nel mondo bizantino* (Bologna: Lo Scarabeo, 2000).

Concina, Ennio, 'Le fortificazioni lagunari fra il tardo Medioevo e il secolo XIX', in Giovanni Caniato, Eugenio Turri and Michele Zanetti (eds), *La laguna di Venezia* (Verona: Cierre, 1995), pp. 249–62.

Fagiolo, Marcello (ed.), *La festa a Roma dal Rinascimento al 1870 (exhibition catalogue)* (2 vols, Turin: U. Allemandi, 1997).

Fagiolo, Marcello, 'L'Effimero di Stato. Dal Conclave al Possesso', in Marcello Fagiolo (ed.), *La festa a Roma dal Rinascimento al 1870 (exhibition catalogue)*, (2 vols, Turin: U. Allemandi, 1997), vol. 2, pp. 8–25.

Fritsch, Corinna, *Der Markuskult in Venedig. Symbolische Formen politischen Handelns in Mittelalter und früher Neuzeit* (Berlin: Dissertation, 2001).

Korsch, Evelyn, *Bilder der Macht. Venezianische Repräsentationsstrategien beim Staatsbesuch Heinrichs III. (1574)* (Berlin: Akademie Verlag, 2013).

Kretschmayr, Heinrich, *Geschichte von Venedig* (3 vols, Gotha: F.A. Perthes, 1905 and 1920; Stuttgart, 1934; reprinted Aalen: Scientia Verlag, 1964).

Madonna, Marialuisa, 'L'ingresso di Carlo V a Roma', in Marcello Fagiolo (ed.), *La festa a Roma dal Rinascimento al 1870 (exhibition catalogue)* (2 vols, Turin: U. Allemandi, 1997), vol. 1, pp. 50–65.

Miller, Dean Arthur, 'The Emperor and the Ritual. Magic and Harmony', in *Byzantine Studies/ Études Byzantines* 6 (1979), pp. 117–28.

Muir, Edward and Ronald F.E. Weissman, 'Social and symbolic places in Renaissance Venice and Florence', in John A. Agnew and James S. Duncan (eds), *The power of place. Bringing together geographical and sociological imaginations* (Cambridge: Cambridge University Press, 1986), pp. 81–103.

Mulryne, J.R., Helen Watanabe-O'Kelly and Margaret Shewring (eds), *Europa Triumphans: Court and Civic Festivals in Early Modern Europe*, (2 vols, Aldershot: Ashgate, 2004), vol. 1, pp. 103–218.

Puppi, Lionello (ed.), *Architettura e utopia nella Venezia del Cinquecento (exhibition catalogue)* (Milan: Electa Editrice, 1980).

Rosand, Ellen, 'La musica nel mito di Venezia', in Manfredo Tafuri (ed.), *'Renovatio urbis'. Venezia nell'età di Andrea Gritti (1523–1538)* (Rome: Officina edizioni, 1984), pp. 167–86.

Samonà, Giuseppe, Umberto Franzoi and Egle Renata Trincanato (eds), *Piazza San Marco. L'architettura, la storia, le funzioni* (Padua: Marsilio, 1970).

Sinding-Larsen, Staale, *Christ in the Council Hall. Studies in the religious iconography of the Venetian Republic* (Rome: L'Erma di Bretschneider, 1974).

Tafuri, Manfredo (ed.), *'Renovatio urbis'. Venezia nell'età di Andrea Gritti (1523–1538)* (Rome: Officina edizioni, 1984).

Trincanato, Egle Renata, 'Rappresentatività e funzionalità di Piazza San Marco', in Giuseppe Samonà, Umberto Franzoi and Egle Renata Trincanato (eds),

Piazza San Marco. L'architettura, la storia, le funzioni (Padua: Marsilio, 1970), pp. 79–91.

Urban, Lina, 'Processioni e feste dogali. "Venetia est mundus"' in *Cultura popolare veneta N. S.*, 14 (Vicenza: Neri Pozza Editore, 1998), p. 187 ff

Urban, Lina, *Venezia e le feste sull'acqua* (Venice: Centro Internazionale della Grafica, 1992).

Urban, Lina Padoan, 'Apparati scenografici nelle feste veneziane cinquecentesche', in *Arte Veneta* 23 (1969), pp. 145–55.

Urban, Lina Padoan, 'Gli spettacoli urbani e l'utopia', in Lionello Puppi (ed.), *Architettura e utopia nella Venezia del Cinquecento (exhibition catalogue)* (Milan: Electa Editrice, 1980), pp. 144–66.

Urban, Lina Padoan, 'La festa della Sensa nelle arti e nell'iconografia', in *Studi Veneziani* 10 (1968), pp. 291–353.

Veblen, Thorstein, *Theorie der feinen Leute. Eine ökonomische Untersuchung der Institutionen*, 6th edn (Frankfurt am Main: Fischer Taschenbuch Verlag, 2000).

Yates, Frances A., *Astraea. The Imperial Theme in the Sixteenth Century* (London and Boston: Routledge and Keegan Paul, 1975).

Chapter 6

Rex Christianissimus Francorum: Themes and Contexts of Henry III's Entry to Venice, 1574[*]

Iain Fenlon

In May 1573, the Polish nobility who controlled the Sejm, the legislature of the recently-created Polish–Lithuanian Commonwealth formed between the Grand Duchy of Lithuania and the Kingdom of Poland, elected Henry of Valois, then Duke of Anjou, as its first monarch. This was the culmination of months of tense negotiation which had followed the death of Sigismund II August, the last monarch of the Jagiellon dynasty, in July of the previous year. The election, which involved an assembly of thousands, took place in a field outside Warsaw and, although the Lithuanians boycotted the election, they were prepared to accept its result. French power might have been on the wane, but a formal alliance with the Valois dynasty seemed, even to the Protestants, to be preferable to the Habsburg alternative. Four months later an official delegation led by the Bishop of Poznań travelled to Paris to present the 'certificate of election', and on 10 September Henry took an oath in the Cathedral of Notre Dame in Paris undertaking to respect Polish liberty and religious toleration.[1] Setting out on his journey to take up his crown Henry reached the Polish borders in January 1574; one month later his coronation took place in Cracow.

These events were of some political interest to the Venetians, always keen to keep abreast of French affairs, and an anonymous four-page pamphlet describing the coronation itself reveals that, together with Ferrara (whose dynastic connections with France were also strong), the Republic was the only Italian state to send an ambassador to the ceremony.[2] Henry's effective reign as King of Poland

---

[*]   The following abbreviations are used in the footnotes:
    ASV: Venice, Archivio di Stato
    BCV: Venice, Biblioteca Correr
    BNM: Venice, Biblioteca Nazionale Marciana
    BNP: Paris, Bibliothèque Nationale
[1]   For Henry's election and its aftermath see Daniel Stone, *The Polish–Lithuanian State, 1386–1795: A History of East Central Europe* (Seattle and London: University of Washington Press, 2001), pp. 116–19.
[2]   *Le allegrezze et solennita fatta in Cracovia citta principale del regno di Polonia* (Venice, 1574), f. A4.

was to be short. Following the death of his elder brother, Charles IX, on 30 May 1574, Henry had been urgently recalled to France to take up the throne by his mother, Catherine de Medici, who had been acting as regent, thus preventing his younger brother, François, duke of Alençon, from doing so in his absence. The Polish nobility had always considered Henry to be untrustworthy, and cultural differences including very different conceptions of the powers of an elective monarchy had caused considerable problems during the new king's brief period in Wawel Castle. The young monarch's indulgent and expensive habits had created a poor impression among the stern Polish nobility, and his foppish sartorial tastes allied to rumours of homosexuality had only made matters worse. Nonetheless, for political reasons, they were opposed to his return to France and Henry was forced to leave surreptitiously under cover of darkness accompanied by a handful of retainers. As could have been predicted, his sudden flight created a power vacuum and provoked a constitutional crisis.[3] This was on 18 June. Following Catherine's advice he went first to Vienna, where he was given hospitality by the Emperor,[4] and from there he began his journey south.[5] At Pontebba he was met by an official delegation of four specially-appointed Venetian ambassadors, who had been charged with accompanying the king from the confines of the state to Venice itself. At Feltre, Belluno and other small towns along the route Henry was welcomed by large crowds, and at Conegliano he made the traditional entry through the main gate of the city and into the main thoroughfare. This had been

---

[3]   Stone, *The Polish–Lithuanian State*, pp. 120–21.

[4]   The main primary sources for Henry's trip through Friuli and the Veneto are Tommaso Porcacchi, *Le attioni d'Arrigo terzo re di Francia et quarto di Polonia descritte in dialogo* (Venice: G. Angelieri, 1574); Nicolo Lucangeli da Bevagna: *Successi del viaggio d'Henrico III christianiss[i]mo re di Francia, e di Polonia, dallasua partita di Cracovia fino all'arrivo in Turino* (Venice, 1574); G. Manzini, *Il glorioso apparato fatto dalla serenissima republica venetiana per la venuta, per la dimora, & per la partenza del christianiss[i]mo Enrico III re di Francia e di Polonia* (Venice: G. Percachino, 1574), BNM MS It. VII. 393 (8647); BNM MS It. VII 73 (8265), ff. 403–408 and the anonymous account in BNP MS Fonds Italien 799 which forms the basis of Pierre De Nolhac and Angelo Solerti, *Il viaggio di Henrico III re di Francia e le feste a Venezia, Ferrara, Mantova e Torino* (Turin, 1890).

[5]   For discussions of the triumphal entries and other ceremonies that took place along the route of Henry's journey to Venice see R.J. Knecht et al., 'The Festivals for Henri III in Cracow, Venice, Orléans and Rouen', in J.R. Mulryne, Helen Watanabe-O'Kelly and Margaret Shewring (eds), *Europa Triumphans: Court and Civic Festivals in Early Modern Europe* (2 vols, Aldershot: Ashgate, 2004), vol. 1, pp. 103–215; Anna Laura Bellina, 'A suon di musica da Cracovia a Lione: i trionfi del cristianissimo Enrico III', in Umberto Artioli and C. Grazioli (eds), *I Gonzaga e l'Impero: itinerary dello spettacolo* (Florence: Le Lettere, 2005), pp. 81–106; Laurie Stras, ' *"Onde havrà'l mond'esempio et vera historia"*: Musical Echoes of Henri III's Progress through Italy', *Acta musicologica* LXXII (2000), pp. 7–41; Iain Fenlon, *The Ceremonial City: History, Memory and Myth in Renaissance Venice* (New Haven and London: Yale University Press, 2007), pp. 193–7.

equipped with two large temporary pyramids painted with the arms of Poland, France and Anjou, and decorated with inscriptions. It was also at Conegliano that a youthful Carlo Pasquali delivered a Latin oration in praise of the King.[6] Both these features of Henry's welcome were entirely traditional, lending both *dignitas* and a touch of *magnificenza* to the occasion, and presage in miniature the arrangements that the king was to encounter in Venice itself. At Lavadina a pontoon bridge decorated with the royal arms and inscriptions had been strung across the river, and at Treviso a ceremonial procession escorted the king under temporary arches decorated with the royal coats of arms, inscriptions and painted scenes showing his victories in France over rebels and heretics.[7] These clear references to the Wars of Religion and to Henry's role as 'Defender of the Faith' in the struggle against the Huguenots, were to become one of the most common themes of the temporary architecture that greeted Henry on his progress through the Veneto, and eventually in Venice itself. From Treviso rapid progress was made to Mestre, and then on to Marghera, where a large crowd of some thirty thousand people was waiting, together with an official deputation of seventy senators dressed in their sumptuous vermilion robes. From there Henry was escorted across the lagoon by some two thousand small craft to the Palazzo Cappello at Murano, where he was lodged for the night. At the island of San Luigi, the party was joined by forty young patricians who had been assigned to the king's service by the Senate for the duration of his stay.[8] Although geographically close to Venice, Murano was governed with a degree of autonomy, as were the towns and cities of the *terraferma*. In purely ceremonial terms its function was similar to that of the Medici villa at Poggio a Caiano outside Florence, or the Villa Madama at Rome, as the final place outside the city from which official entries were launched.

In the course of Henry's journey through the Veneto his entourage was accompanied firstly by the Duke of Nevers and later, at Spilimbergo, by the Duke of Ferrara, Alfonso II d'Este. The former was related to the Gonzaga of Mantua through the marriage of Henriette de Clèves to Lodovico Gonzaga in 1565, while Alfonso, the son of Duke Ercole II and Renée of France, was almost more French than Italian, having spent much of the 1550s at the French court. Famously present at the tournament at which Henri II was mortally wounded (he is reported to have held the king's head as he lay dying), his appearance along the route, together

---

[6]   Caroli Paschali Cuneatis, *Ad Henricum III Francorum regem oratio* (Venice: A. Muschio, 1574).

[7]   See Porcacchi, *Le attioni d'Arrigo terzo*, ff. 19–20; Lucangeli da Bevagna: *Successi del viaggio*, pp. 27–9; Manzini, *Il gloriosissimo apparato*, ff. A3v–A4; *I gran trionfi fatti nella nobil città di Treviso nella venuta del Christianissimo Re di Francia & di Polonia Henrico Terzo* (Venice, 1574).

[8]   They are listed by name in BNM MS. It. VII. 393 (8647), unfoliated. For the details of Henry's crossing to Murano and his stay in Palazzo Cappello see Fenlon, *The Ceremonial City*, p. 197.

with that of Nevers, was both familial and political in motivation.[9] The presence of these two senior Italian princes, one of whom was a blood relation of the King, consolidated the bonds of amity as well as performing the necessary courtesies. Other episodes were also designed to intensify Henry's sense of well-being and familiarity on his journey south. Pasquali, who delivered the welcoming oration at Conegliano, had been a protégé of the magistrate, diplomat and poet Guy de Faur de Pibrac since Pasquali first arrived in Paris from his native Piedmont probably in the late 1560s or early 1570s. Pibrac, who had accompanied Henry on his journey to Poland,[10] was instrumental in securing Pasquali's first royal appointment as extraordinary ambassador to Poland in 1576, a difficult mission which included the task of recovering the collections of classical marbles and precious works of art which the king had left behind. Pasquali subsequently composed a Latin biography of his first patron and, having become a French citizen, went on to a distinguished diplomatic career serving in Germany, Italy and England.[11]

Through such attention to detail, the Venetians attempted to ensure that Henry's entry into Venice constituted the high point of his triumphal return to France.[12] On the day of his entry into the city, the king was rowed to the Lido, which was

---

[9]   On Nevers during Henry's brief period as effective King of Poland see Ariane Boltanski, *Les ducs de Nevers et l'etat royal. Genèse d'un compromis (ca. 1550–ca. 1600)* (Geneva: Droz, 2006), pp. 387–91.

[10]   For the entourage which accompanied Henry, which also included the Duke of Nevers, see Henri Champion: 'La maison et l'entourage de Henri III en Pologne', *Revue d'humanisme et Renaissance*, VII (1940), pp. 286–308.

[11]   The biography, composed in Latin in 1584, the year of Pibrac's death, was subsequently translated as *La vie et moeurs de messier Guy du Faur, seigneur de Pybrac* (Paris: Thibault du Val, 1617); see Katherine M. MacDonald, 'Diplomacy and Biography in the Wars of Religion: Charles Paschal's Life of Guy du Faur de Pibrac (1584)', in Bruno Tribout and Ruth Whelan (eds), *Narrating the Self in Early Modern Europe* (Oxford and Berlin: Lang, 2007), pp. 23–40.

[12]   For the entry and the celebrations in Venice in the days that followed see, in addition to the primary sources mentioned above (footnote 4): Rocco Benedetti, *Le feste e trionfi fatti dalla serenissima signoria di Venetia nella felice venuta di Henrico III Christianissimo Re di Francia et III di Polonia* (Venice, 1574); Rocco Benedetti, *I trionfi et le gran feste fatte dalla Serenissima Signoria di Venetia nella venuta del Christianissimo, et invitissmo Henrico III di Francia et di Polonia* (1574) [NB these are two related but textually distinct accounts both authored by Benedetti]; Marsilio Della Croce, *L'historia della publica et famosa entrata in Vinegia del serenissimo Henrico III di Francia et Polonia con la descrittione particolare della pompa, e del numero, et varieta delli bregantini, paleschermi, et altrivascelli, con la dechiaratione dell'edificio, et arco fatto al Lido* (Venice: [Comin da Trino], 1574). For discussion see Nicolai Ivanoff, 'Henri III a Venise', *Gazette des Beaux-Arts* LXXX (1972), pp. 313–30; David Nutter, 'A Tragedy for Henri III of France, Venice, 1574', in A. Morrogh et al. (eds), *Renaissance Studies in Honor of Craig Hugh Smyth* (2 vols, Florence: Giunti Barbèra, 1985), vol. 1, pp. 591–611; Iain Fenlon, 'Merulo and State Ceremonial: The Visit to Venice of Henri III', in Marco Capra (ed.), *A Messer Claudio, Musico. Le arti molteplici di Claudio Merulo da Correggio (1533–1604) tra Venezia e*

both the actual and symbolic boundary of the city.[13] It was for these strategic and symbolic reasons that the edge of the lagoon, close to the island, was the site of the Doge's annual re-dedication of Venice to the sea on the feast of the Ascension.[14] By this period, distinguished visitors to the city were invariably received at the church of San Nicolò del Lido and the small piazza which served as its forecourt. On this occasion, the most important officials of church and state, supplemented by some of the main elements of the Venetian ceremonial apparatus, welcomed their royal guest onto Venetian soil, and so into the Venetian *civitas*.[15] The main audience for Henry's entry was an impressive flotilla of brigantines, provided and elaborately decorated by the guilds, which represented the economic and commercial foundations of the Republic. At the same time, the incorporation of the representatives of artisanal labour acted as a counterpoint to the elite rituals, given in the presence of a highly select company, that were conducted on the island itself.

The ceremonies enacted at San Nicolò provided the Venetians with the opportunity both to honour their distinguished guest and his achievements, and to instruct all present in the virtues and power of the state. This was achieved through a spectacle of unusual beauty, theatrically enacted at the boundary of land and sea. For Henry's visit two temporary structures, said to have been designed by Andrea Palladio, had been put up on the island.[16] The first was a triumphal arch deliberately modelled, as most commentators reported, on that of Septimius Severus in Rome. Although not the first such structure of its kind to be seen in Venice, it was a typological rarity.[17] Constructed of wood simulated to resemble marble, the arch was adorned with a thematically-related assemblage of statues, inscriptions and paintings. Two traditional themes were prominent in the iconographical scheme of this arrangement: Venice as the dispenser of Peace and Justice and Henry, '*Rex*

Parma (Venice, Parma, Marsilio: Casa della musica, 2006), pp. 261–76; Fenlon, *The Ceremonial City*, pp. 197–215.

[13]   See Evelyn Korsch's chapter in this volume, pp. 79–97.

[14]   Edward Muir: *Civic Ritual in Renaissance Venice* (Princeton, NJ: Princeton University Press, 1981).

[15]   Patricia Fortini Brown: 'Measured Friendship, Calculated Pomp: The Ceremonial Welcomes of the Venetian Republic' in Barbara Wisch and S. Scott Munshower (eds), *'All the World's a Stage ... ': Art and Pageantry in the Renaissance and Baroque* (2 Parts, University Park, Pa: Pennsylvania State University, 1990), Part 2, pp. 137–86.

[16]   M. Della Croce, *L'historia della publica et famosa entrata*, p. 12, states that the design was by Palladio. For a discussion of his responsibility of the two structures see Wolfgang Wolters, 'Le architecture erette al lido per l'ingresso di Enrico III a Venezianel 1574', *Bolletino del centro internazionale di studi di architettura Andrea Palladio* XXI (1979), pp. 280–88. Tracy Cooper, *Palladio's Venice* (New Haven and London: Yale University Press, 2005), pp. 213–27, accepts both as Palladio's work.

[17]   For the earliest example in the city see Maximilian L.S. Tondro, 'The First Temporary Triumphal Arch in Venice (1557)', in J.R. Mulryne and Elizabeth Goldring (eds), *Court Festivals of the European Renaissance: Art, Politics and Performance* (Aldershot: Ashgate, 2002), pp. 335–62.

Christianissimus Francorum', as Defender of the Faith. The first would have been immediately legible by most Venetians, aware of its appearance in the form of an allegorical female figure holding sword and scales; in this guise, the sculpted figure of Justice oversees proceedings in the Piazza San Marco from a number of strategic vantage points including the top of the Porta della Carta. (Fig. 6.1) Even more dramatic is her appearance in a mid-fourteenth-century roundel, usually attributed to Filippo Calendario, on the façade of the Doge's Palace overlooking the Piazzetta. Here she is presented to the patricians who gathered to transact business in the Palace as a composite civic image (Venezia/Giustizia, in which the concept of Justice is merged with the image of Venice itself), holding sword and scales and seated upon a Solomonic throne of lions. In her left hand a scroll reads:

Fortis/Iusta/Trono/Furias/Mare/Sub Pede/Pono

[Enthroned just and strong, I defeat the furies by sea]

thus supplementing the *topos* of Venetian justice guided by wisdom with the imperial dimension of the Republic's domination of the oceans.[18] (Fig. 6.2) The re-invocation of these inter-related themes on the arch at the Lido underlined the symbolic function of the forecourt at San Nicolò as a transposition of the Piazza San Marco itself achieved by a combination of classical forms and the shared language of Venetian auto-celebration.

The second major theme to be elaborated was that of Henry as '*Rex Christianissimus*', a title that resonated with the long and distinctive relationship between the Catholic Church and France, the first modern state to be officially recognised by the Papacy. It had come into common use during the reign of Charles VI, and under his successor, Charles VII, it had been adopted as the exclusive and hereditary title of the Kings of France. Apart from a brief moment in the second decade of the sixteenth century when Pope Julius II, then in dispute with Louis XII of France, considered transferring the title to Henry VIII of England, it had remained indisputably linked to the concept of French monarchy ever since. In the specific context of the religious disturbances which had dominated French affairs since the Massacre of Vassy, which inaugurated the Wars of Religion in 1562, the inherited title took on a heightened significance.

On either side of the arch the arms of France and Venice were mounted, while on top of the structure the royal arms of France were displayed supported by two angels. Below, in the attic, statues of Victory and Peace framed an inscription which ran:

---

[18]   David Rosand, 'Venetia figurata: The Iconography of a Myth', in D. Rosand (ed.), *Interpretazioni veneziane: studi di storia dell'arte in onore di Michelangelo Muraro* (Venice: Arsenale editrice, 1984), pp. 177–96, at pp. 179–80; Debra Pincus, *The Tombs of the Doges of Venice* (Cambridge: Cambridge University Press, 2000), pp. 121–3; David Rosand, *Myths of Venice: The Figuration of a State* (Chapel Hill, NC and London: University of North Carolina Press, 2001), pp. 26–32.

Figure 6.1   Bartolomeo Bon the elder, *Justice*, 1441, Porta della Carta, Ducal Palace. Private collection.

Figure 6.2   Filippo Calendario (?), *Venezia*, c.1345, West façade, Ducal Palace. Private collection.

Henrico III. Franciae atque Poloniae Regi Christianis, & invictiss., Christianae religionis acerrimo propugnatori advenienti, Venetorum Resp. ad veteris benevolentiae, atque observantiae declarationem.

[To Henry III, King of France and Poland, and Most Christian King and most fervent defender of Christianity [offered by] the Republic of Venice on his arrival as a sign of long-standing benevolence and deference.][19]

At the lower level of the arch the façade was articulated by two pairs of Corinthian columns, while above the three openings paintings by Veronese and Jacopo Tintoretto had been placed.[20] Those above the side openings showed the important Catholic victories over the Huguenots at Jarnac and Moncontour. The first of these battles, which had taken place in March 1569, seemingly had been decisive,[21] but when the two armies met again three months later at La Roche-l'Abeille, just south of Limoges, the situation was reversed. In the final analysis this turned out to be a comparatively unimportant episode.[22] At Moncontour, in October, the Catholic forces once again prevailed. Henry, who had taken part in these campaigns, subsequently led the siege of La Rochelle which had begun on 11 February 1573. It is presumably because this massive military assault on the Huguenot city was still in progress (the siege was not lifted until 6 July), that it is absent from the iconographical scheme of Palladio's structure. Further historical scenes showing his election as King of Poland and the reception of the Polish ambassadors in Paris in the summer of 1573 had been placed over the central passageway.[23] Having disembarked from the galley which had brought him from Murano, Henry was welcomed by the Doge and the Cardinal Legate waiting under a baldachin of cloth of gold supported by the six procurators of San Marco accompanied by other dignitaries; it is this moment which is shown in Andrea Vicentino's large-

---

[19]   Reported in most accounts: see Della Croce, *L'historia della publica et famosa entrata*, p. 13; Manzini, *Il gloriosissimo apparato*, f. A4; Porcacchi, *Le attioni d'Arrigo terzo*, f. 24. A shorter version of the inscription is visible in Andrea Vicentino's canvas, *The Arrival of Henri III at the Lido*, painted c. 1593 and installed in the Sala delle Quattro Porte in the Ducal Palace; for the detail showing it see Fenlon, *The Ceremonial City*, p. 192.

[20]   For some difficulties of interpreting the various accounts, particularly in relation to the paintings displayed, see Egon Verheyen, 'The Triumphal Arch on the Lido: On the Reliability of Eyewitness Accounts', in K.L. Selig and E. Sears (eds), *The Verbal and the Visual: Essays in Honor of William Sebastian Heckscher* (New York: Italica Press, 1990), pp. 213–23.

[21]   For the military strategies deployed see Arthur Whiston Whitehead, *Gaspard de Coligny, Admiral of France* (London: Methuen, 1904), pp. 202–8.

[22]   Whitehead, *Gaspard de Coligny*, p. 213.

[23]   See Della Croce, *L'historia della publica et famosa entrata*, pp. 13–14; for the arch see Ivanoff, *'Henri III à Venise'*, pp. 314–15.

scale commemorative canvas that was placed in the Sala delle Quattro Porte some twenty years after the event.[24]

Having passed through the arch, the procession now entered the second temporary structure, a freely designed loggia, where Henry was received by the Patriarch of Venice, Giovanni Trevisan, accompanied by representatives of the Venetian clergy. The significance of the choice, made by two patrician advisers, of this architectural type, would not have been lost on the more alert members of the largely Venetian population that watched the spectacle. In the public realm, such structures were often used as ceremonial spaces, sometimes as places of debate and public discussion, occasionally even with a juridical function. Palladio had used the motif of the free-standing loggia on other occasions, but in quite different contexts, notably in his two related schemes for the Rialto bridge.[25] A more recent and perhaps more relevant experience is his Loggia del Capitaniato in Vicenza,[26] but Sansovino's Loggetta in the Piazza San Marco, an aristocratic forum reserved specifically for members of the ruling class, was the example most familiar to Venetians. With its triumphal iconography, it has been described by one architectural historian as 'the most complete visual representation of the Venetians' view of their own state as the perfect republic',[27] and a changing cast of state officials (the Procurators) who transacted their business inside it, it functioned as a permanent reminder of the rich benefits of Venetian government and of the Republic's dominion over the Adriatic. Palladio's temporary loggia at San Nicolò also served as a '*ritrovo della nobiltà*' ('meeting place for the nobility'), a '*loggia fabricate all'incontro*' ('a loggia designed for meeting') as one observer described it,[28] a reserved space where the King of France, accompanied by the Doge and Papal Legate, was to be received by the official representative of the church in Venice before a socially select audience. In addition, Palladio's structure functioned as the arena for a very particular and highly suggestive piece of ritual, which placed a strong emphasis upon Henry's role and title of 'Most Christian Majesty'.[29]

---

[24]   See Wolters, Wolfgang, 'Le architecture eretta al lido per l'ingresso di Enrico III a Venezianel 1574', *Bolletino del centro internazionale di studi di architettura Andrea Palladio*, 21 (1979), pp. 280–88; Fenlon, *Ceremonial City,* pp. 198–202.

[25]   Bruce Boucher, *Andrea Palladio: The Architect in his Time* (New York and London: Abberville, 1994), pp. 216–29, esp. p. 224.

[26]   See Rudolf Wittkower, *Architectural Principles in the Age of Humanism*, 4th edn (London: Academy Editions, 1973), pp. 86–9; James Ackerman, *Palladio* (Harmondsworth: Penguin, 1966), pp. 120–23; Arnaldo Venditti, *La loggia del capitaniato* (Vicenza: Centro Internationale di Studi di Architettura Andrea Palladio, 1969), pp. 25–7; Boucher, *Andrea Palladio*, pp. 273–6.

[27]   Deborah Howard, *Jacopo Sansovino: Architecture and Patronage in Renaissance Venice* (New Haven and London: Yale University Press, 1975), p. 34.

[28]   Della Croce, *L'historia della publica et famosa entrata*, p. 12.

[29]   Porcacchi, *Le attioni d'Arrigo terzo*, f. 28v.

From a typological point of view Palladio's structure is unconventional as a piece of entry furniture. As it came into view, it was revealed as a tall and airy construction, also painted to imitate marble. The front façade was made up of ten Corinthian columns joined by garlands, while each of the side walls was pierced by an arcade. The rear wall was articulated by columns to form compartments, each of which contained a statue of one of the Virtues, placed beneath a painting. In the central compartment which lay directly in front of the main arcade of the arch, stood an altar placed in a circular niche, while a painting on the ceiling above presented four figures of Victory, their arms raised in the act of coronation with laurel wreaths. The evident reference here was to the four great battles that Henry had won against his enemies, two of which, Jarnac and Moncontour, had already been seen depicted on the ceremonial arch. To complete the scheme a picture of Christ the Redeemer by Jacopo Tintoretto had been placed above the altar.[30] In effect, the loggia was arranged as a temple fit for a Christian apotheosis. For information about the battles at Jarnac and Moncontour the Venetians could have made use of Tortorel and Perrisin's series of forty etchings and engravings showing episodes from the Wars of Religion; this is known to have been complete by September 1570 when it was advertised in Georg Willer's catalogue for the Frankfurt Book Fair of that year.[31] The series was surely available in Venice, one of the hubs of the print trade.[32] It has been suggested that the three principal artists chosen to work at the Lido – Palladio, Tintoretto and Titian – were selected for their ability to collaborate at speed as well as for the quality of their work.[33]

Through its use of classical motifs, the loggia at San Nicolò continued one theme that had already been established by Palladio's arch, that of Venice as the new Rome. In this equation the city was not only equivalent to the ancient capital, but was superior to it, since the triumph of Catholicism, repeatedly referred to in the paintings of both arch and loggia, raised this new civilisation to a higher level than that of pagan antiquity. The focal point for the ritual that confirmed this message was the altar, standing in the centre of this loggia-temple, where Henri now knelt surrounded by the four Victories. The traditional *Te Deum* and other pieces of music were now sung by the choir of St Mark's, and the Patriarch then

---

[30]   Benedetti, *Le feste e trionfi*, f. 6; Della Croce, *L'historia della publica et famosa entrata*, pp. 14–15.

[31]   See Philip Benedict, *Graphic History. The Wars, Massacres and Troubles of Tortorel and Perrisin* (Geneva: Droz, 2007).

[32]   See G.J. Van der Sman, 'Print Publishing in the Second Half of the Sixteenth Century', *Print Quarterly* XVII (2000), pp. 235–47; Bronwen Wilson, *The World in Venice: Print, the City and Early Modern Identity* (Toronto and Buffalo: University of Toronto Press, 2005); Fenlon, *The Ceremonial City*, Chapter 9, 'Republic of Letters, City of Books'.

[33]   Jennifer Fletcher, 'Fine Art and Festivity in Renaissance Venice: The Artist's Part', in J. Onians (ed.), *Sight and insight: essays on art and culture in honour of E.H. Gombrich at 85* (London: Phaidon, 1994), pp. 129–51 at pp. 136–7.

gave his blessing.[34] This solemn moment would have been heard by few as the choir competed with the '*strepito di trombe e di tamburi*' ('cacophony of trumpets and drums') and the noise of artillery described in the accounts.[35] Nonetheless, for those close at hand, this brief ceremony, with its echoes of a coronation, confirmed Henry's role and title of 'Most Christian Majesty'.

These sacred ceremonies finished, the procession descended the steps of the loggia and once more passed under the arch to the sound of artillery.[36] As it did so, it was confronted with a welcoming inscription framed by the complementary statues of Faith and Justice, while the paintings on this side of the arch showed Henry's official reception in Poland and the moment of his coronation, mirrored a few moments earlier in the ceremony in the loggia. The inscription read:

> *Henrico III. Franciae & Poloniae Regi Optimo atque fortissimo, hospiti incomparabili Venetorum Respub. Ob eius adventum foelicissimum.*

> [To Henry III, most superior and strong king of France, incomparable guest of the Venetian republic, on the happy occasion of his entry [into the city.]][37]

Further canvasses showed an expectant France eagerly awaiting the King's return, and the event itself, which was yet to take place.[38] This ingenious intertwining of historical events with present ceremonial critically relies upon the invocation of ritual parallels, in which the King's coronation in Poland was re-enacted on the Lido. Retracing his steps to the quay, with the Cardinal Legate to his right and the Doge to his left, Henry then boarded the *Bucintoro*. As he did so all the church bells of the city began to be rung.[39]

It was at this moment that a newly-commissioned piece of music, 'Sternitur Hadriacum, cui nam tot navibus acquor', composed by Gioseffo Zarlino, *maestro di cappella* at St Mark's Basilica, was performed by the *cappella marciana*. The text, written in elegiac distichs cast in the form of a dialogue between Hospes and a naiad (representing the Republic), had been written for the occasion by Cornelio Frangipane.[40] A lawyer in the service of the Republic, Frangipane was

---

[34]   Porcacchi, *Le attioni*, f. 24v; Benedetti, *Le feste*, f. 5; Lucangeli da Bevagna: *Successi del viaggio*, p. 31; BCV Mariegola 102 (già Cicogna 384), f. 31v.

[35]   Benedetti, *I trionfi e le gran feste*, f. 31v.

[36]   Benedetti, *Le feste e trionfi fatti* (1574), f. 6.

[37]   Reported in Della Croce, *L'historia della publica et famosa entrata*, p. 13. See also Benedetti, *Le feste e trionfi fatti* (1574), f. 4v and Domenico Zenoi's engraving where the inscription, clearly legible, is printed at the head of the sheet. For a reproduction of the latter see Fenlon, *The Ceremonial City*, p. 198.

[38]   Della Croce, *L'historia della publica et famosa entrata*, p. 14.

[39]   Benedetti, *I trionfi*, f. 32; Benedetti, *Le feste e trionfi fatti* (1574), f. 6v.

[40]   The text is given in Lucangeli da Bevagna, *Successi del viaggio*, pp. 31–2; the music does not survive.

also a published writer and poet whose most frequently reprinted work, an oration delivered in his capacity as ambassador of Friuli on the election of Doge Francesco Donato, brings together his professional functions and literary ambitions.[41] The extent to which it, or indeed Zarlino's music, could be heard in the din of artillery fire and the noise of the crowds must be doubted.[42] According to one account, the noise of ordnance and small-arms fire combined as the *Bucintoro* cast off was so great that everything seemed to descend into ruin and destruction.[43] Such practical matters were probably of secondary interest to the choreographers of the occasion; it was more important that a sense of decorum was satisfied, through the performance of a piece in Latin, the language of the educated élite, cast in a form derived from classical literature. In other words, Zarlino's piece (the music itself has not survived) was an appropriate musical response to the resonances of the ancient world evoked by Palladio's temporary structures.

This marked the end of the official rituals at the Lido. Enacted by the highest officers of Church and State, at a symbolically significant site pregnant with historical references that recalled the foundation myths of Venice itself, they achieved their effect through a compendium of cultural forms, visual, literary, musical and ceremonial, that were dense with symbolic meanings. Once Zarlino's dialogue madrigal was finished, Henry was accompanied to the *Bucintoro*, the Doge's ceremonial barge which had been freshly gilded for the occasion, and from there he was taken across the lagoon escorted by the flotilla of small craft that had been drawn up in front of Palladio's temporary structures. (Fig. 6.3) Prominent among them were the brigantines which were maintained at the expense of the trade and craft guilds of the city;[44] their involvement was a traditional feature of the official welcome given to distinguished guests, as well as an important element of the *Sensa* [ritual for the marriage of the sea]. It had been on the Doge's instructions that, on 6 July, the representatives of the guilds had been summoned before the treasurer of the *giustizia vecchia* to be given details of how their craft should be decorated and manned for the entry.[45] This included the specification that the oarsmen were to be dressed in livery adorned with the fleur-de-lis, and that there were to be twelve halberdiers on each brigantine; the overall effect was to be that of a ceremonially-attired, aquatic, armed guard. Failure to comply with these

---

[41]   Cornelio Frangipane, *Oratione ... nella creation del ... Principe Donato* (Venice, [1545]), subsequently reprinted in Francesco Sansovino, *Dell' orationi recitate a Principe di Venetia ... libro primo* (Venice: F. Sansovino, 1562) and in its subsequent editions.

[42]   Benedetti, *I trionfi*, f. 32; Benedetti, *Le feste e trionfi fatti*, f. 6v.

[43]   Della Croce, *L'historia della publica et famosa entrata*, p. 15: 'movendosi il Bucintoro diedero nelle trombe, e tamburi, e nelle varsi dal Lido quivi li Castelli, tutte le Galee, Fuste, Bregantini, Palaschermi, e barche armate fecero cosi stupenda, et maravigliosa salva d'artigliera, d'archibugi, e moschetti, con tanta corrispondenza in un' istesso tempo, che per tremendo strepito pareva ogni cosa ruinasse, e cadesse'.

[44]   BCV 1897, unfoliated.

[45]   BCV, MS Mariegola 102 (già Cicogna 384), ff. 29v–32.

Figure 6.3   Master G.M., *The Reception of Henry III at the Lido*, engraving. Private collection.

guidelines would result in a fine. In practice there was considerable competition between the different guilds to achieve the most spectacular results. The craft fitted out by the silk merchants was said to be particularly elegant,[46] while one of the chroniclers singled out for special mention the brigantine of the mirror-gilders, which was festooned with examples of their work to catch the reflections of the sun.[47] With the official reception at the Lido finished, this extraordinary armada now accompanied the *Bucintoro* and its royal guest through the lagoon to the *bacino* from where Henry was taken down the Grand Canal to his allotted residence at Ca' Foscari.[48] During the days that followed Henry was lavishly entertained with a visit to the Arsenal, another to St Mark's Basilica, and a ball

[46]   Richard S. Mackenney, *Tradesmen and Traders: The World of the Guilds in Venice and Europe, c. 1250–c. 1650* (London and Sydney: Croom Helm, 1987), p. 144.

[47]   Porcacchi, *Le attioni d'Arrigo terzo*, f. 24v.

[48]   Henry and his retainers occupied both Ca' Foscari and the two adjoining Giustiniani palaces, which made it easy to pass from one to the other; see BNM MS. It. VII. (2585) (*olim* Philipps MS. 2514), p. 254. All three had been prepared at public expense; see BNM MS. It. VII. 73 (8265), f. 405v.

in the Ducal Palace.[49] Almost nightly he was treated to music performed from a temporary pontoon moored outside his lodgings,[50] and on his final day in the city the king was accompanied to the Ducal Palace where mass was heard and he took his leave. In a gilded barge the royal party went first to Padua, and then to Mantua, Ferrara and finally Turin, from where he mounted his return to France.

When, in the spring of 1573, less than two years after the victory of the Holy League over the Turks at Lepanto in October 1571, the Venetians contracted a separate peace treaty with the Ottomans, there was anger, disgust and embarrassment, but no great surprise. Philip II, on hearing of the Republic's decision from the two Venetian ambassadors in Madrid, replied with an almost imperceptible and ironic movement and the words: 'You have replied exactly as they told me you would'.[51] Once again, as in 1540, the Venetians had behaved according to type. Despite Spanish anger, Papal disapproval, and even the discomfort of some Venetian ambassadors abroad, reduced to listening to condemnations of the Republic, the Venetians rode the storm. Cyprus had been lost and the size of the indemnity which had to be paid was high, but in return the prized trading agreements which guaranteed access to the markets in the Levant were restored. The bonds which had bound together the members of the League, which in truth had never been strong, were now shattered. In the months which followed the separate peace treaty, Venice had need of friends.

The visit of Henry III could not have occurred at a more felicitous juncture. In addition to meeting the post-Lepanto mood, it also put the seal on an alliance which the Republic had been carefully fostering for decades, at least since the Treaty of Cateau Cambrésis of 1559 which had effectively installed Habsburg Spain as the masters of Italy, while France abandoned all claims to Italy and surrendered Corsica, a major strategic base in the Mediterranean.[52] This left Savoy and Venice as the only truly independent entities on the Italian peninsula. When, on passing through Turin on his way back to France, Henry presented the fortresses

---

[49]   For the events of the following days see Nutter, 'A Tragedy for Henri III'; Rebecca A. Edwards, 'Claudio Merulo: Servant of the State and Musical Entrepreneur in Later Sixteenth-Century Venice' (PhD dissertation, Princeton University, 1990), pp. 223–8; Robert C. Davis, 'The Spectacle Almost Fit for a King: Venice's Guerra de' canne of 26 July 1574', in Ellen E. Kittell and Thomas F. Madden (eds), *Medieval and Renaissance Venice* (Urbana and Chicago, Il: University of Illinois Press, 1999), pp. 181–212; Fenlon, *The Ceremonial City*, pp. 204–15.

[50]   Some of the music performed has survived; see David Bryant, 'Andrea Gabrieli e la musica di stato', in *Andrea Gabrieli, 1585–1985* (Venice: Biennale di Venezia, 1985), pp. 29–45 at p. 38; Nutter, 'A Tragedy for Henri III', p. 596; Stras, *'Onde havrà'l mond'esempio'*, pp. 19–21; Fenlon, *The Ceremonial City*, pp. 205–8.

[51]   Mario Brunetti and Eligio Vitale (eds), *La corrispondenza da Madrid dell' ambasciatore Leonardo Donà (1570–73)* (2 vols, Venice and Rome: 1963), 2/262 at p. 680.

[52]   For a balance-sheet, which includes assessment of the English dimension, see Fernand Braudel, *The Mediterranean and the Mediterranean World in the Age of Philip II*, trans. S. Reynolds (2 vols, London: Collins, 1975), vol. 2, pp. 945–9.

of Pignerolo and Savigliano to the Duke of Savoy, it seemed to the outraged Duke of Nevers, who had accompanied the king from the moment that he had set foot in the Veneto, that Henry had opted 'to close the door for ever on [going] to Italy, after seeing with his own eyes the beauty of that land'.[53]

To many Venetians the decade of the 1570s must have seemed a time of reckoning with the Almighty. Both the victory at Lepanto and the visit of Henry III were celebrated as signs of God's favour towards a Chosen People, but these moments of triumph and glory, underpinned with all the resources of the state ceremonial apparatus, were framed by disasters. In the process of mythogenesis that was designed to obfuscate and obscure as much as to celebrate, the arts were engaged in a way that is highly revealing of Venetian sensibilities and political processes in these troubled years. Music, liturgy and ceremony, literature, architecture and painting were all brought into service as the Venetian ruling class attempted to inscribe the events of the post-Lepanto years into an heroic narrative that effectively underplayed political realities. In this context Henry's visit was seen not only as an opportune moment to strengthen an important alliance but also a much-needed sign of the special status of the Republic in the eyes of the Almighty, and of its imperial image. In the event it was an impression that was to be short-lived as, in the following summer, the plague that inflicted Venice for two years and carried off one quarter of the population, took hold. As Doge Mocenigo recognised in a speech made to the Senate in 1576, this epidemic was one of a sequence of calamities that had afflicted the Republic since the War of Cyprus, all of them portents of divine wrath.[54] Against this background, the visit of Henry III was a brief and exuberant diversion from reality.

Bibliography

Primary Sources

Manuscripts
BCV, MS Mariegola 102 (già Cicogna 384), ff. 29v–32.
BNM MS. It. VII. 73 (8265), f. 405.
BNM MS. It. VII. 365 (7934), f. 60.
BNM MS. It. VII. 393 (8647); BNM MS It. VII 73 (8265), ff. 403–8 and the anonymous account in BNP MS Fonds Italien 799.
BNM MS. It. VII. 2585 (*olim* Philipps MS. 2514).

---

[53] Braudel, *The Mediterranean and the Mediterranean World*, vol. 2, pp. 946–7.
[54] BNM MS. It. VII. 365 (7934), f. 60.

Printed

Benedetti, Rocco, *I trionfi et le gran feste fatte dalla Serenissima Signoria di Venetia nella venuta del Christianissimo, et invitissmo Henrico III di Francia et di Polonia* (1574).

Benedetti, Rocco, *Le feste e trionfi fatti dalla serenissima signoria di Venetia nella felice venuta di Henrico III Christianissimo Re di Francia et III di Polonia* (Venice, 1574).

Caroli, Paschali Cuneatis, *Ad Henricum III Francorum regem oratio* (Venice: A. Muschio, 1574).

Da Bevagna, Nicolo Lucangeli, *Successi del viaggio d'Henrico III christianiss[i]mo re di Francia, e di Polonia, dalla sua partita di Cracovia fino all'arrivo in Turino* (Venice, 1574)

De Nolhac, Pierre and Angelo Solerti, *Il viaggio di Henrico III re di Francia e le feste a Venezia, Ferrara, Mantova e Torino* (Turin, 1890).

Della Croce, Marsilio, *L'historia della publica et famosa entrata in Vinegia del serenissimo Henrico III di Francia et Polonia con la descrittione particolare della pompa, e del numero, et varieta delli bregantini, paleschermi, et altrivascelli, con la dechiaratione dell'edificio, et arco fatto al Lido* (Venice: [Comin da Trino], 1574).

Frangipane, Cornelio, *Oratione ... nella creation del ... Principe Donato* (Venice, [1545]; reprinted in Francesco Sansovino, *Dell'orationi recitate a Principe di Venetia ... libro primo* (Venice: F. Sansovino, 1562).

I gran trionfi fatti nella nobil città di Treviso nella venuta del Christianissimo Re di Francia & di Polonia Henrico Terzo (Venice, 1574).

La vie et moeurs de messier Guy du Faur, seigneur de Pybrac (Paris: Thibault du Val, 1617).

Le allegrezze et solennita fatta in Cracovia citta principale del regno di Polonia (Venice, 1574).

Manzini, G., *Il gloriosissimo apparato fatto dalla serenissima republica venetiana per la venuta, per la dimora, & per la partenza del christianiss[i]mo Enrico III re di Francia e di Polonia* (Venice: G. Percachino, 1574).

Porcacchi, Tommaso, *Le attioni d'Arrigo terzo re di Francia et quarto di Polonia descritte in dialogo* (Venice: G. Angelieri, 1574).

Sansovino, Francesco, *Dell'orationi recitate a Principe di Venetia ... libro primo* (Venice: F. Sansovino, 1562).

Secondary Sources

Ackerman, James, S., *Palladio* (Harmondsworth: Penguin, 1966).

Artioli, Umberto and C. Grazioli (eds), *I Gonzaga e l'Impero: itinerary dello spettacolo* (Florence: Le lettere, 2005).

Bellina, Anna Laura, 'A suon di musica da Cracovia a Lione: i trionfi del cristianissimo Enrico III', in Umberto Artioli and C. Grazioli (eds), *I Gonzaga e l'Impero: itinerary dello spettacolo* (Florence: Le Lettere, 2005), pp. 81–106.

Benedict, Philip, *Graphic History. The Wars, Massacres and Troubles of Tortorel and Perrisin* (Geneva: Droz, 2007).

Boltanski, Ariane, *Les ducs de Nevers et l'etat royal. Genèse d'un compromis (ca. 1550–ca. 1600)* (Geneva: Droz, 2006).

Boucher, Bruce, *Andrea Palladio: The Architect in his Time* (New York and London: Abberville, 1994).

Braudel, Fernand, *The Mediterranean and the Mediterranean World in the Age of Philip II*, trans. S. Reynolds (2 vols, London: Collins, 1975).

Brown, Patricia Fortini, 'Measured Friendship, Calculated Pomp: The Ceremonial Welcomes of the Venetian Republic' in Barbara Wisch and S. Scott Munshower (eds), *'All the World's a Stage ...': Art and Pageantry in the Renaissance and Baroque* (2 Parts, University Park, Pa: Pennsylvania State University, 1990), Part 2, pp. 137–86.

Brunetti, Mario and Eligio Vitale (eds), *La corrispondenza da Madrid dell' ambasciatore Leonardo Donà (1570–73)* (2 vols, Venice and Rome, 1963).

Bryant, David, 'Andrea Gabrieli e la musica di stato', in [No named editor], *Andrea Gabrieli, 1585–1985* (Venice: Biennale di Venezia, settoremusica, 1985), pp. 29–45.

Capra, Marco (ed.), *A Messer Claudio, Musico. Le arti molteplici di Claudio Merulo da Correggio (1533–1604) tra Venezia e Parma* (Venice, Parma, Marsilio: Casa della musica, 2006).

Champion, Henri, *'La maison et l'entourage de Henri III en Pologne', Revue d'humanisme et Renaissance*, VII (1940), pp. 286–308.

Cooper, Tracy E., *Palladio's Venice: architecture and society in a Renaissance Republic* (New Haven and London: Yale University Press, 2005).

Davis, Robert C., 'The Spectacle Almost Fit for a King: Venice's Guerra de' canne of 26 July 1574', in Ellen E. Kittell and Thomas F. Madden (eds), *Medieval and Renaissance Venice* (Urbana and Chicago, Il: University of Illinois Press, 1999), pp. 181–212.

Edwards, Rebecca A., 'Claudio Merulo: Servant of the State and Musical Entrepreneur in Later Sixteenth-Century Venice' (PhD dissertation, Princeton University, 1990).

Fenlon, Iain, 'Merulo and State Ceremonial: The Visit to Venice of Henri III', in Marco Capra (ed.), *A Messer Claudio, Musico. Le arti molteplici di Claudio Merulo da Correggio (1533–1604) tra Venezia e Parma* (Venice, Parma, Marsilio: Casa dellamusica, 2006), pp. 261–76.

Fenlon, Iain, *The Ceremonial City: History, Memory and Myth in Renaissance Venice* (New Haven and London: Yale University Press, 2007).

Fletcher, Jennifer, 'Fine Art and Festivity in Renaissance Venice: The Artist's Part', in J. Onians (ed.), *Sight and insight: essays on art and culture in honour of E.H. Gombrich at 85* (London: Phaidon, 1994), pp. 129–51.

Howard, Deborah, *Jacopo Sansovino: Architecture and Patronage in Renaissance Venice* (New Haven and London: Yale University Press, 1975).

Ivanoff, Nicolai, 'Henri III a Venise', *Gazette des Beaux-Arts* LXXX (1972), pp. 313–30.

Kittell, Ellen E. and Thomas F. Madden (eds), *Medieval and Renaissance Venice* (Urbana and Chicago, Il: University of Illinois Press, 1999).

Knecht, R.J., et al., 'The Festivals for Henri III in Cracow, Venice, Orléans and Rouen', in J.R. Mulryne, Helen Watanabe-O'Kelly and Margaret Shewring (eds), *Europa Triumphans: Court and Civic Festivals in Early Modern Europe* (2 vols, Aldershot: Ashgate, 2004), vol. 1, pp. 103–215.

MacDonald, Katherine M., 'Diplomacy and Biography in the Wars of Religion: Charles Paschal's Life of Guy du Faur de Pibrac (1584)', in Bruno Tribout and Ruth Whelan (eds), *Narrating the Self in Early Modern Europe* (Oxford and Berlin: Lang, 2007), pp. 23–40.

Mackenney, Richard S., *Tradesmen and Traders: The World of the Guilds in Venice and Europe, c. 1250–c. 1650* (London and Sydney: Croom Helm, 1987).

Morrogh, Andrew, et al. (eds), *Renaissance Studies in Honor of Craig Hugh Smyth* (2 vols, Florence: Giunti Barbèra, 1985).

Muir, Edward, *Civic Ritual in Renaissance Venice* (Princeton NJ: Princeton University Press, 1981).

Mulryne, J.R. and Elizabeth Goldring (eds.), *Court Festivals of the European Renaissance: Art, Politics and Performance* (Aldershot: Ashgate, 2002).

Mulryne, J.R., Helen Watanabe-O'Kelly and Margaret Shewring (eds), *Europa Triumphans: Court and Civic Festivals in Early Modern Europe* (2 vols, Aldershot: Ashgate, 2004).

Nutter, David, 'A Tragedy for Henri III of France, Venice, 1574', in A. Morrogh et al. (eds), *Renaissance Studies in Honor of Craig Hugh Smyth* (2 vols, Florence: Giunti Barbèra, 1985), vol. 1, pp. 591–611.

Onians, J. (ed.), *Sight and insight: essays on art and culture in honour of E.H. Gombrich at 85* (London: Phaidon, 1994).

Pincus, Debra, *The Tombs of the Doges of Venice* (Cambridge: Cambridge University Press, 2000).

Rosand, D. (ed.), *Interpretazioni veneziane: studi di storia dell'arte in onore di Michelangelo Muraro* (Venice: Arsenale editrice, 1984).

Rosand, David, *Myths of Venice: The Figuration of a State* (Chapel Hill, NC and London: University of North Carolina Press, 2001).

Rosand, David, 'Venetia figurata: The Iconography of a Myth', in D. Rosand (ed.), *Interpretazioni veneziane: studi di storia dell'arte in onore di Michelangelo Muraro* (Venice: Arsenale editrice, 1984), pp. 177–96.

Selig, K.L. and E. Sears (eds), *The Verbal and the Visual: Essays in Honor of William Sebastian Heckscher* (New York: Italica Press, 1990), pp. 213–23.

Stone, Daniel, *The Polish–Lithuanian State, 1386–1795: A History of East Central Europe* (Seattle and London: University of Washington Press, 2001).

Stras, Laurie, '"Onde havrà'l esempio et vera historia": Musical Echoes of Henri III's Progress through Italy', *Acta musicologica* LXXII (2000), pp. 7–41.

Tribout, Bruno and Ruth Whelan (eds), *Narrating the Self in Early Modern Europe* (Oxford and Berlin: Lang, 2007).

Tondro, Maximilian L.S., 'The First Temporary Triumphal Arch in Venice (1557)', in J.R. Mulryne and Elizabeth Goldring (eds), *Court Festivals of the European Renaissance: Art, Politics and Performance* (Aldershot: Ashgate, 2002), pp. 335–62.

Van der Sman, G.J., 'Print Publishing in the Second Half of the Sixteenth Century', *Print Quarterly* XVII (2000), pp. 235–47.

Venditti, Arnaldo, *La loggia del capitaniato* (Vicenza: Centro Internationale di Studi di Architettura Andrea Palladio, 1969).

Verheyen, Egon, 'The Triumphal Arch on the Lido: On the Reliability of Eyewitness Accounts', in K.L. Selig and E. Sears (eds), *The Verbal and the Visual: Essays in Honor of William Sebastian Heckscher* (New York: Italica Press, 1990), pp. 213–23.

Whitehead, Arthur Whiston, *Gaspard de Coligny, Admiral of France* (London: Methuen, 1904).

Wilson, Bronwen, *The World in Venice: Print, the City and Early Modern Identity* (Toronto and Buffalo: University of Toronto Press, 2005).

Wisch, Barbara and S. Scott Munshower (eds), *'All the World's a Stage': Art and Pageantry in the Renaissance and Baroque* (2 Parts, University Park, PA: Pennsylvania State University, 1990).

Wittkower, Rudolf, *Architectural Principles in the Age of Humanism*, 4th edn (London: Academy Editions, 1973).

Wolters, Wolfgang, 'Le architecture erette al lido per l'ingresso di Enrico III a Venezianel 1574', *Bolletino del centro internazionale di studi di architettura Andrea Palladio*, 21(1979), pp. 280–88.

Chapter 7

Water Policy and Water Festivals: the Case of Pisa Under Ferdinando de' Medici (1588–1609)

Maria Ines Aliverti

The Sequence of Festivities in 1588–89

When Ferdinando de' Medici made his triumphal entry into Pisa on 31 March 1588, he had only recently become Grand Duke of Tuscany.[1] Significantly, after the funeral of Francesco I in December 1587 and Ferdinando's proclamation as Grand Duke, Pisa provided the frame for the first important ceremony of his government. When read carefully, Ferdinando's entry into Pisa confirms the reinforcement of the Tuscan territorial state, combining the necessary theme of the continuity of Medici power with a personal political agenda, almost as a signal of the fact that the Grand Duke had long been preparing for this debut. For Ferdinando, as

---

[1]   Exceptionally two printed descriptions were produced on this Pisan entry: Giovanni Cervoni da Colle, *Descrizzione de la felicissima entrata del Serenis. D. Ferdinando de' Medici cardinale, gran duca di Toscana nella città di Pisa. Con tutti gli archi trionfali, portoni, apparati, imprese, e motti, con le loro interpretazioni, e significati; e con le loro composizioni, che ci si son fatte: con le feste, lumi, fuochi artifiziali, et altri segni d'allegrezze* (Florence: Giorgio Marescotti, 1588); Francesco Dini da Colle, *Trionfi e feste fatte nella città di Pisa. Per l'enrrata [sic!] fatta in essa dal serenissimo Gran Duca di Toscana, il signore don Ferdinando cardinale Medici* (Florence: Francesco Dini da Colle, 1588). Although shorter, Dini's account is more informative in some notable details. There is an anonymous and incomplete manuscript report: *Entrata solenne del G. Duca Ferdinando a Pisa* (Archivio di Stato di Firenze, Mediceo del Principato, 6377, fols 61–4), whose central sheets were missing before numbering. See also: Anna Maria Testaverde, 'Feste medicee: la visita, le nozze e il trionfo', in Marcello Fagiolo (ed.), *La città effimera e l'universo artificiale del giardino* (Rome: Officina, 1980), pp. 69–97; Stefano Renzoni, 'Pisa tra mito e storia nelle feste granducali cinque-seicentesche', in *La festa, la rappresentazione popolare, il lavoro: Momenti della cultura e della tradizione in territorio pisano, XVI–XIX sec.* (Pisa: Archivio di Stato, 1984), pp. 59–75, and 'Documenti', pp. 76–94; Maria Ines Aliverti, 'Pisa: la scena urbana', in Marcello Fagiolo (ed.), *Atlante tematico del Barocco in Italia. Le capitali della festa: Italia centrale e meridionale* (2 vols, Rome: De Luca, 2007), vol. 2, pp. 141–9, with a map showing the itinerary of the entry and the location of the apparati (p. 142).

had been the case for Cosimo I and Eleonora in Siena (28 November 1560),[2] the entry into a subject city could act as a symbolic demonstration of the power of the prince, with the important difference that for Ferdinando the entry into Pisa closely followed his proclamation as his brother's successor. In his entry into Pisa, having retained the office of cardinal-deacon of the Holy Roman Church, he wore the cardinal's robes (Fig. 7.1) that he would only cast off at the end of November 1588, and rode under a canopy on the back of a white mule. A few months later, in April 1589, his bride Christine of Lorraine arrived by sea, sailing from Marseilles on the flagship of the Santo Stefano [St Stephen] fleet decorated for the occasion. When she disembarked at Livorno (24 April), she was welcomed by splendid ceremonies in Pisa (24–27 April), and then she was celebrated in the magnificent festivities in Florence in May.[3]

This significant festival sequence along the Pisa–Florence axis has always been underestimated if not ignored,[4] overshadowed by the Florentine magnificence and by a reading that has focussed, from Warburg onwards, on the importance of neo-Platonic themes, understood as the main vehicle of political expression and interpreted magnificently in the well-known *intermezzi* during the comedy *La pellegrina* performed at the Teatro degli Uffizi, on 2 and 15 May 1589. This paper intends to put forward a different reading, which does not call into question previous findings, but aims to establish more correctly the significance of a politically relevant fact such as the Pisa–Florence axis in order to understand fully what I would call the sequence of festivities in 1588–89: a sequence in which the theme of water played an important role.

---

    [2]   Anna Maria Testaverde Matteini, 'La decorazione festiva e l'itinerario di "rifondazione" della città negli ingressi trionfali a Firenze tra XV e XVI secolo (II)', *Mitteilungen des Kunsthistorischen Institutes in Florenz*, 34 (1990), pp. 165–98: pp. 166–73; I am preparing a critical edition of printed and manuscript sources concerning Ferdinando's entry, in collaboration with Donatella Fratini.
    [3]   On the festivities in Pisa see the printed source of Giovanni Cervoni da Colle, *Descrizzione de le pompe, e feste fatte ne la città di Pisa. Per la venuta de la sereniss. madama Christierna de l'Oreno gran duchessa di Toscana [...]* (Florence: Giorgio Marescotti, 1589). The bibliography on the 1589 festival in Florence is enormous. Two studies are immensely valuable for accurately recording manuscript, printed and iconographical sources and for bibliographical references: Anna Maria Testaverde, 'L'officina delle nuvole. Il Teatro Mediceo nel 1589 e gli Intermedi del Buontalenti nel Memoriale di Girolamo Seriacopi', *Musica e Teatro. Quaderni degli Amici della Scala*, 7 (June–October 1991), monographic issue; James M. Saslow, *Medici Wedding of 1589: Florentine festival as Theatrum Mundi* (New Haven and London: Yale University Press, 1996).
    [4]   Both Testaverde, 'Officina delle nuvole' and Saslow, *Medici Wedding of 1589*, exclusively focus upon Florentine festivities. The Livorno–Pisa–Florence axis in Ferdinand's political thought and in the correspondent festival policy is not taken into consideration in the recent catalogue of a Florentine exhibition *Ferdinando de' Medici 1549–1609: Maiestate Tantum* (Lavorno: Sillabe, 2009).

Figure 7.1   Alessandro Allori, *Ferdinando de' Medici Grand Duke of Tuscany in his cardinal's robes*, 1588, oil on canvas. Pisa, Museo Nazionale di Palazzo Reale. © Soprintendenza per i Beni Architettonici, Paesaggistici, Artistici, Storici ed Etnoantropologici per le province di Pisa e Livorno.

The Meanings of Water in the Sequence of Festivities in 1588–89

The theme of water had already been afforded considerable space in many important artistic and festive productions commissioned by the Medici, especially in the gardens of their villas (the work of Tribolo in Villa Castello, for example, or that of Buontalenti in the Parco di Pratolino and the Boboli Gardens): hydraulic science and the government of waters, conducted expertly to sprinkle gardens, combined with the celebration of water as a vital force symbolized by the personifications of rivers and springs and by the endless gushing of fountains.

It is no coincidence that Tribolo intended to represent the statue of *Fiorenza*, on the top of the fountain in the garden of Castello (1538–50), as a Naiad (or a Venus Anadyomene) wringing her long hair, from which a stream of water flowed.[5] Her left foot rested on a large urn, similar to that which characterized river deities: a reference to the Arno, but also to other rivers and streams which cross the whole of Tuscany. A bronze ring at the base of the statue bore the symbols of several Tuscan cities, including Pisa. This creation symbolized exactly the synthesis of a triple dominion: Fiorenza, the waters and the territory, in which Fiorenza played the dominant role.

The theme of water was by now an almost codified feature. On the ceiling decoration of the Salone dei Cinquecento various panels show views of the Tuscan cities and countryside in association with the allegorical figures of their rivers. This association signified an inseparable union: power over cities was strictly linked to government of the territory, and the government of the territory meant above all the government of the waters, ensuring the fertility of the land and the success of harvests. The festivals and entries of the Medici were no exception. In 1539, after the banquet for the wedding of Cosimo I and Eleonora di Toledo in the second courtyard of the Palazzo Medici, a musical representation was staged featuring personifications of Tuscan cities and rivers. They were called upon to pay their homage to the bride.[6] However, in relation to the theme of water, the sequence of festivities in 1588–89 presented several important developments, full of political significance and intended to demonstrate both the continuity of Ferdinando's rule

---

[5] The statue is known in the version by Giambologna (1572 ca.), Villa La Petraia, Castello, near Florence. On the iconographical theme of Tuscan rivers and cities represented by Tribolo in the fountain, see Cristina Acidini Luchinat and Giorgio Galletti, *Le ville e i giardini di Castello e Petraia a Firenze* (Pisa, 1992), pp. 193–5. On the successful motif of the goddess wringing out her hair see Enrico Maria Dal Pozzolo, *Colori d'amore* (Treviso, 2008), pp. 86–111.

[6] Pier Francesco Giambullari, *Apparato et feste nelle noze dello illustrissimo signor duca di Firenze, & della duchessa sua consorte, con le sue stanze, madriali, comedia, & intermedij, in quelle recitati* (Florence: Benedetto Giunta, 1539), pp. 41–64; Angeli Ubaldo, *Personificazione delle città, paesi e fiumi di Toscana festeggianti le nozze di Cosimo I ed Eleonora di Toledo* (Prato: n. p., 1898).

with Cosimo's and Francesco's policies, and his precise direction with regard to the rule and administration of the territory, the fruit of his long experience in Rome.

In the festivities in Pisa and Florence in 1588 and 1589 we once again find allegorical figures of Tuscan cities and rivers expressed in ephemeral decorations, street and theatrical entertainments. This type of representation took on special importance in the street procession of Neptune and river Gods (*Mascherata dei fiumi*) organized in honour of the Grand Duchess Christine of Lorraine on 28 May 1589, probably an intentional reminder of the festivities of 1539. An engraving by Epifanio d'Alfiano features the God Neptune on a chariot and Rivers carrying cornucopias and urns in front of the Palazzo Pitti.[7] Among the ephemeral decorations set up for Christine's entry in Florence (30 April), the monochrome painting by Ligozzi, at the centre of the façade of Palazzo Vecchio, was the 'most significant statement about Medici rule in the entire entry'.[8] It represented the allegorical crowning of modern Tuscany by Cosimo I (Fig. 7.2): here the personification of Tuscany in regal dress was encircled by the allegorical figures of Tuscan rivers (Arno, Magra, Tevere, Arbia), sea (Tirreno) and mountains (Appennini), to signify the borders of the territorial dominion of the Grand Duchy.[9]

The continuity with Cosimo's policies was also embodied in the organization of the two *naumachiae* of 1589, the first great spectacles of this kind in Tuscany: the one (the 'Battle of Galleons') fought on the Arno in Pisa to celebrate the arrival of Christine on 24 April and the other (the 'Sea Battle') fought in the courtyard of the Palazzo Pitti in Florence on 11 May.[10] In line with Cosimo's policy, Ferdinando wanted to underline the importance of the maritime dominion of Tuscany and of the

---

[7]   Saslow, *Medici Wedding*, catalogue 88, p. 261.

[8]   Roy C. Strong, *Art and Power: Renaissance Festivals, 1450–1650* (2nd ed.,Woodbridge: Boydell Press, 1984), p. 132.

[9]   The painting is now lost, but we can refer to the preparatory drawing (400 x 290 mm), London, British Museum, no. 1874-8-8-3 (Figure 2) and to the engraving after Ligozzi's composition by Cherubino Alberti, *Diadema Porsenae Regis negligentia amissum* (265 x 255 mm), Bartsch vol. 17, n. 157, reproduced in Testaverde, *Decorazione festiva*, p. 193. An etching, also after Ligozzi, illustrates the printed description by Raffaello Gualterotti, *Della descrizione del regale apparato fatto nella nobile città di Firenze per la venuta, e per le nozze della serenissima madama Cristina di Loreno moglie del serenissimo Ferdinando Medici terzo gran duca di Toscana. Libro secondo* (Florence: Antonio Padovani, 1589), pp. 168–70, reproduced in Strong, *Art and Power*, ill. n. 86. There is an ideologically relevant inconsistency between Ligozzi's allegorical composition and the printed description (p. 168), but it will not be discussed in the present chapter. In Ripa's *Iconologia*, Tuscany is associated with the river Arno ('the main river that passes through half of Tuscany and receives many benefits from it'), and that by metonymy indicates the abundance of waters ('seas, rivers and springs') that characterizes the land of this fortunate and 'regal' region, Cesare Ripa, *Iconologia*, ed. Piero Buscaroli (Milan: TEA, 1992), pp. 209–11.

[10]   See J.R. Mulryne's chapter in this collection, pp. 143–75.

Figure 7.2   Jacopo Ligozzi, *The allegorical crowning of Tuscany by Cosimo I*, 400 × 290 mm, drawing, London, British Museum, Department of Prints & Drawings, no. 1847-8-8-3. © The Trustees of the British Museum.

Maritime Military Order of Santo Stefano founded in 1562,[11] although in terms of festive typology the revival of this classical nautical celebration was also undoubtedly related to the desire to pay homage to the tradition of the Valois festivals.

A demonstration of skill in naval combat is especially evident in the Pisan battle of 24 April, which was a full-fledged military spectacle, without any allegorical-festive characteristics, except for the costumes of the 'Arab' and 'Turkish' combatants. The fake battle was conceived as a varied succession of boardings and moments of pure combat.[12] Under festive appearances, the show signified

---

[11]   Franco Angiolini, *I cavalieri e il principe: L'ordine di Santo Stefano e la società toscana in età moderna* (Florence: Edifir, 1996).

[12]   These two *naumachiae* have been recently studied by Maria Alberti who has demonstrated their close parallelism with real war practice. See Maria Alberti, 'Battaglie navali, scorrerie corsare e politica dello spettacolo: Le Naumachie medicee del 1589', *Californian Italian Studies Journal*, 1(1), pp. 1–33, retrieved from http://www.escholarship. org/uc/item/8553h705, publication date: 17 February 2010. The influence of real war tactics is detectable also in the invention of other contemporary games (i.e. the Florentine Calcio

the Grand Duke's strategic plan, that is, his desire to win regal sovereignty for Tuscany as the second Italian state after the Republic of Venice, counting precisely on maritime ports and shipyards and on the prestige of the Order of Santo Stefano, that is, on Livorno and Pisa respectively. This political strategy is displayed in an iconological synthesis, by Volterrano, as a posthumous celebration of Ferdinando I. In this fresco from the series of the so-called 'Fasti Medicei', at the Villa Petraia, Tuscany in regal dress advances towards the sea accompanied by the allegorical personifications of Livorno and Pisa, the latter as a woman carrying the escutcheon of Santo Stefano's Knights.[13]

The theme of maritime power was also hinted at in the fifth intermedio of *La pellegrina*, on the stage of the Teatro degli Uffizi. The episode of the *Rescue of Arion*, drawn from Plutarch's *Moralia*, was intended to illustrate the effect of music on the soul (*musica humana*) in relation to the element of water, just as in the remaining intermedi the instances of *musica humana* (intermedi 2 and 3) and *musica mondana* (the cosmic significance of music: intermedi 1, 4 and 6) were associated with the elements of air, earth and fire, according to the Neoplatonic theory of the whole cycle.

In the fifth intermedio the scene in the Uffizi '*si coperse tutta di scogli marittimi, e 'l palco divenne mare ondeggiante, circondato da quegli scogli, che pareano dirocciati monti*' ('was covered entirely in sea rocks and the stage became an undulating Sea, surrounded by cliffs that seemed to be rocky mountains').[14] This scenery is approximately visualized in the etching by Epifanio d'Alfiano (Fig. 7.3), from the famous series of six prints by the same d'Alfiano and Agostino Carracci, illustrating Buontalenti's *Intermedi*. On the rocky shores in the background of the stage set, we notice various towers, a clear reference to maritime fortifications. In my opinion, this background pointed to a specific and recognizable place: the stretch of Tuscan coast which was at this moment a burning political issue. This association is particularly evident if we compare the preparatory drawing by Andrea Boscoli,[15] with the contemporary views and maps of the Tuscan coast. The

---

and the Gioco del Ponte) into which the tradition of popular *battagliole* and the courtly practise of armed entertainments merged.

[13]   Baldassarre Franceschini called Il Volterrano, *Allegory of the Maritime Glory of Tuscany*, 1637 ca. Villa Petraia, Castello near Florence. See Riccardo Spinelli, 'Gli affreschi di Baldassare Franceschini, il Volterrano a Villa "La Petraia": iconografia medicea e orgoglio dinastico', in Mina Gregori (ed.), *Fasto di corte: La decorazione murale nelle residenze dei Medici e dei Lorena* (4 vols, Florence: Edifir, 2005–09), vol. 2 (2006), *L'età di Ferdinando II de' Medici (1628–1670)*, pp. 13–30.

[14]   Bastiano de' Rossi, *Descrizione dell'apparato e degli intermedi. Fatti per la commedia rappresentata in Firenze. Nelle nozze de' serenissimi don Ferdinando Medici e madonna Cristina di Lorena gran duchi di Toscana* (Florence: Anton Padovani, 1589), p. 55.

[15]   The drawing, 223 x 347 mm (Paris, Louvre, Cabinet des Dessins, n. 866), a copy after Buontalenti's lost scene sketch, was made by Andrea Boscoli in view of being engraved. Its reproduction is accessible on http:// www.photo.rmn.fr. (Fig. 7.3) is reversed

Figure 7.3   Bernardo Buontalenti designer. Epifanio d'Alfiano engraver, *The Rescue of Arion*, etching, 245 × 350 mm, 1589. Pisa, Private collection. © Maria Ines Aliverti (Dipartimento di Storia delle Arti – Università di Pisa).

scenic perspective view, corresponding to the central part of the stage set, shows the coast from the Piombino channel towards Livorno and Pisa. Proceeding from the back onwards, it features the two towers of the ancient Pisan harbour (the Torracce) between the continental coast and the isles of Gorgona and Capraia, represented in perspective as a double imposing mass of escarped rocks. Further afield, a lighthouse situated on a small rocky island near the continental coast is recognizable as the Torre del Fanale outside the port of Livorno. The watch tower on the left, flanked by an overhanging cliff, suggests a view of the north-east coast of the isle of Elba: the tower here could signify the fortified Medicean harbour of Portoferraio, through a reference to the Torre della Linguella, or even the East Elba iron-mines district which the Medici exploited by concession, through a reference to the Torre degli Appiani watching the little harbour of Rio. This synthetic view summarized the prevailing theme of Ferdinando's political aspiration to maritime power, featuring symbols of the three Medicean maritime towns and strongholds: Pisa, Livorno and Portoferraio or Rio. Buontalenti who had directed the fortifications of Livorno and Portoferraio, carefully adapted his

from Boscoli's drawing. Saslow, *Medici Wedding*, pp. 234–6 and illustrations 54 and 55. About the contribution of Boscoli to 1589 festivities see Nadia Bastogi, *Andrea Boscoli* (Florence: Edifir, 2008), pp. 67–78.

scenic view of the Tuscan coast to the needs of a stage perspective, limiting it to the background area, and not encroaching on the practicable part of the stage, where the mythical and allegorical subject of the intermezzo was displayed.[16] At the same time, this urgent political theme was emphasized by being placed at the centre of the scenic composition under the eyes of a multitude of illustrious international guests who attended the wedding ceremonies. Actually as soon as he became Grand Duke, Ferdinando showed his strong aspirations to represent a maritime power, starting the works for a new spacious basin (Grande Darsena)[17] in the port of Livorno and enlarging the fortified area of the town.

By means of various diplomatic initiatives, he attempted to assert his interests concerning control over the maritime channel of Piombino. These initiatives triggered a strong political threat to Spanish maritime power, thus rekindling the still open controversy concerning the Stato de' Presidi. The crisis peaked when Ferdinando ordered a lighthouse to be built on the Meloria island in 1599, thus clearly asserting his claims to Tuscan territorial waters.[18] Was this striking political significance also embodied in the Arion's myth? Shall we see Ferdinando as a new Arion spoiled by greedy Spaniards and saved in his waters by a French Amphitrite?

Right from the beginning, the Medici–Florence equation was undoubtedly too narrow for Ferdinando's aspirations to a modern state policy, while the Florence–Pisa and Livorno axis responded more fully to a state-based territorial strategy that also reinforced the continuity of his political view especially with that of Cosimo I. This symbolic constellation, which places emphasis on the entire territory and the wealth of its marine and aquatic resources, is particularly evident in the importance assumed by the Arno in the sequence of festivities in 1588–89, in which it is one of the main protagonists. In Pisa in its dual role as a spectacular set – the beautiful water stage where the Naval Battle and the Battle of the Bridge took place – and as a vital resource for the territory, and in the Florentine festivities as the centre of the scene of *La pellegrina*.

---

[16]　The acting area was flanked by three *periaktoi* on both sides of the stage, easily recognizable in the series of escarped cliffs in the foreground. Scenic and poetical constraints also explain why maritime fortifications in the background were limited to few symbolic items. For instance even if representing on the left of the scene the Appiani tower in Rio was more correct, considering its location on the Elba island, Buontalenti could have intended to set there the more significant Torre della Linguella. A wide selection of maps and views of the coast near Livorno is consultable in Comune di Livorno and others, *Livorno: progetto e storia di una città tra il 1500 e il 1600* (Pisa, 1980) and in the website *Atlante storico iconografico delle città toscane*, Lucia Nuti (ed.), http://asict.arte.unipi.it/index.htlm .

[17]　The first idea for the location of the new basin, subsequently abandoned, just concerned the sheet of water adjacent to the Torre del Fanale.

[18]　Franco Angiolini, 'Sovranità sul mare ed acque territoriali. Una contesa tra granducato di Toscana, repubblica di Lucca e monarchia spagnola', in Elena Fasano Guarini and Paola Volpini (eds), *Frontiere di terra Frontiere di mare: La Toscana moderna nello spazio mediterraneo* (Milan: Franco Angelini, 2008), pp. 244–97.

It is no coincidence that the comedy by Girolamo Bargagli, chosen for the most important of the Florentine productions, is set in Pisa. On the exemplary value of this stage design I have already written elsewhere, proposing a schematic reconstruction based on the printed description by Bastiano de' Rossi.[19] The elaborate perspective scenery shows the river on the longitudinal axis from the sea to the mountains and the Lungarni towards the central bridge. The river is thus the centre of the composition, beginning from the close-up of a bank of land: a way of representing the river that was not unknown in views of Pisa, but which does not seem to have been used previously in stage designs.[20]

The Entry Into Pisa: the Invention and Sequence of the Apparati

The entry into Pisa in 1588 closely looks to the personal political strategy adopted by Ferdinando to enhance the quality of territorial administration. If, in the iconography adopted by Tribolo and Giambologna, Fiorenza was based on the image of a Venus Anadyomene, Pisa was depicted by Giambologna and Francavilla as a Venus crouching, in reality a beautiful, destitute young mother, raised by the hand of the Grand Duke, who rescues her and the children from starvation. The iconographic reference is both to *Caritas* and to Vasari's fresco in Palazzo Vecchio which shows Cosimo I raising a Pisa–Flora accompanied by her river.[21] It is a political iconography of powerful expressive impact the statue can still be seen in Pisa, though not in its original location.

The personification of Pisa, depicted as 'a gracefully dressed woman' with two putti, appears at the beginning of the route of Ferdinando's entry in a large painting above Porta San Marco, and provides the inaugural message of the whole sequence of apparati. A strikingly original feature of the sequence is that – rather than the exaltation of the inevitable dynastic themes – it underlines in particular the personality and the biography of the protagonist, both to highlight his qualities as a prince and his aptitude for government, and to present a political and administrative programme addressed partly to the solution of urgent problems that required courageous initiatives. From this point of view it was a highly original entry, which on the one hand recalls the concrete nature of the policies expressed

---

[19]   de' Rossi, *Descrizione dell'apparato*, p. 33; Aliverti, 'Pisa: la scena urbana', p. 144.

[20]   It may be compared by contrast with the famous view of Pisa from the Central Bridge (Pons Vetus), by Domenico Beccafumi, considered as the *Stage set for the comedy "L'Amor costante"*, 1536 [?], drawing, 186 x 388 mm, in the Collection of Sir John Pope-Hennessy.

[21]   Giovanni Bologna and Pietro Francavilla, *Pisa raised by the hand of Ferdinand I*, 1594, marble, Pisa, Piazza Carrara; Giorgio Vasari and assistants, *Cosimo I raising Pisa*, 1558–62, vault of the ceiling, Sala di Cosimo I, Palazzo Vecchio, Florence.

in the *tableaux vivants* of medieval entries, and on the other anticipates the modern significance of political campaigns.

The urgent problem was the government of the waters in the Pisan territory: Ferdinando would devote great effort to its resolution throughout his rule, in line with his management of the Campagna Romana during his time as cardinal. As we know, he ordered the major works for the redirection of the Arno mouth, and in the last years of his rule he undertook the vast project of the Pisan aqueduct. In April 1587, as soon as he assumed power, he immediately reformed the Magistratura and the Ufficio de' Fossi (Office of Rivers and Ditches) of Pisa, which had already been reformed by his brother Francesco, only few years before (1583). This impelling political scheme is implicitly expressed by Alessandro Allori (Fig. 7.1), who portrays Ferdinando in 1588 still wearing his cardinal's robes and against the background of a river landscape, very probably the Serchio valley at the point – the borders (the castle and walls of Ripafratta as they stood at the time) between the Republic of Lucca and the Grand Duchy – where the river began, and still begins, to flow in the Pisan land. Besides new administrative directions, Ferdinando placed at the head of the Ufficio de' Fossi his own men, Davide Fortini and Raffaello di Zanobi da Pagno, as chief engineers.[22] A soft spoils system, which saw the arrival of these experienced technicians who had worked for him in Rome and at the Villa Medici. Fortini, a skilled master builder and hydraulic engineer, son-in-law to Tribolo, was an expert of the Pisan area where he had already worked as chief engineer under Cosimo I and Francesco I.[23] For the gifted Bernardo Buontalenti, whose ability as hydraulic and military engineer was firmly established, it meant a *promoveatur ut amoveatur*. Dismissed as chief engineer of the Arno, he was entrusted by Ferdinando with a role more suited to his inventive genius as an architect and stage designer: the artistic direction of the Florentine festivities of 1589. This absorbing and prestigious employment amply repaid the aging Bernardo.[24] We cannot argue whether he played a role in the design of the apparati for Ferdinando's entry into Pisa. In this respect neither documents nor descriptions provide us with help. The scholar who monopolized the role of advisor, as Vincenzo Borghini had done with Cosimo I, was Pietro Angeli da Barga called Il Bargeo, a multitalented academic from the University of

---

[22]   Ranieri Fiaschi, *Le Magistrature Pisane delle Acque* (Pisa: n. p., 1938), pp. 127–40, 163. Zanobi da Pagno was appointed in March 1588, succeeding to Davide Fortini.

[23]   Fiaschi, *Magistrature Pisane*, pp. 97, 121–3; Emanuela Ferretti, 'Maestro Davide Fortini: dal Tribolo al Buontalenti, una carriera all'ombra dei grandi', in Niccolò Pericoli, Elisabetta Pieri and Luigi Zangheri (eds), *Niccolò detto il Tribolo tra arte, architettura e paesaggio* (Poggio a Caiano: Il Commune, 2001), pp. 73–85. Ferretti's contribution is lacking regarding Fortini's activities in Pisa.

[24]   Franco Borsi, *L'architettura del Principe* (Florence: Edifir, 1980), pp. 82–3. Ferdinando intended to show a sign of discontinuity with his brother Francesco's water policy.

Pisa who had been closely bound to Ferdinando since 1574 and who had also been his mentor for the Villa Medici.[25]

This uncertainty regarding artists is almost complete except for Giovanni Stradano who was certainly involved in the apparato of the façade of the church of Santo Stefano dei Cavalieri.[26] For other apparati we can make hypotheses based on our knowledge of artists who were active in Pisa in those years: besides Buontalenti himself, Allori, Boscoli and Stradano and those who had returned with Ferdinando from Rome to Florence. What seems quite clear is that the organization of the festivities saw the participation of two teams, albeit already united by close relations[27]: the Barga team, under the leadership of Angeli and the Colle Val d'Elsa team, commanded by Ferdinando's secretary, monsignor Pietro Usimbardi, bishop of Arezzo and a native of Colle Val d'Elsa, who brought with him the two chroniclers of the festivities: Giovanni Cervoni and Francesco Dini, also both from Colle Val d'Elsa.[28] What place remained for those who did not belong to those two groups, is difficult to say. Also uncertain, therefore, is the author of the most significant and original ephemeral apparato of the whole entry, commissioned by the Ufficio de' Fossi and intended to make clear to the public the new course of the administration of the territory.

[25]   On Angeli's role in relation to Medicean policies see Giovanni Cipriani, 'Pietro Angeli da Barga e la politica culturale di Cosimo, Francesco e Ferdinando de' Medici', in Carla Sodini (ed.), *Barga medicea e le "enclaves" fiorentine della Versilia e della Lunigiana* (Florence: Olschki, 1983), pp. 101–25. Morel investigated Angeli's role as ideologist and inventor of the decorative programme displayed at Villa Medici, and pointed up his collaboration to 1589 Florentine festivities and the influence of his thought on the Intermedi: Philippe Morel, 'Le Parnasse astrologique. Les décors peints pour le cardinal Ferdinand de Médicis. Etude iconologique', in André Chastel and Philippe Morel (eds), *La Villa Médicis* (3 vols, Rome: Académie de France à Rome, 1989–), vol. 3 (1991), pp. 291–307. On Angeli's academic career in Pisa see the many references in *Storia dell'Università di Pisa. 1343–1737*, (ed.) Commissione rettorale per la storia dell'Università di Pisa (Pisa, 1993), vol. 1 (1–2).

[26]   Alessandra Baroni, *Jan van der Straet detto Giovanni Stradano flandrus pictor et inventor* (Milan: Jandi Sapi, 1997), p. 172.

[27]   Pietro Angeli, Giovanni Cervoni da Colle and artists such as Andrea Boscoli also met in the Pisan academic circle of the Risvegliati. Possibly the Bargeo provided the iconological programme for a fresco cycle on Ovid's *Metamorphoses* painted by Boscoli, in 1592, in the Villa Agostini at Corliano (Pisa), see Bastogi, *Andrea Boscoli*, pp. 83–115.

[28]   See note 1. Lovanio Rossi, 'Aspetti della cultura colligiana tra la fine del Quattrocento e la prima metà del Seicento', in *Colle di Val d'Elsa nell'età dei granduchi medicei: "La terra in città et la Collegiata in Cattedrale"* (Florence: Centro Di, 1992), pp. 243–57; Marcello Fantoni, 'Dalla provincia alla capitale: gli Usimbardi di Colle alla corte medicea', in Pietro Nencini (ed.), *Colle Val d'Elsa: diocesi e città tra '500 e '600* (Castelfiorentino, 1994), pp. 117–37.

The Ephemeral Landscape

This apparato, 'beautiful and most cheerful to the sight', was an artificial reconstruction of a natural marsh landscape, a highly original installation destined to remain unique in festive apparati. As was also stated in Cervoni's description, the apparato mounted in one of the city's squares, and animated by living creatures, represented the hills, planes and waters of the Pisan countryside, proving that the salubrity of the air and the fertility of the land depended on the government of the waters: *Aeris salubritas et agrorum procurata fertilitas.*

In the Piazza in front of the Ufficio de' Fossi, which now no longer exists, the brilliant ingenuity of an architect had created a water environment, which I have schematically outlined in collaboration with Maria Grazia Cacciapaglia (Fig 7.4).[29] Against the backdrop of dense greenery that covered the houses around the square was a land with its green, flowering meadows and its wisely governed waters: a watercourse flowing within its banks, and with its slopes flowering, a swamp with its marsh flora, a beautiful grotto with spring-water and a fountain, a floodgate, a water-mill, etc. Abundant live fauna (birds, aquatic animals and turtles) had been brought to indicate the prosperity of the land, on which several men could also be seen intent on hunting and fishing. Two sequences of painted scenes were placed within this naturalistic apparato: at the centre of the first sequence (south side of the Piazza) the coat of arms of the Grand Duke was flanked by the two allegories of the Serchio and the Arno rivers. Inscriptions and images clearly explained the importance of a correct water policy.

The contemporary beholder could easily identify this landscape as the Lake of Bientina, the lake/marsh between the two rivers Serchio and Arno which partly was under the dominion of the Republic of Lucca. Once again this was a question of borders, an old controversy mainly for the various communities living on the shore of the lake.[30] The apparato set up for Ferdinando's entry featured the part of the lake pertaining to the Grand Duchy. The layout of this area in a map of the Lake,[31] dated 1624, shows the same elements of the apparato in a similar location: the reinforced embankment (*Argin grosso*), the great meadow adjacent to the marsh (*Prato Grande*), the effluent flowing from the lake into the Arno dug in 1560, the bridge on the way connecting the village of Bientina to that of Vicopisano, the cataract (*Cateratte di Riparotta*). The marsh/lake of Bientina, as other important areas of the Pisan plain, was subject to the Grand Duke's legislation on the environment, aimed to preserving the wildlife for fishing and hunting: the

---

[29] For details see the *Explanatory Note*, by Maria Grazia Cacciapaglia, pp. 135–7.

[30] Andrea Zagli, 'Acque contese: questioni di frontiera nelle aree umide interne della Toscana (secoli XVI–XVIII)', in Guarini and Volpini (eds), *Frontiere di terra*, pp. 132–70.

[31] See the map of the Lake of Bientina and its surroundings showing the border between the two States of Lucca and Florence, drawn by Alessandro Bartolotti in 1624, Archivio di Stato di Firenze, *Consiglio di Reggenza*, 363, reproduced and commented upon in Zagli, 'Acque contese'.

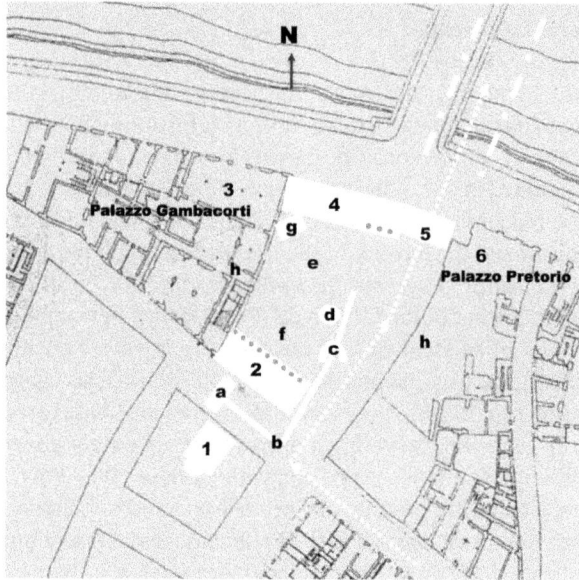

Figure 7.4   *The apparato of the Ufficio de' Fossi in 1588: a schematic reconstruction on the basis of a contemporary urban map.* © Maria Ines Aliverti, Maria Grazia Cacciapaglia.

Ferdinand's progress from Via San Martino • • • • • ▶
Pons Vetus: central bridge in Pisa ━ • ━ • ━▶

The permanent buildings:

1   Church of San Sebastiano.
2   Ufficio de' Fossi with Loggia.
3   Palazzo Gambacorti.
4   Bargello, Loggia dei Catalani and private houses.
5   Volta del Commissario: vaulted passage.
6   Palazzo Pretorio.

The ephemeral landscape

a   floodgate
b   watercourse
c   bridge
d   water-mill
e   marsh
f   meadow
g   grotto
h   greenery

so-called *bandite di caccia e di pesca*.[32] Naturalists and botanists were also used to frequent this humid area for observing the fauna and the natural phenomena, and for collecting various specimens of plants.

The Grand Duke's tastes and interests and his political programme seem to combine in this happy invention. The pastime of hunting, as well as being one of the Medici's favourite occupations in Pisa and a great passion of Ferdinando I in particular, was not extraneous to festive productions, both in public and in the court, and had been represented abundantly in artworks. As antecedents of the artificial 'Pisan Hunt', we might cite in particular the hunts represented in Florentine festivities. The most famous was the popular bull-hunt, a type of bullfight also widespread in Venice and other cities, and often organized in the squares of Florence. In 1589 one such hunt was held in the Piazza Santa Croce on 8 May. However, the Pisan event more closely resembles the hunt created by Buontalenti both with real and fake animals on the occasion of the baptism of Filippo de' Medici on 1 October 1577.[33]

As for artworks, we need only mention the well-known series of *Le cacce*, the tapestries after cartoons by Giovanni Stradano and by Alessandro Allori originally for the Villa di Poggio a Caiano.[34] Woven in the 1560s and 1570s, they depict scenes of the hunting of land and aquatic animals (in particular the *uccellagione*, that is the marsh-birds' hunt). In these cartoons the meticulous attention to the hunting theme is combined with a naturalistic and scientific interest in animal species, and with a taste for landscapes and serene, light-filled, atmospheres.

The Pisan apparato is, however, the fruit of the combination of a taste for landscape and gardens and of the naturalistic, zoological, botanical and geological interests that were an extremely important component of Medici culture. Under Cosimo I and Francesco I this culture had found ample expression in the administration of the estates and in the creation of the gardens, aviaries and menageries. In Pisa, as in Florence, it had also found scientific application with the foundation of the Botanical Gardens and the impulse given by Cosimo I to the study

---

[32]   Fauzia Farneti, 'La legislazione medicea sulle bandite, la caccia e la pesca', in Giovanni Cascio Pratili and Luigi Zangheri (eds), *La legislazione medicea sull'ambiente* (Florence: Olschki, 1994), pp. 95–118.

[33]   Vincenzo Borghini, *La descrizione della pompa, e dell'apparato fatto in Firenze, nel battesimo del serenissimo principe di Toscana* (Florence: Giunti, 1577), pp. 28–30.

[34]   Lucia Meoni, *Gli arazzi nei musei fiorentini: La collezione medicea. Catalogo completo* (2 vols, Livorno: Silabe, 1998–2007), vol. 1, *La manifattura da Cosimo I a Cosimo II (1545–1621)*, pp. 210–27. See also the three series drawings (1567) by Giovanni Stradano engraved after the tapestries between 1570 and 1576, and the series of the *Venationes Ferarum, Avium, Piscium*, also by Stradano, engraved by Philip Galle (various issues between 1578 ca. up to 1596). See Baroni, *Jan van der Straet*, pp. 354–5 (n. 684 and n. 685) and pp. 371–88 (n. 693).

of the Natural Sciences at the University of Pisa.[35] The marriage of naturalistic interests and decorative stage designs that had characterized the creations of Tribolo and Buontalenti had found new and even more refined solutions at the Roman court of Cardinal Ferdinando, under the erudite direction of Pietro Angeli. In the garden of the Villa Medici on the Pincio hill, the wooded part, the artificial *Montagnola*, had been created by Raffaello da Pagno and Davide Fortini for the pastime of hunting.[36] Very probably invented by one of these masters – I suggest Fortini – in collaboration with Giovanni Stradano, the Pisan apparato seems to be conceived of as the creation of a full-fledged *theatrum naturae*, following a web of sophisticated and classical references that led from the work of Ulisse Aldrovandi back to Pliny's *Naturalis Historia*. It contains a trace of the search for naturalistic precision and scientific encyclopaedism that characterized the iconographic programme of Pietro Angeli at the Villa Medici. In particular, Angeli had shown his interest in hunting with a long Latin poem that set out the techniques of bird hunting.[37] Published in Florence in 1566 and republished in Rome in 1585, it is one of the sources for the drawings by Stradano that were executed both in the above-mentioned tapestries and series of engravings.

In conclusion it is important to note the special care for the lacustrian environment shown in the *theatrum naturae* of Ferdinando's entry. It is an expression of the beauty of the natural landscape, and of the joy of water as a resource for man, which is matched in the contemporary frescos in the Loggetta of Palazzo Pitti, executed between 1587 and 1589 by Alessandro Allori and his helpers, and commissioned by Ferdinando in expectation of his bride.[38] Against the backdrop of the fake sky of the Loggetta where birds soar freely, the young maid who wrings her wet hair, like Tribolo's Fiorenza before her, also represents the precious fount of water and the felicity of the Tuscan people.

[35]   Fabio Garbari, Lucia Tongiorgi Tomasi and Alessandro Tosi, *Giardino dei Semplici. Garden of Simples* (Pisa: Edizioni Plus, Università di Pisa, 2002).

[36]   Suzanne B. Butters, '"Magnifico, non senza eccesso": Riflessioni sul mecenatismo del cardinale Ferdinando de' Medici', in Michel Hochmann (ed.), *Villa Medici. Il sogno di un cardinale: Collezioni e artisti di Ferdinando de' Medici* (Rome: De Luca, 1999), pp. 23–45.

[37]   Pietro Angeli, *De aucupio. Liber primus ad Franciscum Medicem* (Florence Bernando Giunta, 1566); (original Latin text and Italian trans.) in Giuliano Innamorati (ed.), *Arte della caccia: Testi di falconeria, uccellagione e altre cacce* (2 vols, Milan: Edizioni II, 1965), vol. 2, pp. 119–191.

[38]   Serena Padovani, 'Il quartiere dei cardinali e principi forestieri', in Marco Chiarini (ed.), *Palazzo Pitti: L'arte e la storia* (Florence: Nardini, 2000), pp. 43–53; Nicola Bastogi, 'Il quartiere dei Cardinali e principi Forestieri', in Mina Gregori (ed.), *Fasto di corte*, vol. 1 (2005), *Da Ferdinando I alle reggenti (1587–1628)*, pp. 75–97.

Appendix: An Explanatory Note on the Piazza of the Ufficio de' Fossi and the Associated Ephemera, by Maria Grazia Cacciapaglia (see Fig. 7.4)

The Piazza on the south bank of the Arno, where the Ufficio de' Fossi set up the apparato to celebrate Ferdinando's entry, no longer exists. The demolitions and the edification of the Logge dei Banchi, built between 1603 and 1605 by Cosimo Pugliani on a design by Bernardo Buontalenti, have completely cancelled the previous urban layout of this area. The Piazza which was, since 1475, the point where merchants and financers met for their business, had evolved under Cosimo I and Francesco I into a political and administrative centre. Unfortunately, documentary and iconographic records concerning this urban area at the end of the sixteenth century are extremely rare and confused. The two printed accounts of Ferdinando de' Medici's entry into Pisa, giving accurate descriptions of the ephemeral setting, provide us with some reliable information on the buildings which faced the square.[39] So, interpreting the apparato also implied proceeding to a hypothetical reconstruction of the Piazza. The resulting map (Figure 7.4, above) illustrates the square and the ephemeral decorations on the basis of both Cervoni's and Dini's *livrets*.

South Side

This was closed off by the fifteenth-century building hosting the Magistratura dei Fossi. The façade of this building was characterized by a loggia resting on ten columns of about 8 m in height, each arch having a span of about 3.5 m.[40] The ephemeral apparato completely disguised the architectural character of this façade. It was composed by nine panels on a broad band of about 3 m in height, elevated above the columns: each of them was richly decorated, in imitation of different sorts of marbles and precious materials, and displayed in the centre an allegorical picture or a landscape.[41] The width of each panel encompassed the underlying intercolumniation; vertical elements of division corresponded to supporting elements below. The architrave on which the decorated band ran was certainly

---

[39] Cervoni, *Descrizzione*, pp. C6r–D8r; Dini, *Trionfi e feste*, pp. 5r–6r.

[40] Measures given by Dini in his report are expressed in *braccia*; he presumably adopted the measurement unit called *braccio fiorentino*, equal to 0.583 m.

[41] The paintings represented: 1. Pisa *in maestà* as a young woman with two putti and a lyocorn; 2. The marshy landscape near Livorno (Stagno) with the god Pan playing the syrinx; 3. A Cibele on her chariot pulled by lions, lying face downwards as a sign of starvation and misery; 4. The figure of the Arno River and a landscape in the background; 5 (central painting). The Grand Duke Ferdinando de' Medici's coat of arms; 6. The figure of the Serchio River and a landscape in the background; 7. A seated Juno with her two peacocks; 8. A scantily dressed Venus sitting on her chariot pulled by two doves; 9. A crane standing watchful, as a symbol of Vigilance (see Ripa's, *Iconology*, pp. 466–7).

part of the ephemeral structure: it was raised up on ten pillars, with fluted herms on the front, which disguised the correspondent columns behind. As we can gather from a rough sixteenth-century plan,[42] the rear of the building was overlooking the last part of Via San Martino (today via Toselli), on the same site where the Church of San Sebastiano stood, before its demolition in 1944. Consequently this was the first glimpse that the Grand Duke, who was coming from Via Fiorentina through Via san Martino, could have of the Palazzo de' Fossi, before turning to the right and taking the street (Carraia Pontis Veteris) towards the Piazza and the bridge (Pons Vetus).

East Side

Houses and shops bordered the east side of the square, along the Carraia Pontis Veteris. The last building standing towards the Arno was the Palazzo Pretorio, hosting the Florentine Magistratura of the 'Commissario'.

West Side

The fourteenth-century Palazzo Gambacorti, with its imposing mass, stood on this side of the square. From 1430 it was the seat of Consoli del Mare as well as the custom-house (Dogana). It is still standing,[43] while other less important edifices, in part owned by a cadet branch of the Gambacorti family, were pulled down around 1620.

North Side

As attested by one of the rare engravings showing the sixteenth-century Lungarno[44], the Piazza was bordered on this side by a close-knit curtain of buildings overlooking the river. They were pulled down when the Pons Vetus collapsed (1637) and a new bridge had to be built.[45] The most relevant of these buildings was the Palazzo del Bargello with the joined prisons. It was connected to

---

[42]   Archivio di Stato di Pisa, *Fiumi e Fossi*, 155, fol. 121, in Ornella Pagni, *Pisa negli anni del Granducato di Ferdinando I (1587–1609)*, degree thesis (University of Pisa, 2005–06), supervisor: Prof. Lucia Nuti.

[43]   It is now the seat of Comune di Pisa (the town-hall).

[44]   It illustrates the Gambacorti's genealogical tree on the background of the Lungarno di Pisa, in Scipione Ammirato, *Delle famiglie nobili napoletane* (Florence: n. p., 1580), pp. 174–5.

[45]   After the edification of a second bridge and a new collapse in a short span of time, two areas free of building were realized, on the project of Bernardo Contini, at both ends

the Palazzo Pretorio (East Side) through an aerial passage. This large vault known as 'la volta del Palazzo del Commissario', is detectable in some ancient plans of Pisa.[46] On this north side of the square, up against the Bargello, there was a rather small structure, resting on four columns,[47] known as the Loggia dei Catalani. According to both the descriptions, two pictures decorated this loggia, achieving the iconographic programme displayed on the opposite Loggia of the Ufficio de' Fossi. These allegoric compositions[48] flanked on both sides a white marble statue of the Virgin, already on the site above the central span of the loggia. Here again the four columns were disguised by four pillars with herms.

The whole of the Piazza was occupied by the ephemeral marshy landscape with its flora and fauna: southwards the green, flowering meadows, the watermill and the grotto, northwards, in the other half of the square, the marsh. Along the east side, parallel to the street leading to the bridge (Carraia Pontis Veteris), was running the stream, banked-up and crossed by a small bridge. All the buildings overlooking the square and placed along the east side of the Carraia were covered by a thick and beautifully arranged greenery (*'d'una bellissima verzura'*),[49] through which it was still possible to see the paintings on the two loggias. Green ornamentation was also installed in the inside of the loggias: a wood of verdant trees which made the most beautiful view (*'una selva d'arbori freschi, et verdeggianti, che faceva vista bellissima'*).[50] We suppose that it continued on the rear side of the Palazzo de' Fossi: here, between the Palazzo and the Church of San Sebastiano, where a floodgate was built on the stream. It announced, to the progressing Grand Duke, the view of the artificial landscape.

---

of the new bridge (the third), built slightly westwards and designed by Francesco Nave (1659–61).

[46]   Emilio Tolaini, *Forma Pisarum: Storia urbanistica della città di Pisa problemi e ricerche* (Pisa: Nistri-Lischi, 2nd edn., 1979), plates XXXIX (Soli, about 1600), XL (Meisner, about 1620), XLIV b (De Rossi, 1643), XLVI (Merian, 1640) e XLVIII (Lucini). Achille Soli's plan, published by Matteo Florimi in Siena at the beginning of the seventeenth century, served as prototype for designing many plans of Pisa in that period. 'La volta del Palazzo del commissario' is detectable also in a beautiful etching by Anton Francesco Lucini from Stefano della Bella, representing the Gioco del Ponte: *Ecco su l'Arno la Pisana gente [...]*, 1634.

[47]   Dini clearly specifies the number of supporting elements (four) of the apparato, and consequently of the loggia, while Cervoni's description is more obscure in this respect. We draw here upon Dini's account.

[48]   The paintings represented: 1.The figure of Concorde with a cornucopia and a landscape with a castle/fortress in the background; 2.The figure of Nemesis with wings extended, on her chariot flying over a landscape.

[49]   Cervoni, *Descrizzione*, p. C7v.

[50]   Dini, *Trionfi e feste*, p. 6r.

Bibliography

Primary Sources

Ammirato, Scipione, *Delle famiglie nobili napoletane* (Florence: n. p., 1580).
Angeli, Pietro, *De aucupio. Liber primus ad Franciscum Medicem* (Florence: Bernando Giunta, 1566); (original Latin text and Italian trans.) in Giuliano Innamorati (ed.), *Arte della caccia: Testi di falconeria, uccellagione e altre cacce* (2 vols, Milan: Edizioni II, 1965), vol. 2, pp. 119–91.
Anon., *Entrata solenne del G. Duca Ferdinando a Pisa* (Archivio di Stato di Firenze, Mediceo del Principato, 6377), fols 61–4.
Borghini, Vincenzo, *La descrizione della pompa, e dell'apparato fatto in Firenze, nel battesimo del serenissimo principe di Toscana* (Florence: Giunti, 1577).
Cervoni da Colle, Giovanni, *Descrizzione de la felicissima entrata del Serenis. D. Ferdinando de' Medici cardinale, gran duca di Toscana nella città di Pisa. Con tutti gli archi trionfali, portoni, apparati, imprese, e motti, con le loro interpretazioni, e significati; e con le loro composizioni, che ci si son fatte: con le feste, lumi, fuochi artifiziati, et altri segni d'allegrezze* (Florence: Giorgio Marescotti, 1588).
Cervoni da Colle, Giovanni, *Descrizzione de le pompe, e feste fatte ne la città di Pisa. Per la venuta de la sereniss. madama Christierna de l'Oreno gran duchessa di Toscana [...]* (In Fiorenza: appresso Giorgio Marescotti, 1589).
Dini da Colle, Francesco, *Trionfi e feste fatte nella città di Pisa. Per l' enrrata [sic!] fatta in essa dal serenissimo Gran Duca di Toscana, il signore don Ferdinando cardinale Medici* (Florence: Francesco Dini da Colle, 1588).
Giambullari, Pier Francesco, *Apparato et feste nelle noze dello illustrissimo signor duca di Firenze, & della duchessa sua consorte, con le sue stanze, madriali, comedia, & intermedij, in quelle recitati* (Florence: Benedetto Giunta, 1539).
Gualterotti, Raffaello, *Della descrizione del regale apparato fatto nella nobile città di Firenze per la venuta, e per le nozze della serenissima madama Cristina di Loreno moglie del serenissimo Ferdinando Medici terzo gran duca di Toscana. Libro secondo* (Florence: Antonio Padovani, 1589).
Ripa, Cesare, *Iconologia*, ed. Piero Buscaroli (Milan: TEA, 1992).
Rossi, Bastiano de', *Descrizione dell'apparato e degli intermedi. Fatti per la commedia rappresentata in Firenze. Nelle nozze de' serenissimi don Ferdinando Medici e madonna Cristina di Lorena gran duchi di Toscana* (Florence: Anton Padovani, 1589).

Secondary Sources

Acidini Luchinat, Cristina and Giorgio Galletti, *Le ville e i giardini di Castello e Petraia a Firenze* (Pisa: Pacini, 1992).

Alberti, Maria, 'Battaglie navali, scorrerie corsare e politica dello spettacolo: Le Naumachie medicee del 1589', *Californian Italian Studies Journal*, 1(1), February 2010, pp. 1–33, http://www.escholarship.org/uc/item/8553h705

Aliverti, Maria Ines, 'Pisa: la scena urbana', in Marcello Fagiolo (ed.), *Atlante tematico del Barocco in Italia. Le capitali della festa: Italia centrale e meridionale* (2 vols, Rome: De Luca, 2007), vol. 2, pp. 141–9.

Angiolini, Franco, *I cavalieri e il principe: L'ordine di Santo Stefano e la società toscana in età moderna* (Florence: Edifir, 1996).

Angiolini, Franco, 'Sovranità sul mare ed acque territoriali. Una contesa tra granducato di Toscana, repubblica di Lucca e monarchia spagnola', in Elena Fasano Guarini and Paola Volpini (eds), *Frontiere di terra Frontiere di mare: La Toscana moderna nello spazio mediterraneo* (Milan: Franco Angelini, 2008), pp. 244–97.

Baroni, Alessandra, *Jan van der Straet detto Giovanni Stradano flandrus pictor et inventor* (Milan: Jandi Sapi, 1997).

Bastogi, Nadia, *Andrea Boscoli* (Florence: Edifir, 2008).

Bastogi, Nicola, 'Il quartiere dei Cardinali e principi Forestieri', in Mina Gregori (ed.), *Fasto di corte*, (4 vols, Florence: Edifis, 2005–9) vol. 1 (2005), *Da Ferdinando I alle reggenti (1587–1628)*, pp. 75–97.

Borsi, Franco, *L'architettura del Principe* (Florence: Edifir, 1980).

Butters, Suzanne B., ''Magnifico, non senza eccesso': Riflessioni sul mecenatismo del cardinale Ferdinando de' Medici', in Michel Hochmann (ed.), *Villa Medici. Il sogno di un cardinale: Collezioni e artisti di Ferdinando de' Medici* (Rome: De Luca, 1999), pp. 23–45.

Cascio Pratilli, Giovanni and Luigi Zangheri (eds), *La legislazione medicea sull'ambiente* (Florence: Olschki, 1994).

Chastel, André and Philippe Morel (eds), *La Villa Médicis* (3 vols, Rome: Académie de France à Rome, 1989–), vol. 3 1991.

Cipriani, Giovanni, 'Pietro Angeli da Barga e la politica culturale di Cosimo, Francesco e Ferdinando de' Medici', in Carla Sodini (ed.), *Barga medicea e le "enclaves" fiorentine della Versilia e della Lunigiana* (Florence: Olschki, 1983), pp. 101–25.

Comune di Livorno and others, *Livorno: progetto e storia di una città tra il 1500 e il 1600* (Pisa: Nistri-Lischi Pacini, 1980).

Dal Pozzolo, Enrico Maria, *Colori d'amore* (Treviso: Canova, 2008).

Exhibition Catalogue, *Ferdinando de' Medici 1549–1609: Maiestate Tantum* (Lavorno: Sillabe, 2009).

Exhibition Catalogue, *La festa, la rappresentazione popolare, il lavoro: Momenti della cultura e della tradizione in territorio pisano, XVI–XIX sec.* (Pisa: Archivio di Stato, 1984), pp. 59–94.

Fagiolo, Marcello (ed.), *Atlante tematico del Barocco in Italia. Le capitali della festa: Italia centrale e meridionale* (2 vols, Rome: De Luca, 2007).

Fagiolo, Marcello (ed.), *La città effimera e l'universo artificiale del giardino* (Rome: Officina, 1980).

Fantoni, Marcello, 'Dalla provincia alla capitale: gli Usimbardi di Colle alla corte medicea', in Pietro Nencini (ed.), *Colle Val d'Elsa: diocesi e città tra '500 e '600* (Castelfiorentino: Società storica della Valdelsa, 1994).

Farneti, Fauzia, 'La legislazione medicea sulle bandite, la caccia e la pesca', in Giovanni Cascio Pratilli and Luigi Zangheri (eds), *La legislazione medicea sull'ambiente* (Florence: Olschki, 1994), pp. 95–118.

Fasano Guarini, Elena and Paola Volpini (eds), *Frontiere di terra Frontiere di mare: La Toscana moderna nello spazio mediterraneo* (Milan: Franco Angeli, 2008).

Ferretti, Emanuela, 'Maestro Davide Fortini: dal Tribolo al Buontalenti, una carriera all'ombra dei grandi', in Niccolò Pericoli, Elisabetta Pieri and Luigi Zangheri (eds), *Niccolò detto il Tribolo tra arte, architettura e paesaggio*, (Poggio a Caiano: Il Commune, 2001), pp. 73–85.

Fiaschi, Ranieri, *Le Magistrature Pisane delle Acque* (Pisa: n. p., 1938).

Garbari, Fabio, Lucia Tongiorgi Tomasi and Alessandro Tosi, *Giardino dei Semplici. Garden of Simples* (Pisa: Edizioni Plus, Università di Pisa, 2002).

Gregori, Mina (ed.), *Fasto di corte: La decorazione murale nelle residenze dei Medici e dei Lorena* (4 vols, Florence: Edifir, 2005–09).

Hochmann, Michel (ed.), *Villa Medici. Il sogno di un cardinale: Collezioni e artisti di Ferdinando de' Medici* (Rome: De Luca, 1999).

Meoni, Lucia, *Gli arazzi nei musei fiorentini: La collezione medicea. Catalogo completo* (2 vols, Livorno: Sillabe, 1998–2009).

Morel, Philippe, 'Le Parnasse astrologique. Les décors peints pour le cardinal Ferdinand de Médicis. Etude iconologique', in André Chastel and Philippe Morel (eds), *La Villa Médicis* (3 vols, Rome: Académie de France à Rome, 1989–) vol. 3 (1991), pp. 291–307.

Nencini, Pietro (ed.), *Colle Val d'Elsa: diocesi e città tra '500 e '600* (Castelfiorentino: Società storica della Valdelsa, 1994).

Nuti, Lucia (ed.), *Atlante storico iconografico delle città toscane*, http://asict.arte. unipi.it/index.htlm

Padovani, Serena, 'Il quartiere dei cardinali e principi forestieri', in Marco Chiarini (ed.), *Palazzo Pitti: L'arte e la storia* (Florence: Nardini, 2000).

Pagni, Ornella, *Pisa negli anni del Granducato di Ferdinando I (1587–1609)*, unpublished degree thesis (University of Pisa: unpublished thesis, 2005–06).

Pericoli, Niccolò, Elisabetta Pieri and Luigi Zangheri (eds), *Niccolò detto il Tribolo tra arte, architettura e paesaggio*, (Poggio a Caiano: Il Commune, 2001).

Renzoni, Stefano, 'Pisa tra mito e storia nelle feste granducali cinque-seicentesche', in Exhibition Catalogue, *La festa, la rappresentazione popolare, il lavoro: Momenti della cultura e della tradizione in territorio pisano, XVI–XIX sec.* (Pisa: Archivio di Stato, 1984), pp. 59–75.

Rossi, Lovanio, 'Aspetti della cultura colligiana tra la fine del Quattrocento e la prima metà del Seicento', in *Colle di Val d'Elsa nell'età dei granduchi medicei: "La terra in città et la Collegiata in Cattedrale"* (Florence: Centro Di, 1992).

Saslow, James M., *Medici Wedding of 1589: Florentine festival as Theatrum Mundi* (New Haven and London: Yale University Press, 1996).

Sodini, Carla (ed.), *Barga medicea e le "enclaves" fiorentine della Versilia e della Lunigiana* (Florence: Olschki, 1983).

Spinelli, Riccardo, 'Gli affreschi di Baldassare Franceschini, il Volterrano a Villa "La Petraia": iconografia medicea e orgoglio dinastico', in Mina Gregori (ed)., *Fasto di corte: La decorazione murale nelle residenze dei Medici e dei Lorena* (4 vols, Florence: Edifir, 2005–09), vol. 2 (2006).

Storia dell'Università di Pisa. 1343–1737, ed. Commissione rettorale per la storia dell'Università di Pisa (Pisa, 1993).

Strong, Roy C., *Art and Power: Renaissance Festivals, 1450–1650*, 2nd edn (Woodbridge: Boydell Press, 1984).

Testaverde, Anna Maria, 'Feste medicee: la visita, le nozze e il trionfo', in Marcello Fagiolo (ed.), *La città effimera e l'universo artificiale del giardino* (Rome: Officina, 1980), pp. 69–97.

Testaverde, Anna Maria, 'La decorazione festiva e l'itinerario di "rifondazione" della città negli ingressi trionfali a Firenze tra XV e XVI secolo (II)', *Mitteilungen des Kunsthistorischen Institutes in Florenz*, 34 (1990), pp. 165–98.

Testaverde, Anna Maria, 'L'officina delle nuvole. Il Teatro Mediceo nel 1589 e gli Intermedi del Buontalenti nel Memoriale di Girolamo Seriacopi', *Musica e Teatro. Quaderni degli Amici della Scala*, 7 (June–October 1991), monographic issue.

Tolaini, Emilio, *Forma Pisarum: Storia urbanistica della città di Pisa problemi e ricerche* (Pisa: Nistri-Lischi, 2nd edn., 1979).

Ubaldo, Angeli, *Personificazione delle città, paesi e fiumi di Toscana festeggianti le nozze di Cosimo I ed Eleonora di Toledo* (Prato: n. p., 1898).

Zagli, Andrea, 'Acque contese: questioni di frontiera nelle aree umide interne della Toscana (secoli XVI–XVIII)', in Elena Fasano Guarini, and Paola Volpini (eds), *Frontiere di terra Frontiere di mare: La Toscana moderna nello spazio mediterraneo* (Milan: Franco Angelini, 2008), pp. 132–70.

Chapter 8

Arbitrary Reality: Fact and Fantasy in the Florentine *Naumachia*, 1589[1]

J.R. Mulryne

Among *naumachiae*, not a vastly numerous *genre* though increasingly studied, perhaps the best known is the entertainment that featured as the concluding event of a festival staged in Florence in the first days of May 1589 – a festival, celebrated at the time and in retrospect, marking the wedding of Grand Duke Ferdinando of Tuscany and his Grand Duchess Christine of Lorraine, granddaughter of the formidable French queen Catherine de' Medici.[2]

The events of that unprecedented month are remembered especially for the superb *intermedi*, ultra-sophisticated works of musical and scenic art interspersed between the acts of Girolamo Bargagli's comedy *La pellegrina*. So intense has been subsequent interest in the *intermedi*, their lavish use of resources and their artistic achievements, that attention has been diverted from the rest of the festival programme. Even in 1589 Raffaello Gualterotti, the festival's principal chronicler, while giving detailed accounts of the *intermedi*, abandoned his task before the festival's end and the concluding *naumachia*.[3] It may be that print deadlines had

[1] I am grateful to the following scholars and colleagues who have generously assisted with the preparation of this essay, in several cases by sharing their scholarship in extended email correspondence: Maria Ines Aliverti, Arthur R. Blumenthal, Suzanne B. Butters, Kathleen Coleman, Felicia Else, John Hoenig, Michael Holden, Lucia Nuti, Jonathan Pearson and James M. Saslow. In addition I have learned a great deal from published scholarship, as acknowledged in footnotes, but especially from Malcolm Campbell's, Anna Maria Testaverde's and Maria Alberti's works. I am grateful also to the editor of this volume, Margaret Shewring, for her assistance and encouragement.

[2] A handful of subsequent celebrations followed the *naumachia* at irregular intervals, including repeat performances of the *intermedi*, a tournament and an allegorical parade, but these look like opportunist left-overs from an otherwise completed design. For a comprehensive list of the festival's events see James M. Saslow, *The Medici Wedding of 1589: Florentine Festival as 'Theatrum Mundi'* (New Haven and London: Yale University Press, 1996), p. 19. Saslow's book offers the most accessible account in English of the events of the festival.

[3] Rafaello Gualterotti, *Della Descrizione del regale apparato fatto ... per le nozze della Serenissima Madama Cristina di Loreno moglie del Serenissimo Don Ferdinando Medici terzo Gran Duca di Toscana* (Florence: Padovani, 1589).

something to do with this, but Gualterotti's haste to publish his account comes across nonetheless as a negative value judgment on the festival's final large-scale event.

My proposal in this chapter is that the festival as a whole can be seen as not merely concluding with, but driving towards, the *naumachia* – a remarkable undertaking on any estimate – that was staged in the *cortile* of the Palazzo Pitti, the Medici's newly-acquired and refurbished residence, on Thursday 11 May. Bernardo Buontalenti, the scenic genius, and hydraulic engineer, who stood behind the *intermedi*, as behind so much else in the festival, also devised the programme for the *naumachia*, an indication that this final occasion may well have been conceived as the artistic or artistic-and-ideological culmination of an integrated series of events. Its significance and timeliness as an index of Medici image-making and self-definition, together with its scale and expense, the staging resources it commanded, the technical challenges it presented and its ambitious historical contextualisation, combine to underscore its place in the planning and delivery of the most lavish festival Florence had yet seen.[4]

The *naumachia*, depicting a Christian–Turkish naval battle with an assault on a Turkish fortress, may be viewed as no more than a noisy spectacle before a crowded and it seems unruly, or at the least, emotional audience of invited guests. Turks and Christians regularly served as the predictable and increasingly iconic antagonists in a nexus of fact rapidly turning into myth – a process stimulated by recollection of the celebrated Christian victory of Lepanto in 1571, as mentioned below. A pedigree such as this, supplemented by, and conflated with, Florentine ambitions for a powerful naval presence in the Mediterranean, gave rise to the *naumachia*'s air of local triumphalism and, no doubt, to the communal if élite enthusiasm with which the show was greeted.

From a different but not unrelated angle, however, the show may be seen not merely as spectacle but as evoking and graphically expressing embedded preoccupations that in 1589 were especially pertinent for a Medici ruler. Ferdinando was perceived, and perceived himself, as rescuing by means of his marriage and the exercise of strong government the political fortunes of a dynasty that had very recently experienced a distinct loss of esteem. This came about as a result of his brother Francesco's less than politically-committed or savvy regime, and in particular following his derided second marriage to his Venetian mistress Bianca Cappello. The notoriety that attached to the almost simultaneous deaths of the married pair two years before the 1589 festival, and the widely-dispersed tabloid suspicions that Ferdinando, the successor Duke, was implicated in their poisoning – speculation that filled contemporary gossip literature – left Ferdinando with an uphill task of

---

[4]   The extraordinary scale of the preparations, the expense entailed, the managerial expertise deployed, the length of the run-up period (stretching back to the final months of 1588) and the urgency, not to say panic, of the days before the spectacle was staged, are fully documented by Saslow, *Medici Wedding*, and in an even more complete way by Testaverde (see note 6 below). Both draw on archival material not otherwise accessible.

recuperation, of which the *naumachia* may be seen as a notable, and costly, element.[5] Each of these aspects will be touched on in the discussion which follows.

The Sources and Their Characteristics

Gualterotti's failure of nerve or haste has resulted – in a publishing climate where festival books were rushed into print, and due perhaps to the interval of a few days between the other main events and the *naumachia* – in only three printed descriptions of the events in the courtyard of the Pitti palace surviving, those by Simone Cavallino, Giuseppe Pavoni and Vittorio Benacci, incorporated within their general accounts of the festival.[6] These books are comparatively rare, with few copies available even among major libraries, a fact that accounts in part, one may assume, for the relative absence of scholarly assessment of the events they uniquely record.

It may be helpful to pick out briefly the leading characteristics of Cavallino's writing and Pavoni's before considering their presentation of the *naumachia*. Like all journalists, Cavallino and Pavoni write with one eye on their readership, so that a modern interpreter attempting to uncover what actually took place in 1589 has to make allowances for conventions of festival description familiar to, and expected by, contemporary readers.[7] Cavallino describes the festival's '*cose maravigliosi*' ('extraordinary events'), as he calls them, including the *naumachia*,

---

[5]   For information relating to the gossip disseminated as far as England about the allegedly scandalous deaths see J.R. Mulryne (ed.), *Thomas Middleton 'Women Beware Women'* (Manchester: Manchester University Press, 2007), Revels Student Editions, especially Introduction pp. 4–7 and references, and my earlier edition of the same play (Manchester: Manchester University Press, 1975) esp. Introduction pp. xxxviii–xliv and Appendix I, pp. 168–79.

[6]   Simone Cavallino, *Raccolta di tutte le solennissime feste nel sponsalitio della serenissima gran dvchessa di Toscana, fatte in Fiorenza il mese di Maggio 1589* (Rome: Blado, 1589) and Giuseppe Pavoni, *Diario Descritto da Givseppe Pavoni delle feste celebrate nelle solennissime nozze delli serenissimi sposi, il sig. Don Ferdinando Medici, & la sig. Donna Christina di Loreno Gran Duchi di Toscana* (Bologna: Rossi, 1589). I am indebted to Maria Ines Aliverti, and her research student Emanuele de Luca, for making both books available to me in photocopied and virtual form. A sprightly brief summary of the *naumachia* (and of the animal hunt) is given in the third printed account: Vittorio Benacci, *Le Ultime Feste et Apparati Superbissimi fatti in Fiorenza nelle Nozze del Serenissimo Gran Duca di Toscana* (Bologna, 1589).

[7]   Aside from secondary material, the only further source known to me of information about the *naumachia* is to be found in the Medici archives in Florence, and here I am largely reliant on Saslow's indispensable *Medici Wedding* and on Anna Maria Testaverde Matteini's hugely detailed and scholarly *L'officina delle nuvole. Il Teatro Mediceo nel 1589* (Milan: Edizione degli Amici della Scala, 1991), especially chapter VII, pp. 137–47 and Appendix pp. 185–99.

with what might generously be described as an engaging naivety. Two matters particularly fascinate him. He marvels, first, at the scale of the entire enterprise and its lavish expense. Coming from ancient but by now provincial Viterbo, it was perhaps natural for him to wonder at Medici extravagance in big-city Florence, and to be eager to report his astonishment to the brothers Giasone and Pompeo Vizani, to whom he addresses his book. He's amazed, he says, by the number of performers in the *intermedi* and their costuming. The Fifth *intermedio*, he tells us, has '*grandissima copia de demonij, & tanti fanciullini ignudi*' ('a huge company of demons, and as many naked little children'). Gods crowd on to clouds, by his account, like passengers on a Calcutta train, though obviously this is not the analogy he uses. Second, he repeatedly returns to the interface between theatrical device and real world. In the Sixth *intermedio*, as he describes it, a city is transformed '*in un voltar d'occhi*' ('in the blink of an eye') into a '*tempestoso mare*' ('storm-tossed sea'), the waves of which '*faceuano quelle spume, che suole il vero mare*' ('made such [an appearance of] foam that it seemed a real sea'). In the *Inferno* episode he is transfixed by a '*Plutone si brutto che diede grandissimo spavento e stupore riguradanti*' a ('Pluto so foul that he instilled huge fear and wonder among the spectators'). The audience present at the last *intermedio* were teased, he tells us, into mistaking the '*pioggia d'oro*' ('golden shower') for a rainfall of actual gold, and rushed forward to acquire their cut – thus colluding, like Cavallino, in the confounding of fact in fiction. Such an overheated description may prepare us for Cavallino's discussion of the *naumachia*, a discussion that is less than documentary in its aims and execution.

Cavallino's relish for astonishing spectacle and his enjoyment of fantasy continue throughout his book. His account of the '*caccia belissima*' ('the very beautiful hunt') in the Piazza di Santa Croce on 8 May serves as a typical example. The slaughtered victims of this noble enterprise add up, he informs us, to a menagerie of dumb beasts that includes two buffalo, badgers, hares, hounds, birds 'in great numbers', goats, deer, swans – and many more. Wolves, mastiffs and '*Liompardi*' ('leopards', probably) were impelled to wreak havoc on a whole range of two and four-legged creatures in a staged combat that lasted half an hour. Some of the animals were unsurprisingly reluctant to fight. At least one escaped into town. The comprehensive destruction of animal life thus evoked evidently appeals to Cavallino's sensibility, though scarcely to that of the modern reader.[8]

Cavallino's fascinations carry over, as might be expected, into his account of the *naumachia*, where he revels in the simulated violence and the staged loss of life, with the din and the gun-smoke that blots out everything. He's particularly taken by what he judges to be, in a re-run of his naïve response to the *intermedi*, the pervasive realism of the events and the convincingness of the scenography. The cries of the wounded and drowning Turkish sailors, to take a single example,

---

[8]   For a vivid description of the carnage of the *caccia* in Florence see Samuel Berner, 'Florentine Society in the Late Sixteenth and Early Seventeenth Centuries', *Studies in the Renaissance*, 18 (1971), pp. 203–46, p. 226.

made use he claims of the 'Turkish' language, though it's far from clear how he could distinguish the language, or even hear it, in the surrounding cacophony. It seems that Cavallino's susceptible imagination is attributing to the spectacle a 'real-life' quality which a more detached observer might wish to discount.

Pavoni is an altogether cooler commentator than his rival, less excitable, and scrupulous to a fault over matters of etiquette and, as he sees it, truth-telling. Yet he too delights in the slaughter in the Piazza Croce, if not quite with Cavallino's lip-smacking relish. He too gets carried away by the quasi-realism of the *naumachia*, including specifying the types of vessels taking part – a feature that is at odds, as we shall see, with our only visual representation. At the same time, he fails to take account of the practicalities of introducing full-sized craft into a restricted, if ample, performance space.[9] Pavoni's degree of specificity proves open to question, though a few scholars have occasionally led evidence to endorse it, at least partially. Both writers are fixated on marvels and are gullible, or relaxed, about the boundaries of fact and fiction, a stance that can make accessing and interpreting the real events problematic.

The Lure of Lepanto

If we step back from contemporary accounts and their idiosyncrasies, we might ask what meaning the events of the *naumachia* and their narrative of Christian–Turkish conflict held for Grand Duke Ferdinando and, importantly, for his invited audience. These last were a privileged group whose entry to the Pitti Palace for the *naumachia* was controlled by ceramic tokens specially made for the occasion – though French and Florentine ladies and French gentlemen were exempt from this provision, a procedure resting somewhere between chivalry and diplomatic nicety. Diplomacy in particular was essential in a situation where French opinion-formers, Christine's countrymen, were especially welcome.[10] As many as 1700 guests from across the Italian city states and beyond had to be accommodated

---

9   See Pavoni, *Diario*, p. 40: '*diciotto vasselli tra grandi, e piccolo, tra i quali vi era vn Galeoncino con tre fano, quattro Galere grosse, & il restante Galere sottili, con altri vasselli & vna fregata*' ('eighteen ships, some large, some small, among which were a *galeoncino* [a type of large galleon] with three masts, four large galleons, and the remainder lesser galleons, with other vessels and a frigate').

10   The provision of porcelain tokens and the formality of the reception party are noted by Pavoni, *Diario*, p. 36: '*persona alcuna, se prima non mostrava il segno di Porcellana, che per tale effetto erano stati dispensati, e si passava per tre corpi di guardie, stando nella terza, ultima, il Serenissimo Gran Duca in persona ...*'. Pavoni goes on to report (p. 36) that '*alle Gentildonne Francesi, e Fiorentine, e anco all' Signori Francesi era libera l'entrata.*' ('each person had to show first a porcelain token which had been distributed for this purpose, and then pass three companies of guards, among the third of which stood the Grand Duke himself ... entry was free for French and Florentine gentlewomen, and for French gentlemen').

in Florence over the festival as a whole, lodging in the case of the most elevated in the Pitti Palace itself, with less high-profile individuals fanning out to noble residences across the city.[11] In effect, these civic and house guests formed a cadre of potential ambassadors for Ferdinando and Tuscany, primed, if the festivities proved sufficiently magnificent, to take home a message of Florentine greatness, with wealth, scholarship and administrative, artistic and technological know-how, it was hoped, the most admired characteristics. The fact that Ferdinando personally received the guests as they arrived for the *naumachia* argues the high value he placed on the occasion and the messages it and the preceding Barriers were hoped and expected to communicate.[12]

The Turkish–Christian theme of the naval battle may, however, have conveyed messages to informed observers that were more complex than simple propaganda. In a recent article Maria Alberti, developing earlier scholarship, makes a case for implicit allusions in the *naumachia* to the famed battle of Lepanto, accepted by contemporaries as a compelling index of Christian naval power in the face of a sustained 'Turkish' or Muslim threat – the terms are not rigorously differentiated in the literature of the period. By implication, through staging the *naumachia*, Ferdinando and Tuscany sought to take on the mantle of Christian nautical-military prowess. There can be no doubt that an intention of recruiting Lepanto to the Florentine cause was in the minds of those who oversaw the programme of the festival as a whole. One of the series of triumphal arches that greeted Christine, in this case at the Canto de' Bischeri, celebrated the great Christian victory, along with other military and maritime successes.[13] Yet in the real world Florentine participation in the battle was limited to no more than twelve galleys. This was out of, on one count, a total Christian fleet of 600 vessels.[14] Alberti attributes such

---

[11]   See Leon Satkowski, 'The Palazzo Pitti: Planning and Use in the Grand-Ducal Era', *Journal of the Society of Architectural Historians*, 42 (December 1983), pp. 336–49, p. 338: 'The highest-ranking visitors, the Duke and Duchess of Mantua, and their retainers, were lodged at the Pitti, but extraordinary solutions were employed to house many of the 1700 guests ... The entire city of Florence was pressed into service as visitors were billeted in the Palazzo Vecchio, and in the palaces of the city's leading families — the Medici, Strozzi, Bardi, and Niccolini.'

[12]   Etchings and engravings, most of them by Orazio Scarabelli, representing the courtyard prepared for foot combat and the processions, chariots and static displays that occupied the space for the earlier part of the evening, are most conveniently viewed in Saslow, *Medici Wedding*, catalogue numbers 71–86, pp. 248–59.

[13]   The arch celebrates, however, the Habsburg dynasty, either as a diplomatic attempt to soften Florence's turning in the present marriage towards France, or as a gesture of family loyalty to Ferdinando's mother, Eleonora of Toledo, or perhaps as a gesture of sympathy to Joanna of Austria, Francesco's spurned first wife. It also anachronistically describes the occupiers of the Holy Places, ousted by a Lorraine ancestor, as 'Turks', in keeping with an emergent theme of the triumphal arches and subsequently of the *naumachia*.

[14]   See Roger Crowley, *Empires of the Sea: The Final Battle for the Mediterranean, 1521–1580* (London: Faber and Faber, 2008), p. 265.

puny involvement – for a city state as wealthy as Florence – to Philip II's ban on Florentine participation in the Holy League's 'crusading' enterprise, on the grounds that Pius V's award of Grand Ducal status to Tuscany, and therefore to the rulers of Florence, constituted an insult to the Emperor.[15] However that may be, there was ground to be made up on Florence's part if Ferdinando's regime was to be measured against leading European states with respect to the prestige conferred by Lepanto. This may be even further the case if one is to take at face value a note preserved in the Medici archive, and now accessible on-line, which suggests that the twelve galleys were not a freely-given contribution to the Holy League's war effort, but were rented to the Pope at the going rate.[16]

We may take it that some at least of the more knowledgeable spectators entertained irreverent thoughts when they were asked to associate Florence with Lepanto, and with the more than bullish account of Christian prowess the *naumachia* offered. It might even have occurred to them that Ferdinando not only had military ground to make up on behalf of the Medici, but a half-guilty sense of failure – of commitment, loyalty and resources – for which to atone. In this regard, it may be worth noting as implicit confirmation that Gualterotti, describing the festival's Canto de' Bischeri arch, has the grace to attribute the victory at Lepanto to the '*lega del Pontefice, del Re and de Veneziani*', and only to add, a little shamefacedly, that it was '*non senza gloria del Gran Duca Cosimo, e di nostra Città*' ('the Holy League of the Pope, the King [of Spain] and the Venetians … [and] not without renown for Grand Duke Cosimo and our city').[17] The gap between hype and desert is, that is to say, implicitly recognised – as we may suppose it was by at least the better-informed of Ferdinando's *naumachia* invitees.

Intriguingly, an engraving dated 1590 depicting the battle of Lepanto, based on the work of the Medici court artist Johannes Stradanus, may cast further light on the association of Lepanto with Ferdinando's marriage celebrations. The engraving, made at Antwerp by Adriaen Collaert just one year after the *naumachia*, is dedicated to Don John of Austria and Philip II of Spain, as might be expected, but is also said in a Latin inscription running across the upper margin to record the '*laetitia*' ('joy') of the people of Florence on the arrival among them of Christine of Lorraine.[18] It looks from this as though a particular association grew up, or

---

[15]   Maria Alberti, 'Battaglie navali, scorrerie corsare e politica dello spettacolo: Le Naumachie medicee del 1589', *California Italian Studies Journal*, I (2010), pp. 1–33, http://escholarship.org/uc/item/8553h705, p. 16. Pp. 16–17 fn. 48 cites a considerable bibliography in support of Alberti's view. Grand Ducal status was awarded by Pope Pius V in response to lobbying on behalf of Cosimo I, though it was not finally conferred until two years after Cosimo's death.

[16]   See *Medici Archive Project: MdP2131, DocID12787.* The document was despatched by an unknown sender to an unknown recipient, 1571.

[17]   Gualterotti, *Della Descrizione*, pp. 140–41.

[18]   A copy of the engraving is held by the British Museum: BM 1873, 0712.35. The inscription running along the upper margin refers to '*Florentiae civitatis laetitia, cum in*

was deliberately cultivated, between Ferdinando's marriage with Christine and the celebration of Lepanto, a possibility worth bearing in mind when interpreting the *naumachia*'s meanings for contemporary observers.

Florence and the Order of Santo Stefano

The Christian military response to 'Turkish' maritime and land-based incursions into Europe and the Mediterranean involved more, however, than the technicolour victory of Lepanto. In particular, the Turks' siege of Vienna (1529), cast a long shadow over the European imagination, constituting as it did a menacing threat to the West's political integrity. Repeated instances of outrageous cruelty in subsequent years by the Turks, rumoured as well as real and reciprocated by the Christians, instilled widespread anxiety.[19] The Turkish menace had, however, altered its nature by the date of Ferdinando's *naumachia*. As the historian Fernand Braudel explains, by 1589 the years of overtly state-sanctioned Christian–Turkish warfare were past, and had been for the previous 15 years. Yet, as he also remarks, 'by some apparently general law, warfare simply took on new forms, reappearing and spreading' as piracy.[20]

It was principally to this new threat that Ferdinando's real-life anti-Turkish efforts were addressed, and it may well be that these, rather than Lepanto, should be seen as the *naumachia*'s immediate frame of reference. Much of the Grand Duke's abundant energy was devoted to reviving and promoting the military-chivalric Order of Santo Stefano, of which his father Cosimo had been the founding Gran Maestro. This was an office to which Ferdinando himself succeeded when taking the habit of the Order on 26 December 1588, while preparations for the marriage festivities were already in hand.[21] The Order was not forgotten during the festive period, with ten new Knights being installed as one of the programme's significant occasions only days before the *naumachia*.[22] A prime objective of the Order lay in repelling the Turkish 'corsairs' or pirates that threatened the Tuscan littoral, and this anti-Turkish activity, yoked implicitly with the Christian principles enunciated in the Order's regulations and ceremonial, will have been, one would suppose, in an audience's mind as it watched events unfold in the courtyard of the Pitti Palace.

Saslow may be a little too graphic in writing that the Order of Santo Stefano was seen 'as little more than a pious front for piracy' on Ferdinando's part, though

---

ea primum Magna Hetruriae Dux Christina Lotharingia ingrederetur' ('the joy of the city state of Florence when Christine of Lorraine entered the city for the first time as Grand Duchess of Tuscany').

[19] Crowley, *Empires, passim.*

[20] Fernand Braudel, *The Mediterranean and the Mediterranean World in the Age of Philip II*, trans. Siân Reynolds (2 vols, London: Collins, 1972–73), vol. 2, p. 865.

[21] Cosimo founded the Order on 30 January 1562.

[22] On 7 May, only four days before the *naumachia* took place.

he qualifies his phrase by ascribing it to the Turkish enemy.[23] Detlef Heikamp is more direct: the Order's 'principal occupation,' he writes, 'consisted in little more than outright piracy.'[24] Braudel himself refers to the 'restless voyages' of the Order's fleets in search of plunder and glory.[25] It is also true that alongside their opportunistic raids the Tuscans managed a small number of solid military achievements. In 1564, within a few years of its inauguration, the Order had captured two large Turkish vessels and, in the decade or so following the *naumachia*, its vessels attacked and seized the Turkish fortress of Chios, and a little later (1605 and 1607) the fortresses of Prevesa (Greece) and Bona (Algeria).[26]

Yet these military successes were crossed with motives that were more commercial than crusading. The Order's port of Leghorn (or Livorno), despite Tuscan professed, as well as real, animosity towards the Turks, was thrown open to all comers, including Turks, a provision that had trading interests, not ideology, behind it.[27] In a more general way, the homes of the period, including those of the Grand Duke's subjects in Florence, were filled with Turkish and Turkish-influenced goods.[28] J.R. Hale writes tellingly of 'the atmosphere of double-think'

---

[23]   Saslow, *Medici Wedding*, p. 157.

[24]   Detlef Heikamp et al. (eds), *Palazzo Pitti: La Reggia Rivelata* (Florence: Giunti, 2003), p. 59.

[25]   Braudel, *Mediterranean*, vol. 2, pp. 876, 877.

[26]   Cosimo 'built a small but powerful fleet of war galleys' and engaged as time went on in naval expansion; Ferdinando pursued the same policy. For details, see J.R. Hale, *Florence and the Medici: the Pattern of Control* (London: Thames and Hudson, 1977, paperback 1983), p. 130. And see Heikamp et al., *Palazzo Pitti* p. 229 for subsequent Medici successes. Turkish naval banners of the period are displayed in the Pisan Church associated with the Order of Santo Stefano. See Franco Cuomo, *Gli Ordini Cavallereschi nel mito e nel storia* (Rome: Newton and Compton, 2004), where the banners are said to come from the battle of Lepanto. Ferdinando's pride in the Order remained strong. Only a few years before his death he commissioned Bernardo Poccetti to create frescos in the *Appartamento dei Forestieri* of the Pitti Palace commemorating the main achievements of the Order as part of an ambitious political programme of Medici self-aggrandisement. See Stefania Vasetti, 'I fasti granducali della Sala di Bona: sintesi politica e culturale del principato di Ferdinando' in Heikamp et al., *Palazzo Pitti*, pp. 229–39.

[27]   Hale, *Florence*, p. 147 writes amusingly of Francesco's naïveté – or perhaps duplicity – when assuring Mohammed Pasha that Turkish ships could use the port of Leghorn, despite the galleys of the Order of Santo Stefano being dedicated to attacking the Turkish galleys that docked there. Francesco explained, Hale says, that 'these galleys belonged to an independent order ... for whose vows (though he had taken them himself) he was in no way responsible'.

[28]   This was especially true of homes in Venice, but not only in Venice, where relationships with Turkish art and culture were numerous. See Marta Ajmar-Wollheim and Flora Dennis (eds), *At Home in Renaissance Italy*, Exhibition Catalogue (London: Victoria and Albert Museum Publications, 2006), p. 309. For an informed and nuanced account of Lepanto and its significance from a Venetian perspective, see Iain Fenlon, *The Ceremonial*

that at the time pervaded the Christian West in regard to the Turks, with one strand of the binocular view 'focused upon monstrous inhumanity; the other on high standards of material well-being'. 'Religion', Hale crisply observes, 'had little to do with either'.[29] One might suppose that the more sophisticated observers of the *naumachia* would respond with a degree of scepticism to an event that, from one perspective, could be seen as an '*efficace instrumentum regni*' ('an effective tool of power')[30] and in another as an opportunity for civic and dynastic self-glorification amid a welter of, in the case of the *naumachia*'s spectators in 1589, alcohol-fuelled triumphalism. The tension between fact and fantasy, by now familiar as an embedded characteristic of the *naumachia*'s, and the Festival's, processes, is once again in evidence.

Naumachia and Classical Precedent

For Ferdinando, one motive for staging the *naumachia* was undoubtedly a wish to align his city with the classical world and with Rome in particular – a frequent matter of policy among the competing principalities of the time, offering an inviting and by no means arduous method of garnering prestige. Ferdinando, it appears, may well have had personal reasons as well as political for including a *naumachia* among his marriage entertainments, an event without precedent at this date among Florentine festivities.[31] His residence while still a Cardinal – before, that is, he forsook his Cardinal's habit for the Grand Ducal coronet (28 November 1588) – had been Rome's magnificent Villa Medici on the *Collis Hortulorum*. The Villa's garden lay in immediate proximity to a site said by antiquarians to be linked with a *naumachia* staged in order to impress the citizens of imperial Rome. Ferdinando, for his part, claimed direct authorship of the scheme for flooding the Pitti courtyard in 1589, a claim that may well be justified, and one that draws yet closer his personal patronage of the festival programme.[32]

City: History, Memory and Myth in Renaissance Venice (New Haven and London: Yale University Press, 2007), esp. pp. 172 ff and 263 ff.

[29]   See J.R. Hale, *The Civilization of Europe in the Renaissance* (London: Harper Collins, 1993), pp. 39–43, p. 41. Hale reproduces an image of a bronze medal showing Charles V supported by an angel, with Sultan Suleiman in the background (British Museum) – an image capable of being read as that of two equal or collaborating potentates.

[30]   The phrase is Alberti's in 'Battaglie navali', p. 1.

[31]   The detailed programme was overseen by Buontalenti and a numerous band of expert craftsmen, artists, engineers and designers, but in keeping with the principles of Renaissance patronage the prince laid down or at the very least approved the overall scheme.

[32]   See Archivio di Stato, Modena, AF 31, letter 7, 13 May 1589, from ambassador Girolamo Gilioli in Florence to Alfonso II d'Este, duke of Ferrara, written two days after the *naumachia*: '*[la festa] comparve benissimo et fece bellissima vista, et con bell'ordine passò questa battaglia, et con grandissima sodisfattione del Granduca per esser stato*

There is a further intriguing if superficially trivial detail. Ferdinando had acquired while in Rome the nickname 'Titus', that is to say the name of the Emperor responsible, as will be mentioned below, for a strikingly ambitious *naumachia*, one of a series of entertainments celebrating the inauguration of the Roman Colosseum in AD 80. It is improbable that court circles in Florence, or invited members of noble houses, were unaware of the nickname's flattering association of Ferdinando with a Roman emperor, or of its current pertinence. Ferdinando's *naumachia*, like its model at the Colosseum, could be seen, moreover, as celebrating the completion of a notable building project. In the modern instance this comprised the extended and beautified Pitti Palace, made over for the first time as the seat of Government, though a Medici possession for some years past. The newly-developed building complex included the Ammannati courtyard where the *naumachia* took place, as well as the remarkable *corridoio* Vasari running from the Grand Duke's private quarters in the Pitti to the Uffizi and the Palazzo Vecchio, and thus knitting the Pitti decisively into the life of the city. The *corridoio* was reaching its final form between October 1588 and May 1589, on the very brink of Ferdinando's marriage entertainments.[33]

Ferdinando may have expected the more informed among his invited guests to recognise the Colosseum *naumachia*, a very high-profile occasion, as precedent for its Florentine successor. Some may have come across relevant passages in their

---

lui l'inventore della festa navale.' ('[the festival] worked brilliantly and offered a very beautiful experience; the battle went well and gave great satisfaction to the Grand Duke in that he had been the inventor of the naval event'). I am indebted to the very generous help of Professor Suzanne Butters for this reference, and for drawing my attention to her published articles relevant to the festival and the *naumachia.* See Suzanne B. Butters, 'Magnifico, non senza eccesso: riflessioni sul mecenatismo del cardinal Ferdinando de' Medici' in *Villa Medici. Il sogno di un cardinal: collezioni e artisti di Ferdinando de' Medici*, exhibition catalogue, Rome: Académie de France à Rome, 17 November 1999–5 March, 2000 (Rome: De Luca, 1999), pp. 22–45; Suzanne B. Butters, 'Contrasting Priorities: Ferdinando I de' Medici, Cardinal and Grand Duke', in Mary Hollingsworth and Carol M. Richardson (eds), *The Possessions of a Cardinal: Art, Piety and Politics, 1450–1700* (University Park, Pa: Penn State Press, 2010), pp. 185–225; Suzanne B. Butters, 'Princely Waters: An Elemental Look at the Medici Dukes', in Arturo Calzona and Daniela Lamberini (eds), *La Civiltà delle Acque tra Medioevo e Rinascimento* (2 vols, Florence: Olschki, 2010), vol. 1, pp. 389–411; and Suzanne B. Butters et al. in the series *La Villa Médicis* dir. André Chastel, vol. 5 (Rome: Académie de France à Rome, École française de Rome, Académie des Beaux-Arts, 2010), p. 348.

[33]   For details of building work at the Palazzo Pitti, in particular the 'Ammannati courtyard' and the completion of the Vasari *corridoio* see for example Satkowski, 'The Palazzo Pitti', p. 339; and Michael Kiene, *Bartolomeo Ammannati 1511–1592* (Milan: Electa, 1995), pp. 88, 100, 104. An earlier phase of the *corridoio* had been completed in some haste for the wedding in 1565 of Francesco and his first wife Giovanna of Austria. See Richard Goy, *Florence: the City and its Architecture* (London: Phaidon, 2002), pp. 149–50, and Felicia Else, 'Giulio Ballino and the Florentine Corridoio', *MAPLINE*, 92 (Winter 2000–01): pp. 1–5 (http://www.newberry.org/smith/Mapline/92/92feature.html).

reading – in the Florentine Academy, the Studio Fiorentino or Studio Pisano – of Cassius Dio, Martial or Suetonius, each of them offering a partial description of what took place at the Colosseum. Others may have acquired a broad knowledge of the ancient events through the writing of contemporary antiquarians.[34] The scholars who oversaw the programme of the marriage entertainments, and the *naumachia* in particular, will certainly have understood – prompted perhaps by the Grand Duke's own directions – how Ferdinando's *naumachia* shared with the celebrated ancient event much of the technological daring, audacious casting, staged violence and allusive narration that rendered the earlier occasion so memorable.

The crucial passage in the ancient texts comes in the *Roman History* of Cassius Dio:

> Titus had suddenly filled this same theatre [Greek *theatron*, i.e. the Colosseum] with water … He also brought in people on ships … they engaged in a naval battle there representing the Corcyreans versus the Corinthians. Others gave a similar display outside the city [in another location, the *stagnum Augusti*] … There, too … on the third day [was held] a naval battle involving three thousand men, followed by an infantry battle: the 'Athenians' conquered the 'Syracusans' (these being the designations the men fought under) landed on the island, and stormed and captured a wall that had been built around the monument.[35]

---

[34] I am grateful to Simon Gilson of the University of Warwick for suggesting the reference to the Accademia and the two Studios. The relevant texts are: Marcus Valerius Martialis, *Liber Spectaculorum* II and XXIV trans. K.M. Coleman (Oxford: Oxford University Press, 2006), intro. pp. lxviii–lxx and Epigram 27, pp. 195–9; Gaius Suetonius Tranquillus, *The Twelve Caesars*, trans. R. Graves (Baltimore, Md: University of Maryland Press, 1962), esp. p. 290 and Lucius Dio Cassius, *Roman History*, vol. 8 (Cambridge MA: Harvard University Press, 1925), XXV. There has been debate as to whether the Colosseum was the location for the Roman *naumachia* in question, but this matter has been effectively settled by the research of Kathleen Coleman, reported in her essay, 'Launching into History: Aquatic Displays in the Early Empire', *The Journal of Roman Studies*, 83 (1993), pp. 48–74. Coleman discusses a range of Roman *naumachiae* and their locations, including the so-called *stagnum Augusti*, an excavated arena filled with water for the occasion. The practicalities of using the Colosseum have been demonstrated by Rossella Rea et al., 'Sotterranei del Colosseo. Ricerca preliminare al progetto di ricostruzione del piano dell'arena', *Mitteilungen des Deutschen Archäologischen Instituts (Römische Abteilung)* 107, (2000), pp. 311–39 and by Martin Crapper, 'How Roman Engineers could have flooded the Colosseum', *Proceedings of the Institution of Civil Engineers – Civil Engineering*, 160 (2007), pp. 184–91. Crapper's calculations were questioned by John Porter in a subsequent issue; his reply with revised figures is given in the University of Edinburgh's on-line journal *Environmental Engineering Research* for 18/04/2008, www. see.ed.ac.uk/MIE/research/environ.

[35] Cassius Dio, *Roman History* LXVI. 25.2–4, cited and translated by Coleman, 'Launching into History', p. 48. The passage (here further abridged) makes clear that the *naumachiae* described took place in two separate locations, the Colosseum and the *stagnum*

The parallels with the 1589 *naumachia* are readily apparent, especially when one recognises that a precedent can be effective without precise duplication. In this instance we may notice the 'suddenness' with which the theatre space was flooded, the noise and mimed or real violence of the naval battle, the watery combat between two named antagonists (anticipating the 'Christians' and 'Turks' of Ferdinando's spectacle), the very large numbers of sailors involved, and the final storming of a fortification on an 'island'. All of these find echoes, spelled out below, in the *naumachia* of 1589.

The Harvard scholar Kathleen Coleman sees in the ancient *genre* of *naumachiae* 'the propaganda motif of "no expense and effort spared"' and notes the strong preponderance of 're-enactments from Greek history'; she comments on the 'life-and-death element' in the spectacles, saying they were 'in grim earnest in the sense that people were meant to get killed'; she refers to the emperor Titus who became through the successful promotion and presentation of the Colosseum *naumachia* 'the heir of Rome's new dynasty, destined for apotheosis'.[36] All of these motives and characteristics find echoes, deliberately and expensively featured, in the 1589 show. There may even be a real if concealed irony, though it is one which Ferdinando's programme planners would not want to be apparent to an audience. As Coleman remarks, 'why stage [at the Colosseum] a replay of an historical event (in this case the Athenians' unsuccessful attack on Syracuse in 414 BC), only to allow the outcome [victory for the Athenians] to contradict the facts of history?'[37] It is improbable that the victory of Lepanto, or the exploits of the Santo Stefano marauders, were already being seen in an equivocal light in Medicean Florence. Much more likely is that Ferdinando, Buontalenti and their scholarly advisers were consciously following ancient precedent by staging a battle that was based on history and that involved antagonists – Christians and Turks – in relation to whom audience sympathies were predictable, ensuring that the result was gratifying in a partisan fashion. Everything in the Florentine *naumachia*, both practical and emotional, is on a smaller scale than the spectacle in the Colosseum: in physical terms, the Colosseum arena measures approximately 54 metres at the widest point of its ellipse by 87 metres in length, dwarfing even the huge Pitti courtyard (approximately 42.8 metres by 38 metres when prepared for the *naumachia*), and no-one, so far as we know, got killed amidst the hullabaloo of the Florentine occasion.[38] Yet, however scaled down, the sixteenth-century *naumachia* shares genetic characteristics with its ancient predecessor, together with similar motives and anticipated results. Ferdinando's advisers would want to pick up the kudos associated with doing as the Romans did – and were prepared to pay for the comparison.

Augusti, though it seems probable that the Colosseum show incorporated both of Dio's narratives. Those drawing up the 1589 programme would not be averse, in any case, to conflating the two.

[36]   Coleman, 'Launching into History', pp. 69, 73, 74.

[37]   Ibid., p. 49.

[38]   For the courtyard dimensions see note 40 below.

Ancient Practicalities

Coleman, like scholars before her, worries about the sheer practicality of staging a *naumachia* in the vast spaces of the Colosseum as they have survived today. Painstaking research of a textual, archaeological and technical kind by a series of recent scholars, including Rossella Rea and her collaborators and the hydraulics expert Martin Crapper, have gone some considerable way to demonstrating that solutions were available to Roman engineers and entertainment organisers.[39] The *hypogeum* or lowest level of the Colosseum amphitheatre, it emerges, probably did not have at the date of the inaugural *naumachia* the ground-level walled divisions that are today such a prominent feature of the monument's structure. The building may have featured instead, according to Rea and her colleagues, an undivided excavated area, perhaps 1.5 metres in depth, beneath a removable wooden floor. The arena could have been flooded for the show – traces of supports and drainage channels survive. Coleman questions whether, given local water supplies, the 'suddenness' of flooding the arena, emphasised in ancient accounts, together with convenient subsequent drainage, could have been managed. Crapper and others have suggested that a branch supply from the Acqua Claudia aqueduct may have been called into service, perhaps supplemented by pipework from the Caelian Hill. Crapper's figures, based on detailed calculations of water-flow and pipework dimensions, show after revision that it would have proved possible to fill the arena in times between approximately 30 minutes and one hour – a timescale that may well have been considered 'sudden'.

Coleman has been doubtful, too, about the dimensions and the practical character of the boats employed in the ancient *naumachia*, concluding that only 'miniaturised' ships could have been used, since 'it would have been impossible to get full-scale ships through the entrances to the arena'. 'Miniature replicas' would necessarily, she concedes, have had to be large enough to accommodate several crew members.[40]

These issues of practicality and scale will need to be considered in relation to the 1589 *naumachia*, given that the modern event faces many of the same challenges of preparation and staging as its Roman precedent. If the parallels between the ancient and modern *naumachiae* were indeed deliberately cultivated, we should expect the overcoming of similar challenges to be a positive aspect of the event's appeal to the sixteenth-century as to the ancient spectators.

How Did Ferdinando's People Do It?

The courtyard of the Pitti Palace is, as a stage space, a vast arena, if not as extensive as the Colosseum. The human figures at the top left of the photograph

---

[39]   See Rea et al., 'Sotteranei del Colosseo' and Crapper, 'Roman Engineers'.
[40]   Coleman, 'Launching into History', pp. 59, 61.

reproduced here (Plate 1), looking like toy miniatures, offer a sense of the courtyard's impressive scale. As measured by Michael Holden, making allowance for the water-proofed boarding associated with the *naumachia*, this extends, as noted above, to 42.8 metres by 38 metres, an area of approximately 1,626 square metres. If we accept, for the moment, the suggestion in a contemporary document of a depth of five feet or so for the *naumachia*, flooding the courtyard would entail an influx of around 2,480 cubic metres of water. Even on a more realistic estimate of water depth at around 1,200 mm or approximately four feet, the capacity of the 'tank' constructed within the courtyard would be roughly 1,950 cubic metres.[41] On either measure, taking into account that a cubic metre of water weighs one ton, a considerable engineering challenge is entailed.

Advice from hydraulics expert Dr Jonathan Pearson of the University of Warwick gives some sense of the extent of the practical requirements. In order to provide, in response to the higher estimate of capacity, something like 3,000 cubic metres of water in order to flood the *cortile* (to take a round figure), a typical domestic supply would require, Pearson says, 35 days. Even at the lesser estimate of depth, the time-scale from a domestic supply would occupy, say, 24 or 25 days. At the greater depth of five feet or so, to offer another indicator of scale, a modern fire engine using four hoses, fed from a lake or pond, would require something like 12.5 hours. Even with scaling-down to the shallower depth, eight hours or so of fill-time would be needed. Pearson, stressing that his figures are approximate, remarks that 'it could be quite challenging to achieve' the implied fill-rate of 500 litres a second, or even at the shallower depth proportionately less, within the 3 hours' interval occupied by the banquet which intervened between the preliminary pageantry in the courtyard and the *naumachia* itself – unless, for example, the full flow of a river was diverted. Pearson has experimentally achieved the higher rate of flow in 1.5 hours, but 'the pipe was 1 metre in diameter and the pump

---

[41]   Michael Holden, private email, 1 May 2011. Holden's measurements take into account the existence of a kerb, originally about 100 mm in height, against which it is presumed the retaining wall would be braced. The measurements also allow for the kerb running about 1.2 m in front of the Boboli gardens façade. A measurement of the water's depth as five feet accords with Pavoni, *Diario*, pp. 35–6, where the *serraglia* is measured at 3 *braccia* (or approximately 5 feet). However, taking into account the necessary gap between the surface of the water and the edge of the tank it is more probable that the water depth would be in the range of four feet. The same passage in Pavoni offers further details of the preparation of the courtyard for the *naumachia*: '*divanti a detti palchi vi era una serraglia alta tre braccia, che circondava tutto il Cortile, quale era bittumata in modo, che havea nessun spiraglio, fatti cosi a posta, per farvi una battaglia navale*' ('in front of the said seating for the ladies was an enclosing wall three *braccia* in height that encircled the entire courtyard, treated with bitumen so that there was no gap, and made in this way to hold a naval battle'). Testaverde (*L'officina*, p. 163) defines a *braccio* as '*circa m. 0,583*' or approximately 20 inches.

was huge'.[42] The question of how a similar outcome could be achieved in late sixteenth-century Florence is, at the least, an intriguing one.

Cavallino's account of flooding the courtyard expresses with some fervour (and characteristic naivety) the astonishment of the invited audience when they returned to their seats after their three-hour absence to find the *cortile* suddenly transformed into '*veramente il mare*' ('the real sea'):

> *Sgombrossi ogni cosa dal campo, & immantinente apparve cosa stupenda e maravigliosa, che si come era apparechiato, si riempi tutto il campo d'acqua, & crebbe all' altezza di quarto [quattro] braccia, cosa dilettevolissima con tante onde che sembrava veramente il mare ...*

> [Everything had been cleared from the courtyard, and at once there appeared an astounding and wonderful thing, that when the courtyard had been prepared the whole space had been filled with water, it was said to the depth of four *braccia*, a most delightful phenomenon with so many waves that it appeared truly the sea ...][43]

Given the engineering feat achieved while their backs were turned and their stomachs filled, the audience was without question justified in the astonishment attributed to them by the chronicler. They may well have been unaware, however, in most if not all cases, of echoing in this respect the acclaim and amazement expressed by the Colosseum audience and the chroniclers of the time at the speed of flooding their own vast arena. It is unlikely that Ferdinando or Buontalenti, on the contrary, were unaware of the comparison, given the challenge the whole spectacle threw out to classical precedent. Ferdinando's deployment, through Buontalenti's agency, of extraordinary resources of time, cost and expertise in realising the seemingly impossible demands of the *naumachia* would have foregrounded such a comparison of ancient and modern for those sufficiently knowledgeable to appreciate its pertinence.[44]

By the date of the *naumachia*, the Medici considered technology an arm of government as well as a source of prestige. Cosimo had shown a deep interest in shipbuilding, metallurgy and irrigation; Francesco conducted experiments on the properties of minerals; Ferdinando maintained continuing support for irrigation

---

[42]   The quotations are from a private email of 8 March 2010. Pearson emphasises the difficulty of giving exact figures in the absence of precise details of the *cortile* and the contours of the surrounding land.

[43]   Cavallino, *Raccolta*, p. 44. Pavoni, *Diario*, p. 40, is characteristically more succinct, but no less emphatic, saying the spectators '*restarono tutti attoniti & stupefatti*' ('all became astonished and amazed').

[44]   For details see, for example, Saslow, *Medici Wedding* and Testaverde, *L'officina delle nuvole*.

and the construction of canals at Pisa and elsewhere.[45] The achievements of ancient and contemporary Rome in hydraulic engineering and the harnessing and distribution of water supplies must have invited both envy and emulation from the relatively new-come Medici regime.[46] A bronze medal by Pier Paolo Galeotti struck in 1565 shows on the obverse Grand Duke Cosimo with, on the reverse, a fountain surmounted by a figure of Neptune with an aqueduct stretching away into the distance, in this fashion giving permanent and widely distributed expression to one aspect, hydraulic engineering, of the Medici's technological expertise. The successful management of the more-than-considerable technical challenges of the 1589 *naumachia* must have formed part of the event's meaning, for the Medici themselves and for those they wished to impress.

The Medici might take things one step further. Water supply could be represented as, and indeed was, not merely an index of technological know-how, but a matter of benevolent, and prestige-conferring, concern for public health. Grand Duke Cosimo, celebrated by 1589 as the founder of the new Medici dynasty, regarded the Neptune fountain in the Piazza Ducale, bringing fresh water for drinking and washing to the city's population, as one of the great achievements of his reign.[47] When a new aqueduct system was installed in Florence in the 1630s, his Medici successors took pains to create the illusion that the health-giving waters streamed into the city from the Boboli Gardens (annexed to the Pitti Palace). It was thus notionally possible to cast the Medici in their Grand Ducal dwelling as the source of the people's health. The overcoming of technical challenges associated with water management could be seen, that is to say, not only as placing the Medici on the same pedestal as ancient and modern Romans – aqueduct technology in modern Rome was celebrated like its ancient precursor – but more generally understood as an aspect of socially-conscious and beneficent rule.[48]

---

[45]   See J.R. Hale, *Florence and the Medici: the Pattern of Control* (London: Thames and Hudson, 1977, pb. 1983), p. 145: 'Cosimo had taken a close interest in technology, especially in connection with shipbuilding, metallurgy and irrigation. Francesco, too, was drawn to applied science …'. For Francesco's interests see Luciano Berti, *Il Principe dello studiolo: Francesco I dei Medici e la fine del Rinascimento fiorentino* (Florence: Edam, 1967).

[46]   For discussion and illustration of contemporary Roman advances in the construction of aqueducts and the science of hydraulics see Pamela O. Long, 'Hydraulic Engineering and the Study of Antiquity, 1557–70', *Renaissance Quarterly*, 61 (2008), pp. 1098–1138. Long notes that it was Pius V, the Pope cultivated by Cosimo when pursuing the title of Grand Duke, who successfully restored the ancient Acqua Vergine (1570), bringing 'thousands of gallons of water to the city daily' (p. 1100).

[47]   Claudia Lazzaro, *The Italian Renaissance Garden* (New Haven and London: Yale University Press, 1990), p. 191.

[48]   The Florentine water projects also had their historic aspect in referring to the ancient Roman aqueducts and could be seen as parallel to the successful project in modern Rome by Pius V to restore the ancient 'Acqua Virgine'. See Long, 'Hydraulic Engineering' and Malcolm Campbell, 'Hard Times in Baroque Florence: The Boboli Gardens and the

It is difficult to measure the extent of the technical challenges posed by the *naumachia*, and even more difficult to establish the means by which they were met. The preparation of the courtyard is well enough described, at least in outline, by the two published chronicles. Pavoni refers to the construction of a *serraglia* or retaining wall about five feet in height encircling the courtyard. This was *bittumata* ('caulked') so that there was no gap left anywhere.[49] Information transcribed by Testaverde from the archives confirms, as we should expect, that this retaining wall was braced against the pressure of the water by blocks of wood prepared for the purpose under Buontalenti's direction. She also draws on archival sources to question the height of the retaining wall, positing a structure less than one metre (90 cm) in height, far lower than the chroniclers claim they saw. Her evidence poses a difficulty for interpreting the preparation of the arena and Buontalenti's overcoming of the practicalities of the naval battle, as will appear below.[50]

The Visual Source

The one illustration we have of the *naumachia*, which might resolve some of these questions, is the well-known etching by Orazio Scarabelli (Fig. 8.1). There are, however, reasons for being cautious about its accuracy as a record of events. Yet again, it would seem, we face a contradiction between what was actually seen and what was represented. The first reason for doubting the etching's accuracy is that it has been dated by Arthur R. Blumenthal to 1592, three years *after* the *naumachia*.[51] Testaverde, for her part, writes that it was '*eseguito alcuni anni dopo sul ricordo*

Grand Ducal Public Works Administration' in John Dixon Hunt (ed.), *The Italian Garden: Art, Design and Culture* (Cambridge: Cambridge University Press, 1996), pp. 160–201, pp. 194, 195. See also the review of Hunt's book by Corinne Mandel in *Sixteenth Century Journal*, XXVIII (Autumn 1997), pp. 879–82, p. 882.

⁴⁹   For the full quotation see note 41 above.

⁵⁰   See Testaverde, *L'officina*, pp. 141–2, esp. p. 141: '*Le dettagliate richieste per i quantitativi legname per gli steccati e le paratie laterali referiscono che l'altezza base era pari a cm 90 (br. 1 e 2/3), contraddicendo dunque le misure variabili citate dai cronisti.*' ('the detailed requests for quantities of wood required for the retaining walls and the side walls imply that the basic height was the equivalent of 90 cm (one and two thirds *braccia*), thus contradicting the various measures given by the chroniclers'). Testaverde, p.141, n. 12, says that the anonymous description edited by Baldini agrees with this conclusion, in contradiction to Pavoni's measurements.

⁵¹   Arthur R. Blumenthal, *Theater Art of the Medici* (Hanover, NH and London: Dartmouth College Museum and Galleries and University Press of New England, 1980), p. 25. Blumenthal, director emeritus of the Cornell Fine Arts Museum, explains (private email, 7 April 2011) that, to his recollection, 'Agostino Caracci and Orazio Scarabelli engraved and etched the print after Buontalenti's designs … in 1592', noting that the date 1592 is 'on all the prints of the 1589 *intermezzi* in the Metropolitan Museum in New York'. I am grateful to Professor Blumenthal for his scholarly assistance.

Figure 8.2   Orazio Scarabelli, *Mock Naval Battle in the Pitti Palace*, 1589. ©
The Trustees of the British Museum.

dell' episodio' ('drawn some years after as a souvenir of the event'). Does the
etching represent an accurate visual account of what took place, recollected in
tranquillity, or does it show what might, or could, have happened, but did not
necessarily happen in this particular way?[52] How far is Scarabelli influenced by
existing and traditional depictions of naval battles, rather than by on-the-spot
observation? The answer to these questions will of course considerably influence
how the etching is interpreted.

Questions about the etching's veracity might plausibly focus on the ships'
appearance. Nicholas Rodger, an international authority on early-modern
shipping, says that, as depicted, the Christian galleys are unconvincing even as
approximations of contemporary vessels. They represent, he writes robustly, 'one
of the absurd stock of images distantly based on widely-circulated engravings or
woodcuts which served in the sixteenth and seventeenth centuries for a public

---

[52]   For a telling discussion of the reliability of contemporary illustrations and their
relationship to the accompanying texts, see Elizabeth Cropper, Giovanni Perini and
Francesco Solinas (eds), *Documentary Culture: Florence and Rome from Grand Duke
Ferdinand I to Pope Alexander VII* (Bologna: Nuova Alfa Editoriale, 1992), especially
Elizabeth Cropper, 'Introduction', pp. 7–21 and Annamaria Petrioli Tofani, 'L'Illustraziionè
Teatrale e il Significato dei Documenti Figurativi per la storia dello Spettacolo', pp. 49–62.

grossly ignorant of what ships looked like'.[53] One example of such an image, showing ridiculously-conceived ships not dissimilar to those in our etching (ridiculous to modern eyes at least), is a drawing after Polidoro da Caravaggio, BM 1868,0612.1374, dated by the British Museum 1540–60. The ultimate source for the drawing seems to be the naval battle depicted on Trajan's column (Rome, second century AD). How accurately Scarabelli represents the ships that made an appearance in the Pitti courtyard in 1589 should therefore be seen as open to question, in the light of customary visual images and Professor Rodger's comments. It would be mistaken to place too great a reliance on the etching in attempting to reconstruct the actual *naumachia*.

There are other features of the etching to consider. The ships' sails billow as though wind-filled, but in bafflingly contrary directions. Close inspection, furthermore, raises questions about the depth of water when calibrated against the pillars of the courtyard, suggesting that Scarabelli has poor warrant for the detail of his drawing, though arguably he is accurate in this particular regard.[54] It is difficult to accept, in addition, that the marine traffic in the etching could be manoeuvred in practice so as to mimic a battle, or tell the story of an assault on a fortress, or indeed sail in any direction (Fig. 8.2). It is true that galley warfare in the period was characterised, as depicted or at least suggested in the etching, by ramming and boarding an enemy and engaging in hand-to-hand combat. This is how the Christian–Turkish battle is described in Cavallino's and Pavoni's texts, and represented in a whole series of contemporary paintings, most famously Vicentino's *Lepanto* in the Doge's palace.[55] The motorway pile-up of the etching might be interpreted as a contemporary's impression of the 1589 event, influenced by the violence and din described by the chroniclers, by gossip and printed texts reporting the realities of Lepanto or another sea battle, and by what had become a convention of artistic representation.

---

[53]   Private email, 5 November, 2009.

[54]   A private email from Michael Holden (1 May 2011) offers reasons for assessing the water depth depicted by Scarabelli as 'a little over 1,200 mm deep (4 ft)'.

[55]   For an excellent scholarly account of contemporary naval warfare see J.R. Hale and Michael Mallett, *The Military Organisation of a Renaissance State: Venice c. 1400–1617* (Cambridge: Cambridge University Press, 1984). Hale notes in another essay the chaos of the battle of Lepanto: 'The crash of broken oars, the rattling explosions of arquebuses and grenades, the war-notes of the Christian trumpets and the Turkish drums, the clash of swords, the shouts and yells of the combatants rose in a deafening din'. *The Project Gutenberg eBook of Famous Sea Fights* (2008), p. 96, www.gutenberg.org/files/25088/25088-h/25088-h.htm.

Figure 8.2   A detail of the etching by Orazio Scarabelli (Fig. 8.2) showing the 'Turkish' fortress under attack, with invited spectators lining the galleries and the sails of attacking ships in the foreground.

Buontalenti's Vessels

How and where were the ships acquired or manufactured? Were they old vessels or new-built? Saslow tells us they were commandeered in widespread sweeps across the Tuscan countryside during the previous six months.[56] His further investigations, however, modify this conclusion, based on a re-reading of documents drawn up by and for Francesco di Jacopo Rabbatini ('apparently the administration's "boat consultant"').[57] As the tale emerges from surviving evidence, including Testaverde's transcriptions from the Medici archives, it becomes evident that Buontalenti and his team proved uncertain about how to acquire the boats needed for the *naumachia*, and resorted to seeking estimates for both new and refurbished craft.[58] A carpenter at the Pitti palace, Antonio Fossetta, a specialist in constructing new boats, seems to have made a prototype. Cost considerations favoured newly manufactured craft,

---

[56]   Saslow, *Medici Wedding*, pp. 168–9.

[57]   Saslow's second thoughts about the evidence were set out in a private email (25 June 2010), to which I am greatly indebted. See also Saslow, *Medici Wedding*, p. 97 and note 51 for the quoted colourful phrase and for reference to the archival source for Girolamo Seriacopi's logbook and Rabattini's correspondence.

[58]   Testaverde, *L'officina*, p. 146 and private email from Maria Ines Aliverti, 29 May 2011 with detailed references to Testaverde.

on the grounds that refurbished boats would be almost as expensive, would require maintenance, and would be hard to re-sell. These are conclusions that accord with those reached by Maria Ines Aliverti who, after reviewing Testaverde's edition of the *Memoriale*, and consulting her colleague Lucia Nuti, came to the view that Buontalenti used for his eighteen-strong mimic fleet 'a model from Livorno; six boats from Pisa (new or refurbished); and some new boats made in the Florentine workshop' possibly by the craftsman-carpenter Fossetta.[59]

What becomes clear from archival and other sources, contrary to some published speculation, is that practical vessels were used in the *naumachia*, crewed by sailors recruited for the purpose, and not merely pantomime craft carried into the arena by crew members. This is a conclusion that makes sense of Pavoni's claims that boats capable of being read as real craft were employed, from a three-masted *Galeoncino* to large and 'narrow' galleys – even if it remains difficult, for practical reasons of scale and depth of water, to credit in any detail Pavoni's precise identifications.[60] These considerations place a question mark against Testaverde's suggestion, mentioned above, that a much lower retaining wall was employed to encircle the courtyard: the boats, new or refurbished, would require a considerable depth of water in which to float and manoeuvre. The same considerations, more importantly, undermine the veracity of Scarabelli's etching, with its boats looking scarcely convincing as the naval craft he claims them to be. The etching seems unreliable as documentary even if, as suggested below, its evocation of the atmosphere of the occasion remains suggestive.

---

[59]   Private emails 29 and 31 May 2011. Aliverti addresses the question of how the relevant boats could have been transported from Pisa and Livorno to Florence. Butters in Calzona and Lamberini, *La Civiltà*, vol. 1, p. 392 notes that 'straight new canals were dug to facilitate the transport of goods by water [from Pisa] to and from the very edge of Florence, and between Pisa and Livorno'. The known dates of these canals are 1592 and 1603, but there are implications that some at least of the network was in place before the earlier date, so that transport by water to Florence may have been available for the *naumachia*'s newly-constructed or refurbished craft.

[60]   Pavoni, *Diario*, p. 40, and see note 9 above. Pavoni is in no doubt that he saw, on the night, authentic or at the very least recognisable boats, specifying among the 18 vessels 'both large and small' a three-masted *Galeoncino*, four large *Galere*, *Galere sottili* ('narrow' galleys) plus other ships and a *fregata* ('frigate'). Saslow, *Medici Wedding*, p. 260 refers to 'small boats decorated to resemble seagoing battleships', a view his more recent reconsideration endorses. Professor Rodger's criticism of the boats depicted in the Scarabelli etching remains valid: Scarabelli was drawing conventional types of craft, not offering an eye-witness sketch. Alberti, 'Battaglia navali', p. 22 footnote 74, states firmly that pantomime craft cannot have been used: '*Numerosi sono i passi del 'Memoriale' che smentiscono definitivamente la vecchia ipotesi che voleva le imbarcazioni montate su carri*' ('there are numerous passages in the *Memoriale* which refute the old hypothesis which suggested that the boats were mounted on cars').

Practical Preparations

It is necessary at this stage to tackle, as far as surviving evidence will permit, some of the more perplexing questions about the technology on which Buontalenti and his colleagues drew in making the *naumachia* of 1589 a practical reality. We have left unanswered the puzzle of how the courtyard could be flooded with such a huge volume of water within such a limited period of time, in implicit homage to the extraordinary *naumachia* in the Roman Colosseum. This is a puzzle which, at present, it has proved possible to answer only in part. The Medici, from Grand Duke Cosimo on, had shown compelling interest in ambitious water projects, including those in Duke Francesco's famous gardens at Pratolino – gardens replete with remarkable water features, which provided, according to Valleriani and Büttner writing for the Max Planck Institute, in addition to visitor appeal, a noted instance of a 'high-tech [and integrated] hydraulic system'.[61] Ferdinando, for his part, maintained the Medici interest in water technology, continuing during the early years of his Grand Dukedom to be directly interested in the supply of water to the gardens of his Villa in Rome, including petitioning Clement VIII for permission to bring water for irrigation from relatively distant Montecavallo.[62] Throughout his reign, he took a deep interest in irrigation projects and in the construction of aqueducts at and near Pisa. This technological commitment to water-engineering by successive Medici Grand Dukes – Francesco's experiments at Pratolino were famed equally for ambition and posturing – unquestionably forms a pertinent background to the technical showmanship of the *naumachia* of 1589. As the inaugural high-profile event of Ferdinando's rule the *naumachia* must have seemed the perfect occasion for the new Grand Duke to make his mark as the promoter of innovative technology in an especially public and international forum.

The Boboli Gardens, immediately adjacent to the Pitti courtyard, featured several fountains and a reservoir which together were the only plausible source for flooding the *naumachia* space. Malcolm Campbell's 'Giambologna's Oceanus Fountain' and 'Hard Times in Baroque Florence' offer a summary of the Gardens' layout, illustrating the discussion in the latter case with an eighteenth-century plan by Agostino Ruggieri that clearly identifies the Gardens' water features at that date, from the statue of *Dovizia* (Abundance, commissioned 1600), the Vivaio Grande (the reservoir at the top of the central *allée*), the Oceanus Fountain and Stoldo

---

[61]   See Matteo Valeriani and Hochen Büttner, 'Pratolino: The History of Science in a Garden', Max Planck Institute for the History of Science, on-line resource http://mpiwg-berlin.mpg.de/en/research/projects/DEPT1_Valle; and Webster Smith, 'Pratolino', *Journal of the Society of Architectural Historians*, 20 (1961), pp. 155–68; also Montaigne, *Journal de voyage* p. 186 as quoted by Webster Smith, 'Pratolino', p. 157: Francesco de' Medici 'would seem to have selected expressly an inconvenient site, sterile and mountainous, nay even without springs, in order that he might have that honour of going to fetch them five miles away'.

[62]   *The Medici Archive Project* documents 407 and 16727 dated 1591/2.

Lorenzi's Neptune Fountain to the Fontana del Carciofo adjacent to the palace courtyard.[63] A sufficient gradient existed, and exists, in this area of the Gardens not only to make possible eye-catching effects when the fountains played but to achieve at the very least a substantial flow of water to the *cortile* when and if the supply was diverted for this purpose, perhaps by way of a newly-excavated channel. There was in existence, moreover, close to the site of the *naumachia*, a network of underground pipes supplying various water features, among them the Grotta dell'Ammannati (or Grotta di Mosè) at the Gardens end of the *cortile* as well as the so-called Buontalenti Grotto (a short distance from the *cortile*) commissioned by Francesco in 1583. A supply of water to the *cortile*, calling on the resources of fountains and underground pipes in order to meet the requirements of the mimic sea-battle, would accord with the rather unspecific reference in Pavoni's chronicle to '*certi sotteranei acquedotti*' ('certain underground channels') which 'rose up' ('*sorgevano*') to fill the arena on the occasion of the *naumachia*.[64] It would also accord with a reference in Gherardo Silvani's *Life* of Buontalenti to '*due cateratoloni*' ('two small sluicegates') which, he says, were opened during the dining interval in order to flood the courtyard to a depth equivalent to a man's height.[65]

It may be that considerable reconstruction and excavation took place in the Boboli Gardens at the time of the *naumachia*. Cristina Acidini Luchinat charts the changes of position of the Neptune fountain within the Boboli Gardens over the later years of the century, concluding tentatively that the return of the fountain to a vantage point overlooking the palace courtyard may have been associated with Ferdinando's plans for celebrating his marriage. Re-location work of this kind may conceivably form part of the technical arrangements needed to make the *naumachia* possible.[66]

---

[63]   Campbell, 'Giambologna's Oceanus Fountain', in Cristina Accidini Luchinat and Elvira Garbero Zorzi (eds), *Boboli 90 ...* (Florence: Edifir, 1991), pp. 89–106 and 'Hard Times in Baroque Florence: The Boboli Garden and the Grand Ducal Public Works Administration', in Hunt, *Italian Garden*, pp.160–201. For a detailed discussion of the provision of water in the Boboli Gardens see Lazzaro, 'The Source for Florence's Water', *Renaissance Garden*, pp. 191–214. The exact positioning of fountains in 1589 remains subject to debate, but the provision of abundant supplies of water is evident.

[64]   Pavoni, *Diario*, p. 40. For a discussion of work on the Grotto Grande during the 1580s see Litta Maria Medri, 'Considerazioni intorno alle prima fasi della Grotta Grande nel Giardino di Boboli', in Isabella Lapi Ballerini and Litta Maria Medri (eds), *Artifici d'Acque e Giardini*, Atti del V Convegno Internazionale su Parchi e Giardini Storici (Florence, 1999), pp. 215–27.

[65]   Testaverde, *L'officina* p. 185, notices among entries in the Florentine archives a reference to 'two large streams' feeding water to the courtyard, which she associates with two statues she identifies in the passages leading to the *cortile* from the Boboli Gardens in Scarabelli's etching; these, she says, were probably connected to the hydraulic arrangements for flooding the courtyard.

[66]   Cristina Acidini Luchinat, 'La Fontana del Nettuno: Viaggi e Metamorfosi', in Luchinat and Zorzi (eds), *Boboli 90*, pp. 33, 42.

A more difficult question is how and at what volume the Vivaio Grande and therefore the fountains were fed. The jets produced by some of the water features both here and in other Medici locations were capable, with the controlling stop-cocks fully open, of displaying astonishing force. The Neptune fountain in the Piazza della Signoria, hard by the Palazzo Vecchio, commissioned by Cosimo and designed by the architect of the *cortile*, Bartolommeo Ammannati in 1560–75, was capable when fed by two aqueducts of producing a geyser known as the *vela* (or sail) which could reach roughly 71.5 feet above pavement level.[67] Felicia Else identifies three aqueducts in the city in and after the time of Cosimo, speculating in a private email that two of them may have been called on for the *naumachia*: the "Pitti aqueduct", which crossed the Arno via the Ponte Vecchio in tandem with the Vasari *corridoio*, and the "Fonte alla Ginevra", which made the river crossing by the Ponte Rubaconte, modern Ponte alle Grazie.[68] The first of these aqueducts is known to have supplied the Vivaio Grande reservoir in the Boboli Gardens. Judging from the fact that this aqueduct when coupled with the Fonte alla Ginevra went on to supply the spectacular geyser-producing Neptune fountain with its multiple jets, it would seem that, with stop-cocks shut to all outlets except the *cortile*, a very considerable volume of water would be available to Buontalenti and those who assisted him in flooding the courtyard rapidly and to the required depth. This is, I believe, as far as we can go at present in accounting for the dramatic phenomenon that so astonished Ferdinando's invited audience by its sudden appearance and its depth.[69]

---

[67]   Felicia Else, 'Water and Stone: Ammannati's Neptune Fountain as Public Ornament' (PhD diss., Washington University, St. Louis, 2003), esp. pp. 255–8; Malcolm Campbell in Hunt, *Italian Garden*, pp. 195–6, considers the source of the Neptune Fountain's spectacular performance, noting that at its most astonishing it may have benefited from the hydraulic engineering installed under Ferdinando II in the 1630s.

[68]   Else, 'Water and Stone', chapter 4; L. Paglianti, *Ferdinando I e l'acquedotto di Pisa. Techniche di approvvigionamento idrico urbano in Toscana fra '500 a '600* (Firenze: Università di Firenze, Facolta di Architettura, 2006–07), pp. 138–40; Else, 'Giulio Ballino', p. 3, and private email 6 June 2011. See also Felicia Else, 'Controlling the Waters of Granducal Florence: A New Look at Stefano Buonsignori's View of the City', *Imago Mundi: The International Journal for the History of Cartography*, 61 (2009), pp. 168–85; Paglianti, *Ferdinando I*, pp. 138–40.

[69]   Recent work under the auspices of the Soprintendenza per i Beni Ambientali e Architettonici per le provincie di Firenze, Prato e Pistoia has restored a mile-long aqueduct between the spring 'della Ginevra' and the Boboli Gardens, extended to the Palazzo Vecchio, but I have been unable to estimate the water-flow this would have provided. See Giorgio Galletti, 'Le genesi della Grotta Grande di Boboli' in Ballerini and Medri, *Artefici d'Acque'*, pp. 228–39.

The *Naumachia* in Performance

It remains to consider the performance conditions in which Ferdinando's extraordinary show took place. After all the technology was assembled, and in the light of the bravado of the preparations, the political intentions and the references to classical precedent, we may ask how the setting and its dressing for the occasion affected the emotional and aesthetic experience of the invited audience. What was it like to be present?

The Pitti Palace *cortile* served in 1589 as what today would be called 'found space': a location not normally used for theatrical purposes but employed for its performance advantages, and because it carries messages for its audience. The courtyard was sufficiently ample for the naval battle; it could be flooded to a sufficient depth in the time available, whatever the technical difficulties; and it could accommodate a very large number of spectators, as Scarabelli's etching shows and the chroniclers, perhaps with exaggeration, confirm. The experience of attending the performance was conditioned by each of these factors, including the sense of special privilege among the invited guests, the crowded arena and the novelty of the experience (even though the courtyard had been used ten years before for a dry-land show).

Testaverde's work on the Medici archives allows us further glimpses of the conditions, for performers and spectators, in which the *naumachia* took place. It is reported that the night was far gone before the banquet finished and the invited guests returned to witness the naval spectacle. Their excitable state must have been ratcheted up by the atmospheric arena they entered. Over the huge space, and part-way down the courtyard walls, a canvas covering supported on ropes was stretched, a feature of the improvised arena since the beginning of the day's proceedings. Such an arrangement no doubt alluded, for those with the requisite knowledge, to the *velarium* that similarly covered the Colosseum for the Roman *naumachia.* On both occasions, the ancient occasion and 1589, the considerable technical and physical feat of erecting, bracing (and dismantling) the huge spread of canvas – more extensive than all but the largest of modern marquees – was managed by hardened sailors, a group of men equipped to undertake the task by experience and skill – and to generate the sense of excitement to which today's circus-goers respond. In the case of the Pitti Palace event the sailors had seen service on the Grand Duke's galleys at Livorno and Pisa, a further implied allusion, it may be, to Medici success in building-up maritime power. More to the point, the costume sign-out sheets, as Saslow and Testaverde have shown, indicate that the numerous sailors, more than 130 in number, engaged for the *naumachia* came from across the Mediterranean world, including in some cases from lands under Turkish control, and were costumed in national garments, a circumstance which, as Alberti notes, conferred '*maggiore vivacità e realismo allo spettacolo*' ('greater liveliness and realism to the spectacle').[70] Employing this diverse, battle-hardened

---

[70]   Alberti, 'Battaglie navali', p. 23. Saslow, p. 169, citing the costume sign-out sheet, counts '120 assailants in 17 boats' on the Christian side, but only 14 defenders on the

and gaudily-costumed cast will have boosted to a marked degree the visual and physical excitement of the entertainment.

There probably was nothing approaching a dress rehearsal, as today's theatre practitioner would understand the term, since the *cortile* is unlikely to have been flooded twice, for rehearsal as well as performance. The result must have been a largely improvised show employing at best a loosely defined narrative. It is scarcely surprising therefore that contemporary accounts stress the violence of the proceedings, the cacophony of explosions and cries of anger and anguish, together with the smoke that drifted everywhere and obscured the action. Scarabelli's etching may be inaccurate in many details, but it does convey the disorder that must have characterised the *cortile* performance, to the excitement and in some cases at least the anxiety of spectators.

It is possible to infer some further aspects of the experience. The *velarium* covering the whole arena was, we learn, coloured red (it is described as a '*tela rossa*'), a feature likely to add to the sheer intensity of the emotional experience in a covered, enclosed space. Great care was taken to ensure that the *velarium* was sufficiently robust and sufficiently well suspended and braced to withstand foul weather, including a '*furia impetuosa de'venti*' ('raging fury of wind') in the vivid words of the archive. This proved a sensible precaution, since on performance day, as Cavallino reports[71], a fierce rainstorm with high winds did indeed blow up, resulting in premature, if shallow, flooding of the *cortile* – flooding that had to be cleared by hurried and ingenious deployment of '*200 sacchi di semola*' ('200 sackfuls of bran') before the earlier proceedings got under way. It is easy to suppose that on a gusty day, as 11 May turned out to be, the flapping of the awning in the darkness of night must have added to the sense of excited threat that faced returning spectators, a feature of their heightened experience that perhaps accounts in part for the amazement and fear to which all the chroniclers refer.[72]

There were other aspects of the *mise-en-scène* that would have contributed to the glamorous and melodramatic atmosphere of the occasion. Under the red-coloured awning the paintings and *papier mâché* ornaments that decorated the improvised space were executed '*con un predominio dei colori giallo, rosso e carboncino*' ('with a predominance of yellow, red and charcoal colours'), a gaudy palette to complement the violent action. Lighting was a matter of considerable attention. Right up to the brink of performance the number of torches illuminating the arena was being augmented day on day, with as many as eighty wood and *papier*

Turkish side, together with 'one battleship'. Alberti, 'Battaglie navali' p. 23, cites Seriacopi, *Memoriale*, ed. Testaverde p. 237, to support Pavoni's account of crew members coming from Pisa (*Diario*, p. 40): '*sono venuti da Pisa quelli che hanno a combattere il castello e vogare*'.

[71]   Cavallino, *Diario*, p. 41.

[72]   Francesco Gurrieri and Judith Chatfield, *Boboli Gardens* (Florence: Editrice Edam, 1972), p. 32 emphasise the astonishment and near-panic generated among the audience returning after the banquet.

mâché torches originally set up being increased by additional lights re-deployed from a recent 'commedia', probably Bargagli's *La pellegrina*. Still further lights were added at the request of the 'quartermaster', Girolamo Seriacopi's assistant Francesco Gorini. These numerous and constantly flickering lights will have both dispersed and intensified the gloom that, at this hour of the night, would otherwise occupy the arena. Added to the damp atmosphere resulting from the flooding of the space, Buontalenti's improvised lighting rig must have created conditions that made an audience uneasy – even if a late-sixteenth-century audience would have been considerably more adjusted to dark nights, flickering torches and damp conditions than cosseted modern spectators.[73]

It should be no surprise that Christina, after enduring the 1589 *naumachia*, arranged that the *naumachia* of 1608, celebrating her son Cosimo's wedding, would take place in the altogether more public, less cramped, less atmospheric and less potentially threatening confines of the river Arno – and in daylight. She ordered moreover that less violence should be used as compared with the 1589 event and that licensed arms only should be carried '*sotto pena della vita*' ('under threat of execution').[74] The vessels created to carry the pantomime Argonauts for this later *naumachia*, an event that took its place in a long tradition of Arno-based pageants, were in several cases bizarre, including barges resembling a peacock and a giant lobster, but the fable underlying the occasion was respectably classical and the leading vessel carrying prince Cosimo was a dignified and elegant barge modelled on the Venetian *bucintoro*.[75] Decorum was therefore observed to an extent strongly contrasting with what must have been the near anarchy of the 1589 *naumachia*.

Political Mannerism

The 1589 *naumachia* provides a remarkable window into the culture of Ferdinando's Florence at a moment when the Grand Duke was seeking to establish his regime in the face of political reverses and loss of esteem. The show's convergence of place, scholarship, advanced technical daring and theatrical flamboyance, together with

---

[73]   Details throughout this paragraph are taken from Testaverde's indispensable *L' officina*, pp. 139–47.

[74]   See Testaverde, *L' officina*, p. 147. A secondary allusion may also be suspected to the *Barriers* for the marriage of Francesco de' Medici and Bianca Cappello, which took place in the *cortile* ten years earlier using a canvas covering similar to that employed in 1589. Ferdinando might be seen as out-doing his errant brother with a grander and more classically authentic show to celebrate a legitimate marriage.

[75]   For illustration of the barges in the 1608 *naumachia*, and scholarly commentary, see Blumenthal, *Theater Art*, pp. 35–86. Paolo Ventrone offers analysis of the staging of the 1608 event and previous occasions: 'L'Arno come "Luogo Teatrale" tra Medioevo e Rinascimento', in Arturo Calzona and Daniela Lamberini (eds), *La Civiltà delle Acque Tra Medioevo e Rinascimento* (2 vols, Florence: Leo S. Olschki, 2010), vol. 1. pp. 589–611.

hard-headed political networking, adds up to a cultural fix that, to borrow John Shearman's term, may be called Mannerist in inspiration and execution. Shearman identifies Mannerism with the *virtù* that arises from the conquest of difficulty, foregrounds ingenuity as a leading characteristic, and notes the 'insatiable appetite for the spectacular which made Mannerism possible'. Mannerist scenography, he adds, aimed at achieving 'the stupendous'. All of these features are present in the Buontalenti *naumachia* which, to use Shearman's words, 'in a somewhat extravagant way illustrates the qualities of surprise, variety, ostentatious ingenuity and expertise emblematic of Mannerism'.[76] If the commentaries by Pavoni and Cavallino are 'unreliable', their inaccuracies arise from exaggerations of language and tone that reflect the authors' emotional engagement with the events they witnessed. Scarabelli's etching displays as much invention as reportage, yet its characteristics go some way towards conveying the emotional reality that presence in the Ammannati courtyard on the night of 11 May 1589 entailed. For a modern interpreter, the surviving printed and visual documents both impede and provide access to the real events. For this reason they reward extended analysis and interpretation – even if the analysis and interpretation offered here are necessarily limited and provisional.

Bibliography

Primary Sources

Benacci, Vittorio, *Le Ultime Feste et Apparati Superbissimi fatti in Fiorenza nelle Nozze del Serenissimo Gran Duca di Toscana* (Bologna, 1589).
Cavallino, Simone, *Raccolta di tutte le solennissime feste nel sponsalitio della serenissima gran dvchessa di Toscana, fatte in Fiorenza il mese di Maggio 1589* (Rome: Blado, 1589).
Dio Cassius, Lucius, *Roman History*, vol. 8 (Cambridge, Ma: Harvard University Press, 1925), XXV and LXVI.
Gilioli, Girolamo, 'Letter to Alfonso II d'Este, 13 May 1589', Archivio di Stato, Modena, AF 31, letter 7.
Gualterotti, Rafaello, *Della Descrizione del regale apparato fatto ... per le nozze della Serenissima Madama Cristina di Loreno moglie del Serenissimo Don Ferdinando Medici terzo Gran Duca di Toscana* (Florence: Padovani, 1589).
Martialis, Marcus Valerius, *Liber Spectaculorum* II and XXIV, trans. K.M. Coleman (Oxford: Oxford University Press, 2006).

---

[76] John Shearman, *Mannerism* (Harmondsworth: Penguin Books, 1967), *passim*, pp. 111, 112. Ludovico Zorzi remarks that the scenography of the *cortile* for the *naumachia* represents '*espressione tipica e calzante del gusto del tardo manierismo fiorentino*' ('a typical and apt expression of late mannerist taste in Florence'), *Il Teatro e la Città: Saggi sulla Scena Italiana* (Florence: Giulio Einaudi Editore, 1977), p. 233 footnote 207.

Pavoni, Giuseppe, *Diario Descritto da Givseppe Pavoni delle feste celebrate nelle solennissime nozze delli serenissimi sposi, il sig. Don Ferdinando Medici, & la sig. Donna Christina di Loreno Gran Duchi di Toscana.* (Bologna: Rossi, 1589).

Suetonius, Gaius Tranquillus, *The Twelve Caesars*, trans. R. Graves (Baltimore, Md: 1962).

Secondary Sources

Ajmar-Wollheim, Marta and Flora Dennis (eds), *At Home in Renaissance Italy*, Exhibition Catalogue (London: Victoria and Albert Museum Publications, 2006).

Alberti, Maria, 'Battaglie navali, scorrerie corsare e politica dello spettacolo: Le Naumachie medicee del 1589', in *California Italian Studies Journal*, I (2010), pp. 1–33; on-line resource http://escholarship.org/uc/item/8553h705

Berner, Samuel, 'Florentine Society in the Late Sixteenth and Early Seventeenth Centuries', *Studies in the Renaissance*, 18 (1971), pp. 203–46.

Berti, Luciano, *Il Principe dello studiolo: Francesco I dei Medici e la fine del Rinascimento fiorentino* (Florence: Edam, 1967).

Blumenthal, Arthur R., *Theater Art of the Medici* (Hanover, NH and London: Dartmouth College Museum and Galleries and University Press of New England, 1980).

Braudel, Fernand, *The Mediterranean and the Mediterranean World in the Age of Philip II*, trans. Siân Reynolds (2 vols, London: Collins, 1972–73).

Butters, Suzanne B., 'Contrasting Priorities: Ferdinando I de' Medici, Cardinal and Grand Duke', in Mary Hollingsworth and Carol M. Richardson (eds), *The Possessions of a Cardinal: Art, Piety and Politics, 1450–1700* (University Park, Pa: Penn State Press, 2010).

Butters, Suzanne B., '"Magnifico, non senza eccesso": riflessioni sul mecenatismo del cardinal Ferdinando de' Medici', in *Villa Medici. Il sogno di un cardinal: collezioni e artisti di Ferdinando de' Medici*, Exhibition Catalogue, Rome: Académie de France à Rome, 17 November 1999–5 March 2000 (Rome: De Luca, 1999).

Butters, Suzanne B., 'Princely Waters: An Elemental Look at the Medici Dukes', in Arturo Calzona and Daniela Lamberini (eds), *La Civiltà delle Acque tra Medioevo e Rinascimento* (2 vols, Florence: Olschki, 2010), vol. 1, pp. 389–411.

Butters, Suzanne B., et al., *La Villa Médicis*, vol. 5 (Rome: Académie de France à Rome, École française de Rome, Académie des Beaux-Arts, 2010).

Büttner, Valeriani and Hochen Büttner, 'Pratolino: The History of Science in a Garden', Max Planck Institute for the History of Science, on-line resource http://mpiwg-berlin.mpg.de/en/research/projects/DEPT1_Valle

Campbell, Malcolm, 'Giambologna's Oceanus Fountain', in Cristina Accidini Luchinat and Elvira Garbero Zorzi (eds), *Boboli 90: Atti del Convegno*

Internazionale di Studi per la salvaguardia e la valorizzazione del Giardino (Florence: Edifir, 1991).

Campbell, Malcolm, 'Hard Times in Baroque Florence: The Boboli Gardens and the Grand Ducal Public Works Administration' in John Dixon Hunt (ed.), *The Italian Garden: Art, Design and Culture* (Cambridge: Cambridge University Press, 1996), pp. 160–201.

Coleman, Kathleen, 'Launching into History: Aquatic Displays in the Early Empire', *The Journal of Roman Studies*, 83 (1993), pp. 48–74.

Crapper, Martin, *Environmental Engineering Research*, University of Edinburgh on-line journal, 18/04/2008, http://www.see.ed.ac.uk/MIE/research/environ

Crapper, Martin, 'How Roman Engineers could have flooded the Colosseum', in *Proceedings of the Institution of Civil Engineers – Civil Engineering*, 160 (2007), pp. 184–91.

Cropper, Elizabeth, Giovanni Perini and Francesco Solinas (eds), *Documentary Culture: Florence and Rome from Grand Duke Ferdinand I to Pope Alexander VII* (Bologna: Nuova Alfa Editoriale, 1992).

Crowley, Roger, *Empires of the Sea: The Final Battle for the Mediterranean, 1521–1580* (London: Faber and Faber, 2008).

Cuomo, Franco, *Gli Ordini Cavallereschi nel mito e nel storia* (Rome: Newton and Compton, 2004).

Else, Felicia, 'Controlling the Waters of Granducal Florence: A New Look at Stefano Buonsignori's View of the City', in *Imago Mundi: The International Journal for the History of Cartography*, 61 (2009), pp. 168–85.

Else, Felicia, 'Giulio Ballino and the Florentine Corridoio', *MAPLINE*, 92 (Winter 2000–01); on-line journal http://www.newberry.org/smith/Mapline/92/92feature.html

Else, Felicia, 'Water and Stone: Ammannati's Neptune Fountain as Public Ornament' (unpublished PhD diss., Washington University, St. Louis, 2003).

Fenlon, Iain, *The Ceremonial City: History, Memory and Myth in Renaissance Venice* (New Haven and London: Yale University Press, 2007).

Galletti, Giorgio, 'Le genesi della Grotta Grande di Boboli', in Isabella Lapi Ballerini and Litta Maria Medri (eds), *Artifici d'Acque e Giardini*, Atti del V Convegno Internationazionale su Parchi e Giardini Storici (Florence, 1999).

Goy, Richard, *Florence: the City and its Architecture* (London: Phaidon, 2002).

Gurrieri, Francesco and Judith Chatfield, *Boboli Gardens* (Florence: Editrice Edam, 1972).

Hales, J.R., *Florence and the Medici: the Pattern of Control* (London: Thames and Hudson, 1977, pb. 1983).

Hale, J.R., *The Civilization of Europe in the Renaissance* (London: Harper Collins, 1993).

Hale J.R., in *The Project Gutenberg eBook of Famous Sea Fights* (2008), p. 96, on-line resource www.gutenberg.org/files/25088/25088-h/25088-h.htm

Hale, J.R. and Michael Mallett, *The Military Organisation of a Renaissance State: Venice c. 1400–1617* (Cambridge: Cambridge University Press, 1984).

Heikamp, Detlef, et al. (eds), *Palazzo Pitti: La Reggia Rivelata* (Florence: Giunti, 2003).

Hunt, John Dixon (ed.), *The Italian Garden: Art, Design and Culture* (Cambridge: Cambridge University Press, 1996).

Kiene, Michael, *Bartolomeo Ammannati 1511–1592* (Milan: Electa, 1995).

Lazzaro, Claudia, *The Italian Renaissance Garden* (New Haven and London: Yale University Press, 1990).

Long, Pamela O., 'Hydraulic Engineering and the Study of Antiquity, 1557–70', *Renaissance Quarterly*, 61 (2008), pp. 1098–1138.

Luchinat, Cristina Acidini, 'La Fontana del Nettuno: Viaggi e Metamorfosi', in Cristina Acidini Luchinat and Elvira Garbero Zorzi (eds), *Boboli 90* (Florence: Edifir, 1991), pp. 33–42.

Luchinat, Cristina Acidini and Elvira Garbero Zorzi (eds), *Boboli 90* (Florence: Edifir, 1991).

Mandel, Corinne, 'Review of John Dixon Hunt (ed.), *The Italian Garden: Art, Design and Culture*' in *Sixteenth Century Journal*, XXVIII (Autumn 1997), pp. 879–82.

Medri, Litta Maria, 'Considerazioni intorno alle prima fasi della Grotta Grande nel Giardino di Boboli', in Isabella Lapi Ballerini and Litta Maria Medri (eds), *Artifici d'Acque e Giardini*, Atti del V Convegno Internationazionale su Parchi e Giardini Storici (Florence: 1999), pp. 215–27.

Mulryne, J.R. (ed.), *Thomas Middleton 'Women Beware Women'* (Manchester: Manchester University Press, 1975).

Mulryne, J.R. (ed.), *Thomas Middleton 'Women Beware Women'*, Revels Student Editions (Manchester: Manchester University Press, 2007).

Paglianti, L., *Ferdinando I e l'acquedotto di Pisa. Techniche di approvvigionamento idrico urbano in Toscana fra '500 a '600* (Firenze: Università di Firenze, Facolta di Architettura, 2006–07).

Rea, Rossella, et al., 'Sotterranei del Colosseo. Ricerca premliniare al progetto di ricostruzione del piano dell'arena', *Mitteilungen des Deutschen Archäologischen Instituts (Römische Abteilung)* 107, (2000), pp. 311–39.

Saslow, James M., *The Medici Wedding of 1589: Florentine Festival as 'Theatrum Mundi'* (New Haven and London: Yale University Press, 1996).

Satkowski, Leon, 'The Palazzo Pitti: Planning and Use in the Grand-Ducal Era', *Journal of the Society of Architectural Historians*, 42 (December 1983), pp. 336–49.

Shearman, John, *Mannerism* (Harmondsworth: Penguin Books, 1967).

Smith, Webster, 'Pratolino', *Journal of the Society of Architectural Historians*, 20 (1961), pp. 155–68.

Strozzi, Beatrice Paolozzi and Dimitrios Zikos (eds), *L'Acqua, La Pietra, Il Fuoco: Bartolomeo Ammannati Scultore* (Florence: Giunti, 2011).

Testaverde Matteini, Anna Maria, *L'officina delle nuvole. Il Teatro Mediceo nel 1589* (Milan: Edizione degli Amici della Scala, 1991).

Tofani, Annamaria Petrioli, 'L'illustraziione Teatrale e il Significato dei Documenti Figurativi per la storia dello Spettacolo', in Elizabeth Cropper Giovanni Perini and Francesco Solinas (eds), *Documentary Culture: Florence and Rome from Grand Duke Ferdinand I to Pope Alexander VII* (Bologna: Nuova Alfa Editoriale, 1992), pp. 49–62.

Treadwell, Nina, *Music and Wonder at the Medici Court: The 1589 Interludes for 'La pellegrina'* (Bloomington, IN: Indiana University Press, 2008)

Ventrone, Paolo, 'L'Arno come "Luogo Teatrale" tra Medioevo e Rinascimento', in Arturo Calzona and Daniela Lamberini (eds), *La Civiltà delle Acque Tra Medioevo e Rinascimento* (2 vols, Florence: Leo S. Olschki, 2010).

Zorzi, Ludovico, *Il Teatro e la Città: Saggi sulla Scena Italiana* (Florence: Giulio Einaudi Editore, 1977).

Chapter 9

Lepanto Revisited: Water-fights and the Turkish Threat in Early Modern Europe (1571–1656)

Marie-Claude Canova-Green

From the fifteenth to the seventeenth century, the Ottoman peril hung over Europe. The conquest of Constantinople in 1453 had cemented the status of the empire as the dominant power in south-eastern Europe and the eastern Mediterranean. In the face of its policy of conquest and aggression Venice felt particularly vulnerable as its seagoing trade routes were contested and its possessions occupied one after the other. In 1570 the Ottomans attacked Cyprus and Crete, the last Venetian outposts in the eastern Mediterranean, from where they could now launch attacks upon the Italian coast. To challenge Ottoman naval strength in the Mediterranean, in the spring of 1571, on the initiative of the Papacy, a Holy League was formed between Venice, Rome and Spain. The victory of the allied fleet under the command of Don Juan of Austria at the battle of Lepanto on 7 October 1571 was a startling blow to the myth of Ottoman invincibility. It gave fresh hopes that its continental and Mediterranean expansion could be stopped and also that Islam would finally be defeated. This enthusiasm however was short-lived. Within six months the Turks had rebuilt their navy and resumed their policy of expansion on land, while disagreement and disunion prevailed amongst the victors of Lepanto.

The celebrations of the victory were enthusiastic but were soon muted by these disagreements.[1] However, on receiving the news, twelve days after the battle,[2] Venice was illuminated for three days. Shops and houses were hung with fine tapestries and decorated with trophies from the battle, *Te Deum*s were sung in various churches, and the city was alive with the sound of concerts and fireworks:

---

[1]   See Iain Fenlon, '*In Destructione Turcharum*: the Victory of Lepanto in Sixteenth-Century Music and Letters', in Francesco Degrada (ed.), *Andrea Gabrieli e il suo tempo* (Florence: Olschki, 1987), pp. 293–317.

[2]   The news of the victory reached Venice on 19 October and Rome during the night of 21 to 22 October.

Furono subito serrate tutte le botteghe, e per tre giorni continui si sonarono le campane di tutte le Chiese, tenendosi lumiere su tutti i campanili sino à mezza notte, & facendosi per i campi fuochi, feste, & allegrezze.[3]

[All the shops were immediately closed, and, for three consecutive days, all the church bells rang, and all the church towers were lit until midnight, and there were fireworks, rejoicing and happiness in all the squares.]

On 4 December the papal commander Marco Antonio Colonna made his triumphal entry into Rome, preceded by horsemen dragging Turkish standards in the dust and herding 500 Turkish slaves dressed in red and yellow. Scenes from the battle decorated the Porta Capenna where the procession entered the city:

La onde si vedeva da una parte une gran copia d'archi, di frecce, di dardi, di scimitarre, turbante, & altre cose tali. Dall'altra si scorgevano timoni, remi, antenne, galere fracassate, artiglierie, & cose appartenenti a conflitto navale.[4]

[There, on one side, one could see an abundance of bows, arrows, javelins, scimitars, turbans, and other such things. On the other side, one could see tillers, oars, masts, broken vessels, pieces of artillery, and things pertaining to a naval battle.]

At the Campidoglio the procession was met by a statue of a gladiator, holding a bare sword in one hand and the bloody head of the Sultan in the other, as if to indicate

che l'Imperio de'Turchi haveva già ricevuto un colpo mortale, & che in virtù de la medesima spada indi à poco doveva perire.[5]

[that the Turkish empire had already been dealt a deadly blow, and that it would shortly perish by the same sword.]

For the following Carnival, Venice staged an elaborate *mascherata* in Piazza San Marco, which included a procession of 100 participants costumed as Turkish slaves. Five out of the 13 *carri* (chariots) used in the procession displayed allegories relating to the victory at Lepanto. On the first chariot Faith could be seen trampling on the Turkish serpent in chains, while personifications of Rome,

---

[3]   *Ragguaglio delle allegrezze, solennità, e feste fatte in Venetia per la felice vittoria* (Venice: Gratioso Perchaccino, 1517).

[4]   *I trionfi, feste, et livree fatte dalli Signori conservatori, & Popolo Romano, & da tutte le arti di Roma, nelle felicissima, & honorata entrata dell'Illustrissimo Signor Marcantonio Colonna* (Venice, 1571).

[5]   Ibid. The entry is represented on a painted frieze in one of the rooms of the citadel in Paliano (reproduced in G.B. Borino, A. Galieti and G. Navone, 'Il trionfo di Marc'Antonio Colonna', *Miscellanea della R. Deputazione Romana di Storia Patria* (Rome, 1938), vol. 12).

Spain and Venice followed on the next three chariots. Finally came Victory, in red velvet and crowned with laurel, with a Turkish slave under her feet. Her chariot, decorated with Turkish spoils '*il carro strassinava bandiere Turchesche, & era adornato de archi bellissimi, carcassi, frezze, simitere, & altre spoglie turchesche*' ('the chariot dragged Turkish banners and was decorated with very fine bows, quivers, arrows, scimitars, and other Turkish spoils'), was in the shape of a serpent cut into two, with its wings broken, to symbolise '*il Turco offeso, e vinto*' ('the wounded and defeated Turk').[6]

Although the victory at Lepanto had only been a temporary repulse of the Ottoman onset, its value as an illustration of the vulnerability of the hosts of Islam might explain its continued popularity as a topic for festivals, and in particular *naumachiae*, for the next fifty years. However, as the nature of naval encounters in the Mediterranean changed in the wake of the battle, the staging of mock battles between Christian and Turkish ships for princely festivals also took on a new significance.[7] Lepanto resulted in a shift in the expansionist policies of the Ottoman Empire, which redirected its efforts towards central Europe and the near East. The Turks slowly withdrew from the Mediterranean, which ceased to be the scene of large-scale confrontations (with the exception of the war of Candia in 1645–69). Instead it became the stage for ever more daring acts of piracy. Deprived of the support and protection of the Turkish navy, Barbary pirates continued their activity and even expanded it, taking advantage of lighter, swifter and more manoeuvrable ships to develop new tactics and even venture into the Atlantic. It is in fact this detestation of Barbary pirates and the fear of their depredations, rather than the Ottoman peril, which lies behind the spectacular water-fights featuring the taking of fortresses or the capture of Turkish ships in early-seventeenth-century France and England.

Valencia 19 January 1586[8]

Fifteen years after the victory of the League at Lepanto, on 19 January 1586, the Spanish town of Valencia staged a reconstruction of the battle for the triumphal entry of King Philip II into the city,[9] testifying to the long-lasting impact of the event. This, however, was not a real water engagement, but an illusionistic performance on a stage. The entry, which concluded the monarch's tour of Catalonia and Valencia, had a military flavour and focused on his and Spain's

---

[6]   *Ordine, et dechiaratione di tutta la mascherata Fatta nella Città di Venetia la Domenica di Carnevale M.D.LXXI Per la Gloriosa Vittoria contra Turchi* (Venice: Giorgio Angelieri, 1572).

[7]   This new significance was further encouraged by the frequent confusion at the time between Turks and Moors, as well as between Turks and Saracens.

[8]   I am grateful to David Sánchez Cano for bringing this entry to my attention.

[9]   This was Philip II's third and last visit to Valencia.

greatest achievements in war. At his entrance into the city, Philip was greeted at the Portal de los Serranos by five nymphs representing five victories: S. Quintin, Peñón de Vélez, Malta, Granada and a *batalla naval*, which the accompanying octet inscribed on the arch immediately identified as the battle of Lepanto. Each of these battles was represented *al vivo* on a platform further along the entry route. The original plan had been for seven nymphs to welcome the king but the two representing Portugal and the Portuguese island of Terceira were dropped so as not to offend Philip's new Portuguese subjects. However the design for the hill-shaped structure to be erected in the Plaza de Predicadores was retained and now depicted the succour of Malta occupied by the Turks in the spring and summer of 1565. Six *naves* and two galleys were supplied to simulate the action of the relief fleet led by the Spanish Admiral, Don García.[10]

The design for the structure representing the battle of Lepanto was just as elaborate. It, too, came alive as the king approached:

> *pasa per lo Mercat y davant lo monestir de les Madalens hi havia un grandissim cadafal y en aquell se representava la batalla naval ab gran multitut de galeres axi de moros com de christians y les galeazes, y al pasar Sa Magestat se mogue la pelea, y totes les galeres, dins les quals hi havia homens armats en cada una de aquelles, corrien per lo dit cadafal ab cert artifici que verdaderament parexia que corrien per la mar, y al millor de la pelea caygue per desastre gran part del cadafal y moltes de les dites galeres ab los homens que dins elles estaven caigueren que verdaderament pareixia que per pelea les havien llanzades a fondo, lo qual dona molt gran gust a Sa Magestat y al Sor Princep e Infanta, y en lo canto del dit cadafal estava lo fort de Lepanto en lo qual estaven afixes les seguents octaves.*[11]

[He passed through the market, and in front of the Magdalen convent there was a very large platform on which the naval battle was represented with a great multitude of galleys both Moorish and Christian and galeasses, and when his Majesty arrived the battle was set in motion, and all the galleys, on each of which there were armed men, moved about on the said platform with such artifice that it truly seemed that they were moving on the sea, and in the midst of the battle a large part of the platform disastrously collapsed and many of the said galleys together with the men which were on board fell down, so that it truly

---

[10]   See Salvador Carreres y Zacarés, *Ensayo de una bibliografía de libros de fiestas en Valencia* (2 vols, Valencia, 1926), vol. 1, p. 153. See too C.A. Marsden, 'Entrées et fêtes espagnoles au XVIe siècle', in Jean Jacquot (ed.), *Les Fêtes de la Renaissance*, (3 vols, Paris: Editions du C.N.R.S., 1956–75), vol. 2 (1960), *Fêtes et cérémonies au temps de Charles Quint*, pp. 389–411.

[11]   Salvador Carreres y Zacarés (ed.), *Libre de memories de diversos sucesos e fets memorables e de coses senyalades de la ciutat e regne de Valencia (1308–1664)* (2 vols, Valencia, 1935), vol. 2, p. 973.

looked as if they had been sunk in the battle, the which gave great pleasure to his Majesty and the Lord Prince [Don Felipe] and the Infanta [Isabel Eugenia Clara], and on the edge of the said platform was the fortress of Lepanto on which the following octaves were affixed.]

However, on the express orders of the king, and for fear of accidents, no gunfire was used in the fighting.[12]

Together with Peñón de Vélez,[13] both the succour of Malta and the battle of Lepanto were allied victories, in which the Spaniards had played a decisive part. In fact Lepanto itself had only been possible because for once Spain had thrown its entire weight in the fight against the Turks. But, as has often been noted, Spain had not seriously endeavoured to pursue the struggle. In 1585 it even signed a peace treaty with the Ottoman Empire; and, as Philip II ascended the Portuguese throne in 1581, Spanish foreign policy became less interested in Mediterranean affairs and more focused on the Atlantic.[14] So why remind Philip of these Mediterranean successes? Was it only conventional panegyric of the monarch as victorious? Could there have been perhaps another agenda? As shown by local celebrations of the allied victory in November and December 1571, when Valencia was illuminated for four days,[15] Lepanto seems to have been regarded, at least by some, as a Valencian achievement. Together with their captain Don Miguel de Moncada, a number of Valencian soldiers had taken part in the battle. The victory was even attributed to the intervention of Our Lady of Remedies, who was revered in Valencia and to whose service Don Juan had dedicated himself. Furthermore, it was on her day that the battle had been fought and won.[16]

Was the choice of topics also a plea for royal support or intervention in the substitute war being waged in the Mediterranean against the Turks and their Moorish allies, one in which Valencia, like Valetta or Livorno, was particularly

---

[12]　See Carreres y Zacarés, *Ensayo de una bibliografía*, vol. 1, p. 164 ('*todas las invenciones que hemos descrito funcionaron a su paso; pero por expreso mandato de Felipe II se efectuaron sin disparo de armas de fuego, por temor fuera ello causa de alguna desgracia entre la mucha gente congregada en las calles*'). However the structures were later reused for the fireworks.

[13]　Peñón de Vélez was a small island, which was captured by Spain in September 1564 (an unsuccessful attempt had been made in August 1563).

[14]　See Fernand Braudel, *The Mediterranean and the Mediterranean World in the Age of Philip II*, trans. Siân Reynolds (2 vols, Berkeley, Los Angeles, London: University of California Press, 1995), vol. 2, p. 1184.

[15]　See Carreres y Zacarés, *Ensayo de una bibliografía*, vol. 1, p. 139 and vol. 2, document LXX.

[16]　In memory of the victory Don Miguel had the League banner hung in the central nave of the Church of the Virgen del Remedio, while the habit worn by the Turkish Admiral Alí on the day was made into a cover for the main altar (see D. José March y Labores, *Historia de la marina Real española* (Madrid, 1854); quoted by Carreres y Zacarés, *Ensayo de una bibliografía*, vol. 1, p. 139).

active?[17] Urban privateering, already important in the mid-sixteenth century, had dramatically increased in the years following Lepanto. Valencian seamen were known to operate off the coast of Algiers, and in the last decades of the century some even joined daring operations to rescue Christian captives from their prisons or to set fire to ships in the harbour. Besides, Valencia and Catalonia, together with Provence, were at the mercy of repeated pirate raids from Algiers, now in full expansion.[18] Under the guise of eulogy, the organisers of the entry might very well have used historical references to Lepanto and Malta to allude to more pressing concerns of their own.

Florence 11 May 1589

Three years later, as part of the wedding festivities of Duke Ferdinando de' Medici and Christine de Lorraine, Florence also staged a re-enactment of the iconic battle (see Figure 8.1).[19] On 11 May 1589, in the flooded *cortile* of the Palazzo Pitti, a fleet of eighteen or so boats representing the Christian forces launched an attack upon a Turkish castle defended by Turkish galleys and a number of defenders on land, all dressed in trousers *alla greca*, and armed with bows and arrows.[20] After

---

[17]   Was it simply a coincidence that in 1578 Venice had succeeded in obtaining from Philip II a ban on privateering in part of the Mediterranean?

[18]   According to Saint-Sulpice, in 1563, during one of Philip II's previous visits to the city, 'all the talk is of tournaments, jousting, balls and other noble pastimes, while the Moors waste no time and even dare to capture vessels within a league of the city, stealing as much as they can carry' (quoted in Fernand Braudel, *The Mediterranean*, vol. 2, p. 882). In fact Philip's stay in Valencia ended on 14 February 1586 with a visit to the fortress overlooking the sea (see Henrique Cock, *Relación del viaje hecho por Felipe II, en 1585, á Zaragoza, Barcelona y Valencia*, ed. Alfred Morel-Fatio and Antonio Rodriguez Villa (Madrid, 1876), p. 256).

[19]   See J.R. Mulryne's chapter, above, pp. 143–75.

[20]   Bows and arrows were the customary weapons of the elite *Azappi*, or galley archers. As Cesare Vecellio explains: 'It has always been the custom among the Turks to train as well as possible in the use of the bow. So they arm their galleys with many *Azappi*. These are soldiers [...] They wear a short *dulimano*, knee-length, in whatever color they like, open in front up to the belt to allow greater freedom of movement. Their sleeves are slightly more than elbow-length. They attach a scimitar and a quiver of arrows to a strap that hangs from their neck to their hip and, as can be seen, they also wear a bow. On their heads they wear a small cap in the same color as the *dulimano*, in felt or some other fabric, and trousers and shoes, in the Turkish style'. (Margaret F. Rosenthal and Ann Rosalind Jones (eds), *The Clothing of the Renaissance World: Europe. Asia. Africa. The Americas: Cesare Vecellio's Habiti Antichi et Moderni* (London: Thames & Hudson, 2008), p. 398). The superior firepower of the Christian fleet at Lepanto was real, but festival organisers exploited the contrast between the cannon and artillery of the Christians and the bows and arrows of the Turks for their own aesthetic and propagandistic aims. On the one hand,

a conventionalised combat lasting several hours, during which '*si sentiva gridare in Turchescho quelli che erano feriti, e quelli, che cascavano in acqua*' ('those who were wounded or fell in the water could be heard to shout in Turkish'), the Christian forces overcame the Turkish ships, with great losses on the enemy side:

> *Finalmente l'armata cristiana superò la turchesca, dissipando di mala maniera i loro vasselli, talché si vedevano per il mare diverse reliquie, come: timoni, antenne, pavesi, remi et altri simili instrumenti, con degli uomini attaccati, per non affogarsi, che nuotavano ritirandosi ogn'uno verso i suoi.*[21]

> [Finally the Christian fleet overcame the Turks, and routed their ships so badly that various pieces of wreckage could be seen all over the sea, such as tillers, masts, flags, oars, and other such items, with men clinging on to them, for fear of drowning, and swimming back towards their mates.]

After fresh rounds of artillery bombardments and further pretended loss of life, the castle was stormed, the enemy standard taken and brought as a final tribute to the new Duchess.

The *naumachia*, a novelty at the Medici court, did not make use of an existing lake or river, but nothing had been spared to give the spectators an illusion of reality. The crowded space, the noise, smoke and commotion of fireworks and artillery bombardments, the splashing about and shouting of the injured or panicked sailors were reminiscent of real encounters. Besides, most of the participants seem to have been professional sailors from various Mediterranean locales, who had no doubt been hired while they were on shore at Livorno. Nevertheless, however illusionistic the show might have been, it could not pretend to be a direct imitation of the events on 7 October 1571. For instance no Turkish castle had been stormed on the day[22] and equal numbers of Christian and enemy ships had taken part in

---

it increased the spectacular nature of the entertainment and offered a pleasing variety of weapons, on the other hand it helped to undermine the standing of the enemy and neutralise – at least in imagination – the threat they still represented.

[21] Giuseppe Pavoni, *Diario descritto da Giuseppe Pavoni delle feste celebrate nelle solennissime nozze delli Serenissimi Sposi il Signor Don Ferdinando Medici e la Signora Donna Cristina di Loreno Granduchi di Toscana* (Bologna: Giovanni Rossi, 1589); quoted in Sara Mamone, *Il teatro nella Firenze medicea* (Milan: Mursia, 1981), pp. 125–6.

[22] A number of contemporary maps and paintings of the battle, notably the mural in the Palace of the Marquises de Santa Cruz in Ciudad Real (reproduced in Fernand Braudel, *The Mediterranean*, vol. 2, n. p.), did in fact feature a fort in the background, which might have represented the Venetian citadel dominating the town of Lepanto. But the storming of a castle or fortress, followed by its destruction amidst fireworks, was also a common motif of Renaissance festivals, which, together with parades and jousts, points to their roots in chivalric warfare traditions.

the battle.[23] Lepanto had been an encounter between two large fleets off the Bay of Lepanto. Even allowing for the reduced scale of a dramatic re-enactment, the *naumachia* did not represent the battle as such, it only acted as a reminder. But it was also a generic battle which embodied all past, present and future encounters between Christians and Muslims. In the minds of the spectators of the *naumachia*, as of most contemporaries, Turks stood for all 'Infidels', including Moors and of course Saracens. In many respects the victory at Lepanto and its commemoration in Florence were still embued with the spirit of the Crusades.

Above all, like the entry of Christine into the city which preceded it, the *naumachia*, besides being an engineering feat, was an exercise in self-aggrandisement on the part of the Florentines and the Medici. Both events reminded the spectators of the part that their rulers had played in the war against the Turks. Large paintings of the battles of Lepanto and Linz, to both of which victories Duke Cosimo, the current Duke's father, had contributed, decorated the arch after Ponte Santa Trinità, which was dedicated to the bride's family, but also extolled the glorious deeds of the Florentines. As the inscription read:

> *Qui pare, che in un certo modo finiscano le cose sacre, perchè l'una, e l'altra vittoria, fu contra l'infideli, e non senza gloria del granduca Cosimo, e di nostra Città, che ancora delle Turchesche spoglie in più luoghi sta adorna [...].*[24]

> [We see here the way that sacred things end, because both victories were against the Infidels, and to the glory of the Grand Duke and our city, which is still decorated with Turkish spoils in many places.]

Duke Cosimo had originated the Florentine fleet. In 1562, he had also founded the crusading order of San Stefano, whose knights were pledged to take part, or pay others to take part, in galley warfare against the Turks, and made their first *sortie* in 1564. He had finally drawn attention to the ability to defend Tuscany from the sea and started the development of Livorno, which was soon to become one of the great Italian ports on the Mediterranean. Cosimo's policies were continued by his two sons, notably Ferdinando, whose statue on the waterfront at Livorno represented him astride Turkish captives.

The double depiction of the battle of Lepanto not only celebrated past achievements of the Medici dynasty, it also testified to contemporary concerns

---

[23]	Fernand Braudel lists 230 ships on the Turkish side and 208 on the Christian side, with six powerful Venetian *galleasses* reinforcing the galleys of Don Juan of Austria (*The Mediterranean*, vol. 2, p. 1102).

[24]	Raffaelo Gualterotti, *Della Descrizione del regale apparato fatto nella nobile città di Firenze per la venuta, e per le nozze della Serenissima Madama Cristina di Loreno moglie del Serenissimo Don Ferdinando Medici terzo Gran Duca di Toscana* (Florence: Antonio Padouani, 1589), p. 141. The bronze of Ferdinando's equestrian statue in Piazza Santissima Annunziata came from captured Turkish guns.

and the current Duke's continued participation in the fight against the Turks. From 1574 onwards there had been a visible increase in the activity of the Florentines in the Levant. Admittedly, as J.R. Hale has pointed out, the galleys of San Stefano were sent against the Turks as pirates rather than as crusaders, and the loot brought back from successful Tuscan raids served to fill the coffers of Duke Ferdinando.[25] The Medici rulers were bankers after all! Unlike the *intermedi* given in the Teatro degli Uffizi, which did not mention current affairs, the entry of Christine and the *naumachia* at the Palazzo Pitti were more open to contemporary reference, which they used to promote the regime and to exalt Medici policies in the eyes of Florence and the world.

London 13 February 1613

Twenty-four years later, when it came to devising celebrations for the wedding of James I's daughter to the Elector Palatine, the English court drew upon the same source of inspiration and mounted its own Christian–Turkish encounter on the Thames. Given the links between the late Prince Henry and the Medici court, the water-fight on the Thames unsurprisingly reflected the 1589 *naumachia* in the *cortile* of the Palazzo Pitti,[26] although the choice of the battle of Lepanto as a topic could also be read as an homage to James I, who had penned a long epic poem in 1585 in honour of the allied victory.[27]

On 13 February 1613 no less than thirty-eight vessels were engaged in a mock battle which was considerably noisier and more physical than the Florentine occasion. Seventeen Turkish galleys were seen to attack two Venetian ships and a Spanish *galliaza*, which were taken after a short resistance and carried as booty to a fort said to represent the castle of Algiers. Before long, however, they were challenged by English pinnaces and forced to seek refuge in their haven, where they surrendered after a fierce and prolonged battle:

---

[25]   J.R. Hale, *Florence and the Medici* [1977] (London: Phoenix Press, 2001), p. 164.

[26]   See J.R. Mulryne, 'Entries and Festivals in Late Sixteenth and Early Seventeenth Century Florence as Precedents for Court and Theatre in England 1600–1620', in M.-C. Canova-Green and J. Andrews, with the collaboration of M.-F. Wagner (eds), *Writing Royal Entries in Early Modern Europe* (Turnhout: Brepols, 2013), pp. 357–73.

[27]   James seemed to have thought highly of this work: he included it in *His Majesties Poeticall Exercises at Vacant Houres* in 1591, together with a translation into French by Du Bartas, and subsequently republished it in 1603, when he acceded to the English throne. This might seem surprising given his lifelong aversion to both figurative and literal military exploits, which contrasted with the chivalric and bellicose *persona* adopted by his son. But like so many other instances of James's ambivalent attitude, the 'Lepanto' seems to have exemplified his strategy of balancing Catholic interests against Protestant ones. See Peter C. Herman, 'Authorship and the Royal 'I': King James VI/I and the Politics of Monarchic Verse', *Renaissance Quarterly*, 54/4, part 2 (Winter 2001), pp. 1495–1530.

At last the [Turkish] galleys, being overcharged with long and forward encounters of the English Navie, for refuge and shelter made now into the Castle, which began likewise to play bravely upon the English, and their thundering ordinance made as it were the ground to shake. The King's Navie to answere them was not backward in performance, but made the ayre gloomie with fire and smoke roreing from their loude-mouthed cannons. The fight for a time continued fiercely, the victorie leaning to neither side, either of them attempting to assault and board each other, but at last the gallies, being sore bruised and beaten, began to yeeld, whereupon the English Admirall fell down, and cast anker before the Castle, and then spared not in the best manner to thunder off their ordnance, whereat the Turks yielded both Castle and gallies, and submitted to the conquest of the English Admirall, who fiered many of the said gallies, sacked the Castle, and tooke prisoner the Turke's Admirall, with divers Bashawes and other great Turkes, and also recovered the Venetian and Spanish shippes before taken by the gallies.[28]

In a further departure from the historical battle at Lepanto, the English fleet succeeded where the real victors of Lepanto were shown to have failed. The water-fight on the Thames was evidently not a re-enactment of a past event. It was a demonstration of the strength and capabilities of the English navy, as evinced by the sight of the English admiral coming to the rescue of the allied Christian fleet. Although England had not been involved in the fighting at Lepanto, it had won an equally significant sea battle a few years later. As John Taylor reminded the reader in his account of the entertainment,

This was the manner of the happy and famous battell of Lepanto, fought betwixt the Turks and the Christians in the year of grace 1571; in this bloody manner was the memorable battaile betwixt us and the invincible (as it was thought) Spanish Armada in the yeare 1588.[29]

For Taylor the victory of the alliance at Lepanto and the defeat of the Spanish Armada at the hands of the English became one and the same.

If the English presence at Lepanto was as much a historical anomaly as the Florentine show of strength, English naval superiority somehow justified it. But in the spring of 1613, a small Florentine fleet under the command of the Earl of

---

[28]   *The Magnificent Marriage of the Two Great Princes Frederick Count Palatine, &c. and the Lady Elizabeth, Daughter to the Imperial Majesties of King James and Queen Anne, to the Comfort of All Great Britain*, in *The Progresses, Processions and Magnificent Festivities of King James the First, His Royal Consort, Family and Court*, ed. John Nichols (4 vols, London, 1828), vol. 2, pp. 540–41.

[29]   John Taylor, *Heaven's Blessing and Earth's Joy; or, a True Relation of the Supposed Sea-Fights and Fire-Workes as Were Accomplished Before the Royall Celebration of the All-Beloved Marriage of the Two Peerlesse Paragons of Christendome, Fredericke and Elizabeth*, in Nichols, vol. 2, p. 529.

Candale launched an assault on the fortress at Agliman and captured it.[30] Florence was only an aspiring naval power but their achievements outdid the somewhat lukewarm efforts of the English against the Turks in the eastern Mediterranean. The boasts of the Pitti *naumachia* were spectacularly vindicated.

The water-fight on the Thames offered a fictionalised version of the battle which testified to national ambitions, but also revealed tensions between the monarch and his son, the late Prince of Wales, who had had a hand in devising both the water-fight and the fireworks following it. What was the *naumachia* propaganda for? Was it for the English navy trumped up as both the nemesis and the saviour of the Spanish fleet? In reality the English navy was no longer the unrivalled sea-power it had been under Elizabeth. With James's foreign policy of peace and mediation, it had fallen on hard times. On the other hand Henry, who saw that sea power was central to the country's power and prosperity, wanted to restore it to its former glory. He championed its reform, supported Sir Walter Raleigh imprisoned in the Tower since 1604, and invested in a number of schemes of discovery and colonisation.[31] In this respect the water-fight on the Thames was a public allusion to the late Prince's preoccupations with all things nautical.

As an image of war, the water-fight also reminded the spectators of Henry's militaristic stance in European affairs. In the years leading to his death he had developed a reputation as a strong Protestant leader and, unlike his father, had favoured a policy of active intervention on the Continent. The hope was that he would even lead a Protestant army against the strengthening power of the Catholic Habsburgs in the not too distant future. Could the fight against the Turks have been an acceptable form of intervention for England in the international arena, a symbolic transposition of the prince's Christian zeal,[32] which had, in the first instance, been directed against European Catholicism? Was it even an overture to real warfare? Was Henry joining the call for an international crusade against the East, seen as one hostile force, threatening Christendom? This interpretation

---

[30]   The *Mercure François* gave a full account of the Florentine expedition (*Le Mercure François, ou, la Suitte de l'Histoire de la Paix* (25 vols, Paris: Estienne Richer, 1611–48), vol. 3 (1616), pp. 81–94).

[31]   See Roy Strong, *Henry, Prince of Wales and England's Lost Renaissance* (London: Thames & Hudson, 1986), p. 60.

[32]   In the *Barriers* given at Whitehall on 6 January 1610 the prince had appeared as *Meliadus*, a name which emphasised his desire to use his arms in the service of God (it was an anagram of *Miles a Deo*, Soldier for God) and also hinted at the political role which Henry seems to have wanted to play on the Continental stage. As Drummond noted in a marginal note to his 'Teares on the Death of Meliades' (1613): 'The *Name*, which in these Verses is given Prince HENRIE, is that which he himselfe in ye Challenges of his Martial Sports, & Mascarads, was wont to use, *Meliades Prince of the Isles*, which in *Anagramme* maketh *Miles* A DEO' (quoted in *Ben Jonson: Works*, ed. C.H. Herford and Percy and Evelyn Simpson (11 vols, Oxford: Clarendon Press, 1925–52), vol. 10 (1950), p. 515).

appears to be borne out by the poem 'To the World' published by Thomas Campion soon after the prince's death:

> … Mourne all you soules opprest under the yoake
> Of Christian-hating Thrace; never appear'd
> More likelyhood to have that blacke league broke,
> For such a heavenly prince might well be fear'd
> Of earthly fiends […].[33]

As devised, at least partly, by the prince, the water-fight on the Thames could be said to claim a leading role for Britain in the defence of the true faith.

London 6 June 1610

The recurring motif of the assault on a Turkish castle by Christian forces in the Florence and London *naumachiae* pointed in fact to a significant shift in the way the Turkish threat was now perceived in Western Europe. And consequently in the way water-fights were devised. After the strategic redeployment of Ottoman forces in the wake of Lepanto, danger in the Mediterranean no longer came from the Turkish fleet, but from the quick sudden raids of Barbary pirates, now operating alone from the harbours of Tunis, Algiers and Sallee in Morocco. Indeed three years before the mock encounter on the Thames for the Palatinate wedding, another water-fight was given in London to celebrate the investiture of Henry as Prince of Wales and his return from Richmond. This too was an appropriate tribute to the prince of an island nation who had a close interest in nautical matters. As far as can be judged from Anthony Munday's account of the occasion, the intention was to stage a petty act of piracy rather than a large-scale confrontation between Christian and Turkish ships. This was a topical reminder that, although now deprived of Turkish protection, Barbary pirates were still a formidable nuisance and a constant menace to merchantmen. This explains the fear and detestation in which they and renegade English pirates were held in England at the time, whereas English privateers who attacked and plundered Spanish vessels seem to have had the sympathy of their fellow countrymen.

On 6 June 1610, Londoners witnessed a 'verie fierce and dangerous fight' between

> A Turkish pirate prowling on the seas, to maintaine a Turkish castle (for so their armes and streamers described them both to be) by his spoyle and rapine of merchants and other passengers, sculking abroad to finde a bootie,

---

[33] Thomas Campion, 'To the World', *Songs of Mourning bewailing the untimely death of Prince Henry* (London: Printed [by Thomas Snodham] for John Browne, 1613).

and two merchant ships, which put up a bold resistance but had eventually to be succoured by two men-of-war cruising nearby. After more fierce fighting,

> now the fighte grewe on all sides to be fierce indeed, the castle assisting the pirate very hotly, and the other withstanding bravely and couragiously; divers men appearing on either side to be slayne and hurlled over into the sea […].

the pirates were eventually defeated and the fort destroyed:

> In conclusion, the merchants and men of warre, after a long and well-fought skirmish, prooved too strong for the pirate, they spoylde bothe him and blewe up the castle, ending the whole batterie with verie rare and admirable fire-workes, as also a worthie peale of chambers.[34]

Munday's account explicitly placed the encounter within the referential framework of an economic war. No mention was made either of Christian assailants or of Infidel defenders. The pirates and the castle providing assistance were merely said to be Turkish, that is, Moorish. Moreover the presence of a castle and the implicit allusion to such pirates' dens as Algiers or Sallee helped to maintain the fiction of a Mediterranean setting. Unsurprisingly the pirates were defeated. Mock merchant ships and men-of-war were seen to succeed where their real-life counterparts often failed. Moreover, in a satisfactory reversal of the common kidnapping of English men and women by real pirates, the water-fight concluded with the taking and formal presentation of Turkish prisoners, all suitably dressed in conventional oriental garb. According to the author of *The Magnificent Marriage*, these 'were conveyed to the King's Majestie as a representation of pleasure, which to his Highness moved delight, and highly pleased all there present'.[35] Representation became a form of compensation for an otherwise disappointing reality, a commitment perhaps for the future.[36]

---

[34] Anthony Munday, 'London's Love to the Royall Prince Henrie, Meeting Him on the River Thames at His Returne from Richmonde, with a Worthie Fleete of her Citizens, on Thursday the Last of May 1610. With a Briefe Reporte of the Water-Fight and Fire-Workes', in Nichols, vol. 2, p. 323.

[35] *The Magnificent Marriage of the Two Great Princes*, p. 541.

[36] Interestingly, one year earlier, in June 1609, a combined Franco–Spanish attack on La Galetta in Tunis, in which the English had planned but failed to take part, had dealt a heavy blow to the pirates. A large number of their ships had been set alight in the harbour. But, instead of following up the victory to try and rid the Mediterranean of pirates once and for all, the Spaniards turned on the Moriscos of Andalusia, who were massively deported to North Africa only to give new impetus to the activities of the pirates (see Samuel C. Chew, *The Crescent and the Rose. Islam and England during the Renaissance* (New York: Oxford University Press, 1937), p. 358). The show also coincided with English schemes to capture the renegade English pirate John Ward (Ibid., pp. 347–54).

Bristol 7 June 1613

A similar show was enacted on the River Severn on the occasion of Queen Anne's visit to Bristol in early June 1613. In this new skirmish between Christian and Turkish forces, a single English ship was engaged with two Turkish galleys. Again nothing was spared to make the fighting look realistic. As a local chronicler reported:

> a ship came up under sail and cast anchor, and drew their ensigns upon their top-masts, making obeisance to the Queen. After that they spread their flag again; and up came two gallies of Turks and set upon the ship, and there was much fighing and shooting, three bands of soldiers being placed, one on each side of the two rivers, having apparel for the time. The Turks boarded the ship, and were put off again with loss of men; some of them running up the main-mast to pull down the flag, were thrown overboard into the river, while the ship's side did run over with blood. At length the gallies were beaten off and fled, and some of the Turks remained prisoners [...].[37]

Naturally, the English ship came off triumphant. After the battle the Turkish prisoners were presented to the Queen, 'who laughingly said, that they were not only like Turks by their apparell, but by their countenances'. She became part of the drama much as the French Queen would in the entertainment at La Rochelle in 1632.

This latest mock battle was in fact a re-enactment of one of these sudden pirate raids which so terrified coastal populations in Europe and from which even Bristol suffered. The use of lighter and more manoeuvrable boats had given a new impetus to Barbary pirates and facilitated their increasingly daring ventures into the Atlantic. Unlike the two previous *naumachiae* on the Thames, the water-fight on the Severn was not the stylised enactment of an iconic battle or the dramatic staging of a generic Mediterranean encounter, but the reconstruction of a now common occurrence, a pirate raid on British shores. Four years later, in October 1617, a Moorish pirate vessel was even taken in the Thames estuary.[38]

The author of the verse account of the Queen's visit, one Robert Naile, was at pains to remind his readers that the Turks had captured many Christian merchantmen and condemned them to endless bondage as galley-slaves, as if to encourage public support for James I's efforts to suppress piracy by a reminder of Moorish atrocities. A number of punitive expeditions in the Mediterranean were being planned, although one gets the impression that nothing short of a crusade would have satisfied Robert Naile. His lines are an impassioned call to Christian monarchs to unite and fight a holy war:

Ye Christian Kings and Potentates, joyne both your hearts and hands,

---

[37]   See Naile's 'Entertainment of the Queen at Bristol', in Nichols, vol. 2, pp. 645–6.

[38]   See *C.S.P., Dom.*, 1611–18, p. 427. Mentioned in Chew, *The Crescent and the Rose*, p. 363.

To chase this off-scumme Scithian brood from you and all your lands;
Unite your forces Christian-like from Europe to expell
Proud Ottoman, too dangerous a neighbour neare to dwell;
Whose moony standards still attend, expecting but a prey,
To satisfie their greedy lusts impatient of delay.[39]

No expedition however took place until the late summer of 1621. Needless to say, it was not a crusade. It was a flat failure, which only resulted in a new outbreak of piracy.[40]

Interestingly, in the 1610s, French court festivals were also calling for a crusade against the Turks and the recovery of the Holy Land. In the *Ballet du Triomphe de Minerve*, which was given at court in March 1615, on the eve of Princess Elisabeth's marriage to the future King of Spain, Etienne Durand exhorted the young Louis XIII to avail himself of the Habsburg alliance to

> *Parmi les bataillons fouler, vainqueur, la race*
> *Des Ottomans aux pieds, souverain prendre place,*
> *Où seoit Constantin, avec tes douces fleurs,*
> *Du monde Oriental abreger les douleurs,*
> *Et d'un acier tranchant eslever à l'Eglise,*
> *En ces lieux esloignés une seure franchise.*[41]

> [Amidst the battalions, victorious,
> To trample upon the Ottoman race, to reign supreme
> Where Constantine sat, with your sweet-smelling flowers,
> To ease the pain of the Eastern world,
> And with a sharp-edged sword, to create for the Church,
> In these distant lands, a safe sanctuary.]

Nationalistic prejudices and rivalries between the various European powers, however, spoke louder than eschatological dreams or the sense of a common peril.

---

[39]   Robert Naile, *A Relation of the Royall, Magnificent, and Sumptuous Entertainment Given to the High and Mightie Princess Queen Anne, At the Renowned Citie of Bristol [...] Together with the Oration, Gifts, Triumphes, Water-Combats and Other Showes There Made*, in Nichols, vol. 2, pp. 660–61.

[40]   See *C.S.P., Dom.*, 1619–23. Mentioned in Chew, *The Crescent and the Rose*, p. 365.

[41]   *Ballets et mascarades de cour de Henri III à Louis XIV (1581–1652)*, ed. Paul Lacroix (6 vols [1868–70], (Geneva: Slatkine rpts, 1968), vol. 2, p. 80. The rhetorical dimension of these texts is obvious. These exhortations are *topoi* in all royal panegyrics. Moreover the mention of the fight against the Turks, which is linked here to the recovery of the Holy Land, also serves to ground the dynastic claims of the Bourbons, who claimed descent from both Charlemagne and Saint-Louis. In addition it serves to illustrate and justify the epithet of *Très-Chrétien* commonly given to the French monarch.

As a result any plans for united action were almost always inevitably thwarted. French kings had had a resolutely pro-Turkish policy since the sixteenth century, not only because it was commercially advantageous to do so, but also because the Ottoman Empire could act as a counterbalance to the Spanish monarchy, whose power rivalled the French on the Continent. Unsurprisingly France had refused to join the Holy League between Venice, Rome and Spain in 1571. In England, too, commercial interests were stronger than religious convictions and, notwithstanding popular sentiments, Elizabeth I and James I had encouraged the creation of commercial and diplomatic links with the Sublime Porte. With *realpolitik* stronger than Christian ideals, the hoped-for crusade against the Turks could wait.

La Rochelle 22 November 1632

Turkish affairs were nonetheless followed with keen interest in France as can be gauged from the dramatic rise in pamphlets dealing with the war or the renewed prophetic activity after the victory at Lepanto. Yet this renewed interest does not appear to have led to the performance of specific celebratory or commemorative spectacles of the battle. Turks and Moors were popular characters on the court stage, but, as far as I am aware, the only *naumachia* to enact a French–Turkish encounter dates from November 1632.[42] Even so it did not feature the Turkish fleet, but a single pirate ship from Algiers:

> *L'Armée Angloise ayant gaigné le haut, parut un grand Navire Turc entrant par Antioche. Il portoit sur le Perroquet, & au derriere le Croissant d'argent dans un Pavillon Rouge, estoit pavoizé tout de mesme, & vint jetter le fer à la grande rade hors la portee du Canon de l'armée Françoise. Deux legers vaisseaux de Rame en façon de Galeres, & douze Chaluppes sont envoyées pour recognoistre*

---

[42]   A number of water-fights had been given in France since the turn of the century, but none enacted a French–Turkish encounter. The *naumachia* given for Henry IV in Rouen, on 19 June 1588, featured *Negres tous nuds qui avec leurs arcs & fleches bien empennées, firent bien autant de mal que la milliace de canomnades [sic] qui fut lors tirée* (Negroes all naked, who, with their bows and feathered arrows, wrought as much havoc as the thousands of shots that were fired at the same time), see *Brief Discours sur la Bonne et Joyeuse Reception faicte à la Majesté du Roy par ses tres fidelles & obeïssants sujects de la ville de Rouen* (Rouen: Pierre Courant, 1588), n. p.; whereas the one given a few days later, on 27 June, showed a fort standing in the middle of the river and representing La Rochelle. The third *naumachia*, also given in Rouen, on 24 October 1596, simply featured *deux galleres & une galleotte estrangeres* (two foreign galleys and a galiot), see *Discours de la Joyeuse et Triomphante Entrée de [...] Henry IIII [...] en sa ville de Rouen [...] le mercredy saizieme jour d'octobre M.D.XCVI* (Rouen: R. du Petit Val, 1596, p. 73). As to the water-fight which concluded the wedding festivities of Louis XIII and Anne of Austria in Bordeaux, on 15 December 1615, it was a mock assault on the Russian ambassador's ship.

de plus pres, & si la chose dit le surprendre ou bien le forcer. Les François trouvent que c'est un Pyrate d'Alger [...] & comme ces Navires sont tousjours forts d'hommes, qu'il estoit maneuvré par nombre de Gens ayant le Turban, la Veste & les Botines, qui les acceuillent [sic] à coups de fleches: de sorte que sans marchander on fait brusler la pouldre aux Soldats pour nettoyer les ponts, gaigner s'il est possible les costez, se couvrir de l'Artillerie & tapper à bord franchement.[43]

[As the English fleet retreated, there appeared a large Turkish ship, arriving from Antioch. The ship bore, on the top gallant sail and behind, the silver crescent on a red flag, and was decked out with these flags. It came and put down anchor in the harbour, out of the range of the cannon of the French army. Two light rowing vessels like galley ships and twelve shallops were sent to carry out reconnaissance at close quarters and to see whether or not they could take the boat by surprise or by force. The French found that it was a pirate ship from Algiers [...]. These ships are always well-equipped with men, and they found this one to be operated by a number of men wearing turbans, jackets and boots, who welcomed them with flights of arrows, in such a way that, without hesitation, the soldiers were commanded to open fire in order to clear the decks and, if possible, to reach the ship's sides, covered by artillery, and boldly storm the ship.]

For the French, too, the immediate danger was not so much from the Ottomans as from the Barbary pirates, whose raids terrorised Provence. Besides, more favourable circumstances in the 1620s[44] had led to a renewal of negotiations with Algiers with a view to curbing piracy in the Mediterranean. A treaty was signed in September 1628, which would have guaranteed greater security to French commerce, had it been properly implemented. Another treaty signed soon afterwards authorised the re-establishment of French trading posts, notably the *Bastion de France* and La Calle.[45]

For the first time the French–Turkish encounter given at La Rochelle in honour of the Queen's visit was not the *pièce de résistance* of the occasion. It was only the epilogue to another, far more important show, which re-enacted, on a life-size scale, out at sea, an actual battle between the French and the English fleets. The battle had taken place in September 1628 when the English fleet unsuccessfully tried to break the blockade at La Rochelle. The French had come off triumphant.

---

[43]   Daniel Defos, 'Relation de ce qui s'est passé à l'Entrée de la reyne en la Ville de la Rochelle. Au mois de Novembre mil six cens trente-deux', ed. M.-C. Canova-Green, in J.R. Mulryne, Helen Watanabe-O'Kelly and Margaret Shewring (eds), *Europa Triumphans. Court and Civic Festivals in Early Modern Europe* (2 vols, Aldershot: Ashgate, 2004), vol. 2, p. 228.

[44]   A peace treaty between France and Algiers was signed in Marseille in March 1619.

[45]   On these negotiations, see H.-D. de Grammont, *Relations entre la France et la Régence d'Alger au XVIIe siècle*, 4 parts (Algiers: Adolphe Jourdan, 1879–85).

Four years later they – literally – re-enacted their victory: Cardinal Richelieu, who had devised and paid for the Queen's entry, had enlisted the participation of the *Royale* with its ships and experienced crews in the mock battle.[46] Against such a fearsome opponent, the Algiers pirate did not stand much of a chance! His men were quickly overcome, his ship seized, and himself taken prisoner and brought to the Queen, who graciously pardoned him. He was then said to have decided to remain in France and to have converted to Christianity:

> *On dit qu'il fut bien tost apres Baptizé parmy les Chrestiens & nommé Roulerie,*
> *comme en effect il avoit bien roulé du monde avant de s'arrester.*[47]

[It is said that soon afterwards he was baptized a Christian and renamed 'Roulerie' since, before being stopped, he had indeed run around the world.]

Although given as fact in the text, the story is obviously fabricated. And yet, some details are reminiscent of the life of one Soliman Rays, a renegade pirate from La Rochelle, who had recently died fighting for the French. According to Père Dan, in his *Histoire de Barbarie et de ses corsaires*, this Huguenot sailor was captured by Barbary pirates, taken to Algiers, where he turned pirate and scoured the Mediterranean for several years before he was finally caught by the Sieur de Beaulieu, near Hyères, in 1621. He was freed after five years as a galley slave, offered his services to the French, recanted and converted to Catholicism. He died a while later, fighting the Turks near Rhodes.[48] An edifying story, if ever there was one!

The sea-battle given at La Rochelle to entertain Queen Anne on 22 November 1632 was obviously meant to demonstrate the strength of the French navy and the military and diplomatic successes of the regime. The English fleet had been thwarted in their attempt to succour the besieged La Rochelle. Barbary pirates had been forced to show respect – or so it seemed – to the French king; they had been compelled to sign a peace treaty giving France greater privileges; some had even been brought into the Catholic fold. Reality however was different. The English fleet had indeed been defeated and forced to sail back to England, but the weather had been on the side of the French. Above all Barbary pirates resisted these optimistic fictions and continued to pose a threat to the security of French commerce.[49] Once again representation turned into creative reconstruction.

---

[46]   The involvement of the French fleet in the encounter might even allude to Richelieu's decision in the 1620s to put an effective end to privateering by only allowing navy ships to wage war against pirates. The decision however was reversed by Louis XIII in 1635.

[47]   Defos, *Relation*, p. 228.

[48]   R.P. Pierre Dan, *Histoire de Barbarie et de ses corsaires* (Paris: Pierre Rocolet, 1637), pp. 350–54.

[49]   In fact, according to Père Dan, 80 French vessels and 1,331 sailors and passengers were captured by the Algerians between 1629 and 1634 (*Histoire de Barbarie*, p. 286).

Representation of Conflict with the Turks

The water-fights discussed in this paper reveal that the representation and the significance of the fight against the Turks changed during the first half of the seventeenth century. In France as in England, these shows hardly ever enacted or even referred to the iconic battle of Lepanto. Or if they did, as in the show on the Thames in February 1613, the reference was instrumentalised and put in the service of national interests. Similarly, in the sea battle fought at La Rochelle, in 1632, the demonstration of French naval power prevailed over any other consideration. The battle of Lepanto was not even mentioned and the only historical reference was to a recent victory of the French against the English. Most of the time, however, these mock encounters featured acts of piracy rather than large-scale national confrontations. So-called Turks were now Barbary pirates. Indeed for local populations terrified by their audacious raids on Mediterranean and increasingly on Atlantic shores, these pirates were a far more real danger than Ottoman advances on the fringes of Europe. This might also explain why the motif of the Algiers castle and the implied Mediterranean setting of the encounter were eventually dropped and replaced by the mimicking of raids in the Severn estuary or the Saintonge shoreline.

The significance of these shows also changed. In the years following the battle of Lepanto, their function had been to celebrate or commemorate a significant, although short-lived, victory. Later on, with all reference to Lepanto gone, it rather became one of compensation. Punitive expeditions against Barbary pirates were cherished dreams rather than real historical facts. Encounters were more likely to result in the taking and plundering of merchant ships than in the routing of pirates. The demonstration of naval power on the part of the French or the English that these shows represented was in fact an exercise in national self-aggrandisement, a form of propaganda, designed to reassure populations and no doubt impress foreign observers.

Bibliography

Primary Sources

Ballets et mascarades de cour de Henri III à Louis XIV (1581–1652), (ed.) Paul Lacroix (6 vols [1868–70], Geneva: Slatkine rpts, 1968).
Brief Discours sur la Bonne et Joyeuse Reception faicte à la Majesté du Roy par ses tres fidelles & obeïssants sujects de la ville de Rouen (Rouen: Pierre Courant, 1588).
Campion, Thomas, 'To the World', *Songs of Mourning bewailing the untimely death of Prince Henry* (London: Printed [by Thomas Snodham] for John Browne, 1613).
C.S.P., Dom., 1611–18.

Dan, R.P. Pierre, *Histoire de Barbarie et de ses corsaires* (Paris: Pierre Rocolet, 1637).

Defos, Daniel, 'Relation de ce qui s'est passé à l'Entrée de la reyne en la Ville de la Rochelle. Au mois de Novembre mil six cens trente-deux', ed. M.-C. Canova-Green, in J.R. Mulryne, Helen Watanabe O' Kelly and Margaret Shewring (eds), *Europa Triumphans. Court and Civic Festivals in Early Modern Europe* (2 vols, Aldershot: Ashgate, 2004).

Discours de la Joyeuse et Triomphante Entrée de [...] Henry IIII [...] en sa ville de Rouen [...] le mercredy saizieme jour d'octobre M.D.XCVI (Rouen: R. du Petit Val, 1596).

Gualterotti, Raffaelo, *Della Descrizione del regale apparato fatto nella nobile città di Firenze per la venuta, e per le nozze della Serenissima Madama Cristina di Loreno moglie del Serenissimo Don Ferdinando Medici terzo Gran Duca di Toscana* (Florence: Antonio Padouani, 1589).

I trionfi, feste, et livree fatte dalli Signori conservatori, & Popolo Romano, & da tutte le arti di Roma, nelle felicissima, & honorata entrata dell'Illustrissimo Signor Marcantonio Colonna (Venice, 1571).

Le Mercure François, ou, la Suitte de l'Histoire de la Paix (25 vols, Paris: Estienne Richer, 1611–48).

Munday, Anthony, 'London's Love to the Royall Prince Henrie, Meeting him on the River Thames at his Returne from Richmonde, with a Worthie Fleete of her Citizens, on Thursday the Last of May 1610. With a Briefe Reporte of the Water-Fight and Fire-Workes', in John Nichols (ed.), *The Progresses, Processions and Magnificent Festivities of King James the First, His Royal Consort, Family and Court* (4 vols, London, 1828).

Naile, Robert, 'A Relation of the Royall, Magnificent, and Sumptuous Entertainment Given to the High and Mightie Princess Queen Anne, At the Renowned Citie of Bristol [...] Together with the Oration, Gifts, Triumphs, Water-Combats and Other Showes There Made', in John Nichols (ed.), *The Progresses, Processions and Magnificent Festivities of King James the First, His Royal Consort, Family and Court* (4 vols, London, 1828).

Ordine, et dechiaratione di tutta la mascherata Fatta nella Città di Venetia la Domenica di Carnevale M.D.LXXI Per la Gloriosa Vittoria contra Turchi (Venice: Giorgio Angelieri, 1572).

Pavoni, Giuseppe, *Diario descritto da Giuseppe Pavoni delle feste celebrate nelle solennissime nozze delli Serenissimi Sposi il Signor Don Ferdinando Medici e la Signora Donna Cristina di Loreno Granduchi di Toscana* (Bologna: Giovanni Rossi, 1589).

Ragguaglio delle allegrezze, solennità, e feste fatte in Venetia per la felice vittoria (Venice: Gratioso Perchaccino, 1517).

Taylor, John, 'Heaven's Blessing and Earth's Joy; or, a True Relation of the Supposed Sea-Fights and Fire-Workes as Were Accomplished Before the Royall Celebration of the All-Beloved Marriage of the Two Peerlesse Paragons of Christendome, Fredericke and Elizabeth', in John Nichols (ed.), *The*

Progresses, Processions and Magnificent Festivities of King James the First, His Royal Consort, Family and Court (4 vols, London, 1828).

'The Magnificent Marriage of the Two Great Princes Frederick Count Palatine, &c. and the Lady Elizabeth, Daughter to the Imperial Majesties of King James and Queen Anne, to the Comfort of All Great Britain', in John Nichols (ed.), *The Progresses, Processions and Magnificent Festivities of King James the First, His Royal Consort, Family and Court* (4 vols, London, 1828).

Vecellio, Cesare, *The Clothing of the Renaissance World: Europe. Asia. Africa. The Americas: Cesare Vecellio's Habiti Antichi et Moderni*, eds Margaret F. Rosenthal and Ann Rosalind Jones (London: Thames & Hudson, 2008).

Secondary Sources

Borino, G.B., A. Galieti and G. Navone, 'Il trionfo di Marc'Antonio Colonna', *Miscellanea della R. Deputazione Romana di Storia Patria*, 12 (Rome, 1938).

Braudel, Fernand, *The Mediterranean and the Mediterranean World in the Age of Philip II*, trans. Siân Reynolds (2 vols, Berkeley, Los Angeles, London: University of California Press, 1995).

Carreres y Zacarés, Salvador, *Ensayo de una bibliografía de libros de fiestas en Valencia*, (2 vols, Valencia, 1926).

Carreres y Zacarés, Salvador (ed.), *Libre de memories de diversos sucesos e fets memorables e de coses senyalades de la ciutat e regne de Valencia (1308– 1664)* (2 vols, Valencia, 1935).

Chew, Samuel C., *The Crescent and the Rose. Islam and England during the Renaissance* (New York: Oxford University Press, 1937).

Cock, Henrique, *Relación del viaje hecho por Felipe II, en 1585, á Zaragoza, Barcelona y Valencia*, eds Alfred Morel-Fatio and Antonio Rodriguez Villa (Madrid, 1876).

Degrada, Francesco (ed.), *Andrea Gabrieli e il suo tempo* (Florence: Olschki, 1987).

Fenlon, Iain, '*In Destructione Turcharum*: the Victory of Lepanto in Sixteenth-Century Music and Letters', in Francesco Degrada (ed.), *Andrea Gabrieli e il suo tempo* (Florence: Olschki, 1987), pp. 293–317.

Grammont, H.-D. de, *Relations entre la France et la Régence d'Alger au XVIIe siècle*, 4 parts (Algiers: Adolphe Jourdan, 1879–85).

Hale, J.R., *Florence and the Medici* [1977] (London: Phoenix Press, 2001).

Herford, C.H. and Percy and Evelyn Simpson (eds), *Ben Jonson: Works* (11 vols, Oxford: Clarendon Press, 1925–52).

Herman, Peter C., 'Authorship and the Royal 'I': King James VI/I and the Politics of Monarchic Verse', *Renaissance Quarterly*, 54/4, part 2 (Winter 2001), 1495–1530.

Mamone, Sara, *Il teatro nella Firenze medicea* (Milan: Mursia, 1981).

March y Labores, D. José, *Historia de la marina Real espanola* (Madrid, 1854).

Marsden, C.A., 'Entrées et fêtes espagnoles au XVIe siècle', in Jean Jacquot (ed.), *Les Fêtes de la Renaissance* (3 vols, Paris: Editions du C.N.R.S., 1956–75), vol. 2 (1960), *Fétes et ceremonies au temps de Charles Quint.*

Mulryne, J.R., 'Entries and Festivals in Late Sixteenth and Early Seventeenth Century Florence as Precedents for Court and Theatre in England 1600–1620', in M.-C. Canova-Green and J. Andrews, with the collaboration of M.-F. Wagner (eds), *Writing Royal Entries in Early Modern Europe* (Turnhout: Brepols, 2013).

Mulryne, J.R., Helen Watanabe-O'Kelly and Margaret Shewring (eds), *Europa Triumphans. Court and Civic Festivals in Early Modern Europe* (2 vols, Aldershot: Ashgate, 2004).

Strong, Roy, *Henry, Prince of Wales and England's Lost Renaissance* (London: Thames & Hudson, 1986).

Chapter 10

Mary, Queen of Scots' Aquatic Entertainments for the Wedding of John Fleming, Fifth Lord Fleming to Elizabeth Ross, May 1562

Pesala Bandara

During her six-year personal reign in Scotland from 1561 to 1566, Mary, Queen of Scots, presided over a range of festivities which were designed to ratify her royal status, expound the splendour of her personal court and strengthen Scotland's various foreign alliances. However, in terms of critical scholarship in the field of the early modern festival, there is hardly any work on Mary's theatrical agency during her reign in Scotland. In fact, in the rare instances when Mary's Scottish court festivities are mentioned, they are usually branded as recreational and apolitical.[1] I believe that the modern critical reluctance towards recognizing Mary's Scottish court entertainments as a plausible scholarly topic can be ascribed to two fundamental reasons. Firstly, there is the dominant critical consensus that Mary was an unsuccessful monarch. Secondly, our retrospective awareness of the ill-fated later years of Mary's reign has prompted many critics to brand Mary's earlier court festivals as trivial.

However, our knowledge that Mary's reign in Scotland was doomed should not stop us from attempting to understand how, for Mary, court festivities were an integral part of government and an important vehicle for communicating her royal authority. Perhaps we should also reassess our definition of a monarch's success. As it is, Mary's reign in Scotland cannot strictly be deemed a total failure. After all, Mary's son still became the next king (James VI) of Scotland even after her deposition. Additionally one of Mary's chief dynastic aspirations – to inherit the English throne – was accomplished when her son also became King James I of England on Queen Elizabeth's death.[2] These achievements are due in no small way to Mary's earlier efforts to appear monarchical and, in particular, to her court spectacles, many of which were designed to convey the power and legitimacy of her royal line to both her national and international audiences.

---

[1]   Retha M. Warnicke, *Mary, Queen of Scots* (London: Routledge, 2006), p. 300.

[2]   Carter Lindberg, *The European Reformations*, 2nd edition (Chichester: Wiley-Blackwell, 2010), p.320.

During her reign, Mary inaugurated an array of public, civic, familial and court theatricals and festivities. These included fêtes for half-brother James Stewart's wedding in February 1562, a series of Shrovetide banquets in the Scottish court in 1564, masque entertainments for the French ambassador Rambouillet in February 1566 and grand baptismal celebrations for her son and heir, the future James VI of Scotland in December of that same year. Yet, perhaps the most extraordinary festivities she arranged during her Scottish reign were the aquatic entertainments she organized for the wedding of John Fleming, fifth Lord Fleming, to Elizabeth Ross. As the illegitimate child of Mary Queen of Scots' father, King James IV of Scotland and his mistress Agnes Stewart, John Fleming was Mary's cousin.[3] Elizabeth Ross meanwhile was the daughter of Robert, master of Ross, and Agnes Moncrieff.[4] Robert Lindsay of Pittscottie – who provides the most detailed record of the festivities that took place at Fleming's and Ross's wedding on 14 May 1562 – tells us that all 'the quens grace and the nobilietie [were] present' at this event.[5] However Lindsay also significantly indicates that the courtly entertainments that Mary staged were also 'done befor the ambassadour of Swadin'.[6] The unusual presence of the Swedish ambassador in the audience suggests that Mary's matrimonial celebrations for Fleming and Ross had a twofold importance: they were devised to have an impact on both a national and international scale.

The festivities for the wedding featured a water battle: 'thair was maidwpoun the locht of Airthour saitt gaillayis and ane castell maid alsua thair of tymmer and greit artaillzeschot in everiesyde.'[7] With the entertainments she provided at Fleming's and Ross's wedding, Mary effectively imported the festive *naumachia*, the mock water battle, to the royal court of Scotland. However, other than a passing reference to this waterborne festivity by Carpenter in her essay 'Performing Diplomacies: The 1560s Court Entertainments of Mary, Queen of Scots', this groundbreaking move by Mary in terms of sixteenth-century festival culture has not attracted any critical attention.[8] I will demonstrate how Mary deployed this *naumachia* in May 1562 as a vehicle for her foreign policy.

As mentioned, Mary did not stage a water battle in May 1562 for the admiration of the Scottish nobility only, but also for the approval of the Swedish ambassador whose presence in Fleming's and Ross's audience was an unusual one. The reasons behind the Swedish ambassador's visit to Scotland in May 1562

---

[3]   John Simmons, 'Fleming, John, fifth Lord Fleming (*d.* 1572)', *Oxford Dictionary of National Biography* (2004): http://www.oxforddnb.com/view/article/9701 (accessed 26 July 2010).

[4]   Ibid.

[5]   Lindsay, Robert, *The Historie and Cronicles of Scotland* (2 vols, London: Blackwood and Sons, 1899–1911; first pub. Edinburgh, 1728), vol. 2 (1899), p. 176.

[6]   Ibid., p. 176.

[7]   Ibid., p. 176.

[8]   Sarah Carpenter, 'Performing Diplomacies: The 1560s Court Entertainments of Mary, Queen of Scots', *The Scottish Historical Review*, 88/2 (2003), p. 203.

are important to an understanding of why Mary presented this *naumachia* to him and of the intended purpose of this waterborne display.[9] From the letters written by the English Ambassador in Scotland, Thomas Randolph, to Queen Elizabeth I of England's Secretary of State, William Cecil, we can gauge that the Swedish ambassador's visit to Scotland in 1562 was shrouded in secrecy and was the object of much speculation by Elizabeth's English government. At Cecil's request, Randolph itemizes meticulously the various furtive discussions between Mary and the Swedish ambassador and contemplates the reasons for their meetings. On 29 May for example, Randolph writes how 'On Wednesday afternoon, the Swedish ambassador talked long with the Queen … Their purposes are not yet come to light.'[10] Randolph did discover one of the motives for Mary's meeting with the ambassador. On 3 June, Randolph wrote to Cecil that: 'On Sunday last, the ambassador took leave of the [Queen] without "longe purposes", he received letters to his master, with safe conduct for the king [Eric XIV of Sweden] with 60 ships to arrive on any "coste" of her [Mary's] realm, for the space of 2 years.'[11]

Mary's meetings with the ambassador were organized to establish a treaty by which Swedish ships and naval troops would arrive in Scotland as a measure of added security if necessary. This agreement was perhaps made in the light of erupting religious and political strife in Scotland and Europe. The French Wars of Religion had effectively commenced with the Siege of Rouen a few days before Fleming's wedding.[12] Indeed Lindsay contextualizes Mary's 1562 *naumachia* by reference to the political climate in France, suggesting that her staging of the entertainment was in some way shaped by the situation in France. Lindsay describes how 'At this tyme the congregation of France raise and destroy it the haill imagis an alteris of Rowan'.[13] There was also some restlessness towards Mary amongst the Highland nobility in Scotland, many of whom owned their own private naval troops.[14] This restlessness would culminate in the rebellion of George Gordon, Earl of Huntly, in October 1562,[15] an uprising which would coincidentally be crushed by John Fleming. At the successful settlement of the Scots–Swedish agreement, Randolph reports how Mary presented the ambassador and his staff with '"ij fayer basins and

---

[9]   For information on the link between Scotland and Sweden in the sixteenth century, see Alexia Grosjean, *An Unofficial Alliance: Scotland and Sweden 1569–1654* (Leiden: Brill, 2003) and T. Christopher Smout, *Scotland and Europe, 1200–1850* (Edinburgh: John Donald, 1986).

[10]   Letter from Randolphe to Cecil, 29 May 1562, *Calendar of the State Papers, Scotland*, ed. J. Bain (Edinburgh, 1990), p. 628.

[11]   Ibid., pp. 629–30.

[12]   R.J. Knecht, *The French Wars of Religion 1559–1598* (London: Longman, 1996), p. 2.

[13]   Lindsay, *Historie*, vol. 2, p. 176.

[14]   Susan Doran, *Mary, Queen of Scots: An Illustrated Life* (London: The British Library, 2007), p. 71.

[15]   Ibid., p. 71.

eauers, ij broode cuppes, and two standing peeces of silver"... a chain worth 40 crowns and to the secretary another worth 100'.[16]

However, the primary reason for the meetings between Mary and the Swedish ambassador in May 1562 – the reason which Cecil and the English government suspected and worried about – was the potential arrangement of a marriage treaty between Mary and King Eric XIV of Sweden. Urged by Cecil, Randolph rooted around for proof of possible marriage negotiations between the two. Randolph cautiously wrote to Cecil that Mary extended to the Swedish ambassador 'the honour to "banckquet" six of the Queen's chief ladies, as I hear, very "honorablye" treated'.[17] Randolph also notes that:

> to one of them [the Queen's Ladies] (I know not yet to which) he [the Swedish ambassador] gave the King's picture to be presented to the Queen, 'the verrie whole boddie, as I thynke your honour have seen the lyke'. However she likes it we cannot yet [say], but I am assured it is placed in her 'secrete cabinet' among things she esteems, 'either for antiquetie, noveltie, or that she dothe tayke pleasure in.' This I write to none but your self, being committed to me in assurance of my silence.[18]

This exchange of portraits – a common procedure in sixteenth-century politically-based matchmaking – would have pointed towards marriage talks between Mary and Eric.[19] Elizabeth stubbornly insisted on having a decisive involvement in Mary's choice of marriage suitors: she did not want Mary's prospective husband to strengthen her claim to the English throne.[20] The prospect of Mary's wedding to a powerful foreign suitor like Eric, without her consent, would have brought little assurance to Elizabeth. A Scottish–Swedish marital alliance could effectively make England vulnerable to attack. The possibility of Mary's marriage to Eric would have been more distressing given that he had just recently very publicly pursued marriage with Elizabeth. The Swedish matrimonial proposal had gone so far as Elizabeth entertaining Eric's brother, Duke John of Finland and a Swedish ambassador. Elizabeth and Eric had also exchanged miniatures, with Elizabeth sending the Flemish artist Steven van der Meulen to Stockholm to paint Eric.[21]

---

[16]   Letter from Randolphe to Cecil, 3 June 1562, *Calendar*, p. 630.

[17]   Ibid., p. 630.

[18]   Ibid., p. 630.

[19]   Patricia Fumerton, '"Secret" Arts: Elizabethan Miniatures and Sonnets', in Stephen Jay Greenblatt (ed.) *Representing the English Renaissance* (Berkely and London: University of California, 1988), p. 93.

[20]   Jenny Wormald, *Mary, Queen of Scots: political, passions and a kingdom lost* (London: Tauris Parke, 2001), p. 150.

[21]   Peter Brimacombe, *All the Queen's Men: the world of Elizabeth I* (New York: St Martin's Press, 2000), p. 108.

Elizabeth's council, particularly Cecil and Sir Nicholas Throckmorton, had strongly supported Eric as a match for Elizabeth.[22] Moreover, there was much enthusiasm regarding a marriage between Elizabeth and Eric amongst the English public. It prompted a surge in new publications about Swedish history and culture and London stationers also began selling illustrations of Elizabeth and Eric side by side.[23] Eric was a powerful suitor: he was King of Sweden and, after 1561, also King of Estonia.[24] As a Lutheran, Eric's religious inclination also recommended him to the Protestant English public. Furthermore an Anglo–Swedish marital alliance would have had great commercial benefits: opening up opportunities in terms of Baltic trade for English merchants.[25] However as a result of Elizabeth's ultimate failure to show any real indication of wanting this courtship with Eric to progress, the Swedish King grew impatient and diverted his attention to seeking Mary's hand in marriage instead.[26] Scotland could now potentially, Elizabeth must have feared, reap the benefits from a marital alliance with Sweden.

Given the basis for the Swedish ambassador's visit to Scotland, the 1562 waterborne festivities probably had two main purposes. Firstly, the *naumachia* was intended to celebrate and express the value of the agreement of Swedish naval assistance in Scotland for the next two years. Secondly, it was probably directed towards steering the Swedish matrimonial proposal further: to convince the Swedish ambassador of the Queen of Scots' rank as a worthy marriage suitor and assert the international power of the Scottish crown. Perhaps inherently there was also the wish to convey, through the *naumachia*, an image of Mary's Scottish realm as equal, or indeed superior, to Elizabeth's England.

Lindsay describes the aquatic entertainments performed at Fleming's and Ross's wedding, suggesting their political connotations:

Wpoun the 14 day of May the quene come to Edinburgh and great triumph was maid be ressone of the ambassadour of Swadin. Wpoun the xx day of May the ambassadour of Swadin gaif presentis to the quens grace weill accompanist witht the burgessis of Edinburgh and was honourabill eressawit in the abbay of Hallierudhouse and the same day me lord Fleming was marieit witht great triumph maid, to wit, thair was maid wpoun the locht of Airthour saitt gaillayis and ane castell maid alsuathair of tymmer[27] and greit artaillzeschot in everie

22   Ibid., p. 109.
23   Susan Doran, *Monarchy and Matrimony: the courtships of Elizabeth I* (London: Routledge, 1996), p. 33.
24   Gary Dean Peterson, *Warrior Kings of Sweden: the rise of an empire in the sixteenth and seventeenth centuries* (Jefferson NC and London: McFarland and Co., 2007), p. 66.
25   Doran, *Monarchy*, p. 34.
26   Ibid., p. 34.
27   'Tymmer': meaning timber. See 'Tymmer', *Ancient laws and customs of the burghs of Scotland* (2 vols, Edinburgh: Scottish Burgh Records Society, 1868–1910), vol. 2, p. 220.

side, the quens grace and the nobilietie present, quhilk was done befor the ambassadour of Swadin conforme to the fegour of the Seige of Leytht.[28]

Lindsay mentions that the water festivities were performed on 'the locht of Airthour'.[29] The wedding ceremony took place at Holyrood Park, as *A Diurnall of Remakable Occurents* recounts: 'Fleyming was maryit in the quenis park'.[30] This probably indicates that 'the locht of Airthour' refers to what we now know as Duddingston Loch,[31] which lies immediately to the south of the Park. As one of the smallest lochs in Scotland, it has a circumference of only one and a half miles and a depth of only ten feet.[32] Duddingston Loch's small size would have made it easy for an audience to gather around to watch the water-battle show. Lindsay relates how the loch was filled with galleys. There followed a pyrotechnic fort-holding exercise with a 'castell maid alsuathair of tymmer' and afterwards an elaborate naval assault on the fort took place with 'greit artaillzeschot in everiesyde'.[33] This waterborne military display proves Scotland's advanced expertise in terms of early modern firework-theatre techniques.[34]

Lindsay remarks that the *naumachia* was intended to be evocative of a real naval battle of the recent past: the 1560 Siege of Leith. Following the death of King James V in 1542, Henry VIII had repeatedly attempted to invade Scotland and force a marriage between the Queen of Scots and his son, the future Edward VI, thereby unifying England and Scotland. This drove Mary's mother and Regent of Scotland, Mary of Guise, to make a settlement with France in 1548, in which French naval troops would arrive at the port of Leith and fortify it as a measure of national security.[35] Over the next decade, Protestant Scottish factions grew anxious at the increasing number of French troops in Leith fearing that they would have an inordinate Catholic influence in Scotland. With the assistance of English troops sent by Elizabeth, the Protestant party carried out a fierce assault on the French troops at Leith.[36] After a series of water and land attacks, the siege came to an end in 1560 when Scotland, England and France drew up the Treaty of

---

[28]   Lindsay, p. 176.

[29]   Ibid., p. 176.

[30]   Ibid., p. 176.

[31]   Ibid., p. 176.

[32]   Alexander Francis Lydon, *Scottish Loch Scenery* (London: John Walker and Co., 1882), p. 10; Bruce Gittings, 'Duddingston Loch', *The Gazetteer for Scotland*, 2010, http://www.scottishplaces.info/features/featurefirst7881.html (accessed 28 July 2010).

[33]   Lindsay, vol. 2, p. 176.

[34]   Carpenter, 'Performing Diplomacies', p. 203.

[35]   Jan Glete, *Warfare at sea, 1500–1650: maritime conflicts and the transformation of Europe* (London: Routledge, 2000), p. 151.

[36]   Ibid., p. 151.

Edinburgh which secured the departure of French and English troops from Leith.[37] Given that the Siege had disappointingly resulted in the withdrawal of French troops from Scotland, it may seem strange that Mary chose to recreate this military event in her 1562 waterborne festivity. However, Mary's *naumachia* appears to allude specifically to a battle during the Siege in which Scottish and French troops were victorious.[38] The battle, in January 1560, took place after Mary of Guise had ordered the port of Leith to be further fortified and eight sophisticated protecting bastions to be built.[39] Over 6,000 Scottish and English troops attacked the newly strengthened fort and were unsuccessful.[40] Mary of Guise's troops went on in fact to raid and gain control of Glasgow and Linlithgow.

The evocation of this particular naval battle, even the evocation of the entire Siege of Leith in Mary's *naumachia*, was a way of assuring the Swedish ambassador of the value and solidity of the treaty providing for Swedish naval assistance to arrive in Scotland. Undoubtedly, the nautical theme of the festivities acted as a way of celebrating the agreement that Mary and the ambassador were in the process of making. The *naumachia*'s representation of the successful partnership between Scotland and France in the water-battle of January 1560 also had positive implications for the prospective Scottish–Swedish alliance. The *naumachia* depicted the confidence and strength of Scotland's international relationships and indirectly presaged the same political success for Sweden and Scotland.

The relocation of the Siege of Leith in this splendid festivity proved an effective device. It redefined this entire military event as a victorious one, as proof of Scotland's ability to face international threats like this English attack and ward it off. The *naumachia* assured the Swedish ambassador of the stability and security of the Scottish realm, and thus the constancy of any treaty made between the two countries. It would also have served as a reassuring and powerful courtly spectacle for Mary and her nobility. The example of Scotland's safe recovery from the Siege implied that the realm would survive the current dangers both to its own shores and on the continent. Indeed, as mentioned, Lindsay contextualizes Mary's 1562 *naumachia* alongside the siege of Rouen a few days earlier on the fifth of May.[41] This suggests that Mary's court *fête* was demonstrably responding to these contemporary upheavals and reinforcing Scotland's strength against any potential threats.

The main purpose of the 1562 *naumachia* was most probably, however, to advance the possibility of a marriage treaty between Mary and Eric further, by showing the Scottish crown as an internationally powerful one to which to be

---

[37]   Charles Knight, *Popular history of England: an illustrated history of society and government from the earliest period to our own times* (9 vols, London: 1856–82), vol. 3 (London: Bradbury and Evans, 1857), p. 121.

[38]   Carpenter, 'Performing Diplomacies', p. 203.

[39]   Antonia Fraser, *Mary, Queen of Scots* (London: Weidenfeld and Nicolson, 1994), p. 129.

[40]   Ibid., p. 129.

[41]   Lindsay, vol. 2, p. 176.

conjugally allied. The spectacle of Scotland's enacted naval triumph over England in Mary's *naumachia* was designed by extension to assert Scotland's status and authority on the continent. A performance of Scotland's command of the sea was not just a general exhibition of the country's place among nations. For centuries, the Scottish monarchy had considered its naval strength as being a dominant component of the country's political and military power in Europe. For Mary's grandfather King James IV of Scotland, the strengthening of the country's sea power was one of his most keenly advocated national programmes.[42] He had even made personal requests to Venice and the papacy for support of his naval ambitions.[43] The galley would emerge as the most potent symbol of royal power by the end of the sixteenth century in Europe.[44] However the Scottish crown had recognized the prestige of the galley as far back as the beginning of the century.[45] James IV was responsible for building the largest ship of his time with the construction of the one thousand ton *Michael* in 1511.[46] The Scottish monarchy's navies were also known to be far superior to the Highland nobility's naval resources.[47] France also prized their alliance with Scotland, especially during the period of civil conflict in 1562, as Scotland boasted excellent sea communications in terms of the transportation of troops and provisions.[48] The Scottish crown had long appreciated the importance of sea power and the potential influence that becoming one of the leading maritime nations would confer in Europe. The naval historian Ken Booth has shown the importance of navies and sea warfare to small countries like Scotland in the Renaissance because of a navies' threefold diplomatic, policing and military function.[49]

Mary's *naumachia* directly and specifically conveyed Scotland's potency as a nation to the Swedish ambassador. Indeed King Eric XIV of Sweden and his father, King Gustav I of Sweden, appreciated the importance of sea power and

---

[42]   Miles Glendinning, Ranald MacInnes and Aonghus MacKechnie, *A History of Scottish Architecture: from the Renaissance to the Present Day* (Edinburgh: Edinburgh University Press, 1996), p. 7.

[43]   Ibid., p. 7.

[44]   John B. Hattendorf and Richard W. Unger, *War at sea in the Middle Ages and the Renaissance* (Woodbridge: Boydell, 2003) p. 237.

[45]   Julian Goodare, *State and society in early modern Scotland* (Oxford: Oxford University Press, 1999), p. 165.

[46]   Glendinning, MacInnes and MacKechnie, *Scottish Architecture*, p. 7.

[47]   Jane E.A. Dawson, *The politics of religion in the age of Mary, Queen of Scots: the Earl of Argyll and the struggle for Britain and Ireland* (Cambridge: Cambridge University Press, 2002), p. 54.

[48]   Stuart Carroll, *Noble power during the French wars of religion: the Guise affinity and the Catholic cause in Normandy* (Cambridge: Cambridge University Press, 1998), p. 48.

[49]   Ken Booth, *Navies and Foreign Policy* (London: Croom Helm, 1977), pp. 24–5.

keenly pursued a policy of expanding Swedish naval warfare.[50] The *naumachia*'s demonstration of Scotland's maritime authority must have also appealed to the Swedish monarchy's own conception of power. Furthermore, the *naumachia*'s performance of Scotland's past naval victory over England would have presented the Scottish crown as a formidable force against the English crown. It thus portrayed to Eric Mary's superiority as a marriage prospect in comparison to Elizabeth. Coincidentally, England's seaborne defeat in Mary's *naumachia* in May would be re-enacted in reality only a few months later in September. Elizabeth sent several ships and troops to support the French Huguenots in Le Havre and maintain the English garrisons there.[51] However the sea-assault was unsuccessful and resulted in the English crown losing their garrisons in both Le Havre and Dieppe.[52] The *naumachia* that Mary staged for the Swedish ambassador must have been an impressive display of Scotland's power and value as an ally, especially given the fact that it secured the treaty for extra naval support from Sweden. Moreover even after the Swedish ambassador's departure from Scotland, Eric would continue to pursue Mary as a bride.[53] Believing a more powerful suitor could be found for Mary, it was the Scottish court that would ultimately put an end to the marriage negotiations with the Swedish king.[54]

Bibliography

Primary Sources

Letter from Randolphe to Cecil, 29 May 1562, *Calendar of State Papers, Scotland*, ed. J. Bain (Edinburgh, 1990), p. 628.
Letter from Randolphe to Cecil, 3 June 1562, *Calendar of State Papers, Scotland*, ed. J. Bain (Edinburgh, 1990), pp. 629–30.

Secondary Sources

Ancient laws and customs of the burghs of Scotland (2 vols, Edinburgh: Scottish Burgh Records Society, 1868–1910).
Black, Jeremy (ed.), *European warfare, 1494–1660* (London and New York: Routledge, 2002).
Booth, Ken, *Navies and Foreign Policy* (London: Croom Helm, 1977).

---

[50]   Mark Konnert, *Early Modern Europe: The Age of Religious War, 1559–1715* (Plymouth: Broadnew Press, 2002), p. 229.
[51]   Jeremy Black (ed.), *European warfare, 1494–1660* (London and New York: Routledge, 2002), p. 182
[52]   Ibid., p. 182.
[53]   Doran, p. 35.
[54]   Ibid., p. 35.

Brimacombe, Peter, *All the Queen's Men: the world of Elizabeth I* (Stroud: Sutton Press, 2000).

Carpenter, Sarah, 'Performing Diplomacies: The 1560s Court Entertainments of Mary, Queen of Scots', *The Scottish Historical Review*, 88/2 (2003), pp. 194–225.

Carroll, Stuart, *Noble power during the French wars of religion: the Guise affinity and the Catholic cause in Normandy* (Cambridge: Cambridge University Press, 1998).

Dawson, Jane, E.A, *The politics of religion in the age of Mary, Queen of Scots: the Earl of Argyll and the struggle for Britain and Ireland* (Cambridge: Cambridge University Press, 2002).

Doran, Susan, *Monarchy and Matrimony: the courtships of Elizabeth I* (London: Routledge, 1996).

Doran, Susan, *Mary, Queen of Scots: An Illustrated Life* (London: The British Library, 2007).

Fraser, Antonia, *Mary, Queen of Scots* (London: Weidenfeld and Nicolson, 1994).

Fumerton, Patricia, '"Secret" Arts: Elizabethan Miniatures and Sonnets', in Stephen Jay Greenblatt (ed.), *Representing the English Renaissance* (Berkeley and London: University of California Press, 1988), pp. 93–134.

Gittings, Bruce, 'Duddingston Loch', *The Gazetteer for Scotland*, http://www.scottish-places.info/features/featurefirst7881.html (28 July 2010).

Glendinning, Miles, Ranald MacInnes and Aonghus MacKechnie, *A History of Scottish Architecture: from the Renaissance to the Present Day* (Edinburgh: Edinburgh University Press, 1996).

Glete, Jan, *Warfare at sea, 1500–1650: maritime conflicts and the transformation of Europe* (London: Routledge, 2000).

Goodare, Julian, *State and society in early modern Scotland* (Oxford: Oxford University Press, 1999).

Greenblatt, Stephen J. (ed.), *Representing the English Renaissance* (Berkeley and London: University of California Press, 1988).

Grosjean, Alexia, *An Unofficial Alliance: Scotland and Sweden 1569–1654* (Leiden: Brill, 2003).

Hattendorf, John B. and Richard W. Unger, *War at sea in the Middle Ages and the Renaissance* (Woodbridge: Boydell, 2003).

Knecht, R.J., *The French Wars of Religion 1559–1598* (London: Longman, 1996).

Knight, Charles, *Popular history of England: an illustrated history of society and government from the earliest period to our own times* (9 vols, London, 1856–82), vol. 3 (London: Bradbury and Evans, 1857).

Konnert, Mark, *Early Modern Europe: The Age of Religious War, 1559–1715* (Plymouth: Broadnew Press, 2002).

Lindberg, Carter, *The European Reformations*, 2nd edn (Chichester: Wiley-Blackwell, 2010).

Lindsay, Robert, *The Historie and Cronicles of Scotland* (2 vols, London: Blackwood and Sons, 1899–1911; first pub. Edinburgh, 1728).

Lydon, Alexander Francis, *Scottish Loch Scenery* (London: John Walker and Co., 1882).

Peterson, Gary Dean, *Warrior Kings of Sweden: the rise of an empire in the sixteenth and seventeenth centuries* (Jefferson, NC and London: McFarland and Co., 2007).

Simmons, John, 'Fleming, John, fifth Lord Fleming (*d.* 1572)', *Oxford Dictionary of National Biography* (September 2004). http://www.oxforddnb.com/view/article/9701.

Smout, T. Christopher, *Scotland and Europe, 1200–1850* (Edinburgh: John Donald, 1986).

Warnicke, Retha M., *Mary, Queen of Scots* (London: Routledge, 2006).

Wormald, Jenny, *Mary, Queen of Scots: politics, passions and a kingdom lost* (London: Tauris Parke, 2001).

Chapter 11

Looking Again at Elvetham: An Elizabethan Entertainment Revisited

H. Neville Davies

One of the last stages, or 'gesses', of Queen Elizabeth's late summer progress in 1591 was a three-night visit to Elvetham, a modest estate in the north-east corner of Hampshire that belonged to Edward Seymour, Earl of Hertford. It was not until 20 September, however, that the queen eventually arrived there, already high time for her and her itinerant court to return to the royal palaces. Furthermore, we should realize that had our Gregorian calendar then been in operation the visit would have crossed the threshold into what is now regarded as October; and the full implications of that ought to be taken into account when we consider the viability of outdoor entertainments commissioned by a host anxious to demonstrate, in every available way, both his nobility and the strength of his allegiance. More than three centuries later, and after the mid-eighteenth-century adjustment of the British calendar, the poet John Keats (who was enjoying 'chaste weather – Dian skies' in Hampshire) was already noting on 21 September a 'temperate sharpness' in the Hampshire air, and feeling the need for a parlour fire in the evening. Yet Keats's 21 September was effectively ten days earlier than an Elizabethan 21 September and, appropriately enough, the Winchester poem he had been inspired to compose just two days before was an ode 'To Autumn' in which 'gathering swallows' prepare for migration to warmer climes.[1] So, at the end of the royal visit, with the rain bucketing down onto the queen's coach as Elizabeth left Elvetham, a poet attired in black to betoken mourning, and presumably dripping wet and soaked to the skin, addressed her majesty with words to which the weather added the commiserations of the pathetic fallacy:

[1]   Letters to J.H. Reynolds and to Richard Woodhouse, 21 September 1819, *The Letters of John Keats, 1814–1821*, ed. Hyder Edward Rollins (2 vols, Cambridge Mass: Harvard University Press, 1958), vol. 2, pp. 167 and 169.

O see sweete Cynthia, how the watery Gods,
Which ioy'd of late to view thy glorious beames,
At this retire doe waile, and wring their hands,
Distilling from their eies salt showers of teares;
To bring in Winter with their wet lament:
For how can Summer stay when Sunne departs?[2]

Never was actor better served by stage manager and the Special Effects Department than was Hertford's rain-drenched poet by the precipitation from on high.

But not only was it late in the year for the queen's visit, there were also serious misgivings troubling the earl about the suitability of the venue itself. Elizabeth's father had spent a night there way back in October 1535 as the guest of Hertford's father, the Duke of Somerset who became Protector in the reign of Edward VI, and King Henry had been there again the following year;[3] yet, as Hertford was acutely aware in 1591, the ancient residence at Elvetham was not one of his 'chiefe mansion houses' and its restricted park was 'but of two miles in compasse, or thereabouts' (p. 570). Indeed, almost a decade earlier, in 1582, when the earl had considered hosting a royal visit that ultimately failed to materialize, it was to have been not at unsuitable Elvetham but at the better provided Tottenham Lodge, his home by Savernake Forest at Great Bedwyn near Marlborough in Wiltshire.[4] He had recently had it enlarged and refurbished.

Fortunately, despite the problems that had to be overcome, and some 'foule', even 'stormie' weather (p. 581), all went well at Elvetham, or so it seems. And as the queen passed through the park gate on that wet morning of her departure, and after a succession of festivities that had evidently given great pleasure throughout the visit, the final touch was provided by two highly regarded singers, accompanied by a consort secreted in a bower, where, one can only hope, valuable musical instruments received adequate shelter from the rain. Her majesty graciously halted the coach to listen to their accomplished performance of an enticing invitation that repeatedly implored her to '*Come againe*' (p. 595), although ten years later, in 1601, when she had every intention of revisiting Hertford, it was Tottenham in Wiltshire not Elvetham in Hampshire that the queen had in mind. The evidence comes from one of John Chamberlain's letters, but both John Nichols, who quotes

---

[2]   Quotations are from my edition in *John Nichols's The Progresses and Public Processions of Queen Elizabeth I: A New Edition of Early Modern Sources*, eds Jayne Elisabeth Archer, Elizabeth Clarke and Elizabeth Goldring (5 vols, Oxford: Oxford University Press, 2013), vol. 3, 563–95 (p. 594). For 'the great raine', see p. 595, sidenote.

[3]   See *Letters and Papers, Foreign and Domestic, of the Reign of Henry VIII* (21 vols, London: Longman, Green, Longman and Roberts, 1862–1932), vol. 9, pp. 619–20; *The Victoria History of the County of Hampshire and the Isle of Wight* (6 vols, London: Constable, 1900–14), vol. 4, ed. William Page (1911), p. 75.

[4]   J.E. Jackson, 'Wulfhall and the Seymours', *Wiltshire Archaeological and Natural History Magazine*, 15 (1875), p. 200.

from the letter, and Chamberlain's modern editor have assumed that a return to Elvetham was envisaged.[5] It is clear, nevertheless, from the way that Chamberlain associates Hertford's residence with Littlecote, the neighbouring Wiltshire seat of Sir John Popham only some half dozen miles from Tottenham Lodge, that far distant Elvetham is not alluded to. In the event, because of the need to receive the duc de Biron's French embassy, the planned progress was to be curtailed anyway before it could reach Wiltshire. The following year, to make up for this, and to collect the 'jewells and presents' that would have been bestowed upon her in 1601, the queen once again hoped to visit Tottenham Lodge. But it was not to be, then or ever, with bad weather and fear of smallpox taking the blame this time.[6] In 1603 the new king and queen were to fulfil Elizabeth's unrealized intention, spending four days at Tottenham Lodge at the beginning of September. James added a second visit in July 1620.[7] The 1591 visit to Elvetham, therefore, had no successor, and no Elizabethan precursor. It was a one-off, memorable because it reflected some of the earlier extravagance of Kenilworth, and because it anticipated developments associated with the Jacobean court masque. It is significant, too, because it included the only Elizabethan progress entertainment of which there is a contemporary pictorial record.

Antiquarian Editors, 1779–1823: Richard Gough and John Nichols

Virtually everything that we know about the visit and the diverse entertainments that made it remarkable comes from one or other version of the anonymously authored and elegantly produced commemorative pamphlet, entered in the Stationers' Register a mere eight days after the queen's departure. Under the title of *The Honorable Entertainement gieuen to the Queenes Maiestie in Progresse, at Eluetham in Hampshire, by the right Honorable the Earle of Hertford. 1591*, and printed by John Wolf, this official account, undoubtedly commissioned by the earl himself, must have been published either before the end of that year or before 25 March 1592.[8] When, in 2001, I undertook to edit it for inclusion in a

---

[5]   John Nichols, *Progresses ... of Elizabeth I* (3 vols, London: J.B. Nichols, 1823), vol. 3, p. 568; *Letters of John Chamberlain*, ed. Norman Egbert McClure (2 vols, Philadelphia, Pa: American Philosophical Society, 1939), vol. 1, p. 131. Similarly, June Osborne, *Entertaining Elizabeth I: The Progresses and Great Houses of her Time* (London: Bishopsgate Press, 1989), p. 94, and Katherine Duncan-Jones, 'Elizabeth I and her "Good George"', in Peter Beal and Grace Ioppolo (eds), *Elizabeth I and the Culture of Writing* (London: British Library, 2007), p. 31.

[6]   Chamberlain, *Letters*, vol. 1, pp. 156–7 and 160.

[7]   John Nichols, *Progresses ... of James the First* (4 vols, London: J.B. Nichols, 1828), vol. 1, p. 250 and vol. 3, p. 613.

[8]   Wolf's association with Hertford went back at least six years. In 1585 Wolf had been responsible for issuing Marcantonio Pigafetta's *Itinerario*, published in London and

new edition of the early modern sources of that venerable and still indispensable collection, John Nichols's *Progresses and Public Processions of Queen Elizabeth I*, my initial task was to sort out the tangled bibliographical confusion bequeathed by my editorial predecessors, though I little realized then what a ramshackle house of cards they had erected. The post-Elizabethan process of editing had begun, as I discovered, with John Nichols's friend Richard Gough who, under the pseudonym of 'A Constant Reader', serialized a reprint of this 'curious (tho' little known) publication' in the *Gentleman's Magazine* in 1779.[9] His copy text was most probably the Lambeth Palace quarto, which has the advantage of including a fold-out sheet with a hand-coloured woodcut depicting the waterborne entertainment presented before Elizabeth late in the afternoon on the second day of her visit (Plate 2). The account explains that to compensate for the deficiencies of Elvetham, Hertford had had a crescent-shaped lake or 'pond' specially created for the occasion, and that this, with its three distinctive islands, provided the setting for an ambitious aquatic pageant. The woodcut duly shows the lake, the ship isle with its three mast-like trees, the fort isle, and the snail isle with its winding spiral of privet hedging; and it shows too some performers and some boats, including a pinnace, scaled down of course, but still large enough to accommodate at least eight performers, and sufficiently seaworthy to be towed by an elaborately accoutred group of swimmers and waders across the lake during the performance, those swimmers and waders impersonating the 'watery Gods' who were later, with their 'wet lament', to deplore the queen's departure.[10] The only feasible way of presenting this sixteenth-century woodcut to readers of the *Gentleman's Magazine* was to print from a hand-copied woodcut reproduction and to forgo the luxury of colour. The result, as Figure 11.1 demonstrates, was disastrous. T.G., whose initials convict the perpetrator, had taken the inexcusable liberty of converting a pictorially enhanced site-map into something approaching an eighteenth-century illustrative scene, up-dated with a liberal supply of anachronistic union jacks, the Elizabethan pinnace remodelled as an eighteenth-century man-of-war, and the park freshly landscaped with a generous planting of smart new trees. Replete with their tiny oarsmen and musicians, the graceful toy barges that replaced the single-scull skiffs crudely

---

dedicated, probably at Wolf's instigation rather than the author's, 'All'Illustrissimo ed Eccellentissimo Signore il Signor Eduardo Seymer Cavaliere, Conte d'Hertford e Signore di Beauchampe'. See the editions of Pigafetta's book, ed. Daria Perocco (Padua: Poligrafo, 2008), p. 72 and ed. Michela Petrizzelli (Vicenza: Biblioteca Civica Bertoliana, 2008), p. 18. The heraldic woodcut displaying Hertford's arms on the title page of the 1585 *Itinerario* was reused by Wolf in 1591 for the title page of *The Honorable Entertainement*.

[9]   February–March, pp. 81–5 and 121–5 Digitized at http://books.google. com/books?id=zXxIAAAAYAAJ&dq=the%20gentleman's%20magazine%20 elvetham&pg=PA81#v=onepage and http://books.google.com/books?id=zXxIAAAAYAAJ&dq=the%20 gentleman's%20magazine%20elvetham&pg=PA121#v=onepage respectively.

[10]   There are many discrepancies between what the text records and what the picture shows, but it would be wrong to hold a diagrammatic picture too strictly to account.

Figure 11.1   The pond at Eluetham as depicted in the *Gentleman's Magazine*, 1779.

depicted in the original even suggest the microform pomp and circumstance of a Lilliputian version of Handel's Water Music. Indeed, truly proportionate to the diminutive size of the Augustan homunculi on board these vessels would be the minuscule semi-hemi-demi-semiquavers and facetiously contrived 3/32 time signature of the *Lilliputsche Chaconne* from Telemann's Gulliver Suite. For by imposing a more consistent sense of scale, the make-over introduces a process of systematic miniaturization more redolent of Mistress Masham's Repose than of Elvetham in 1591. The picture has also been reversed so that east and west have confusingly exchanged places.

The next reprint of the pamphlet, by Nichols in his 1788 edition of the *Progresses of Queen Elizabeth*, soon followed. The text was independent of Gough's, but to show the waterborne entertainment Nichols economized by reusing T.G.'s by then rather worn, somewhat damaged block, and one unfortunate result is that T.G.'s wilfully divergent image has, in our time, too often been reproduced from Nichols as though it were an authentic Elizabethan picture. For instance, to cite but a single example, the compilers of the forthcoming Hampshire volume in the widely respected *Records of Early English Drama* series do precisely this in an interim survey that they have published.[11] The unrevealing caption they supply to accompany the illustration gives no indication that the source is an eighteenth-century publication. It merely alludes to 'Hampshire Record Office, 15M84/ Z3/37', while the appended bibliography fallaciously identifies this archival item as a book dated 1591. In fact, the original Elizabethan woodcut has never

---

[11]   Jane Cowling and Peter Greenfield, *Monks, Minstrels and Players: Drama in Hampshire before 1642*, Hampshire Papers 29 (Winchester: Hampshire County Council, 2008).

been reproduced in colour, and since the colour was hand-painted over the inked impression, the composite image is one that cannot successfully be represented by black-and-white photography. Transparent washes, like the blue of the pond, cause no problem, but opaque washes, like those in the foreground, simply register as unsightly blemishes, while more dense body colour entirely obscures underlying graphic detail that in the original just about manages to remain visible. Furthermore, the colouring is not, as might be thought, cack-handed embellishment added in some idle moment by the book's misguided owner (or by the owner's well-meaning children) but an in-house up-grade already present when the book was first acquired, and so an essential part of the intended impact.

Only two examples of the woodcut survive, one in the Lambeth Palace copy of *The Honorable Entertainement* and one, which is similarly coloured, in the Cambridge University Library copy. The Lambeth print is very slightly damaged in that a small section of the framing border has been shaved, but this damage does not impinge on the pictorial inset. The Cambridge copy, on the other hand, is seriously impaired, for the bottom 15 mm of the picture have been sheared off. Not that one would ever guess this, however, from Jean Wilson's silently doctored reproduction of it in her book *The Shakespeare Legacy: The Material Legacy of Shakespeare's Theatre*.[12] There the imposition of a continuous border that neatly frames the truncated illustration effectively conceals the cropped edge, and consequently the defective condition, of the inappropriately chosen original.

More disturbingly, what readers and editors who know Nichols's work only through the later and more commonly consulted 1823 edition of the *Progresses* frequently fail to realize is that even the engagement with the text of *The Honorable Entertainement* was far from straightforward. For having printed off what he regarded, understandably enough, as an acceptable text – although, by good chance, before the printed sheets were finally assembled and published in 1788 – Nichols came across a second quarto edition, dated on the title page, like the first edition, 1591, but with the words '*Newlie corrected, and amended*' appended to the title. The discovery presented him with a dilemma. For it was clear that although there is interesting material in the first edition that was excluded from this second edition, it was that corrected and emended text that would have constituted his prime

---

[12]   Jean Wilson, *The Shakespeare Legacy: The Material Legacy of Shakespeare's Theatre* (Godalming: Bramley Books, 1995), p. 130. For black-and-white reproductions of the woodcut in the Lambeth Palace copy, see W.W. Greg, *A Bibliography of the English Printed Drama to the Restoration* (4 vols, London: Printed for the Bibliographical Society at the University Press, Oxford, 1939–59), vol. 1, pl. xxxi; G.B. Harrison, *An Elizabethan Journal: Being a Record of those Things Most Talked of During the Years 1591–1594* (London: Routledge, 1938), facing p. 56; and Ruth Samson Luborsky and Elizabeth Morley Ingram, *A Guide to English Illustrated Books, 1536–1603* (2 vols, Tempe, Ariz: Medieval and Renaissance Texts and Studies, 1998), vol. 2, fig. 99. The suspected loss, from *both* surviving copies of the fold-out sheet, of letterpress printed below the woodcut is discussed in my edition (pp. 563 and 572 n. 196).

authority had he known of its existence before he had ventured into print.[13] Yet he was unwilling to write off what he had already produced and to start all over again, so he added a make-do postscript, explaining what had happened and detailing what he considered to be the significant Q2 variants. By far the most exciting variant was a vastly more revealing and sophisticated illustration of the aquatic entertainment. And by this time, possibly as a result of sharpened awareness gained through comparing the two 1591 illustrations, it had been realized just how embarrassingly ill-judged was T.G.'s adaptation of the Q1 woodcut. So, when Nichols then included in the postscript a specially commissioned engraving of the newly discovered and fascinatingly detailed Q2 replacement picture, he accompanied this spectacular additional plate (Fig. 11.2) by the reassuring assertion that it had been 'exactly copied'.[14] Whether that claim was legitimate is a question to which we shall return.

Some 35 years later, in 1823, Nichols published a radically revised version of his pioneering collection, and rightly seized the opportunity to tidy up the makeshift presentation of *The Honorable Entertainement* that he had been forced to adopt in 1788. He decided on a conflation of Q1 and Q2, but unfortunately produced the new recension without going back to the quartos themselves. Instead, he simply conflated his not entirely reliable 1788 reprint of Q1 with the Q2 variants that he had incompletely recorded in his 1788 postscript, and recorded so confusingly, as it turned out, that he confused even himself. The result is a textual mishmash that is far from satisfactory. Two particularly glaring examples of what went wrong show just how detrimental the procedure was. The 'Come againe' song, sung as Elizabeth departed, has four two-line stanzas in Q1 and similarly four two-line stanzas in Q2, although the worked-over song in Q2 is much revised. By process of unregulated accretion, Nichols's 1823 mishmash allowed an all-inclusive *eight-*stanza song (i.e. all four stanzas from Q1 plus all four from Q2) to accumulate, with consequent elements of repetition and partial repetition in it that no one had ever intended or sanctioned, and that no one could regard as desirable.[15] Yet this Nichols version, patently garbled though it is, has gained undeserved currency. Equally absurd is the way that the words 'Here follows', used by Nichols at one point in his 1788 postscript to indicate where a particular Q2 addition properly belongs, have

---

[13]   The particulars of the Wednesday banquet are the most notable omission.

[14]   Vol. 2, section E, p. 25. Precisely whose dissatisfaction in 1591 with the Q1 woodcut was responsible for the commissioning of the Q2 replacement is matter for speculation, but the improvement certainly resulted in an illustration more in accord with Wolf's experience of European publishing and the model of the continental festival book, as well as with Wolf's developing position as the leading London printer of books that included maps. See Maria Grazia Bellorini, 'Le pubblicazioni Italiane dell'editore Londinese John Wolfe (1580–1591)', *Miscellanea*, 1, ed. Manlio Cortelazzo (Udine: Arti Grafiche Friulane, 1971), pp. 17–65 and Laurence Worms 'Maps and Atlases', in John Barnard and D.F. MacKenzie, with the assistance of Maureen Bell (eds), *The Cambridge History of the Book in Britain*, (7 vols, Cambridge: Cambridge University Press, 1999–2011), vol. 4 (2002), p. 235.

[15]   *Progresses* (1823), vol. 3, p. 121.

Figure 11.2   The pond at Eluetham from J. Nichols (ed.), *The Progresses and Public Processions of Queen Elizabeth* (3 vols, 1788), vol. 2, section E, p. 25.

themselves been incorporated into the 1823 text, and subsequently been accepted unquestioningly by later editors as authentic.[16] We should be glad, however, that Nichols now dropped T.G.'s travesty of the Q1 woodcut and chose to include only the more elaborate Q2 illustration. To do this required the preparation of a new plate, but again it was copied, with inevitable degeneration, from 1788, not afresh from 1591.

Literary Editors, 1902–80: Warwick Bond and Jean Wilson

The next noteworthy edition was by Warwick Bond in his *Complete Works of John Lyly*,[17] eccentrically included in that enterprise because Bond had conceived the totally fanciful notion that Lyly was both the 'deviser' and 'the practical stage-manager' of the Elvetham entertainments and that Lyly had then collaborated with an anonymous retainer of the earl of Hertford in compiling and writing the

---

[16]   *Progresses* (1823), vol. 3, p. 102.

[17]   R. Warwick Bond (ed.), *Complete Works of John Lyly*, (3 vols, Oxford: Clarendon Press, 1902).

commemorative pamphlet.[18] It is an edition with genuinely scholarly pretensions, but, alas, the impressive looking textual apparatus is as whimsical as the unconvincing attribution of the entertainments to Lyly. That there are exemplars of Q1 at Lambeth and at Cambridge has already been noted in connection with remarks about the Q1 woodcut, but there is also a third exemplar, unavailable to either Gough or Nichols, that as yet has not been mentioned because it does not include (and probably never did include) the woodcut.[19] It is now in the British Library, having been acquired by the British Museum in 1868, where it conveniently provided Bond with his copy text. But, quite apart from the absence of the woodcut, it raised a problem, for Bond noticed disturbing differences between Nichols's published text and this particular quarto. In fact, there are two easily explicable reasons for such divergence. One is that Nichols was none too fastidious when it came to minor matters like preserving the vagaries of old spelling and Elizabethan punctuation, and the other is that a few press variants are to be found in the three surviving examples of Q1. None of those copies duplicates either of the other two, and none of them can be regarded as ideal because no single one of them incorporates both outer forme B and inner forme D in a corrected state. The Cambridge copy is unique in having an error on its title page.

Bond understood nothing of this. He had not collated the three copies and, moreover, simply assumed, quite wrongly, that Nichols transcribed with unerring accuracy and had printed a text without any editorial intervention. Thus Bond jumped to the mistaken conclusion that the textual discrepancies he had observed showed that Nichols must have had access to an edition that was distinct from that exemplified by the British Library's quarto. This figment of his editorial imagination Bond christened 'Q2', despite having himself never laid hands on any actual example of the phantom he had postulated. The real Q2 he shunted down the line of succession and rechristened 'Q3'. Moreover, to make matters worse, this 'Q3' as he called it (though it is really Q2) had gone missing. Nobody knew where Nichols had consulted it. The only record of it was Nichols's postscript of 1788, and not a solitary soul seemed to have seen it since. Regrettably, the enduring legacy of Bond has been uncritical belief in the three-edition theory, still alive and flourishing, though utterly indefensible. And one consequence of that has been the unwarrantable assumption that *The Honorable Entertainement*, with supposedly so many editions called for, must have been something of an

---

[18]   Vol. 1, pp. 406 and 522. Bond's unconvincing attribution of the entertainments to Lyly still occasionally resurfaces, e.g. Susan Watkins, *Elizabeth I and her World* (London: Thames and Hudson, 2007), p. 80. An abbreviated edition of *The Honorable Entertainement* had been included in R.H. St Maur's *Annals of the Seymours* (London: Kegan Paul, Trench, Trubner and Co., 1902), but is too confused and inaccurate to merit attention.

[19]   Reasons for supposing that the fold-out sheet was probably never included in the BL copy are to be found in my edition (pp. 563–4). The BL copy has been digitized as part of the library's Renaissance Festival Books series, and is available on-line at http://special-1.bl.uk/treasures/festivalbooks/BookDetails.aspx?strFest=0234.

Elizabethan best seller.[20] There has even been loose talk of 'an aggressive rhetoric, a public relations move' on Hertford's behalf being bolstered by such surprisingly vigorous and persistent marketing.[21]

After Bond's *Lyly* the next significant scholarly edition of *The Honorable Entertainement* was Jean Wilson's in her *Entertainments for Elizabeth I* (Woodbridge: Brewer, 1980), regarded by many as the standard edition.[22] By then, of course, bibliographical studies had moved on. With the publication in 1939 of the first volume of Greg's *Bibliography of the English Printed Drama to the Restoration*, which magisterially established the fact that Q1 had been corrected during the print run, the three-edition theory ought to have been heard of no more. However, it received a new lease of life when Wilson (who most unwisely seems not to have consulted Greg) tacitly adopted it, although she knew that as long ago as 1923 E.K. Chambers had shown a degree of caution.[23] It goes without saying that she ought to have collated the three known Q1 copies, but she failed to do so. This may have been because in her textual introduction she claimed that her work was based not on any of those three texts but on the '*Newlie corrected, and amended*' quarto which, blindly clutching Bond's rope of sand, she identified as 'Q3'.[24] Unfortunately, the sad truth is that Wilson had never actually seen the elusive text she was supposedly following, any more than Bond had seen it. In reality, her copy text was that unsatisfactory old standby, Nichols's 1823 mishmash, which she imagined to have been a reprint of the '*Newlie corrected, and amended*' quarto. But then, at what seems to have been a late stage in the production of her book, a note has been inserted on the blank verso of an unpaginated leaf that serves as a section divider. It confesses that the quarto itself had 'proved impossible to trace'.[25]

---

[20] E.g. Ernest Brennecke, 'The Entertainment at Elvetham, 1591', in John H. Long (ed.), *Music in English Renaissance Drama* (Lexington, Ky: University of Kentucky Press, 1968), p. 171 n. 5.

[21] Suzanne Westfall, '"He who Pays the Piper Calls the Tune": Household Entertainments', in Richard Dutton (ed.), *The Oxford Handbook of Early Modern Theatre* (Oxford: Oxford University Press, 2009), p. 275.

[22] The edition by T.F.R. for FitzRoy Anstruther-Gough-Calthorpe (London: Hatchards, [1926]) may be passed over since it is extracted from *Progresses* (1788).

[23] E.K. Chambers, *The Elizabethan Stage* (4 vols, Oxford: Clarendon Press, 1923), vol. 4, p. 66. In his 1971 discussion of *The Honorable Entertainement*, David M. Bergeron, in *English Civic Pageantry, 1558–1642* (London: Edward Arnold, 1971) refers readers to Greg (Bergeron, p. 57).

[24] Jean Wilson, *Entertainments for Elizabeth I* (Woodbridge: Brewer, 1980), p. 99.

[25] Ibid., facing p. 61.

Recent Editions, 1999–2011

The three latest editions, namely Arthur F. Kinney's (1999), which has been found so pervasively unreliable that it has been withdrawn from a revised edition of the anthology in which it appeared, Alessandra Ruggiero's attractive bilingual Italian and English edition (2002) and the enterprisingly annotated edition by Donald Stump and Susan M. Felch (2009), plus the substantial extracts included in Albert Chatterley's edition of Thomas Watson's *English Poems* (Norwich, 2003) and in Dana F. Sutton's hypertext edition of Watson's *Complete Works* (posted 29 November 2010, revised 4 May 2011) have all unavoidably been prepared without recourse to the '*Newlie corrected, and amended*' quarto lost to us since 1788.[26] Moreover, four of these five editors, led astray by reliance on Wilson, accept Bond's three-edition theory unaware that Greg totally discredited it in 1939. Commentators too, myself included, have made the same mistake.[27] Like some virulent disease the error has been transmitted ineluctably from one publication to the next.

A particularly unhappy consequence of having lost trace of the revised quarto has been the impossibility of judging how faithful to its replacement illustration are the versions published by Nichols in 1788 and 1823. One or other of those versions – they can be distinguished most easily by counting the lateral gun ports on the pinnace: 1788 has six, 1823 has five – is frequently reproduced, but as often as not captioned in ways that obscure the disturbing snag that this renowned representation of courtly festivity is not taken directly from an Elizabethan book. I would guess that many people who have encountered the image on numerous occasions, and have long grown familiar with it, have never paused to consider that what we have frequently been led to regard as a reproduction of an authentic

---

[26]   Arthur F. Kinney (ed.), *Renaissance Drama: An Anthology of Plays and Entertainments* (Malden MA and Oxford: Blackwell, 1999), pp. 140–54; Alessandra Ruggiero (ed.), *The Honorable Entertainment Gieven to the Queene's Majestie, in Progresse, at Elvetham in Hampshire, by the Right Hon'ble the Earle of Hertford, 1591*, Angelica 5 (Naples: Liguori Editore, 2002); and Donald Stump and Susan M. Felch (eds), *Elizabeth I and Her Age: Authoritative Texts, Commentary and Criticism* (New York and London: W.W. Norton, 2009), pp. 417–33, which omits the Latin version of the welcoming oration spoken by the Poet. Sutton's edition is to be found at www.philological.bham.ac.uk/watson/elvetham/text.html but it is much in need of further revision.

[27]   These include Brennecke, 'The Entertainment at Elvetham, 1591', p. 34; H. Neville Davies, '"To Sing and Revel in these Woods": Purcell's *The Fairy-Queen* and *The Honourable Entertainment at Elvetham*', *Renaissance Journal*, 1/6 (June 2002), p. 7; Ulrich Suerbaum, 'Performing Royalty. The Entertainment at Elvetham and the Cult of Elisa', in Günter Ahrends et al. (eds), *Word and Action in Drama: Studies in Honour of Hans-Jürgen Diller* (Trier: Wissenschaftlicher Verlag Trier, 1994), p. 56. Curt Breight, 'Realpolitik and Elizabethan Ceremony: The Earl of Hertford's Entertainment of Elizabeth at Elvetham, 1591', *Renaissance Quarterly*, 45 (1992), pp. 25–6, exceptional in having consulted all three extant copies of Q1, is careful to refer to 'two or three surviving texts (depending on which critic is right)'; but it is a pity that Breight seems not to have consulted Greg.

Elizabethan picture might be better thought of as a modern photographic or digitized reproduction of a nineteenth-century lithograph of an eighteenth-century engraving that had been commissioned to replicate an Elizabethan woodcut, now apparently lost, of what must have been originally an Elizabethan drawing; and with goodness knows what distortions introduced during the process of protracted transmission. If one turns, for instance, to the frontispiece to Jean Wilson's collection of *Entertainments*, it is, at two removes from the 1591 woodcut, the 1823 version that will be found, but stripped of the identifying inscription that, in accordance with the provisions of the so-called 'Hogarth Act', included the telltale date of November 1822. The caption supplied by Wilson simply says 'The Entertainment at Elvetham 1591'. In Susan Doran's *The Tudor Chronicles* on the other hand, it is the 1788 version, slightly trimmed on two sides, that is reproduced, while there the accompanying caption specifically states that the picture is from *The Honorable Entertainement* published in 1591.[28] Richard Rex's *The Tudors*[29] and Timothy Mowl's *Elizabethan and Jacobean Style*[30] similarly reproduce the 1788 version, and with no acknowledgement that an eighteenth-century publication is the source.[31] Thus misleading information, or lack of information, regularly suppresses or obscures the questionable status of the image.

A New Edition (2013)

So we come to my edition. Like others before me I searched for the lost quarto but was no more successful in my quest than anyone else had been. In these circumstances I proposed to attempt to reconstruct the lost text in so far as that was possible. Despite the limitations that constrained me, there was at least the opportunity to exclude arrant nonsense like the reduplicative eight-stanza version of 'Come againe' and the mistakenly interpolated 'Here follows' instruction. By reasonable conjecture and intelligent patchwork I believed I could restore some of what had been lost. I completed my assignment, it was approved by the general editors, and I turned to other preoccupations as I waited for proofs. The intended date of publication came and went. And then one Saturday, three years

---

[28]   Susan Doran, *The Tudor Chronicles* (London: Quercus, 2008), p. 372.

[29]   Richard Rex, *The Tudors* (Stroud: Tempus, 2009).

[30]   Timothy Mowl, *Elizabethan and Jacobean Style* (London: Phaidon, 1993), p. 198.

[31]   Mowl's caption invites the reader to see 'The inevitable naval assault on a fort and Triton's musical serenade – illustrated as simultaneous events' (p. 78). But although tritons can be seen noisily sounding their instruments, they are not performing anything that approximated even remotely to the music of a serenade; nor is there the slightest sign of any naval assault. Equally misleading is Mowl's claim that 'the lakeside stronghold' (by which presumably he means the island fort) was 'besieged for Elizabeth's amusement' (p. 110). The armed men – unfortunately not depicted in the illustration – who 'enuironed' the fort were there to guard it, not to besiege it.

after I had last had anything to do with my edition, there was a sale of surplus or decommissioned music books at the City Library in Birmingham. Had I known quite what crowds of people would be attracted I doubt whether I would have gone, but in the fray I picked up several bulky items I was glad to have, and joined the queue for the till. As I waited I noticed the spine of a little pocket book: '*The English Madrigal* – Fellowes'. It was not one of Edmund H. Fellowes's important scholarly works but a brief introductory account aimed at the general reader, first published in 1925. I was not aware that Fellowes had written such a survey and I was curious. I bought it for less than £1, more because I was still fumbling with it than for any better reason. At home I paid no attention to this extra little item for some days. I was much more interested in the other volumes and rather thought I had been foolish to burden myself with a book that had outlived its usefulness.

When eventually I got around to looking it over I was mildly surprised to find a reproduction of the famous Q2 Elvetham picture, not an obvious choice for a book on the madrigal; but when I took a proper look at the illustration I was stunned to see it was manifestly not reproduced from Nichols. It could therefore, I immediately realized, derive only from the lost Q2 itself and, on this occasion, the caption that included the words 'From the engraving in the original edition printed by John Wolfe in 1591' evidently meant what it said. I read the couple of pages dealing with the Elvetham entertainments. They included a few short quotations that I soon established must have come directly from Q2 and, as further confirmation, a disparaging passing allusion to the inaccuracy of the Nichols text.

Clearly the lost quarto, supposedly unsighted since 1788, had survived at least until the 1920s, and had been seen by Fellowes. So much for Greg's assertion in 1939 that after 1788 'of this second edition nothing further seems ever to have been heard' (p. 98). If it had after all survived undetected for that long there seemed a very good chance it was still extant even though it had eluded two generations of STC compilers, bibliographers in general, historians and literary scholars. The Fellowes book was without notes or acknowledgements of any sort and yielded no additional clues. Fellowes himself had died in 1951. But I knew of him as an indefatigable musicologist and editor who used a wide range of libraries, private as well as public, in Britain, on the continent and across the Atlantic, and knew too that he had haunted the salesrooms as well as having been in touch with private collectors. That cast the net very wide, and my only real clue was that if the book had survived it was presumably not in a major library or its existence would be common knowledge. I made two guesses: the library of St George's Chapel, Windsor, for Fellowes had lived at Windsor where, since 1900, he had been a minor canon of St George's, and the now dispersed library formerly at St Michael's, Tenbury, that Fellowes had catalogued in the early 1920s, and of which the catalogue cards are preserved in the Bodleian. No luck with either. Perhaps Fellowes's autobiography, his *Memoirs of an Amateur Musician* (London, 1946), would reveal which out-of-the-way collections he had used in that period of his life. I turned at once to the index, and found that 'Elvetham' and other obvious trigger words were not there. So, as I read the book, the best that I could hope for was that among his reminiscences Fellowes would have referred to libraries and book collectors it could be worth investigating. I did not, of course, expect to encounter any disclosure quite as direct as this one:

> In 1923 the Oxford University Press approached me to write a short book on *The English Madrigal* for a series called *The World's Manuals*. It included a few illustrations, among which was ... an engraving of an elaborate entertainment of the Queen at Elvetham Hall, in Hampshire, taken from a unique book in the royal library at Windsor (p. 137).

So on 21 April 2008, I visited the Royal Library at Windsor and, while I examined this record of entertainments for Elizabeth I, a military band outside the window played music to entertain the present owner of the volume, Queen Elizabeth II, on the occasion of her birthday. I too had reason to celebrate, although my ill-fated edition, with its painstakingly-argued but now redundant conjectures was, of course, a pinnace holed below the waterline. The only question was could I withdraw it or would I have to be content, rather like Nichols in 1788, with adding a postscript. Fortunately the answer was good news. There was still just enough time for me to prepare an entirely new edition based on the unique Windsor text, and for it to replace my previous work.

The Windsor Quarto

With the recovery of the unique Windsor Q2 it becomes possible at long last to answer the question: How faithful was the copy of the woodcut commissioned by Nichols more than two centuries ago, and upon which scholars have perforce relied ever since? Unlike the *Gentleman's Magazine* version of the earlier Q1 woodcut, the 1788 engraving is, in fact, in most respects remarkably accurate; and, although some people may be surprised to find that the long-lost image (Plate 3) now gives them tuppence coloured where they expected penny plain, it certainly has to be acknowledged that the exuberantly animated illustration published in 1591 had not been up-dated into an eighteenth-century engraving of dull sobriety.[32] Nevertheless, Nichols's claim that the original was 'exactly copied' is not strictly true. Nichols's engraver realized that his 1591 predecessor must surely have been working from a drawing that included the *whole* of the lake, that would have included the word SOUTH at the bottom extremity of the picture to match WEST, NORTH and EAST at the other extremities, and that would not have shown torsos deprived of their legs at the bottom of the picture. Indeed, the putative drawing might well have extended

---

[32]   In both his 1788 and 1823 editions Nichols had in fact informed readers that the Q1 and the Q2 woodcuts were coloured. Fellowes ought not to have referred in his 1925 caption and in his autobiography to the Q2 woodcut as an 'engraving'. It was, though, as an engraving that Nichols was to have it reproduced.

further on all four sides. To improve on the work of his predecessor, therefore, the eighteenth-century engraver has added to the bottom of the picture an intelligent and convincing but entirely conjectural extra strip (see Fig. 11.2).

Between them, the Q2 illustration of 'the great *Pond*' and the account of events given in the two quartos of *The Honorable Entertainement* present many teasing problems, although only now has it become possible to confront them with the help of properly established textual evidence, and with the assurance of knowing that the rediscovered and unique Windsor woodcut provides the most reliable graphic record that we can ever reasonably expect to find. Above all, nagging doubts about the wisdom of relying on the work of an eighteenth-century copyist that hitherto bedevilled any close scrutiny of the evidence as published by Nichols, whether pictorial or textual, can, thankfully, be set aside. And prominent among the issues that now need to be addressed, given that Hertford's artificial lake disappeared long ago and his old house no longer stands, is the problem of determining how the pictorial and textual evidence can be mapped onto and reconciled with the topography of Elvetham.

Locating the Great Pond

In 1982 a collaborative article on 'The Site of the Elvetham Entertainment' by David R. Wilson, Curator in Aerial Photography at Cambridge University, and Jean Wilson, whose edition of *The Honorable Entertainement* had been published two years previously, appeared in the journal *Antiquity*.[33] Since then it has been accepted that their findings are reliable, so that when, for instance, Paula Henderson in her authoritative *The Tudor House and Garden: Architecture and Landscape in the Sixteenth and Early Seventeenth Centuries*[34] remarks that 'the crescent-shaped lake is sometimes visible [at Elvetham] as parch marks in very dry conditions', it is on the say-so of the two Wilsons rather than on any observation of her own that she relies. There are, however, several considerations that make it necessary to challenge an investigation that was seriously flawed, although Henderson's 'very dry conditions' requirement and her use of the term 'parch marks' are elaborations that misrepresent the technicalities of what had actually been reported. The Wilson undertaking involved low-altitude aerial reconnaissance of Elvetham on 15 April 1981, and thereafter the examination of an aerial photograph to look for any

---

[33]   David R. Wilson and Jean Wilson, 'The Site of the Elvetham Entertainment', *Antiquity* (1982), pp. 46–7 and plates IIb and III. Prior to that, Jean Wilson had supposed the lake to have been created by damming the River Hart ('Queen Bess's Three Days in Wonderland', *Times*, 10 January 1981, p. 12), although quite where that would have placed the lake is unclear.

[34]   Paula Henderson, *The Tudor House and Garden: Architecture and Landscape in the Sixteenth and Early Seventeenth Centuries* (New Haven and London: Yale University Press, 2005), p. 128.

markings that might vaguely suggest a crescent shape, a procedure that without validating support is all too reminiscent of cloud gazing and imagining that one sees camels, weasels or whales: 'By th'mass, and 'tis very like a camel indeed' ... Methinks it is like a crescent pond. What the published report fails to do is to correlate the tenuous photographic evidence with any firm cartographic evidence, and with any practical on-site investigation. Loftily flying over in an aeroplane is all very well, but on its own no substitute for poring over maps and walking the terrain. R.H. Tawney's advice about the historian's need for a stout pair of boots deserves to be taken seriously.

Quite apart from the dubious nature of the crescent shape discernible in the evidential photograph that accompanied the report, there are five principal objections to the Wilson theory.[35] The first arises from the discrepancy between the orientation of the shadowy crescent supposedly revealed in the photograph and the orientation clearly indicated in the woodcut. Whereas the axis or fold-line that would divide the crescent into symmetrical halves in the Q2 illustration is a north-south line, the site proposed by the Wilson partnership would have an axis skewed by about 45°, making it roughly NE–SW in alignment. The second objection concerns landmarks at Elvetham. In the woodcut, the area of land to the north of the water, that is, between the eastern and western horns of the crescent, is shown as the site of two substantial buildings, one identified as the premises in which the queen was housed (presumably Elvetham House itself) and the other a church-like structure that temporarily served as 'Her Maiesties wardrop' (p. 573). Neither of those buildings survives today, but the present Elvetham Hall, a Victorian mansion that currently functions as a hotel, was built on the site that was occupied by the house that stood in 1591, while a church, erected in 1840, that has now been adapted for use as a squash court, occupies the site of an ancient church that it replaced.[36] Furthermore, we know that the ship isle and the snail mount were

---

[35]   Besides the unfortunate circumstance that there was a predisposition to identify a crescent shape anyway, and evidently without much regard to its size, it is pertinent to bear in mind the caution that David Wilson has recommended elsewhere: 'The careful archaeologist will always hesitate to interpret from a single [aerial] photograph ... [for] there are so many possibilities for misunderstanding and error in a single view that to rely on that alone must be counted a desperate expedient' (*Air Photo Interpretation for Archaeologists*, rev. edn, Stroud: Tempus, 2000, p. 212).

[36]   http://www.elvethamhotel.co.uk provides photographs of the buildings and the grounds, and there are photographs by Mark Fiennes in Watkins, *Elizabeth I*, pp. 181–2. The Hall itself is the work of Samuel Sanders Teulon with later additions, while St Mary's Church was the work of Sir Henry Roberts with additions by Teulon. Interior and exterior decorative features at the Hall recall Elizabeth's visit to Elvetham as well as recalling Walter Scott's *Kenilworth*. An 1839 map (Hampshire Record Office 21M65/F7/79/2), prepared in accordance with the Tithe Act of the previous year, shows the position of the old church and the old manor house (the latter destroyed by a fire in 1840), while the house alone is depicted in an engraving from 1792, together with a ground floor plan dated 1788, in *Progresses*, vol. 3 (1805), facing p. 74. The position of house and church is also shown in

'neere vnder the prospect of [the queen's] Gallerie window' (p. 580). Were we to be guided by the Q2 illustration we would, therefore, expect the site of the earl of Hertford's lake to be 'in the bottome' (p. 571), that is in the low ground, more or less due south of, and overlooked by, the present mansion and deconsecrated church. The site proposed by the Wilson partnership, however, envisages the horns of the crescent embracing high ground further east where there is no reason to think that buildings ever stood. The third objection comes from a consideration of the contours of the landscape, for a pond in the Wilson position would be in part a very deep pond, requiring a daunting supply of water and the construction of a formidable embankment and dam to contain the arc of its south-western perimeter. In a lake so positioned there would have been differences in depth of some 5 meters. Wading 'brest-high' (p. 582) would not have been an option at the deep end, while at the shallow end, where no more than ankle-deep paddling would have been possible, there would have been, without an implausible amount of excavation, insufficient clearance for a vessel like the pinnace to begin its voyage from the 'Bower' (marked, but not keyed, on the Q2 woodcut as M).[37] The fourth objection relates to the surface area of a lake as large and elongated as that postulated by the Wilsons.[38] As a *mise-en-scène* for the entertainment presented before Elizabeth it would have been impractical for both visual and auditory reasons, the action would have been too dispersed, and the voyage of the pinnace would have taken too long to sustain the interest of onlookers, including the queen herself. Besides, it was already 'aboute foure of the clocke' when she took her seat (p. 581). By then the light must already have been beginning to fade, with little more than an hour and a half before sunset. Moreover, the task of towing the pinnace almost the whole length of such a lake would probably have been overwhelmingly arduous anyway. The fifth objection, insofar as it is different from the fourth, concerns shape. The Wilson crescent, extending up the valley and away from 'the bottome', seems to have a more gentle curve than the tighter shape depicted in the woodcut, and it is that tighter shape that would have provided the more suitably cohesive performance space.

---

the 'Reduced Plan of Elvetham, Hants, 1822' (Hampshire Record Office 50M63/C28). The Q2 woodcut has repositioned the church somewhat to the south of its true location. Harry H. Boyle, 'Elizabeth's Entertainment at Elvetham: War Policy in Pageantry', *Studies in Philology*, 68 (1971), p. 147, is, I believe, mistaken in supposing that these two buildings were erected for the queen's visit.

[37]   At the western end of the ship isle the water was sufficiently deep for a spectacular dive to be executed by one of the 'Sea-gods' accompanying Nereus, but, rather closer to the queen, sufficiently shallow for Nereus to deliver his oration while he was standing in the water.

[38]   David Wilson has himself warned archaeologists that 'a sense of human scale ... is easily lost in the bird's-eye view' and may need to be re-established by fieldwork (*Air Photo Interpretation*, p. 213).

Much of the area where we might expect to find lingering traces of the pond as it is depicted in the woodcut was redeveloped at the end of the nineteenth century to provide an extended and raised garden for the Victorian mansion, and this radical reshaping of that part of the landscape necessarily obliterated pre-existing features. But fortunately, before that happened, the 1871 Ordnance Survey of Elvetham had taken place, and the result was a detailed map published in 1872 that shows two ponds (numbered 186 and 188 on the map). Because they are placed exactly where we would expect Hertford's lake to have been, they must be either remnants of his work or ponds that had already existed and were expanded on his instructions to form the larger pool he wished to create. The *Book of Reference* that accompanies the map gives their area as 0.193 and 0.201 acres respectively (i.e. 8,407.08 sq. ft/781.043 m^2 and 8,755.56 sq. ft/813.418 m^2; the equivalent in size, though not in form, of circles with diameters of approximately 103.5 and 105.5 feet), while the map itself, with its lavish 25.344 inches to the mile (i.e. scaled at 1:2,500), shows their position and irregular shapes in a way that enables us to see how they could have formed part of a crescent. If these two ponds are transposed onto a modern OS map, it will be found that the location of the western part of the marginally larger of them is now principally under the south-east corner of the raised garden and close to where a tennis court is situated. By good chance, this tennis court, with its standard line markings either side of the net, happens to provide a useful indication of relative size, and this is particularly helpful if aerial views like those available on Google Earth are accessed on-line.[39] The field drains shown on the map and still plainly evident on site as ditches that converge just outside the corner of the brick wall that retains the raised garden may be assumed to follow, roughly speaking, the course taken in wet weather in Elizabethan times by small rivulets that would have emptied into the two ponds. Certainly the wishful thinking represented by Hamlet's whales and weasels must be resisted, yet the mapped outline of the ponds is suggestively consistent with their being part of a larger crescent-shaped waterscape that would have conformed reasonably well with the natural contours of the landscape as it must have been before the present garden was created.[40]

---

[39]   The sidelines on a doubles court are 36 ft apart; the distance from the base line to the net is, at 39 ft, just short of the 40 ft (or 12.192 m) measurement (along with its half and its double) that is particularly relevant to the islands. The smaller of the two ponds had an area equivalent to just less than that of three doubles courts.

[40]   The shape and size of the ponds must have varied according to season and rainfall. In dry summer weather no water would have remained, and that is probably why the very detailed 1839 tithe map shows no ponds in that position, while the 1860 'Plan of Elvetham Estate shewing Recommended Diversion of course of stream' (Hampshire Record Office 26M62/Box/3/(iii)) shows a single pond, corresponding in location to no. 188 on the 1872 OS map, but different in shape. The 'Reduced Plan' (1822) also shows a single pond, but yet again rather different in shape.

The picture that emerges is less grandiose than the one it replaces. Hertford's pond was smaller than has been supposed, even though its precise dimensions cannot be determined. However, we know the dimensions of the three islands that were its chief features. The western ship isle was 100 ft by 40 ft, and since it was ship-shaped it must be supposed that the beam measurement of 40 ft narrowed towards the bows and, less so, towards the stern. The central fort isle was 20 ft square. The eastern conic snail-mount (rising to a height of 20 ft) had, at its base, a circle with a diameter of either 40 ft or 80 ft. Q1 specifies 'fortie foote', but Q2 revises and doubles this dimension to 'fourscore foote' (p. 572). Since there are also other instances of Q2 revising a Q1 number, it seems reasonable to suppose that the revisions are deliberate corrections and therefore likely to be more reliable than the readings they supersede. The trouble is that if one imagines the mount rising from the water's edge to the apex of a pointed summit, the Q2 measurements produce a gentle gradient of only 25°, hardly the profile of a would-be snail, and not at all like the mounts that were a recognized feature of renaissance gardens. In marked contrast the Q1 measurements generate a much steeper gradient of 45°. But perhaps what we ought to imagine is a combination of the two: a circular island that had Q2's 80 ft diameter, and a mount that occupied (somewhat as depicted in the Q2 woodcut) only the central part of that island platform. In this way Q1's 40 ft diameter might be regarded as the diameter of the base of the mount, a mount that would have risen steeply to an apex at its 20 ft high summit (as in the woodcut) or slightly more steeply to a flattened summit of the same height.[41]

In addition to knowing the size of the three islands we are told that they were placed with great regard to symmetry. Thus 'equallie distant from the sides of the ponde' all three were evidently placed midway between the north and south arcs of the crescent (p. 572). There was also equal spacing between the islands and, as Q2 punctiliously adds, this equal spacing applied as well to the distance between the ship isle and the western end of the pond and between the snail isle and the eastern end of the pond. If only we knew what that distance was we would (by also taking into account the island measurements) be able to calculate the approximate extent of the pond. But even without that missing information we can arrive at something like a minimum size; and by paying regard to the mapped position of the two ponds surveyed in 1871 and the lie of the land as it still was at that date make plausible conjectures about where the islands were probably positioned, and what the limits of the crescent probably were.

---

[41] Even so, a diameter of 80 ft seems rather out of keeping with the dimensions of the other two islands. With a 40 ft diameter the surface area occupied by the snail isle would have been roughly comparable with that of the ship isle.

Preparations at Elvetham

Envisaging a lake of an appropriate size, and substantially more compact than
the one proposed by the two Wilsons, is important if the water pageantry that
entertained Elizabeth in 1591 is to be imaginatively appreciated more than
four centuries later. But it is also essential if we are to understand the sort of
preparations made by the earl of Hertford in order to entertain his sovereign.
Practical questions like, how much prior notice did the earl have of the queen's
intention to visit Elvetham? and, how could the earl be sure that there would be
sufficient water to fill his specially created lake if the summer were a dry one?
inevitably arise. *The Honorable Entertainement* tells us a little in answer to the first
question, explaining that the earl was dependent upon two sources of information:
'the ordinarie Gesse' and 'his honourable good friends in the Court, neare to her
Maiestie' (p. 570). The first of these has been comprehensively misunderstood.
Editors who modernize spelling turn 'Gesse' into 'guess', while editors who retain
old spelling either leave the word unglossed, presumably because they suppose it
to be a form of 'guess', or gloss it as 'conjecture'.[42] Ruggiero's Italian translation
is '*dovuto intuire*' (p. 71). But the word has no connection with guessing, as its
proper pronunciation indicates. It should be spoken like the first three letters of
'jest', not like the first four letters of 'guest'.[43] In the plural form, as used in the
opening sentence of this paper, it means 'the various stages of a journey, esp. of a
royal progress' (*OED2*, †gest, *sb.*[4] *Obs.*), but it can also mean, as here, an itinerary,
drawn up by the lord chamberlain, listing the places at which the queen intended to
reside or stop during a progress (cf. *OED2*, †gist, *sb.*[1] *Obs.*), and it is to just such
an 'ordinarie' (customary and generally accessible) document that *The Honorable
Entertainement* refers.[44]

---

[42]   Eight-year-olds being introduced to this old-spelling text are told, in a schoolbook
on *Life in Tudor Times* (Winchester, n.d.) published by Hampshire Record Office, that 'the
ordinarie gesse' means 'good guessing' (p. 14).

[43]   The pronunciation is made clear in John Norden's *A Progress of Piety, whose
Jesses lead into the Harborough of heavenly Hearts-ease*, a work first published in the
same year as *The Honorable Entertainement*. No copy of that first edition of Norden's book
survives, but the Parker Society editor (Cambridge, 1847) had access to an imperfect copy
now lost and to Lowndes's transcript of the title. These sources reveal that the word 'jess'
or 'jesses', used metaphorically, was applied repeatedly in that lost text to the eight stages
of a devotional journey or spiritual progress. But even in the 1590s readers may have been
baffled by the word, for the 1596 edition systematically excluded it, leaving (probably by
accident) only one vestigial instance. Misunderstanding the word and failing to appreciate
its relevance to the concept of a royal progress, the Parker Society editor was to gloss it
incorrectly as 'a check, or pause. Properly, the strap tied about the hawk's leg' (p. 47).

[44]   See Mary Hill Cole, 'Monarchy in Motion: An Overview of Elizabethan
Progresses', in Jayne Elisabeth Archer, Elizabeth Goldring and Sarah Knight (eds), *The
Progresses, Pageants, and Entertainments of Queen Elizabeth I* (Oxford: Oxford University
Press, 2007), p. 33 and Ian Dunlop, *Palaces and Progresses of Elizabeth I* (London: Cape,

The point being emphasized by the writer of *The Honorable Entertainement* is that Hertford did not benefit from preferential treatment by being given warning of the impending visit in advance of that information becoming known at court. As late as 10 July, only some 12 or 13 days before the queen expected to set out, Henry Carey, Lord Hunsdon, in his capacity as chamberlain of the royal household, was still trying to finalize details about where the progress could be accommodated; and it was not until that date that he wrote to Sir William More informing him that her majesty had resolved 'to come to your house'.[45] But because the start of the 1591 progress was then to be delayed until the very end of the month, there proved to be slightly more preparation time than would otherwise have been the case. Yet even so, less than four weeks after Hunsdon dispatched his letter, the queen and her enormous entourage had arrived at Loseley House, near Guildford, where More lived, and was to be entertained there for four nights. Precisely when the 'ordinarie Gesse' was issued is not known, but in view of the last-minute nature of some of the planning it seems that it cannot have been issued much in advance of the commencement of the progress, and would have given Hertford less than two months to prepare. However, this period was no doubt a little extended by earlier intimations from 'his honourable good friends in the Court'.

In the limited time available, there was much to be done at Elvetham, with temporary buildings to be erected and equipped, the house itself to be extended, provisions to be bought in, entertainments to be devised, costumed and rehearsed, fireworks to be organized, suitable gifts to be acquired, as well as a lake and islands to be created, and the mud and earthworks involved in that transformation to be decently covered over. Furthermore, boats had to be provided for the lake. In particular, a convincing-looking, practicable pinnace had to be constructed (built by Hampshire shipwrights from the Solent?), and navigational strategies contrived for its hauling and handling, strategies that must have been thoroughly tried and tested before the queen's arrival. This was not a matter that could be left for inspired improvisation on the day. A demanding timetable must have been rigorously adhered to, so that, for instance, the creation of the lake itself, and the establishment of a sustainable water-level, were goals that must have been achieved before boats could be launched and performers could begin to learn how to cope with the challenges posed by 'faire Shewes, and Pastimes' of an aquatic kind. To realize the vital necessity of well rehearsed coordination, one has only to consider the hazardous manoeuvre of turning a flotilla of three vessels round within a confined space, under the very nose of the queen, and without fouling the heavy, sodden cables of the towing lines.

We may guess that members of the earl's own company of players, which was active around 1591, would have been deployed at Elvetham, and it seems

---

1962), p. 119, for accounts of the usual preparatory process. Routine procedures for vetting and preparing houses to receive the queen are highlighted in Zillah Dovey, *An Elizabethan Progress: The Queen's Journey into East Anglia, 1578* (Stroud: Alan Sutton, 1996).

[45] *Progresses ... New Edition*, vol. 3, p. 547.

likely that the earl's foresters or huntsmen who would have been accustomed to pursuing a quarry when it went 'to soil', that is, when it took to the water, and who would have been skilled in the sounding of hunting calls, would have provided the 'fiue Tritons brest-high in the water … all fiue cheerefully sounding their trumpets', and who would also be required to sound 'a point of warre'.[46] But *The Honorable Entertainement* valuably supplements such reasonable speculation by several revealing statements about the earl's retainers. A 'Traine well mounted, to the number of two hundred and vpwardes, and most of them wearing chaines of golde about their neckes' rode out with the earl to meet the queen and conduct her on her way to Elvetham;[47] and the banquet of a thousand dishes, 'al in siluer and glasse', that followed a firework display on the evening of the third day was served by 'two hundred of my Lord of Hertfords Gentlemen' lit by 'an hundred torch-bearers'.[48] The number of artificers employed in construction work – though whether that included the creation of the lake is unclear – is given as 'two hundred or thereabouts' (p. 570), but had a large additional workforce been employed just in creating the lake and its islands the compiler of *The Honorable Entertainement* would probably have wanted to record their number as yet further evidence of the magnitude of the preparations.[49] All in all, bearing in mind the timescale, the information about available manpower, the range of work that had to be undertaken to accommodate the queen and her whole entourage (not to mention the measures needed to cope with an influx of 'neer tenne thousand' sightseers, (p. 574), and what can be deduced by combining pictorial and mensural information from Q2 with cartographic evidence, it is impossible to believe that the Elvetham lake, impressive and uniquely ambitious though it undoubtedly was, justifies Roy Strong's exaggerated description of it as 'vast'.[50] Compared with the great

---

[46]   Ibid., pp. 582 and 587. For the earl's players, see John Tucker Murray, *English Dramatic Companies, 1558–1642* (2 vols, London: Constable, 1910), vol. 1, pp. 317–18, and vol. 2, p. 332. For his eldest son's players, see vol. 2, pp. 24–5.

[47]   Ibid., pp. 573–4. The Q1 number of '3. hundred' was revised in Q2.

[48]   Ibid., p. 590. Because the description of the banquet was excluded from Q2, the associated statistics are unconfirmed.

[49]   Q2, p. 1; modified from 'three hundred' in Q1. It should not be forgotten that harvest time was a busy period anyway, making heavy demands on labour.

[50]   Roy C. Strong, *The Renaissance Garden in England* (London: Thames and Hudson, 1979), p. 125. The information about sightseers is a Q2 addition unrecorded by Nichols, and therefore unknown to commentators until now. Breight, 'Realpolitik', presents the lake as 'huge' (p. 26). Trea Martyn, who describes the lake as 'enormous', does so on the basis of wildly supposing that Elizabeth was entertained with a *naumachia* waged between floating islands, and that 'no one had staged the defeat of the Armada more winningly' (*Elizabeth in the Garden: A Story of Love, Rivalry and Spectacular Design* (London: Faber and Faber, 2008, pp. 242–3)). Her account is an absurd travesty, although the strange misconception that the islands floated (erroneously imported from Jonson's *Masque of Blacknesse*?) is one she shares with others, e.g. Westfall, p. 274 and Brennecke, 'The Entertainment at Elvetham', p. 36, as is the equally mistaken and persistent notion

artificial lake at Kenilworth it was, surely, a modest affair. Dudley, however, did not need to create the historic Kenilworth Mere when he entertained Elizabeth in 1575. Unlike Hertford, he had been able to make use of a truly extensive resource that already existed.

Measured Proportion: Lake and Performance

The great virtue of Hertford's lake, conceived and created in honour of Elizabeth as 'Faire *Cinthia* the wide Oceans Empresse', was not its extent, but its careful and significant design, its 'cressent forme' figuring 'the rich increase/ Of all that sweete *Elisa* holdeth deare', and the three component islands each delightfully offering symbolic invention in different but complementary ways (p. 583).[51] The ship isle, explained as the vessel in which 'gold-brested *India*' had brought a jewel to present to the queen, allowed Elizabeth to be eulogized both as the awe inspiring sovereign who so daunted India that she abandoned ship and fled, and as the life-giving potentate whose 'gracious lookes' miraculously restored verdancy to the masts and tackle that had once again become the living trees they originally were (pp. 583–4). The snail mount is explained as the threat represented by the Spanish Armada three years previously, and here envisaged as an 'vglie monster creeping from the South', now immobilized and metamorphosed into a harmless snail by the potency of Elizabeth's presence (p. 584). Both islands imaginatively embodied narratives of metamorphosis. The fort isle, on the other hand, is explained as a demonstration of Neptune's authority as divine protector of Elizabeth's realm.

But in addition to this rich texture of interwoven conceits, *The Honorable Entertainement* also stresses the significant symmetry invested in the *mise-en-scène*, an ordered setting that had been created with due regard to 'iust measured proportion' (p. 572). It is an aesthetic that is mirrored by that of the pageantry itself, with the spatial organization of the pond matched by that of the entertainment

---

that a *naumachia* was 'staged' on the lake, e.g. Stump and Felch's edition, p. 416, Luborsky and Ingram, *A Guide*, vol. 2, p. 353, Henderson, *The Tudor House and Garden*, pp. 128 and 203, Doran, *The Tudor Chronicles*, p. 372, Janette Dillon, *The Language of Space in Court Performance, 1400–1625* (Cambridge: Cambridge University Press, 2010), p. 64 and James M. Sutton, *Materializing Space at an Early Modern Prodigy House: The Cecils at Theobalds, 1564–1607* (Aldershot: Ashgate, 2004), p. 52. Similarly, Strong's presentation of the firework display on the lake the following evening in terms of a battle (p. 126) seems to me unwarranted over-interpretation. Vis-à-vis descriptions of the lake as 'enormous', 'vast' or 'huge', it is noteworthy that three months before the Cambridge aerial photograph was taken, Jean Wilson had described the lake as 'small', suggesting that it measured 'about 200 by 100 yards' ('Queen Bess's Three Days', p. 12).

[51]   Suerbaum, in his perceptive and persuasive 'Performing Royalty', remarks that 'the main emphasis' at Elvetham 'was not on size and splendour but on the essential meaning of a royal visit as a celebration of a subject's love and duty towards his sovereign, and of the sovereign's responding grace' (p. 56).

presented before the queen late in the afternoon on her second day at Elvetham. Modern readers insufficiently sensitive to figurative design have generally disregarded the coherently organized nature of an entertainment that could well be given the title *The Earl of Hertford's Masque of the Three Gifts to Cynthia*. Its design is of a synoptic kind we fail to appreciate if we take account only of the requirement, commonly associated with such strongly temporal art forms as the drama and the novel, for a steadily developing plot.

Hertford's masque does not enact a narrative, but instead combines two contrasting and interlaced elements, one being the solemn and ceremonious presentation of gifts to Cynthia, the other being the slapstick humiliation of Sylvanus, a disruptive, satyr-like figure whose nature and role can be seen with hindsight as anticipating aspects of the antimasque that Ben Jonson was to develop in the following decade, but was probably regarded in 1591 as an appropriation from Kenilworth where his namesake had been impersonated by George Gascoigne. The performance began with the approach, across the lake, of marine deities, 'a pompous araie of sea-persons' hauling behind them a handsomely equipped and beflagged pinnace and all making their way, wading and swimming, towards the enthroned queen, herself duly envisaged by the conceit of the masque as Cynthia (p. 581). The impressive spectacle of this magnificent entry was accompanied by the sounding of trumpets, blown by tritons standing in the water, and by the music of cornetti played by 'three Virgines' conveyed, along with singers and a lutenist, in the pinnace (p. 582). The music from the pinnace was answered by echo ensembles placed in two other vessels that also formed part of this waterborne procession. At the end of the masque this processional pageantry became recessional pageantry as the 'sea-persons' and the boats retired back across the lake, and again the spectacle was accompanied by the sounding of trumpets and the music of cornetti, echoed and re-echoed over the water.

The second phase of the masque was focused on 'waterie *Nereus*', the leader of the procession, and his delivery of an oration to Cynthia, in which he presented the queen, on behalf of Hertford, with India's 'Iewell', before introducing the performance of a song in praise of 'dread *Eliza* that faire Dame' (pp. 584–5). The piece was 'sung dialogue wise' with double echoes by Thetis' 'Musick-maides', the principal singers being on board the pinnace and the echo singers responding from the two other vessels transporting the supplementary musicians.[52] And just as the processional commencement of the masque was symmetrically balanced by the recessional conclusion, this second phase was symmetrically balanced by a penultimate phase in which Nereus's companion Neæra similarly delivered an oration (though in her case from the pinnace) in which she presented the queen with Neptune's gift, 'a Sea Iewel, bearing the forme of a fan' (p. 587).[53] Like

---

[52]   The countess of Hertford's gift had been presented earlier in the day.

[53]   Strangely, as depicted in the Q2 illustration, Neæra's gift seems to look like an hourglass rather than a fan. Since Nereus's gift was also conveyed in the pinnace, it was probably safeguarded by Neæra during the voyage.

her male counterpart Nereus, Neæra introduced a performance, but this time the performer was the star of the show, Elizabeth herself, appealed to as 'A sea-borne Queene, worthie to gouern Kings' and as a 'sacred *Sybill*', her performance taking the form of a ship-naming ceremony in which 'HER MAIESTIE NAMED THE PINNACE THE *BONADUENTURE*' (p. 588).

The third and fourth phases of the masque, flanked by the twin halves of the Nereus/Neæra pairing, featured the entry and the exit of Sylvanus and his followers. So, in the third phase, the sylvans emerged by land from a wooded area to the west of the pond, and behind the canopied chair of state where Elizabeth was seated. On reaching the queen Sylvanus delivered an oration expressing his 'vnfained reuerence', and as his act of homage presented Apollo's gift: a 'sacred scutchion' inscribed '*Detur dignissimæ*' ('Let it be given to the worthiest lady'). The performance associated with this phase was comic, Sylvanus being revealed as a passionate but rejected suitor of Neæra. For his presumption he is tricked by Nereus and pulled into the water 'where all the Sea-gods laughing, did insult over him' (p. 587).[54] This third phase or episode was symmetrically balanced by (and passes into) the antepenultimate (and fourth) phase in which Sylvanus was to cry revenge. The associated performance this time was therefore a 'skirmish' or pitched battle between the sylvans armed with darts and the sea-gods armed with squirts, a rumbustious mêlée concluded when Sylvanus and his followers retreated to the woods, it having been declared that her majesty was 'a friend alwaies to peace, and enemie to warre' (p. 587).

Artfully disposed in three concentric pairs, the recessed symmetry of these six phases of the masque (ABC::CBA) frames a triumphal centre in which Elizabeth's pre-eminence among her sex (*dignissima*) was honoured by the Latin verses of Apollo's escutcheon. They awarded her precedence over the Muses and the nymphs of Diana, and declared her more beautiful than the goddesses of the deep sea. But by being composed in the reduplicated, chiastic form of an elaborately extended palindrome or antimetabole, the Apollonian portentousness of their rhetorical symmetry ingeniously encapsulates in concentrated and concentred form the ordered symmetry of the masque as a whole:

      Detur dignissimæ
  Aönijs prior, & Diuis es pulchrior alti
   Equoris, ac Nymphis es prior Idalijs.
  Idalijs prior es Nymphis, ac æquoris alti.
  Pulchrior es Diuis, & prior Aönijs

---

[54] If Neæra's rejection of Sylvanus is seen as an endorsement of Elizabeth's rejection of her successive suitors, it must be remembered that the entertainment presented the following morning, and enthusiastically encored by the queen, was to feature a coy mistress who eventually relented.

One does not even have to translate this pair of highly contrived elegiac couplets in order to take the rhetorical point. Their structure is what matters. And the centre was also a double centre, for at precisely the same time that Elizabeth was perusing the chiastic verses, her triumphal ascendancy was being burlesqued by the antithetical humiliation of Sylvanus as he was 'duckt'. Writers of texts organized in the concentric manner of the Elvetham masque often employed, in this period, the simple device of repeating, just after the centre, words or a motif that had been used just before the centre. In this way the centre is highlighted, and readers are provided with a signal to indicate that from this point onward the out-going sequence will be one that responds in reverse order to the in-coming sequence already established. In the case of *The Honorable Entertainement*, it is the recapitulated phrase *Detur dignissimæ* that acts as the conventional marker either side of the turning point. Although only spectators lucky enough to be present could enjoy the immediate excitement of an occasion in which the queen was both performer and recipient, the retrospective of the pamphlet account is able to reveal structure and significance to thoughtful readers in a way that mere performance never could. For instance, in live performance it seems that no one other than their royal recipient was privileged to scrutinize the Apollonian verses. So it is that an essential purpose of *The Honorable Entertainement*, besides recalling in times to come the honourable glories that once were, and the occasion as it was experienced by onlookers, whether courtiers or 'countrey people', was to reveal the enduring substance that underlay and gave meaning to an otherwise evanescent spectacle.[55] Like the printed text of a Jonsonian masque the Elvetham commemorative account provides what Barbara Ravelhofer has characterized as a 'timeless performance', a record or recording presented in a mode able to transcend the limitations of the vanished moment.[56]

In the opening sentence of *The Honorable Entertainement* readers are warned that a prerequisite for a 'better vnderstanding of euerie part & proces' of the entertainments themselves is an appreciation of the Elvetham setting, including what had been achieved there 'by art and labour' in preparation for the queen's visit. In view of this, and prompted by the symbolism and 'iust measured proportion' of the artfully contrived pond and its islands, it becomes appropriate to understand the manner in which the three gifts of the masque that honours Cynthia should be seen as corresponding to the three islands of the pond that similarly honours Cynthia (and even perhaps to the three trees of the ship isle, the three-part composition of the music, and the three boats of performing musicians). The waterborne gifts presented by Nereus and Neæra are positioned in the structure of the masque either side of Apollo's gift, and thereby mirror the way that the two islands supposedly created by Elizabeth's metamorphic power had been disposed either side of Neptune's protective fort. Similarly, the ordered symmetry of the

---

[55] Ben Jonson, in his preface to *Hymenaei*, was to develop and theorize this distinction.

[56] Barbara Ravelhofer, *The Early Stuart Masque: Dance, Costume, Music* (Oxford: Oxford University Press, 2006), p. 265.

specially created landscape in which the sequence of '*western pond bank* →
(water) → *ship isle* → (water) → *fort isle*' balanced by the corresponding mirror-
sequence of '*fort isle* ← (water) ← *snail isle* ← (water) ← *eastern pond bank*' is
reflected in the proportionate and symmetrically ordered structure of the masque.
All is as harmonious as it should be.

With the coming of the queen, a hitherto unremarkable Hampshire park had
marvellously become the local habitation of benign deities, its woods, waters and
gardens transformed into a poetry of imaginatively allusive settings for fantastical
shows. In the process, boundaries between the fabulous and the factual, the literal
and the metaphorical, the supernatural and the familiar had dissolved, making
the concordant diversity of the Elvetham entertainments a gloriously honourable
celebration: the royalty of a loved (albeit vain) sovereign acclaimed by the loyalty
of a loving (albeit anxious) host. But, impelled by the notion of 'a courtly culture
accustomed to search for covert messages', academic studies seem to feel a need
to reveal or, in effect, impose more provocative, more hazardous, more daringly
manipulative designs; and it has been well said that 'Elizabethan progresses seem
to demand – and defy – interpretation'.[57]

Masque of the Three Gifts to Cynthia

Claims that the *Masque of the Three Gifts to Cynthia* (as I have elected to call
it) was really 'a kind of drama' in which 'topical allegory' represents Howard of
Effingham as Nereus, in which Neæra 'personifies profit and the spoils of war',
Sylvanus represents Sir John Norris, Neptune represents Lord Thomas Howard,
and the somersaulting diver somehow manages to represent both 'rich booty' and
the earl of Hertford, have been rightly dismissed by Curt Breight as ungrounded
speculation, as have the contentions that Sylvanus's cry of 'Revenge!' was an
allusion to the sinking of the galleon of that name, and that the choice of the
name *Bonadventure* for Neæra's pinnace was an allusion to the similarly named
ship then lying off the Azores.[58] But Breight's own argument that the masque
was a 'mini-drama' in which Sylvanus represents Hertford in his youth, and that
Sylvanus's humiliation alludes to the episode of some thirty years earlier in which,
as a result of a clandestine marriage to Lady Catherine Grey, young Hertford had
aroused Elizabeth's fury and been convicted of the serious offence of deflowering
a virgin of the blood royal is equally speculative.[59] The attempt to foist *realpolitik*

---

[57]   Breight, 'Realpolitik', p. 32; Jayne Elisabeth Archer and Sarah Knight, in Jayne
Elisabeth Archer, Elizabeth Goldring and Sarah Knight (eds), 'The Riddle of the Progresses',
in *The Progresses, Pageants, and Entertainments of Queen Elizabeth I* (Oxford: Oxford
University Press, 2007), p. 1.

[58]   Boyle, 'Elizabeth's Entertainment', pp. 147–9, 152–8. Breight, p. 24.

[59]   Breight, pp. 23, 31–7. Issue is taken with Breight by Michael Leslie, '"Something
Nasty in the Wilderness": Entertaining Queen Elizabeth in her Progresses', *Medieval and*

significance of an unwarrantably precise and contentious kind onto a performance where it would have been dangerously out of place is misconceived. So too is Kevin Sharpe's tentative suggestion that the 'Scottish Gigges' played on their cornetti by the 'Musick-maides' of Thetis might have been 'a gesture to Elizabeth's triumph over Mary, Queen of Scots'.[60] What an extraordinarily intrusive and unwelcome gesture that would have been! Even Sharpe's assertion that Neæra tells her auditors that it is on Elizabeth that the future of the ship of state depends is mistaken, for Sharpe has misread the text and, having confused direct and reported speech so that a possessive pronoun is fatally misunderstood, he wrenches a simple reference to Neæra's pinnace ('thy boat') into a supposedly much more significant allusion to the metaphorical ship of state.[61] The same sort of carelessly tendentious approach had allowed Boyle to identify the ship isle as an 'emblem' of England. He quotes the words 'See where her [England's] ship remaines ...', but the antecedent he parenthetically supplies for the possessive pronoun is incorrect.[62] It ought to have been 'India', and with that correction his whole argument about the symbolism of the three islands instantly founders.

Altogether more appropriate than such misdirected attempts to discover far-fetched and 'covert' significance in these entertainments is the linking of texts and their Elvetham setting. It is to be hoped that the recovery of the Windsor quarto with its revised text and unique illustration will give fresh impetus to that worthwhile endeavour.

Bibliography

Primary Sources

Bond, R. Warwick, *Complete Works of John Lyly* (3 vols, Oxford: Clarendon Press, 1902).

Davies, H. Neville, 'The Entertainment at Elvetham', in *John Nichols's The Progresses and Public Processions of Queen Elizabeth I: A New Edition of Early Modern Sources*, ed. Jayne Elisabeth Archer, Elizabeth Clarke and Elizabeth Goldring (5 vols, Oxford: Oxford University Press, 2013), vol. 3, pp. 563–95.

Renaissance Drama in England, 10 (1998), pp. 47–72.

[60]   Kevin M. Sharpe, *Selling the Tudor Monarchy: Authority and Image in Sixteenth-Century England* (New Haven and London: Yale University Press, 2009), p. 438. For the nature of Scotch gigs, see for example annotations on Shakespeare's *Much Ado about Nothing*, II. 1.

[61]   Confidence in Sharpe's reading of *The Honorable Entertainement* is not increased by his assertion that the three islands in the pond were 'shaped after a fish, a fowl and a snail' (p. 437).

[62]   Boyle, p. 151.

Gough, Richard (ed.), 'Queen Elizabeth's Entertainment by Ld. Hertford at Elvetham', *Gentleman's Magazine*, 49 (1770), pp. 81–5 and 121–5.

John Norden's A Progress of Piety, whose Jesses lead into the Harborough of heavenly Hearts-ease, ed. anonymously (Cambridge: Parker Society, 1847).

Letters and Papers, Foreign and Domestic, of the Reign of Henry VIII (21 vols, London: Longman, Green, Longman and Roberts, 1862–1932).

Letters of John Chamberlain, ed. Norman Egbert McClure (2 vols, Philadelphia, Pa: American Philosophical Society, 1939).

Nichols, John (ed.), *Progresses and Public Processions of Queen Elizabeth* (3 vols, London: J. Nichols, 1788–1805).

Nichols, John (ed.), *The Progresses and Public Processions of Queen Elizabeth I* (3 vols, London: J.B. Nichols, 1823).

Nichols, John (ed.), *The Progresses, Processions and Magnificent Festivities of King James the First* (4 vols, London: J.B. Nichols, 1828).

Pigafetta, Marcantonio, *Itinerario*, ed. Daria Perocco (Padua: Poligrafo, 2008).

Pigafetta, Marcantonio, *Itinerario*, ed. Michela Petrizzelli (Vicenza: Biblioteca Civica Bertolina, 2008).

Ruggiero, Alessandra (ed.), *The Honorable Entertainment Gieven to the Queene's Majestie, in Progresse, at Elvetham in Hampshire, by the Right Hon'ble the Earle of Hertford, 1591*, Angelica 5 (Naples: Liguori Editore, 2002).

The Letters of John Keats, 1814–1821, ed. Hyder Edward Rollins (2 vols, Cambridge, Mass: Harvard University Press, 1958).

Watson, Thomas, *Complete Works* (hypertex ed.) Dana F. Sutton, www.philological. bham.ac.uk/watson/elvetham/text.html (Nov. 2010; rev. May 2011).

Watson, Thomas, *English Poems Transcribed from Original Prints*, (ed.) Albert Chatterley (Norwich: Marion Hopkins, 2003).

Wilson, Jean, *Entertainments for Elizabeth I* (Woodbridge: Brewer, 1980).

Secondary Sources

Ahrends, Günter, et al. (eds), *Word and Action in Drama: Studies in Honour of Hans-Jürgen Diller* (Trier: Wissenschaftlicher Verlag Trier, 1994).

Anon., *Life in Tudor Times* (Winchester: Hampshire Record Office, n.d.).

Archer, Jayne Elisabeth and Sarah Knight, in Jayne Elisabeth Archer, Elizabeth Goldring and Sarah Knight (eds), 'The Riddle of the Progresses' in *The Progresses, Pageants, and Entertainments of Queen Elizabeth I* (Oxford: Oxford University Press, 2007), pp.1–26.

Archer, Jayne Elisabeth, Elizabeth Goldring and Sarah Knight (eds), *The Progresses, Pageants, and Entertainments of Queen Elizabeth I* (Oxford: Oxford University Press, 2007).

Barnard, John and D.F. MacKenzie, with the assistance of Maureen Bell (eds), *The Cambridge History of the Book in Britain* (7 vols, Cambridge: Cambridge University Press, 1999–2011), vol. 4 (2002).

Beal, Peter and Grace Ioppolo (eds), *Elizabeth I and the Culture of Writing* (London: British Library, 2007).

Bellorini, Maria Grazia, 'Le pubblicazioni Italiane dell'editore Londinese John Wolfe (1580–1591)', *Miscellanea*, 1, ed. Manlio Cortelazzo (Udine: Arti Grafiche Friulane, 1971). [*Miscellanea*, 1 is at the same time also Pubblicazioni della Facultà di Lingue e Letterature straniere con Sede in Udine, Università di Trieste, no. 1.]

Bergeron, David M., *English Civic Pageantry, 1558–1642* (London: Edward Arnold, 1971).

Boyle, Harry H., 'Elizabeth's Entertainment at Elvetham: War Policy in Pageantry', *Studies in Philology*, 68 (1971), pp. 146–66.

Breight, Curt, 'Realpolitik and Elizabethan Ceremony: The Earl of Hertford's Entertainment of Elizabeth at Elvetham, 1591', *Renaissance Quarterly*, 45 (1992), pp. 25–6.

Brennecke, Ernest, 'The Entertainment at Elvetham, 1591', in John H. Long (ed.), *Music in English Renaissance Drama* (Lexington, Ky: University of Kentucky Press, 1968).

Chambers, E.K., *The Elizabethan Stage* (4 vols, Oxford: Clarendon Press, 1923).

Cole, Mary Hill, 'Monarchy in Motion: An Overview of Elizabethan Progresses', in Jayne Elisabeth Archer, Elizabeth Goldring and Sarah Knight (eds), *The Progresses, Pageants, and Entertainments of Queen Elizabeth I* (Oxford: Oxford University Press, 2007), pp. 27–45.

Cowling, Jane and Peter Greenfield, *Monks, Minstrels and Players: Drama in Hampshire before 1642*, Hampshire Papers 29 (Winchester: Hampshire County Council, 2008).

Davies, H. Neville, '"To Sing and Revel in these Woods": Purcell's *The Fairy-Queen* and *The Honourable Entertainment at Elvetham*', *Renaissance Journal*, 1/6 (June 2002), pp. 3–14.

Dillon, Janette, *The Language of Space in Court Performance, 1400–1625* (Cambridge: Cambridge University Press, 2010).

Doran, Susan, *The Tudor Chronicles* (London: Quercus, 2008).

Doubleday, Arthur H. and William Page (eds), *The Victoria History of the County of Hampshire and the Isle of Wight* (6 vols, London: Constable, 1900–14), vol. 4, (ed.) William Page (1911).

Dovey, Zillah, *An Elizabethan Progress: The Queen's Journey into East Anglia, 1578* (Stroud: Alan Sutton, 1996).

Duncan-Jones, Katherine, 'Elizabeth I and her "Good George"', in Peter Beal and Grace Ioppolo (eds), *Elizabeth I and the Culture of Writing* (London: British Library, 2007), pp. 29–42.

Dunlop, Ian, *Palaces and Progresses of Elizabeth I* (London: Cape, 1962).

Dutton, Richard (ed.), *The Oxford Handbook of Early Modern Theatre* (Oxford: Oxford University Press, 2009).

Fellowes, Edmund H., *Memoirs of an Amateur Musician* (London: Methuen, 1946).

Fellowes, Edmund H., *The English Madrigal* (London: Oxford University Press, 1925).

Greg, W.W., *A Bibliography of the English Printed Drama to the Restoration* (4 vols, London: Printed for the Bibliographical Society at the University Press, Oxford, 1939–59).

Harrison, G.B., *An Elizabethan Journal: Being a Record of those Things Most Talked of During the Years 1591–1594* (London: Routledge, 1938).

Henderson, Paula, *The Tudor House and Garden: Architecture and Landscape in the Sixteenth and Early Seventeenth Centuries* (New Haven and London: Yale University Press, 2005).

Jackson, J.E., 'Wulfhall and the Seymours', *Wiltshire Archaeological and Natural History Magazine*, 15 (1875), pp. 140–207.

Kinney, Arthur F. (ed.), *Renaissance Drama: An Anthology of Plays and Entertainments* (Malden MA and Oxford: Blackwell, 1999).

Leslie, Michael, '"Something Nasty in the Wilderness": Entertaining Queen Elizabeth in her Progresses', *Medieval and Renaissance Drama in England*, 10 (1998), pp. 47–72.

Long, John H. (ed.), *Music in English Renaissance Drama* (Lexington, Ky: University of Kentucky Press, 1968).

Luborsky, Ruth Samson and Elizabeth Morley Ingram, *A Guide to English Illustrated Books, 1536–1603* (2 vols, Tempe, Ariz: Medieval and Renaissance Texts and Studies, 1998).

Martyn, Trea, *Elizabeth in the Garden: A Story of Love, Rivalry and Spectacular Design* (London: Faber and Faber, 2008).

Mowl, Timothy, *Elizabethan and Jacobean Style* (London: Phaidon, 1993).

Murray, John Tucker, *English Dramatic Companies, 1558–1642* (2 vols, London: Constable, 1910).

Osborne, June, *Entertaining Elizabeth I: The Progresses and Great Houses of her Time* (London: Bishopsgate Press, 1989).

Ravelhofer, Barbara, *The Early Stuart Masque: Dance, Costume, Music* (Oxford: Oxford University Press, 2006).

Rex, Richard, *The Tudors* (Stroud: Tempus, 2009).

Sharpe, Kevin M., *Selling the Tudor Monarchy: Authority and Image in Sixteenth-Century England* (New Haven and London: Yale University Press, 2009).

St Maur, R.H., *Annals of the Seymours* (London: Kegan Paul, Trench, Trubner and Co., 1902).

Strong, Roy C., *The Renaissance Garden in England* (London: Thames and Hudson, 1979).

Stump, Donald and Susan M. Felch (eds), *Elizabeth I and Her Age: Authoritative Texts, Commentary and Criticism* (New York and London: W.W. Norton, 2009).

Suerbaum, Ulrich, 'Performing Royalty. The Entertainment at Elvetham and the Cult of Elisa', in Günter Ahrends et al. (eds), *Word and Action in Drama:*

Studies in Honour of Hans-Jürgen Diller (Trier: Wissenschaftlicher Verlag Trier, 1994).

Sutton, James M., *Materializing Space at an Early Modern Prodigy House: The Cecils at Theobalds, 1564–1607* (Aldershot: Ashgate, 2004).

Watkins, Susan, *Elizabeth I and her World* (London: Thames and Hudson, 2007).

Westfall, Suzanne, '"He who Pays the Piper Calls the Tune": Household Entertainments', in Richard Dutton (ed.), *The Oxford Handbook of Early Modern Theatre* (Oxford: Oxford University Press, 2009).

Wilson, David R., *Air Photo Interpretation for Archaeologists*, rev. edn (Stroud: Tempus, 2000).

Wilson, David R. and Jean Wilson, 'The Site of the Elvetham Entertainment', *Antiquity* (1982), pp. 46–7, and plates IIb and III.

Wilson, Jean, 'Queen Bess's Three Days in Wonderland', *Times*, 10 January 1981, p. 12.

Wilson, Jean, *The Shakespeare Legacy: The Material Legacy of Shakespeare's Theatre* (Godalming: Bramley Books, 1995).

Worms, Laurence, 'Maps and Atlases', in John Barnard and D.F. MacKenzie, with the assistance of Maureen Bell (eds), *The Cambridge History of the Book in Britain*, (7 vols, Cambridge: Cambridge University Press, 1999–2011), vol. 4 (2002), pp. 228–45.

Chapter 12

The Ice Festival in Florence, 1604

Mary M. Young

Through their sponsorship of elaborate celebrations and festivals in the sixteenth and seventeenth centuries, the Medici grand dukes of Tuscany eagerly seized opportunities to glorify themselves, Florence and the Medicean principate through the commemoration of weddings, baptisms, funerals, visits of foreign dignitaries and annual civic events such as Carnival and the Feast of St John the Baptist. Intended for a select audience of Florentine nobility and distinguished guests, private spectacles were usually held in the Salone dei Cinquecento in the Palazzo Vecchio, the Medici Theatre in the Uffizi, the Palazzo Medici, or the grand hall or courtyard of the Palazzo Pitti. The Medici *feste* that were available to the general population were typically held in Piazza Santa Croce, Piazza Santa Maria Novella, or Piazza della Signoria. For these public festivities, all Florentines had the opportunity to experience a variety of entertainments including football games, animal baiting, horse ballets and various types of *palii* and jousts.[1]

In late December 1604, the Arno River became the setting for an unusual public celebration when a rare weather event in Florence created an opportunity for a member of the Medici court to stage an extraordinary ice festival. When the river

---

[1]   There are numerous studies of Medici festivals, including Arthur R. Blumenthal, *Theater Art of the Medici*, exhibition catalogue (Hanover, N.H: Dartmouth College Museum/ University Press of New England, 1980); Heidi L. Chrétien, *The Festival of San Giovanni: Imagery and Political Power in Renaissance Florence* (New York: Peter Lang, 1994); J.R. Mulryne, Helen Watanabe-O'Kelly and Margaret Shewring (eds), *Europa Triumphans: Court and Civic Festivals in Early Modern Europe* (Aldershot, England and Burlington, VT: Ashgate, 2004); Giovanna Gaeta Bertelà and Annamaria Petrioli Tofani, *Feste e apparati Medicei da Cosimo I a Cosimo II*, exhibition catalogue (Florence: Leo S. Olschki, 1969); Pietro Gori, *Le Feste Fiorentine Attraverso i Secoli, Le Feste per San Giovanni* (Florence: R. Bemporad & Figlio, 1926; reprint 1989); A.M. Nagler, *Theatre Festivals of the Medici, 1539–1637*, trans. George Hickenlooper (New Haven: Yale University Press, 1964); Michel Plaisance, *Florence in the Time of the Medici: Public Celebrations, Politics, and Literature in the Fifteenth and Sixteenth Centuries*, trans. and (ed.) Nicole Carew-Reid (Toronto: Centre for Reformation and Renaissance Studies, 2008); James M. Saslow, *The Medici Wedding of 1589: Florentine Festival as 'Theatrum Mundi'* (New Haven: Yale University Press, 1996); Angelo Solerti, *Musica, Ballo e Drammatica alla Corte Medicea dal 1600 al 1637* (Florence, 1905; reprint, New York and London: Benjamin Blom, 1968); Roy C. Strong, *Art and Power: Renaissance Festivals, 1450–1650* (Woodbridge: Boydell Press, 1984).

froze unexpectedly, a section of the ice-covered waterway was transformed into a festival space where people engaged in animal hunts, a pageant procession and a variety of competitions. But unlike other *feste* that required lengthy planning and organization, the Florentines had to act quickly for these entertainments. At the time of the Ice Festival, Grand Duke Ferdinando I de' Medici was away from Florence. Having left the city in mid-December, the grand duke was travelling with his court between various residences before settling in Pisa where he typically spent the Carnival season. However, one prominent member of the Medici family remained in Florence. Through his leadership and support, the Florentines had the opportunity to experience a carnival-like celebration early in the season.

To appreciate the 1604 Ice Festival within a cultural and political context, this chapter will examine two contemporary sources, a commemorative festival book and a Medici court diary. Providing an official account of the icy amusements, *Relazione delle feste fatte in Firenze. Sopra il ghiaccio del fiume d'Arno l'vltimo dì di Dicembre MDCIV* presents captivating details of unusual activities on the frozen river.[2] Describing a *'memorabil giornata'* ('unforgettable day'), the text was meant to stir the memories of those who experienced it and recreate it for those who were absent.[3] Undeniably entertaining, this work communicates an atmosphere of gaiety and humor surrounding the *festa*. With references to events that occurred *'il giorno avanti di hieri'* ('the day before yesterday') and *'hiermattina'* ('yesterday morning'), the author indicates that the text was written soon after the Ice Festival took place.[4] Published in 1604, the work was certainly composed within a relatively short time frame. Considering the date of the Ice Festival (31 December) and the Florentine calendar (the New Year began on 25 March), there was an interval of approximately

---

[2]   *Relazione delle feste fatte in Firenze. Sopra il ghiaccio del fiume d'Arno l'vltimo dì di Dicembre MDCIV* (Florence: Bartolomeo Sermartelli, 1604) [accessed at http://special-1. bl.uk/treasures/festivalbooks]. All quotations from this festival book are referenced by the page numbers on the British Library website. From the more than 2,000 books in its Renaissance festival collection, the British Library has scanned 253 works and made these primary source documents available on the Internet. [These 253 books were photographed, annotated and made responsive to digital keyword search terms as part of an AHRC-funded project led by J.R. Mulryne, co-investigator Margaret Shewring.] This text was reprinted by Alessandro Guiducci in Florence with slight variations in spelling and punctuation. *Relazione delle feste fatte in Fiorenza sopra il ghiaccio del fiume d'Arno l'ultimo di di dicembre MDCIV* (Florence: Alessandro Guiducci, 1604), see http://warburg.sas.ac.uk/ mnemosyne/DigitalCollections.htm. Regarding authorship, see Gaeta Bertelà, *Feste*, p. 211 and Solerti, *Musica*, p. 35. In their brief references to the 1604 Ice Festival, both works refer to Cammillo Guidi as the author of the work. While the Warburg text has the name of Cammillo Guidi handwritten on the front page, the one in the British Library does not contain a reference to an author.

[3]   *Relazione*, p. 16.

[4]   Ibid., p. 4.

three months for the writing and publishing of this text.[5] With his accounts of births, marriages, deaths, political affairs and entertainments, the diary of Cesare Tinghi is an invaluable resource for information about Medici court life. As '*aiutante di camera*' ('Groom of the Chamber') to Ferdinando, the diarist was well acquainted with the grand duke, his family and followers, and his daily activities. Through regular and often detailed entries, Tinghi documents the interests and movements of the grand duke and his entourage.[6]

Following a sketch of the principal elements of the *festa*, this paper will explore the features that distinguish the 1604 festival from other Medici sponsored celebrations and then consider its effect on Carnival activities in Pisa. In light of references to a visiting Spanish dignitary in the official festival book, the event will also be explored in terms of political relations between Ferdinando I and Philip III.

The Setting

Bisecting the city of Florence, the Arno River is a defining feature of the city. When considering the Florentines' lighthearted response to the unexpected weather event, one should keep in mind the uncertainty and dangerous potential of the river. Florence's history is replete with accounts of destructive floods and droughts during all seasons. Just three years before the Ice Festival, in January 1601, the Arno flooded and caused serious damage to the city.[7] Well aware of the destructive power of nature, the Florentines harnessed this frozen anomaly in 1604 and used it to their advantage.

Instead of the long ribbon of water that flowed through the city a section between two bridges, the Ponte Santa Trinita and the Ponte alla Carraia, was transformed into a frozen piazza in a setting '*che per esser vestito de più belli edifizii, et ragguarde vole delle piu graziose vedute della Città*' ('that is dressed with the most beautiful buildings, and notable for the most lovely views of the city').[8] Apart from any embellishment by the author of the festival book, this neighbourhood became popular

---

[5]   All references to years in this chapter are written in the modern style. Many festival books were written in advance of a celebration. Helen Watanabe-O'Kelly, 'Festival Books in Europe from Renaissance to Rococo,' *The Seventeenth Century*, 3 (1988), 194–5 and 'The Early Modern Festival Book: Function and Form', *Europa Triumphans*, vol. 1, pp. 3–17.

[6]   Cesare Tinghi, *Diario di Ferdinando I e Cosimo II gran Duca di Toscana scritto da Cesare Tinghi da' 22 luglio 1600 sino a' 12 settembre 1615* (Biblioteca Nazionale Centrale di Firenze. Fondo Gino Capponi 261, vol. 1). With regard to Tinghi's unusual orthography, I have substituted words for his symbols, such as 'per'. I am grateful to Professor Mark Rosen at the University of Texas at Dallas for his support and observations.

[7]   Regarding the floods of 1589 and 1601, see Samuel Berner, 'Florentine Society in the Late Sixteenth and Early Seventeenth Centuries', *Studies in the Renaissance*, 18 (1971), p. 210 and J.R. Hale, *Florence and the Medici* (London: Thames and Hudson, 1977; London: Phoenix Press, 2004), p. 160.

[8]   *Relazione*, p. 4.

among the aristocracy after the relocation of the Medici court to the Palazzo Pitti in the 1550s and the construction of Bartolomeo Ammannati's Ponte Santa Trinita in the 1560s.[9] Used for annual water festivities in celebration of the Feast of San Jacopo on 25 July, this particular segment of the river also provided the stage for the spectacular *Argonautica* during the wedding festivities for Cosimo II de' Medici and Maria Magdalena in 1608 (Fig. 12.1).[10]

An examination of Stefano Bonsignori's map from the late sixteenth century may explain the reason for this preferred location.[11] There were obstructions above the Ponte Vecchio and below the Ponte alla Carraia (shallow water and weirs), and structures abutting the riverbank on the Oltrarno side between the Ponte Vecchio and the Ponte Santa Trinita (Fig. 12.2). With street access (Lungarno Guicciardini and Lungarno Corsini) on either side of the area between the Carraia and the Santa Trinita bridges, this section allowed access from all four sides of the river for spectators.

At the beginning of the festival book, the author describes the *festa* in terms of weather when winter suddenly arrived '*con tanto rigore*' ('with much force'), causing the Arno to solidify after five or six days of freezing temperatures.[12] According to the text, it had been sixty years since the river froze in such a manner. This may be a reference to an icing incident in January 1546 that allowed for informal festivities on the ice-covered river.[13] In his diary, Tinghi confirms the bitter cold with numerous descriptions of chilly Tuscan days '*il tempo cativo*' ('bad weather') and '*un gran freddo*' ('a great cold') throughout the winter months.[14] Commenting on the Ice Festival, he explains that the lack of rain led to a low water level that allowed the water to freeze solidly: '*piu di cento venti giorni senza pioggia ... et per questa secita il fiume era tanto Basso*' ('more than one hundred and twenty days without rain ... the river was so low because of this drought').[15]

---

[9]   Designed by Bartolomeo Ammannati, the Ponte Santa Trinita was built in 1567–69 following a flood in 1557. Chrétien, *Festival*, pp. 90–91; Eve Borsook, *The Companion Guide to Florence* (London: Collins, 1988), p. 180; Hale, *Florence and the Medici*, p. 155.

[10]   Concerning the elaborately decorated ships for the 1608 *Argonautica*, see Blumenthal, *Theater Art of the Medici*, pp. 35–7, 57–86.

[11]   Stefano Bonsignori's map was printed in 1584 and reprinted in 1594. The reproduction of the work in this chapter is of the second version. Felicia M. Else, 'Controlling the Waters of Granducal Florence: A New Look at Stefano Bonsignori's View of the City (1584)', *Imago Mundi*, vol. 61:2 (June 2009), pp. 168–85.

[12]   *Relazione*, p. 3.

[13]   Plaisance, *Florence*, p. 103.

[14]   Tinghi, *Diario*, 117v, 118v, 119v and 122. One contemporary description notes that the Arno River remained frozen until 20 February. 'Diario Istorico Fiorentino d'Autore Anonimo Dal 1600 al 1640', in *Notizie Istoriche Italiane scritte e compilate da M.R.* vol. 3 (Florence: Antonio Benucci, 1781), p. 120.

[15]   Tinghi, *Diario*, p. 117.

Figure 12.1   Matthias Greuter, *The Argonautica in the Arno River*, detail, 1608
Collection of Mary M. Young, Photograph: Daniel Mendenhall

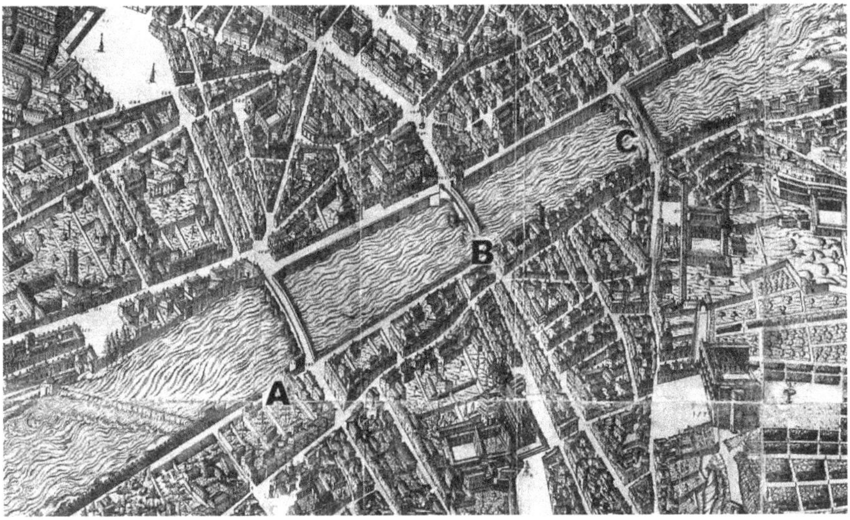

Figure 12.2   Stefano Bonsignori, *Nova pulcherrimae civitatis Florentiae topographia accuratissime delineata*, detail. [1584], 1594 A. Ponte alla Carraia; B. Ponte Santa Trinita; C. Ponte Vecchio © British Library Board, Maps *23480 (21)

The Organizer

On the first page of the book, the reader is introduced to Don Virginio Orsini as the organizer of these public entertainments since his uncle the grand duke was absent from Florence: '*qualche publica ricreazione come per obligo in assenza di loro Altezze*' ('some public recreation in the absence of their Highnesses).[16] Recognized by the author for '*la solita affabilita*' ('usual affability'), Don Virginio was the son of Isabella de' Medici and Paolo Giordano I Orsini, and was the nephew of Grand Duke Ferdinando I.[17] When his father died in 1585, he inherited the title of Duke of Bracciano. Born in 1572 and raised in the Medici palace in Florence, Don Virginio grew up at his uncle's court and enjoyed a privileged relationship with the grand duke. Despite a difference in age of twenty-three years, they were married the same year and their children were close in age. For Ferdinando's wedding in 1589, Don Virginio played an integral role in the celebrations as team leader for the '*giuoco di calcio*' ('soccer') in Piazza Santa Croce and as coordinator of the grand procession prior to the *sbarra* tournament at the Palazzo Pitti.[18] As a participant in the parade, Don Virginio's display was the most extravagant of all, presenting him as 'a surrogate crown prince'.[19]

Tinghi's journal details the particularly close bond between Don Virginio and the grand duke. His diary is filled with entries that describe numerous shared activities – attending mass, hunting expeditions, travelling to Livorno, Pisa and various Medici country villas, as well as countless outings '*in cochio*' ('coach rides'). A frequent companion to his uncle at court and civic events, Don Virginio accompanied Ferdinando to observe the annual water *festa* on the Arno, '*il palio di navicelli*' ('boat race'), on 25 July 1604, five months before the Ice Festival.[20]

In the festival text, the author explains that Don Virginio was in Florence for a reason related to his wife: '*rimasa à Firenze per la freschezza del parto si trovava in questa Città, et non alla Corte*' ('stayed in Florence and did not travel with the court because of the recent birth of a child').[21] This pregnancy is the subject of several entries in Tinghi's journal. On 17 November 1604, the diarist notes that the Duchess of Bracciano left Ambrogiana with her children to return

---

[16]   *Relazione*, p. 3.

[17]   In the festival book, Don Virginio Orsini is listed as Don Virginio Orsino. In his diary, Tinghi often refers to him as Don Verginio. See The Medici Archive Project for basic biographical information, http://www.medici.org. For Don Virginio's journey to England in 1601, see Michael Wyatt, *The Italian Encounter with Tudor England, A Cultural Politics of Translation* (Cambridge: Cambridge University Press, 2005), pp. 130–34, 308. Wyatt also discusses the murder of Don Virginio's mother by his father, a scandal that was the basis for John Webster's 1612 play, *The White Devil*.

[18]   Saslow, *The Medici Wedding*, p. 171.

[19]   Ibid., p. 168.

[20]   Tinghi, *Diario*, p. 100.

[21]   *Relazione*, p. 3.

to Florence and await the approaching childbirth. Demonstrating concern for her welfare, he writes '*che Dio la conservi felice*' ('may God keep her blessed').[22] On 14 December, Tinghi comments that '*S.A. La matina ebbe nuova che la pasata notte la duchessa di Braciano aveva Partorito un figlio Mastio [sic] et S.A. ne senti un gran contento*' ('His Highness received news in the morning that the Duchess of Bracciano had given birth to a son the night before and His Highness felt a great contentment').[23] The very next day, Tinghi records that the new father was once again travelling '*in cochio*' ('in a coach') with the grand duke. At the time of the Ice Festival, Don Virginio was most likely in high spirits because of his recently delivered son.

The Event

According to the festival text, the Florentines were initially afraid to step onto the frozen surface of the river. But after watching those brave enough to venture forth and being reassured that the ground was safe ('*sodo et da reggere*' ('solid and secure')), townspeople crowded the ice and used the area as '*una grande, et stabile piazza*' ('a large and stable square').[24] While the festival book mentions a '*gioco di pallone*' ('ball game') and '*caccie*' ('hunts') with cats and rabbits, it is clear that the writer's primary interests are the '*mostra*' ('parade') and the subsequent three competitions. When all participants were in place, the *mostra* began with the emergence of six drummers and six trumpeters beneath the Santa Trinita arch nearest Santo Spirito. They were followed by three groups of contestants. With the participants '*vestiti alla Carnovalesca, et alla Comica*' ('dressed in Carnival and humorous style'), the first assembly involved a large number of people who would compete in a '*palio à piè ignudo*' ('barefoot race').[25] The next group consisted of persons dressed as nymphs and seated on '*seggiolette*' ('low chairs'). Adapted for the ice competition, this type of chair required the participants to position and propel themselves in an unusual way:

> ... *à sedere con le gambe alte distese à maniera di gottosi, che con due bastonetti appuntati in mano si sospingevano avanti et sdrucciolavano a modo di storpiati, che faceva bellissima, et ridicola vista, il servirsi delle braccia per gambe, et lo star in una postura cosi stravagante.*[26]

---

[22]   Tinghi, *Diario*, p. 112. Don Virginio's wife, Flavia Damasceni Peretti di Montalto-Orsini, died less than two years later, on 14 September 1606. Ibid., p. 164v.

[23]   Ibid., p. 114v. Tinghi refers to Ferdinando as 'S.A.' or 'S.A.S.' meaning '*Sua Altezza*' or '*Sua Altezza Serenissima*'.

[24]   *Relazione*, p. 3.

[25]   Ibid., p. 5.

[26]   Ibid.

[sitting with the legs extended like those with gout, with two sticks held in their hands, they pushed themselves forward and glided in the manner of disabled persons, and the strange use of the arms for the legs made a most beautiful and ridiculous view.']

The final assembly involved the '*giostratori*' ('jousters'), members of the aristocracy who were seated on '*slitte*' ('sleds'), '*carri bassi, et lunghetti*' ('low, long carts') that were pulled or pushed by a crew of people and were decorated with beautiful designs '*à modo di quadrighe antiche*' ('in the style of ancient chariots').[27] Wheels were removed from carts and lengths of board and metal strips were placed beneath the bases to enable them to slide more easily on the ice. After '*una sella che non si vedeva*' ('a saddle unlike any ever seen before') was placed upon each pageant sled, the *slitta* became a unique all-in-one means of transportation – '*di Cavallo, di Cocchio, et di Barca*' ('a horse, a coach, and a boat').[28] Of the fourteen pages of text in the festival book, ten describe the procession of allegorical figures and pageant sleds for seventeen men of nobility.[29] With a detailed account of each aristocrat, the author includes the verses that were presented to the crowd as well as a thorough description of their costumes and *imprese*.

Apart from some obscure allegorical references, the pageantry provided the spectators with an impressive visual display. While Cammillo Suarez and Francesco Martelli appeared as savages with riotous beards and hair, Filippo Valori came dressed as a Turkish woman in a red garment trimmed in jewels and pearls, and displayed an elaborate hairstyle. Giulio Riario and Bardo Corsi came as sorcerers with long beards and great turbans with jewels and feathers. Their *slitta* was painted colourfully with touches of gold and silver and pulled by a large fire-breathing dragon. Dressed as Pluto, Manfredi Malespina's sled was another dragon that spewed fire and was propelled by four devils carrying silver pitchforks and dressed in garments that were decorated with flames. Accompanied by ten attendants, Don Virginio appeared as a Bascià Ottomanno (Turkish viceroy) '*con più ragguardevole et più sublime apparato*' ('with the most notable and sublime apparatus'). Wearing a feather plume of nearly six feet in height, he rode in a golden *slitta* that was shaped like two birds with swan wings.[30]

The 15 jousters were followed by two brothers, Ridolfo and Niccolò della Fonte, who appeared on a *barca* with '*fuochi lavorati*' ('fireworks') and a '*girandola*' ('Catherine wheel') on top of the mast.[31] After the procession around the frozen

---

[27]   Ibid.

[28]   Ibid.

[29]   In order, they are Cammillo Suarez, Francesco Martelli, Don Fernando Suarez, Bartolommeo Bettini, Antonio Magalotti, Piero Guicciardini, Alessandro del Nero, Carlo Soderini, Filippo Valori, Tommaso Capponi, Niccolò Giugni, Don Virginio Orsini, Giulio Riario, Bardo Corsi, Marchese Manfredi Malespina, Ridolfo della Fonte and Niccolò della Fonte.

[30]   *Relazione*, pp. 11–12.

[31]   Ibid., p. 14.

piazza, the three groups gathered beneath the three arches of the Ponte Santa Trinita and awaited their competitions. The first contest was the *palio de discalzi* where the runners slipped, stumbled and fell on the ice because of their bare feet. Describing it as '*uno di piu graziosi et ridicoli spettacoli che si sia visto giamai*' ('one of the most graceful and ridiculous spectacles that has ever been seen'), the author comments on the '*mescuglio*' ('jumble') of tangled bodies.[32] Tired from so much laughter, the spectators apparently could not easily determine the winner.

After this spirited and chaotic contest, the next activity was an equally entertaining '*Palio delle seggiolette*' ('chair race'), that involved similar slippery action on the ice: '*che anch' esso fece vista non punto men bella per la strana foggia com' eran posti, e per la stravagante forza che si vedevan far di braccia, di capo, & di spalle*' ('it made a view no less beautiful for the odd manner that it was arranged and for the extravagant effort that was made by the arms, heads, and shoulders [of the participants]').[33] The final competition was a joust where '*I Cavalieri cominciarono à correre et à romper le lancie al Saracino*' ('the *Cavalieri* began to run and target their lances at a mock Saracen'). Placed on a *slitta*, the mannequin was pushed by four men wearing shoes that were '*ben ferrati, et tenaci*' ('well made of iron'). Sliding around on the ice, many of the participants tumbled from their seats and broke their lances. Noting the potential for injury to the participants, the author describes the overturned *slitta* carrying the Saracen: '*molti di essi gettaron à terra non solo il Saracino ma rovesciaron la Slitta con gran pericolo di quei ch' eran dietro à tenerla*' ('many were thrown to the ground, not only the Saracen but the sled overturned with great danger to those who were holding on behind').[34]

Following this tournament, the author describes the appearance of Alessandro '*saltatore celebre et facilmente il piu raro de nostri tempi*' ('celebrated tumbler and easily the most exceptional of our time') who demonstrated an impressive dexterity on the slippery ice.[35] A renowned performer of acrobatics, including performances on horseback ('*molti salti al cavallo*'), Alessandro is noted as an entertainer for the grand duke and his court at various times during Carnival in Pisa.[36] The festival text ends with a description of fireworks and objects that referred to grand ducal rule, identifying six barrels that suggested the Medici *palle* and a representation of the royal crown with a lily.

Throughout the festival book, the author comments on the '*strettezza del tempo*' ('limited time') to prepare for an event that was so '*transitoria*'.[37]

---

[32] Ibid., p. 14–15.

[33] Ibid, p. 15.

[34] Ibid.

[35] Ibid.

[36] Tinghi writes of performances by Alessandro for court entertainments during Carnival in Pisa on 2 March 1604 and 26 February 1606. Tinghi, *Diario*, pp. 84v and 175v. He also performed on 7 August 1604. Ibid., p. 101v.

[37] *Relazione*, p. 4.

Apparently, some of the nobility could not participate in full regalia '*alcuni senza invenzioni et alcuni con esse imperfette*' ('some without devices and some with unfinished ones') because of '*la brevità del tempo*' ('the brevity of time').[38] And yet, the account describes an extraordinary production. Considering the elaborate pageantry, it would seem reasonable that many of the costumes and devices involved recycled items from prior *feste*. One might also assume that someone other than Don Virginio would have supervised the technical aspects of the production such as the elaborate fireworks arrangement. In view of the '*fuochi lavorati*' ('fireworks') and the '*girandola*' ('Catherine wheel') on the pageant ship and during the finale with the impressive grand ducal imagery, one candidate might be Bernardo Buontalenti. Associated with the *girandola*, Buontalenti was the grand duke's engineer and architect who directed the arrangements for many court-sponsored spectacles. Though he was nearing the end of his career, Tinghi does refer to '*Bernardo Buontalenti detto delle girandole*' at least twice in his diary in the six months preceding the ice *festa*.[39]

As described in the commemorative text for the 1604 Ice Festival, the overall notion of a procession, allegorical references, tournaments with members of the nobility as principal participants and use of fireworks is consistent with other grand ducal celebrations. Among the many festivities for Ferdinando's wedding in 1589, there were a '*giuoco di calcio*' ('soccer') and two jousts in Piazza Santa Croce. The pageant procession prior to the *sbarra* at the Palazzo Pitti involved trumpeters leading a parade of chariots with fantastic characters and themes – one displayed a complete garden, a dragon pulled another and one float presented a crocodile and a sorcerer atop a mountain. As a participant in this parade, Don Virginio came costumed as Mars on an elaborate pageant cart, surrounded by nymphs and satyrs (Fig. 12.3).[40]

The '*palio delle seggiolette*' ('chair race') in the Ice Festival may have reminded the spectators of a style of competition that was introduced by Cosimo I in 1563 as

---

[38]   Ibid., pp. 4, 10.

[39]   In his diary Tinghi writes of a meeting on 20 June 1604 between the grand duke and Buontalenti ('*suo ingeniere*') regarding '*Molti Belli ordini*'. On 6 August 1604, the diarist refers to '*Bernardo Buontalenti detto delle girandole*' Tinghi, *Diario*, pp. 97v, 100v. Considering that he lived until 1608, it is possible that Bernardo Buontalenti, or even his successor Giulio Parigi, may have been involved with the Ice Festival. See Saslow, *The Medici Wedding*, regarding Buontalenti. For Buontalenti's involvement with the 1600 wedding festivities for Marie de' Medici and Henry IV, see Strong, *Art and Power*, pp. 147–8.

[40]   Don Virginio's presentation involved multiple, elaborate floats with many attendants. Saslow notes that Buontalenti did the arrangements for the procession. Regarding the parade, see Saslow, *The Medici Wedding*, pp. 165–9, 171 and 248–60; Blumenthal, *Theater Art of the Medici*, pp. 17–25; Strong, *Art and Power*, p. 143.

Figure 12.3   Orazio Scarabelli, *Chariot of Don Virginio Orsini as Mars*, detail
© The Metropolitan Museum of Art (Harris Brisbane Dick Fund,
1931, no. 31.72.5)

part of the festivities for the feast of San Giovanni: the *Palio de' Cocchi*.[41] Tinghi
comments on the grand duke viewing '*il palio de Cochi*' ('the coach race') in the
Piazza Santa Maria Novella on 23 June each year. And yet, for the Ice Festival,
people instead of horses propelled the *slitte*.

The final frosty contest was a *giostra al saracino*, a tournament that involved
combatants aiming their lances at a Saracen mannequin. This style of joust was
performed in Piazza Santa Croce for the wedding of Francesco I de' Medici
and Bianca Cappello in 1579 as well as for Ferdinando in 1589.[42] In the months
preceding the Ice Festival in 1604, Archduke Maximilian von Habsburg '*Ha voluto
correre al Saracino*' ('wanted a Saracen joust') during his visit to Florence in April
1604 and a '*giostra al saracino*' was held on 31 August 1604.[43] Though there was a
Florentine tradition of the Saracen joust, the manner in which it was implemented
for the Ice Festival was novel. Instead of competing on horseback, the *giostratori*

---

[41]   Henk Th. van Veen, *Cosimo I de' Medici and His Self-representation in Florentine
Art and Culture*, trans. Andrew P. McCormick (Cambridge: Cambridge University Press,
2006), p. 149; Chrétien, *Festival*, pp. 45–6; Gori, *Le Feste Fiorentine*, pp. 230–42.

[42]   Gaeta Bertelà, *Feste*, p. 55; Blumenthal, *Art of the Medici*, p. 15; Saslow, *The
Medici Wedding*, p. 171.

[43]   Medici Archive Project, http://www.medici.org/ MdP 3124, Folio 178, DocID
11202 (May 1604). See also Tinghi, *Diario*, pp. 91v, 103v and Solerti, *Musica*, p. 33.

rode astride their unusual horse-coach-boat *slitte*. Even the author of the festival text acknowledges '*faceva gentilissima vista la nuova et strana maniera del correre*' ('the new and strange manner of the race made a most pleasant sight').[44] The frozen river provided a different field condition that fundamentally altered the structure and nature of a traditional parade and competitions.

While the individual entertainments can be appreciated for their novel elements, it is important to remember the ice-covered piazza as a unique festival space: '*col concorso di popolo innumerabile che haveva calcato le sponde, le strade, le finestre, e le tetta, sin dove arrivava la vista, faceva il più nobile et più raro amphiteatro che si sia veduto giamai*' ('the gathering of countless people who crowded the riverbanks, the streets, the windows and the rooftops from where they could see the view. It made the most noble and rare amphitheatre that one has ever seen').[45] Though this section of the river was traditionally used for San Jacopo celebrations, this was a different setting for a Saracen joust and *palii* that did not involve boats. This uncommon '*agghiacciati arringhi*' ('frozen tiltyard') most likely added an exciting new dimension to the festival experience, for participants as well as spectators.[46] Any recycled pageant costumes or *invenzioni* would have been appreciated differently in this atypical venue and manner of parade and competitions. In his diary, Tinghi frequently uses the phrase '*in luogho solito*' ('in the usual place') in reference to customary event locations such as the *Palio de Cochio* in Piazza Santa Maria Novella.[47] There was nothing *solito* about the setting or the activities of the 1604 Ice Festival.

Throughout the festival book, the author conveys a carnival-like atmosphere with his descriptions of amusing disorder and '*tante risa delli spettatori*' ('lots of laughter from the spectators').[48] In his diary, Tinghi comments on comic performances that were commonly arranged for the pleasure of the grand duke and his family, the court and visiting nobility. On 27 April 1604 for the visit of Archduke Maximilian, there was '*una comedia all'improviso*' ('improvised comedy'), and to help celebrate a wedding in the second week of December 1604, Ferdinando arranged for the presentation of several comedies, one of which was with young Florentines '*al improviso*'. These were probably performances of *commedia dell'arte*, a popular form of entertainment that was not necessarily extemporaneous.[49] On 31 December 1604, the frozen field on the Arno became

---

44   *Relazione*, p. 15.

45   Ibid., pp. 4–5. One should also consider that the space on the Arno is larger than Piazza della Signoria and the piazzas in front of Santa Maria Novella and Santa Croce.

46   *Relazione*, p. 16.

47   Tinghi, *Diario*, pp. 11, 33v, 66.

48   *Relazione*, p. 15.

49   Tinghi, *Diario*, pp. 91, 114. The wedding was for Francesco Maria Malaspina and Ippolita Malaspina. See also Solerti, *Musica*, p. 34. Regarding comedies during Carnival and Carnival activities in Florence, see Plaisance, *Florence*, pp. 32–4, 104–12. Regarding the notion of improvisation and *commedia dell'arte*, see Saslow, *The Medici Wedding*,

the setting for an ice comedy that was truly improvisational, one that involved unscripted performances by professional as well as non-professional actors.

Impact of the Ice Festival on Pisa's Carnival

According to Tinghi's diary, Ferdinando left Florence on 18 December and travelled with his court between a number of Medici country villas for the next few weeks. On the day of the Festival, 31 December, the grand duke was in Pescia where he planned '*il festino di Ballare*' ('dance'), a common amusement for the nobility.[50] On 3 January he received information about the *festa* in Florence. In his journal, Tinghi writes:

Et adi 3 di genaio conparse nuove a S.A. come il Sig. Don Verginio sendo a firenze et sendo per si gran freddo giaciato di sexte anno che Sua Ecelenza insieme con Molti gentiluomini avevono in suldiaccio fatto caccie d'animali di lepre conigliate inzocholi gioste al saracino corso il palio da uomini scalzi et fatto saltare al cavallo in tre o quarto giorni et di Molte altre cose di grandisimo gusto et gran piaceri et con tanto popolo che Mai a tempi nostri se vide tal cosa et per gio sendo stato per fino a oggi piu di cento venti giorni senza pioggia se non una volta sola et per questa secita il fiume era tanto Basso che il diaccio auto forza di a sodarsi sendo tanto gran freddo che e grandissima Meraviglia.[51]

[On 3 January, His Highness received news about Don Virginio who was in Florence. Because of the great freezing cold that had not happened in sixty years, his Excellency, together with many gentlemen, arranged on the ice over three or four days an animal hunt of hares, rabbits, cats, hoofed creatures; a Saracen joust; a barefoot race; and tumbling on horseback; and many other things of enormous taste and great pleasure, and with so many people who have never seen such a thing in our time, and until today there has been more than

---

p. 37 and Pierre Béhar and Helen Watanabe-O'Kelly, *Spectaculum Europaeum: Theatre and Spectacle in Europe (1580–1750)/Histoire du Spectacle en Europe (1580–1750)* (Wiesbaden: Harrassowitz, 1999), p. 82. *Commedia dell'arte* could involve acrobatic performers like Alessandro. M.A. Katritsky, 'The Diaries of Prince Ferdinand of Bavaria: *Commedia dell'Arte* at the Wedding Festivals of Florence (1565) and Munich (1568)', in J.R. Mulryne and Margaret Shewring (eds), *Italian Renaissance Festivals and their European Influence* (Lewiston: Edwin Mellen Press, 1992), p. 151–2.

[50]   Tinghi, *Diario*, p. 116.

[51]   Ibid., p. 117. It is curious that Tinghi does not mention the '*palio delle seggiolette*'. In his brief remarks about this Ice Festival, Solerti asserts that Ferdinando was in Pisa preparing for Carnival at the time of the festival. Solerti, *Musica*, p. 35. Tinghi, however, writes in his diary that the grand duke was in Pescia.

one hundred and twenty days without rain and the river was so low because of this drought that the ice hardened with such a great cold. It is a great wonder.]

With his fondness for comic entertainment, one can imagine the grand duke's disappointment in missing the Florentine festivities.[52]

Despite bad weather, on 7 February, Ferdinando and his court travelled to Pisa where they would spend the Carnival season: '*sendo il tempo cativo S.A. dopo desinare si parti da livorno con tutta la Corte et se ne venne a pisa in carroza a fare il Carnovale*' ('in bad weather, His Highness left Livorno with all the court after dining, and he went to Pisa in his coach for Carnival').[53] Though there were days when the grand duke spent time hunting and dealing with '*negoti importanti*' ('important business matters'), Carnival festivities were celebrated over a fifteen-day period (8–22 February), longer in duration than in the immediately preceding and following years. A review of the principal civic entertainments from 1602–08 reveals a shift in court-sponsored Carnival activities in Pisa where more public events occurred after the Ice Festival in December 1604 (Table 12.1).[54]

Table 12.1   The principal civic entertainments in Pisa from 1602–1608. © Mary M. Young.

Event	1602	1603	1604	1605	1606	1607	1608
Battaglia del Ponte	✓	✓	✓	✓	✓	✓	✓
Giostra alla "Cintana"	✓		✓	✓			
Giostra al "Saracino"				✓	✓	✓	✓
Palio				✓			✓

[52]   Saslow, *The Medici Wedding*, pp. 123–4, 160.

[53]   Tinghi, *Diario*, p. 119v.

[54]   Tinghi began his diary on 22 July 1600. For the first year, he did not write on a daily basis. His first entry regarding Carnival in 1601 is a meagre acknowledgment that the grand duke travelled to Pisa, '*a fare il Carnovale*' on 22 February (Tinghi, *Diario*, p. 9v). For Carnival in 1605, Tinghi devotes eight pages to descriptions of the entertainments. In his discussion of the jousts that were held in the piazza between the grand duke's palace and the church of San Nicola, Tinghi makes a clear distinction between the '*Correre alla Cintana*' on 17 February and the '*visare il seracino*' on 21 February. After its introduction in 1604, the *giostra al saracino* seems to have replaced the '*giostra alla Cintana*' in the following three years. Tinghi, *Diario*, pp. 120v, 121v. See Plaisance, *Florence*, p. 106 note 20 regarding '*chintana*' and '*quintana*'. In his study of the 1589 wedding, Saslow notes that there were two different jousts, one '*alla quintana*' and a '*corso al saracino*'. Saslow, *The Medici Wedding*, pp. 164, 171.

Event	1602	1603	1604	1605	1606	1607	1608
Palio-Navicelli				✓			✓
Caccia				✓			

Having missed the *festa* on 31 December, the grand duke may have ordered an expansion of court-sponsored activities in Pisa in response to the spectacular nature of the Ice Festival in Florence. In his journal, Tinghi notes the presence of Florentines in Pisa for Carnival: '*Molte fiorentine, Dame fiorentine le quali erono venute a pisa a fare il Carnovale*' ('many Florentines, Florentine women who came to Pisa for Carnival').[55] One might assume that those Florentines who had observed, or participated in, the recent ice *festa* would make a comparison of the two celebrations. At least two nobles were involved in both, Bartolomeo Betini and Don Virginio.[56] Regardless, it appears that Pisan citizens benefited from the 1604 Florentine festival, with more activities planned for the amusement of the public.

In the three years before the ice *festa* in Florence, Tinghi comments on Carnival entertainment in terms of pleasure for the aristocracy: '*al Gran Principe, nobilita, gentildonne et gentil[u]omini*' ('the Great Prince, the nobility, gentlewomen and gentlemen').[57] In 1605, however, his language changes to include remarks about the public as spectators, as he notes the grand duke's desire to provide pleasure to all the people: '*dare un poco di piacere al popolo pisano*', '*... a tutti il popolo Pisano*', '*... alla cita*' ('give a little pleasure to the people of Pisa, to all the people of Pisa, to the city') and the public's appreciation of those efforts '*con grandisimo gusto d' tutto il popolo*', '*il popolo ebbe gran piacere*' ('with the greatest enthusiasm of all the people', 'the people had great delight').[58] The diarist's attention to *il popolo* evokes the language of the Ice Festival text that emphasizes the '*publica ricreazione*' and the amusement of *il popolo*.[59] Despite fewer public activities for Carnival in the following two years, Tinghi writes enthusiastically about Carnival in 1608, a spirited season with many entertainments that were enjoyed by '*tutto il popolo di Pisa*'.[60] This was the grand duke's last Carnival. He died on 7 February 1609.

[55] Tinghi, *Diario*, pp. 120, 120v.

[56] Bartolomeo Betini was in the '*saracino*' joust on 21 February and Don Virginio was in the '*sbarra*' on 22 February. Tinghi, *Diario*, pp. 121v and 123.

[57] Ibid., pp. 23, 48, 49.

[58] Tinghi discusses the Carnival season and the entertainments on pages 119v–123.

[59] Regarding '*publica ricreazione*', see *Relazione*, p. 3. Acknowledgement of '*il popolo*' is throughout the festival text. Tinghi notes that the grand duke was interested in entertainment for the people when he wanted to provide a *palio* for the citizens for the Feast of Saint Bartholomew on 24 August 1604 – '*dare un poco di piacere et spasso al popolo ... il quale cosi si fece con gran gusto del Popolo*' ('gave a little pleasure and recreation to the people ... which was done with the great enthusiasm of the people'). Tinghi, *Diario*, p. 103.

[60] Tinghi, *Diario*, p. 203. Tinghi also comments on the attendance and enjoyment of '*tutto la cita d'Pisa*' at the Saracen joust in 1606, 150v. He describes only three days of

The Message of the Ice Festival

Like many festival books that were commissioned by European courts, the 1604 text conveyed a message of political propaganda. In the case of the ice *festa*, the successful entertainments communicated to the reader that the citizens could respond to an unpredicted weather event and enjoy a spontaneous celebration. The swift and clever response of the Florentines was certainly a positive reflection on Ferdinando and his city. As the grand duke's stand-in, Don Virginio effectively orchestrated a festival that would have likely pleased his uncle.[61] In his study of this Florentine ruler, Samuel Berner asserts that Ferdinando was 'a shrewd merchant-prince who directs his expenditures only into conspicuous areas which will assure him stature and prestige. At the same time, with little or no cost to himself, he is able to play the rôle of a patron to popular causes ... In Duke Ferdinand, ostentatiousness and frugality were not mutually exclusive'.[62] In financial terms, the Ice Festival is consistent with the grand duke's thrifty approach in executing political strategy. Because this public *festa* was arranged at short notice, the participants probably recycled old costumes, accessories and pageant carts. With the ice as a platform for free entertainment, costs were kept to a minimum.

Apart from the official message that Florence was an organized and harmonious society, the festival and festival book may also reflect Medici foreign policy. Early in the text, the author notes the unexpected arrival of a foreign dignitary, Don Antonio di Sandoval, an emissary for the Spanish ambassador in Rome ('*mandato dal Signor Marchese di Vigliena Ambasciador di S. Maestà Cattolica in Roma*').[63] Though arrangements for a festival may have been underway when the Spanish visitor arrived in Florence, it is apparent that Don Antonio di Sandoval was an important guest. The author refers to him in the text on several occasions,

---

Carnival events for the year 1607.

[61]   For information on Ferdinando I, see Samuel Berner, 'Florentine Society in the Late Sixteenth and Early Seventeenth Centuries', *Studies in the Renaissance*, 18 (1971), pp. 203–46; Suzanne B. Butters, 'Ferdinando de' Medici and the Art of the Possible', *The Medici, Michelangelo, and the Art of Late Renaissance Florence* (New Haven; Detroit: Yale University Press; in association with the Detroit Institute of Arts, 2002), pp. 66–75; Hale, *Florence and the Medici*, pp. 150–65; Hibbert, *The Rise and Fall*, pp. 279–81; Saslow, *The Medici Wedding*, pp. 10–16. Saslow writes that there is no complete biography of Ferdinando, p. 268 note 15.

[62]   Berner, 'Florentine Society', pp. 208–10. See also Saslow, *The Medici Wedding*, pp. 33, 45, 178. Berner and Saslow cite Robert Dallington's 1596 assessment of Ferdinando: 'sparing is a great revenue'. In his discussion of Ferdinando's 1589 wedding, Saslow notes that the nobility underwrote the costs for pageant floats and chariots.

[63]   *Relazione*, p. 4. According to the festival text, Florence was a brief stop for Don Antonio di Sandoval on his journey between Rome and Parma. See the Medici Archive Project regarding Juan Fernández Pacheco, Marquis of Villena and Duke of Escalona, who became the Spanish ambassador in Rome in 1603 and was the viceroy of Sicily from 1607–10.

including his arrival and stay at the Palazzo Pitti, his specific location for viewing the activities on the ice, and his invitation to a celebratory feast at the end of the evening with Don Virginio at the home of Carlo di Bardi. At the time of the Ice Festival, Ferdinando was in particular need of the Spanish king's acknowledgment of his rights with regard to Siena and Portoferraio, privileges that were initially secured by Cosimo I in 1557 from Philip II. Because the investiture only applied to Portoferraio on Elba, the rest of the island was under the direct authority of Spain.[64] After he became grand duke following the death of his brother in 1587, Ferdinando received notice that the Spanish king had renewed the investiture in June 1588.[65] But when Philip II died in 1598, the grand duke again needed his authority to be recognized by the Spanish king's successor, Philip III. This did not happen until 26 March 1605, in Valladolid, in a formal procedure that was administered by the Duke of Lerma.[66]

In the months leading up to the investiture, Ferdinando made numerous overtures to the Spanish court through a calculated program of gifts.[67] In letters to Sallustio Tarugi, the Medici ambassador in Spain, the grand duke discusses the many and varied offerings that he wanted to bestow upon members of the Spanish court in order to influence and hasten the investiture. In one dated 20 December, Ferdinando refers to tapestries, linens, jewelry, money and even the home of his deceased brother Pietro de' Medici.[68] One of the Spanish recipients was Don Francisco Gómez de Sandoval y Rojas, Duke of Lerma. Wielding great influence over Philip III, the Duke of Lerma was known to promote members of his own family within the Spanish court.[69] Considering that Sandoval was the name of the

---

[64]   Eve Borsook, 'Art and Politics at the Medici Court I: The Funeral of Cosimo I de' Medici', *Mitteilungen des Kunsthistorischen Institutes in Florenz* (December 1965), pp. 35–6. In addition to Siena and Portoferraio, Borsook notes the rights to the Maremma. She also writes that Ferdinando's brother, Francesco I, received the investiture on 19 May 1575, a little over a year after Cosimo I's death on 21 April 1574. Hale, J.R., *Florence and the Medici: The Pattern of Control* (London: Thames and Hudson, 1977), p. 132.

[65]   The Medici Archive Project, MdP 4919, Folio 359, Doc ID 8287 (23 June 1588).

[66]   Edward L. Goldberg, 'Artistic Relations between the Medici and the Spanish Courts, 1587–1621: Part I', *The Burlington Magazine*, vol. 138, no. 1115 (February 1996), pp. 105–114, especially 105, 108–9.

[67]   Ibid., Goldberg discusses the increase in gifts to encourage the investiture. See also Edward L. Goldberg, 'Artistic Relations between the Medici and the Spanish Courts, 1587–1621: Part II', *The Burlington Magazine*, vol. 138, no. 1121 (August 1996), pp. 529–40.

[68]   The Medici Archive Project, MdP 4936, Folio 322, Doc ID 14609 (2 October 1604); MdP 4936, Folio 377, Doc ID 14617 (20 December 1604). Regarding interest in the investiture of Siena and Portoferraio, see also, MdP 5080, Folio 331, Doc ID 9976 (1604). Tinghi notes that Tarugi left on 19 July 1604 on his journey to Spain as the Grand Duke's new ambassador to the Spanish court. Tinghi, *Diario*, p. 99v.

[69]   Antonio Feros, *Kingship and Favoritism in the Spain of Philip III, 1598–1621* (Cambridge: Cambridge University Press, 2000), pp. 94–5.

Spanish dignitary in Florence at the time of the Ice Festival, it is plausible that the visitor named throughout the festival text was related to the Duke of Lerma.[70]

In a letter dated 14 February 1605, Ferdinando demonstrates his frustration to Tarugi over the seeming futility of his offerings to the Spanish court with regard to the investiture.[71] Additionally, the grand duke expressed a concern over the building of a fortress in Porto Longone (today Porto Azzurro) on Elba by the Spanish viceroy of Naples. The proposed fortification, after seventy years of planning (according to Ferdinando), is the subject of much interest in correspondence between the grand duke and Tarugi as well as his brother Giovanni de' Medici.[72] Finally, on 22 April 1605, Tinghi comments on the arrival of a communication from Spain regarding the investiture: '*un corriero venuto di Spagnia da quella Corona che portava e privilegi a S.A.S. della investiture dello stato di Siena et la investitura di porto ferraio nel isola del elba*' ('a messenger from the Spanish ruler brought the privileges of the investiture of the state of Siena and Portoferraio on the island of Elba'). Along with news of the birth of Philip III's son (the future Philip IV), the long awaited achievement was celebrated in jubilant style by the grand duke as well as the citizens of Pisa: '*S.A. per alegreza fece fare fuochi luminare et gran salva dartigliere alla fortezza di pisa e per 3 sere continue con gran alegria di tutto il popolo*' ('out of joy, His Highness arranged fireworks and a great artillery salute at the fortress of Pisa and this continued for three nights to the great delight of the people').[73] At the time of the Ice Festival, Ferdinando was probably feeling political pressure with the delayed investiture and the proposed fortress on Elba. The grand duke would have certainly seized any opportunity to demonstrate good will toward the Spanish court. Considering his close relationship with his uncle and his involvement in Ferdinando's political affairs, Don Virginio would have probably known of Ferdinando's eagerness to secure the investiture. In light of the escalation of gifts to the Spanish court, Don Antonio di Sandoval's prominent recognition in the official festival book might then be considered as an additional offering to Philip III.[74]

---

[70]   The family connection cannot be firmly established for this paper.

[71]   The Medici Archive Project, MdP 4936, Folio 441, Doc ID 14624 (14 February 1605).

[72]   Ibid., MdP 4936, Folio 402, Doc ID 17291 (1604); MdP 4936, Folio 404, Doc ID 17292 (1604); MdP 5157, Folio 43, Doc ID 8627 (25 February 1604); MdP 4936, Folio 405, Doc ID 942 (12 January 1605); MdP 4936, Folio 434, Doc ID 17311 (6 February 1605); MdP 4936, Folio 419, Doc ID 17300 (1605).

[73]   Tinghi, *Diario*, p. 130.

[74]   See Berner, 'Florentine Society', p. 209, for his discussion of the grand duke's generosity toward foreign dignitaries.

Conclusion

An unforeseen occurrence, the frozen Arno River, presented an opportunity for a public celebration and a promotion of the Florentine state. The combination of unexpected weather, the involvement of a prominent member of the Medici family and the surprise arrival of a distinguished guest, provided an unusual opportunity to stage a winter carnival. An examination of the 1604 festival book reveals that this celebration was consistent with Medici grand ducal festival practices, a strong tradition that allowed for the success of this winter *festa* as a spontaneous event. The procession of exotic pageant carts and nobles dressed as allegorical figures, the inclusion of tournament games, fireworks and a commemorative book reflect basic elements of established grand ducal celebrations. And yet, the slippery field created an occasion for the Florentines to demonstrate their adaptability and express their creativity with innovative forms of equipment and competitions. The frozen piazza became a stage for public theatre, a rare space for new forms of pageantry, competition and comedy.

Beginning with the first sentence of the festival book, the author acknowledges the power of nature and its role in creating a '*maraviglia*' ('wonder'): '*La stagione asciutta, et senza piover già tanti mesi, et il verno entrato con tanto rigore cagionarono in questo fiume d'Arno una maraviglia non più accaduta nel corso di circa 60 anni*' ('The dry season, and without rain for many months, and winter arrived with much severity and caused in this Arno River a marvel that had not happened in about sixty years').[75] While Florentines may have harnessed nature's '*accidente prodigioso*' ('wonderful accident') in late December 1604 and used it to their advantage, the slippery ice still governed the activities.[76] As understood from the festival text, much of the success of this event stemmed from the comic disorder that arose from the participants' lack of control over their environment. In the case of the ice festivities, nature enhanced the activities and the spectacle. Nature's unpredictability is what made this celebration so extraordinary. A study of the festival book and the Medici court diary suggests that the Ice Festival may have influenced Carnival activities in Pisa and presented an opportunity for an important diplomatic gesture. Regardless of any cultural or political consequences concerning Pisa or Spain, the entertainments were a serendipitous gift to the Florentines. For one remarkable day in the winter of 1604, the Arno River was transformed into a delightful, icy festival playground. Though all traces of the *festa* would disappear with the melting ice, the festival book ensures that '*la memoria sarà portata per l'età*' ('the memory will be carried through the ages').[77]

---

[75]   *Relazione*, p. 3.

[76]   Ibid., See Saslow, *The Medici Wedding*, pp. 123, 135, 148, for his discussion of 'art and nature' and the notion of 'theater as a space of controlled artifice'.

[77]   *Relazione*, p. 16.

Bibliography

Primary Sources

Florio, John, *Queen Anna's New World of Words, or Dictionarie of the Italian and English Tongues, Collected, and newly much augmented by Iohn Florio, Reader of the Italian vnto the Soueraigne Maiestie of Anna, Crowned Queene of England, Scotland, France and Ireland, &c. And one of the Gentlemen of hir Royall Priuie Chamber. Whereunto are added certaine necessarie rules and short observations for the Italian tongue* (London, 1611). <http://www.pbm.com/~lindahl/florio>.

Relazione delle feste fatte in Fiorenza sopra il ghiaccio del fiume d'Arno l'ultimo di di dicembre MDCIV (Florence: Allessandro Guiducci, 1604) <http://warburg.sas.ac.uk/mnemosyne/DigitalCollections.htm>.

Relazione delle feste fatte in Firenze. Sopra il ghiaccio del fiume d'Arno l'vltimo dì di Dicembre MDCIV (Florence: Bartolomeo Semartelli, 1604) <http://www.bl.uk/treasures/festivalbooks/homepage.html>.

Tinghi, Cesare, *Diario di Ferdinando I e Cosimo II gran Duca di Toscana scritto da Cesare Tinghi da' 22 luglio 1600 sino a' 12 settembre 1615* (Biblioteca Nazionale Centrale di Firenze. Fondo Gino Capponi 261, vol. 1).

Secondary Sources

Béhar, Pierre and Helen Watanabe-O'Kelly, *Spectaculum Europaeum: Theatre and Spectacle in Europe (1580–1750)/Histoire du Spectacle en Europe (1580–1750)* (Wiesbaden: Harrassowitz, 1999).

Berner, Samuel, 'Florentine Society in the Late Sixteenth and Early Seventeenth Centuries', *Studies in the Renaissance*, 18 (1971), pp. 203–46.

Blumenthal, Arthur, R., *Theater Art of the Medici*, exhibition catalogue (Hanover, NH: Dartmouth College Museum and the University Press of New England, 1980).

Borsook, Eve, 'Art and Politics at the Medici Court I: The Funeral of Cosimo I de' Medici', *Mitteilungen des Kunsthistorischen Institutes in Florenz* (December 1965), pp. 31–54.

Borsook, Eve, *The Companion Guide to Florence* (London: Collins, 1988).

Brucker, Gene, *Florence: The Golden Age, 1138-1737* (Berkeley and Los Angeles: University of California Press, 1998).

Butters, Suzanne B., 'Ferdinando de' Medici and the Art of the Possible', *The Medici, Michelangelo, and the Art of Late Renaissance Florence* (New Haven; Detroit: Yale University Press; in association with the Detroit Institute of Arts, 2002), pp. 66–75.

Chrétien, Heidi L., *The Festival of San Giovanni: Imagery and Political Power in Renaissance Florence* (New York: Peter Lang, 1994).

Cochrane, Eric W., *Florence in the Forgotten Centuries, 1527-1800: A History of Florence and the Florentines in the Age of the Grand Dukes* (Chicago: University of Chicago Press, 1973).

'Diario Istorico Fiorentino d'Autore Anonimo Dal 1600 al 1640', in *Notizie Istoriche Italiane scritte e compilate da M.R.* vol. 3 (Florence: Antonio Benucci, 1781).

Else, Felicia M., 'Controlling the Waters of Granducal Florence: A New Look at Stefano Bonsignori's View of the City (1584)', *Imago Mundi*, vol. 61:2 (June 2009), pp. 168–85.

Feros, Antonio, *Kingship and Favoritism in the Spain of Philip III, 1598–1621* (Cambridge: Cambridge University Press, 2000).

Franceschini, Pietro, *Relazione delle Feste Fatte in Firenze sopra il Ghiaccio del Fiume Arno il 31 Dicembre 1604* (Florence: Libreria Popolare, 1885).

Gaeta Bertelà, Giovanna and Annamaria Petrioli Tofani, *Feste e apparati Medicei da Cosimo I a Cosimo II:* exhibition catalogue (Florence: Leo S. Olschki, 1969).

Goldberg, Edward L., 'Artistic Relations between the Medici and the Spanish Courts, 1587–1621: Part I', *The Burlington Magazine*, vol. 138, no. 1115 (February 1996), pp. 105–114.

Goldberg, Edward L., 'Artistic Relations between the Medici and the Spanish Courts, 1587–1621: Part II', *The Burlington Magazine*, vol. 138, no. 1121 (August 1996), pp. 529–40.

Gori, Pietro, *Le Feste Fiorentine Attraverso i Secoli, Le Feste per San Giovanni* (Florence: R. Bemporad & Figlio, 1926; reprinted 1989).

Hale, J.R., *Florence and the Medici* (London: Thames and Hudson, 1977; London: Phoenix Press, 2004).

Hibbert, Christopher, *The Rise and Fall of the House of Medici* (New York: William Morrow & Co., 1975).

Medici Archive Project. < http://www.medici.org/>.

Mulryne, J.R. and Elizabeth Goldring (eds), *Court Festivals of the European Renaissance Art, Politics, and Performance* (Aldershot: Ashgate, 2002).

Mulryne, J.R. and Margaret Shewring (eds), *Italian Renaissance Festivals and their European Influence* (Lewiston: Edwin Mellen Press, 1992).

Mulryne, J.R., Helen Watanabe-O'Kelly and Margaret Shewring (eds), *Europa Triumphans: Court and Civic Festivals in Early Modern Europe* (Aldershot and Burlington, VT: Ashgate, 2004).

Nagler, A.M., *Theatre Festivals of the Medici, 1539–1637*, trans. George Hickenlooper (New Haven: Yale University Press, 1964).

Plaisance, Michel, *Florence in the Time of the Medici: Public Celebrations, Politics, and Literature in the Fifteenth and Sixteenth Centuries*, trans. and (ed.) Nicole Carew-Reid (Toronto: Centre for Reformation and Renaissance Studies, 2008).

Saslow, James M., *The Medici Wedding of 1589: Florentine Festival as 'Theatrum Mundi'* (New Haven: Yale University Press, 1996).

Solerti, Angelo, *Musica, Ballo e Drammatica alla Corte Medicea dal 1600 al 1637* (Florence, 1905; reprint New York and London: Benjamin Blom, 1968).

Strong, Roy C., *Art and Power: Renaissance Festivals, 1450–1650* (Woodbridge: Boydell Press, 1984).

Testaverde, Anna Maria, 'Spectacle, Theater, and Propaganda at the Court of the Medici', *The Medici, Michelangelo, and the Art of Late Renaissance Florence* (New Haven; Detroit: Yale University Press; in association with the Detroit Institute of Arts, 2002), pp. 122–31.

Trexler, Richard C., *Public Life in Renaissance Florence* (Ithaca and London: Cornell University Press, 1991; Originally Published New York and London: Academic Press, 1980).

Veen, Henk Th. Van, *Cosimo I de' Medici and His Self-representation in Florentine Art and Culture*, trans. Andrew P. McCormick (Cambridge: Cambridge University Press, 2006).

Watanabe-O'Kelly, Helen, 'Festival Books in Europe from Renaissance to Rococo', *The Seventeenth Century*, 3 (1988), pp. 181–201.

Watanabe-O'Kelly, Helen and Anne Simon, *Festivals and Ceremonies: A Bibliography of Works Relating to Court, Civic, and Religious Festivals in Europe 1500–1800* (London and New York: Mansell, 2000).

Wyatt, Michael, *The Italian Encounter with Tudor England, A Cultural Politics of Translation* (Cambridge: Cambridge University Press, 2005).

Chapter 13

The Thames *en Fête*

Sydney Anglo

On 10 January 1608, the River Thames invaded James I's brand new Banqueting House at Whitehall. Flooding was, and remained, a common enough occurrence there: indeed Pepys later noted, after an exceptionally high tide in December 1663, that all Whitehall had been 'drowned'.[1] In 1608, however, the river had not overflowed its banks but was simply 'personated by Master Thomas Giles', dancing master, who – crowned with flowers, and wearing a blue cloth of silver – leaned upon an urn that did, indeed, flow with water. The occasion was Jonson's *Masque of Beautie* in which Vulturnus, a south-easterly wind, addressed the Thames thus:

> Rise, aged Thames, and by the hand
> Receive these Nymphes, within the land:
> And, in those curious Squares, and Rounds,
> Wherewith thou flow'st betwixt the grounds
> Of fruitfull Kent, and Essex faire,
> That lend thee gyrlands for thy hayre;
> Instruct their silver feete to tread,
> Whilst we, againe to sea, are fled.

There followed a 'most curious Daunce, full of excellent device, and change', which ended in the 'figure of a Diamant'. Then a second dance – 'more subtle, and full of change, then the former' – was so exquisitely performed that the King demanded an encore.[2]

Of course, I am stretching a point because, while this particular Thames rose, flowed and reached the sea, and was clearly part of a *fête*, it was a dancing master and the masquers (not the river itself) who were *en fête*. Precisely how the flow of the river was choreographed remains a matter for conjecture: but the virtuosic dances clearly constituted the principal feature of the entertainment; and they especially interested King James who could be bored to a frenzy by Jonson's

---

[1]   *The Diary of Samuel Pepys: a new and complete transcription*, ed. Robert Latham and William Matthews (11 vols, London: Bell, 1970–86), vol. 4 (1971), p. 406.

[2]   Ben Jonson, *Works*, ed. C.H. Herford and Percy and Evelyn Simpson (11 vols, Oxford: Clarendon Press, 1925–52), vol. 7 (1941), pp. 191–2.

versifying.[3] But the difficulty with court masques, as has often been noted, is that we are too dependent upon surviving texts. Scenographic sources are inadequate; masque music is only fitfully available; and the hieroglyphic dances – such as the mysterious movements of the Thames – can scarcely be reconstituted at all. The masque has been left prey to literary gentlemen; and poets and poetasters have assumed a prominence which would have astonished contemporaries for whom costume, spectacle and dancing were pre-eminent. All this is common knowledge: but it is a necessary prolegomenon because, although I should like to discuss the Thames *en fête*, some important aspects of the subject are poorly documented – or, perhaps I should say, have not been documented at all.

For John Taylor, the McGonagall of Stuart England, no river in the world was superior to the Thames:

> What doth it doe, but serves our full contents,
> Brings food, and for it, takes our excrements.[4]

A beautiful sentiment! The river certainly was London's sewer; but it was also its main highway. The great royal palaces – Greenwich, Hampton Court, Richmond, Sheen, Westminster and Whitehall – were situated along its banks, and barges were the favoured mode of transport when monarchs moved from one palace to another. Royal barges, the barges of lesser dignitaries, and those used by important foreign visitors, were regularly seen on the Thames as, for example, in 1586 when Henry Ramelius, the Danish Ambassador, 'during the time of his tariance had the Queenes Majesties barges and servants imploied about him' back and forth from Greenwich to London.[5] Spectacles of this sort were colourful and attractive, but so usual that contemporaries took them for granted and scarcely bothered to describe them.

Londoners were inevitably more stirred by the rare and exotic. Mock battles and firework displays on the Thames attracted a good deal of attention, and there are some spirited accounts of shows such as the pre-coronation river procession of Elizabeth of York in November 1486, when the *Bachelers Barge*, 'garnysshed and apparellede, passing all other' carried a 'great red Dragon spowtyng Flamys of Fyer into Temmys'.[6] Three years later there was a similar display for the creation of Arthur as Prince of Wales. Henry VII entered his barge at Sheen and proceeded down the river, picking up *en route* numerous dignitaries with their trumpeters and

---

[3]   The prime example of this is James's response to Jonson's *Pleasure Reconciled to Virtue*, when he gave vent to his 'natura colerica' and cursed the masquers roundly for not getting on with the dancing. See Herford and Simpson, vol. 10 (1950), p. 583.

[4]   John Taylor, *The Praise of hemp-seed ... Concluding commendations of the famous river of Thames* (London, 1620), sig. F3v.

[5]   John Nichols, *The Progresses and Public Processions of Queen Elizabeth* (3 vols, London, 1823), vol. 2, pp. 458, 460.

[6]   John Leland, *De Rebus Britannicis Collectanea*, ed. Thomas Hearne (6 vols, London: G. and J. Richardson, 1770), vol. 4, pp. 18–34.

minstrels. These were then joined at Chelsea by the Mayor's barge together with 'all the Craftes in their Barges, empareilled with Banyeres and Penons royally beseene'; and there was a further augmentation at Lambeth when the Spanish ambassadors and 'many Marchauntes of their Nacion in Ship Bottes', joined the show, 'shutting Gownnes in greate Nombre. And after, casting Apples as it had bene in fighting on the See with Targes, all in Rejoyshing of the Princes Comyng.'[7] It does not sound very serious: though the impact of a pippin on the ear might have been painful. And accidents did happen as when, in June 1536, there were 'ordained two Lighters made like ships to fight upon the water, one of which brast in the midst, whereby one Gates, gentleman, a servant of Master Knevets was drowned in his harness … [and] In the other, a gunn brast her chamber, and maimed two of the mariners'.[8] Exciting as such spectacles must have been, they were unusual: perhaps only eight or so between 1487 and 1612.[9]

Even rarer were the strangest Thames shows of all when the river was frozen over and a great frost fair could be held on the ice, as in 1608, which is described in a pamphlet, *The Great Frost. Cold doings in London*;[10] and again in 1621, immortalized by John Taylor in his inimitable fashion:

> The liquid Thames each where from shore to shore,
> With colde bak'd Paste, all pastycrusted o're …
> But once againe, Ile turne me to my Theame,
> Of the conglutinated Frozen streame:
> Upon whose Glassie face both too and fro,
> Five hundred people all at once did goe.[11]

However, the problem for us lies elsewhere and is highlighted by the shows accompanying the inauguration of each Lord Mayor. This was the London festival *par excellence*, with an almost unbroken history from the fourteenth century onwards; and, from 1422 (when Sir William Walderne was the first Mayor to travel to Westminster by barge) right up to 1856, the progress through the city

---

[7]   Ibid., vol. 4, pp. 250–53.

[8]   Robert Withington, *English Pageantry: an Historical Outline* (2 vols, Cambridge, Mass: Harvard University Press, 1918–26; repr. New York: B. Blom, 1963) vol. 1, p. 98, citing Harleian MS. 540, fol. 9v.

[9]   There were, for example, water battles in 1550, before Edward VI at Deptford; in 1610, for Prince Henry's creation as Prince of Wales; and in 1612 for the Palatine marriage. See *Literary Remains of King Edward the Sixth*, ed. John Gough Nichols (2 vols, London: J.B. Nichols and Sons, 1857), vol. 2, p. 279; John Nichols (ed.), *The Progresses, Processions, and Magnificent Festivities of King James the First* (2 vols, London, 1828), vol. 2, pp. 322–3, 536–41.

[10]   *The Great Frost. Cold doings in London, except it be at the lotterie* (London, 1608).

[11]   John Taylor, *The colde tearme, or, the frozen age, or, The metamorphosis of the River Thames* (London, 1621).

was preceded by a brilliant procession of livery barges on the Thames. It was an annual event: but it is not well documented. Here, for example, is the diarist Henry Machyn on the Lord Mayor taking to the water in October 1555:

> There were ij goodly pennes [pinnaces] deekyd with gones and flages and stremars, and am. penselles [pennons], the penes pentyd on whyt and bluw, and thodur yelow and red, and the oars and gownes lyke coler; and with trumpets and drumes, and alle the craftes in barges and stremars; and at the ix of the cloke my nuw lord mayre and the shreyffes and the althermen toke barge at the iij Cranes with trumpets and shalmes, and the whetes playhyng; and so rod to Westmynster, and toke ys othe in the cheyker; and all the way the penoys shutyng of gones and playhyng up and done; and so after cam backe to Powlles warffe, and landyd with gret shutyng of gownes and playng.[12]

This passage is frequently cited, but it does not tell us very much; and, while it is true that Machyn was an undertaker and better on funerals than festivals, it must be conceded that no contemporary did any better.

What, in fact, was there to say? The water processions were splendid, of course, but they were always more or less the same, so that when you have described one flotilla with flying pennons and the noise of trumpets, gunshot and so forth, you have described them all. They really were the Thames *en fête*: but historians have, on the whole, concentrated attention on those occasions after 1585 for which texts survive: and in those printed accounts of mayoral pageantry, the processions of barges are usually ignored, and the water shows tend (paradoxically) to be swamped by those on land. Nonetheless, there was almost always an introductory speech and an opening pageant or two which, as the pamphlets noted, were set 'on the water' – that is on flat-bottomed barges or rafts (literally 'floats') – and these had some relevance to water in general or, more specifically, to the Thames itself.[13] A few examples should serve to demonstrate the limitations of words when it comes to conveying the essence of these public spectacles.[14]

---

[12]   *The Diary of Henry Machyn, citizen and merchant-taylor of London, from A.D. 1550 to A.D. 1563*, ed. John Gough Nichols (London: J.B. Nichols and Son, 1848), p. 96.

[13]   These floats are clearly shown in Dirck Stoop's etching of the Lord Mayor and Corporation of London meeting Charles II and Catherine of Braganza on their arrival at Whitehall from Hampton Court on 23 August 1662. The show, *Aqua Triumphalis*, was devised by John Tatham. The scene at Whitehall is clearly reproduced in Kenneth Nicholls Palmer, *Ceremonial Barges on the River Thames. A History of the Barges of the City of London Livery Companies and of the Crown* (London: Unicorn Press, 1997), p. 10.

[14]   On the Lord Mayors' pageants, see Withington, *English Pageantry*; and David M. Bergeron, *English Civic Pageantry 1558–1642* (London: Edward Arnold, 1971). The study of the printed texts has been hugely facilitated by their availability via *Early English Books Online*.

The earliest text (recording George Peele's show for 1585) unfortunately only prints the speeches without any scene-setting, so we cannot tell whether the nymph, representing the River Thames, spoke her verse on land or water – although the latter is more likely:

> With silver glide my pleasant streames doo runne,
> Where leaping fishes play betwixt the shores;
> This gracious good hath God and kinde begun,
> For Londons use with help of Sailes and Ores.[15]

In 1591, however, a sea nymph *certainly* delivered a speech 'on the water' at the Lord Mayor's embarking for Westminster; and in 1611 there were not only speeches when the Mayor took to his barge, but also sea-fights and skirmishes 'actively performed both in the passage on to Westminster, and back again'.[16] Thomas Dekker devised the next show, *Troia-Nova Triumphans* (1612), and included spectacles on the water: although, as he writes dismissively at the end of the printed pamphlet:

> The Title-page of this *Booke* makes promise of all the Shewes by water, as of these on the Land; but Apollo having no hand in them, I suffer them to dye by that which fed them; that is to say Powder and Smoake. Their thunder (according to the old gally-foyst-fashion) was too lowd for any of the Nine Muses to be bidden to it.[17]

Much more interesting is the show for the inauguration of Sir Thomas Hayes, Draper, in 1614. This was the work of Anthony Munday (himself a member of the Drapers' Company) and purports to describe the origin of the water procession. Until the year 1453, says Munday, the Lord Mayors of London 'used to ride on horsebacke to Westminster at such time as each one went to take his oath'. But then Sir John Norman (like the current Mayor, a Draper) decided to build, at his own expense, a 'very goodly Barge for himself and his Brethren, to be rowed therein by water, and so to continue for a yearely custome.' The vessel was expensive, and the oars were said to be covered in silver: 'in memorie

---

[15]   George Peele, *The Device of the Pageant borne before Woolstone Dixi lord maior of the citie of London* (London, 1585), sig. A3.

[16]   George Peele, *The Device of a Pageant, borne before M. William Web, Lord Maior of the Citie of London* (London, 1591), sig. A4; Anthony Munday, *Chruso-thriambos. The Triumphes of Golde, At the inauguration of Sir James Pemberton* (London, 1611), sig. A3.

[17]   Thomas Dekker, *Troia-Nova Triumphans. London Triumphing* (London, 1612), sig. D1v. On the galley-foist (a small square rigged gun-boat) see David Carnegie, 'Galley-foists, Lord Mayors' Shows, and Early Modern English Drama', *Early Theatre*, 7/2 (2004), pp. 48–71.

whereof, and the honest benefite yerely found thereby, the Watermen made a pleasant song called *Rowe thy Boate Norman*'.[18] This was, as a matter of fact, the *second* time a Mayor had been rowed to his inauguration, although it is true that Norman was the first to have a barge especially built for his company's use.[19] In any case, the story gave Munday a good introduction for his show:

> This honour, beginning likewise in the Draper, and falling out so fitly to help our invention: in a goodly faire Barge, made meete for the purpose, attendeth the supposed shadow of Sir John Norman, with the seaven liberall Sciences (all attired like graceful Ladies) sitting about him, untill such time as the Lord Maior commeth to take water.

The ghost of Sir John Norman summarizes the history of his innovation, before 'divers sweet singing youths', choristers of St Paul's, 'sing a most sweet dittie of Rowe thy Boate Norman' as they pretend to propel the barge towards Westminster with their silver oars.[20]

In the following year (1615), Munday again devised the show for another Draper (Sir John Jolles) who was greeted on the water by two vessels. The first, 'rowed by divers comely Eunuches', was a 'goodly Argoe, shaped so neere as Art could yeeld it, to that of such auncient and honourable fame as convaied Jason and his valiant Argonautes of Greece to fetch away the golden fleece from Colchos'. This was obviously appropriate to the Drapers' Company; although Jolles may have been puzzled by Medea playing with Jason's 'love-lockes and wantoning him in all pleasing dalliance'. I wonder what they did?[21] It is also worth noting, *en passant*, that novelty was not Munday's strongest suit. He dished up another Argo for a Draper Mayor in 1623, and he had a marked predilection for defunct civic dignitaries.[22] In 1615 the second vessel, provided by Neptune and the Thames, was a sea chariot shaped like a whale, wherein sat the ghost of yet another Draper, Sir Henry Fitz-Alwain who, in the reign of Richard I, had become the first Mayor of London and who now addressed his successor in a 'Speech on the Water'.

---

[18]   For the London chronicles reporting the origins of the song, see A.H. Thomas and I.D. Thornley (eds), *The Great Chronicle of London* (London: George W. Jones, 1938), pp. 186–7, 425. There have been several attempts to recover the words of the ditty: but none offer more than mere, and unconvincing, conjecture.

[19]   In 1422 Sir William Walderne was the first Mayor to travel to Westminster by barge. On the Thames barges, see Palmer, *Ceremonial Barges on the River Thames*.

[20]   Anthony Munday, *Himatia-Poleos. The triumphs of old draperie* (London, 1614), pp. 9–10.

[21]   Anthony Munday, *Metropolis coronata, the triumphes of ancient drapery; or Rich cloathyng in England* (London, 1615), sig. A3v–4.

[22]   On Munday's second Argo, see *The Triumphs of the Golden Fleece* (London, 1623), sig. A3v–4.

The 'ancient and right worshipful Company of Fishmongers' provided the next Mayor but – presumably because there was no versifying fishmonger to be found – Munday duly obliged with *The Golden Fishing* in which, true to form, he conjured up another apparition. This time it was Sir William Walworth, the fighting Fishmonger, who had, in 1381, slain the insurgent Wat Tyler.[23] The shows 'upon the water first' had depicted a 'Fishing busse' in which fishermen were 'seriously at labour drawing up their nets, laden with living fish, and bestowing them bountifully among the people'; and then, symbolic of the Company, there was a crowned Dolphin, ridden by Arion 'a famous Musician and Poet', because the dolphin is 'a fish inclined much (by nature) to Musique'.

There were two 'presentments' on the water in 1620 in the pageants devised by John Squire for the new Mayor, Sir Francis Jones – a text which, unusually, includes the words and music for a song sung by the Muses on Mount Parnassus.[24] Similarly, in 1624, John Webster provided 'for the more amplefying the shew upon the water, two Eminent Spectacles, in maner of a Sea-Triumph'. The first of these was a conventional affair which included Thetis, the Thames, the Medway and Oceanus (who had already appeared four years earlier). But the second was a 'Terrestiall Globe with seaven of our most famous Navigators', that is to say Drake, Hawkins, Frobisher, Gilbert, Cavendish, Carleill and Davis, 'who have made England so famous in remotest partes of the world'.[25]

For my last two examples of Lord Mayors' shows, I return to Thomas Dekker who, in 1628, tried his hand again with *Britannia's Honor*, the 'first salutation' of which was on the water and 'furnished with persons and properties fitting the quality of that Element'. Atop an artificial rock, flanked by two mermaids, sat Amphitrite, 'Queene of the Seas', wearing fantastic headgear 'made out of a Fishes writhen shell' and surmounted by 'an Artificiall moving Tortoyse'.[26] Then, in the following year (1629), Dekker provided a speech for the Sea God, Oceanus, who cannot say enough in praise of London's river. Even the Rhine, Volga, Ganges, Nile, 'long haired Euphrates' and the Tagus whose 'golden handes claspe Lisbone walles':

> Were they all here, they would weepe out there eyes,
> Madde that new Troys high towers on tiptoe rize
> To hit Heauens Roofe: Madde to see Thames this day
> (For all his age) in wanton windinges play …
> That Grand Canal where stately once a yeare
> A fleete of bridal Gondoletts appeare,
> To marry with a golden ring (thats Hurld,
> Into the sea) That minion of the world

23   *Chrysanaleia. The Golden Fishing: or Honour of Fishmongers* (London, 1616), sig. D1.

24   John Squire, *Tes Irenes Trophaea, or, The Tryumphs of Peace* (London, 1620), sigs. B1v–2.

25   John Webster, *Monuments of Honour* (London, 1624), sig. A3v.

26   Thomas Dekker, *Britannia's Honor: Brightly Shining in severall Magnificent Shewes or Pageants* (London, 1628), sig. A4r–v.

> Venice to Neptune, – A poore Lantscip is,
> To theis full Braveries of Thamesis.[27]

'Presentments' on the water were organized year after year. Their themes were conventional; and the poets continued to trundle out their platitudinous classical allusions without telling us much about the appearance or scale of the shows. However, Dekker's comparison between the festivals on the Thames and those of Venice may not be as far-fetched as it seems. Dirck Stoop's etching of the 1662 river spectacle for Catherine of Braganza suggests that Londoners had a capacity for brilliant displays on their river which the written texts simply do not convey.

Bibliography

Primary Sources

Anon., *The Great Frost. Cold doings in London, except it be at the lotterie* (London, 1608).

Dekker, Thomas, *Britannia's Honor: Brightly Shining in severall Magnificent Shewes or Pageants* (London, 1628).

Dekker, Thomas, *Londons Tempe, or, The Feild of Happines* (London, 1629).

Dekker, Thomas, *Troia-Nova Triumphans. London Triumphing* (London, 1612).

Jonson, Ben, *Works*, ed. C.H. Herford and Percy and Evelyn Simpson, (11 vols, Oxford: Clarendon Press, 1925–52).

Leland, John, *De Rebus Britannicis collectanea*, ed. Thomas Hearne (6 vols, London: G. and J. Richardson, 1770).

Machyn, Henry, *The Diary of Henry Machyn, citizen and merchant-tailor of London, from A.D. 1550 to A.D. 1563*, ed. John Gough Nichols (London: J.B. Nichols and Son, 1848).

Middleton, Thomas, *The Triumphs of Truth* (London, 1613).

Munday, Anthony, *Chruso-thriambos. The Triumphes of Golde. At the Inauguration of Sir James Pemberton* (London, 1611).

Munday, Anthony, *Chrysanaleia. The Golden Fishing: or Honour of Fishmongers* (London, 1616).

Munday, Anthony, *Himatia-Poleos. The triumphs of old draperie* (London, 1614).

Munday, Anthony, *Metropolis coronata, the triumphes of ancient drapery; or Rich cloathyng in England* (London, 1615).

Munday, Anthony, *The Triumphs of the Golden Fleece* (London, 1623).

Nichols, John (ed.), *The Progresses and Public Processions of Queen Elizabeth* (3 vols, London, 1823), vol. 2.

Nichols, John (ed.), *The Progresses, Processions and Magnificent Festivities of King James the First* (2 vols, London, 1828), vol. 2.

---

27   Thomas Dekker, *Londons Tempe, or, The Feild of Happines* (London, 1629), sig. B1.

Nichols, John Gough (ed.), *Literary Remains of King Edward the Sixth* (2 vols, London: J.B. Nichols and Sons, 1857), vol. 2.

Peele, George, *The Device of a Pageant, borne before M. William Web, Lord Maior of the Citie of London* (London, 1591).

Peele, George, *The Device of the Pageant borne before Woolstone Dixi lord maior of the citie of London* (London, 1585).

Pepys, Samuel, *The Diary of Samuel Pepys: a new and complete transcript*, eds Robert Latham and William Matthews (11 vols, London: Bell, 1970–86), vol. 4 (1971).

Squire, John, *Tes Irenes Trophaea, or, The Tryumphs of Peace* (London, 1620).

Taylor, John, *The colde tearme, or, the frozen age, or, The metamorphosis of the River Thames* (London, 1621).

Taylor, John, *The Praise of hemp-seed ... Concluding commendations of the famous river of Thames* (London, 1620).

Thomas, A.H. and I.D. Thornley (eds), *The Great Chronicle of London* (London: George W. Jones, 1938).

Webster, John, *Monuments of Honour* (London, 1624).

Secondary Sources

Bergeron, David M., *English Civic Pageantry 1558–1642* (London: Edward Arnold, 1971).

Carnegie, David, 'Galley-foists, Lord Mayors' Shows, and Early Modern English Drama', *Early Theatre*, 7/2 (2004), 48–71.

Palmer, Kenneth Nicholls, *Ceremonial Barges on the River Thames. A History of the Barges of the City of London Livery Companies and of the Crown* (London: Unicorn Press, 1997).

Withington, Robert, *English Pageantry: an Historical Outline* (2 vols, Cambridge, Mass: Harvard University Press, 1918–26; repr. New York: B. Blom, 1963).

Chapter 14

Royal River: The Watermen's Company and Pageantry on the Thames

Michael Holden

The first volume of a *History of the Company of Watermen and Lightermen* was published in London in 1869, covering the period 1209 to 1699.[1] It provides a journal style history of the Thames, including some unique information, as seen from a waterman's perspective.[Figure 14.1]The *History* also records a number of royal processions and those of the nobility and the merchant companies of the City of London. These processions were expressions of status, and opportunities for royalty and nobility to raise their profile, as well as gain popularity and support amongst the citizenry of this, the largest city in England and one of the largest in Europe.

This chapter briefly illustrates the way in which the many waterborne processions and a small number of *naumachiae* are recorded in the *Watermen's History* for the sixteenth century.[2] While the *History* goes into little detail with regard to events which were repeated year on year, such as the Lord Mayor's annual procession to Whitehall, it does transcribe one source offering a description of a waterborne procession for the accession of Lady Jane Grey, which, if it can be authenticated, may add something to our existing knowledge of this two-week period for which no state and few private records are extant.

The *History's* reliability has to be regarded with some scepticism as the Company's own records were all lost in the fire of London in 1666 and the *History* is a compilation drawn from other sources by a mid-nineteenth-century Clerk of the Company, Henry Humpherus. These sources include parliamentary records, written histories such as Stow, Machin and the Greyfriars Chronicle and manuscripts at the Society of Antiquaries and the British Library, though the quotations tend to be attributed only intermittently. Originally intended to record the Acts of Parliament and other Statutory Regulations relevant to the Company,

---

[1]   Humpherus, Henry, *History of the Origin & Progress of the Company of Watermen and Lightermen of the River Thames with Numerous Historical Notes*, published by the Company in 1874, reprinted 1981 and again in 1999, the edition used here.

[2]   *Naumachiae* are recorded in the entries for 1549 at Deptford, 1561 at Greenwich, 1610 at Westminster, 1613 at Whitehall with a battle staged between Turks and Christians, and 1684 where a pageant includes ships and castles though no sham battle is recorded. Waterborne jousting, using the rushing water beneath London Bridge to propel the boats, is recorded in the 1390 entry.

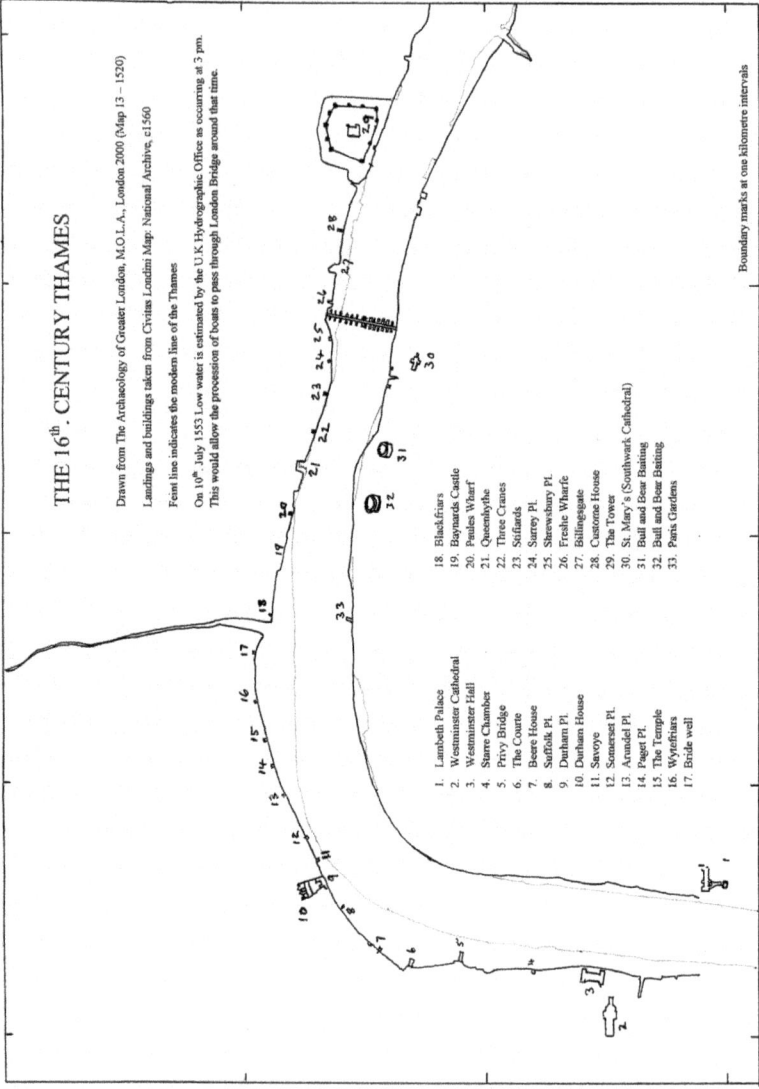

THE 16th CENTURY THAMES

Drawn from The Archaeology of Greater London, M.O.L.A., London 2000 (Map 13 – 1520)

Landings and buildings taken from Civitas Londini Map: National Archive, c1560

Feint line indicates the modern line of the Thames

On 10th July 1553 Low water is estimated by the U.K Hydrographic Office as occurring at 3 pm.
This would allow the procession of boats to pass through London Bridge around that time.

1. Lambeth Palace
2. Westminster Cathedral
3. Westminster Hall
4. Starre Chamber
5. Privy Bridge
6. The Courte
7. Beere House
8. Suffolk Pl.
9. Durham Pl.
10. Durham House
11. Savoye
12. Somerset Pl.
13. Arundel Pl.
14. Paget Pl.
15. The Temple
16. Wytefriars
17. Bride well

18. Blackfriars
19. Baynards Castle
20. Paules Wharf
21. Queenhythe
22. Three Cranes
23. Stilliards
24. Surrey Pl.
25. Shrewsbury Pl.
26. Froshe Wharfe
27. Billingegate
28. Custome House
29. The Tower
30. St. Mary's (Southwark Cathedral)
31. Bull and Bear Baiting
32. Bull and Bear Baiting
33. Paris Gardens

Boundary marks at one kilometre intervals

Figure 14.1   The River Thames in London in the sixteenth century. Drawing. © Michael Holden.

the 1869 (first) edition is a paper-bound book dealing largely with the statutory regulation of Watermen from 1209 to 1666.The interest in this pamphlet was such that the Company asked Humpherus (then about 50 years old) to compile a much more detailed history drawing on a wider range of sources. This was published in 1874 as a three-volume work, with the first volume covering the same period as the 1869 pamphlet and two further volumes taking the *History* to 1845. A photo-lithographic copy of the 1874 edition was published by the Watermen's Company in 1981.No subsequent history has been written and the majority of the Company's surviving records are now held in the City of London Guildhall Library.

The *History*'s format is that of an annual journal, each year having an entry with one or more notable items recorded. Each volume is furnished with a detailed index. For the sixteenth-century period the text notes the increasing traffic on the river, including the barges of noblemen whose houses began to line the river's north bank in the first half of the century. It notes that the Livery Companies of the City increasingly purchased their own barges during this period and also describes the way in which barges were hired from, for instance, the Archbishop's barge master, so giving us a glimpse of the possessions of a major household of the period.

> … in this year the Drapers' company agreed with Edmond Wade, the bargeman of the Archbishop of Canterbury, "For his grete barge, at such tyme as we shall have need to occupy it, either with the mayer or shrives, or for any other business, he to have for himself xxxviij oars furnished, and cysshons for the said barge, at every voyage when we shall have need thereof, with our compaignie in the livery the sum of xxxs.[3]

The increasing ownership of barges by the city companies underscores the burgeoning wealth of London. The *History* suggests in fact that ownership of a decorated barge to use in full public gaze on the Thames became one of the most evident displays of wealth and social standing. It must be remembered that the Thames was the best highway through London from the seat of Government at Westminster to the eastern boundary of the City at the Tower of London. A waterborne procession on the Thames thus had the same impact on the community as a land procession would have had along the principal road of another city. The *History* frequently notes the use of a foist or wafter (a smaller boat than a barge) able to act in part as a tug to assist the manoeuvring of the larger vessel and also as a means of getting the normal traffic of the Thames out of the barge's path.

A passage from the *History*'s account of the early years of the century notes an increasing royal and noble trend towards extravagant display. The entry for 1529 states that 'the number of barges kept by the nobility on the river increased in the reign of Henry VIII, and processions were very frequent. Cardinal Wolsey … kept

---

[3]   Entry for 1534, p. 84.

numerous barges for his use, as well as a retinue of watermen'.[4] Humpherus goes on to cite a quotation from Cavendish's *Life of Wolsey*:

> He used also every Sunday to resorte to the Courte, then being for the most parte of all the yeere at Greenwiche, with his former triumphs, taking his barge at his own stairs, furnished with yeomen, standing upon the bayles, and his gentlemen being within a boat, and landed again at the Three Cranes in the vintree, and from thence he rode upon his mule, with his crosses, his pillars, his hat, and the broad seal carried before him on horseback, through Thames street until he came to Billingsgate, and there took his barge againe, and so rowed to Greenwiche, where he was nobly received, &c.[5]

Clearly this was not a casual journey but an ostentatious procession designed to affirm Wolsey's status. The mention of his gentlemen in a boat suggests that the river procession included at least a barge and a further boat with perhaps a foist to assist the barge and to clear its passage on the busy river. The transfer to land at the City's Vintree ward would avoid the risky passage through London Bridge where, except at high and low water, the river's tidal flow caused the bridge to act as a weir and made passage through the arches dangerous. Taking the barges and boats through the Bridge when the tide was running was undertaken by a special class of watermen called 'Bridge Shooters'. The 1529 entry goes on to quote a stanza from a poem by John Leland:

> Yet here we may not longer stay,
> But shoot the bridge and dart away,
> Though with resistless fall, the tide
> Is dashing on the bulworks' side;
> And roaring torrents drown my song
> As o'er the surge I drift along.[6]

The Tudor monarchs, with the exception of Mary, appear to have consciously used river processions to confirm their own exalted position, but also with an eye to the inclusion of commoners of importance (notably the Mayor and Livery Companies) in order to seek the citizens' general approval and support. Thus the *History*'s 1533 entry states that Henry, at the particularly controversial moment of Anne Boleyn's coronation, invited the mayor and citizens to fetch her from

---

[4]   Ibid., p. 80.

[5]   Cavendish, *Life of Cardinal Wolsey*, in manuscript from about 1558. A bowdlerised version was printed in 1645 but a copy printed from the manuscripts in 1810 is presumed to be the reference here.

[6]   John Leland, *Cygnea cantio* written in 1545. Humpherus may have transcribed the stanza from the manuscript, hence the nineteenth-century spelling. He attributes the poem to 'Lelland' rather than Leland.

Greenwich to the Tower. Humpherus cites a description of the procession from Hall's *Chronicles*:

> First before the mayor's barge was a foist or wafter, full of ordnance, in which was a great dragon, continually moving and casting wild fire, and rounde about stood terrible monsters, and wild men, casting fire, and making hideous noises; this vessel served to clear the way for the mayor's barge, which was garnished with many goodly banners and streamers, and richly covered, in which barge were shalmes, shagbushes, and divers other instruments, which continually made goodly harmony. Next after the mayor followed his fellowship, the Haberdashers, next after them the Mercers, then the Grocers, and so every company in his order, and last of all the mayor's and sheriff's officers, every company having melody in his barge by himself, and goodly garnished with banners, and some garnished with silk, and some with arras, and rich carpets, and in that order they rowed downward to Greenwich towne, and there cast anchor, making great melody.

The phrase 'and so every company in his order' hides a considerable jockeying for position. Whilst the companies were generally accorded status by the date of their formation, there were some perceived incongruities resulting from differences in the wealth and size of the companies.As the entry for 1483 shows, in a summary by Humperus, competitiveness between the companies was of long standing:

> From the commencement of the mayor's procession by water, the question whether the Merchant Tailors or Skinners' company should have precedence in the procession had been a matter of dispute; a great feud having existed between those companies, one barge always attempting to get before the other barge; this year the rival companies came to blows, which resulted in bloodshed and loss of life. In consequence of this the matter was referred to the mayor for arbitration, whereupon he decided that for the future the two guilds should alternately have precedence, and that each year on approaching Westminster, they should lash their two barges together and drink as a toast "The Merchant Taylors and Skinners; Skinners and Merchant Tailors; root and branch may they flourish for ever.

There were also, it seems, traditional practices of some antiquity. The historical precedent had long been established that a new monarch would process by water to the Tower, the strategic strong point of the City and its principal symbol of power, and then proceed by land to Westminster for the coronation. This practice was followed by all the Tudors, even Mary, who first arrived as queen at the Tower of London by land from the north on 3 August 1553. After the debacle of the attempted accession of Lady Jane Grey, Mary needed to 'hold' the Tower to show her position and power. Rather later she went to St James's Palace and then Whitehall, before taking her barge in procession to the Tower on 27 September, two days before her Coronation procession by land through the City to Westminster.

The *History* records with disdain that Mary used chariots in her land-based coronation procession, one for herself and another for Princess Elizabeth and the Lady Anne of Cleeves. This is said to be the beginning of the use of carriages, a use which, according to the 1553 entry, 'subsequently proved so injurious to the bargemen of the nobility, watermen &c.'. Though carriages became more common in Queen Elizabeth's time she escapes criticism because she seems to have used the river whenever possible. In his 1559 entry Humpherus describes her waterborne procession to the Tower to mark her accession:

> Queen Elizabeth having succeeded to the throne, removed on the twelfth of January from her palace at Westminster to the Tower, a change preparatory to her passage through the city of London. She went by water and was attended by the Lord Mayor and aldermen, in their barges, and all the citizens, with their barges, decked and trimmed with targets and banners of their mysteries. The batchellers barge of the Lord Mayor's companie, to wit, the Mercers, had their barge, with a foist trimmed with three tops, and artillery a boord, gallantlie appointed, to wait upon them, shooting off lustily as they went, with great and pleasant melodie of instruments, which plaied in most sweet and heavenlie manner. Her grace shot the bridge at about two of the clocke in the afternoon, at the still of the ebbe, the Lord Mayor and the rest following her barge, until her Majesty landed at the privy stairs, at the Tower wharf. The Lord Mayor,&c., returning and landing at the Three Cranes in the Vintry.

It will be noted how carefully the procession was planned: down river from Westminster to the Tower on the falling tide, in order to reach London Bridge at the end of the ebb, so that passage could be made through the bridge without risk to the royal barge. There is a clearly organised order to accommodate the many barges and boats of the entourage. The return journey for the mayor and attendant boats is made on the beginning of the flood tide, before the passage of the bridge becomes difficult, so that the Mayor may land at Three Cranes, his most convenient landing. Thus the barges travelled with the flow of the tides rather than rowing against them.

In the same 1559 entry Humpherus offers an unattributed description:

> The XXV day of April was St. Marke's day, the Quen's grace supt at Beynards Castyll, at my Lord of Pembroke's place and after super the Quen's grace rowed up and down the Temes, and a C bottes a boute her grace, with trumpettes, and drumes, and flutes, and gones, and squybes, horlyng on hi to and fro tyll x at nyght, er her grace depertyd, and all the water syd, with a M pepull lokyng on her grace.

A magnificent procession such as this with its one hundred boats was of course a popular way for the new Queen to establish herself in the eyes of her people, evoking a peaceful holiday mood in contrast to the years of Mary's reign. Clearly it was thought to be a useful show since on the eleventh of June in the same year the *History* records her as being 'rowed in her barge along bankside, and afterwards on the city side, about eight o'clock in the evening, for pleasure'.

Judging by the 1568 entry it appears that Elizabeth also continued her father's public relations theme of requiring the City to receive distinguished visitors:

> …consulting the honour and grandeur of the nation, and in particular of the city of London, ordered the Lord Mayor, aldermen, &c., and the several companies to receive in their formalities all strangers of high distinction, ambassadors, &c., who arrived by water at Gravesend, and to attend them in their barges to the metropolis.

A practice such as this, it may be remarked, must have saved the Royal Exchequer the cost of many processions, necessary to the dignity of the occasion, at a time when attempts were being made to reduce the burden of debt with which the reign had begun.

An entry for 1549 incorporates a transcription from the diary of Edward VI, drawn from the *Cottonian MS*.[7] As will have been noted thus far, Humpherus tends to use old spelling when he is directly quoting and modern spelling when he uses a later source or a translation. This entry may allow us to judge the accuracy of his quotations, a feature that will become important later in this discussion. The square brackets indicate substantive variations in the manuscript from the printed *History*. Some spelling variations and almost all the punctuation are attributable to Humpherus but these variations have not been noted here. The printed *History* makes two insertions '(Thames)' to clarify the manuscript's 'temps' and '(to take)' to clarify the narrative:

> In the diary of King Edward VI …in His Majesty's own handwriting, is an account of Lord Clinton being made Admiral of England, and of the sham fight, &c., at Deptford on the nineteenth June. The particulars given by His Majesty are as follows:

> 'I went to Detford, being bedden to supper by the L Clinton, where, before souper [soup], I saw certaine men stand upon [th'end of] a bote without hold of anything, and rane one at another till one was cast into the water. At supper, Mons. Vieedam and Henadey supped with me. After supper, was ther a fort made upon a great lighter on the temps, (Thames) which had three walles and a watch towre, in the meddes of wich Mr. Winter was captain, with forty or fifty other soldiours, in yelow and blake. To the fort also apperteined a galery [galey] of yelow color, with men and municion in it for defence of the castel; wher farther cam four [4] pinesses with ther men in wight, ansomely dressed, wich entending to geve assault to the castill, first drove away the yellow piness, and aftir with clods [cloddes], scuibs, canes of fire, darts made for the nonce,

---

7   British Library, Cotton MS, Nero CX, 8b. Seen on Microfilm 2529.

and bombardes, assaunted [assaulted?] the castel, [and at] length came with ther pices [peces], and burst the utter walles of the castill, beating them of the castill into the seconde ward, who after issued out and droue away the penessis [pinesses], sinking one of them, out of wich, at[al]the men in it, being more than twenty, leaped out, and swamme in the temps. Then came th' Admiral of the navy, with three others pinessis [penessess],and wanne[wane] the castle[castil] by assault, and burst [in] the tope of it doune, and toke the captain and under captain. Then the Admiral went forth (to take) the yelow ship, and at length [lenght] clasped with her, toke fier [her], and assaulted also her toppe, and wane [wonne] it by compulcion, and so returned home.'

There are misreadings and omissions in Humpherus's transcription but not such as to distort the content. However his transcription places the event in 1549 when in fact it took place on 19 June, 1550, a mistake that clearly arises from the page in Edward's manuscript diary being headed '1549' (using old style dating) in reference to March of what we would now call 1550. In his entry introducing Edward's diary extract Humpherus conflates the appointment of Lord Clinton as Admiral of England, which took place on 4th May 1550, six weeks before, with the *naumachia* itself. The *History*, it seems, is accurate in broad content but may lack accuracy in detail.[8]

The accuracy of the *History*'s 1549 record becomes important for the entry referring to 1553 where a description of the procession to mark the accession of Lady Jane Grey may have been translated from another language, resulting in a mix of unusual phrasing, *lacunae* and nineteenth-century English:

On the death of King Edward VI, [there occurred] the unfortunate attempt to place the Lady Jane Grey on the throne of England, by the Duke of Northumberland, (whose son the Lord Guildford Dudley [the Lady Jane] had married) and her father, the Duke of Suffolk, and other noblemen; great rejoicings took place. At the mansion of the Duke of Northumberland, a gallant train issued from [the house?] and descended the stairs leading to the river, where, appointed for their conveyance were drawn up a squadron of fifty superbly gilt barges, some decorated with banners and streamers, some with cloth of gold and arras, embroidered with the devices of the civic companies, others with innumerable silken pennons, to which were attached small silver bells, making a goodly noise and a goodly sight as they waved in the wind, while others, reserved for the more important personages of the ceremony, were covered on the sides with shields, gorgeously emblazoned with the armonial [armorial?] bearings of the different noblemen and honourable persons composing the Privy Council, amid which the cognizance of the Duke of Northumberland, 'a lion rampant *or* double

---

8   It may be of interest to note that in the 1561entry another similar *naumachia* is described on the Thames at Greenwich, including the information that Elizabeth watched it 'from a bank with ii tope (castles) for the Queens grace to be in'.

quevee *vert*', appeared proudly conspicuous. Each barge was escorted by a light galley, termed a foist or wafter, manageable either by oar or sail, as occasion demanded, and attached to its companion by a stout silken tow-line. The Lady Jane embarked in a magnificent barge, with two large banners, beaten with the royal arms, planted on the foreship; its sides were hung with metal escutcheons, alternately emblazoned with the cognizances of the Queen and her consort, and its decks covered with the richest silks and tissues. It was attended by two smaller galleys, one of which designated the batchelor's barge, was appropriated to the younger sons of the nobility, the other was devoted to the maids of honour. In the galleys, besides the rowers, whose oars were shipped and in readiness to be dropped at an instant's notice into the tide, and the men-at-arms, whose tall pikes, steel caps, and polished corslets, flashed in the sunbeams, sat bands of minstrels, provided with sackbuts, shalms, cornets, rebecs, &c. The conduct of the whole squadron was entrusted to six officers, whose business it was to prevent confusion, and who in the small swift wherries appointed to their use, rowed rapidly from place to place, endeavouring by threats and commands to maintain order, and keep off the crowd of boats and craft of all sorts hurrying towards them from every quarter of the river. The procession was a brilliant and busy one, and might be supposed a joyous and inspiriting one, more especially as the object which had called together this assemblage was the conveyance of a young and lovely sovereign to her throne within the Tower; it being then the custom for the monarchs of England to spend the first few days of their reign within that ancient fortress.

A few days afterwards, when Queen Mary arrived at the Tower, Lady Jane Grey was made prisoner, but escaped and was conveyed in a small boat to Sion House, Isleworth, where on the following day she was discovered, and conveyed back to the Tower, the scene of her recent grandeur, in the Royal barge, by torchlight, unattended and unnoted. The Duke of Northumberland and other noblemen were afterwards conveyed from the Tower, in barges, to Westminster Hall, and after their conviction conveyed back in the same manner to the Tower, preparatory to their execution.

This description of a traditional, and magnificent, waterborne procession for Lady Jane Grey from Durham House to the Tower, and her subsequent escape from the Tower following Queen Mary's triumph, appears in none of the histories I can identify. The language may suggest that Humpherus had access to a source which has escaped others. If so it may have been a Spanish source for he was married to a Catherine Barriero and their first children were called Catherine Barriero and Henry Domingos, suggesting a possible Spanish ancestry.[9] The introductory reference to an 'unfortunate attempt' might also indicate a catholic

---

[9]   The names are given as enumerated in the 1851 Census.

stance. A search of records relating to the modern family has found no written material on which Humpherus might have drawn for his work.

The detail in the description suggests an observer actually present at the event, and one who was conversant with boats. The use of the word 'foreship' for the location of the royal banners, the description of the oars as 'shipped' and the knowledge of oar and sail for the foist, point to someone with a maritime background. There is no description of Jane's procession, so far as I am aware, in any of the many romantic accounts of her life which began to circulate from the early part of the seventeenth century, with increasing fictional additions from the nineteenth century. The phrase 'beaten with the royal arms' would suggest the banners were decorated with gold leaf and although poetic in expression, is comprehensible. By contrast the term 'silken tow-line' seems poetic rather than realistic and so may hint at a later, fictional, account.

Could the description be reasonably accurate? The barges certainly existed and were probably gilded in their carved and decorated parts, as shown in engraved and painted illustrations of livery and state barges dating from a century later. The heraldry was also in common use, and the armed attendants with their corslets and pikes would have carried the shields serving as the escutcheons decorating the barges. The UK Hydrographic Office confirms that low water on 10 July 1553 was about 3pm, so that the waterborne procession could have passed through the bridge at the time indicated. Indeed lunch at Durham House may have been arranged to wait for the tide whilst enjoying the earlier stronger ebb for the journey from Syon House in Isleworth to Durham House in Westminster. Other histories confirm that Lady Jane was taken, probably on 9 July from Chelsea to Syon House, situated opposite the Palace of Richmond across the Thames. On 10 July she travelled downstream to Durham House for lunch and from thence to the Tower.[10] It is this last journey which is described. Some references suggest she came from Richmond rather than Syon House, but the proximity of house and palace makes this confusion understandable.

A procession such as that in the *History* would have taken time to organise, and may be part of the reason for the announcement of Edward's death (on 6 July) being delayed until 10 July. It would be in keeping with the public role of pageantry on the Thames for the procession to be both an announcement and a confirmation of Jane as Queen.

By contrast to the splendid account of Lady Jane Grey's procession, that of Mary from Whitehall to the Tower on 28 September, is accorded only a sparse description. The *History* (1553 entry again) describes it as follows:

> The XXviij day of September the Queen's grace removed from St. James and so to Whyt hall, and ther her grace took her barge unto the Towre, and there all the craftes, and the mare and the aldermen in bargurs [barges], with streamers

    [10]   Nichols, J.G. (ed.), *The Chronicle of Queen Jane and of two years of Queen Mary*, Camden Society Old Series 48, 1850.

and mynstrels, as trumpets, wettes[waits], shaines, [?shawmes] and regalls [?rebecs}, and with a gret shooting of gunes, tyll her grace cam in to the Towr.

For the Tudors, waterborne procession on the Thames became both a confirmation of attaining the crown and a means of drawing the increasingly wealthy city livery companies into accord with the monarchy. For Elizabeth at least, it was a means of drawing closer to her ordinary subjects at a point when it was important to be popular – the first appearance of the now familiar royal walkabout, in Elizabeth's case waterborne.

Appendix: Schedule of Processions and Pageants noted in the *History of the Company of Watermen*

1215	Runnemeade [*sic*], Magna Carta, the river blocked with the splendid barges of the nobility.
1253	Quainton played on the river (? At London Bridge) with description of the game.
1415	Return of Henry V from Agincourt, mayor and aldermen in procession with pageants on the bridge.
1422	Mayor and Sheriffs process to Westminster to swear for Henry V by boat rather than by land.
1445	Marriage of Henry VI and Margaret of Anjou, pageants on London Bridge watched by boats on river.
1454	Lord Mayor's procession by Barge for first time, Sir John Norman (Draper) in new gilded barge. Waterborne Lord Mayor's processions continued (with slight intermissions) until 1856.
1455	Lord Mayor from Carpenters Company who had had a barge for some years.
1461	Edward IV processes from Westminster to London [?Tower] on his proclamation as king.
1467	Visit of Count de la Roche met at Greenwich by Constable of England, lords, knights, aldermen and commoners who made procession to London.
1471	Barges hired for funeral procession of Henry VI from Blackfriars to Chertsey.
1476	A procession to receive Edward IV, out of France, to London.
1480	Bargemen's clothing decorated for coming of Margarette of Bourgoigne to London.
1483	Richard III processes to the Tower by water, proclaimed as king.
1485	Henry VII received with public rejoicing, Mayor and Companies meet him in barges.

1487   Coronation procession of Elizabeth of York, included Mayor, sheriffs and aldermen. Mention of the Batchelor's barge (both Royal and City barges) with explanation.

1494   Royal feast at Westminster Hall, Lord Mayor and aldermen process by water.

1501   Wedding of Arthur and the Infanta Catherine, procession from Baynards Castle to Westminster.

1519   High Admiral and Bishop of Paris to Greenwich where they were received with great pageants etc.

1520   After the Field of the Cloth of Gold, French nobles conveyed to Tower and thence to Richmond.

1522   Visit of Charles V, Emperor of Germany, procession of 30 barges from Gravesend to Greenwich and thence to Westminster.

1527   Bishop of Bayenne in London to ratify the Treaty of Amiens by barge to Greenwich and also Richmond and Hampton Court.

1533   Anne Boleyn brought from Greenwich to the Tower for her coronation by Mayor and Aldermen etc.

1540   Lord Mayor and city companies process with Henry VIII and Anne of Cleeves in the royal barges from Greenwich to Westminster.

1541   Henry VIII and his Queen process by water to Westminster.

1551   Procession with great pomp for the Lord of Misrule from Greenwich to the Tower and return as part of the Christmas festivities.

1553   Accession processions of Lady Jane Grey, with description, and Queen Mary

1554   Lord Mayor's procession to Westminster described.

1555   Princess Elizabeth from the Tower to Greenwich in the Queen's barge and retinue of 6 boats. Lord Mayor's procession described.

1556   Lord Mayor's procession, costumes described.

1557   Princess Elizabeth from Somerset House to Richmond with a retinue of 6 boats. Lord Mayor's procession.

1558   Elizabeth I on her proclamation as Queen to the Tower, then to Somerset House.

1559   Elizabeth I procession from Westminster to the Tower prior to coronation.

1560   Duke of Holstein received and by water to Somerset House. Several processions on the river for his amusement.

1561   Two waterborne processions by Lord Mayors, to Westminster described.

1562   Lord Mayor's procession described.

1567   Lord Mayor's procession with a note of seven hundred pounds of gunpowder bought for the occasion.

1572   Visit of the Duke of Montmorencie received and Lord Mayor and city procession to Somerset House and after to the Court with the Earl of Essex etc.

1575   Lord Mayor's procession this year was very grand; a full description was published by William Smythe.

1581   Francis Bourbon and ambassadors by water from Gravesend to Westminster. Processions, pageants, triumphs, fireworks on the river and plays at the Steel yard carried out for their entertainment.

1591   Lord Mayor's procession.

1594   Visit of Prince of Russia. Tranships to 15 barges for his procession to Greenwich and then the Tower.

1606   Visit of King of Denmark. 35 barges go to receive him and a special barge with windows made like a castle for him, it was towed by another barge with 30 oars. Several processions to see London.

1610   Lord Mayor and companies in 54 barges to Putney to receive Prince Henry on his way to Whitehall. There is a long quotation from a published description of the event.

1611   Lord Mayor's procession described with reference to Anthony Munday's poem *Chruso-thriambos.*

1612   Visit of the Count Palatine received at Gravesend and by barges to Whitehall. The Lord Mayor's procession having 4 or 5 pageants was stopped by great winds forcing the barges to run aground.

1613   Gentlemen maskers of Inner Temple and Gray's Inn by night and lit by torches from Winchester steps to Whitehall (against the tide) with warlike galleys to attend them and thence with the King to Temple gardens. The King, Queen, Prince Charles, the Palsgrave and the Lady Elizabeth from Whitehall to Greenwich on the Lady Elizabeth's departure to Holland. The Lord Mayor's procession this year included moored boats decorated as islands and as chariots with Neptune and other characters in them.

1614   Visit of the King of Denmark, royal processions to receive him at Gravesend.

1615   Lord Mayor's procession with references to the classical gods.

1616   His Majesty rowed from London to Queensborough on his way to Germany. The Lord Mayor's procession and pageants in the form of moored boats decorated as islands. Prince Charles created Prince of Wales with a royal procession by barge from Barn Elms to Whitehall is described.

1617   Visit of the King of Sweden to London in the King's barge but not in that barge for the return. The Lord Mayor's procession as extravagant again, costing the Grocer's Company more than £800.

1620   Lord Mayor's procession more elaborate and classical in theme but now also with presentations on land. Visit of the French Ambassador, the *Marquess de Cadenet* received at Gravesend by some twenty barges.

1625   Arrival of Henrietta Maria procession from Gravesend with the King and Queen in the royal barge, with many other barges of honour and many thousands of boats to Whitehall.

1634   The Lord Mayor's procession written by John Taylor who after published a description.

1637   Arrival of Ambassadors for the Emperor of Morocco. Received at Gravesend, then to Greenwich where they stayed four hours until the king's barge arrived with Lord Kenwell and 12 men of the Privy Chamber to take them to the Tower by torch light.

1650   Arrival of Mynheer the Comm.ʳ Schape from Holland, received by 'the barges of state' at Gravesend.

1655   Lord Mayor's procession recommenced (it had been discontinued in 1639).A descriptive poem quoted.

1658   Lord Mayor's procession saluted by guns as they pass down the Thames but no note of pageantry.

1661   Charles II processed by water to Westminster previous to his coronation and reference is made to a description in "Neptune's address to his most sacred King Charles etc." The annual procession of the Lord Mayor returns to its previous form with Neptune and pageants.

1662   A great waterborne procession from Hampton Court to Whitehall to carry the new Queen Catherine of Portugal. There appear to have been upwards of 1,000 barges and boats. Description published as *Aqua Triumphalis.*

1663   Lord Mayor's procession briefly noted with the various Company barges setting off from different stairs.

1671   Lord Mayor's procession by water to Westminster commenced again (discontinued since 1664 on account of plague and the Great Fire). Pageants on the Thames and the return landing at Baynards Castle with a land procession made to look as much like a water one as possible. Reference to Thomas Jordan's *Londons Resurrection to joy and Triumph etc.*

1672   Funeral procession of the Earl of Sandwich to Westminster. Lord Mayor's as for the previous year.

1675   Lord Mayor's procession recorded by Thomas Jordan, Gent., *in Triumphs of London, etc.,*

1677   Lord Mayor's procession increasingly placing the pageantry in the land part of the procession.

1678   Lord Mayor's procession only noted as being much as the previous year.

1680   Lord Mayor's procession returns its concentration to the water with a full rigged ship in the procession. Description in Thomas Jordan, Gent., in *London's glory etc.*

1681   Lord Mayor's procession recorded by Thomas Jordan in *London's Joy etc.*

1683   Lord Mayor's procession recorded in Thomas Jordan's *The Triumphs of London etc.*

1684   Lord Mayors procession noted with no details.
        On 16th November, the Queen's birthday, fireworks on the Thames before Whitehall with pageants, castles, forts and other devices and a multitude of boats and barges.

1686	Lord Mayor's procession recorded by Mr Taubman in *London's Jubilee etc.,*
1687	The Lord Mayor, Sir John Shorter was presented with a ship by his company the Goldsmiths, fully laden and manned at his procession day. A note of the procession being also on land.
1688	A single barge for King James as he left London for exile.
1689	Lord Mayor's procession includes a ship laden with spices, emblematic of the Mayor as a Turkey merchant. Particulars in Matthew Taubman's *London's Great Jubilee etc.*
1691	Lord Mayor's procession carried out in the usual form. Recorded by Elkanah Settle.
1692	Lord Mayor's procession again recorded by Elkanah Settle.
1694	Lord Mayor's procession carried out at great expense by the Clothworkers, recorded by the City Poet, Elkanah Settle.
1695	Lord Mayor Sir John Houblon (Grocer) carried out with great magnificence. Particulars recorded by city poet E. Settle in *Triumphs of London &c.*
1697	The King returns after the Treaty of Ryswick with France to Gravesend and is met "as usual" by the Lord Mayor and Aldermen who escorted him over London Bridge with great pomp, the river being covered with boat, barges &c., crowded with people.
1698	Lord Mayor's procession noted as embarking at Three Cranes and landing at Dorset stairs (Blackfriars).
1699	Lord Mayor's procession takes the same route and is recorded by E. Settle in *Triumph of London &c.*

Bibliography

Humpherus, Henry, *History of the Origin & Progress of the Company of Watermen and Lightermen of the River Thames with Numerous Historical Notes*, published by the Watermen's Company in 1874 (reprinted 1981 and 1999).

Nichols, J.G.(ed.), *The Chronicle of Queen Jane and of two years of Queen Mary*, Camden Society Old Series 48, 1850.

Chapter 15

The Ambassador's Reception: The Moroccan Embassy to London of 1637–1638 and the Pageantry of Maritime Politics

Iain McClure

Pageantry is the art of the moment. It is a form of culture that, despite its often marvellous materiality, is inscribed upon transitory occasions of celebration and ephemeral instances of spectacle. This is especially so with pageants enacted upon the rivers and seas of Early Modern Europe. Here the very location of such displays forcibly reminds us of the obscuring force of mutability: these are dramas written on water. Thus, it is the task of the cultural historian of these phenomena to renew an understanding of an easily lost context, to recover those fissile moments of splendour and significance long eclipsed by time and by tide. In this discovery of what can easily be forgotten, it may prove interesting to unite the study of waterborne spectacle with another forgotten context: English relations with Islamic powers in the Early Modern Period. We can bring these two neglected sources into confluence by examining how nautical pageantry, and related pageantry on the theme of maritime power, became an integral part of the English reception of the Moroccan embassy to Charles I that lasted from the autumn of 1637 to the spring of 1638.

It is clear this embassy had a significant place in Caroline foreign policy. The activities of 'Barbary' or 'Turkish' pirates operating out of Algiers, Tangiers, Tunis, Tripoli, Salé and other pirate citadels caused extensive disruption to international trade in both the Atlantic and the Mediterranean throughout the Early Modern Period. Of course, English shipping was not immune to these depredations, and particular anxiety was caused by the capture and forced conversion of English mariners by such 'Barbary corsairs'. Whilst the King of England increasingly viewed North African pirate citadels as an impediment to commercial expansion and an insult to national pride, the Sultan of Morocco considered them a threat to his assumed pre-eminence in the region, classifying them either as treacherous rebels against his suzerainty or forward operating bases of the hostile Ottomans. Thus, it became progressively more desirable in the early decades of the seventeenth century to institute some form of Anglo–Moroccan alliance in order to rout mutual and troubling enemies. Undeniably, there were considerable impediments to this union. To the alarm of the English, some of their sailors languished as captives in Moroccan prisons, in addition to those enduring slavery in the outlaw ports of Barbary; to the annoyance of the Moroccans, English diplomats and merchants were more than willing to deal pragmatically with those 'subjects' of the Moroccan Emperor who rebelled against his authority. However, nostalgia could be allied to realpolitik, and both parties often invoked the collaboration between Elizabeth I and Ahmad Al-Mansur, as confirmed by the visit of Abd el-Ouahed ben Messaoud to London in 1600, as a glorious precedent for such collaboration.[1]

Admittedly, England was slow to move towards this state of amity. The late 1620s abound with attempts at English conciliation with the 'rogue states' of the Maghreb. Accordingly, we discover documents detailing a royal proclamation calling on all His Majesty's subjects to refrain from violence against Algiers, Tunis and Salé; royal demands that letters of marque entail co-operation with these cities; accounts of the gracious royal farewell accorded to an ambassador from Algiers; the cordial receipt of English ordnance by the Dey of Algiers and his request for a subsequent gift of ammunition; Sir John Harrison's negotiation of a treaty with the secessionist Republic of Bou Regreg.[2] All these proceedings suggest anxious, even fearful, attempts to placate and persuade. Yet, by the 1630s, English opinion became markedly more 'hawkish' towards Barbary pirates and solicitous of a regional ally. This was partly because the years 1629–36 saw some 53 English ships taken by North African vessels.

Certainly, the infamous raid upon Baltimore in western Ireland in 1631, which saw dozens carried off into bondage, accelerated demands for retributive action. Ambitious schemes began to emerge, with the sanguine plan to reduce all Barbary ports 'to waste burne and spoyle' being approved in principle by the Privy Council in 1632. By 1636, fuelled by speculation about the uses of Ship Money, such discussions had crystallised into a resolution that 'Algiers must certainly be taken by a compounded force of Christians', with Sir Thomas Roe championing an even more elaborate proposal to send 'a strong fleet' as far eastwards as Alexandria.[3] Such plans reached partial fruition in William Rainborow's relatively successful expedition to Salé in the summer of 1637. In this operation an English marine task force, assisted by the Machiavellian Sidi Al-Ayachi, managed to inflict extensive damage on the resident corsairs' vessels, redeem more than three hundred European captives and cement cordial relations with the Sultan of Morocco amid the shifting sands of Maghrebi politics. Immediately after this incomplete but welcome victory, Rainborow took charge of conveying both the freed hostages

---

[1]   Khalid Ben Srhir, *Britain and Morocco during the embassy of John Drummond Hay*, translated Malcolm Williams and Gavin Waterman (Abingdon: Routledge Curzon, 2004), p. 11. George Glover, *The Arrivall and Intertainements of the Embassador Alkaid Jaurar Ben Abdella with his associate Mr R. Blake, from the high and mighty Prince, Mulley Mahamed Sheque, Emperor of Morocco, King of Fesse and Suss* (London: 1637), p. 19.

[2]   Kenneth R. Andrews, *Ships, Money and, Politics: seafaring and naval enterprise in the reign of Charles I* (Cambridge: Cambridge University Press, 1991), pp. 167–70. Geoffrey Fisher, *The Barbary legend: war, trade and piracy in North Africa, 1415–1830* (Oxford: Clarendon Press, 1957), pp. 202–204.

[3]   Fisher, pp. 204–206.

and a diplomatic party (including the Moroccan Ambassador and the English emissary to Morocco, Robert Blake) to London.[4] It is clear that the Moroccan embassy of 1637–38 was an attempt to celebrate and consolidate existing military co-operation between Stuart London and Saadian Marrakech, and to expand upon this nascent alliance.

In this attempt to advance these designs, the waterborne pageant of the Ambassador's arrival in London, is worth especially close scrutiny. We have a detailed account of this ceremonial entrance, on a date in the autumn of 1637 that the records do not reveal, from George Glover's *The Arrivall and Intertainments of the Embassador Alkaid Jaurar ben Abdella* (1637). Significantly, this work begins by offering a summary of the ideology that underpins this event. In consequence, Glover's notes how such an episode 'makes peace, love, and amity with Princes and Potentates, though they are remote from each other in Religions, Realmes, Regions and Territories'. To this reconciliatory purpose, Glover also offers not only an account of the Salé expedition, but also a sympathetic account of the Ambassador's compatriots and their religion:

> For their Religion, they are strict observers of the Law of Mahomet; they say Christ was a great Prophet, borne to be the Saviour of the World, (but not incarnate) that hee was the Breath of God, that hee was borne of a Virgin, and that the Iewes should have beleev'd him.

Reducing confessional differences to parentheses, this author seems intent on discovering common ground that unites those who are separated by custom and geography. It is striking that Glover also chooses to emphasise the patrician status of the Ambassador himself. Despite the potentially humiliating fact that he was 'by birth a Portugall ... taken Captive in his Child-hood' and 'distesticled, or Eunch'd', this English writer is keen to stress that the Moroccan Ambassador is the Emperor's 'chiefest favourite'. Noting that 'the high stile and title of Alkaid, or Lord' conveys immense prestige, he also comments that 'there is no higher degree under the Emperor' and that this great man's office is comparable to being both 'Lord great Chamberlain and Lord Privy Seal'. The princely status of this figure is confirmed by his possession of 'lands and revenews fit and correspondent for so eminent a calling'.[5] In an intensely hierarchical society, the establishment of the Ambassador's aristocratic character seems fitting before we are treated to an account of his inclusion in English, regal spectacle.

It is no surprise to discover that the Ambassador's progression down the Thames was an event charged with spectacle and significance. The ritualised nature of this procession is highlighted by the fact that 'Sir John Finnet, Knight, Master of Ceremonies' was dispatched to be the Ambassador's ceremonial pilot from Gravesend to London. It is also noteworthy that this party 'had no sooner taken

---

[4] Andrews, pp. 176–80.
[5] Glover, pp. 2–3, 5, 34–5.

their Barges' than they were greeted by 'an expression of Love and Welcome' that resounded 'in thundering manner out of the mouths of the great Ordnance'. Given the fundamentally military ambitions that lie behind this embassy, it is hardly remarkable that the engines of war are seen as the ideal interlocutors of 'Love and Welcome'.[6] Despite the cultured confections of peace erected around this diplomatic mission, state spoke to state through the violent dialect of 'shock and awe'. From its outset, this ceremonial procession acted as a canvas upon which the pretentions of Charles I to formidable armed strength could be given shape and form.

This maritime pageant next passed close by another piece of floating propaganda. It is entirely natural that the Ambassador's journey down the Thames should pass close by to 'his Majesties new great Ship (the Eighth Wonder of the World)'.[7] Although increasingly engaged with all naval matters, the King's 'most personal and ambitious project of all' was undoubtedly this prodigious ship. Although designed by Phineas Pett in 1634, and constructed over the next three years at Woolwich, this colossal triple-decked, 1,522-ton, 102-cannoned giant was very much the product of the King's own imagination. Indeed, Charles frequently interfered in this process of construction, usually in order to increase the armaments or decoration borne by this leviathan. This ship was so gargantuan Charles's own naval advisors issued troubled warnings: 'the strength of men could not wield her cables'; 'anchors and cables could not hold a ship of this bulk in a storm'; 'the art of wit of men cannot build a shipp fit for service with three tier or ordnance'; 'there is no port in the kingdom can harbour this ship'.[8] In military terms, this vessel was clearly designed to operate as an early modern super-dreadnought, intimidating all-comers with overwhelming firepower. The total exchequer expenditure on this vessel is now impossible to calculate, however contemporary opinion estimated the amount spent on *The Sovereign* as equivalent to 'a whole years Ship-Money'.[9] Interestingly for the honoured guest from Morocco, Captain Rainborow, the champion of the raid on Salé, was given command of this ship for forthcoming sea-trials. In highlighting such a piece of military hardware in the itinerary of the Ambassador's formal progress, the interconnections between Caroline naval power and developing foreign alliances were clear for all to see.

However, as well as being an impressive piece of military equipment, *The Sovereign* was also sumptuously decorated. As a guide through the thickets of iconography exhibited on this ruinously expensive craft, Thomas Heywood's *A True Description of his Majesties Royall Ship* (1637) proves invaluable. In

---

[6]   Ibid., p. 8.

[7]   Ibid, p. 8.

[8]   Evelyn Berckman, *Creators and destroyers of the English Navy* (London: Hamilton, 1974), pp. 79–81.

[9]   James Howell, *Epistolæ Ho Elianæ ... Familiar Letters domestic and forren; divided into six sections: partly historicall, politicall, philosophicall, upon emergent occasions. By J. H.* (London: 1645), p. 222.

particular, Heywood's detailed scrutiny of the use of the Anglo–Saxon King Edgar in *The Sovereign*'s adornments sheds light on the political ambitions behind the construction of this ornate colossus. Thus, we should note that Heywood describes how this ship's 'Beak-head', or transom, carries a likeness of 'royall King Edgar on horseback, tramping on Seven Kings'. Such regal puissance is repeated in Heywood's assertion that Edgar was 'the first who could truely write himself an absolute ruler of this Iland' and the observation that, despite a naturally irenic nature, Edgar first established a kingly navy in order to 'secure navigations from, Enemies and Rovers'. It is interesting to note that Heywood pays some attention to the 'most princely barge' used by Edgar and its use in his royal progresses; through such a vessel, it appears that the ancient monarch 'let the world know he was Lord and king'. Of course, Heywood views Charles as 'the True and Lawfull hereditary successor' to Edgar; more intriguingly, he also sees Charles as the inheritor of his claim to be 'Rex Marium'. This title may seem to be a typical piece of Caroline hyperbole. However, this designation refers to Charles I's attempt to exert an unprecedented degree of legal control over the waters surrounding his Kingdom. This doctrine was formally advanced on behalf of the Crown by "the learned Mr [John] Selden, in the exquisite and absolute work of his called *Mare Clausum*" and posited the monarch's ability to control all shipping within the coastal waters of his realm.[10] Selden's rejection of the legal status quo not only claimed 'the very shores and ports of the neighbouring sovereigns on the other side of the sea are the bounds of the maritime dominion of Britain'. His tenuous arguments also imagined royal power extending into the 'open and vast ocean to the north and west' of these islands.[11] The Latin mottoes on *The Sovereign*'s transom carving ('Ab Egdaro quator Maria Vindico') and larger cannon ('Carolus Edgari Sceptrum Stabilibit Aquarum') were designed to support this early modern claim to exercise an ancient right far in excess of that commonly considered due to European monarchs.[12] With such a vessel, Charles I could not only enact his newly ambitious naval policy, but exhibit this ideology of an absolute maritime monarchy extending beyond the horizon. In the 'pleasing and contenting Admiration' with which this vessel was viewed by the Moroccan emissary, we can see the King's guest gratifyingly assenting to both the spectacle and ideology presented to him.[13]

After this moment of wonder, this maritime procession moved onwards to more memorable scenes. Admittedly, the ambassadorial party sojourned 'at the Rose and Crowne for foure Houres'. However, progress upstream was soon resumed

---

[10] Thomas Heywood, *A true Description of His Majesties Royall Ship, built this yeare 1637, at Wooll*-witch (London, 1637), pp. 29–39.

[11] R.P. Anand, *Origin and Development of the Law of the Sea* (The Hague and London: Martinus Nijhoff, 1983), p. 106.

[12] Alan R. Young, *His Majesty's royal ship: a critical edition of Thomas Heywood's A true description of His Majesties royall ship* (New York and London: AMS Press, 1990), p. xxvii.

[13] Glover, p. 8.

when Jauhar Ibn 'Abd Allah boarded 'the Kings Barge with the Lord Kenwell and 12. Gentlemen of his Majesties Privy Chamber', and was then rowed 'to Tower-wharfe' with 'Trumpets sounding before them all the way'. As this party reached the north shore of the Thames, the crowd that met it disembarking was composed of 'Thousands, and tens of Thousands of spectators'. The Ambassador was conveyed to 'his Majesties Coach' with 'at least 100. Coaches more, and the chiefest of Citizens' in attendance. The City of London had marshalled its forces to welcome this honoured guest; accordingly, the full complement of 'the Sheriffes and Aldermen of London in their Scarlet Gownes' gathered in greeting. Moreover, a squadron of 'Barbary-Merchants bravely mounted on horseback, all richly apparelled, every man having a Chain of Gold about him', were also present on the distinguished shoreline. Having set out from Greenwich 'an houre before Night', the final reception of 'this brave and noble Embassador' took place in darkness. However, there was such an abundance of 'Torches and Links, that thought it were Night, yet the Streetes were almost as light as Day'.[14] It seems that such ceremonies could transform the shadowy thoroughfares of London into a stage on which a radiant, almost magical, display of international concord was performed.

Crucially, these episodes of maritime spectacle did not end with the Ambassador's initial reception in London. The notebooks of John Finet inform us that 'The Moroccan Ambassador and his associate Mr Blake' attended the presentation of a Court masque on 'Twelfthnight' in early 1638 in the recently renovated Banqueting House at Whitehall. Interestingly, Finet tells us that these guests 'were there seated with the better sort of person in attendance in a compartment capable of a dozen persons at the left hand behind his majestyes seate'.[15] From this privileged viewing point, they would have been able to enjoy William Davenant's *Britannia Triumphans*, the first masque performed at Court since 1636. Furthermore, this location would have allowed these envoys a superior view of the 'ceiling since richly adorn'd with pieces of painting of great value' by Peter Paul Rubens, commemorating 'the acts of King James I of happy memory'. The declared subject of the masque was of immediate relevance to the King's wider maritime and naval policy:

> Britanocles, the glory of this world, hath by his wisdom, valour and piety, not only vindicated his own, but also far distant seas, infested with pirates, and reduc'd the land, by his example, to a real knowledge of all good acts and sciences.

In the heightened, allegorical language of the masque, Charles I is declared to be the victor over lawless seas and the wise ruler of his own people. In the decoration around the stage on which this drama will be performed, this political message was repeated and amplified. Thus, we should pay attention to two emblematic figures:

---

[14]　Ibid., pp. 8–9.

[15]　John Finet, *The Ceremonies of Charles 1: the notebooks of John Finet, 1628–1641*, (ed.) Alfred J. Loomie (New York: Fordham University Press, 1987), p. 242.

On the right hand a woman in a watchet drapery, heightened with silver, on her head a *Corona Rostrata* with one hand holding the rudder of a ship, and in the other a little winged figure with a branch of palm, and a garland: this woman represented Naval Victory. Opposite to this on the other neech sate the figure of a man bearing as sceptre … his foot treading on the head of a serpent. By this figure was signified right government.[16]

The spectacle to be viewed is, in consequence, framed by an idealised vision of true kingship and maritime military potency.

The action of the masque itself also engages with this theme of naval ambition. When Britanocles appears, 'Fame' and an attendant chorus of ancient poets eulogise this model monarch in language that clearly asserts the newly forceful Caroline naval policy.

What to thy power is hard or strange? Since not confined unto land;
The sceptre to a trident change! And straight unruly seas thou canst command!
How hath thy wisdom rais'd this Isle? Or thee, by what new title shall we call?
Since it were less'ning of thy style, If we should name thee Nature's Admiral.

Later, this masque transports us to 'the farthest part of the ocean' with the backdrop 'terminating the sight with the horizon'. From these waters 'the sea-nymph Galatea … on the back of a dolphin, in a loose white garment' appears. She, too, extols the model monarch's virtues in 'Reducing what was wild' in the oceans, ensuring that 'That fairest sea-nymphs leave the troubled main / And haste to visit him on shore'. As Galatea departs, we next see 'ships that were discern'd sailing afar off in several ways' transform into 'a great fleet'. This fleet is then carried by 'a prosperous gale' safely into 'a haven with a citadel', with this spectacle 'continuing to entertain the sight whilst the dancing lasted'.[17] Thus, it seems that royal power can change dangerous waters into a calm place suitable for trade, and bring those who do business on those waters into a place of security and protection. For all spectators, including the envoy from the Empire of Morocco, the meaning of this nautical fantasia was clear: Charles I, absolute ruler of this island and all seas, was to be an actor of global significance in maritime affairs.

The continuity of form and message between varied forms of spectacular entertainment now seems apparent. The coastal batteries had already announced Caroline aspirations to naval supremacy with their volleys of ordnance over the Moroccan Ambassador's barge; the ornate immensity of *The Sovereign of the Seas* had attempted to imprint these desires in the imagination of this same diplomat through the shipwright and carver's art; the commanders of early modern, international capitalism had been luminously mustered on the Thames in support of the 'Rex

---

[16]   William Davenant, *Dramatic Works* (5 vols, Edinburgh: Paterson, 1872–78), vol. 2, pp. 265–6.
[17]   Ibid., pp. 285–9.

Marium'; finally, the honoured guest from the Maghreb saw Caroline ambitions to rule the waves dramatised in the resplendent theatricality of Court masque. Each of these phenomena, placed on true or pretended waves, deployed a related vocabulary of emblems and symbols that are entirely consonant with contemporary royal ambitions. Moreover, in the Court of Charles I, all locations seem to have become a kind of stage, all events a species of symbolic drama, all persons of consequence both actors and spectators in one form of pageant of another. Not only were forms of waterborne pageantry essential to the way Charles I's monarchy represented itself during this period, such pomp and ceremony was also seamlessly fused into the wider cultural, political and military practices of his regime.

However, we must not be too easily seduced by the striking allure and apparent coherence of such cultural propaganda. We should recall that many of the enterprises associated with this diplomatic mission ended unfortunately. Charles I was clearly keen to impress the Ambassador's master with his representations of regal power: not only did his parting gift to the Ambassador include 'fair Denmark horses', 'a coach to be lined with crimson velvet', 'the finest broad cloths' and '100 lances' but also 'the king and queens pictures drawne after the Vandikes originals'.[18] However, the great images of authority fabricated in London and sent to Morocco seemed to change little. No sustained military alliance ever materialised, commerce in the waters of North Africa did not flourish and Englishmen in chains were not triumphantly set at liberty. Indeed, Nabil Matar has argued that the persistent failure of the Crown to protect English shipping and mariners crucially antagonised the mercantile élite of London in the years of discontent that acted as prologue to civil war.[19] According to Matar, it is telling that *The Grand Remonstrance* of 1641 makes much of the fact that the 'unheard-of tax of ship-money', despite raising 'near L 700, 000 some years' still left mercantile traffic 'naked to the violence of the Turkish pirates' and thousands still 'in miserable captivity'.[20] The opposition of Parliament, the natural ally of the mercantile class, to the unbounded ambitions of the Crown may have been partly prompted by the disappointments of the King's North African misadventures. Similarly, *The Sovereign of the Seas* did not see active service in any great pacification of distant waters; rather this monstrosity became the occasion of new enmities, with John Evelyn offering the opinion that the extravagant expenditure on this ship 'cost his Majestie the Affections of his subjects'.[21] It is with a grim irony that *Britannia Triumphans* included an anti-masque of 'rebellious Leaders in war' that included 'Cade, Kett, Jack Straw and their soldiers'.[22] It was in the Banqueting House at Whitehall, the venue for this

---

[18]   Finet, pp. 249–50.

[19]   Nabil Matar, 'The Barbary Corsairs, King Charles I and the Civil War', *The Seventeenth Century*, 16, no. 2 (2001), pp. 239–58.

[20]   Ibid., p. 246.

[21]   John Evelyn, *Diary*, ed. E.S. De Beer (6 vols, Oxford: Clarendon Press, 1955), vol. 1, p. 22.

[22]   Davenant, vol. 2, p. 274.

masque, that Charles I would be executed by order of his seditious subjects. Yet, in all of the maritime shows, performances and pageants associated with the visit of the Moroccan embassy of 1637–38, we observe the assumption of present concord and victory, and the expectation of yet greater fame for the King in the years to come. Amid so much complacency, the real or imagined waters of pageant yielded no sign of the shipwreck that lay ahead.

Bibliography

Printed Primary Sources

Davenant, William, *Dramatic Works* (5 vols, Edinburgh: Paterson, 1872–78).
Evelyn, John, *Diary*, ed. E.S. De Beer (6 vols, Oxford: Clarendon Press, 1955).
Glover, George, *The Arrivall and Intertainements of the Embassador Alkaid Jaurar Ben Abdella with his associate Mr R. Blake, from the high and mighty Prince, Mulley Mahamed Sheque, Emperor of Morocco, King of Fesse and Suss* (London, 1637).
Heywood, Thomas, *A true Description of His Majesties Royall Ship, built this yeare 1637, at Wooll-witch* (London, 1637).
Howell, James, *Epistolæ Ho Elianæ ... Familiar Letters domestic and forren; divided into six sections: partly historicall, politicall, philosophicall, upon emergent occasions. By J.H.* (London, 1645).
Srhir, Khalid Ben, *Britain and Morocco during the embassy of John Drummond Hay*, trans. Malcolm Williams and Gavin Waterman (Abingdon: Routledge Curzon, 2004).

Secondary Sources

Anand, R.P., *Origin and Development of the Law of the Sea* (The Hague and London: Martinus Nijhoff, 1983).
Andrews, Kenneth R., *Ships, Money and, Politics: seafaring and naval enterprise in the reign of Charles I* (Cambridge: Cambridge University Press, 1991).
Berckman, Evelyn, *Creators and destroyers of the English Navy* (London: Hamilton, 1974).
Finet, John, *The Ceremonies of Charles 1: the notebooks of John Finet, 1628–1641*, (ed.) Alfred J. Loomie (New York: Fordham University Press, 1987).
Fisher, Geoffrey, *The Barbary legend: war, trade and piracy in North Africa, 1415–1830* (Oxford: Clarendon Press, 1957).
Matar, Nabil, 'The Barbary Corsairs, King Charles I and the Civil War', *The Seventeenth Century*, 16, no. 2 (2001), pp. 239–58.
Young, Alan R., *His Majesty's royal ship: a critical edition of Thomas Heywood's A true description of His Majesties royall ship* (New York and London: AMS Press, 1990).

Chapter 16

The Savoy *Naumachia* on the Lake Mont Cenis: A Site-specific Spectacle in the 'Amphitheatre' of the Alps

Melanie Zefferino

The Mont Cenis Pass is an ancient doorway to the Alps, famous for having been used as the main passage for the descent of Constantine the Great to Italy in spring 312 as well as Charlemagne's invasion in 773. Few know, however, that this harsh route connecting Savoy's Maurienne Region to Piedmont's Susa Valley became part of a festival path taking a princely couple to Lake Mont Cenis, just across the pass, where a *naumachia* was staged in 1619. The aim of this chapter is to give an account of this waterborne festival, set up to bring the past into the present while celebrating the marriage of Victor Amédée I of Savoy, Prince of Piedmont and Marie Christine de Bourbon, Princess of France, part way through their triumphant journey from Chambery to Turin.

The converging political strategies of France and Savoy in the second decade of the seventeenth century culminated with the nuptials of Victor Amédée I of Savoy and Marie Christine de Bourbon. As a matter of fact, this dynastic marriage revived the alliance established in April 1610 with the Treaty of Bruzolo, signed by Charles Emanuel I, Duke of Savoy and Henry IV, King of France, with its agreement to the marriage of their offspring, Victor Amédée I and Elisabeth de Bourbon respectively. Things went wrong, however, when Henry IV was murdered nearly one month later and the Regent Maria de' Medici countermanded the agreement. As a consequence, Elisabeth de Bourbon was married to Philip IV of Spain in 1615, whilst Victor Amédée I was sent to Madrid to renew the frayed political ties with his Spanish relatives.[1] Savoy's reconcilement with Spain did not last, however: soon after taking over his mother's regency as ruling king of France, Louis XIII received a new proposal for the marriage of his sister Marie Christine de Bourbon to Victor Amédée I of Savoy.[2]

---

[1]   Victor Amédée I of Savoy (1587–1637) was the second born but eldest surviving son of Charles Emanuel I, Duke of Savoy (1562–1630) and the Infanta Catalina Michaela of Spain (1567–97).

[2]   *Matrimonio tra il Principe di Piemonte Vittorio Amedeo Io e Cristina di Francia figlia di Enrico 4 e Sorella di Lodovico 13, Re di Francia*, Mazzo 26, no. 2, '*Minuta d'istruzione del Duca Carlo Emanuele al Presidente Fresia, e Barone di Marcieux per*

Historic documents in the Italian State Archives of Turin reveal that the negotiations between Louis XIII and Cardinal Charles Maurice, Prince of Piedmont, on behalf of his brother Charles Emanuel I and his nephew Victor Amédée I of Savoy, went on for more than a year.[3] Finally, the marriage agreement was signed on 11 January 1619. A petition asking the Pope's dispensation for the French princess to marry at the age of 13 was presented on 17 January 1619,[4] and the marriage was celebrated on 10 February that same year.[5] Marie Christine de Bourbon was not pleased with the choice made by her brother, because marrying the future Duke of Savoy[6] she would never have become queen, yet she did acquire the honorary title of Queen of Cyprus by way of this marriage. Nonetheless, she would have used the title *Madame Royale*, indicating her status at the French Court, even when she ruled Savoy as regent from 1638 to 1648 and, *de facto*, until her death in 1663.[7]

In September 1619 Victor Amédée I and Marie Christine, who had earlier left Paris, departed from Tours bound for Lyon.[8] According to the sources, their

portarsi alla Corte di Francia, e farvi la proposizione del Matrimonio di Madama Cristina sorella secondogenita del Re col Principe di Piemonte', 1617 (Turin, State Archives).

[3] Ibid., Mazzo 26, no. 3, *'Procure del Duca di Savoia Carlo Emanuele Primo e del Principe di Piemonte Vittorio Amedeo Primo di lui figlio primogenito in capo del Cardinale Morizio di Savoia per portarsi in Pariggi a trattare, e conchiudere il matrimonio del ditto Principe di Piemonte con Maria Cristina di Francia, figlia d'Enrico il Grande'*, 20 and 28 October 1618; no. 5, *'Capitoli proposti per parte di Ludovico 13 Re di Francia per il Matrimonio di Maria Cristina di Francia sua sorella col Principe di Piemonte Vittorio Amedeo. Colle risposte fatte dal Principe Carlo Maurizio di Savoja'*, 1618; and no. 6, *'Riflessi del Presidente a Favore sovra li Capitoli proposti per parte del Re di Francia per lo Matrimonio di Vittorio Amedeo I con Maria Cristina di Francia'*, 1618 (Turin, State Archives).

[4] Ibid., Mazzo 26, no. 7, *'Contratto di matrimonio tra il principe di Piemonte Vittorio Amedeo Figlio del Duca Carlo Emanuele Primo di Savoja, e Maria Cristina di Francia figlia del Re Enrico 4o e Sorella di Lodovico 13o'*, 11 January 1619; no. 8 – *'Procura del Principe di Piemonte Vittorio Amedeo I a motive di ottenere la dispensa del Papa per la celebrazione del Matrimonio tra esso, e la Principessa Cristina di Francia'*, 17 January 1619 (Turin, State Archives).

[5] *Les Pompes et magnificences faites au Mariage du Prince Victor aisné de la Maison de Savoye & Madame Christine fille de France. Espousez le Dimanche au soir dixiesme Fevrier mil six cens dixneur. Ensemble de la reception desdicts sieurs Princes dans le Louvre* (François Yurat, Lyon 1619) in Turin, Biblioteca Reale, Misc. 298/7. See also *Relation du Grand Ballet du Roy dance en la sale du Louvre le 12 février 1619 sur adventure de Tancrède en la forest enchantée* (Paris : Jean Sara, 1619) in Paris, *Bibliothèque Nationale de France*, Lb 36–116).

[6] Andrea Merlotti, 'Politique dynastique et alliances matrimoniales de la Maison de Savoie au XVIIe siècle', *Dix-septième siècle*, 2009/2, n. 243, pp. 239–53.

[7] See Samuel Guichenon, *Le Soleil en son apogée ou l'histoire de la vie de Chrestienne de France* (Turin, Biblioteca Reale, MSS. St Patria, 911).

[8] *Grande et celebre magnificence, faites à Madame Christine de France, Princesse de Piedmont à son arivée dans Thurin. Avec la forme de sa reception, nombre des Princes Signeurs*

original plan was to continue their journey towards Avignon, and then make their triumphal entry into Chambery. A hand-written *minuta* now in the State Archives of Turin bears witness to a night-time tournament and lavish fireworks organized for the occasion, on 23 October 1619, and followed by a stag hunt also involving *Madame Royale*.[9] For the couple's triumphal entry into Chambery, the Duke of Savoy's knights wore amaranthine velvet jackets with silver embroideries and light blue silk lining; scarlet cavalry dresses; and white, amaranthine and carnation helmet plumes. According to the missive sent to the House of Savoy to announce that their marriage proposal had been accepted (and thus disclosing 'the colours of the bride') white, carnation, light blue and amaranthine were the princess's favourite hues. Of course, these colours carried symbolic meanings: white epitomized faith; carnation was an allusion to virtue; amaranthine, the colour of Turin, represented strength; whilst light blue, the colour of Savoy, hinted at nobleness.[10] Marie Christine de Bourbon's dowry inventory reveals that carnation may well have been her favourite colour as two of her 15 dresses and other clothing were made of *encarnadin* silk. Only one dress and a mantle were white, but she had four silver threaded silk dresses, the richest of which is described as '*Une robe de brocard à fonds de trame d'argent relevée de fleurs d'argent avec manches pendants et manches de toile d'argent garnie de boutons et passementerie d'argent*' ('A brocade dress with silver threads in the weft, silver flowers in relief, pendant sleeves, and sleeves of silver toile with silver buttons and trimming'). Silver and gold embroidery also ornamented four black silk dresses and a blue one.[11]

From Chambery, *Madame Royale* and Victor Amédée I were supposed to go to Nice, pass the autumn there '*come in una Primavera*' ('as if it were spring'), and thence reach Turin.[12] But the autumn was mild that year and there was no snow on the near mountains, so the programme was changed: after a short stay in Chambery, the couple made their way to Turin through Novalesa, Susa, Rivoli, Moncalieri and Chieri after passing by Lake Mont Cenis.

& *Grandes Dames, qui s'y sont trouvés, les jouxtes & tournois, & autres actes de resiouissance y representez* (Paris: Silvestre Moreau en sa Boutique en la Cour du Palais, 1619).

[9] *Matrimonio* ..., Mazzo 26, no. 11, '*Relatione delle feste fatte d'ordine del Duca Vittorio Amedeo Primo a Maria Cristina di Francia sua Consorte nel di lei passaggio del Moncenisio, e dell'entrata che fece nella Citta di Torino il 15 marzo 1620*' (Turin, State Archives).

[10] *Relatione della correria all'Huomo armato fatta dal Sereniss.o Prencipe di Piemonte*, (Turin, Luigi Pizzamiglio, 1619) in Turin, Biblioteca Reale, Misc. 300/13.

[11] 'A brocade dress of raised woven silver and silver flowers, with hanging sleeves of cloth, decorated with buttons and silver trimming.' *Matrimonio* ..., Mazzo 26, no. 10, '*Inventario de' mobili, argenterie ed abiti portati da Pariggi da Maria Cristina di Francia Moglie del Duca di Savoja Vittorio Amedeo Primo*' (Turin, 1619).

[12] *Relatione della festa fatta fare da S. A. Sereniss. a Madama nel passare, che fece del Moncenisio alli 9 di Novembre, 1619*, (Turin: Luigi Pizzamiglio Stampator Ducale, 1619).

Favourable weather conditions not only underpinned the change in the originally planned route, but also allowed the Duke of Savoy to have what we may call in today's terms a 'site specific' show staged in a natural amphitheatre on the Alps, described as follows in the *Relatione della festa fatta fare da S. A. Sereniss. a Madama nel passare, che fece del Moncenisio alli 9 di Novembre 1619*:

> *Il sito è nobilissimo et conspicuo tra tutti gl'altri del Mondo; è in mezo delle Alpi che dividono la Savoia dal Piemonte e l'Italia dalla Gallia, ov'è una pianura che è lunga da sei a otto miglia Italiani e larga circa quattro, che si va però restringendo nelle punte in forma d'ovato oblungo. Ha in mezo un lago amplissimo, chiaro et fertile d'ogni sorte di pesci, et massime di trutte grandi oltre misura, et d'altre picciole saporitissime. S'ha un fiume, che precipitandosi nella caducità dell'altezza del monte verso il Piemonte entra nella Dora a Susa: il nome suo è Cenisio, et lo pigliò, overo lo diede al monte. Intorno a questa gran piana fanno corona sei altissimi monti, tutti pascoli eccellentissimi et ripieni d'armenti d'ogni sorte, alla cima poi de quali s'elevano in tanti scogli aguzzi sei punte piramidali a cui le famose d'Egitto devono cedere d'assai. La prima a mandestra nella salita d'Italia è il monte di nostra Signora di Rocchiamelone, overo della Neve, dove vi è una capella fatta fabricare da uno de' Signori della Casa Rovera centinaia d'anni sono; et è di grandissima divotione, concorrendovi il giorno della festa, che è alli cinque d'Agosto, popolo innumerabile, et dalla Savoia et dal Piemonte. Segue poi a quella stessa mano il gran Moncenisio, et indi il Monte Iseran al primissimo dove nasce l'Isera, fiume navigabile. Continuando poi l'ovato dall'altra parte, confina con questo la Vanoysa, monte che è sopra Laneborgo et dal quale si può andare in Tarantasa. A questo segue il picciol Moncenisio, che è di rispetto del grande, et poi quello di Giaglione, che confina col Delfinato e mira quello di nostra Signora di Rocchiamelone; et così si vede compito il circolo dell'ovato.*

[The site is sublime, and remarkable among all others in the world. It is in the middle of the Alps that divide Savoy from Piedmont and Italy from Gaul. There's a plain here, measuring from six to eight Italian miles in length and nearly four in width, which has an oblong shape, like that of an oval with narrowing edges. In the middle of this plain there is a wide and clear lake inhabited by a huge variety of fish species, especially trout, mainly large-sized, but also small-sized and very tasty. There also is a river that runs down from the height of the mountain into Piedmont, and merges into the Dora River at Susa: its name is Cenis – taken from, or rather given to, the mount. The wide plain mentioned earlier is crowned by six high mountains: all are grasslands swarming with many kinds of herds, and all culminating in rocky peaks which, in the distance, look like six sharp edges of as many pyramids, by far higher than the famous ones in Egypt. From the climbing route on the Italian side, the first mountain on the right is Our Lady of Rocciamelone or Our Lady of the Snows, where there's a chapel that was built hundreds of years ago by order of a nobleman of the House of Rovere. It is an important place of worship in that lots of people come here from Savoy and Piedmont on the patron's day, that is the fifth of August. Looking further from right to left we may see the great peak of Mont Cenis and then Mount Iseran, the headwaters of the Isera, a navigable river. Moving forward to the other side of the oval shape, we may see the Vanoise, a mount overseeing Lanslebourg, from which it is possible to go to the Tarentaise Valley. Then, there's the small peak of Mont Cenis, facing the great one. And lastly there is the peak Giaglione, bordering on the Dauphiné and facing the mount of Our Lady of Rocciamelone. Hence, the oval outline is complete.][13]

The anonymous author of the festival book supposes that the Duke of Savoy wished to entertain Marie Christine of France with a sumptuous feast and so relieve her from the tiresome route through the Alps, and would thus have brought Europe's most curious and remarkable products into such a harsh mountain scene. For this purpose, he commissioned the construction of an ephemeral castle overlooking the lake, yet not too far from the route. Designed by the architect Carlo di Castellamonte, the castle 'was finished perfectly and so quickly that, considering the short time available, it nearly seemed to have been made by magic'.[14] The rooms at the first floor had crimson red velvet wall tapestry with grotesque-motif embroideries; they were decorated with Chinese silk drapery, Flemish tapestries depicting scenes from Ovid's *Metamorphosis*, and frescoes on the vaulted ceilings. From these rooms *Madame Royale*, the Savoy family and the court would have seen a dazzling re-enactment of Amédée V of Savoy's expedition to Rhodes, undertaken in 1315 to aid the Knights of St John defending the island of Rhodes against the Turks.

The House of Savoy was bound by the marriage agreement[15] to welcome Marie Christine with receptions fitting for her princely status, and yet the huge effort required to realize such a challenging project offers a clue suggesting that there were further aspects of this *naumachia* that made it of value to Charles Emanuel I. With regard to the subject, we may bear in mind that Honoré d'Urfé (1567–1625) was likely to have completed his *Savoysiade* during his long sojourn in Piedmont, from the year of his knighting by the Duke of Savoy in 1618, to 1620.[16] D'Urfé's epic poem, in which one of the most significant episodes is the expedition of Amédée

---

[13]   Ibid.

[14]   Ibid., '*fu finito di tutto punto et così presto che, rispetto alla brevità del tempo, parve quasi un incanto*'.

[15]   *Matrimonio ...*, Mazzo 26, no. 7, '*Contratto di matrimonio tra il Principe di Piemonte Vittorio Amedeo Figlio del Duca Carlo Emanuele Primo di Savoja, e Maria Cristina di Francia figlia del Re Enrico 4o e Sorella di Lodovico 13o*', 11 January 1619 (Turin, State Archives).

[16]   Nicolas Ducimetière, 'La bibliothèque d'Honoré D'Urfé: histoire de sa formation et de sa dispersion à travers quelques exemplaires retrouvés', *Dix-septième siècle*, 2010/4, n. 249, pp. 747–73.

V to Rhodes,[17] celebrates the history of the House of Savoy, emphasizing the fact that this dynasty – unlike the Medici or the Farnese – had ruled since the Middle Ages, and could boast dynastic ties with royal houses such as the Habsburg and the Bourbon since 1313 and 1355 respectively.[18] In staging the deeds of Amédée V (1249–1323), therefore, Charles Emanuel I would have celebrated the glory of the House of Savoy, bringing the past into the present, as explicitly asserted in the description of the *naumachia*.[19]

Also according to this source, the geographical conformation of the site made the Lake Mont Cenis a suitable scene for the re-enactment of the Greek island's rescue since 'in the middle of the lake, although a little closer to the southern part, there is an island with a concave shore forming a beautiful harbour, similar to that of Rhodes, as we may see it in the pictures depicting it'.[20]

The Duke of Savoy's dream came true on 9 November 1619, when the Lake Mont Cenis and its island were transformed into the Aegean Sea and the island of Rhodes, for the pleasure of those seeing the spectacle:

> *Et si scoprì nello spuntar del giorno tutta l'Isola torregiante et cintà di muraglia merlata d'ogni intorno, et col suono delle trombe et de' tamburri si vide ripiena di Cavalieri di S. Giovanni, le cui Croci et armi lampeggiavano d'ogni parte. Poi si vedeva l'armata Turchesca da una parte dell'Isola vicina ad un cavo del Lago, poco discosto da Rhodi, uscire con buon ordine tutta biancheggiante di turbanti, et vistosa d'habiti rossi, con mezze lune argentate tanto nelle bandiere, fiamme et stendardi ch'altri ornamenti loro. Et sopra uno rilevato dalla parte del Lago verso ponente si vedeva l'Artiglieria del Campo de' Turchi; che nello sparare contra la Città faceva ribombare questi monti d'intorno. D'altra parte, un poco più à mano dritta del Palazzo, si vedeva ancho uscire l'Armata de'*

---

[17]   G. Bosco, 'L'Epico D'Urfé, cortigiano sabaudo', in M. Masoero, S. Mamino and C. Rosso (eds), *Politica e Cultura nell'età di Carlo Emanuele I*, Papers of the International Conference held in Turin on 21–24 February 1995 (Florence, 1999), pp. 263–73.

[18]   See Franco Angiolini, 'Medici e Savoia. Contese per la precedenza e rivalità di rango in età moderna', in P. Bianchi and L.C. Gentile (eds), *Dinastie, poteri, élites in Piemonte e Savoia tra tardo medioevo e prima età moderna* (Turin, 2006), pp. 435–80.

[19]   *Relatione della festa ...*, 'Et faccia Dio, che sicome quel Gran Amedeo riportò da un'attione così heroica quel bel titolo di FORTITUDO EIUS RHODUM TENIT et la Croce bianca per le sue armi, così il nostro Buono Vittorioso Amedeo, havendo una Regal Christiana per guida, con i magnanimi et generosi suoi Fratelli non solo Rhodi soccorri, ma l'espugni et lo togli dalla mano di quelli infedeli, con Gierusaleme insieme'* ('May God permit that our noble Victor Amédée – like Amédée the Great, who was awarded the prestigious title of *Fortitudo Eius Rhodum Tenit* for his deeds, and took the White Cross [on a red background as his coat of arms] – could not only help Rhodes, but rather rescue it from those infidels and also rescue Jerusalem').

[20]   Ibid., *'Nasce in mezo del lago, però un poco più vicino alla riva dalla parte di mezo giorno, un'isola, la quale ha in mezo un seno incavato che fa un porto bellissimo, et appunto come quello che si vede figurato di Rhodi'*.

Christiani del Serenissimo Amedeo in bonissimo ordine, con stendardi, fiamme, bandiere, et sopraveste turchine, colore di Savoia, con argento, che si faceva una leggiadrissima vista. Et dall'altra parte del Palazzo, a mano sinistra, si scorgeva ancora benissimo un essercito di Terra de Christiani. Et molto più lontano, dalla parte di Levante e mezzo giorno, un altro de' Turchi, i quali poco a poco s'andavano approssimando.

[And so, at dawn, we discovered that the island was covered with towers surrounded by crenellated walls, and full of Knights of St John, whose crosses and weapons were gleaming everywhere at the sound of trumpets and drums. Then, from one part of the island, near an inlet on the lake that is not very far from 'Rhodes', we saw the Turks marching in line, all wearing white turbans and striking red clothes; they carried torches, banners and other ensigns, all with silvery half moons thereon. The Turkish camp's artillery, whose shooting at the city made these mountains roar, was on top of an eminence on the western side of the lake. On the other side, slightly to the right of the palace, the Christian soldiers of Duke Amédée, all wearing silver embroidered cloaks of turquoise, the colour of Savoy, marched up in line carrying banners, torches and flags; and all this was utterly pleasing to see. To the left of the palace we could also see very clearly the ground forces of the Christians; and, in the distance, the Turkish ground troops approaching slowly from South-East.][21]

As far as we can glean from this description, the show had already started when the princely couple – followed by Charles Emanuel I, the cavalry, the Duke's brothers Charles Maurice, Philibert and Thomas of Savoy (on horseback) and the nobles – arrived at the lake surrounded by a festive crowd. Indeed, the show continued while a banquet was given in the castle, and gained momentum by the time the meal had finished, as we may assume from the following passage:

Fra tanto ... le armate tanto di mare, per così dire, che di terra s'erano già approssimate tanto, che mettendosi Madama alla finestra si vide prima le maritime venir alle mani, le quali ostinatamente combattettero da tutte le parti per un buon prezzo, al fine però vinse il Serenissimo Amedeo con li Christiani, che messi in fuga una parte de vascelli et gli altri presi, et remurciandoli fecero un giro per il Lago voltando verso Rhodi, come per il trionfo, e lo liberarono dall'assedio. In questo mentre quelle di terra fecero anco l'istesso, et cominciarono prima gl'Arcobuggieri a cavallo delle guardie delle loro Altezze ad attaccar la scaramuccia, hora dando et hora pigliando la carica fino che gli squadroni delle lancie s'andarono loro accostando, scontentandosi così gli uni et gl'altri fin tanto che, usciti dalle dette squadre alquanti Cavalieri che il Signor Prencipe Tomaso havea seco, et il Marchese di Cigliano dall'altra parte, come per una particolar sfida s'incontrarono gl'uni et gl'altri. Et così a campo aperto

---

[21]   Ibid.

ruppero alcune lancie benissimo, ma frà gl'altri, che si segnalarono più, tanto nel romper delle lancie che delle livree, fu il detto Serenissimo Prencipe Tomaso col Signor di Parela, che ruppero eccellentemente. Così anco il Marchese di Cigliano, il Conte di Masino, il Conte di Montuè, il Conte di Vische, il Cavalier Cavorreto, il Signor Tagliacarne, il Conte Arduino Valperga, il Signor Forno, tanto che riunitisi con li squadroni vennero al fatto d'armi, che durò poco poiché li Turchi pigliarono la fuga et il Campo restò de' Christiani.

[In the meantime ... the 'marine forces', if I may call them so, and the ground forces, had already approached. Henceforth, looking out of the window, Madame Royale saw the sea army fighting on all sides for quite a while. At last, however, the Duke Amédée and the Christians triumphed: after making the enemy flee and taking some of their ships, the rowing vessels of the rescuers sailed across the lake towards 'Rhodes', as if in a Triumph, and broke the naval siege. While all this was going on, the ground troops were also fighting: at first the cavalrymen of the Savoy guard fired their arquebuses, which they continued to load and fire until the lancer squadrons came closer and started a skirmish. Then, some of these lancers – led by Prince Thomas of Savoy on one side, and the Marquis of Cigliano on the other – engaged in military contest. And so in open combat they all broke their lances, but those who excelled for their jousting skills and in their liveries were Prince Thomas of Savoy with Sir Parela, who tilted with their lances very well, and so did the Marquis of Cigliano, the Count of Masino, the Count of Montuè, the Count of Vische, the lord of Cavorreto, Sir Tagliacarne, the Count of Arduino Valperga, and Sir Forno. Once the joust had finished, the knights re-joined their squadrons and fought a battle with the enemy, which didn't last long because the Turks fled and the Christians took over the battlefield.][22]

Finally, the nobles and knights exited the fictional space and came into the real space – that of their audience – as they had to escort Marie Christine of France on her way to the Benedictine Abbey of Novalesa, a stronghold of Christianity. Strangely, it seems they would not even then stop throwing spears and engaging in short skirmishes.[23]

With regard to the audience's reception of the show, the author of the celebratory report tells us that nothing could have pleased *Madame Royale* more than seeing the representation of a victory against those 'infidels' also defeated many times by her Christian ancestors. This kind of binary opposition actually engaged the European audiences of the time, and the theme recurs in epic poems as well as other forms of artistic expression. This one in particular ended before

---

[22] Ibid.

[23] Early seventeenth-century arquebuses, spears, jousting armours and cavalry banners of Savoy and Piedmont as well as Charles Emanuel I of Savoy's armour can be seen at the Royal Armoury of Turin.

sunset, and is remembered as 'marvellous and beautiful by virtue of the subject, the audience, the site and the season, in that the mountains are usually covered with snow at that time of the year, yet the weather was so mild that 'Autumn seemed like Summer".[24]

Bibliography

Primary Sources

Anon., *Grande et celebre magnificence, faites à Madame Christine de France, Princesse de Piedmont à son arivée dans Thurin. Avec la forme de sa reception, nombre des Princes Signeurs & Grandes Dames, qui s'y sont trouvés, les jouxtes & tournois, & autres actes de resiouissance y representez* (Paris: Silvestre Moreau en sa Boutique en la Cour du Palais, 1619).

Anon., *Les Pompes et magnificences faites au Mariage du Prince Victor aisné de la Maison de Savoye & Madame Christine fille de France. Espousez le Dimanche au soir dixiesme Fevrier mil six cens dixneuf. Ensemble de la reception desdicts sieurs Princes dans le Louvre* (Lyon: François Yurat, 1619) in Turin, Biblioteca Reale, Misc. 298/7.

Anon., *Matrimonio tra il Principe di Piemonte Vittorio Amedeo Io e Cristina di Francia figlia di Enrico 4 e Sorella di Lodovico 13, Re di Francia*, Mazzo 26, no. 2, '*Minuta d'istruzione del Duca Carlo Emanuele al Presidente Fresia, e Barone di Marcieux per portarsi alla Corte di Francia, e farvi la proposizione del Matrimonio di Madama Cristina sorella secondogenita del Re col Principe di Piemonte*', 1617 (Turin, State Archives).

Anon., *Matrimonio tra il Principe di Piemonte Vittorio Amedeo Io e Cristina di Francia figlia di Enrico 4 e Sorella di Lodovico 13, Re di Francia*, Mazzo 26, no. 3, '*Procure del Duca di Savoia Carlo Emanuele Primo e del Principe di Piemonte Vittorio Amedeo Primo di lui figlio primogenito in capo del Cardinale Morizio di Savoia per portarsi in Pariggi a trattare, e conchiudere il matrimonio del ditto Principe di Piemonte con Maria Cristina di Francia, figlia d'Enrico il Grande*', 20 and 28 October 1618.

Anon., *Matrimonio tra il Principe di Piemonte Vittorio Amedeo Io e Cristina di Francia figlia di Enrico 4 e Sorella di Lodovico 13, Re di Francia*, Mazzo 26, no. 5, '*Capitoli proposti per parte di Ludovico 13 Re di Francia per il Matrimonio di Maria Cristina di Francia sua sorella col Principe di Piemonte Vittorio Amedeo. Colle risposte fatte dal Principe Carlo Maurizio di Savoja*', 1618.

---

[24]   *Relatione della festa …*, '*maravigliosa et bella, tanto per il soggietto come per gli spettatori et il luogo et sito dove è seguita, et parimente per la stagione nella quale sogliono questi monti esser ordinariamente carichi di neve, et in questo giorno vi era la polvere in ogni parte, con un tempo quietissimo, che pareva più d'Estate, che d'Autonno*'.

Anon., *Matrimonio tra il Principe di Piemonte Vittorio Amedeo Io e Cristina di Francia figlia di Enrico 4 e Sorella di Lodovico 13, Re di Francia*, Mazzo 26, no. 6, '*Riflessi del Presidente a Favore sovra li Capitoli proposti per parte del Re di Francia per lo Matrimonio di Vittorio Amedeo I con Maria Cristina di Francia*', 1618 (Turin, State Archives).

Anon., *Matrimonio tra il Principe di Piemonte Vittorio Amedeo Io e Cristina di Francia figlia di Enrico 4 e Sorella di Lodovico 13, Re di Francia*, Mazzo 26, no. 7, '*Contratto di matrimonio tra il principe di Piemonte Vittorio Amedeo Figlio del Duca Carlo Emanuele Primo di Savoja, e Maria Cristina di Francia figlia del Re Enrico 4o e Sorella di Lodovico 13o*', 11 January 1619 (Turin, State Archives).

Anon., *Matrimonio tra il Principe di Piemonte Vittorio Amedeo Io e Cristina di Francia figlia di Enrico 4 e Sorella di Lodovico 13, Re di Francia*, Mazzo 26, no. 8, '*Procura del Principe di Piemonte Vittorio Amedeo I a motive di ottenere la dispensa del Papa per la celebrazione del Matrimonio tra esso, e la Principessa Cristina di Francia*', 17 January 1619 (Turin, State Archives).

Anon., *Matrimonio tra il Principe di Piemonte Vittorio Amedeo Io e Cristina di Francia figlia di Enrico 4 e Sorella di Lodovico 13, Re di Francia*, Mazzo 26, no. 10, '*Inventario de' mobili, argenterie ed abiti portati da Pariggi da Maria Cristina di Francia Moglie del Duca di Savoja Vittorio Amedeo Primo*' (Turin, 1619).

Anon., *Matrimonio tra il Principe di Piemonte Vittorio Amedeo Io e Cristina di Francia figlia di Enrico 4 e Sorella di Lodovico 13, Re di Francia*, Mazzo 26, no. 11, '*Relatione delle feste fatte d'ordine del Duca Vittorio Amedeo Primo a Maria Cristina di Francia sua Consorte nel di lei passaggio del Moncenisio, e dell'entrata che fece nella Citta di Torino il 15 marzo 1620*' (Turin, State Archives).

Anon., *Relation du Grand Ballet du Roy dance en la sale du Louvre le 12 février 1619 sur adventure de Tancrède en la forest enchantée* (Paris: Jean Sara, 1619) in Paris, *Bibliothèque Nationale de France*, Lb 36–116.

Anon., *Relatione della correria all'Huomo armato fatta dal Sereniss.o Prencipe di Piemonte*, (Turin, Luigi Pizzamiglio, 1619) in Turin, Biblioteca Reale, Misc. 300/13.

Anon., *Relatione della festa fatta fare da S. A. Sereniss. a Madama nel passare, che fece del Moncenisio alli 9 di Novembre, 1619* (Turin: Luigi Pizzamiglio Stampator Ducale, 1619).

Guichenon, Samuel, *Le Soleil en son apogée ou l'histoire de la vie de Chrestienne de France* (Turin, Biblioteca Reale, Mss. St Patria, 911).

Secondary Sources

Angiolini, Franco, 'Medici e Savoia. Contese per la precedenza e rivalità di rango in età moderna', in P. Bianchi and L.C. Gentile (eds), *Dinastie, poteri, élites in Piemonte e Savoia tra tardo medioevo e prima età moderna* (Turin, 2006), pp. 435–80.

Bianchi, P. and L.C. Gentile (eds), *Dinastie, poteri, élites in Piemonte e Savoia tra tardo medioevo e prima età moderna* (Turin, 2006).

Bosco, G., 'L'Epico D'Urfé, cortigiano sabaudo', in M. Masoero, S. Mamino and C. Rosso (eds), *Politica e Cultura nell'età di Carlo Emanuele I*, Papers of the International Conference held in Turin on 21–24 February 1995 (Florence, 1999), pp. 263–73.

Ducimetière, Nicolas, 'La bibliothèque d'Honoré D'Urfé: histoire de sa formation et de sa dispersion à travers quelques exemplaires retrouvés', *Dix-septième siècle*, 2010/4, n. 249, pp. 747–73.

Masoero, M., S. Mamino and C. Rosso (eds), *Politica e Cultura nell'età di Carlo Emanuele I*, Papers of the International Conference held in Turin on 21–24 February 1995 (Florence, 1999).

Merlotti, Andrea, 'Politique dynastique et alliances matrimoniales de la Maison de Savoie au XVIIe siècle', *Dix-septième siècle*, 2009/2, n. 243, pp. 239–53.

Chapter 17

Naumachiae at the Buen Retiro in Madrid

David Sánchez Cano

Rivers and water seem, symbolically and physically, to have played only a minor role in festivals on the Iberian peninsula in the Renaiassance and Early Modern periods. A survey of the major bibliographies of Spanish festivals quickly confirms this: *naumachiae*, naval battles, regattas, waterborne decorations are all but missing, festival books dedicated to them non-existent, images of them extremely rare and those that exist mostly from later centuries. In fact, it seems that the only image of a mock naval battle from Spain is an engraving from Valencia of a naval spectacle staged in 1753 between two bridges on the river Turia, obviously modelled on the famous Pitti Palace *naumachia* of 1589 in Florence.[1] In 1586 Valencia honoured the visiting Philip II with decorations incorporating five mock battles, including the key naval victory of Lepanto, but all were performed as *tableaux vivants* on stages along the entry route.[2] The term *naumachia* scarcely appears in Spanish festival literature, one rare example being in the festival book on Anna of Austria's entry in Burgos in 1570, where it is used to describe a mock naval battle. Yet contrary to the claim of reviving ancient Roman *naumachiae*, the spectacle actually re-enacted episodes from the chivalric epic *Amadis of Gaul* and was performed on a dry city square.[3] Few other naval battles were staged

---

[1]   On this spectacle see Victor Minguez, 'La Naumaquia del Turia del 1755. Un hito en el espectaculo barroco valenciano', in *Millars Geografia-Historia*, 12 (1988–89), pp. 55–69.

[2]   The decorations are described in Henrique Cock, *Relacion del viaje hecho por Felipe II, en 1585, á Zaragoza, Barcelona y Valencia*, ed. Alfred Morel-Fatio and Antonio Rodriguez Villa, (Madrid, 1876), pp. 227–33 and in *Libre de memories de diversos sucesos e fets memorables e de coses senyalades de la ciutat e regne de Valencia (1308–1664)*, ed. Salvador Carreres y Zacarés (2 vols, Valencia: Acción Bibliográfica Valenciana, 1935), vol. 2, p. 973.

[3]   '*Relacion verdadera del recebimiento que la muy noble y muy mas leal ciudad de Burgos, Cabeça de Castilla, y Camara de su Magestad hizo a la Magestad Real de la Reyna nuestra señora, doña Anna d'Austria ...*' (Burgos, 1571), p. 52v: '*Era la traca, & inuencion de la fiesta de aquel dia, represntar vna parte de Amadia de Gaula d. esta manera. Embarcaronse en el Galeon, dos Galeras, y Fragata la Reyna Sardamira, y el Principe Salustanquidio, y otros romanos, con muy ricos vestidos, tocados, y adereços a la antigua, de tela de oro, terciopelos, y damascos muy bordados de telas, y passamanos de oro y plata, y los baxeles llenos de caualleros muy bien armados, que despues auian de tornear, y ansi entraron en la plaça, con tan grande triumpho y aparencia, que se pudieran muy*

in Spain, notably in Madrid in 1570[4] and Zaragoza in 1599,[5] which although performed on bodies of water were essentially aquatic versions of the popular ritual combat between Muslims and Christians ('*moros y cristianos*'). The aquatic entertainments held at the Buen Retiro palace during the reign of Philip IV were similarly not full-fledged *naumachiae* but, rather, courtly entertainments. They stand out, however, for the claims made of reviving ancient Roman spectacles – and for their connection with a series of paintings commissioned for the Buen Retiro at that time.

El Buen Retiro as Pleasure Palace

The Buen Retiro palace was located on the eastern outskirts of Madrid and occupied an area equivalent to about two thirds of the city. It was erected between 1632 and 1640 in a piecemeal and haphazard manner by adding to the original apartments adjoining the monastery of San Jerónimo. The palace was the brainchild of Philip IV's favourite, the Count-Duke of Olivares, its primary function being to amuse the king and distract him from affairs of state, as epitomised in its name El Buen Retiro, the 'Good Retreat'. Almost completely destroyed in the War of Independence, 1808–13, the palace has been virtually and eloquently reconstructed in the well-known monograph by Brown and Elliott.[6]

The Buen Retiro was an austere, utilitarian brick building with monotonous, almost unadorned façades of identical rows of simple windows, as we can observe in a painted view of the palace from approximately 1637 (Plate 4). Its main attractions were the extensive gardens with several small so-called hermitages – actually secular retreats – set in the parks, the many canals and ponds, as well as the lavish decorations inside the palace itself. These decorations included furniture,

---

bien comparar a aquellas Naumachias, o juegos Nauales, que los Emperadores romanos en el tiempo passado celebraron, con gastos tan excessiuos, como ingeniosos.' ('The idea and the invention of the spectacle for that day was to represent a part of *Amadis of Gaul* in the following manner. Queen Sardamira and Prince Salustanquidio, and other Romans, attired in very fine clothes, headdresses, and dressed in the antique manner, with goldcloth, velvets, damask silks embroidered with cloth, gold and silver braids, boarded the galleon, two galleys and frigate. The ships were full of very well armed gentlemen, who afterwards were to engage in the tournament, and they entered the square with great triumph and display, which could very well be compared with those *naumachie*, or naval games, which the Roman emperors celebrated in past times with great fantasy at such excessive costs.')

[4]   Juan Lopez de Hoyos, *Real apparato, y svmtvoso recebimiento con qve Madrid (como casa y morada de su M.) rescibio ala Serenissima reyna D. Ana de Austria ...* (Madrid, 1572) p. 24v.

[5]   Vicencio Blasco de Lanuza, *Historias ecclesiasticas, y seculares de Aragon* (2 vols, Zaragoza, 1622), vol. 2, p. 404.

[6]   Jonathan Brown and John H. Elliott, *A Palace for a King. El Buen Retiro and the Court of Phillip IV* (New Haven: Yale University Press, 1980).

sculptures, tapestries and various specifically commissioned series of paintings for the palace, such as the twelve battle paintings for the Hall of Realms and a series on ancient Roman spectacles, which will be examined below.

One reason for the palace's plain architectural style was that it was initiated as a venue for festivals, to provide an enclosed square for staging them. In the 1637 painting of the Retiro we can see several courtyards, from where spectators could look down on games of *cañas* ('cane throwing'), bullfights, costumed processions and other such entertainments and spectacles. The first festivals held at the Buen Retiro were staged on 5 December 1633 to inaugurate the completed sections of the building.[7] The most sumptuous, however, were the series of festivals celebrated during Carnival between 15 and 24 February 1637 to celebrate the election of Philip's brother-in-law as King of Hungary and to mark the arrival of the Princess of Carignan a few months previously, with such entertainments as a masquerade, allegorical wagons, a tournament and a burlesque academy.

However, for the most part, the Buen Retiro was used only during Carnival for a few weeks each year and otherwise only occasionally, as the venue for bullfights, *cañas* games, literary contests, banquets, dances and especially theatrical plays, as well as Carnival entertainments. One such amusement was the throwing of gilded or silver-plated eggs filled with perfumed water; in some years there are payments for up to 28,000 such eggs.[8] The construction of the 'Coliseo', a proscenium theatre at the Buen Retiro, as well as the lavish stage machinery and sets by the Florentine stage designers Cosimo Lotti and later Baccio del Bianco, contributed to the development of elaborate plays employing music, ballets, masques, costumes and spectacular mechanical transformations. All in all, the Buen Retiro was unquestionably a true '*Lustschloß*' ('a pleasure palace').

Aside from the courtyards and gardens one of the venues for such festivities and entertainments was the '*Gran Estanque*' ('Great Lake'), which we can see in a detail from Teixeira's map of 1656 (Fig 17.2). Payments from the Simancas archive indicate that in February 1634 construction was initiated by the engineer Juan de Ramesdique, who was in charge of levelling the ground, and by the contractor Cristóbal de Aguilar, who laid out the actual lake. Work was finished by 1635 on the Great Lake as well as on three other pools, including a round one to keep the boats, a small island in the middle of the Great Lake and a long canal.[9] In 1637 four waterwheels are mentioned at the corners. In 1638 it was noted that the Great Lake should measure 1,000 by 450 feet, instead of the (unspecified) smaller dimensions it had previously; to compensate for this Cristóbal de Aguilar

---

[7]   They are described in *Copiosa relacion de las grandiosas fiestas, que la Catolica Magestad del Rey nuestro Señor mandó hazer en la villa de Madrid, assistiendo a ellas su Real persona, y los demas principes que assisten en la Corte, a honra del Palacio, y plaça nueva: lunes cinco de diziembre deste presente año de 1633* (Seville, 1633).

[8]   José Maria Azcárate, 'Anales de la construcción del Buen Retiro', *Anales del Instituto de Estudios Madrileños*, 1 (1966), pp. 99–135, p. 122.

[9]   Ibid., pp. 113–16.

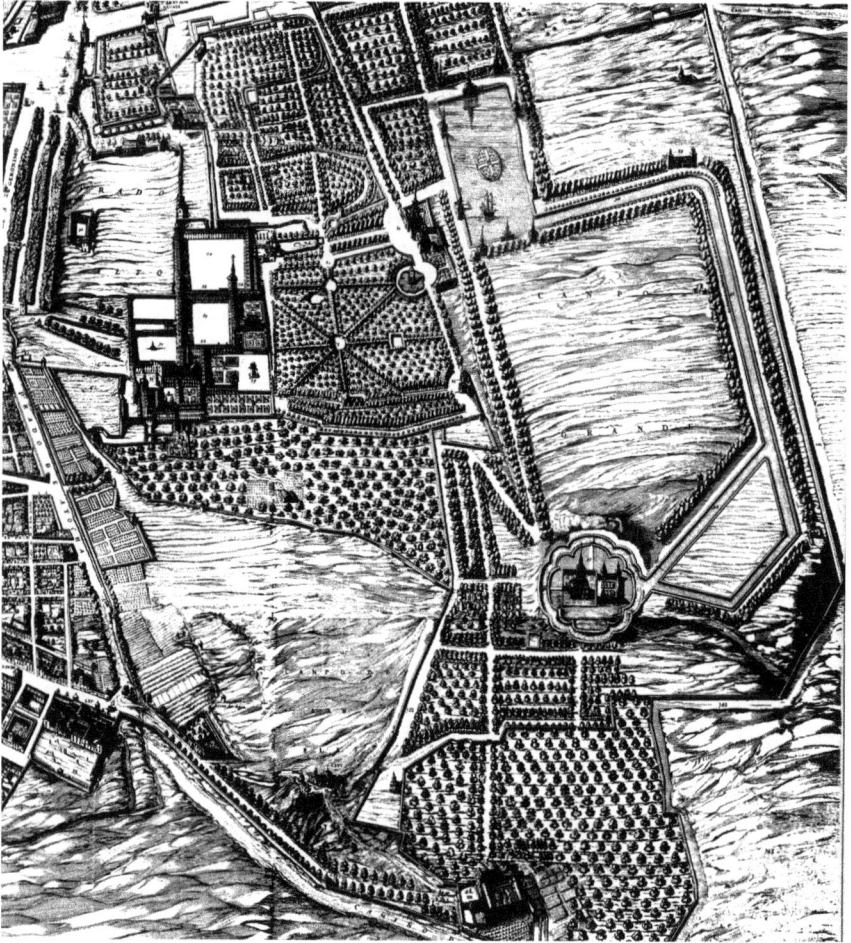

Figure 17.1   Pedro Teixeira, *Mantua Carpentanorum Sive Matritum Urbs Regia*
(Antwerp, 1656).

was obliged to dig out (or possibly extend) the canal by 1,000 feet. Four bridges to
access the island and a shipyard for the boats are mentioned that same year, 1638,
as well as 210 pounds of live fish that were deposited in the Great Lake and six
small pavilions at its edges to fish from.[10]

Fishing at the Great Lake was apparently an Arcadian pastime organised for the
members of the court, but this recreation was to be undertaken from the comfort of
the pavilions. In the detail from Teixeira's map we can see the Great Lake with the
six pavilions at the edges of the lake and the four watermills, the small island in its
middle, as well as the canal leading to the hermitage of San Antonio with its ornate

---

[10]   Ibid., p. 115 (1635), p. 119 (1637), p. 121 (1638).

moat. Another pool is located next to the hermitage of San Isidro just behind the palace. The lakes and canals served not only to irrigate the extensive gardens and as fishing grounds, but also as waterways for boating. In modified form the Great Lake still exists today in Madrid's Retiro Park.

The Royal 'Fleet of the Lake'

The archival records excerpted by Azcárate indicate that between the 1630s and 1660s various types of boats were built, or ordered, for the Buen Retiro's waterways. Two years after the Buen Retiro was inaugurated ten '*barquillos*' ('small boats') and three '*barcos*' ('ships') were painted in 1635 and mentioned as forming the so-called '*Flota del Estanque*' ('Fleet of the Lake'). In 1638 a 'large ship', a '*bergantin*' ('brig') and a '*falúa*' ('felucca'), the latter 20 feet long by six feet wide, were constructed. Eight further boats are mentioned while a large boat, 40 feet long, also appears in the slightly later records of 1640. Gerardo Quin, most likely from the Low Countries, is mentioned as both shipbuilder and captain of this fleet, while in 1643 seven sailors from Naples are dismissed; they presumably arrived with the gilded gondolas sent from Naples by the Viceroy there, the Duke of Medina de Torres, which allegedly cost over 352,000 ducats.[11]

The inventory of the Buen Retiro made in 1701 still lists numerous cushions, chairs, backrests, curtains, canopies, banderoles and various other types of standards and banners, all belonging to the various boats. Twelve different sets of uniforms, for crews of four, eight, as well as one of 40 sailors, still existed at that time.[12] The set of four uniforms for the 'sailors of the Royal Gondola' were made of gold cloth with silver embroidered flowers and consisted of a doublet, bonnet, white silk stockings and garters with mother-of-pearl ornaments.[13] One set of 40 uniforms of white damask could not be appraised, since 'they were in tatters'.[14] Another set of four uniforms was destined for the 'gondola of his Highness the Prince'.[15] Thirty-six small and large pieces of artillery are also mentioned by the inventory, some of which possibly belonged to the boats.

---

[11]   Jose Pellicer y Tovar, *Avisos históricos que comprenden las noticas y sucesos más particulares ocurridos en nuestra Monarquía desde 3 de enero de 1640 a 25 de octubre de 1644*; Biblioteca Nacional Madrid, Mss. 7692 and 7693; reprinted in *Semanario erudito, que comprehende varias obras ineditas, criticas, morales, instructivas ...*, (ed.) Antonio Valladares de Sotomoyar, (34 vols, Madrid, 1790), vol. 32, pp. 9–10.

[12]   Gloria Fernández Bayton, *Inventarios reales. Testamentaria del Rey Carlos II 1700–1703* (2 vols, Madrid: Museo del Prado, 1985), vol. 2, pp. 238–44, items 163–74 and 208–11.

[13]   Ibid., p. 238, item 165.

[14]   Ibid., p. 238, item 164.

[15]   Ibid., p. 238, item 166.

In 1653 a galley is mentioned as being built and a new galley and two gondolas were constructed three years later by Carlos Ravasquier in 1657. This large galley was decorated with a coat of arms, banners and banderoles and was rowed by '*moros*' ('Moors'), the term commonly employed in Spain for North African Muslims. In 1658 uniforms are mentioned for the galley's captain Oliver Paradis, for the shipwright Carlos Ravasquier and a further four anonymous officers. Paradis's and Ravasquier's names suggest that they are the 'Dutch captains' mentioned in 1660 in connection with the large galley, who were assisted by Jaime Gandolfo, summoned from the shipyards in Barcelona to help in the construction.[16]

The crew of the galley also included 20 'Moors' and 18 slaves, according to these same archival records. We know from parish records that in the second half of the seventeenth century the majority of slaves in Madrid were Muslims from North Africa, followed in number by so-called 'Turks' (in reality Greek and Balkan Christians) and a few Africans.[17] Clothing, the building of a new sleeping room for the 'moors' and even a priest to catechise the Christian slaves appear in the records, in addition to some child slaves mentioned as musicians. The so-called 'Moors' then were almost certainly also Muslim slaves, called so to distinguish them in the documents from (often forcibly baptised) Christian slaves, and are explicitly said to serve in the great galley. 172 oars were supplied from Barcelona and the Basque province in 1661, while a large galley, a brig and four new galleys are mentioned.

These archival fragments attest to what lengths those responsible at the Buen Retiro went to make the 'Fleet of the Lake' as authentic as possible. Presumably the authenticity of these galleys went so far as to include slave rowers, just as the real Spanish galleys in the Mediterranean between 1530 and 1748 were driven by Muslim as well as Christian slaves, together with prisoners of war and convicts.[18] We can imagine the members of the court idly floating along the Great Lake and the canals amid the gardens, while slaves propelled the galleys forward. Some of the ships just described might be the ones depicted in an engraving by Louis Meunier showing the Great Lake, 'where the King of Spain amuses himself in galleys and boats', as the legend explains (Fig. 17.2). The image depicts the fishing pavilions, three sailboats and a galley and provides us with a relatively clear idea of the architecture and lake, but we must be cautious about the size of the ships as well as of the staffage, as they are wholly disproportionate. As in his other engravings of Madrid, Meunier exaggerated the dimensions of streets and buildings and portrayed the accessory human figures as minuscule.

---

[16]   Azcárate, 'Anales de la construcción', p. 128 (1653), p. 129 (1657), p. 130 (1658) and p. 131 (1660).

[17]   Claude Larquié, 'Les esclaves de Madrid a l'epoque de la décadence (1650–1700)', *Revue Historique*, 244 (2002), pp. 41–74 (p. 59).

[18]   Félix Sevilla y Solanas, *Historia Penitenciaria Española (La Galera). Apuntes de Archivo* (Segovia: El adelantado de Segovia, 1917), p. 51.

Figure 17.2   *View of the Great Lake at the Buen Retiro*, Louis Meunier, in: *Differentes veues des Palais et Jardins de plaisance des Rois despagne dedie a la Reine* (Paris, 1665–68), copper engraving, 13.3 × 24.7 cm.

Santo Rey Don Fernando

By far the most spectacular of the boats was one named the *Santo Rey Don Fernando*. It was built in the Alcazares Reales royal palace of Seville in 1638 on the initiative of the palace's vice governor Antonio Manrique, as a gift to Olivares and the King, 'to serve the King our Lord on the lake of the Buen Retiro'.[19] In that same year the boat was first launched and tested on the Guadalquivir river in Seville and then transported on a large custom-built wagon to Madrid. According to the archival documents published by Gestoso,[20] the ship was a luxurious affair: decorated with sculptures of snakes, two lions, masks, coats of arms, six mermaids and a figurehead on the prow of Fernando III, the canonised king and Christian conqueror of Seville. Its interior was panelled with mahogany and cedar, gilded and festooned with silks, banners and standards; most famously the ship included paintings, probably allegorical, by one of the greatest Spanish painters of the seventeenth century, Francisco de Zurbarán. Unfortunately, no other evidence, material, visual or archival, exists of Zurbarán's contribution nor of the ship itself.[21]

---

[19]   José Gestoso y Pérez, *El Navío 'El Santo Rey D. Fernando'. Memorias Históricas sevillanas del siglo XVII* (Sevilla: Oficina Tip. De Gironés y Orduña, 1890), pp. 23–4. On the boat see also Nicolás Sentenach, 'Francisco de Zurbarán. Pintor del Rey', *Boletin de la Sociedad Española de Excursiones*, 17/2 (1909), pp. 194–8.

[20]   Gestoso, *El Navio 'El Santo Rey D. Fernando'*, docs 1–20, pp. 20–31.

[21]   Ibid., Document 15, p. 26; on Zurbarán's work for this ship see also Odile Delenda, *Francisco de Zurbarán. 1588–1664 Catálogo Razonado y Critic* (2 vols, Madrid: Museo

This ship was fully navigable with an unspecified number of masts and sails as well as four gilded oars; cords were attached from a mahogany and crimson damask throne on the deck to the helm, so that someone – presumably the king himself – could steer the vessel in comfort. The ship even carried ten pieces of small, bronze, functioning artillery. Eight persons could be comfortably accommodated, in addition to the crew of three, which consisted of Captain Lucas Guillén de Beas as well as a carpenter/sailor and a young cabin boy; damask uniforms were tailored for the crew. Captain Guillén helped build the ship and was sent, along with the rest of his little crew, from Seville to Madrid in order to ceremoniously present the boat to the king. In a letter dated 22 February 1639 to Manrique he describes how the king, the prince and Olivares enjoyed sailing in the boat on the Great Lake in the mornings and afternoons.[22] In July 1638 Guillén had previously mentioned how the boat was well received by the king and Olivares, 'although it arrived at the highpoint of the wars'.[23]

The cautious understatement in Guillén's letter to his superior alludes to the probable indignation among Madrid's populace aroused by the toy fleet at the Buen Retiro, at a moment when Spain was at war against the French and Dutch and precisely when naval forces were suffering from an acute lack of funds. This indignation is mentioned by contemporary authors of letters and news reports in Madrid. One writer noted in 1658 that the king was depressed by events in Flanders and did 'not realise that he would do better to use his money for soldiers than in plays with stage machinery or in a bullfight, which costs more than 80,000 ducats each time one is held'.[24] Such reporters repeatedly mention festivals, entertainments and spectacles and the expenses incurred by them; in fact, they name specific sums for individual items such as dances, costumes, or stage decorations, meaning that such financial information openly circulated around the court and the public sphere surrounding it in Madrid.[25] Although not revolutionaries by any means, they occasionally lamented the decadence of an extravagant court while the populace suffered from the economic crisis, particularly when funds for the war effort were difficult to find. Naturally, the images of courtiers and king sailing in a toy ship with real artillery on the Great Lake, or being propelled by slaves in galleys along the canals, or of hundreds of pounds of expensive live fish being

---

Nacional del Prado Fundación Arte Hispánico, 2009), vol. 1, p. 62.

[22]　Gestoso, *El Navio 'El Santo Rey D. Fernando'*, doc. 20, pp. 30–31.

[23]　Ibid., doc. 19, p. 29.

[24]　Jerónimo Barrionuevo de Peralta, *Avisos de Madrid de los Austrias y otras noticias*, ed. José María Díez Borque (Madrid: Castalia, 1986), letter of 1 July 1658, p. 86: '*[...] ni acaba de dar en cuenta que le está mejor gastar su dinero con soldados que no en comedias de tramoyas ni en cada fiesta de toros 80.000 ducados y mas cada vez que se corren.*'

[25]　See the contemporary anonymous news reports in *La Corte y Monarquía de España en los años de 1636 y 37*, (ed.) Antonio Rodríguez Villa (Madrid, 1886): report of 22–29 November 1636, p. 67; 15–20 February 1637, p. 98 and p. 101. See also Barrionuevo de Peralta, *Avisos de Madrid*, letter of 4 July 1657, p. 181.

dumped into the Great Lake so that courtiers could play at fishing, all raise the clichés of a decadent court in the midst of national squalor. Nevertheless, and even if the *Santo Rey Don Fernando* was a gift – just like the gondolas from Naples – the toy fleet at the Buen Retiro unquestionably embodied the injustices of an absolutist political regime.

Water Entertainments

All the investments in ships, fleet, lakes and canals were not used for extraordinary water festivals, but rather for regular courtly entertainments. The only news we have of these entertainments in fact are a few scattered, fragmentary mentions, primarily in contemporary letters and news reports; it is surprising that so few descriptions were ever written or published of them. In June 1637 for example a Jesuit letter-writer very briefly mentions a '*rehata*', that is a regatta, in the Buen Retiro.[26] During the festivities held at the Buen Retiro in February 1637 one small component of them was a ride in boats on the pool at the Hermitage of San Isidro, to the accompaniment of three different ensembles of music on 18 February 1637.[27] The chronicler Jose Pellicer details the plans for a *comedia* to be held on the first day of Corpus Christi celebrations in June 1639, to be performed on a floating stage on the Great Lake, lit by over 3,000 torches and watched by the king and courtiers from gondolas, on which they were also to be served supper. As ill-luck would have it, a strong wind arose during the performance which blew out the lights, turned over some of the gondolas and terrified the young Prince, leading to the abrupt cancellation of the fiesta.[28]

The same Pellicer writes that on 16 June 1639 a 'very solemn' festival was represented at the Buen Retiro, 'which was an imitation of those *naumachiae* of the Romans'.[29] This is one of the very few examples known to me of the term *naumachia* in Spain as used for such aquatic spectacles, but it is hardly surprising from a chronicler who was engaged in establishing parallels between the entertainments at the Buen Retiro and Roman spectacles, as we shall see below. The unspecified spectacle was repeated three times, for the royal family on Thursday, for the Council of Castile on Friday and on the following Monday for the religious orders and general public, with free admission that day. Pellicer

---

[26] 'Cartas de algunos PP. de la Compañia de Jesús', in *Memorial Histórico Español. Colección de documentos, opúsculos y antigüedades, que publica la Real Academia de la Historia* (50 vols, Madrid, 1862) vol. 13, p. 139.

[27] Andres de Sanchez Espejo, *Relacion aiustada en lo possible, a la verdad, y repartida en dos discvrsos. [...] El segundo, de las fiestas que se celebraron en el Real palacio del buen Retiro, à la eleccion de Rey de Romanos* (Madrid, 1637), p. 20r.

[28] Pellicer y Tovar, *Avisos historicos*, letter of 14 June 1639, p. 29.

[29] Ibid., letter of 21 June 1639, p. 33; '*que fue una imitación de aquellas Naumachias de los romanos*'.

also mentions that a festival book or pamphlet will be published on this event, of which unfortunately there is no trace. That same month Pellicer briefly relates how the King celebrated the Eve of Saint John (24 June 1639) with boats and music on the lakes of the Buen Retiro till one in the morning, but provides no more detail.[30]

Just like Pellicer, the letter-writer Jerónimo de Barrionuevo succinctly mentions aquatic entertainments at the Buen Retiro for a later period, from 1654 to 1658. He however takes a more overtly critical stance towards the court. Thus on the Eve of Saint Peter's feast (29 June) 1657 he reports how a pasquinade appeared on the doors of churches and monasteries in Madrid, announcing that the king would that night:

> *que se embarca esta noche en la armada que ha hecho en el Retiro contra Cromwell, y va a verse con él y a descercar a España por mar.*

> [embark on the armada that he has assembled at the Buen Retiro against Cromwell, and he will sail forth to battle him and break the naval blockade of Spain].[31]

The pasquinade was well timed, since that night aquatic entertainments were indeed held at the Buen Retiro. Barrionuevo describes a large galley which can accommodate 60 persons, sirens and nereids accompanying the galley on other boats, all to the sound of artillery salutes and the playing of Moorish musicians – presumably those child slaves mentioned above in the archival records. The king and queen, reports Barrionuevo, will enjoy floating along the canals and lakes of the Buen Retiro till the middle of August.[32] They did this apparently without paying any heed to the pasquinade and its criticism.

That same July 1657, when a hot summer reduced water supplies, Barrionuevo describes how the royal galley, the *Real de España*, ran aground on the Great Lake and how the boat was dragged by force, breaking eight oars.[33] On another day – when apparently enough water was available – he describes the use of the boats:

> *Los Reyes se solazan en la galera el día que no le da la cuartana a Liche. Van delante las góndolas y navío. Parece una armada, y en la popa, sentados en un tapete, el Valido y su hijo a los reales pies. Fingen escaramuzas, juegan el artillería y mosquetes, dan tres o cuatro vueltas, llega la noche y todo se acaba. Es cosa de ver y entretenimiento gustoso y poco cansado.*

> [The king and queen take their leisure in the galley [...] The gondolas and ship sail before them. It looks like an armada, at the stern, seated on a carpet, are the favourite and his son, at the royal feet. They pretend to skirmish, play at artillery

---

30   Ibid., letter of 5 July 1639, p. 38.
31   Barrionuevo de Peralta, *Avisos de Madrid*, 4 July 1657, p. 181.
32   Ibid., p. 181.
33   Ibid., 11 July 1657, p. 181.

and muskets, do three or four turns, night arrives and everything is over. It is something to be seen, a pleasurable entertainment and hardly tiring.][34]

Barrionuevo's description emphasises the element of courtly leisure as well as that of the members of the court playing at war in their toy fleet. Given the historical context of the indignation and the wars going on at that time, did he also want to imply a little irony?

The Model: Roman Spectacles Series

These few scanty fragments demonstrate that *naumachiae*, naval battles or aquatic spectacles of any kind – except for theatre performances – hardly took place on the Buen Retiro's lakes, pools and canals. Rather, the financing, designing and building of these waterways served primarily for the entertainment of the court itself. Floating and sailing along the water, fishing from the pavilions on the Great Lake, observing the watermills, watching the different kinds of boats, seem to have appealed much more to the king, the favourite and courtiers than mounting water-based spectacles for audiences. As did the charm of a 'toy fleet' of various types of boats, in a similar way to model trains or miniature dollhouses: reality in detail – real cannon firing salutes, real decorations or real galley slaves – but reduced dimensions which allow the observer, who is in fact the owner, to feel as though he or she rules over this miniature world. Captain Guillén, who brought the *Santo Rey Don Fernando* from Seville to Madrid, expressed fascination several times in his letters for the tiny size of the ships comprising the toy fleet. The fascination this toy realm must have held for Philip IV, whose real kingdom was crumbling around him, we can only imagine. In spite of this, attempts were made to equate the festival culture of the Madrid court with ancient Roman spectacles, a common strategy of the epoch. Pellicer for example published a pamphlet describing a spectacle organised 'according to the ancient custom of Rome' to celebrate the birthday of Prince Baltasar at the Alcazar palace on 13 October 1631.[35] A lion, a tiger, a bear, a bull, a horse, a whippet, as well as some smaller animals 'to serve as amusement and entertainment', were pitted against each other in an arena and instigated to fight. Not surprisingly, the bull was – at least according to the author – the heroic victor and was then killed by a single musket shot from the king. The bull here symbolises Spanish valour, but Pellicer also explains that bullfighting, 'the fiesta that was celebrated in the Circus Flaminius', was still practised after the fall of Rome up to the present in Spain.

Similar motives might have been behind an extensive series of large-format paintings made for and hung in the Buen Retiro. They were most likely

---

[34]   Ibid., 18 July 1657, p. 182.

[35]   Jose[ph] Pellicer de Tovar, *Anfiteatro de Felipe el Grande, Rey Catolico de las Españas, Monarca Soberano de las Indias de Oriente y Occidente* … (Madrid, 1632).

commissioned in the second half of the 1630s from 15 Italian artists in Rome and Naples by the Count of Monterrey (ambassador in Rome 1628–31, viceroy in Naples 1631–37) and the Marquis of Castel-Rodrigo (ambassador in Rome 1631–41) while they held their posts in Italy. Differences in the dimensions and formats of the paintings, an absence of coherence or of a unifying argument and the fact that an architectural space was never conceived for these paintings, so that they were distributed in various places and never seen in conjunction, have led many scholars to question whether this group of pictures truly make up a unified series.[36] It seems that just as the Buen Retiro was haphazardly constructed without a master plan, the ambitious undertaking of this series was carried out without an overall iconographic *concetto*, even though some specific instructions must have been issued to such a large number of artists working independently in different places. What is certain is that this group of approximately 34 paintings (of which six have been lost or destroyed) have a certain family resemblance and can be roughly divided into three sub-groups: the heroic deeds of Roman emperors, mythological scenes and 14 paintings of Ancient Roman rites and spectacles. The paintings in this last sub-group demonstrate an antiquarian interest in the civic customs and architectural monuments of Ancient Rome. In the *View of a Roman Amphitheatre*,[37] for example, we see various animals fighting (an elephant, two bulls, a bear, jaguar, boar), recalling the combat of animals described by Pellicer. The amphitheatre is depicted in a cut-away section, an artificial visual device employed solely to present the architecture of the building, just like in the similar *Circus Maximus at Rome*,[38] and demonstrates how scholarly interests were served in these paintings. For many of the pictures we can find direct visual models in antiquarian works of the late sixteenth century or early seventeenth century on Ancient Rome, such as the engravings from Giacomo Lauro's *Meraviglie della Roma antica*, from 1610, or more generally in Onophrio Panvinio's *De Ludis Circensibus*, Paris 1601. Justus Lipsius likely provided the subject for paintings such as the '*Combat of Female Gladiators*'[39] or '*Roman Gladiators Fighting with*

---

[36]   On the series see Andrés Úbeda de los Cobos, 'El ciclo de la historia de Roma Antigua', in *El Palacio del Rey Planeta. Felipe IV y el Buen Retiro* (Madrid, Museo Nacional del Prado, 2005), pp. 169–89 and Samantha Sisignano, *Committenza, opera e 'concetto' nella decorazione plastica e pittorica del Palacio del Buen Retiro* (Naples: degree thesis, Seconda Università degli studi di Napoli, 2003), pp. 111–13.

[37]   Domenico Garguilo (Micco Spadaro) and Viviano Codazzi, ca. 1638 (oil on canvas, 220 x 352 cm, Museo Nacional del Prado, Madrid; deposited in Ministerio de Asuntos Exteriores, Madrid).

[38]   Domenico Garguilo (Micco Spadaro) and Viviano Codazzi, ca. 1638, (oil on canvas, 155 x 355 cm, Museo Nacional del Prado, Madrid).

[39]   Attributed to Andrea Vaccaro, ca. 1635–40, (oil on canvas, 175 x 200 cm, Madrid, Museo Nacional del Prado).

Wooden Swords'[40] in his *Saturnalium sermonum libri duo* (Antwerp, 1598) in which he set up a typology of gladiators defined by geological origin, type of weapon or gender and mentioned their training with wooden swords.

Another subject well-known from textual sources was portrayed by Giovanni Lanfranco,[41] the artist who produced the largest number of works (seven) for this series: '*A Roman Naumachia*' (Plate 5). Panvinio for example describes it in detail in his *De Ludis Circensibus*, while the 1642 edition of *De Ludis Circensibus* even has a *naumachia* on the frontispiece as well as a large double page engraving within the text of a *naumachia* with galleys in a flooded amphitheatre. These engravings appeared in the Padua 1642 edition, after Lanfranco's picture was created, and did not of course serve as direct models for his painting; they illustrate however how *naumachiae* were imagined at that time. In Lanfranco's painting soldiers or gladiators from two boats with rowers battle up close in the foreground, while in the background two further galleys can be seen. They fight before an indistinct audience, possibly meant to depict the Roman Senate, standing on what seems like a permanent stone structure, possibly a flooded amphitheatre. The figure in the water on the far right looking directly at the observer, a common device to draw in the observer, is a self-portrait of Lanfranco.[42] Rather than the antiquarian recreation of Roman spectacle and architecture as in the *View of a Roman Amphitheatre* or the *Circus Maximus at Rome* the focus here – as in many of the other works of this series – is on the portrayal of battling gladiators and their Classical physiques, inspired by ancient statues. A second painting of identical dimensions by Viviano Codazzi and Aniello Falcone, now lost, is mentioned in the 1701 inventory as depicting 'the Thermae of Diocletian with an armada of galleys'. This picture could possibly have been linked in size and content to the series, maybe portraying a staging of a *naumachia* in Roman times, even if not precisely at the Diocletian baths.[43]

It seems apparent that this extensive pictorial catalogue of Roman spectacles was intended to establish a connection between ancient Roman spectacles and

---

[40]   Giovanni Francesco Romanelli, ca. 1635–39, (oil on canvas, 235 x 356 cm, Madrid, Museo Nacional del Prado).

[41]   On Lanfranco and his works for this series see Erich Schleier (ed.), *Giovanni Lanfranco. Un pittore barocco tra Parma, Roma e Napoli* (Milan: Electa, 2001), pp. 27–52.

[42]   Cf. the engraving of Lanfranco by Claude Randon preceeding Lanfranco's biography in Giovan Pietro Bellori, *Le vite de'pittore, scultori e architetti moderni*, (ed.) Evelina Borea (Torino: Einaudi, 1976), p. 376.

[43]   Fernández Bayton, *Inventarios reales*, vol. 2, p. 285, item 112: '*Ottra de quattro Uaras de largo y ttres menos quarta de alto Con Una prespectiua Original de Viuiano y las figuras de Anelo falconi, las termas de Diocleçiano con Una Armada de Galeras con marco tallado y dorado tasada en Cien doblones*' ('Another one of four bars long and two and three fourths high, with an original view by Viviano and the figures by Anelo Falconi of the thermae of Diocletian with an armada of galleys, with a carved and gilded frame, appraised at 100 doubloons'.)

the festivities held at the Buen Retiro. Even though Pellicer specifically named one such planned event at the Great Lake a *naumachia*, as mentioned above, the aquatic entertainments staged at the Buen Retiro hardly qualify as *naumachiae* or naval battles at all; in fact like the other fiestas there they had very little to do with recreating Roman spectacles. The attempt to follow and cite the venerated models of Roman festival culture might have been undertaken to justify the expense of the festivities and entertainments at the Buen Retiro, to defend the idea of a pleasure palace in times of war and economic crisis in the face of contemporary criticism. The disparity however between festival practice and exalted model was deep and immensely wide.

Bibliography

Printed Primary Sources

Anon., *Copiosa relacion de las grandiosas fiestas, que la Catolica Magestad del Rey nuestro Señor mandó hazer en la villa de Madrid, assistiendo a ellas su Real persona, y los demas principes que assisten en la Corte, a honra del Palacio, y plaça nueva: lunes cinco de diziembre deste presente año de 1633* (Seville, 1633).

Anon., *La Corte y Monarquía de España en los años de 1636 y 37*, (ed.) Antonio Rodríguez Villa (Madrid, 1886).

Anon., *Relacion verdadera del recebimiento que la muy noble y muy mas leal ciudad de Burgos, Cabeça de Castilla, y Camara de su Magestad hizo a la Magestad Real de la Reyna nuestra señora, doña Anna d'Austria* ... (Burgos, 1571).

Barrionuevo de Peralta, Jerónimo, *Avisos de Madrid de los Austrias y otras noticias*, ed. José María Díez Borque (Madrid: Castalia, 1986).

Bellori, Giovan Pietro, *Le vite de'pittore, scultori e architetti moderni*, (ed.) Evelina Borea (Torino: Einaudi, 1976).

Blasco de Lanuza, Vicencio, *Historias ecclesiasticas, y seculares de Aragon* (2 vols, Zaragoza, 1622), vol. 2.

Carreres y Zacarés, Salvador (ed.), *Libre de memories de diversos sucesos e fets memorables e de coses senyalades de la ciutat e regne de Valencia (1308– 1664)* (2 vols, Valencia: Acción Bibliográfica Valenciana, 1935), vol. 2.

'Cartas de algunos PP. de la Compañia de Jesús', in *Memorial Histórico Español. Colección de documentos, opúsculos y antigüedades, que publica la Real Academia de la Historia* (50 vols, Madrid, 1862) vol. 13.

Cock, Henrique, *Relacion del viaje hecho por Felipe II, en 1585, á Zaragoza, Barcelona y Valencia*, ed. Alfred Morel-Fatio and Antonio Rodriguez Villa, (Madrid, 1876), pp. 227–33.

Lopez de Hoyos, Juan, *Real apparato, y svmtvoso recebimiento con qve Madrid (como casa y morada de su M.) rescibio ala Serenissima reyna D. Ana de Austria* ... (Madrid, 1572).

Pellicer de Tovar, Jose[ph], *Anfiteatro de Felipe el Grande, Rey Catolico de las Españas, Monarca Soberano de las Indias de Oriente y Occidente* ... (Madrid, 1632).

Pellicer y Tovar, Jose[ph], *Avisos históricos que comprenden las noticas y sucesos más particulares ocurridos en nuestra Monarquía desde 3 de enero de 1640 a 25 de octubre de 1644*; Biblioteca Nacional Madrid, MSS. 7692 and 7693; reprinted in *Semanario erudito, que comprehende varias obras ineditas, criticas, morales, instructivas* ..., ed. Antonio Valladares de Sotomoyar, (34 vols, Madrid, 1790), vol. 32.

Sanchez Espejo, Andres de, *Relacion aiustada en lo possible, a la verdad, y repartida en dos discvrsos. [...] El segundo, de las fiestas que se celebraron en el Real palacio del buen Retiro, à la eleccion de Rey de Romanos* (Madrid, 1637).

Secondary Sources

Azcárate, José Maria, 'Anales de la construcción del Buen Retiro', *Anales del Instituto de Estudios Madrileños*, 1 (1966), pp. 99–135.

Bayton, Gloria Fernández, *Inventarios reales. Testamentaria del Rey Carlos II 1700–1703* (2 vols, Madrid: Museo del Prado, 1985), vol. 2.

Brown, Jonathan and John H. Elliott, *A Palace for a King. El Buen Retiro and the Court of Phillip IV* (New Haven: Yale University Press, 1980).

Delenda, Odile, *Francisco de Zurbarán. 1588–1664 Catálogo Razonado y Critico* (2 vols, Madrid: Museo Nacional del Prado Fundación Arte Hispánico, 2009), vol. 1.

Gestoso y Pérez, José, *El Navío 'El Santo Rey D. Fernando'. Memorias Históricas sevillanas del siglo XVII* (Seville: Oficina Tip. De Gironés y Orduña, 1890).

Larquié, Claude, 'Les esclaves de Madrid a l'epoque de la décadence (1650–1700)', *Revue Historique*, 244 (2002), pp. 41–74.

Minguez, Victor, 'La Naumaquia del Turia del 1755. Un hito en el espectaculo barroco valenciano', in *Millars Geografia-Historia*, 12 (1988–89), pp. 55–69.

Schleier, Erich (ed.), *Giovanni Lanfranco. Un pittore barocco tra Parma, Roma e Napoli* (Milan: Electa, 2001).

Sentenach, Nicolás, 'Francisco de Zurbarán. Pintor del Rey', *Boletin de la Sociedad Española de Excursiones*, 17/2 (1909), pp. 194–8.

Sevilla y Solanas, Félix, *Historia Penitenciaria Española (La Galera). Apuntes de Archivo* (Segovia: El adelantado de Segovia, 1917).

Sisignano, Samantha, *Committenza, opera e 'concetto' nella decorazione plastica e pittorica del Palacio del Buen Retiro* (Naples: degree thesis, Seconda Università degli studi di Napoli, 2003).

Úbeda de los Cobos, Andrés, 'El ciclo de la historia de Roma Antigua', in *El Palacio del Rey Planeta. Felipe IV y el Buen Retiro* (Madrid: Museo Nacional del Prado, 2005).

Chapter 18
Waterfront Entertainments in Saxony and Denmark from 1548–1709

Mara R. Wade

Every Ascension Day until 1798 the Doge sailed in the *Bucentaur* to celebrate the marriage of Venice with the Adriatic sea, and the city celebrated many other civic and religious festivals on the lagoon that were documented in splendid paintings by Canaletto, among others.[1] The *naumachia* staged in the courtyard of the Palazzo Pitti in 1589 for the Medici wedding epitomizes the Renaissance aquatic festival as an element in a dynastic court festival, while Venice ranks foremost among European cities for its venerable tradition of civic sea pageants.[2] In stark contrast to the Italian waterborne pageants, the German and Scandinavian traditions present a largely unwritten history.[3] There are only occasional waterborne pageants, such as the entry of a Danish bride into Dresden in 1602 and the magnificent regatta held a century later in 1709 in Venice for the state visit of King Frederik IV of Denmark. In contrast to that of Venice, the Danish and German traditions of aquatic entertainments consist primarily of fireworks on or near the water, often in conjunction with fictional sieges of castles. This study focuses, therefore, primarily on fireworks that were held at the shore for the courts of Dresden and Copenhagen from 1548–1709. For some early cases graphic materials from other courts are presented to offer images of comparable events.

The castle fireworks event on the water has a long tradition in the Empire and in Denmark. For example, the elaborate castle fireworks ignited for the coronation of the Emperor Mathias II in Frankfurt in 1612 strongly resembled the pyrotechnic display for the Emperor Ferdinand I in 1558.[4] (Fig. 18.1) In the case of Denmark

[1]   See, for example, the exhibition catalogue: *Venice: Canaletto and His Rivals* (London: National Gallery, 2010). http://www.nationalgallery.org.uk/whats-on/exhibitions/ venice-canaletto-and-his-rivals See also Evelyn Korsch's chapter in this volume, pp. 79–97.

[2]   Nina Treadwell, *Music and Wonder at the Medici Court: The 1589 Interludes for La Pellegrina* (Bloomington: Indiana University Press, 2008); James Maxwell Saslow, *The Medici Wedding of 1589: Florentine Festival as 'Theatrum Mundi'* (New Haven: Yale University Press, 1996). See also J.R. Mulryne's chapter in this volume, pp. 143–75.

[3]   Simon Werret, *Fireworks. Pyrotechnic Arts and Sciences in European History* (Chicago: University of Chicago Press, 2010).

[4]   Gotthard Arthus, *Electio Et Coronatio Sereniss. Potentiss. Et Invictiss. Principis Et Dn. Dn. Matthiæ I. …* ([Frankfurt, Main]: Officina de Bry, 1612). http://diglib.hab.de/

Figure 18.1 *Castle Fireworks for the Coronation of Emperor Matthias, Frankfurt, 1612.* Courtesy of the Herzog August Bibliothek, Wolfenbüttel, 36-11-1-geom-2.

these displays underscored the close association with military prowess and the nation's role as a major seafaring power. In the sixteenth century, Danish fireworks often also had a strongly anti-papal theme, while in the empire the displays often involved capturing a 'Turkish' fortress. These Danish and German pageants are noteworthy because from a very early period they represented pyrotechnic dramas that became increasingly elaborate over time and fully exploited their location at the shore and upon the waters.

Firework Manuals in Denmark

The courts of Dresden and Copenhagen mounted firework displays for courtly entertainments from as early as the 1540s. In both Germany and Denmark, as elsewhere, there is a close association between fireworks for war and those for entertainment, between *Kriegsfeuerwerk* and *Lustfeuerwerk*.[5] The incendiary

---

drucke/36-11-1-geom-2f-2/start.htm

[5] Helen Watanabe-O'Kelly, 'Entries, Fireworks, and Religious Festivals in the Empire', in Helen Watanabe-O'Kelly and Pierre Béhar (eds), *Spectaculum Europaeum*,

arts were extremely important to European courts as they were closely related to the ability to wage war and thus to the success and defeat of armies. Books of pyrotechnic knowledge were extremely valuable, and access to information about how to mount fireworks was often closely controlled. Frederik II (1534–1588), King of Denmark and Norway from 1559 until his death, had the munitions book by Joachim Arentsehe (Arentsch) printed in 1578 on parchment in a single copy for his son Christian IV (1577–1648).[6] The manuscript is beautifully bound; it is truly a gift for a king. Christian's own notations in the margins of the text confirm that the precious volume was both read and used. Several other manuscript volumes on fireworks attest to King Frederik's enduring interest in pyrotechnics. The Royal Library, Copenhagen, owns two nearly identical fireworks manuscripts from the second half of the sixteenth century by Rudolph von Deventer; one is dedicated to King Frederik II[7] and one to the nobleman Christoffer Valkendorf (1525–1601).[8] One of the illustrations presents a fireworks fortress typical of those in Denmark and German-speaking lands at the time. This anti-papal fireworks display features a burning effigy of the pope on the left with monks self-immolating at the four corners of the platform. Connected to the scaffold by a little bridge is a larger, covered edifice on the right from which emerges a moving figure dressed as a Danish nobleman holding a fiery pyrotechnic sword. Rockets fly from both buildings, while two monsters breathe flames from the back wall of the larger edifice. (Fig. 18.2) The technological expertise of the moving figures and of the fireworks that were clearly intended to burn in controlled stages confirms the tendency from an early period to enact pyrotechnic dramas.

Carl Christmann's manuscript fireworks manual, 'Artilleri-og Fyrværkeri-Atlas', from around 1650 confirms the continued interest of the Danish court in pyrotechnical books.[9] Christmann's lavishly illustrated volume provides a very clear model of the so-called blockhouse fireworks – a perennial feature of early

---

Wolfenbütteler Arbeiten zur Barockforschung, 31 (Wiesbaden: Harrassowitz, 1999), pp. 721–39.

[6]   *Ein Buch zusammen gezogen aus vielen probierten Künsten und Erfarungen, wie ein Zeughausz sampt aller Munition anheimisch gehalten werden sol* ... (Copenhagen: Benedicht, 1578) Shelfmark LN 367 2o.

[7]   Rudolf von Deventer, *Bericht vom Pulver und Feuerwerken* (Royal Library, Shelfmark NKS 101 2o). There are other early fireworks manuscripts in the Royal Library, for example, *Ein Buch von einem grossberühmten Kriegs-Erfarnen, aus vielen probierten Khünsten unnd Erfahrungen zusammengezogen* (Shelfmark GKS 351 2o, later printed in Copenhagen by Lorentz Benedicht, 1578) and *Verzeichniss, wie man gut Schies-Pulver machen soll*, 1576 (Shelfmark GKS 1861 4o).

[8]   Rudolf von Deventer, *Kunstbuch von aller handt Kunsten der Argkaley, Geschütz und Feuerwerk zu Wasser und zu Lande. Subjicitur ad calcem: Bericht von Pulver zu machen* (Shelfmark Thott 273, 2o). Christoffer Valkendorf was an extremely important official at the Danish court; under Christian IV he was *Rigshofmester*, or Steward of the Realms.

[9]   Shelfmark GKS 352 2o.

Figure 18.2   Rudolff von Deventer, *Anti-Papal Castle Fireworks*. Courtesy of the Royal Library, Copenhagen, Thott 273 2o.

tournaments and court festivals during the preceding century in Northern Europe. (Fig. 18. 3) Christmann's portrayal of how to 'dress' a castle fireworks, that is, how to cover the explosive devices so that the resulting edifice looks like a fortress, depicts wild men on the right and Roman heroes on the left, all with torches to ignite the explosives. The two stories of the edifice with its five towers further indicates that the fireworks were intended to be burned in stages – first the small towers, then the large central one, and so on. The picture suggests that this was a design for a mock siege and a pyrotechnic drama. Variations of the blockhouse fireworks dominated German and Danish displays from 1548–1719.

Building on the early work of Torben Krogh, I have suggested elsewhere that the manuscripts preserved in the Royal Library are records of actual fireworks held at the Danish court during the reigns of Frederik II and Christian IV, that is, in the period roughly spanning the century from 1550–1650.[10] For example, two figures from Christmann's manuscript, 'Babylonia' or the Whore of Babylon (Fig. 18.4) and 'Invidia' (Fig. 18.5), strongly correlate to firework figures ignited at Christian IV's coronation in 1596. Beginning with the unique imprint of the fireworks manual for Christian IV at his birth through his coronation and into his late reign,

---

[10]   Mara R. Wade, *Triumphus Nuptialis Danicus: German Court Culture and Denmark: The "Great Wedding" of 1634* (Wiesbaden: Harrassowitz, 1997) (also Wolfenbütteler Arbetien zur Barockforschung, vol. 27), pp. 120–46. See also Torben Krogh, 'Optogbilleder fra Christian IV's Kroningsfest', *Musik og Theater* (Copenhagen: Munksgaard, 1955), pp. 1–11. Rpt. from *Tilskuerne* 2 (1938), pp. 187–98.

Figure 18.3   Carl Christman, 'Bekleidung des Castels,' ca. 1650. Courtesy of the
Royal Library, Copenhagen, GKS 352 2o.

Figure 18.4   Carl Christman, 'Babylonia,' ca. 1650. Courtesy of the Royal Library, Copenhagen, GKS 352 2o.

Figure 18.5   Carl Christman, 'Invidia,' ca. 1650. Courtesy of the Royal Library, Copenhagen, GKS 352 2o.

there is steady documentary evidence of the Danish monarch's abiding interest in pyrotechnics. His funeral sermon specifically states that Christian IV understood fireworks and artillery, and that he himself designed fireworks displays:

> With great industry he devoted himself in the same manner [as he did to fortifications and ship building] to the artillery and to the pyrotechnic arts, such that he understood the guns ['pieces'] together with their proportions and several times put together fireworks on his own without the help of a single master of the artillery.[11]

The lavish manuscript volumes in Denmark offer splendid examples of the pyrotechnic arts, confirming that the fireworks were at an advanced stage there no later than 1578 and, in all likelihood, well before that time. The Christmann manuscript attests to the enduring interest of the court in fireworks through the next century. The long tradition of fireworks in Denmark coincides with the enthusiasm for pyrotechnics at the dynastically closely related court in Dresden. An obligatory component of every court festival in both Denmark and Electoral Saxony was an elaborate fireworks display, normally in conjunction with a mock battle, usually designed as the siege of a castle, often a 'Turkish' fortress.

Fireworks in Saxony

The Saxon Prince Electors assiduously archived the descriptions, accounts, drawings, paintings, material objects, manuscripts and imprints concerning their own festival traditions from 1547 with the establishment of the Albertine line, and today these materials can be found in prominent Dresden collections. The most important documents concerning fireworks for festivals are located in the Dresden State Archives in the division called the *Oberhofmarschallamt*, while printed texts can be found mainly in the Dresden State and University Library and extensive pictorial materials are in the cabinet of prints and drawings. With only rare exceptions did the Dresden court engage in the printing of massive festival

---

[11] 'Umb die Artiglierie und Feurwerckerkunst/ hat er sich gleicher gestalt mit grossem Fleiß angenommen/ also daß er die Stücke mit ihrer proportion vorstanden und etliche mahl Feurwercke allein und ohne eintziges Meisters Zuthun verfertiget', (94). Stefan Klotz, *Geistliche Cypressen Kräntzlein* ... (Lübeck: Wettstein, 1669), (HAB: Stolberg 2396). The funeral sermon for Christian IV of Denmark is called: *Andre Leich-Predigt. Des Königs David schöne Ehren-Crone ... Zum unsterblichen Nachruhm ... Christian des Vierdten ... zu Flensburg den 18. Nov. Anno 1648.* This funeral sermon is part of a much larger collection by Klotz and is found in the fourth 'Decas' on pp. 41–104.

works typical of some of the other German courts,[12] such as at Stuttgart, yet the archival record confirms a continuous interest in pyrotechnics.

Fireworks were a required element of court weddings from at least 1548 and constituted a significant part of the first major celebrations held after the elevation of the Albertine line to the Electorate. There were major firework displays for the weddings of August in 1548, Christian I in 1582, Christian II in 1602, Johann Georg I in 1604 and 1607, Sophie Elisabeth in 1627, Marie Elisabeth in 1630, Magdalena Sibylle (in Copenhagen) in 1634, Johann Georg II in 1638 and for the double wedding for the princes Moritz and Christian in 1650 through the splendid fireworks for the state visit of King Frederik IV of Denmark in 1709.[13] There appears to have been a direct relationship between the increased frequency of fireworks displays in Dresden during the 1630s and the escalating involvement in, and resultant adversity for, Saxony during the Thirty Years' War.

A key figure in the design and organization of fireworks events during this period was the Electoral Prince and later Elector Johann Georg II (1613–80), who exerted a strong influence on pyrotechnic displays at the Saxon court with a particular focus on the themes of Jason and Hercules.[14] A splendid fireworks manuscript preserved in Berlin, *Verzeichnuß und Ordnung der Feuerwergke ...*, documents the fireworks that Johann Georg organized as Electoral Prince, that is, until 1656.[15] While there were fireworks in Dresden before 1634, Johann Georg II visited Denmark in that year for the wedding of his sister Magdalena Sibylle (1617–68) and experienced the lavish pyrotechnic displays ignited on this occasion. My research suggests that his exposure to the Danish firework tradition with its pyrotechnic dramas gave fresh impetus to his fascination with fireworks and to organizing displays himself. As for King Christian IV of Denmark, the role as organizer and designer of court fireworks was for Johann Georg II the royal privilege of the ruler.

---

[12]   The exception is the massive volume documenting a meeting of all the Saxon brothers in Dresden in 1678. See Gabriel Tzschimmer, *Durchlauchtigste Zusammenkunft* (Nürnberg: Hofmann, 1680). See also Helen Watanabe-O'Kelly, 'Gabriel Tzschimmer's *Durchlauchtigste Zusammenkunft* (1680) and the German Festival Book Tradition', *Daphnis*: 22 (1993), pp. 61–72.

[13]   In addition to the nuptial fireworks listed above, Helen Watanabe-O'Kelly, 'Entries, Fireworks, and Religious Festivals in the Empire', lists more fireworks in Dresden in 1635 and 1637 (734). See also Wade, 'Dänisch–sächsische Hoffeste der frühen Neuzeit', pp. 63–9 and Claudia Schnitzer, '"Bey dero höchsterfreulichen Anwesenheit allhier in Dreßden." Die Festlichkeiten anläßlich des Besuchs Frederiks IV. Von Dänemark 1709 in Dresden,' pp. 289–301, both in *Mit Fortuna übers Meer. Sachsen und Dänemark – Ehen und Allianzen im Spiegel der Kunst (1548–1709)* (Dresden: Staatliche Kunstsammlungen, 2009).

[14]   Helen Watanabe-O'Kelly, *Court Culture in Dresden* (Houndsmills, Basingstoke: Palgrave, 2002), pp. 131, 143–8, 152–5, 177 and 235–6.

[15]   *Verzeichnuß und Ordnung der Feuerwergke, So itzige Churfl. Durchl. selbst angegeben und ferttigen laßen, auch theils selbst laboriren helffen und verbrannt*, 1671. (Berlin: Staatsbibliothek Preußischer Kulturbesitz, Ms. Germ 2o 297).

Saxon and Danish Fireworks: Case Studies

Castle fireworks from the German and Danish traditions maintained the close association between war and entertainment with the mock sieges and their connection to the tournament. These fireworks were normally embedded in a programmatic festival and were part of a sequence of festival elements. For example, to celebrate the city of Hamburg's allegiance to King Christian IV in 1603, the tournament procession included a pageant wagon of blockhouse fireworks.[16] (Fig. 18.6) The pageant concludes with a fireworks castle on wheels in which stands a Turk brandishing his sword. The description explains that the pyrotechnic blockhouse, part of the 'tenth invention', was a tournament prize. The tournament concluded with the siege of the 'Turkish' fortress. This pageant was created for Christian IV of Denmark by the equerry Georg Engelhard Löhneysen (1552–1622), a figure closely associated with the courts of Dresden and Wolfenbüttel. In both the German and Danish traditions the tendency to create fireworks dramas was present from the beginning of the documented tradition. Three of the pyrotechnic pageants on the water – from 1548, 1634 and 1709 – for Danish–Saxon dynastic occasions and two waterborne pageants – for the entry of the bride into Dresden in 1602 and for the state visit of Frederik IV of Denmark to Venice in 1709 are discussed below.

The Wedding of Prince Elector August of Saxony and Anna of Denmark at Torgau in 1548

In 1548 for the wedding of Duke, and later Prince Elector, August of Saxony (1526–86) with the Danish princess Anna (1532–85), sister of King Frederik II of Denmark, a mock battle was held on the town square at Torgau.[17] An imposing blockhouse was erected and then stormed by four groups of knights on horseback.[18] The teams were colour-coded, with the Elector Moritz (1521–53) leading the

---

[16]   Georg Engelhard Löhneysen, *Della Cavalleria; Dasist: Gründlicher und außführlicher Bericht, von allem was zu der löblichen Reutery gehörig, und einem Cavallier zu wissen von nöhten: Insonderheit von Tunier- und Ritterspielen* ... (Remling: [Löhneysen], 1624). Inventions 6–10 portray the pageants in Hamburg and are presented here on a single folio opening (62–3); the description of the event is at 70–71. There is also music for the various inventions (74–82) (Wolfenbüttel: Herzog August Bibliothek, 1.5 Bell. 2o).

[17]   These events are briefly described in *Vorzeichnus was vor Chur und Fürsten etc. auff dem Herlichen Beylager und Freud des ... Herrn Augusten Hertzogen zu Sachsen etc. mit der Durchlauchten Fürstin Freulein Anna etc. ... gescheen den siebenden tag Octobris Anno etc. xlviij zu Torgaw/ gewesen, AiijA*. I would like to thank Dr Dorothea Sommer, Halle, for providing me with a copy of this print.

[18]   Rigsarkiv, Copenhagen, Denmark, TKUA, speciel del Sachsen, A II 20, *Akter og Dokumenter vedr. det politiske Forhold til Sachsen. Ægteskabet August og Anna, 1548–54,* '*Sturm eines Hauses/ am platz tzu Torga[u] ...* '.

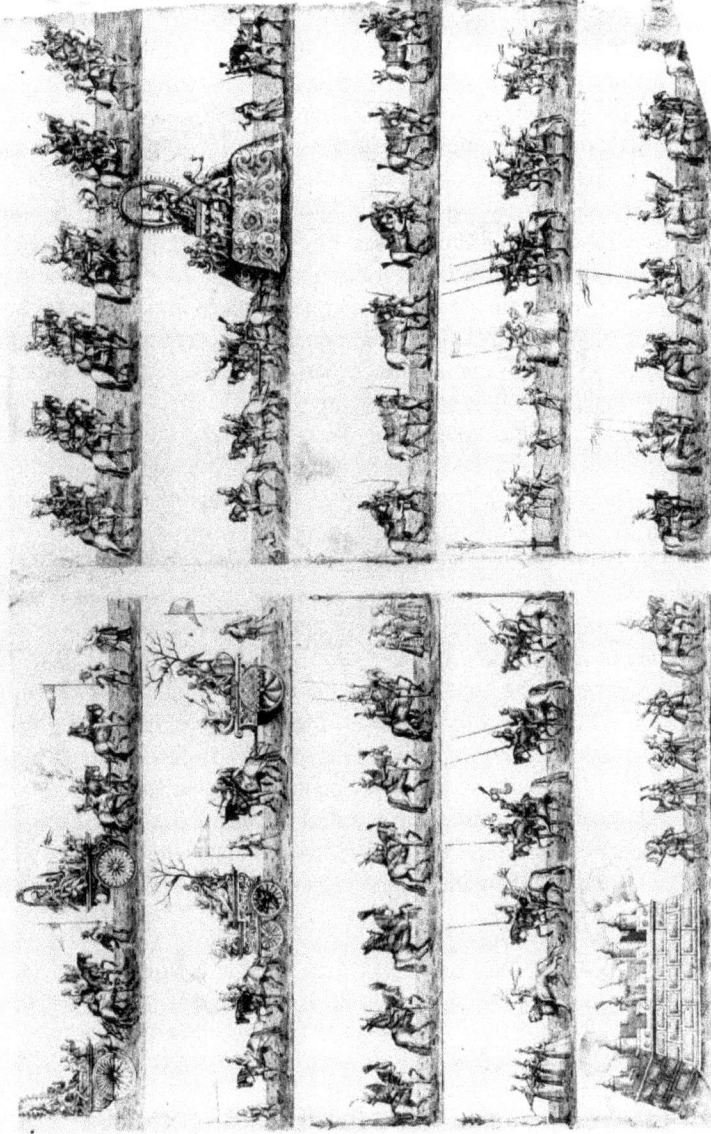

Figure 18.6 Fireworks of a Turkish castle for a tournament, Hamburg, 1603. Georg Engelhard Löhneysen, *Della Cavalleria* … (Remling: [Löhneysen],1624), pp. 62–3. Courtesy of the Herzog August Bibliothek, Wolfenbüttel,1.5 Bell.2°.

red group; his brother, the bridegroom, August, the blue; and two other leading courtiers the yellow and the green teams. Ordnance was fired, and the teams skirmished before three other groups of knights stormed the castle on horseback and on foot.

The following evening the pyrotechnic displays continued the mock battle with the siege of a fireworks castle on the river Elbe. There is a wide bend in the river below the fortress at Torgau, offering an excellent site for the fireworks. The view across the water is very good at this location, and the view from the castle above would have also been spectacular, affording all onlookers the full sensory impressions of light, sound and action. The manuscript and printed descriptions portray the siege as a costumed event, including knights dressed as 'Turks' and 'Tartars' as well as those in traditional German dress. This drama consisted of 'Germans' storming a two-storey blockhouse with towers at each corner held by 'Tartars' and 'Turks'.[19] A skirmish occurred and preliminary fireworks were shot off before the action of the pyrotechnic display began. This consisted of even more elaborate effects and in three separate attacks several ships stormed the castle, which was located on the Elbe. The spectacular pyrotechnic effects increased with each attempt to capture the blockhouse. The 'Turks' had red costumes with white trim, while the attackers were dressed in white and carried little swords and lances. A court trumpeter blew Turkish trumpet calls.[20] This magnificent pyrotechnic display, in which the water's reflection enhanced the fireworks effects of over 2,000 charges placed in the castle alone, lasted over one-and-a-half hours. It is extremely important to note that as early as 1548, the mock battle was carried out as a costumed drama over multiple days and locations, culminating in a pyrotechnic display in several 'acts' on the river.

The 1548 fireworks on the Elbe at Torgau were quite typical for the mid-sixteenth century.[21] While there is no pictorial record of this event, the storming of a pyrotechnic blockhouse on the water was a common festival element in the German empire and in Denmark, and there are contemporary images preserved of similar events. For example, an excellent point of comparison are the fireworks pantomimes that spanned three days for the 1585 wedding of Johann Wilhelm I of Jülich-Kleve-Berg (1562–1609) with Jacobe of Baden (1558–97) in Düsseldorf.

---

[19]   Rigsarkiv, Copenhagen, Denmark, TKUA, speciel del Sachsen, A II 20, *Akter og Dokumenter vedr. det politiske Forhold til Sachsen. Ægteskabet August og Anna, 1548–54, 'Welcher gestalt vff Churfürstlichem Bevelch Hertzog Moritzen zu Sachssen der Oberzeugkmeister Caspar Vogt den Sturm zu Wasser vff ... türckisch bestelt hat ...* '. The following description is based on this account.

[20]   See especially in Claudia Schnitzer, "Das Türkenmotiv im höfischen Fest," Claudia Schnitzer and Holger Schuckelt (eds), *Im Lichte des Halbmonds*, (Dresden: Staatliche Kunstsammlungen, 1995), pp. 227–34.

[21]   For an overview of the culture of firework displays, see Kevin Salatino, *Incendiary Art: The Representation of Fireworks in Early Modern Europe* (Los Angeles: The Getty Research Institute, 1997), pp. 1–46.

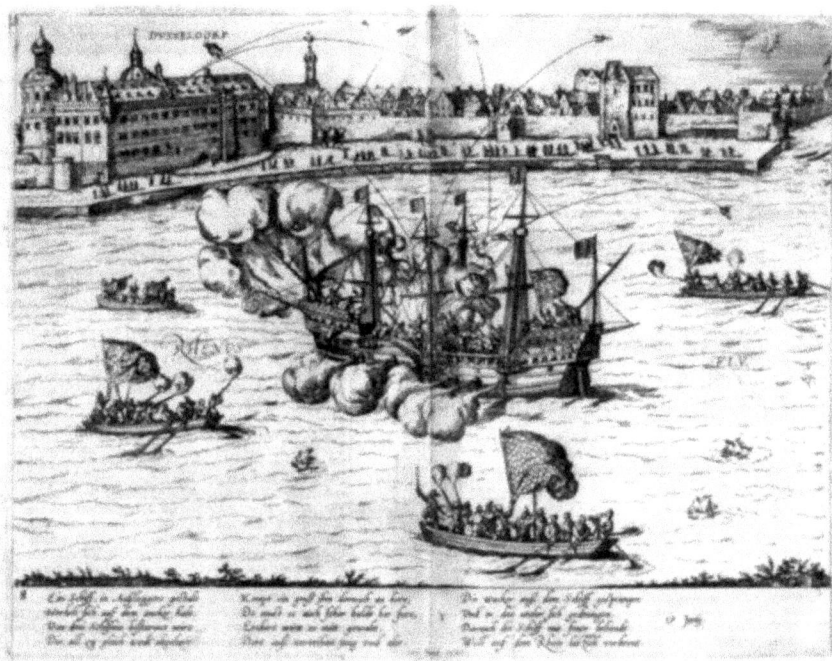

Figure 18.7   Fireworks Ship, Düsseldorf, 1585. Courtesy of the Bayerische
Staatsbibliothek, München, Res/2 Bavar. 381 m.

These well-illustrated events offer appropriate comparisons to the Saxon events.[22]
All three firework displays at Düsseldorf were held on the Rhine. The first evening
presented a pyrotechnic display in the form of a ship (Fig. 18.7),[23] followed the
next evening by fireworks on the labours of Hercules (Fig. 18.8),[24] while the third

---

[22]   Dietrich [Theodor] Graminaeus, *Beschreibung derer Fürstlicher Güligscher u.
Hochzeit/ so im jahr Christi tausent fünffhundert achtzig fünff/ am sechszehenden Junij vnd
nechstfolgenden acht tagen zu Düsseldorff mit grossen freuden/ Fürstlichen Triumph vnd
herrligkeit gehalten worden* (Köln: [Theodor Gras], 1587). The copy consulted for this study
is in the Herzog August Bibliothek, Wolfenbüttel. First mentions in the notes refer to this
copy; parenthetical comments refer to the on-line copy of the Bayrische Staatsbibliothek,
München, Res/2 Bavar. 381 m (BSB, textual description, followed by the firework's image
number in the on-line copy). See http://mdz1.bib-bvb.de/~db/bsb00006424/images/ where
the book can be read online. There is a thumbnail function for browsing and easy navigation
to the images of the fireworks; these are identified by their image numbers below. The book
identifier is VD16 G 2797.

[23]   Graminaeus, *Beschreibung ...*, sig. Kia–Kivb. (BSB, 82–4, image 00081)

[24]   Graminaeus, *Beschreibung ...*, sig. Eeivb–Ggia. (BSB, 152–6, image 154)

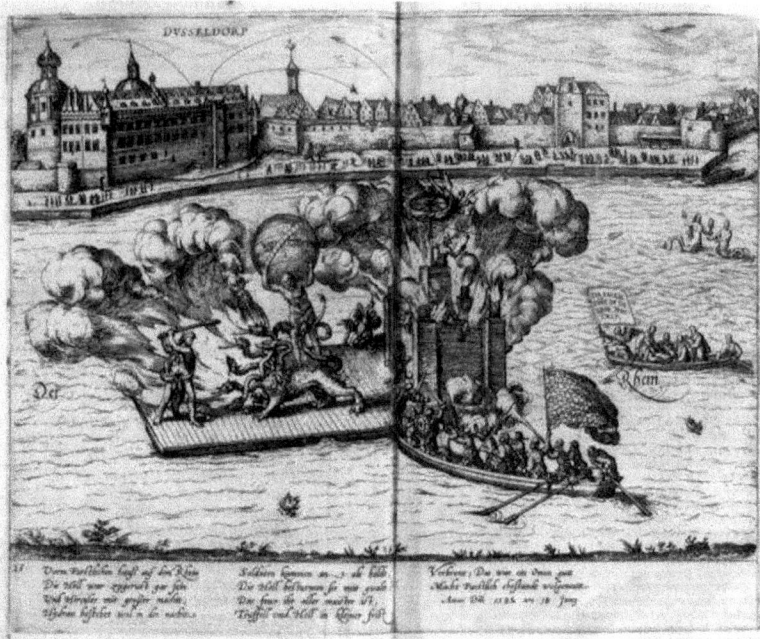

Figure 18.8   Fireworks, the labours of Hercules, Düsseldorf, 1585. Courtesy of the Bayerische Staatsbibliothek, München, Res/2 Bavar. 381 m.

Figure 18.9   Fireworks battle between a whale and a dragon, Düsseldorf, 1585. Courtesy of the Bayerische Staatsbibliothek, München, Res/2 Bavar. 381 m

incendiary event depicted the fight between a whale and a dragon (Fig. 18.9).[25] Helen Watanabe-O'Kelly has posited that this series of fireworks from Düsseldorf marks the beginnings of an early proto-cinematic tradition involving the play of colour and light, mobile figures and a wide audience of awed spectators.[26] The fireworks at Dresden predate the Düsseldorf events by nearly 40 years.

The Dresden Wedding of Prince Elector Christian II and Princess Hedwig of Denmark

A waterborne pageant on the Elbe welcomed the bride Princess Hedwig of Denmark (1581–1641) to her new home in Dresden in 1602. Accompanied by the two highest ranking men in attendance – her brother Duke Ulrik of Holstein (1578–1624) and her soon-to-be husband Prince Elector Christian II (1583–1611) – Hedwig was welcomed by an allegorical water pageant in which sirens swam alongside a magnificent chariot in the form of a whale. Kneeling in the direction of the bridegroom, four sea horses with red manes and white tails pulled a pageant float of Neptune. Glaucus, sounding his trumpet, was also part of this watery procession.[27] Pageants, fireworks and tournaments were held on the days following the wedding on 12 September 1602. While the printed source devotes little space to the water-borne pageant itself, great attention was paid to the ceremony of the bride's entry into the city – the solemn occasion that this aquatic pageant marked. The Saxon court thus paid homage to the new Electress by making her Danish home and seafaring origins visible in an aquatic pageant.

The engraving of a comparable event portrays an aquatic pageant on the River Spree at the Brandenburg court, which was closely related to both the Dresden and Copenhagen courts. (Fig. 18.10) The event depicted is a waterborne pageant with fireworks for the visit of Hedwig's brother, the then minor King Christian IV of

---

[25]   Graminaeus, *Beschreibung ...*, sig. Qqia–Ria. (BSB, 212–14, image 213)

[26]   Helen Watanabe-O'Kelly, "Firework Displays, Firework Dramas and Illuminations – Precursors of Cinema?" *German Life and Letters*, 48 (1995), pp. 338–52.

[27]   Hedwig's wedding to Elector Christian II of Saxony (1583–1611) was celebrated with great pomp in Dresden in September of 1602 with plays, mummings, allegorical tournaments and fireworks, and the allegorical welcome on the Elbe. Many of the archival sources associated with this wedding are believed to have been destroyed in WWII. However, there is ample textual and pictorial documentation concerning the splendid celebrations for the weddings of Christian's younger brother Johann Georg (1585–1656) in 1604 and again in 1607, together with a series of annual carnival festivities during Christian's brief reign. A small number of printed works provide descriptions of the Dresden wedding festivities from this period, so scholars nonetheless have an overview of the nuptial celebrations. See, for example, *Kurtze vnd doch aus führliche Relation vnd wahrhaffte Erzehlung von gehaltenem Beylager/ Des Durchlauchtigsten Hochgebornen Fürsten vnd Herrn/ Herrn Christiani II. Hertzogen zu Sachsen/ des heiligen Römischen Reiches Erztmarschallen/ vnd Churfürsten/ Landgraffen in Düringen/ Marggraffen zu Meissen/ vnd Burggraffen zu Magdeburg/ etc. ...* (Jena: Steinman 1603).

Figure 18.10 Neptune fireworks for the visit of King Christian IV of Denmark to Cölln an der Spree (Berlin), 1595. Courtesy of the Kunstbibliothek, Staatliche Museen zu Berlin-Preußischer Kulturbesitz, OS 2822.

Denmark, to Berlin (Cölln an der Spree) in 1595, in the year before his coronation. The mythological pageant on the River Spree literally flows around the castle walls at Berlin. A loving couple sits in a conch shell decorated with symbols suggesting a prosperous union: the caeducus, the crowned pillar of constancy and Fortuna on her globe with a sail. Neptune, holding a pyrotechnic trident, leads a vessel drawn by three sea horses. Viewers can see smoke and fire emitting from the figures, suggesting an early stage in a fireworks drama. The descending dove indicates that this is a so-called *Schnurfeuerwerk*, a display ignited by a mobile incendiary figure; here the dove descends along a rope to the main display that will then burn up in stages, enacting a drama. Mortars line the front edge of the image, showing that many kinds of pyrotechnic devices were employed for this event. The towers and windows of the Berlin castle are filled with spectators. The union of the elements of earth, air, fire and water must have exerted a strong pull on the viewers, and the senses were overloaded during such a display. Fireworks on the water increased the sensory effects by reflecting the play of lights and colours in the water. The close similarity of the illustration for Berlin pyrotechnic water pageant for Christian IV to the description of the Dresden welcome for his sister Hedwig suggests that these two aquatic displays of Neptune and sea horses were, in fact, very similar.

The Berlin, Dresden and Copenhagen courts nurtured a common festival tradition during this period, and the festival culture of the three courts overlapped in the figure of Giovanni Maria Nosseni (1544–1620). He was officially the court architect at Dresden but often created festivals and pageants for other rulers. In the year following the aquatic pageant for Christian IV at Berlin, the Dresden court allowed its chief festival artist to travel to Copenhagen in 1596 with a pageant 'invention' on the theme of the mountain of virtue.[28] Nosseni thus designed the elaborate display on behalf of the Berlin court for the Danish coronation.[29] These close cultural ties reflect the dynastic relations among the three Protestant courts.

The 'Great Wedding' of 1634, Copenhagen

In the century from 1548 there was an increasing trend toward the dramatization of the pyrotechnic displays for Danish–Saxon dynastic occasions that reached its zenith in the so-called 'Great Wedding' of 1634. While several fireworks displays were held in Copenhagen and environs to celebrate this event, the focus here is on two pyrotechnic allegories that were staged as part of the wedding festivities on the waterfront in front of the Copenhagen castle. The first of these pyrotechnic extravaganzas was a hybrid entertainment, a cross between fireworks and an illumination with immobile, flaming allegories, shooting rockets and Catherine wheels. This pyrotechnic display, called *Fortitudo* in the printed descriptions, was held during the night after the royal wedding, lasting from three until five in the morning.[30] (Fig. 18.11) It was the capstone event of a day of much celebrating.

The engraving of *Fortitudo* presents a largely static display in the sense that the Virtue is surrounded by many fire-spewing obelisks, columns and other pyrotechnic structures, yet immobile. In the foreground two men costumed as Turks with sabres and shields engage in single combat. Although the display was ignited in stages by costumed figures with torches, it was not a drama, but a fixed allegorical illumination on the theme of Fortitude, who holds the pillar of Constancy. This allegory was meant to function at several levels indicating the strength and constancy of the prince in his love for his Saxon bride and of the Danish monarchy against religious foes. Since the event was held after the creation of Knights of the Danish Order of the Elephant, the allusion also suggests strength and constancy in battle. The architectural ordering of this fireworks event places it in the realm of the emblematic, rather than the dramatic.

---

[28] Giovanni Maria Nosseni, *Inventio. Mons virtutis. Tugendberg des Herrn Christiani, Marggraffen zu Brandenburg ... Welcher zum Venturiren auff der Krönung König Christiani des Vierten in Dennemarck zu Koppenhagen ... im Ringrennen zu gebrauchen verordenet, und ins Werck gerichtet worden, Auctore Iohan. Maria Nossenio architect* (Copenhagen: Stockelmann, 1596).

[29] Wade, 45–7, 139–140.

[30] See Wade, 132–3 for a fuller description of the event.

Chriſtophorus Swenckius junior inventor   *fol.20.*

Figure 18.11 *Fortitudo*, emblematic fireworks for the 'Great Wedding,'
          Copenhagen 1634. Courtesy of the Royal Library, Copenhagen, 35-
          276-4o.

The emblem of Fortitude standing steadfast among the flames anticipated the
complex allegory of the 'Tragedy of the Vices and Virtues' that was the theme
of a pyrotechnic morality play in five acts held at the waterfront in front of the
Copenhagen castle. (Fig. 18.12) This was the second major fireworks event held
in Copenhagen for the 'Great Wedding' of 1634; fireworks were also held at
Kronborg and Frederiksborg as the wedding party progressed around the island of
Zealand. The pyrotechnic display of the 'Battle of the Vices and Virtues' assumed
a central position in Danish festival culture as it was printed twice in 1634 –

Figure 18.12 Pyrotechnic 'Tragedy of the Vices and the Virtues', for the 'Great Wedding', Copenhagen 1634. Courtesy of the Royal Library, Copenhagen, 35-276-4o.

once in German and once in Danish.[31] The entire event was repeated in 1636 for the wedding of Christian IV's daughter Leonora Christina (1628–91) to Corfits

---

[31]   See *Tragoedia von den Tugenden und Lastern, beim grossen Fewrwerck agiert Ao. 1634 d. 10. Oct. auff ihre Printzliche Gnaden Beylager* (Copenhagen: Jürgen Holst, 1634). See also *Tragoedia Om Dyder Oc Lastersom udi hans Printzlige Naadis Bryllups Fest, Ao. 1634. d. 10. Oct. hos det store Fyrvæcrk bleff Agerit* (Copenhagen: n.p., 1636). The wedding of Christian IV's daughter Sophie Elizabeth to Christian Penz was held the same day as this fireworks display.

Uhlfeldt (1606–64).[32] As far as I have been able to determine, the printed booklet describing the 'tragedy' with its illustration of the pyrotechnic plot is the first published fireworks play in Europe.

The Copenhagen pyrotechnic tragedy is a *Schnurfeuerwerk* with a bird of prey swooping down to ignite the opulent castle of the Vices with its open arcades in the centre of the image. The rear left depicts the tent of the Virtues. Fireworks pillars mark the four corners of the pyrotechnic stage and more fireworks structures stand at the perimeters. In the right foreground is a gruesome hell mouth into which devils lead the hapless figures of the Vices. Pyrotechnicians dressed as demons hold torches and play bagpipes. This display was divided into five acts, and the printed programme provides the dialogue between the Vices and Virtues. The dramatic structuring of the 'tragedy' allowed for a controlled release in stages of the pyrotechnic effects. The placement of the fireworks next to the shore heightened the visual and acoustic impression of the rockets and their reflections.

Visiting the ships in the harbour created an important parallel to the siege of mock castles and fireworks, and viewing the fleet was a significant element of every court festival in early modern Denmark. Firing cannon in the harbour was a direct military corollary to igniting fireworks for entertainment. The shooting of the ship's cannon for the entry of the guests into Copenhagen and during the visits to the fleet were real-life military parallels to the emblematic illumination and the pyrotechnic drama. During the 'Great Wedding' every major group of foreign ambassadors was taken to the harbour and boarded the ships. Cannon were fired and ordnance detonated. The display was loud and not to be ignored. The attention to both war and entertainment fireworks in aquatic settings for the 'Great Wedding' of 1634, and again for the next Danish wedding in 1636, is striking for its excess. The restaging of the fireworks drama together with the reprinting of the Danish text in 1636 was appropriate, however, since the war continued and the political scene had changed little in the ensuing two years. During the two-week long celebrations in Copenhagen in the autumn of 1634 there were many, many explosions. The focus on pyrotechnics seems to be associated with the organization of the wedding as a summit meeting at the mid-point of the Thirty Years' War.[33] Christian IV was using the wedding to position himself and his heir as the mediators of the German peace. The striking emphasis on martial and pleasurable pyrotechnics in the otherwise peaceful Danish capital simply would not permit the many foreign guests in attendance to forget the wars in Europe.

---

[32]   *Tragoedia Om Dyder Oc Lastersom udi hans Printzlige Naadis Bryllups Fest, Ao. 1634. d. 10. Oct. hos det store Fyrvæcrk bleff agerit. Oc nu paa H. Corvits Ulfelds etc. Bryllup-Høytid anden gang agerit* (Copenhagen: n.p., 1636).

[33]   Mara R. Wade, "'Große Hochzeit' und Gipfeltreffen in Kopenhagen 1634: Dänische Repräsentationspolitik im Dreißigjährigen Krieg," in *Zwischen Alltag und Katastrophe. Der Dreißigjährige Krieg aus der Nähe* (ed.) Hans Medick and Begnina von Krusenstjern, Zusammenarbeit von Patrice Veit (also Veröffentlichungen des Max-Planck-Instituts für Geschichte, vol. 148). (Göttingen: Vandenhoeck & Ruprecht, 1999), pp. 113–31.

The nearly daily explosions repeatedly forced the attendees' attention back to the military and political matters of the day.

Frederik IV of Denmark in Venice 1709

King Frederik IV of Denmark travelled to Italy in the autumn of 1708 and stayed through the carnival season in 1709, which he spent in Venice. There the famous artist in pastels, Rosalba Carriera (1675–1757), drew his portrait.[34] (Plate 6) Two copies exist today, one in the Gallerie Alte Meister, Dresden, and one at the Danish National Museum, Frederiksborg, Denmark. During the nine weeks he spent enjoying the carnival in Venice, Frederik IV visited both the opera and the theatre. Under his *incognito* as the 'Count of Oldenburg' he was entertained lavishly by the highest ranking families of the city. On 4 March 1709, the day before his departure, a splendid regatta was held for the Danish king.[35] Luca Carlevarijs (1663–1730) painted the Venetian water pageant for Frederik IV of Denmark, and the original of this magnificent canvas is held at the National Museum, Frederiksborg, Denmark. (Plate 7) The painting depicts

> in the middle boat, liverymen in red and gold uniforms [who] row the king, dressed in red, toward his waiting hosts at the Palazzo Foscari, seen on the left. They will pass a huge green parade float, decorated with royal, Venetian, and aquatic symbols, that marks the end of the race. At the foot of the float are four different colored [sic] flags; whoever grabs the red flag first is the winning boatman.[36]

Carlevarijs's *vedute* are noteworthy as they were ambassadorial gifts. They vividly portray the grandeur of the city as well as document in lavish detail the splendid occasion of the waterborne pageant.

While in Venice Frederik IV stayed at the residence of the British ambassador extraordinaire Charles Montagu, the 4th Earl of Manchester (1656–1722), whose

---

[34] To view the portrait, see, for example, http://www.denstoredanske.dk/@api/deki/files/67369/=292767.501.jpg

[35] *La magnificenza veneta nella pomposa comparsa delle sontuose poete, che scorsero il Canal Grande nella regata seguita il di 4. marzo 1709 à divertimento di Sua Maestà Federico IV. Rèdi Danimarca, Norvegia etc.* (Venice; n.p., 1709).

[36] *Regatta on the Grand Canal in Honor of Frederick IV, King of Denmark.* The commentary from the Getty website continues: "The view towards the Rialto bridge, seen in the far distance, shows in great detail the facades of buildings alongside the canal, with spectators filling the balconies. Luca Carlevarijs painted many vedute, views of Venice that were popular souvenirs with diplomatic visitors and wealthy foreigners making the Grand Tour of Italy in the 1700's." http://www.getty.edu/art/gettyguide/artObjectDetails?artobj=916 (consulted 22 February 2011).

entry into Venice Carlevarijs had painted in 1707.[37] The English ambassador's residence was located very near the family palace of the Doge Ca'Mocenigo di S. Stae. According to reports, the king 'watched the whole of the regatta from the splendid vessel of the Dolfin family and was afterwards entertained at yet another splendid banquet, this time hosted by Alvito Foscari at Ca'Foscari.'[38] Both the regatta for the Danish king and the painting were well known and copies were made, one now at the Getty and one at the Hermitage in St Petersburg.[39] The fame of the regatta for the Danish King was significantly augmented by the splendid painting, and the aquatic pageant remains one of the most famous of such events held in Venice at the turn of the century.

Frederik IV of Denmark in Dresden

On his return from Italy, Frederik IV spent over a month in Dresden at the court of his cousin, Prince Elector August II (1670–1733), who was known as August the Strong and who was also King of Poland. There were splendid festivities held every day during his visit, including magnificent tournaments on foot and on horseback, a ladies running-at-the-ring, a nocturnal shooting contest, opera, ballets, comedies, banquets and fireworks music on the Elbe.[40] After the ladies running-at-the-ring, an extraordinary pyrotechnic display designed by August the Strong himself was ignited. First, water music was performed on ships close to the Dresden castle. This overture to the fireworks was a 'Serenade' on the theme of Peace and War in supplication before the throne of Glory. The imperial Capellmeister Carlo Agostino Badia (1672–1738) composed his Italian *Serenata, La Pace e Marte supplicanti Avanti al Trono alla Gloria*, in 1700 for the Viennese court; it was used again in Dresden for the Danish monarch's visit. Badia was a prominent Venetian composer who introduced the "stylistic inventions of the late Baroque" to the imperial court, among them works for the King of Denmark's visit and the fireworks. It is also noteworthy that Badia's opera *Gli amori di Circe con Ulisse*, written for the Dresden court, was performed for Frederik's visit.[41] The

---

[37]   Susan Tipton, "Diplomatie und Zeremoniell in Botschafterbildern von Carlevarijs und Canaletto," *RIHA*, 8 (2010), pp. 1–197, here 28–30. http://www.riha-journal.org/articles/2010/tipton-diplomatie-und-zeremoniell

[38]   Patrick Kragelund, "Popes, Kings and the Medici in the Eighteenth-Century *fasti* of the Palazzo Mocenigo di S. Stae in Venice," *Journal of the History of Collections*, 21(2009), pp. 1–15.

[39]   See Kragelund, p. 3.

[40]   Claudia Schnitzer, "'Bey dero höchsterfreulichen Anwesenheit allhier in Dreßden.' Die Festlichkeiten anläßlich des Besuchs Frederiks IV. von Dänemark 1709 in Dresden," pp. 291–4.

[41]   Herbert Seiffert, "Die Rolle Wiens bei der Rezeption italienischer Musik in Dresden," in Günther Stephan and Hans John (eds), *Dresdner Operntraditionen*, (Dresden: Schriftenreihe der Hochschule für Musik Carl Maria von Weber, 1985), pp. 96–105. See

royal fireworks music performed for two kings predated Handel's *Royal Fireworks Music* (1748) by nearly 40 years.

After the music on the Elbe, the pyrotechnic display began with the firing of cannon and hundreds of rockets, while on a fireworks castle in the middle of the Elbe the initials of the Danish king, 'F.4.R.D.' [Fridericus IV Rex Daniae], could be seen in green fire.[42] (Plate 8) In the windows of the fireworks tower blazed the emblems of the Danish Order of the Elephant – the elephant with a castle on its back. Below it the 'Vivat' burned in blue. After this illumination came the fireworks themselves, which were divided into three 'acts', or 'attacks'. Each act involved many more rockets and explosions than the previous one, resulting in a massive display of sound and light. Over 150 years after the wedding of August and Anna in 1548, the mock siege of a fireworks fortress was still a staple of the royal display. In contrast to the fireworks displays of earlier centuries, however, this event was thoroughly modern in its musical setting, the illumination with the king's initial and emblems, and its integration into the overall festival program. Of particular interest here is the emphasis on green fire. This was a completely new innovation and demonstrated August the Strong's superior knowledge and control of pyrotechnics. The Prince Elector and King of Poland paid an enormous compliment to his cousin the King of Denmark by allowing his monogram to blaze in green. The flaming green initials of the monarch were a royal tribute from one king to another.

Conclusion

Early modern theories of the macrocosm and microcosm as well as popular ideas concerning alchemical principles have informed the evolution of fireworks. The pyrotechnic display is an elemental event: the soaring of the rockets through the air, the fire they embody, the water that reflects them and protects the onlookers and the earth on which the viewers stand, all unite the elements in a physical, even corporeal, way that is apprehended sensually. The play of the elements was used strategically in these displays to underscore the primal nature of such events. For example, a fireworks display in Stuttgart in 1616 took the contest between fire and water as its theme, when a fireworks ship was ignited in the tournament area at the

---

also Lawrence E. Bennet, "Badia, Carlo Agostino," *Grove Music Online*: 'In 1709 he was commissioned to write the opera *Gli amori di Circe con Ulisse* for Dresden; the performance took place during a visit by the King of Denmark. It seems unlikely that Badia travelled to Dresden for the performance, which was directed by Baron Francesco Ballerini, one of the most famous singers at the imperial court.' Consulted 22 February 2011.

[42] Moritz Bodenehr, *Eigentlicher Abriß und Beschreibung des Feuer-Wercks welches dem Könige in Dennemark Friedrich IV. in Dreßden der König u. Churfürst zu Sachsen 6. Jun. 1709 verbrennen lassen* (Dresden SLUB Hist.Sax.C.233, 52).

castle, offering an allegorical battle between the elements of fire and water.[43] (Fig. 18.13) After two hours of thundering rockets and pyrotechnic effects, Neptune's ship succumbed to the superior element of fire. This early German display expressed the contemporary interest in the secret nature of the physical world with the competition between opposites and the victory of fire over water. Of particular interest for this nautical pageant is the striking lack of water at the tournament yard at the Stuttgart court. The philosophical underpinnings of the event weighed more heavily than the practical arrangement of the event itself. The theme stresses the importance of fiery pageants at the shore and on the water for early modern court festivals in German-speaking lands and in Denmark.

Pyrotechnical festival events were much more than mere frivolities and were embedded in the political and artistic discourses of the time. One of the striking features of fireworks is their close association with military prowess as even peaceful displays were often portrayed as sieges. The fireworks and mock battles from the Germanic tradition were also invariably held along the water. There are several reasons for this, and most of the arguments align closely with cultural, scientific and artistic discourses of the day. Of course, the most obvious reason for placing pyrotechnics near or at the waterfront is safety. The many reports of persons injured or killed during firework displays attest to the danger of igniting what amounted to weapon grade explosives in front of a large audience of onlookers in a densely populated urban area. The night-time sky and dark waters enhanced the bursts of colour and light, and the thunder of detonating the explosions carried well across the waters. There was compelling reason to situate the pyrotechnics along the water because the reflection of the exploding fireworks in the water, thereby doubled the effect and aesthetic appeal of the brilliant illuminations. With the formation of pyrotechnic castles, giants, moveable flying dragons and other such papier mâché creatures, by indulging in spectacular colour effects and by mirroring reflections in the water, aquatic fireworks pageants showcased the art and science of pyrotechnics and demonstrated the prince's manipulation of the element of fire.

The intent of royal fireworks is to inspire awe in the onlooker and to impress the viewer with the might of the prince launching the pyrotechnics. The technology of the fireworks and the chemistry of saltpetre were all valuable knowledge for both war and peace. This overview of Danish–Saxon pyrotechnic displays suggests that the greater the political dimension of the occasion, the more elaborate the fireworks display.

Fireworks were also embedded in the philosophical and emblematic discourses of the period and demonstrate that there was also an abstract level of meaning of pyrotechnics for the prince. (Fig. 18.14) A fireworks emblem illustrates the ideal of

---

[43]   Esaias van Hulsen, *Repræsentatio Der Fvrstlichen Avfzvg Vnd Ritterspil. So ... bey Ihr. F.G. Neüwgebornen Sohn, Friderich Hertzog zu Württemberg. etc. Fürstlicher Kindtauffen, denn 10. biss auff denn 17 Martij* ... (Stuttgart: Hulsen, [1616]). http:// diglib.hab.de/drucke/36-17-3-geom-2f-1/start.htm (image 91). See also Eberhard Fähler, *Feuerwerke des Barock* (Stuttgart: Metzler, 1974), pp. 25–6.

Figure 18.13 Fireworks Ship, Stuttgart, 1616. Esaias van Hulsen, *Repræsentatio Der Fvrstlichen Avfzvg Vnd Ritterspil*. [Stuttgart: Hulsen], [1616]. Courtsey of the Herzog August Bibliothek,Wolfenbüttel, 36.17.3 Geom. 2° (1).

the good prince with its motto: '*Dum luceam peream*' ('Let me perish, provided I should shine').[44] The fireworks illuminating the sky are an allegory of the prince's good reputation, one he guards and treasures above all else. The act of designing,

---

[44] Diego de Saavedra Fajardo, *Idea de un Principe Politico Christiano* ... (Brussels: Viveni, 1649), symbolum 15, *Emblematica Onlin*,. http://diglib.hab.de/drucke/86-1-quod-2f-1s/start.htm.

Symbola Politica.   115

S Y M B O L U M   XV.

OUam vellem præfentis Emblematis fymbolum
legere mihi liceret in pectoribus omnium
Principum , atque ut quemadmodum ignes miffiles
per aerem volitantes aftrorum imitantur fplendo-
rem , lucentque mox atque emittuntur è manu, do-
nec

Figure 18.14 Emblem 15, 'Dum luceam peream' ('Let me perish, provided I
should shine'), Diego de Saavedra Fajardo, *Idea de un Principe
Politico Christiano* ... 1649. Courtesy of *Emblematica Online*,
University of Illinois and Herzog August Bibliothek, Wolfenbüttel,
Sf 216.

igniting and viewing fireworks was entirely the prerogative of the prince, while the short, but mighty, blasts of sound, colour, quaking earth and twinkling waters, served as a potent allegory to the ruler of his own place in the world. The measure of the prince's life was not how long one lived, but how well. The aquatic pageants and fireworks were part of a complex web of social and political interactions, thrilling, potent displays of the dynasty's hierarchy, visible to all and yet powerful reminders of the fleeting fragility of the human condition.

Bibliography

Manuscript Sources

Anon., *Ein Buch von einem grossberühmten Kriegs-Erfarnen, aus vielen probierten Khünsten unnd Erfahrungen zusammengezogen* (Royal Library, Shelfmark GKS 351 2o, later printed in Copenhagen by Lorentz Benedicht, 1578).

Deventer, Rudolf von, *Bericht vom Pulver und Feuerwerken* (Royal Library, Shelfmark NKS 101 2o).

Deventer, Rudolf von, *Kunstbuch von aller handt Kunsten der Argkaley, Geschütz und Feuerwerk zu Wasser und zu Lande. Subjicitur ad calcem: Bericht von Pulver zu machen* (Shelfmark Thott 273, 2o).

Rigsarkiv, Copenhagen, Denmark, TKUA, speciel del Sachsen, A II 20, *Akter og Dokumenter vedr. det politiske Forhold til Sachsen. Ægteskabet August og Anna, 1548–1554, 'Sturm eines Hauses/ am platz tzu Torga[u] …'.*

Rigsarkiv, Copenhagen, Denmark, TKUA, speciel del Sachsen, A II 20, *Akter og Dokumenter vedr. det politiske Forhold til Sachsen. Ægteskabet August og Anna, 1548–1554, 'Welcher gestalt vff Churfürstlichem Bevelch Hertzog Moritzen zu Sachssen der Oberzeugkmeister Caspar Vogt den Sturm zu Wasser vff … türckisch bestelt hat …'.*

Verzeichniss, wie man gut Schies-Pulver machen soll, 1576 (Royal Library, Shelfmark GKS 1861 4o).

Verzeichnuß und Ordnung der Feuerwergke, So itzige Churfl. Durchl. selbst angegeben und ferttigen laßen, auch theils selbst laboriren helffen und verbrannt, 1671 (Berlin, Staatsbibliothek Preußischer Kulturbesitz, Ms. Germ 2o 297).

Printed Primary Sources

Anon., *Ein Buch zusammen gezogen aus vielen probierten Künsten und Erfarungen, wie ein Zeughausz sampt aller Munition anheimisch gehalten werden sol …* (Copenhagen: Benedicht, 1578. Shelfmark LN 367 2o).

Arthus, Gotthard, *Electio Et Coronatio Sereniss. Potentiss. Et Invictiss. Principis Et Dn. Dn. Matthiæ I …* ([Frankfurt, Main]: Officina de Bry, 1612). http://diglib.hab.de/drucke/36-11-1-geom-2f-2/start.htm

Bodenehr, Moritz, *Eigentlicher Abriß und Beschreibung des Feuer-Wercks welches dem Könige in Dennemark Friedrich IV. in Dreßden der König u. Churfürst zu Sachsen 6. Jun. 1709 verbrennen lassen* (Dresden SLUB Hist.Sax.C.233, 52).

Graminaeus, Dietrich [Theodor], *Beschreibung derer Fürstlicher Güligscher u. Hochzeit/ so im jahr Christi tausent fünffhundert achtzig fünff/ am sechszehenden Junij vnd nechstfolgenden acht tagen zu Düsseldorff mit grossen freuden/ Fürstlichen Triumph vnd herrligkeit gehalten worden* (Köln: [Theodor Gras], 1587). http://mdz1.bib-bvb.de/~db/bsb00006424/images/

Hulsen, Esaias van, *Repræsentatio Der Fvrstlichen Avfzvg Vnd Ritterspil. So ... bey Ihr. F.G. Neüwgebornen Sohn, Friderich Hertzog zu Württemberg. etc. Fürstlicher Kindtauffen, denn 10. biss auff denn 17 Martij ...* (Stuttgart: Hulsen, [1616]).

Klotz, Stefan, *Geistliche Cypressen Kräntzlein ...* (Lübeck: Wettstein, 1669).

Kurtze vnd doch ausführliche Relation vnd wahrhaffte Erzehlung von gehaltenem Beylager/ Des Durchlauchtigsten Hochgebornen Fürsten vnd Herrn/ Herrn Christiani II. Hertzogen zu Sachsen/ des heiligen Römischen Reiches Erztmarschallen/ vnd Churfürsten/ Landgraffen in Düringen/ Marggraffen zu Meissen/ vnd Burggraffen zu Magdeburg/ etc. ... (Jena: Steinman, 1603).

La magnificenza veneta nella pomposa comparsa delle sontuose poete, che scorsero il Canal Grande nella regata seguita il di 4. marzo 1709 à divertimento di Sua Maestà Federico IV. Rè di Danimarca, Norvegia etc. (Venice; n.p., 1709).

Löhneysen, Georg Engelhard, *Della Cavalleria; Dasist: Gründlicher und außführlicher Bericht, von allem was zu der löblichen Reutery gehörig, und einem Cavallier zu wissen von nöhten: Insonderheit von Tunier- und Ritterspielen ...* (Remling: [Löhneysen], 1624).

Nosseni, Giovanni Maria, *Inventio. Mons virtutis. Tugendberg des Herrn Christiani, Marggraffen zu Brandenburg ... Welcher zum Venturiren auff der Krönung König Christiani des Vierten in Dennemarck zu Koppenhagen ... im Ringrennen zu gebrauchen verordenet, und ins Werck gerichtet worden, Auctore Iohan. Maria Nossenio architect* (Copenhagen: Stockelmann, 1596).

Saavedra Fajardo, Diego de, *Idea de un Principe Politico Christiano ...* (Brussels: Viveni, 1649). http://diglib.hab.de/drucke/86-1-quod-2f-1s/start.htm

Tragoedia Om Dyder Oc Lastersom udi hans Printzlige Naadis Bryllups Fest, Ao. 1634. d. 10. Oct. hos det store Fyrvæcrk bleff agerit. Oc nu paa H. Corvits Ulfelds etc. Bryllup-Høytid anden gang agerit. ([Copenhagen]: n.p., [1636]).

Tragoedia von den Tugenden und Lastern, beim grossen Fewrwerck agiert Ao. 1634 d. 10. Oct. auff ihre Printzliche Gnaden Beylager. (Copenhagen: Jürgen Holst, 1634).

Tzschimmer, Gabriel, *Durchlauchtigste Zusammenkunft* (Nürnberg: Hofmann, 1680).

Vorzeichnus was vor Chur und Fürsten etc. auff dem Herlichen Beylager und Freud des ... Herrn Augusten Hertzogen zu Sachsen etc. mit der Durchlauchten Fürstin Freulein Anna etc. ... gescheen den siebenden tag Octobris Anno etc. xlviij zu Torgaw/ gewesen (n. p.; n. p., n. d.))

Secondary Sources

Bennet, Lawrence E., 'Badia, Carlo Agostino', *Grove Music Online* (consulted 2 February 2011).

Exhibition catalogue: *Venice. Canaletto and His Rivals* (London: National Gallery, 2010): http://www.nationalgallery.org.uk/whats-on/exhibitions/venice-canaletto-and-his-rivals

Fähler, Eberhard, *Feuerwerke des Barock* (Stuttgart: Metzler, 1974).

Kragelund, Patrick, 'Popes, Kings and the Medici in the Eighteenth-Century *fasti* of the Palazzo Mocenigo di S. Stae in Venice', *Journal of the History of Collections*, 21 (2009), pp. 1–15.

Krogh, Torben, 'Optogbilleder fra Christian IV's Kroningsfest', *Musik og Theater* (Copenhagen: Munksgaard, 1955), pp. 1–11; reprinted from *Tilskuerne* 2 (1938), pp. 187–98.

Regatta on the Grand Canal in Honor of Frederick IV, King of Denmark: http://www.getty.edu/art/gettyguide/artObjectDetails?artobj=916 (consulted 22 February 2011).

Salatino, Kevin, *Incendiary Art: The Representation of Fireworks in Early Modern Europe* (Los Angeles: The Getty Research Institute, 1997).

Saslow, James Maxwell, *The Medici Wedding of 1589: Florentine Festival as 'Theatrum Mundi'* (New Haven: Yale University Press, 1996).

Schnitzer, Claudia, "'Bey dero höchsterfreulichen Anwesenheit allhier in Dreßden." Die Festlichkeiten anläßlich des Besuchs Frederiks IV. von Dänemark 1709 in Dresden,' in *Mit Fortuna übers Meer. Sachsen und Dänemark – Ehen und Allianzen im Spiegel der Kunst (1548–1709)* (Dresden: Staatliche Kunstsammlungen, 2009), pp. 289–301.

Schnitzer, Claudia, 'Das Türkenmotiv im höfischen Fest', in Claudia Schnitzer and Holger Schuckelt (eds), *Im Lichte des Halbmonds* (Dresden: Staatliche Kunstsammlungen, 1995).

Schnitzer, Claudia and Holger Schuckelt (eds), *Im Lichte des Halbmonds* (Dresden: Staatliche Kunstsammlungen, 1995).

Seiffert, Herbert, 'Die Rolle Wiens bei der Rezeption italienischer Musik in Dresden', in Günther Stephan and Hans John (eds), *Dresdner Operntraditionen* (Dresden: Schriftenreihe der Hochschule für Musik Carl Maria von Weber, 1985), pp. 96–105.

Stephan, Günther and Hans John (eds), *Dresdner Operntraditionen* (Dresden: Schriftenreihe der Hochschule für Musik Carl Maria von Weber, 1985).

Tipton, Susan, 'Diplomatie und Zeremoniell in Botschafterbildern von Carlevarijs und Canaletto', *RIHA*, 8 (2010), pp. 1–197. http://www.riha-journal.org/articles/2010/tipton-diplomatie-und-zeremoniell

Treadwell, Nina, *Music and Wonder at the Medici Court: The 1589 Interludes for La pellegrina* (Bloomington: Indiana University Press, 2008).

Wade, Mara R., 'Dänisch–sächsische Hoffeste der frühen Neuzeit', in *Mit Fortuna übers Meer. Sachsen und Dänemark – Ehen und Allianzen im Spiegel der Kunst (1548–1709)* (Dresden: Staatliche Kunstsammlungen, 2009), pp. 63–9.

Wade, Mara R., '"Große Hochzeit" und Gipfeltreffen in Kopenhagen 1634: Dänische Repräsentations politik im Dreißigjährigen Krieg', in Hans Medick and Begnina von Krusenstjern (eds), *Zwischen Alltag und Katastrophe. Der Dreißigjährige Krieg aus der Nähe*, Zusammenarbeit von Patrice Veit (also Veröffentlichungen des Max-Planck-Instituts für Geschichte, 148). (Göttingen: Vandenhoeck & Ruprecht, 1999), pp. 113–31.

Wade, Mara R., *Triumphus Nuptialis Danicus: German Court Culture and Denmark: The "Great Wedding" of 1634* (Wiesbaden: Harrassowitz, 1997) (also Wolfenbütteler Arbetien zur Barockforschung, 27), 120–46.

Watanabe-O'Kelly, Helen, *Court Culture in Dresden* (Houndsmills, Basingstoke: Palgrave, 2002).

Watanabe-O'Kelly, Helen, 'Entries, Fireworks, and Religious Festivals in the Empire', in Helen Watanabe-O'Kelly, Helen, 'Firework Displays, Firework Dramas and Illuminations – Precursors of Cinema?' *German Life and Letters*, 48 (1995), pp. 338–52.

Watanabe-O'Kelly, Helen, 'Gabriel Tzschimmer's *Durchlauchtigste Zusammenkunft* (1680) and the German Festival Book Tradition', *Daphnis*: 22 (1993), pp. 61–72.

Watanabe-O'Kelly, Helen and Pierre Béhar (eds), *Spectaculum Europaeum*, Wolfenbütteler Arbeiten zur Barockforschung, 31 (Wiesbaden: Harrassowitz, 1999).

Werret, Simon, *Fireworks. Pyrotechnic Arts and Sciences in European History* (Chicago: University of Chicago Press, 2010).

Chapter 19
Sea Spectacles on Dry Land:
The 1580s to the 1690s

Roger Savage

Jean Rousset put it succinctly 50 years ago. There are two forms of marine drama: in one, theatre goes to the water; in the other, water comes to the theatre.[1] Much of this book deals with the first of these. I would like to look briefly at the second, 'dry-land' theatre, or one part of dry-land theatre. Not, that is to say, at the simulations of watery things on the decorated floats of processions and pageants, and not at shows in princely courtyards and ducal playhouses where actual water was occasionally piped in for special events: at Aleotti's Teatro Farnese in Parma, for example. Rather, my concern is with sea- and river-scenes from the 1580s to the 1690s played out on illusionistic indoor stages that were wholly dry, or where the only water to be found was in butts that good theatre-practice required should be kept permanently full backstage in case of fire.[2]

In the late sixteenth century, such spectacles in dry-land theatres could be spectacular indeed, for example the two that the dramatist Giovanni Bardi and scenographer Bernardo Buontalenti included among the interludes between the acts of Bardi's court-comedy *L'amico fido* at Florence in 1586.[3] In one of these an audience sees, at a distance, the dismal, flame-lit underworld city of Dis, accessible only by ferry over a sludgy stream. A hideous ferryman out of Dante brings his boat to the hither shore to collect those malign spirits banished from Florence on account of the splendid dynastic marriage that is being celebrated. Gloomy songs are sung by ferryman and passengers as they embark and cross unsteadily

---

[1]   Jean Rousset, 'L'eau et les tritons dans les fêtes et ballets de cour (1580–1604)', in J. Jacquot (ed.), *Les fêtes de la Renaissance* (2 vols, Paris: CNRS, 1956), vol. 1, pp. 237–8. Rousset's is a rewarding essay, as is J. de La Gorce, 'Un aspect du merveilleux dans l'opéra français sous le règne de Louis XIV', in A. Schnapper (ed.), *La scenografia barocca* (Bologna: CLUEB, 1982), pp. 65–72.

[2]   For fire safety, see Seriacopi (1589) in A. Warburg, 'I costumi teatrali per gli intermezzi del 1589', *Gesammelte Schriften*, (ed.) Fritz Rougemont and Gertrud Bing (Leipzig, 1932), p. 404; Federigo Zuccari (1608) in A. Nagler, *Theatre Festivals of the Medici 1539–1637* (New Haven: Yale University Press, 1964), p. 185; and Galeazzo Sabbattini (1638) in B. Hewitt (ed.), *The Renaissance Stage: Documents of Serlio, Sabbattini and Furttenbach* (Coral Gables, Fl: University of Miami Press, 1958), p. 98.

[3]   Nagler, *Theatre Festivals*, pp. 63–6.

to the dreadful city. In the other interlude, the scene is a rocky, reedy coast with a seascape beyond and ships visible at a distance. The blue-haired goddess Thetis and a troupe of sea-creatures come ashore from the deep. Thetis invokes King Neptune, at which the sea gets rough, the ships seem to dance on the waves, sea-monsters appear and Neptune himself, attended by Naiads, comes up in a great shell-chariot drawn by four pawing and curvetting sea-horses. The god commands that the seas be still; the monsters sink down; the shore becomes a blossoming meadow – an image of the benign effect of the Medici wedding presumably – and the Naiads happily pluck flowers there until they and Neptune go undersea again.

Many members of the audience at the Uffizi Palace in 1586 must have found all of this splendidly 'realistic' and strikingly novel, though a lot of it in fact was less novel than it may have appeared. Graphic hell-scenes stretched back to medieval religious drama, while the prospect of a rough seacoast with an ocean beyond it grew easily out of the permanent 'satyric' scene derived from Vitruvius by Sebastiano Serlio in the mid-sixteenth century. Serlio's illustration of such a scene in his *Second Book of Architecture* has a forest backing and bosky wings. His commentary however mentions 'cliffs and rocks covered with diverse sea shells [and] coral branches of many colors',[4] and it would have been easy to substitute a marine back-piece for his forest-piece and replace the bosky side-pieces with wholly rocky ones. A bustling port, too, could be made by taking the side-pieces of one of Serlio's two urban street-scenes and giving them a marine back-piece, perhaps attaching a wood-and-canvas wave-machine of some sort to it, to give the impression of moving water. Other elements of the Florentine decor were not novel in 1586 either. Scaled-down boats holding real performers, with the boats' stage-wheels generally masked, were to be seen in age-old Passion plays, mystery plays, saints' plays and, more recently, on floats in alfresco pageant-processions. Neptune's shell-chariot had featured in pageants too. Attendant Nereids, Sirens and Tritons were seen singing and dancing in less spectacular Italian interludes and French *mascarades* well before 1586; and as for simulated sea-monsters, 'practicable' beasts of all sorts – whales, dolphins, sea-horses and such – had been constructed for Catherine de' Medici's ambitious water-fête at Bayonne in 1565.

What was more novel in 1580s Florence was Buontalenti's making complex but unified stage-pictures of all these things and his fading them in and out, so to speak, through his virtuoso use of revolvable, scenically-painted *periaktoi* – perhaps also of retractable wing-flats of the kind that would become current in the following century. Such changeable perspectives, set up behind an imposing proscenium arch, not only gave new life to the conjunction of the earlier elements but also created a wing-space invisible to the audience from which he and his team could play their visual toccatas with moveable ground-rows, elaborate trapdoors, rotatable wave-machines and so on.[5]

---

4   Hewitt, *The Renaissance Stage*, p. 32.

5   For water fêtes, see R. Strong, *Splendour at Court: Renaissance Spectacle and Illusion* (London: Weidenfeld and Nicolson, 1973), pp. 134–9. For wave-machines etc., see

Buontalenti and his colleague Bardi played their creative tricks again three years later with the famous set of interludes for the comedy *La pellegrina* at the Medici–Valois wedding of 1589. In the fifth of these, a scenic sea-change ushered in surfacing Tritons and an august Queen Amphitrite attended by sea-girls with blue silk tails. These disported themselves on the waves and paid their respects to the newly-wed royal couple, the '*coppia reale*', in the audience. Then a fine ship (travelling on special grooves, as we know from production manager Seriacopi's notes) performed gallant manoeuvres in honour of the happy pair, after which the mythical musician Arion was revealed on the ship's prow, apparently accompanying himself on a harp-like lyre – in fact a prop made of cardboard – and singing what he thought would be his swan-song: a song with a double echo from behind the scenes. Threatened with the knives of the ship's rapacious crew who were after his gold, he jumped into the sea – 'one saw the water splash up', an eye-witness said – only to be carried off by a music-loving dolphin (four *braccia* long and made of *papier-mâché* and silver paper), while the piratical crew rashly celebrated their coup with a cheerful madrigal. The splash was possibly made using water borrowed from a fire-safety butt, or possibly – some experts recommended this – it too involved silver paper, artfully shredded and blown upwards by a hidden stage-hand through a 'cardboard cornucopia'.[6]

Between them, these *pellegrina* and *Amico fido* interludes of Arion, Neptune and the crossing of the Styx pretty well established the hardware of aquatic scenes in proscenial spaces for the next hundred years or so, though one should add to the devices Buontalenti used in them various sorts of 'flying' machinery that could bring Olympian deities down to sea-level, unleash personified airborne winds from the cave of Aeolus, or allow Perseus flying on Pegasus's back to 'execute an admirable caracole in mid-air' (as one observer put it) after the rescue of Andromeda.[7] There were, of course, technical refinements over the century, notably in the matter of the smooth and simple drawing on and off of scenic flats. There were new effects too: islands and reefs that could surface in the middle of the sea; bridges that could collapse; ships that could sink or indeed be turned to stone (as in Badoaro and Monteverdi's *Ritorno d'Ulisse*); the means for a character to out-jump Arion from a high tower into the sea (as in the Buti-Cavalli

Sabbattini and Furttenbach in Hewitt, *The Renaissance Stage*, pp. 130–46, 239–45. For sea-monsters in Florence at the turn of the century, see M. Ossi, ' "*Dalle machine ... la maraviglia*": Bernardo Buontalenti's *Il rapimento di Cefalo* at the Medici Theater in 1600', in M. Radice (ed), *Opera in Context* (Portland: Amadeus Press, 1998), pp. 29–30.

[6]   Interlude V: Nagler, *Theatre Festivals*, pp. 87–8. Seeing the splash: B. Rossi, *Descrizione dell'apparato e degli Intermedi fatti per la commedia* (Florence, 1589), p. 58. Dolphin, grooves and harp: Warburg, 'I costumi teatrali', pp. 400–401, 405–406. Silver paper: Sabbattini in Hewitt, *The Renaissance Stage*, pp. 142–3.

[7]   P. Corneille, *Andromède* (Paris, 1650), III, iii. For F. Chauvcau's engraving of the scene, see P. Bjurström, *Giacomo Torelli and Baroque Stage Design* (Stockholm: Almqvist and Wiksell, 1961), p. 152.

Ercole amante (*Hercules in Love*)); and cunningly witty scene-painting that could indicate that the action was taking place full fathom five below the surface of the ocean. But broadly, the waterscapes assembled in Florence in the 1580s went on being recycled, modified and developed from the age of Bardi and Jacopo Peri (who composed and sang Arion's part in 1589) to that of John Dryden, Henry Purcell and the last act of their *King Arthur* in the 1690s.[8]

It is true that critics might sometimes take exception to what they saw as bad practice, either because they were sure that no theatre beyond the borders of their own city state could come up with a half decent sea-scene, or because some scenic element or other posed a health and safety risk. And sometimes there was criticism that sprang from a purist–classicist campaign against the foregrounding of picturesque scenic illusion in general, as when Jean de la Fontaine declared that, though such things had a superficial charm, they were not really high art, and besides their machinery had a way of going embarrassingly wrong. Indeed, 'Often the finest chariot is impeded by its counter-weight; a god hangs on a rope and calls to the machinist; part of a forest remains in the sea'.[9] Yet the carpers were at least balanced by the enthusiasts. Some of these, of course, were the official chroniclers of interludes, masques, court ballets or early operas who were duty-bound to report of, say, the *Ballet de Psyché* in 1619 that its sea-decor 'represented the azure waves rising and falling so well that one would not have thought it could be shown without water'.[10] But private citizens too could be enthusiastic: observers like the traveller Barthold von Gadenstedt, who was in the audience for the Medici interludes of 1589 and (though not realising that the sea-sequence in them was connected with the Arion myth) declared that it was an '*intermedium miraculosissimum*' ('a most marvellous interlude'), delighted as he was by the ocean which 'moved as if blown by the wind', by the manoeuvres of the ship and by the tenor-man's death leap. Then there were those connoisseurs who consciously appreciated the joint presence of artifice and illusion. One was the author of the anonymous treatise on staging of around 1630, *Il corago*, who relished the 'curiosity to know how it is all done', which came over him when he saw 'the ocean suddenly appear and in it Tritons, gods, ships and other *trompes l'oeil*'. Another sophisticate was Pierre Corneille, who said in 1650 of the coast scene in the machine-play *Andromède* he had devised with the great scenographer Giacomo Torelli that Nature seemed to contribute more than Art to the cliff set

---

[8]   For repertories of marine scenes and effects available in the 1680s, see C.-F. Ménestrier, *Des représentations en musique anciennes et modernes* (Paris, 1681), p. 172 and *Des ballets anciens et modernes* (Paris, 1682), p. 247.

[9]   *Campanilismo*: see the Florentine Inghirami's coolness about Parmesan sea-scenes in 1628: Nagler, *Theatre Festivals*, pp. 146, 150. Health and safety: see I.-N. du Tralage's 1689 review of *Thétis et Pélée*, quoted in De La Gorce, 'Un aspect du merveilleux', p. 68. La Fontaine: *Epitre á M. Niert sur l'Opera* (1677), pp. 10–21.

[10]   P. Lacroix (ed.), *Ballets et mascarades de cour sous Henri III et Louis XIV (1581–1652)* (Geneva: J. Gay, 1868–70), pp. 205–06.

Torelli had designed. 'It is in this that the artifice of the maker is marvellous', he argued, 'becoming the more apparent the more he takes pains to hide it'.[11]

If the scenography was in a fairly static state in these dry-land sea-pieces, so too was the constellation of myths that provided much of the material for plot and spectacle. Those myths might seem quite diverse and complicated to a modern reader at first blush, but many of their *dramatis personae* – the majority of them Greek albeit with Latinised names – soon become familiar, recurring again and again over the decades. In Renaissance humanist terms there was little that was obscure about them. Apart even from their appearances in the mythological handbooks of the age, a reassuringly large number featured in Lucian's compact, lyrical and delightfully tongue-in-cheek *Dialogues of the Sea-Gods*, and most were to be found with ease somewhere in Homer or Virgil, Ovid or Apollonius Rhodius.[12] (When a Triton joins the action in William Browne's Inner Temple *Masque of Ulysses and Circe* in 1615, Browne is keen to point out that he is 'in all parts as Apollonius, Book Four of the *Argonautica*, shows him'.) In the myths' upper echelons are the two royal couples, Oceanus with Tethys and Neptune with Amphitrite, seconded by Aeolus the wind god, the foam-born Venus and her unpredictable son, and lesser *dieux marins* such as Proteus (shape-changer and shepherd of Neptune's flocks), Glaucus, Thetis and Galatea. Then there are the mortals these salty lovers were linked with – Scylla, Peleus, Acis – and other mortals or semi-mortals who had famous adventures on or near the water: Orpheus and Arion, Andromeda and Ariadne, Jason and Ulysses, and the kingfisher-couple Ceyx and Alcyone. Roman myth-figures with watery connections occasionally appear too: Queen Dido on Carthage wharf for instance; also near-mythical figures like Antony and Cleopatra (who, according to the court ballet *Les amours déguisés* of 1664, were rowed away from the Battle of Actium by Cupids disguised as boatmen). And there are a few farther-fetched characters: the happy natives of the Tobacco Islands, the bridge-building King Xerxes of Persia, Queen Indamora of Narsinga in her chariot drawn by sea-monsters – she appears in William Davenant's *Temple of Love* (1635) – plus quite a few personifications, some of them geographical (of seas and rivers

---

[11]   Gadenstedt: W. Kimmel, 'Deutscher Bericht über die Florentinischen Intermedien des Jahres 1589', *Analecta Musicologica*, 9 (1970), pp. 15–16. *Il corago*: R. Savage, 'Staging an *Intermedio*', in J.R. Mulryne and Margaret Shewring (eds), *Italian Renaissance Festivals and their European Influence* (Lewiston: Edwin Mellon Press, 1992), p. 64. Corneille: *Andromède*, the '*Décoration du troisième acte*', cf. Hédelin d'Aubignac, 'La pratique du théâtre' (1657), in A. Nagler (ed.), *A Source Book in Theatrical History* (New York: Dover, 1959), pp. 172–3.

[12]   There are also occasional paragraphs in late classical novels and Renaissance romances which cram as many sea-supernaturals as they can into one small space, e.g. Apuleius, *Metamorphoses (The Golden Ass)* (c. 158–180 AD), IV. 31 – Venus's ocean cruise near the beginning of the narrative of Cupid and Psyche – and F. Colonna, *Hypnerotomachia Poliphili* – the episode of the voyage with Cupid – see Jocelyn Godwin's English translation (London: Thames and Hudson, 1991), p. 279.

particularly: the demi-gods Tirreno, Thamesis and their like), others embodying abstract concepts.

But it is those Greek mythical figures who dominate in aquatic scenes, reappearing from show to show, accompanied often by Nereids and Tritons, mariners and fisherfolk, pearl-divers and coral-gatherers. What do these mythical and quasi-mythical marine figures signify? This depends on the contexts in which they find themselves. In the full-length *favola maritima* genre that gets under way operatically in the 1610s after the Rinuccini–Monteverdi *Arianna* of 1608, the myths provide material for everyday stories of water-borne or water-connected folk, to be experienced in the way myths can, as pure narrative, as psychological/ symbolist discourse, perhaps as far-off political allegory. Marine fables of this sort run from the operatic *Galatea* of Chiabrera and Orlandi in 1615, where the whole cast apart from the land-lubber Cyclops either swims or fishes, to the kingfisher opera *Alcyone* of Lamotte and Marais 90 years later.[13] One instance from the years between is the *Arione* given in 1628 at the ducal court of Savoy: a court which seems to have had a special fondness for Arion-shows of various kinds in various locales, perhaps because the courtiers there were especially wedded to the idea of Harmony Triumphant or perhaps because they had a particularly fine artificial dolphin which they wanted to see in action again and again. Beyond the *favola maritima* there are sea- and river-scenes in full-length works largely land-based: Orpheus crossing the Styx; Perseus's nick-of-time rescue of the rock-bound heroine from the sea-monster in various danced, spoken and sung *Andromedas*, and the episode of the abduction of the heroine by ship – a real challenge to stage effectively – as in the Quinault–Lully *Alceste* (1672): an episode Quinault seems to have invented himself.

Such things did not have to be solemn. They could be semi-comic, as with the presentations of the ferryman Charon in the Quinault–Lully *Alceste* and in the Striggio–Monteverdi *Orfeo* 65 years earlier, or genially ironic, as with the scenes in Minato and Cavalli's Venetian *Xerse* (1665) where Xerxes gets his troops to admire his splendid new bridge linking Europe and Asia, only for it to collapse when the clownish retainer Elviro tries to cross it.[14] When *Xerse* was revived in France at Louis XIV's court, this Hellespont episode was capped with a comic *entrée* devised by Lully, which derived from the *ballet de cour* tradition and involved a ship's captain, his mariners, some slaves and their agile monkeys. Naturally everyone danced, the monkeys included. And that *entrée* of Lully's can

[13]   Possibly the greatest *favola maritima* of all would have been one that was never completed: Monteverdi's setting of a text by Scipione Agnelli on the marriage of Thetis, which the composer's patron, the Duke of Mantua, decided was surplus to requirements and cancelled in mid-composition. See *The Letters of Claudio Monteverdi*, trans. D. Stevens (London: Faber and Faber, 1980), pp. 114–29.

[14]   David Kimbell, 'Operatic Variations on an Episode at the Hellespont', in E. Bridges, E. Hall and P. Rhodes (eds), *Cultural Responses to the Persian Wars* (Oxford: Oxford University Press, 2007), pp. 209–10, 212–13.

lead discussion from the marine-mythical figures in full-length narratives to those in shorter and more segmented forms: the Italian interlude, the English masque, the *ballet de cour* itself. The aquatic *dramatis personae* in these tend to be more celebratory or encomiastic or straightforwardly allegorical than those in full-scale plays or operas, through their being more directly linked with the social or political life of the audiences watching them. It is as if we were moving from the world of one great painting of the 1620s and 1630s to that of another: from Poussin's iconographically rich but apparently self-contained and wholly 'ancient' *Triumph of Neptune and Amphitrite* to Rubens's *Reception of Marie de Medici at Marseilles*, where the modern queen steps from her boat over a sea-surge peopled by strenuous Tritons, sea-nymphs and a blue-bearded Neptune.

Very broadly, one could say that in these shorter forms myth is harnessed in one of two ways. Either the mythical characters on stage turn their gaze and their songs of congratulation directly to the guests of honour in the audience, or the worlds of mythical characters and audience somehow unite on the stage itself. Where the direct gaze is concerned, Bardi supplies cases in point in the Florentine sea-interludes of 1586 and 1589; there Amphitrite and assorted sea-nymphs come up from the depths especially to sing the praises of the harmonious calm that these Medici marriages will, everyone hopes, ensure. Similarly, about half a century later, in one of Filippo d'Aglié's ballets, *Hercole ed Amore* (1640), emissaries from the court of Venus arrive in a well-filled boat to salute the *Madama Reale* of Savoy seated in state in the auditorium and to link her country with their native Cyprus, while northward across the Alps and English Channel in almost the same year, the Galatea in Davenant's *Britannia Triumphans* comes 'waving forth, riding on the back of a dolphin', her hair richly dishevelled, to sing to Charles I's queen and his assembled court of that prince's greatness:

> So well Britanocles o'er seas doth reign,
> Reducing what was wild before,
> The fairest sea-nymphs leave the troubled main,
> And haste to visit him on shore.[15]

Where it is a case of the world of ancient myth blending on stage with representations of the modern world, there is one especially vivid Medicean instance. The interludes in *Il giudizio di Paride*, mounted in Florence in 1608, include one by Gianbattista Strozzi presenting an exotic Caribbean seascape into which sails the pre-eminent New World explorer where the Medici were concerned, the Florentine Amerigo Vespucci. His ship is crowded with personified virtues, and a further personification, the Lady Tranquillity, rises up on a reef which surfaces from the deep nearby, while in the heavens Aeolus reins in his discordant winds and Apollo celebrates with his Muses. Vespucci has become a modern Argonaut,

---

[15] D'Aglié: see Strong, *Splendour at Court*, p.11; Davenant: M. Lefkowitz (ed.), *Trois masques à la cour de Charles 1er d'Angleterre* (Paris: CNRS, 1970), p. 207.

blessed and protected by the gods. Two interludes in a *mascherata* mounted at Florence in 1611 bring things even nearer home, making the local Tyrrhenian Sea off the accurately painted port of Livorno the site for the epiphanies of a bevy of sea-spirits, notably a pearl-crowned Neptune and a dolphin-borne Venus: a Venus whose son has absconded and set out for the Medici court nearby, sure that he'll be very much at home there.[16] Similarly, in a Stuart masque of the year before, the 13 nymphs attending on Oceanus's queen in Samuel Daniel's *Tethys' Festival* turn out to bear the names of 13 very English and Welsh rivers. Things are taken still further in Ben Jonson's masque *Neptune's Triumph* (prepared for but not actually staged at James I's court in 1624), where Proteus, Apollo and other Greek mythical types are joined on stage by Albion, a demigod who is clearly wholly British – indeed who in some sense 'is' Charles, the Prince of Wales, just as Neptune 'is' Charles's father, King James.

It was much the same when Louis XIV in his youthful dancing days took the role of Neptune in the spectacular aquatic prologue to Molière's '*divertissement royal*' of 1670, *Les amants magnifiques*. Louis must have felt the more comfortable with being Neptune on stage since his royal father's sway over the sea had been celebrated in a pair of ballets 30 or so years before: the *Ballet de la marine* of 1635, where Nereids and sea-gods sing the praises of French naval power and usher in a sequence of *entrées* by Tritons, sailors, soldiers, fishermen and bringers of gifts from distant lands, and the *Ballet de la prospérité des armes de France* (1641), which presents French galleons crippling the Spanish treasure trade with the Americas. It is introduced by three Sirens who are eager to assure their audience that in their songs promising glory and honour to French power they are, for once, actually telling the truth. Court ballets of the 1650s and 1660s in which Louis himself danced did not lose sight of the sea and ships. In the big celebration of the liberal and useful arts that is part of the wedding attended by Olympian and marine gods in *Les noces de Pélée et de Thétis* (1654), 'Navigation' features among the useful ones, its personification doing his dance in a jaunty ship-crowned hat. And the navigator's art returns rather more extensively in the 1663 *Ballet des arts,* where a corsair chief and some pirates strut their stuff in front of picturesque sea-scenery once Thetis has sung a *récit* in praise of navigation – music by Michel Lambert, words by Isaac de Benserade – urging her audience to venture forth and have no fear of shipwreck.[17] Actually, it is specifically the

---

[16]   Nagler, *Theatre Festivals*, pp. 107–8, 116–18. In much the same way, the friendly confrontation in the Neapolitan *'festa a ballo' Delizie di Posilipo boscarecce e maritime* (1620) between the sea-loving Venus (with her Nymphs, Sirens and swans) and the land-loving Pan (with his Satyrs, shepherds and apes) is played out against a stage-simulation of the actual promontory of Posilipo, which was close to the vice regal palace where *Delizie* was given.

[17]   *La marine* and *La prosperite*: Margaret M. McGowan, *L'art du ballet de cour en France, 1581–1643* (Paris: CNRS, 1963), pp. 185–90. *Pélée et Téetis* and *Les arts*: M.-F. Christout, *Le ballet de cour de Louis XIV, 1643–1672* (Paris: A. et J. Picard, 1967), pp. 72–7,

ladies in the audience who are urged to be bold and adventurous, which is typical of a strain in Benserade's ballet *récits* and his accompanying *vers des personages* (as it is later in the opera libretti of Quinault): the eroticising of the marine myth and material they call on. It is as if the sea-scenes staged at the French court are almost as likely to allude to the power of love as they are to the love of power: something their poets would doubtless justify if pressed by drawing attention to Venus's being born in Neptune's realm and Neptune (as is shown in the *Ballet de la naissance de Venus* of 1665) being very proud of the fact.[18]

Meanwhile, in the late 1650s England's sea power features vividly in various plans for music-theatre pieces which use sea-scenery as a way of encouraging the short-lived Protestant republic to go one better in maritime affairs than Catholic-monarchical France or Spain. Naval vistas – fleets 'discovered at a distance' and 'boats rowing to the shore' – play their part in Davenant's pair of theatrical hybrids, *The Cruelty of the Spaniards in Peru* and *The History of Sir Francis Drake*, though the trend apparent in some recent French court ballets is carried to an extreme here in that classical myth's marine *dramatis personae* entirely disappear. The ships and the waves are there, but Sir Francis isn't visibly or even verbally seconded by Neptune or Thetis or a squadron of Tritons. However, though Davenant's contemporary Richard Flecknoe has a similar political agenda, for him there is life left in the traditional myth-figures. Hence, his masque-like operatic text, *The Marriage of Oceanus and Brittania* [sic] (1659), which is described on its title-page as an 'Allegorical Fiction really declaring England's Riches, Glory and Puissance by Sea, To be represented in Musick, Dances, and proper Scenes'. In it, Oceanus – his chariot 'gliding on the wheels of watermills to stem the waves' – is smitten with love for Britannia. She was once betrothed to 'the *Gallic* shore', but, aided and abetted by Tritons and Sirens and by Aeolus's ability to supply favourable winds, the god bestows so much naval and mercantile success on the native Britons that the lady yields to him and – to the great satisfaction of 'Nobility, Gentrie, Citizen, and Honest Swain' – they marry.

Oceanus smiles again at the end of the first English 'semi-opera' (loosely so-called): the part-spoken, part-sung expansion in 1674 of Davenant and Dryden's re-working of the greatest pre-proscenial sea play, Shakespeare's *Tempest*, now subtitled *The Enchanted Island*. In the 1674 version, Prospero, restored to his ducal status in an age when just restoration was on everyone's mind, assures his fellow voyagers that they will have a smooth passage home from the island, and

---

109–10. Navigation's hat: see M.-F. Christout, *Le ballet de cour au XVII siècle* (Geneva: Editions Minkoff, 1987), pl. 52.

[18]   To take two instances out of many: Benserade's *vers* on the Duc de Guise as Neptune in *the Ballet de Psyché* (1656) hint that the Duke's offstage inconstancy as a lover makes it apt that he should be dancing the role of the king of an inconstant element, see Benserade, *Oeuvres* (Paris, 1698), vol. 11, p. 151: and Quinault's libretto for Lully's *Persée* (1682), where the troubled lovers Mérope and Phinée declare during the storm preceding Andromeda's rescue that mortals in love are more tempest-tossed than stormy seas.

calls up a vision to ensure that they do. In fact it is a theatre-masque with words by Thomas Shadwell and music by a panel of five or six composers. Enter Oceanus and Tethys with Neptune and Amphitrite in a chariot drawn by sea-horses. Insisting that Aeolus drive all his 'blusterers' and 'roaring boys' to the ocean floor, the royal couples encourage their Tritons to 'sound a calm' on their conch-shells. The result: the spectacle of a halcyon sea, which is crowned in a final theatrical coup with the sight of Ariel flying out of the rising sun.[19] Similarly, but closer to home, in the same year and the year following, personifications of London's river contribute to the celebrations of apparent Stuart stability in two high Tory allegorical prologues: one to the version of Perrin and Cambert's *Ariadne* given at Drury Lane in 1674, the other to Crowne's court masque *Calisto* in 1675. In *Calisto*, Thames leans on an urn attended by Peace and Plenty and is cheered by the arrival of a naval hero attended by sea-gods and Tritons. In the *Ariadne* prologue she is seen reclining in a great shell with her sisters the Tiber and the Seine, who seem perfectly happy to be told that:

> Cupid himself reigns in this isle
> E'er since Venus resolved to quit
> Her native throne to come to dwell in it.[20]

Ten years later, river- and sea-scenes feature again in *Albion and Albanius*, Dryden's allegorical opera libretto on the restoration of Charles II and the seemingly happy succession of his brother James. The English Channel at Dover and the Thames at London are homes to a chorus of Naiads and a train of rivers, to troupes of dancing Tritons and watermen, to Neptune, Venus, Proteus – and again to the local god Thamesis. Dryden has clearly been looking at his English predecessors in marine allegorising and at his Continental predecessors too. And this is even more strikingly the case in the sea-scene of the 'dramatick opera' that *Albion and Albanius* had been intended to introduce: *King Arthur, or The British Worthy*, for which Purcell would eventually provide a score in 1691. For reasons prospective and retrospective, *King Arthur* makes a fitting final port of call.

When Arthur's wars are over, the magician Merlin ends the show, as the Restoration Prospero did, by conjuring up a masque-vision. Its subject is the history and renown of Britain: 'the Wealth, the Loves, the Glory of our Isle'. First we see the glory of Britain's coming into existence. Fractious winds on wires lour in the heavens over a stage-sea, but Aeolus appears in a cloud and commands them to withdraw. In the calm that follows, he exhorts an island (indeed 'the Queen of Islands') to appear, which – by being thrust up through a trap 'to a soft Tune' – it does. On it sits Britannia. At her feet fishermen keep an eye out for Proteus's herds

---

[19]　Jocelyn Powell, *Restoration Theatre Production* (London: Routledge, 1984), pp. 65–7, 78–82.

[20]　*Ariadne or The Marriage of Bacchus: an Opera, or Vocal Representation* (London, 1674), Prologue.

in the waters around them. A Nereid and the god Pan celebrate Britain's fisheries and sheep farms, and when Comus has led some farmers' lads in a rumbustious Harvest Home, Venus appears and announces that she and her son have come to dwell on this 'Fairest Isle, all Isles Excelling.'[21]

James Thomson surely recalled all this fifty years later in his masque *Alfred*, where the irrepressible 'Rule Britannia' ode begins:

> When Britain first, at heaven's command,
> Arose from out the azure main.

However, just as interesting as that possible looking-forward is the retrospection in Merlin's masque. Take his Aeolus. On a good dozen occasions in earlier interludes, court ballets, machine plays, *divertissements*, semi-operas and all-sung operas – in the Cicognini–Cavalli *Giasone* for instance – a visible Aeolus has raised a storm or dispersed one, or blown ships in one direction or another. Then islands and reefs have risen from the main or have moved about it in the 1608 Vespucci interlude, in the mooted *Neptune's Triumph* of 1624, in the Argonauts' interlude from the Parmesan *Aminta* of 1628, and in the danced prologue to Molière's *Les amants magnifiques* a few decades later. '*Tout ce spectacle est une magnifique galanterie*', says Molière gleefully of his island-machinery there: a *galanterie* which clearly had its influence on Dryden. As for those fishermen at Britannia's feet in the *King Arthur* scene, they are soon to be upstanding and performing a dance, which puts them in the line of the singing fishermen in the Mantuan *Arianna* of 1608 and the Florentine *Andromeda* of 1618 and of the dancing fisherfolk, pearl-divers and coral-gatherers in the *Ballet de la marine* of 1633 as well as in several French and Savoyard ballets of the 1650s, 1660s and 1670s, among them *Les noces de Pélée et de Thétis* (1654) and *L'unione per la pellegrina Margarita* (1660). Proteus, that 'shepherd of the seas', as Jonson calls him in *Neptune's Triumph*, herds his marine flocks picturesquely in the prologue to the big *Ballet de la nuit* of 1653 before characteristically changing shape a few times (as he does again in *Albion and Albanius* and the Quinault–Lully *Phaéton* of 1683). And what of Venus, Cupid and their decision to leave their native Cyprus and make their dwelling in Britain? As we have seen, the anonymous prologue-writer of the London *Ariadne* of 1674 has his Thames report the same thing, and further back in time we have seen emissaries from the Cyprian Grove making enthusiastic landfall in Savoy in 1640, and Cupid in 1611 deciding that Florence is just the place for him. Great Britain may be within sight of gathering a new empire in which Britannia will rule the waves, but in matters of theatrical allegory and machinery, the means for visualising it go back a long way.

---

[21] *King Arthur*, ed. H. Neville Davies in Michael Burden (ed.), *Henry Purcell's Operas: The Complete Texts* (Oxford: Oxford University Press, 2000), pp. 326–30.

Bibliography

Primary Sources

Apuleius (c. 158–180 AD), *Metamorphoses* (*The Golden Ass*).
Ariadne or The Marriage of Bacchus: an Opera, or Vocal Representation (London, 1674).
Benserade, Isaac de, *Oeuvres* (2 vols, Paris, 1698), vol. 2.
Colonna, F., *Hypnerotomachia Poliphili*, trans. Jocelyn Godwin (London: Thames and Hudson, 1991).
Corneille, P., *Androméde* (Paris, 1650).
Hédelin d'Aubignac, 'La pratique du théâtre' (1657), in A. Nagler (ed.), *A Source Book in Theatrical History* (New York: Dover, 1959), pp. 172–3.
King Arthur, (ed.) H. Neville Davies in Michael Burden (ed.), *Henry Purcell's Operas: The Complete Texts* (Oxford: Oxford University Press, 2000).
La Fontaine, *Epitre á M. Niert sur l'Opera* (1677; pub. Paris, 1765).
Ménestrier, C.-F., *Des ballets anciens et modernes* (Paris, 1682).
Ménestrier, C.-F., *Des representations en musique anciennes et modernes* (Paris, 1681).
Rossi, B., *Descrizione dell' apparato e degli Intermedi fatti per la commedia* (Florence, 1589).
Sabbattini, Galeazzo (1638), in B. Hewitt (ed.), *The Renaissance Stage: Documents of Serlio, Sabbattini and Furttenbach* (Coral Gables, Fl: University of Miami Press, 1958), pp. 98–245.
Seriacopi (1589) in A. Warburg, 'I costumi teatrali per gli intermezzi del 1589', *Gesammelte Schriften*, (ed.) Fritz Rougemont and Gertrud Bing (Leipzig, 1932), p. 404.
The Letters of Claudio Monteverdi, trans. D. Stevens (London: Faber and Faber, 1980).
Zuccari, Federigo (1608), in A. Nagler, *Theatre Festivals of the Medici 1539–1637* (New Haven: Yale University Press, 1964), p. 185.

Secondary Sources

Bjurström, P., *Giacomo Torelli and Baroque Stage Design* (Stockholm: Almqvist and Wiksell, 1961).
Bridges, E., E. Hall and P. Rhodes (eds), *Cultural Responses to the Persian Wars* (Oxford: Oxford University Press, 2007).
Burden, Michael (ed.), *Henry Purcell's Operas: The Complete Texts* (Oxford: Oxford University Press, 2000).
Christout, M.-F., *Le ballet de cour au XVII siècle* (Geneva: Editions Minkoff, 1987).
Christout, M.-F., *Le ballet de cour de Louis XIV, 1643–1672* (Paris: A. et J. Picard, 1967).

de La Gorce, J., 'Un aspect du merveilleux dans l'opéra français sous le règne de Louis XIV', in A. Schnapper (ed.), *La scenografia barocca* (Bologna: CLUEB, 1982), pp. 65–72.

Hewitt, B. (ed.), *The Renaissance Stage: Documents of Serlio, Sabbattini and Furttenbach* (Coral Gables Fl: University of Miami Press, 1958).

Kimbell, David, 'Operatic Variations on an Episode at the Hellespont', in E. Bridges, E. Hall and P. Rhodes (eds), *Cultural Responses to the Persian Wars* (Oxford: Oxford University Press, 2007), pp. 209–13.

Kimmel, W., 'Deutscher Bericht über die Florentinischen Intermedien des Jahres 1589', *Analecta Musicologica*, 9 (1970), pp. 15–16.

Lacroix, Paul (ed.), *Ballets et mascarades de cour sous Henri IV et Louis XIII (1581–1652)* (Geneva: J. Gay, 1868–70; repr. Geneva: Slatkine, 1968).

Lefkowitz, M. (ed.), *Trois masques à la cour de Charles 1er d'Angleterre* (Paris: CNRS, 1970).

McGowan, Margaret M., *L'art du ballet de cour en France, 1581–1643* (Paris: CNRS, 1963).

Mulryne, J.R. and Margaret Shewring (eds), *Italian Renaissance Festivals and their European Influence* (Lewiston: Edwin Mellon Press, 1992).

Nagler, A. (ed.), *A Source Book in Theatrical History* (New York: Dover, 1959)

Nagler, A., *Theatre Festivals of the Medici 1539–1637* (New Haven: Yale University Press, 1964).

Ossi, M., ' *"Dalle machine ... la maraviglia"*: Bernardo Buontalenti's *Il rapimento di Cefalo* at the Medici Theater in 1600', in M. Radice (ed.), *Opera in Context* (Portland: Amadeus Press, 1998), pp. 29–30.

Powell, Jocelyn, *Restoration Theatre Production* (London: Routledge, 1984).

Radice, M. (ed.), *Opera in Context* (Portland: Amadeus Press, 1998).

Rousset, Jean, 'L'eau et les tritons dans les fêtes et ballets de cour (1580–1604)', in J. Jacquot (ed.), *Les fêtes de la Renaissance* (2 vols, Paris: CNRS, 1956), vol. 1, pp. 237–8.

Savage, R., 'Staging an *Intermedio*', in J.R. Mulryne and Margaret Shewring (eds), *Italian Renaissance Festivals and their European Influence* (Lewiston: Edwin Mellon Press, 1992), pp. 51–72.

Schnapper, A. (ed.), *La scenografia barocca* (Bologna: CLUEB, 1982).

Strong, R., *Splendour at Court: Renaissance Spectacle and Illusion* (London: Weidenfeld and Nicolson, 1973).

Warburg, A., 'I costumi teatrali per gli intermezzi del 1589', in *Gesammelte Schriften*, (ed.) Fritz Rougemont and Gertrud Bing (Leipzig, 1932), pp. 400–406.

Chapter 20

Sing Again, Sirena: Translating the Theatrical *Virtuosa* from Venice to London

Eric Nicholson

What does Starbucks coffee have to do with the main focus of this chapter, that is to say with the theatrical *virtuosa* of the late sixteenth and early seventeenth centuries, a figure with a role to play in waterborne as well as land-based pageantry? The brief answer is: a shared and ambivalent iconography. A capsule history of the Starbucks logo from the 1970s to the present, featuring an ambiguously-mutating mermaid, would reveal a shift over time towards a politically-correct 'G-rating', first by way of covering the female figure's breasts, then with the editing out of her open 'legs', or rather, fish-tails. Although she is yet to be given a bikini top, *à la* Disney's Little Mermaid, pointed stars have been added, her smile has become more direct and prominent and little remains of the original image, itself based on a fifteenth-century engraving of the legendary, shape-changing Mélusine.[1]

While this coffee-chain censorship may be interpreted as a move towards diluting erotic prurience and a perceived threat to the nation's morals, it also confirms the ambivalence and mutability of this hybrid figure. Whether part-woman and part-bird, or part-woman and part-fish, or sometimes a combination of all three, the Siren figure mixes categories and crosses boundaries. As attested by her frequent association with travellers, the mermaid can thus be understood as an emblem of translation. In Early Modern Europe, the Siren-Mermaid also figured as an emblem of the female singer and public performer, whose seductive voice could, in a phallic way, penetrate the ears of her listeners and ravish their souls, or at least lead their minds astray.[2]

---

[1]   A first version of this paper was drafted for the Conference on 'Waterborne Pageants and Festivities in the Renaissance', held at Warwick University in Venice, Italy, in March 2010. This draft was then delivered as part of a session on 'Translating Female Performance', organized by Natasha Korda and chaired by Jean E. Howard, at the Renaissance Society of America meeting in Venice, Italy, in April 2010. I am grateful for constructive comments made by respondents on this occasion, including those by fellow members of the international working group Theater Without Borders.

[2]   For this and several following points, I am indebted to the fundamental studies of Linda Austern, especially her co-edited volume (with Inna Naroditskaya) on *Music of the Sirens* (Bloomington and Indianapolis: Indiana University Press, 2006), as well as to Murizio Bettini and Luigi Spina for *Il mito delle sirene* (Turin: Einaudi, 2007).

As several scholars have demonstrated, the legendary figure of the siren has undergone changes of form and significance, but since antiquity has consistently represented the irresistible power of melodious song and music. While sirens sometimes evoke heavenly harmonies and spiritual transcendence – the crucial source here is Plato's *Republic*, Book X, describing the Pythagorean 'music of the spheres' – they most often cause disruption and, on occasion, destruction. To take a Shakespearean example, there is Oberon's reminiscence with Puck:

> Thou rememb'rest
> Since once I sat upon a promontory
> And heard a mermaid on a dolphin's back
> Uttering such dulcet and harmonious breath
> That the rude sea grew civil at her song
> And certain stars shot madly from their spheres
> To hear the sea-maid's music?
> (*A Midsummer Night's Dream*, II, i, 148–54)

The sea grows civil, but the stars veer off course: with their own sibilant and mellifluous assonance, these lines themselves enact the ambiguous and transformational effects of mermaids' and sirens' singing. As Austern aptly puts it, 'where there are sirens, there are sea-changes',[3] an interpretation that echoes the invisible sea-nymphs' 'Ding dong bell' song in *The Tempest*.

An Elizabethan and Jacobean listener to Shakespeare's work could also call up the figure of Mélusine, or perhaps Vincenzo Cartari's emblem of Sea-Serpent and Mermaid, imported from Italy, where audiences were already enjoying – but in some cases, also denouncing – the performances of professional female singers and actors. In this campaign of denunciation, *la Sirena* is a recurring figure. Decrying theatres as '*il sacrario di Venere*' ('the shrine of Venus'), where 'vainglorious females' are '*allettamenti della sensualità*' ('enticements to sensuality') and '*l'attrici, gl'intermedi, le galantarie, le musiche, et i balli, son quinta essenza di lascivia*' ('actresses, interludes, gallantries, music and dancing are the fifth essence of lasciviousness'), the early-seventeenth-century Jesuit Jaime Alberto asks: '*Se s'inchioda talmente nell'animo un detto lascivo, anchor che s'ascolti senza badarvi, che sarà essendo in versi di stile elegante et adorno, accompagnato da voci di Sirene, che secondo Lattanzio tanto dilettano che ci trasformano?*' ('If a lewd saying pierces the soul, however faintly it is heard, what will ensue when such lewdness is spoken in elegant and pleasing verses by voices of the Sirens, which according to Lactantius give so much delight that they transform us?')[4]

---

[3]   Linda Austern, '"Teach me to Heare Mermaides Singinge": Embodiments of (Acoustic) Pleasure and Danger in the Modern West', in Austern and Naroditskaya, *Music of the Sirens*, p. 85.

[4]   Ferdinando Taviani, *La Fascinazione del teatro: la commedia dell'arte e la società barocca* (Rome: Bulzani, 1991), pp. 231, 237.

A few years after Alberto, Giovan Domenic Ottonelli, in his extended attack on actresses and female performers, whom he compares to 'infernal Amazons, armed with sword and arrows', and Medusas 'filled with serpents that cause the spiritual ruin of weak-hearted souls', offers in illustration the following terza rima verses by the early-seventeenth-century Bishop Lorenzo Azzolini:

> *Ma se col ragionar l'alme avvelena*
>> *Femminea voce, qual si poscia il rischio*
>> *Quando nel canto e suon sembra Sirena?*
> *Come all'occulte panie alletta il fischio*
>> *Incauto augel; così l'orecchio ingordo*
>> *Trae cantatrice all'amoroso vischio.*
> *Meglio sarebbe all'uom diventar sordo*
>> *Che damigella udir, quando cantilla*
>> *Barzellete d'amor sul Buon accordo.*
> *Un non so che di tenero distilla*
>> *Musica femminil, che l'alme assonna,*
>> *E i cuori a suo voler turba e tranquilla*
> [But if with her words the feminine voice poisons souls,
>> What then will be the risk when with its sounds
>> And its singing that voice doth seem a Siren?
> Just as a whistle lures the careless bird
>> To the hidden lime, so the female singer
>> Leads the voracious ear to the amorous snare.
> Better it were for men to be deaf
>> Than to hear a maiden, when she warbles
>> Harmonious 'Barzellette d'amor'.
> Womanly music distills indescribable
>> Tenderness, that lulls the soul to sleep,
>> And as it will both soothes and troubles hearts.]

Using the rhetorical question format of 'if this, what then' favoured by Jesuit preachers, Ottonelli goes on to insist that: '*Se il canto disonesto e vizioso nuoce tanto, quanto nuocerà quello che oltre al contenere disonesti e viziosi concetti, sarà formato con la voce di donna, e donna vana, e comica impudica?*' ('If immoral and dissolute songs cause great harm, how much more harm will come from those songs which, beyond their immoral and dissolute conceits, will be sung by the voice of a woman, a vainglorious woman, a wanton actress?')[5] As elsewhere, the author recycles earlier anti-actress tracts, such as that of Pedro Hurtado de Mendoza, who argues that spectators are dragged into lewdness and mad love by '*spiritose, abili nella danza e nel canto, esperte nell'arte della recitazione*'

---

[5]   Ibid., pp. 373–9.

('witty women, skilled in dance and song, experts in the art of acting'),[6] and that of Domenico Gori, who claims that lascivious comedies inspire lascivious behaviour, precisely because: '*Le musiche effemminano, le narrative, i gesti etc., tanto che quando arriva la femmina che recita, altrui si trova tanto debole per le precedenti cose, che moralmente è impossibile resistere.*'('Music, and the stories, gestures, et cetera, feminize the audience, so much so that upon the entrance of the actual woman who performs, those already susceptible to the aforementioned things find it morally impossible to resist her').[7] The sirens and their seductive music are one thing when imagined, or described in a book, or even when given visual form in a painting; perhaps such artistic formats could serve to contain or even rationalize the sirens' powers. When, however, real flesh-and-blood women sing live and in public, the sirens' potential threat to reason and moral rectitude – especially of the male-gendered variety – becomes all too palpable and morally contagious.

Yet, in keeping with the deeply ambiguous tradition and associations of this mythological figure, the siren also appears in encomia of early modern Italian actresses and female singers. Tommaso Garzoni, for one, in his compendious journalistic tome *La Piazza Universale di tutte le professioni del mondo* exalts the early *commedia dell' arte* actress Vittoria Piissimi as: '*quella divina Vittoria che fa metamorfosi di se stessa in scena, quella bella maga d'amore ch' alletta i cori di mille amanti con le sue parole, quella dolce sirena ch' ammaglia con soavi incanti l' alme de' suo i divoti spettatori e senza dubbio merita di esser posta come compendio dell' arte*' ('that Divine Vittoria who creates metamorphoses of herself on the stage, that beautiful magician of love who wins the hearts of a thousand lovers with her words, that *sweet siren* whose melodious enchantments catch the souls of her adoring spectators, and certainly deserves to be held the epitome of her profession').[8]

Garzoni's praise of Piissimi dates from the 1580s, but a decade earlier the Jewish playwright and impresario Leone de' Sommi of Mantua had dedicated hundreds of rhapsodic lines to another early Diva of the Italian stage, Vincenza Armani, casting her as 'an immortal goddess', a universally talented performer who like Orpheus could tame wild animals with her '*pregiata lira*' (admirable lyre – most likely the courtly, violin-like '*lira da braccio*') as well as with her singing: '*Di sì dolce Harmonia le note amene/ son colme, e tal dolcezza il suo canto have,/ che d'assai vince i cigni, e le Sirene/ mentre ella accorda con l'acuto, il grave*' ('Her charming notes are filled with such sweet Harmony, and her own singing has such sweetness, that she far outdoes the swans and the Sirens, as she harmonizes both high and low').[9] Seen as potentially fatal seductresses, but also

---

[6]   Ibid., p. 89.

[7]   Ibid., p. 139.

[8]   Tommaso Garzoni, *La piazza universale di tutte le professioni del mondo* (Venice: n. p., 1585), p. 754. The emphasis is mine.

[9]   Leone De' Sommi, *Quattro Dialoghi in materia di rappresentazioni sceniche* (ca. 1575), ed. Ferruccio Marotti (Milan: Edizioni Il Polifilo, 1968), p. 94.

and more admirably as artists, as in other contexts, these early public actresses and musical performers can be associated with the ambivalent figure of the female poet/musician/courtesan. Whether or not she was an actual courtesan, Gaspara Stampa – like her contemporary Tullia d'Aragona – was an accomplished poet, lutenist and singer, and was honoured with the title of *virtuosa* in a letter by Girolamo Parabosco, the first organist of San Marco. Re-working Petrarch's classic exaltation of Laura as '*questa sol fra noi del ciel sirena*', *Canzoniere* 167, ('this only heavenly siren among us') Parabosco also praises Gaspara's '*angelica voce*', her angelical voice that sings '*a guisa di Sirena*' ('like a Siren'). This neo-Platonic eulogy receives confirmation from the contemporary madrigalist, Perissone Cambio, who notes that Stampa's listeners called her a '*divina sirena*'.[10] Those who praised actresses thus reiterated extant positive notions of the harmoniously singing Siren, even as they risked sabotaging their own project through the usage of this same ambiguous and ideologically overloaded figure.

By the late sixteenth century, then, this nexus of Siren/Mermaid to Female Musician/Singer to Courtesan/Actress was firmly established in Italian and even European cultural consciousness. It could appear, quite appropriately, in the text of an anonymous madrigal set to music by the Flemish Adriano Willaert, an innovative composer in mid-cinquecento Venice:

> Love, if it's your will that I take the risk
>> Of hearing and seeing
>> Sirens and Basilisks;
>> Grant me the favor, good sir,
>> Should it chance that the splendour
>> Of two shining eyes melt me,
>> And make me prey to witty speaking,
>> That she who is to blame might see
>> And believe that I am dead by hearing and seeing.
>> Gentle and most excellent pair,
>> He who sees and listens to you,
>> But for one time, 'tis true,
>> And does not of pleasure die,
>> Can bravely go and dare
>> To list' and eye
>> The Sirens of Love and the Basilisks.[11]

---

[10]   Elena Laura Calogero, '"Sweet Alluring Harmony": Heavenly and Earthly Sirens in Sixteenth- and Seventeenth-Century Literary and Visual Culture', in *Music of the Sirens*, p. 150.

[11]   Cited by Bonnie Gordon, 'The Courtesan's Singing Body as Cultural Capital in Seventeenth-Century Italy', in Martha Feldman and Bonnie Gordon (eds), *The Courtesan's Arts: Cross-Cultural Perspectives* (Oxford: Oxford University Press, 2006), p. 195. The translation is mine.

As Bonnie Gordon observes, the lyrics evoke '*La Sirena*' and '*La Basilisca*', two well-known real-life courtesans of Venice mentioned by the contemporary author and actor Andrea Calmo, while their insistence on orgasmic death from combined visual and auditory delight conveys the simultaneous pleasures and perils associated by early modern males with such women performers. The madrigal is itself a witty challenge to young adventurers, who need to practise exceptional self-control, *à la* the classical Ulysses, to survive their visits to courtesan-singers. We encounter once again the anti-theatricalists' favoured trope of the irresistibility of female performance, and the accompanying threat of men being feminized, especially in a public setting where they might also risk their own exposure and humiliation. The 'Renaissance regime of *virtù*', as Guido Ruggiero aptly puts it, meant that publicly performing courtesans, female singers and actresses had the power to enchant their passive male customers and audiences, who in the process risked losing both prestige and their own rational, masculine selves.[12]

The crux of the matter was the female performer's own *virtù*, with the potential specific valency of artistic skill, a conventionally masculine property that could thus give a transgendered sense to the term *virtuosa*. Like the liminal siren, the courtesan and the actress – both known for sometimes performing not only elegant, post-Petrarchan poetry but also 'popular' musical pieces like the '*frottola*' in glamorous, courtly settings – made a nonsense of conventional distinctions and binary opposites. Castiglione and other authors of European conduct books encouraged young aristocratic women to learn and play stringed or keyboard instruments (not percussion nor woodwinds, since the former were too militaristic and the latter were deemed unsightly for the female face). However, they more or less rigorously enjoined that a refined, decorous woman should express her musical talents only behind closed doors, in the private sphere of the home or palazzo. Even there, the dignified musical woman was supposed to wear modest clothing and avoid unnecessary embellishments, and to keep her eyes and body directed away from her listeners' gaze. In short, she was advised against 'playing to the audience'. Courtesans, however, were notorious for doing just the opposite. As evident in a print by Giacomo Franco of the '*Abito delle Cortegiane Prencipale*'[13] (the clothing of the chief courtesans), the spinet player wears a low-cut dress with richly patterned sleeves and a high-coiffed and hair-framing starched ruff. While looking obliquely back at her viewers, she also flirtatiously tilts her head away from them, exposing even more of her bare neck and its shining pearl necklace.[14] While neither the courtesan's hand position nor her spinet are reproduced accurately, actual instruments were often painted with ambiguously erotic mythical scenes,

---

[12]   Guido Ruggiero, 'Who's Afraid of Giuliana Napolitana?' in *The Courtesan's Arts*, p. 285.

[13]   Giacomo Franco, *Habiti d'uomeni et donne venetiane* (Venice: n. p., 1610).

[14]   Drew Edward Davies, 'On Music Fit for a Courtesan: Representations of the Courtesan and Her Music in Sixteenth-Century Italy', in Feldman and Gordon (eds), *The Courtesan's Arts*. pp. 144–6.

such as, for example, a portable octave spinet (ca. 1600) in the Victoria and Albert Museum depicting Arion on a dolphin's back playing a lute, surrounded by naked and sexually active mermaids, mermen and goddesses. Are these marine frolickers chastened and 'held spellbound' by Arion's music,[15] or are they being aroused by it? At first glance, the latter could well appear to be the case. Given the ambiguity of sirens and siren-lore, as well as the amorous connotations of spinet-playing, I would argue that both interpretations are conceivable, especially since readers of Ovid's ever-popular *Art of Love* knew that the music of Arion could also be linked with eroticism and female musical seduction (Ovid, *Ars amatoria,* III, 315–26). For, despite the dangers, positive pleasures and the chance to transform oneself are also possible in this scenario, as Antipholus of Syracuse understands in Shakespeare's *Comedy of Errors*: 'Transform me then, and to your power I'll yield', he declares to Luciana, and pleads to her 'O, train me not, sweet mermaid, with thy note/ To drown me in thy sister's flood of tears;/ Sing, siren, for thyself, and I will dote' (III, ii, 40; 45–7).

By the time of Franco's publication, then, a kind of 'iconography of the Venetian courtesan' had emerged, which frequently accentuates her seductive musical skills (or *virtù)* as well as wealth, beauty and elegance. In Parrasio Micheli's influential oil painting of the 1560s, now in Budapest, the golden-haired, ruby-lipped and open-mouthed lutenist gazes toward heaven in the company of a winged *amorino*: this same cherub, however, holds a music-book, evoking an actual performance made all the more earthly by the precisely rendered lute, together with the woman's pearl necklace, earrings, bracelet, fallen brocaded sleeve and exposed breasts. The laurel wreath around the *amorino*'s arm may suggest immortal poetic and musical fame, again keeping the image poised between worldly sensuality and heavenly transcendence. During the same period, the most famous of all Venice's sixteenth century painters also contributed to the 'musical Venus' iconography of the courtesan: Titian's *Venus with a Lute-Player*, in its Metropolitan Museum of Art version (another, slightly earlier one is in the Fitzwilliam Museum, Cambridge), shows the naked love-goddess holding a recorder next to a *viola da gamba*, perhaps ready to accompany the fully and stylishly clothed, somewhat distracted, male lutenist. Along with a potential allegory of the senses, this image provides an affirmation of music's erotic powers.

Returning to Giacomo Franco's graphic work of the early seventeenth century, and underlining the water-borne theme of this chapter and collection, a particularly revealing image is his illustration of a fleet of gondolas, bearing the caption: '*In questa Maniera la State nei gran caldi si va ai freschi per li canali della città la sera fino a mezzanotte, con musiche di voci, e diversii stromenti, con grandissimo diletto, con le Signore Cortegiane, e spesso anco si cena in barca con mirabil piacere*' ('in this way, during the great heat of the summer, people go to cool themselves on the canals of the city in the evening, until midnight, with music of voices and divers instruments, to their very great delight, accompanied by the

---

[15]   Austern, "Teach me", p, 89.

Lady-Courtesans, and often they dine on the boats with wondrous pleasure'). Most of the gondolas are shown with arched canopies, under which well-dressed patrician ladies or courtesans and their companions can be seen, but in the foreground, a large open gondola holds a small orchestra, including women who play the lute, spinet and possibly a recorder.[16] Are these the courtesans to whom Franco's caption refers, or are they professional women musicians? Whatever the case, their singing and playing for 'very great delight' and 'wonderful pleasure' on the nocturnal water would evoke for listeners and viewers their association with amorous sirens. Drew Edward Davies has suggestively linked this illustration with Adriano Banchieri's 1605 madrigal comedy *Barco di Venetia per Padova,* which features a facetious and musically talented courtesan named Rizzolina, her very name an echo of *the commedia dell'arte 'maschera'* Ricciolina. Finally, in a more explicitly theatrical context, Franco's well-known print of *commedia* players and charlatans in Piazza San Marco includes a lute-strumming female performer, who attracts the attention of Pantalone on the stage, and that of international audience members, some of them identified as 'Turk', 'Spanish' and 'English'.

By 1600 Venice's reputation as a seductive city of glamour and luxury depended to a large extent on the closely linked phenomena of theatre, beautiful courtesans, performing women and aquatic pastimes, including waterborne festivals. Visitors to *La Serenissima* would have directly or at least indirectly heard not only of the extravagantly decorated state gondola or *Bucintoro,* but also of the lavish *Teatri del Mondo,* large circular theatres that were floated down the Grand Canal to the Piazzetta di San Marco on such occasions as the festivities sponsored by the Compagnia della Calza, known as the *'Accesi',* in 1564, the spectacular receptions and shows in honour of the French king Henri III in 1574 and the elaborate inauguration ceremonies for the *'Dogaressa'* Morosina Morosini in 1597. This last-named 'Theatre of the World' was designed by none other than Vincenzo Scamozzi, Palladio's assistant and successor in the establishment of the famous Teatro Olimpico at Vicenza. Like his predecessors, Scamozzi devised a neo-classical structure that could hold dozens of musicians and their privileged audiences – many of them described as *'bellissime gentildonne'* – and would in so doing have evoked the wonders of the sea: in Giacomo Franco's print of this structure, a giant carved Neptune stands prominently behind the central circular theatre, drawn by two giant marine monsters and crammed with a group comprised of richly dressed women.[17] Structures and entertainments such as these floating microcosmic theatres – a kind of ephemeral festive anticipation of the Globe Theatre in Southwark –would have suggested that Venice's status as a supremely magnificent urban stage-set involved alluring, watery and feminine spectacles as much as it did more conventionally 'manly' structures like the triumphal arches

---

[16]   Illustration and commentary in Davies, 'On Music', pp. 154–5.

[17]   Lina Padoan Urban, 'Gli spetta coli urbani e l'utopia', in Lionello Puppi (ed.), *Architettura e Utopia nella Venezia del cinquecento* (Milan: Electa, 1980), pp. 149–63.

erected in 1557 for the *Dogaressa* Zilia Dandolo[18] and again in 1574 for Henri III. The aquatic and sensual world of the sirens can thus be perceived in these particular Venetian playing-spaces, whether private gondolas or large-scale floating 'theatres', which became famous throughout Europe and beyond.

A siren, a courtesan, but above all a musical and theatrical *virtuosa* performing for an international public: this, then, is the female figure which was imported and translated, in a variety of senses, from Venice to London. Particular insight can be gleaned from the well-known passages in Thomas Coryate's *Crudities*, recording his extended visit to Venice in 1608, and his attendance at performances by actresses, as well as his encounter with one of the city's famous courtesans, who:

> will endevour to enchaunt thee partly with her melodious notes that she warbles out upon her lute, which shee fingers with as laudable a stroake as many men that are excellent professors in the noble science of musicke; and partly with that heart-tempting harmony of her voice. Also thou wilt finde the Venetian cortezan (if she be a selected woman indeede) a good rhetorician, and a most elegant discourser, so that if she cannot move thee with all these foresaid delights, shee will assay they constancy with her rhetoricall tongue.[19]

Alluding at least indirectly to the siren threat, Coryate warns the English traveller to 'furnish they self with a double armour, the one for thine eyes, the other for thine eares ... against the attractive inchauntments of their [the courtesans'] plausible speeches'.[20] Coryate's friend, Ben Jonson, wrote witty dedicatory verses for the *Crudities*, as well as his Venetian satirical comedy *Volpone* (1606), in which the English traveller Lady Politic Would-Be is informed that her foolish husband Sir Pol is 'rowing upon the water in a gondola,/ With the most cunning courtesan of Venice' (III, v, 19–20).

I now want to focus briefly on this play, and the Venetian tragedy with which it engages in frequent intertextual dialogue, Shakespeare's *Othello, the Moor of Venice* (produced just the year before *Volpone*, in 1604–05). Like Othello, who gullibly succumbs to Iago's insinuations and takes his innocent wife 'for that cunning whore of Venice', Lady Politic is herself a jealous soul, who readily believes Mosca's false report of her husband's dalliance with a 'cunning courtesan'. An early Grand Tourist, she makes sure to mention, in her own attempted flirtation with the bed-ridden Volpone, her enthusiastic reading of 'all' the Italian poets, including the 'desperate wit' Pietro Aretino. She thus claims to know the

---

[18]   Maximilian L.S. Tondro, 'The First Temporary Triumphal Arch in Venice (1557)', in J.R. Mulryne and Elizabeth Goldring (eds), *Court Festivals of the European Renaissance: Art, Politics and Performance* (Aldershot and Burlington, VT: Ashgate Publishing, 2002), pp. 349–55.

[19]   Thomas Coryate, *Coryate's Crudities* (2 vols, London: n. p., 1611; rept. 2 vols, Glasgow: Maclehose, 1905), vol. 1, p. 406.

[20]   Ibid.

notorious, pornographic *Modi*, where Aretino's 'pictures are a little obscene' –
though like Jonson himself she may confuse the author with the illustrator, Giulio
Romano. She may also refer implicitly to Aretino's *Sei giornate* dialogues among
prostitutes, in which the experienced Nanna teaches her daughter Pippa that few
things excite male customers like cross-dressing.

Back in England, Lady Would-Be may have seen Shakespeare's *Twelfth Night,
or What You Will,* and could also have read the play's Italian source, the *Intronati
di Siena*'s seminal *gl'Ingannati* and the lines spoken by its Viola prototype, the
cross-dressing Lelia, who fears that 'one of these young reprobates might seize
me, and dragging me into some house, try to find out whether I'm male or female',
and is then identified by her confidante Nurse Clemenzia as a potential *'femina
del mondo'*, that is, a roving prostitute.[21] These exciting ambiguities of gender
and social status were also visualized in courtesan iconography, such as in the
well-known print by Pietro Bertelli (ca. 1588), complete with lift-up flap revealing
high platform *'zoccoli'* or chopines and a pair of men's breeches. Perhaps with
this image before her eyes, Lady Would-Be, after having uttered one of the truly
sublime comic lines of all time – 'I pray you lend me your dwarf' (III, vi, 29) –
rushes out toward the Rialto. Finding her husband with the witty English traveller
Peregrine, she complains to the latter:

> I would be loathe to contest publicly
> With any gentlewoman; or to seem
> Forward, or violent; as *The Courtier* says,
> It comes too near rusticity in a lady,
> Which I would shun by all means; and however
> I may deserve from Master Would-Be, yet,
> To have one fair gentlewoman thus be made
> Th'unkind instrument to wrong another,
> And one she knows not, aye, and to persèver,
> In my poor judgment is not warranted
> From being a solecism in our sex,
> If not in manners
>   (IV, ii, 33–44).

Such behaviour would be a 'solecism' indeed, as she assumes that Peregrine is
a cunning courtesan of Venice dressed as a man. It is no wonder that she does:
Peregrine himself, with confirmation from Sir Politic, had earlier alleged that
Lady Would-Be 'lies here in Venice for intelligence/ Of tires, and fashions, and
behaviour,/ Among the courtesans' (II, i, 27–9). Apparently, she knows the tricks of
the trade. Practising decorum, or conceding that Venetian courtesans often sought
to pass for aristocratic ladies, she calls Peregrine a 'gentlewoman', but when he

---

[21]   Academici Intronati di Siena, *Gl'Ingannati*, in Nino Borsellino, *Commedie del
Cinquecento* (2 vols, Milan: Feltrinelli, 1962-67), vol. 1, pp. 212–14.

starts to laugh, and Sir Politic expresses bewilderment, the rhetorical and perhaps actual gloves come off, as Lady Would-Be launches into 'poetic fury and historic storms'. She fumes that 'you provoke me with your impudence/ And laughter of your light land-siren here,/ Your Sporus, your hermaphrodite' (ll. 46–7), and after learning that Peregrine is English, she continues to rail at her husband's patronage, or ironic 'St George'-like protection, of 'a lewd harlot, a base fricatrice,/ A female devil in a male outside' (ll. 55–6), before she physically assaults her target, trying to remove his doublet and shirt with her own hands. Echoing the language of the Italian pro- and anti-theatricalists, Jonson pointedly includes the siren in his all-too-theatrically and erotically conscious character's diatribe. The reference also ironically fits with Sir Politic's claim that he had come to Venice not to know 'men's minds and manners, with Ulysses's (the fabled survivor of the siren's song), but rather to follow 'a peculiar humour of my wife's' (II, i, 10–12). In this regard, Lady Would-Be's frustrated and foolish attempt to 'dis-cover' Peregrine as a 'land-siren' anticipates the famous 'confutation' of the ranting Puritan hypocrite Zeal-of-the-Land Busy by the neuter puppet Dionysius in *Bartholomew Fair* (1614). As in the later play, female theatricality and androgynous performance are linked to sirenic and Circean seduction, and in a way that ridicules the naïve, bigoted literalism of English anti-theatricalists: like their Italian counterparts, these attackers of the supposedly decadent and effeminate public stage link their target with sirens, sometimes even alleging that women who attend plays will do so 'in open sight, themselves to show and vaunt', as 'light-taylde huswives, which like *Sirens* sing,/ And like to *Circes* with their drugs enchant'.[22]

With her aggressive and domineering impulses, and originally played by a male actor on the London stage, Lady Politic is something of a 'hermaphrodite' herself, in a play where the 'actual' hermaphrodite/fool Androgyno performs in a kind of private anti-masque *chez* Volpone. According to the dwarf-presenter Nano, the 'soul of Pythagoras that juggler divine' is now enclosed in Androgyno's body, after having transmigrated through dozens of others, including the courtesan Aspasia. Before shifting to crucial tropes of transmigration, translation and hybridism, the focus now needs to be directed towards Volpone's most jealous and aggressively theatrical/anti-theatrical character, whose conflicting Jonsonian 'humours' of jealousy and avarice make him a self-contradiction. This is the merchant of Venice, Corvino, a loud and greedy raven who first threatens his wife Celia with house imprisonment and then seeks to prostitute her to Volpone in hopes of inheriting the latter's fortune. His two opposed actions, however, derive from a common source: the figuration, or rather the disfiguration, of Celia as a prostitute-actress. No longer an interior space for the playing of Mosca's anti-masque addressed to the carnivalesque mis-ruler Volpone, the stage in Act Two becomes an 'obscure nook of the Piazza' di San Marco adapted for a mountebank's show, of the kind

---

[22]   From John Lane, *Tom Tell-Troths Message and His Pens Complaint* (1600), quoted by Melinda Gough in her outstanding article 'Jonson's Siren Stage', *Studies in Philology* 96, 1 (1999), p. 77.

so richly documented and illuminated by M.A. Katritzky.[23] Volpone, disguised as the historical and internationally renowned *commedia* actor and troupe leader Dionisio Scoto Mantuano, launches into a *tour de force* salesman's pitch, aimed at attracting the attention of Celia, under whose window the Magnifico turned Quack Player has mounted his bank. In a version of the classic *commedia* theatregram of the 'lady at the window',[24] and in a translation both of the actual practice of throwing money wrapped in handkerchiefs to *montimbanchi/*'Dottori'[25] and the various real and imaginary exchanges of Othello's handkerchief, Celia bestows hers upon Volpone/Scoto.

The recipient launches into an impromptu exaltation of a beauty-bringing 'powder that made Venus a goddess (given her by Apollo), that kept her perpetually young', suggesting that he now plays the *commedia maschera* of the *Innamorato* to Celia's *Innamorata* at the window. The enraged Corvino enters to close down the show:

> Come down! No house but mine to make your scene?
> Signor Flaminio, will you down, sir? Down!
> What, is my wife your Francischina, sir?
> No windows on the whole Piazza here
> To make your properties, but mine? But mine?
> 'Heart? Ere tomorrow I shall be new-christened,
> And called the *Pantalone di Bisognosi*
> About the town.
>   (II, iii, 2–9).

Aptly casting himself as the often cuckolded and openly mocked Venetian merchant *maschera* Pantalone, and identifying Volpone/Scoto with the lover *maschera* Flaminio, Corvino demotes his wife to the status of the *serva* Franceschina, played by actresses who exposed their breasts and engaged in sexual *lazzi*, as evoked in the oft-cited scene from John Day's *Travailes of the Three English Brothers* (1607), where the Italian clown Harlequin tells his English colleague Will Kemp that the 'onely practice' of his wife and professional partner is to play 'a whores part or a courtisan'.[26] Corvino also knows that *commedia/*mountebank troupes

---

[23]   M.A. Katritzky, *The art of commedia: a study in the commedia dell' arte, 1560–1620,* (Amsterdam: Rodopi, 2006) and numerous articles and other publications.

[24]   See Louise George Clubb, *Italian Drama in Shakespeare's Time* (New Haven: Yale University Press, 1989) and Jane Tylus, 'Women at the Windows: *Commedia dell'Arte* and Theatrical Practice in Early Modern Italy', *Theatre Journal*, 49 (1997), pp. 323–42.

[25]   Bella Mirabella, '"Quacking Delilahs": Female Mountebanks in Early Modern England and Italy', in Pamela Allen Brown and Peter Parolin (eds), *Women Players in England, 1500–1660* (Aldershot and Burlington, VT: Ashgate Publishing, 2005), pp. 94–5.

[26]   M.A. Katritzky, *Women, Medicine and Theatre, 1500–1750: Literary Mountebanks and Performing Quacks* (Aldershot and Burlington, VT: Ashgate Publishing, 2007), p. 210.

included singing and/or acrobatic female performers – a 'tumbling whore' is Corvino's reference – and with this in mind, he sarcastically and brutally dares Celia to become a professional player:

> Or, let me see,
> I think you'd rather mount? Would you not mount?
> Why, if you'll mount, you may; yes, truly you may –
> And so you may be seen down to the foot.
> Get you a cittern, Lady Vanity,
> And be a dealer with the virtuous man
> (II, v, 17–22).

While the insistent 'mount' pun identifies sexual with theatrical performance, and here also implies that audience members in the piazza would be looking up Celia's dress, the last two lines of the harangue graft the English Morality Play tradition onto the secular, commercial Italian *commedia*, and fittingly deploy a trans-national play on words. In English, 'virtuous' would carry a primarily positive moral sense, but its Italian root also evokes the artistically or musically talented *virtuoso*, here linked with the guitar-playing, publicly performing, female 'dealer' and *virtuosa*. Given this perception of his wife as a money-making tumbler/musician/prostitute/ comedian, Corvino il Pantalone almost inevitably and simultaneously treats Celia as a possession to keep under lock and key, as well as a valuable performing commodity and an instrumental investment towards claiming a lavish inheritance. For at the end of this same scene, the parasite Mosca convinces Corvino to act as a pimp for his own wife, in order to be named Volpone's heir.

Hustled into Volpone's bedroom, Celia will not, however, perform in any way. Rather it is Volpone who sings. As part of his own sudden 'revival', he alludes to his youthful recitation of Antinous, beautiful young lover of the Emperor Hadrian, in 'our comedy' for entertainment of the 'great Valois' Henri III, during the famous Venetian shows and festivities of 1574. He then offers up the melodious air 'Come, my Celia let us prove/ While we can, the sports of love', with lyrics translated from Catullus and music by the Italian composer Alfonso Ferrabosco. This intricate example of hybridism and virtuoso translation thus transfers a command public performance to the private world. In mirror-image fashion, Shakespeare's *Othello* makes a private musical performance become public. In this case, the singer, or at least the singing character, is female, and the effect is deeply, perhaps indissolubly ambivalent. As befits a chaste, modest early modern lady, Desdemona sings her famous 'Willow song' in private, for an on-stage audience of one. At the same time, the actual off-stage theatre audience hears it as well: as elsewhere in the play, we become spies and eavesdroppers, grossly gaping and overhearing, in this case to a scene of intimate undressing and confidential conversation between women. Even here, then, Desdemona is subject to Iago's 'be-whoring' scheme, traducing her and demeaning her from faithful bride to 'common' prostitute. Iago, in effect, anticipates Corvino, through his own paranoiac jealousy, which translates virtue and fidelity into their opposites. With his wit turned the seamy side out, he casts Desdemona as 'a super-subtle Venetian', and declares that 'she's the worse for all this', meaning her artistic, musical and rhetorical talents: she is, as Othello affirms, 'so delicate with her needle, an admirable musician – O, she will sing the savageness out of a bear – of so high and plenteous wit and invention!' (IV, i, 182–5). As Othello elsewhere acknowledges, his 'wife is fair, feeds well, loves company,/ Is free of speech, sings, plays, and dances well –/ Where virtue is, these are more virtuous' (III, iii, 187–9).Taken together, these two speeches suggest that moral virtues and artistic, even magical, *virtù* cohere in the *virtuosa* Desdemona. Before he fully yields to jealousy, Othello might be termed a pro-theatricalist, a man willing to call his convention-defying wife 'a fair warrior' in public, and to defend her freely-shared skills as a performer. His terms closely echo the terms employed by those who praised Italian actresses, like Leone de' Sommi, mentioned above, who had eulogized Vincenza Armani not only for her Orphic ability to sing savageness out of bears, but for her playing 'now the woman on fire with love's passion, now the armed woman warrior'.[27] Desdemona thus carries many attributes of the Italian musical and theatrical diva, and for this very reason she is vulnerable to the misogynist and anti-theatrical disfigurations of Iago.

Further research and analysis is needed on this subject, especially regarding such matters as the dancing skills of the early modern courtesan and actress. It will perhaps suffice to mention here that Tullia d'Aragona was not only a graceful dancer herself, but reputedly had the power to make besotted elderly men dance such sprightly steps as the *rosina* barefoot to her music.[28] Since Othello, a self-professed novice in the arts of love and courtly entertainments, is likely to be at least 20 years older than Desdemona, stories such as these (assuming that Shakespeare and/or his audience knew them) could also augment his insecurity, already fuelled by Iago's racist insinuations: 'Haply, for I am black/ And have not those soft parts of conversation/ That chamberers have, or for I am declined/ Into the vale of years' (III, iii, 266–9). What is evident – as several critics have seen – is Iago's role as a negative, paradoxically anti-theatrical playwright and director. Specific to his Italian context, he possesses many traits of the scheming, competitive and often treacherous *commedia* trickster servant Brighella: in this case, he defeats his superior by devising a final tableau that 'poisons sight', after getting Othello to share his vision of hybrid monsters and translating Desdemona's 'virtue into pitch'. By the end of the play, this talented woman does get to sing, not like a courtesan or a *prima donna*, but rather like her mother's maid Barbary, echoing a song of unrequited love, betrayal, rejection and deathly sorrow. While Desdemona thus resists association with the whore or 'courtesan' figure – hers is not a song of seduction, like those sung by the 'siren' Francischina in Marston's *Dutch Courtesan* (1605) and the Venetian courtesan Imperia in the anonymous (probably Dekker's) *Blurt, Master Constable* (1602) – her own melodious singing,

---

27　De' Sommi, *Quattro Dialoghi*, p. 90.
28　Feldman and Gordon, *The Courtesan's Arts*, pp. 107–8.

suffused as it is with water imagery, evokes the fatal sirens who in various legends were themselves transformed into swans.[29] This role, however, is assigned to Emilia, previously cast by Othello as both a 'bawd' and 'subtle whore', but now redeemed by the playscript as her lady's outspoken defender and Iago's innocent victim: 'I will play the swan,/ And die in music: (*sings*) "willow, willow, willow"' (V, ii, 246–7). Thanks to this swan-song that places Emilia in a love-and-deathbed, first with Desdemona and then with Othello, Iago's destructively jealous, racist and misogynist script is enacted. At the same time, his reduction of women's singing and playing to something whorish and monstrous is both denied and transcended. The stage sirens, translated into swans, may be heavenly after all, whether in Venice, Cyprus, or even in a London theatre.

A postscript, which brings us back to Jonson, and on to Whitehall, may be seen as looking ahead to my further work on this project. Soon after a court performance of *Othello* (on 1 November 1604), Queen Anna of Denmark, already several months pregnant, insisted that she and her court ladies dance in Jonson's first collaboration with Inigo Jones, *The Masque of Blackness*, playing the daughters of the river Niger with their arms, necks and faces fully blackened. As Clare McManus has persuasively argued, though these performing ladies neither sang nor spoke, they still caused some disruption, especially to Jacobean tastes and to the masque's own purported aim to have divine spirit transcend material form.[30] Queen Anna's and the other lady masquers' impersonation of '*blackamores*' was an 'ugly sight' for Sir Dudley Carleton, who also complained that the women's 'Apparell was rich but too light and Curtizan-like for such great ones'.[31] These visually provocative female dancers were thus identified in Carleton's mind into Italianate courtesans; Carleton and others may also have been troubled by the sight and sound of 'a pair of sea-maids, for song' (Jonson, *Blackness*, ll. 29–30), sopranos who sang of the women:

> black in face,
> Yet are they bright,
> And full of life and light,
> To prove that beauty best
> Which not the color but the feature
> Assures unto the creature
> (*Blackness*, ll. 82–7).

The audience's perplexity could have been suggested by Jonson's words themselves, for the Triton who sings and invites the Daughters of Niger to enter the Ocean and thus proceed to Britannia, warns that:

---

[29] Austern, "Teach me", pp. 85–6.

[30] Clare McManus, *Women on the Renaissance Stage: Anna of Denmark and Female Masquing in the Stuart Court (1590–1619)* (Manchester and New York: Manchester University Press, 2002), pp. 15–17.

[31] Carleton, cited by McManus, p. 1

> If you do not stop your ear,
> We shall have more cause to fear
> Sirens of the land, than they
> To doubt the sirens of the sea.
>   (*Blackness*, ll. 271–4).

Over four hundred years later, such doubts, uncertainties and courtesan-like powers still adhere to the singing siren: one can see them worldwide, even in the shadows of a Starbucks café.

Bibliography

Primary Sources

Academici Intronati di Siena, *Gl'Ingannati*, in Nino Borsellino, *Commedie del Cinquencento* (2 vols, Milan: Feltrinelli, 1962-67), vol. 1.

Coryate, Thomas, *Coryate's Crudities* (London: n. p., 1611; rept. 2 vols, Glasgow: Maclehose, 1905).

De' Sommi, Leone, *Quattro Dialoghi in materia di rappresentazioni sceniche* (ca. 1575), ed. Ferruccio Marotti (Milan: Edizioni Il Polifilo, 1968).

Franco, Giacomo *Habiti d'uomeni et donne venetiane* (Venice: n. p.,1610).

Garzoni, Tommaso, *La piazza universale di tutte le professioni del mondo* (Venice: n. p., 1585).

Jonson, Ben, *Volpone*, ed. Brian Parker, revised edition (Manchester: Manchester University Press, 1999).

Lane, John, *Tom Tell-Troths Message and His Pens Complaint* (London: n. p. 1600).

Secondary Sources

Austern, Linda, '"Teach me to Heare Mermaides Singinge": Embodiments of (Acoustic) Pleasure and Danger in the Modern West', in Linda Austern and Inna Naroditskaya (eds), *Music of the Sirens*, (Bloomington and Indianapolis: Indiana University Press, 2006), pp. 85–9.

Austern, Linda and Inna Naroditskaya (eds), *Music of the Sirens* (Bloomington and Indianapolis: Indiana University Press, 2006).

Bettini, Murizio and Luigi Spina, *Il mito delle sirene* (Turin: Einaudi, 2007).

Brown, Pamela Allen and Peter Parolin (eds), *Women Players in England, 1500–1660* (Aldershot and Burlington, VT: Ashgate Publishing, 2005).

Calogero, Elena Laura, '"Sweet Alluring Harmony": Heavenly and Earthly Sirens in Sixteenth- and Seventeenth-Century Literary and Visual Culture", in Linda Austern and Inna Naroditskaya (eds), *Music of the Sirens* (Bloomington and Indianapolis: Indiana University Press, 2006), p. 150.

Clubb, Louise George, *Italian Drama in Shakespeare's Time* (New Haven: Yale University Press, 1989).

Davies, Drew Edward, 'On Music Fit for a Courtesan: Representations of the Courtesan and Her Music in Sixteenth-Century Italy', in Martha Feldman and Bonnie Gordon (eds), *The Courtesan's Arts: Cross-Cultural Perspectives* (Oxford: Oxford University Press, 2006), pp. 144–55.

Feldman, Martha and Bonnie Gordon (eds), *The Courtesan's Arts*: *Cross-Cultural Perspectives* (Oxford: Oxford University Press, 2006).

Gordon, Bonnie, 'The Courtesan's Singing Body as Cultural Capital in Seventeenth-Century Italy', in Martha Feldman and Bonnie Gordon (eds), *The Courtesan's Arts*: *Cross-Cultural Perspectives* (Oxford: Oxford University Press, 2006), p. 195.

Gough, Melinda, 'Jonson's Siren Stage', *Studies in Philology* 96, 1 (1999), p. 77.

Katritzky, M.A., *The art of commedia: a study in the commedia dell' arte, 1560–1620* (Amsterdam: Rodopi, 2006).

Katritzky, M.A., *Women, Medicine and Theatre, 1500–1750: Literary Mountebanks and Performing Quacks* (Aldershot and Burlington, VT: Ashgate Publishing, 2007).

McManus, Clare, *Women on the Renaissance Stage: Anna of Denmark and Female Masquing in the Stuart Court (1590–1619)* (Manchester and New York: Manchester University Press, 2002).

Mirabella, Bella, '"Quacking Delilahs": Female Mountebanks in Early Modern England and Italy', in Pamela Allen Brown and Peter Parolin (eds), *Women Players in England, 1500–1660* (Aldershot and Burlington, VT: Ashgate Publishing, 2005), pp. 94–5.

Mulryne, J.R. and Elizabeth Goldring (eds), *Court Festivals of the European Renaissance: Art, Politics and Performance* (Aldershot and Burlington, VT: Ashgate Publishing, 2002).

Puppi, Lionello (ed.), *Architettura e Utopia nella Venezia del cinquecento* (Milan: Electa, 1980).

Ruggiero, Guido, 'Who's Afraid of Giuliana Napolitana?' in Martha Feldman and Bonnie Gordon (eds), *The Courtesan's Arts: Cross-Cultural Perspectives* (Oxford: Oxford University Press, 2006), p. 285.

Taviani, Ferdinando, *La Fascinazione del teatro: la commedia dell'arte e la società barocca* (Rome: Bulzoni, 1969–91).

Tondro, Maximilian L.S., 'The First Temporary Triumphal Arch in Venice (1557)', in J.R. Mulryne and Elizabeth Goldring (eds), *Court Festivals of the European Renaissance: Art, Politics and Performance* (Aldershot and Burlington, VT: Ashgate Publishing, 2002), pp. 349–55.

Tylus, Jane, 'Women at the Windows: *Commedia dell'Arte* and Theatrical Practice in Early Modern Italy', *Theatre Journal*, 49 (1997), pp. 323–42.

Urban, Lina Padoan, 'Gli spetta coli urbani e l'utopia', in Lionello Puppi (ed.), *Architettura e Utopia nella Venezia del cinquecento* (Milan: Electa, 1980), pp. 149–63.

Chapter 21

Sailing Towards a Kingdom: Ernst August von Braunschweig-Lüneburg (1629–1698) in Venice in 1685 and 1686

Helen Watanabe-O'Kelly

On 25 June 1686 Ernst August, Prince Bishop of Osnabrück and by this time also duke of the territory of Braunschweig-Lüneburg-Calenberg, staged a magnificent regatta on the Grand Canal.[1] The regatta was a sporting contest consisting of a series of competitions between various kinds and sizes of boat rowed standing up in the Venetian manner which raced each other the length of the Grand Canal. In all, 352 oarsmen and 104 boats took part. A foldout plate in Alberti's account, consisting of some 11 sheets stuck together, takes the viewer from the Arsenale, passes in front of St Mark's Square and up through the Grand Canal to Ca' Foscari where Ernst August, his heir Georg Ludwig and other members of his family were staying. Before the sporting part of the proceedings, however, there was a waterborne pageant. The most striking feature of this was a huge structure in the shape of a dolphin surmounted by a kind of grotto on which was balanced another dolphin which in turn bore a shell on which stood a figure of Neptune. (Fig. 21.1) Numerous hippocamps and Tritons swam around this structure in the water. Then came the six decorated boats or *peote* of Venus, Mars, Glaucus, Diana, Juno and Pallas respectively, rowed in each case by ten costumed oarsmen. (Fig. 21.2: *Peota* of Venus). Ernst August himself took part in the procession in a *margherota*, a somewhat smaller boat rowed by eight oarsmen dressed as Venetian gondoliers (Fig. 21.3). There followed a further fifteen decorated *peote* bearing nineteen Venetian patricians whose names are a roll-call of the great families of Venice: Dolfin, Foscari, Zuliani, Loredan, Mocenigo, Pisani, Venier, Manin and Pesaro, to name but some of them (Fig. 21.4). That night, at the end of the regatta, the *machina* with the figure of Neptune on top was illuminated and towed up the Grand Canal until it came to Ca' Foscari where it stopped and the figure of

---

[1] Giovanni Matteo Alberti, *Givochi festivi e militari, Danze, Serenate, Machine, Boscareccia artificiosa, Regatta solenne. Et altri sontuosi Apprestamenti di Allegrezza espositi alla Sodisfattione vniversale Dall Generosità dell' A.S. d'Ernesto Avgusto, Dvca di Brvnsvich, e Lvnebvrgo, Prencipe D'Osnaprvch, etc. Nel tempo di sua dimora in Venetia …* (Venice: Andrea Poletti, 1686). http://special-1.bl.uk/treasures/festivalbooks/BookDetails. aspx?strFest=0229

Figure 21.1   The *machina* of Neptune on the Grand Canal. From: Giovanni
               Matteo Alberti, *Givochi festivi e militari, Danze, Serenate,*
               Machine, Boscareccia artificiosa, Regatta solenne. Et altri sontuosi
               Apprestamenti di Allegrezza espositi alla Sodisfattione vniversale
               Dall Generosità dell' A.S. d'Ernesto Avgusto, Dvca di Brvnsvich,
               e Lvnebvrgo, Prencipe D'Osnaprvch, etc. Nel tempo di sua dimora
               in Venetia ... (Venice: Andrea Poletti, 1686). Reproduction courtesy
               of the Gottfried Wilhelm Leibniz Bibliothek – Niedersächsische
               Landesbibliothek.

Neptune bowed to the Duke who was standing on the balcony. So the regatta was a
very public event, quintessentially Venetian, which demonstrated the high esteem
in which Ernst August was held by the leading families of Venice.

Around the same time as he held the regatta, Ernst August staged what Alberti
calls a '*Serenata Grande*', again on the grand canal in front of Ca' Foscari.
This involved another huge '*machina*', 42 feet wide, 60 feet long and 36 feet
high, representing Proteus with Venus accompanied by the Graces on his back
(Fig. 21.5). A famous musician – Alberti does not name him – sat up in Proteus's
head and provided him with a singing voice. After Venus had performed she
vanishes and Proteus plunges into the waves. Then comes a second floating
machine – a beautiful courtyard with a fountain surrounded by musicians who
perform a serenade to Sincere Love. Five of the musicians represent five European
nations: Adolfo the German, Henrico the Frenchman, Alonso the Spaniard, Flavio
the Italian and Casimiro the Pole. Casimiro is declared the most sincere lover.
Fame then appears in a cloud to proclaim the victories and glories of Venice in
the Orient.

Figure 21.2   The *peota* of Venus. From: Giovanni Matteo Alberti, *Givochi festivi e militari* ... (Venice: Andrea Poletti, 1686). Reproduction courtesy of the Gottfried Wilhelm Leibniz Bibliothek – Niedersächsische Landesbibliothek.

These festivities pose the question as to what a north German prince such as Ernst August was doing in Venice and why he was praising the Republic at the same time as they were honouring him. Ernst August knew Venice very well, for he and his three older brothers, born in 1622, 1624 and 1625 respectively – he himself was born in 1629 – had all first come to Italy as very young men, leaving a Germany still in the throes of the Thirty Years' War and thus experiencing the contrast with Italy all the more vividly.[2] The brothers seized every opportunity from then on to return to Italy but particularly to attend the Carnival in Venice. They all learned Italian and loved Italian culture, above all Italian music. They commissioned many operas, the earliest of which seems to have been Pietro Andrea Ziani's *L'incostanza triofante, overo Il Theseo* of 1658, which is dedicated to Ernst August and his brothers Georg Wilhelm and Johann Friedrich.[3] They also brought Venetian opera and Venetian composers back to their own courts in Germany. Of all the brothers, it was Ernst August who was the greatest connoisseur of music and it was he who, in order to be able to enjoy Venetian opera at home, built an opera house in Hanover in 1688. Through the good offices of the philosopher Gottfried Wilhelm Leibniz, his historiographer, he brought the Venetian Agostino Steffani, composer, Catholic prelate and diplomat, to Hanover as court *Kapellmeister*, where Steffani composed

[2]   Georg Schnath, *Geschichte Hannovers im Zeitalter der neunten Kur und der englischen Sukzession 1674–1714*, vol. I: 1674–92 (5 vols, Hildesheim und Leipzig: August Lax, 1938), p. 377. http://www.gwleibniz.com/ernst_august/ernst_august.html

[3]   Pietro Andrea Ziani, *L'incostanza triofante, overo Il Theseo. Drama per mvsica nel teatro di San Cassano. Consacrato alli serenissimi prencipi Georgio Gvglielmo, Gio. Federico et Ernesto Avgvsto, dvchi di Bransvvich, e Lvnebvrgh, etc* (Venice: Giuliani, 1658).

Figure 21.3 Ernst August in his *margherota*. From: Giovanni Matteo Alberti, *Givochi festivi e militari* ... (Venice: Andrea Poletti, 1686). Reproduction courtesy of the Gottfried Wilhelm Leibniz Bibliothek – Niedersächsische Landesbibliothek.

a whole series of operas.[4] Of course these German princes also enjoyed other pleasures of the flesh while in Venice – both Georg Wilhelm and Ernst August had natural children by Venetian women, for instance. Ernst August's wife, the remarkable Sophie of the Palatinate, only accompanied her husband to Venice once, in 1664–65, refusing to come thereafter. This did not stop Ernst August from spending several months in Venice in 1669–70, 1671–72 and 1680–81, renting Ca' Foscari from its owner and keeping it in permanent readiness for his next visit under the management of a German doctor called Johann Matthäus Alberti – the same Alberti who, under the Italian form of his name, is the author of *Givochi Festivi*.

Ernst August's next visits did not take place until 1685 and 1686. In 1685 he came to Venice on 18 January and remained there until 11 September, spending eight months continuously in the city. Hardly had he got home than he was off again to Venice on 16 December, again spending most of the next eight months of

    [4]   Hans-Peter Schramm, *Hannover und Italien zur Leibniz-Zeit. Aus den Beständen der Niedersächsischen Landesbibliothek Hannover* (Hanover: Niedersächsische Landesbibliothek Hannover, 1984). See also Hannes Razum, 'Theater', in Hans Patze (ed.), *Geschichte Niedersachsens*, vol. 3, part 2, *Kirche und Kultur von der Reformation bis zum Beginn des 19. Jahrhunderts* (Hildesheim: August Lax, 1983), p. 650.

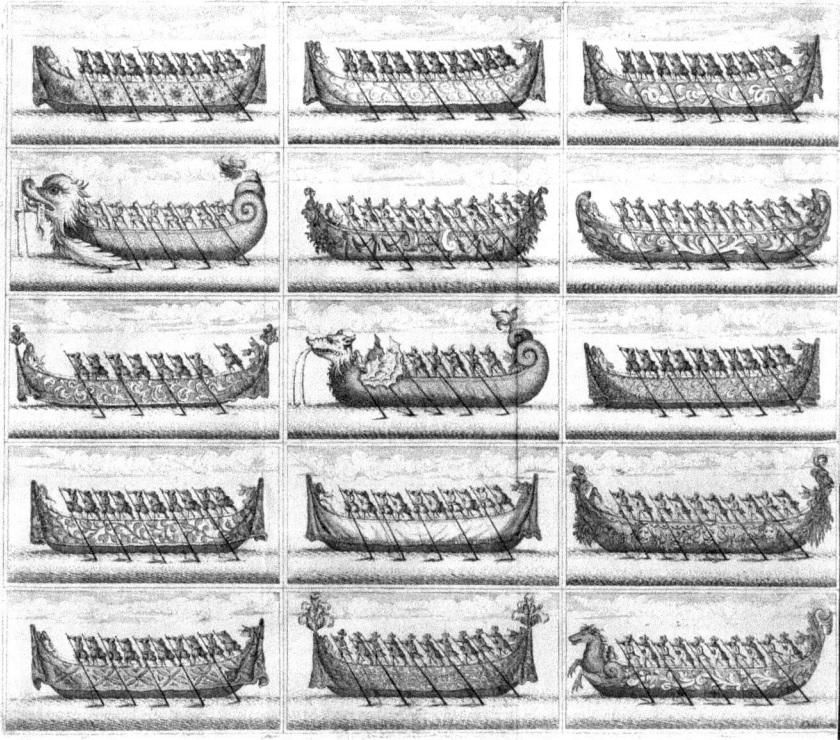

Figure 21.4   Other *peote* in the water pageant. From: Giovanni Matteo Alberti, *Givochi festivi e militari* … (Venice: Andrea Poletti, 1686). Reproduction courtesy of the Gottfried Wilhelm Leibniz Bibliothek – Niedersächsische Landesbibliothek.

1686 in the city, apart from a short period in Rome in April. During what was the best part of two years in Venice, Ernst August was listening to and financing a lot of music. He had his own band of instrumentalists and vocalists, among them the composer Antonio Gianettini.[5] In 1685, he staged a number of musical events. In June he had an opera on the theme of the Judgement of Paris put on at night on a '*sontuosa machina*' resembling a garden erected in front of Ca' Foscari on the Grand Canal and he organised another musical performance on the topic of the glorious victories of Venice in the Levant.

But it is an event held in April 1685 over on the Lido that shows us another side of Ernst August's connections with Venice. For this event he had a great *mole* or raft constructed, 90 feet wide by 60 feet high. This raft bore a substantial structure decorated to resemble a wood but containing rooms and grottoes and an observation area. The purpose of this was to enable Ernst August and his entourage to observe

---

5   Schnath, *Geschichte Hannovers*, p. 380.

Figure 21.5   The *ure* of Proteus. From: Giovanni Matteo Alberti, *Givochi festivi e militari* ... (Venice: Andrea Poletti, 1686). Reproduction courtesy of the Gottfried Wilhelm Leibniz Bibliothek – Niedersächsische Landesbibliothek.

the manoeuvres on dry land of three infantry regiments of Brunswickers led by Maximilian Wilhelm, Ernst August's third son.

The coat of arms at the beginning of Alberti's account gives us a clue as to how and why Ernst August had three regiments of Braunschweig soldiers in Venice. Under the actual coat of arms are the trophies of war and the figures of four manacled Turks. Ernst August was supporting the Venetian Republic with 6,700 troops, led by his son. A year before, in April 1684, the Venetians had taken advantage of the Ottoman struggles with the Habsburgs to the north to declare war against them in Morea, that is, in the southern part of the Peloponnese.[6] The Morean War formed part of a fifteen-year-long conflict between Venice and the Ottoman Empire that lasted from 1684 to 1699. The Venetians could not conquer Morea alone, so they put together a coalition including, among the German states, Saxony and Braunschweig. Francesco Morosini (1616–94), now getting on in years but a distinguished general nonetheless and with experience of war in

---

[6]   Joachim Meier, S.J., *Churfürstl. Durchl. Zu Braunsw. Und Lüneb. Ernest Augusti höchstseeligen Andenkens Geschichts-Calender* (Goßlar: König, 1699), p. 41.

Greece, was chosen as commander. Ernst August's troops were not pressed men but mercenaries, and many of them deserted before they ever got to the field of combat.[7] Three thousand of the more than 6,000 men died in Greece, mostly from disease and hunger, between 1685 and the end of their campaign in 1687. But why was Ernst August supporting Venice's expansionist aims?

The reason was a purely financial one. Ernst August needed to bolster his position and could only do so if he maintained a considerable army. He therefore kept a large troop which, by the period under discussion, was swallowing up almost half of all the income of his territories.[8] By 1683 he had seven cavalry and nine infantry regiments at his disposal. By 1684 this had grown to nine cavalry regiments, two regiments of dragoons and nine infantry regiments. This meant that a population of 160,000 to 200,000 inhabitants was supporting an army of 15,000! Ernst August financed these troops by renting them out to whoever would pay for them. He hoped to make a profit from such a transaction. Even if it only meant that someone else – in this case Venice – took over the cost of feeding, clothing and housing the troops, he would thereby have improved his financial position. Of course Venice – and the Emperor to whom Ernst August was renting out other troops – knew that he needed money and so drove a hard bargain. Any actual profit from the transaction was small and in any case did not come back to Braunschweig or Hannover but was spent by Ernst August in Venice itself. This is the reason why the Venetians were keen to honour him publicly by sailing up the Grand Canal in his wake in 1686 – his troops were fighting their war for them.

They had already paid elaborate tribute to him in 1685. In August of that year Marco Contarini (1631–89), procurator of St Mark's and therefore the second most important man in Venice after the Doge, had invited Ernst August to visit him in his villa in Piazzola on the Brenta, about 45 kilometres west of Venice and about 15 kilometres northwest of Padua.[9] The central portion of the Villa Contarini had been designed by Palladio in the sixteenth century but was greatly extended by Marco Contarini in the seventeenth century by adding two wings to provide a frontage of almost 200 metres. Like his guest, Marco Contarini's great passion was music and he had a theatre holding 400 people erected in the nearby convent called the Luoco delle Vergini where orphan girls were trained as singers. Here too there was a printing press and it is this press that published the account of Ernst August's visit in 1685.[10] For Ernst August's visit Contarini had Domenico

---

[7]   Schnath, *Geschichte Hannovers*, p. 350.

[8]   Schnath, *Geschichte Hannovers*, p. 335.

[9]   For this and other festivals in Piazolla see Olga Visentini, 'Feste, musica e spettacoli in Villa Contarini a Piazzola sul Brenta (1679–86)', in *Atlante Tematico del Barocco in Italia* (8 vols, Rome: De Luca, 2007), vol. I,1, Marcello Fagiolo ed. with the collaboration of Giancarlo Coccioli, *Le Capitali della Festa. Italia settentrionale*, pp. 341–7.

[10]   Francesco Maria Piccioli, *L'Orologio del Piacere: che mostra lore del diletteuole soggiorno hauto dall'altezza serenissima d. Ernesto Augusto, vescouo d'Osnabruc, duca di Bransuich, Luneburgo, &c. Nelluoco di Piazzola di S.E. il signor Marco Contarini,*

Freschi (1634–1710), Master of Music at Vicenza Cathedral, compose six musical offerings as tributes to his guest. These were performed by the young female singers from the nearby orphanage.

So Ernst August with his son and heir Georg Ludwig and his third son Maximilian Wilhelm set off along the Brenta to Piazzola (Fig. 21.6). After they had been received and shown to their extensive apartments, Freschi's opera *L'Ermelinda*, which had been premiered in Piazzola in 1682, was performed in the convent theatre and then supper was served in a *bucintoro* which could seat 80 people. Next came the first of the musical tributes to Ernst August, *Il Vaticinio della Fortuna*, in which three singers representing la Gloria, la Fortuna and Cintia hymn his praises. The next musical work to be performed was *La Schiavitù fortunata di Nettuno*. Neptune riding on his shell boat appeared on the canal bordering the grounds of the villa during supper, accompanied by Eolo and Anfitrite (Fig. 21.7). The next day there was dinner with music, during which a flying monster appeared and sailed into the middle of the room. This was followed by a performance of *Il Ritratto della Gloria donato all'Eternità*, in which the cast consisted of Eternità, Idea, Virtù, Valor and Grandezza. Then came *Il Preludio Felice* followed by a naval battle (Fig. 21.8) in which a Turkish warship, captained by the Turks Amurat Bassa and Ibrain was sunk by the Venetian ship *La Veneta Armata*, captained by General Morosini. The Turks then described how they would encounter on land the troops led by Maximilian Wilhelm. The next event was a race run by Barbary horses and a banquet in the palace courtyard during which the final serenade, *Il Merito Acclamato*, was sung by 24 girls brought in on a triumphal cart drawn by six horses. On the cart were figures of two horses and two hippocamps 17 feet high on which four girls played the trumpet. That evening Freschi's opera *Gli'Amori d'Alidaura* was premiered, again in the Luoco delle Vergini. Next day there was a concert and before he left, Ernst August was presented with a gift of horses.

The festivities were, therefore, a feast of music, and it must have given Marco Contarini great pleasure to have such a knowledgeable guest who could appreciate what he was listening to. But they were also a feast of praise for Ernst August. The six libretti, like the account composed by Francesco Maria Piccioli, are liberally sprinkled with references to Ernesto Augusto, with much play on the name Augusto, and to his sons. Ernst August's virtue, honour and fame are hymned over and over again.

But who was Ernst August? At the time of his stay in Venice he was Prince Bishop of Osnabrück (1661–92) and Duke of Braunschweig-Lüneburg-Calenberg (1679–92), the capital of which is Hanover. The second of Ernst August's two titles is already surprising, but then the man's whole career and rise to greatness is nothing short of astonishing. Ernst August was a member of the Guelph family, Europe's oldest dynasty. Ernst August was the youngest of four sons born to

---

procurator di S. Marco, consacrato all'A. S. Dalla medemma eccellenza/ del dottor Piccioli (Piazzola: Luoco delle Vergine, 1685). http://beinecke.library.yale.edu/ Image ID 1074574. Italian Festivals 112.

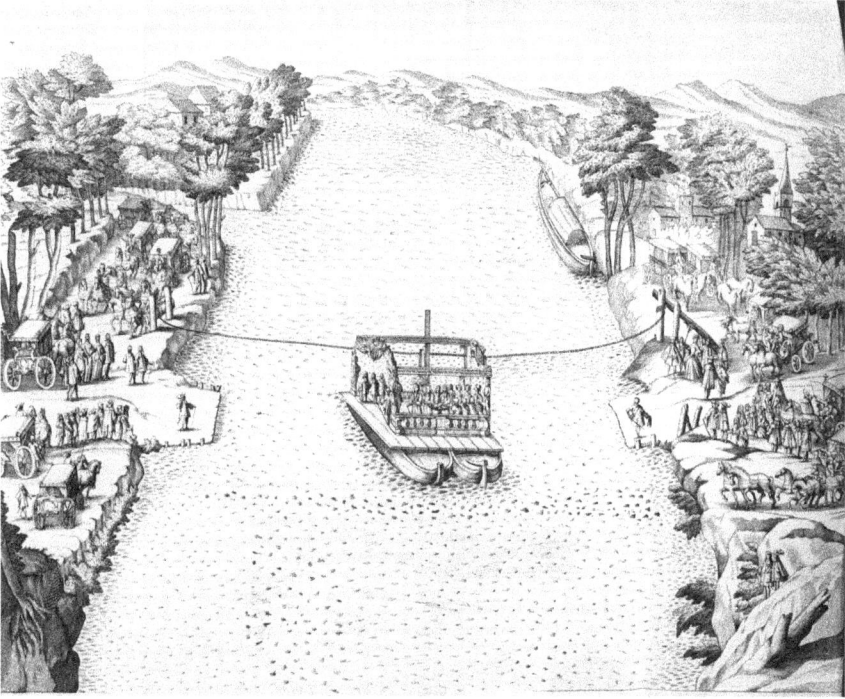

Figure 21.6   Ernst August arrives in Piazzola. From: Francesco Maria Piccioli, *L'Orologio dell Piacere: che mostra lore del diletteuole soggiorno hauto dall'altezza serenissima d. Ernesto Augusto, vescouo d'Osnabruc, duca di Bransuich, Luneburgo, &c. Nel luoco di Piazzola di S.E. il signor Marco Contarini, procurator di S. Marco, consacrato all' A. S. dalla medemma eccellenza/del dottor Piccioli.* (Piazzola: Luoco delle Vergine, 1685). Courtesy of the Herzog August Bibliothek, Wolfenbüttel.

Duke Georg of Calenberg (1582–1641), seemingly destined to play a minor role in history and to come into a very modest inheritance. But Ernst August combined a number of strokes of luck with considerable energy, determination and decisiveness. The first stroke of luck was that, in 1658, he married Sophie of the Palatinate (1630–1714), the twelfth and last child of the Winter King and Winter Queen, that is, Friederich of the Palatinate (1596–1632) and Elizabeth of England (1596–1662). It was a stroke of luck because Sophie turned out to be a woman of exceptional character and intelligence but even more because, over 40 years later, she was declared heir to the British throne in the Act of Settlement of 1701 on the death of Queen Anne – though she died before she could ascend the throne.

Two other strokes of luck were that two of Ernst August's three older brothers predeceased him: the eldest, Christian Ludwig (1622–65) and the third brother

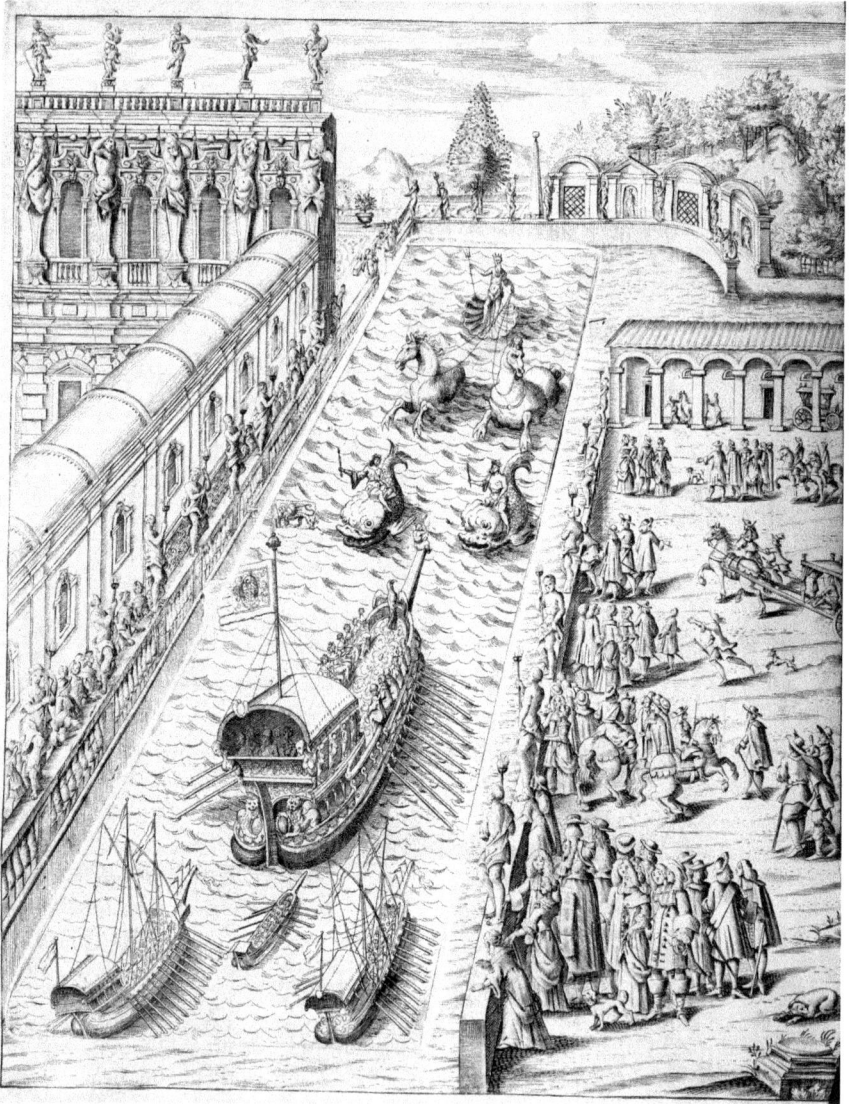

Figure 21.7   The arrival of Neptune. From: Francesco Maria Piccioli, *L'Orologio dell Piacere* ... (Piazzola: Luoco delle Vergine, 1685). Courtesy of the Herzog August Bibliothek, Wolfenbüttel.

Johann Friedrich (1625–79). A further stroke of luck was that his second eldest brother Georg Wilhelm (1624–1705) only had one daughter who could be made to marry her cousin, Ernst August's heir, so as to unite Georg Wilhelm's territory with that of Ernst August. Ernst August's son, therefore, eventually inherited all the territories of the Lüneburg line – Braunschweig, Lüneburg, Calenberg and

Figure 21.8   The *naumachia*. From: Francesco Maria Piccioli, *L'Orologio dell Piacere* ... (Piazzola: Luoco delle Vergine, 1685). Courtesy of the Herzog August Bibliothek, Wolfenbüttel.

Celle – to make up the territory of Hanover. In 1683, Ernst August instituted primogeniture, against the wishes of his younger sons. Having managed by luck and good judgement to reunite the subdivided Guelph territories, he wanted to keep them intact for the future. Indeed, he needed to do so, because his main ambition was to become an elector – that is, one of the most important men in the

Holy Roman Empire – and he could only become an elector if he was the lord of a sizeable territory. He managed finally to have a ninth electorship created for him in 1692. The man who was born a fourth son was now Elector of Hanover.

His ambitions did not stop there, for Ernst August was also working to place his eldest son Georg Ludwig on the British throne. In this too he succeeded, even though he did not live to see Georg Ludwig crowned King of Great Britain and Ireland in 1714 as George I – the first of the Hanoverian monarchs. Keeping his troops under arms by renting them to the Venetians was just one of the important stepping stones on Ernst August's path from younger son to father of a king.

Postscript

Festivals are ephemeral, but the events and the people described in Alberti's and Piccioli's works have all left considerable legacies. Venice is recognisably still what it was in Ernst August's time. The Ca' Foscari is now the University of Venice. The Villa Contarini exists and is still a centre of music-making, now run by the Fondazione G.E. Ghirardi. The Contarini family still has a scion called Marco Contarini and Ernst August, Prince of Hanover, is still the head of the House of Guelph. A direct descendant of the seventeenth century Ernst August still sits on the British throne. But there are other kinds of legacy. Two of the collections that Marco Contarini showed Ernst August in Piazolla in 1685 are in Venetian collections today – the music manuscripts in the Biblioteca Marciana and the musical instruments in the Museo Correr. Alberti's *Givochi Festivi* of 1686, fully digitized and freely available on the British Library website, is one of the legacies bequeathed to scholars by J.R. Mulryne who masterminded the digitization of this and 252 other festival books in that Library. These are the legacies truly valued by historians.

Bibliography

Primary Sources

Alberti, Giovanni Matteo, *Givochi festivi e militari, Danze, Serenate, Machine, Boscareccia artificiosa, Regatta solenne. Et altri sontuosi Apprestamenti di Allegrezza espositi alla Sodisfattione vniversale Dall Generosità dell' A.S. d'Ernesto Avgusto, Dvca di Brvnsvich, e Lvnebvrgo, Prencipe D'Osnaprvch, etc. Nel tempo di sua dimora in Venetia* … (Venice: Andrea Poletti, 1686).
http://special-1.bl.uk/treasures/festivalbooks/BookDetails.aspx?strFest=0229
Joachim Meier, S.J., *Churfürstl. Durchl. Zu Braunsw. Und Lüneb. Ernest Augusti höchstseeligen Andenkens Geschichts-Calender* (Goßlar: König, 1699).
Piccioli, Francesco Maria, *L'Orologio del Piacere: che mostra lore del diletteuole soggiorno hauto dall'altezza serenissima d. Ernesto Augusto, vescouo*

d'Osnabruc, duca di Bransuich, Luneburgo, &c. Nel luoco di Piazzola di S.E. il signor Marco Contarini, procurator di S. Marco, consacrato all' A. S. dalla medemma eccellenza/ del dottor Piccioli (Piazzola: Luoco delle Vergine, 1685). http://beinecke.library.yale.edu/ Image ID 1074574. Italian Festivals 112.

Ziani, Pietro Andrea, *L'incostanza triofante, overo Il Theseo. Drama per mvsica nel teatro di San Cassano. Consacrato alli serenissimi prencipi Georgio Gvglielmo, Gio. Federico et Ernesto Avgvsto, dvchi di Bransvvich, e Lvnebvrgh, etc* (Venice: Giuliani, 1658).

Secondary Sources

Fagiolo, Marcello (ed.), with the collaboration of Giancarlo Coccioli, *Atlante Tematico del Barocco in Italia*, vol. I, 1 (8 vols, Rome: De Luca, 2007).

Razum, Hannes, 'Theater', in Hans Patze ed. *Geschichte Niedersachsens*, vol. 3, part 2, *Kirche und Kultur von der Reformation bis zum Beginn des 19. Jahrhunderts* (Hildesheim: August Lax, 1983).

Schnath, Georg, *Geschichte Hannovers im Zeitalter der neunten Kur und der englischen Sukzession 1674–1714*, vol. I: 1674–92 (5 vols, Hildesheim und Leipzig: August Lax, 1938); http://www.gwleibniz.com/ernst_august/ernst_august.html

Schramm, Hans-Peter, *Hannover und Italien zur Leibniz-Zeit. Aus den Beständen der Niedersächsischen Landesbibliothek Hannover* (Hanover: Niedersächsische Landesbibliothek Hannover, 1984).

Visentini, Olga, 'Feste, musica e spettacoli in Villa Contarini a Piazzola sul Brenta (1679–86)', in *Atlante Tematico del Barocco in Italia* (8 vols, Rome: De Luca, 2007), vol. I,1, Marcello Fagiolo ed. with the collaboration of Giancarlo Coccioli, *Le Capitali della Festa. Italia settentrionale*, pp. 341–7.

Index

The entries in this index include proper names of people, places, allegorical and mythical figures, and titles of plays, ballets, operas and court masques, as well as selected references to festival types and events, particularly those involving ships and waterborne entertainments. Alternative spellings are given when this reflects different spellings within the chapters. Scholars and critics of the twentieth and twenty first centuries are not included in the index, but full details are given in the bibliographies following each chapter.

For Product Safety Concerns and Information please contact our EU
representative GPSR@taylorandfrancis.com
Taylor & Francis Verlag GmbH, Kaufingerstraße 24, 80331 München, Germany